THE GLORY OF THE LORD

Hans Urs von Balthasar

THE GLORY OF THE LORD:
A THEOLOGICAL AESTHETICS

By Hans Urs von Balthasar

VOLUMES OF THE COMPLETE WORK
Edited by Joseph Fessio, S.J., and John Riches

The publishers gratefully acknowledge the support of the
Pro Helvetia Foundation in the preparation of
the English translation.

THE GLORY
OF THE LORD

A THEOLOGICAL AESTHETICS

BY

HANS URS VON BALTHASAR

VOLUME V: THE REALM OF
METAPHYSICS IN THE MODERN AGE

*Translated by Oliver Davies, Andrew Louth,
Brian McNeil C.R.V., John Saward
and Rowan Williams
Edited by Brian McNeil C.R.V. and John Riches*

T&T CLARK, 59 GEORGE STREET, EDINBURGH

Copyright © T&T Clark, 1991
T&T Clark, 59 George Street, Edinburgh EH2 2LQ, Scotland
T&T Clark is an imprint of HarperCollins*Publishers*

Authorised English Translation of
Herrlichkeit: Eine theologische Ästhetik, Band III, 1:
Im Raum der Metaphysik, Teil II: *Neuzeit*
Copyright © Johannes Verlag, Einsiedeln, 1965

All rights reserved. No part of this publication may be reproduced,
stored in a retrieval system, or transmitted in any form or by any
means, electronic, mechanical, photocopying, recording or
otherwise, without the prior permission of T&T Clark.

First Published 1991

British Library Cataloguing in Publication Data
Balthasar, Hans Urs von, *1905*
The glory of the Lord: a theological aesthetics
Vol. 5: The realm of metaphysics in the modern age.
1. Christian theology
I. Title   II. Riches, John *1939—*
230

ISBN 0 567 09576 2

Typeset by Barbers Highlands Ltd, Fort William
Printed and bound in Great Britain by Billing & Sons Ltd, Worcester

CONTENTS

VOLUME V
THE REALM OF METAPHYSICS
IN THE MODERN AGE

2. ELABORATIONS

110994

BALTHASAR, H.
THE GLORY OF THE LORD VOL
110994 01   230.611185

110994

OXFORD BROOKES UNIVERSITY
LIBRARY   HARCOURT HILL

This book is to be returned on or before the last date stamped below.
A fine will levied on overdue books.
Books may be renewed by telephoning Oxford 488222
and quoting your borrower number.
You may not renew books that are reserved by another borrower.

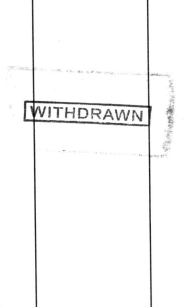

WITHDRAWN

11099401

B. THE AESTHETICS OF TRANSCENDENTAL REASON

1. THE PARTING OF THE WAYS

a. Origins of the Modern Period

What we are offering here is neither a history of philosophy nor a general intellectual history; we are inquiring solely into what became of the classical experience of God's glory over the course of the centuries. And we are conducting this inquiry in such a way that the element of Christian glory within this philosophical survey is excluded as far as possible and reserved for the concluding, biblical section. We have already seen how the Early and High Middle Ages dutifully received and developed the classical experience of a world which reveals God, how they understood the historical salvation-event wholly within a comprehensive and cosmic context, to such an extent that the universal categories of beauty which we find in antiquity served largely as a conceptual language in which the total revelation of God—with its centre in Jesus Christ—was expressed. Admittedly, this monistic vision (Erigena, the Victorines) was undermined by the advancing philosophy of Chartres and Abelard and by the Aristotelian renaissance, but during the period of High Scholasticism the Franciscan and Dionysian wave had once again produced a system of contemplation which transcended Being, in which not only the believing but also the philosophizing Christian felt that he could dare to say that the reflection of eternal goodness and beauty is perceptible in all being. In terms of intellectual history, this precept disappears after Thomas Aquinas. His ontology, upon which it was based, remained without imitators—if this is understood in the sense of an elemental, historical experience of Being. Thomas's experience of Being gathered within itself

and embodied the inheritance of antiquity in its entirety, of
an Aristotle who is always transformed and imbued with a
religious light by Plato (with his historical backgrounds!),
Dionysius and Augustine. For Thomas, to contradict an
experience of this kind would have been to cast doubt on
whether the religious experience of mankind (which had
drawn close to Christianity in its Greek guise) still had an
obligatory character in the present.

It was Averroism, which since 1250 had purported to be
the sole serious and radical interpretation of the sole 'scientific'
philosopher, Aristotle, which brought the turning-point. It
understood itself to be the attempt to ascertain how far human
reason could go in the inquiry into the ultimate grounds of
Being when it excluded and dispensed with all revelatory
knowledge, be it Islamic (Avicenna!) or Christian. The fact
that in 1270 initially fifteen propositions, and then in 1277,
two hundred and nineteen propositions of Averroistic
inspiration were condemned by the Bishop of Paris at first
appeared only to be one event in the struggle between the
secular philosophers and the Christian theologians, and for
the latter it seemed in the broader perspective one which was
by no means unfavourable, in that it stimulated an attempt
(upon which Thomas had already painstakingly embarked)
to draw the boundaries more clearly between philosophy and
Christianity. And the more clearly Christianity, as it moved
into the modern period, distanced itself from philosophy, the
more clearly it had finally to begin to set forth its own
irreducible understanding and possession of glory. In the
background, however, there was a completely different line
of decision: that concerning Plato and the openness to God
which Plato inherits, which can be described as 'mythical'
and which was permitted at least in principle by Aristotle in
his lost *Peri Philosophias*. For now the Averroists placed
philosophy, as the sole comprehensive science, above
theology. The latter was based upon *fabulae* (myths),[1] while
the ultimate science identified reality, rationality and
necessity, with the result that God must create the world,

[1] Condemned theses, quoted following Gilson, *La Philosophie au Moyen-
Age*, 2nd edn. 1952, p. 559, E.T. (1955), p. 406.

which exists from eternity, of course in such a way that he produces only the One Being, which is his own likeness, and which he orders by virtue of subordinate causes in a descending scale from himself to the material plane. This is a God without freedom, without knowledge of creatures, or a true otherness with respect to the world. This is a mental creature which lacks psycho-spiritual individuality (since the *intellectus agens* is only a single—divine—reality), without freedom or immortality. A world (according to Siger of Brabant) of eternal recurrence. This is a man who is characterised in his highest powers of philosophical reasoning as Θεῖον, as is the case in Aristotle: 'Just as we call divine that which is best in the totality of beings, so too we call divine that which is best in man' (Boethius of Dacia).[2] But it is clear to what extent the original Greek opposition between gods and men is lost here in these undifferentiated statements. However much in subsequent ages theologians sought to identify what belonged distinctively to the nature of revelation, nevertheless they were simultaneously inclined to accept as fact and as counterpart the proudly resigned self-limitation of philosophy, and thus largely to renounce the infrastructure of a 'natural revelation' in order merely to cast light from within on the nature of faith for those who already believe.

The late Middle Ages is a time of darkness like few others;[3] the social order is in ruins, war and plague prevail, secular and ecclesiastic façades are collapsing, the face of the visible Church is disfigured beyond recognition, especially through the great schism; and the radiance of the heavenly Jerusalem no longer breaks through the clouds to illumine God's earthly realm. Those realistic, often cynical spotlights on human existence, which have always accompanied the forms and

---

[2] *De summo bono sive de vita philosophi*, ed. Grabmann in: *Arch. Hist. doctr. litt.* MA VI (1932) (*Mittelalterliches Geistesleben*, II, pp. 200–204). As an Aristotelian, Boethius of Dacia can nevertheless feel an 'astonished admiration' of the 'first principle' and 'a love for it' and can find therein 'the highest delight' or bliss of man on earth.

[3] J. Huizinga, *The Waning of the Middle Ages*, E.T. London 1955.

images which transfigure and console—we mentioned at the beginning Archilochus, who repeatedly celebrates resurrections, or Martial, or many cynical and blasphemous wandering minstrels' songs—now take the upper hand in such a way that existence as a whole appears in the image of the dance of death. And just as Socrates and Boethius philosophised in the face of death, now numerous 'books of consolation' from Eckhart[4] to Peter of Blois, John of Dambach[5] and far beyond seek to interpret existence under the rubric of suffering.[6] But it is mostly classical, Stoic and mystical elements which predominate among the reasons for consolation, and only rarely do we find—as, e.g., in Catherine of Siena—that suffering enters so brilliant a Christian light that it can itself be understood as glory. And thus for the first time something is born in the Christian sphere which corresponds to the position of the Greek spirit in the age of tragedy, and the preconditions are created for the emergence of the sole tragedy to attain the metaphysical heights of antiquity during the Christian age: the tragedies of Shakespeare, above all his tragedies of kings.

In Thomas's ontology, the transcendental aesthetics of the classical period (which Dionysius sums up and passes on to Christian theology) achieves a state of balance: Being (*esse*), with which he is concerned and to which he attributes the modalities of the One, the True, the Good and the Beautiful, is the unlimited abundance of reality which is beyond all comprehension, as it, in its emergence from God, attains subsistence and self-possession within the finite entities. Where this balance is not maintained, then there are only two possible ways forward: either to formalise Being to the extent that it becomes the comprehensive concept of reason (which is the case with Scotus), and thus expressly or by

---

[4] In his 'Book of the divine consolation' for Queen Agnes of Hungary who was in mourning for her murdered father, Emperor Albrecht I of Habsburg.

[5] A. Auer, 'Johannes von Dambach und die Trostbücher vom 11. bis 16. Jahrhundert', in: *BGPhThMA*, 1928.

[6] A. Auer, *Leidenstheologie des Mittelalters*, Salzburg 1947; F. Maurer, *Leid*, 1951.

implication to concede to reason the oversight and control of Being. Being then necessarily becomes the category which is both highest and most devoid of meaning, whose syntheses with their ever more concrete forms can be rationally reconstructed or, as in the Idealism which prevails between Kant and Hegel, can be pre-constructed by reason. We see immediately that Being which is formalized to this extent can still just possess the inner modalities of unity, truth and goodness, but no longer that of transcendental beauty. For how should the divine and mysterious *pleroma* radiate from this empty space? Since Scotist formalism provides the model for the scientific thinking of our day, it is to be expected that the consciousness of any transcendental glory must be alien to it, and must become ever more alien.

The other way in which Being can be interpreted after Thomas is simply to identify it (once again) with God, as Meister Eckhart does, thus setting his stamp upon the conceptual model of late-medieval mysticism and to a large extent upon that of its spiritual descendants. Plotinus had avoided this identification and characterised the primal ground beyond Being as the Good. Dionysius followed him in this, but Erigena already inclined towards interpreting the God-world relation in terms of complication and explication, and for the school of Chartres, especially for Gilbert, God appeared as the form of Being which determines all else. This is the tradition which Eckhart continues, and Nicolas of Cusa will take up Erigena's scheme at the end of the medieval period. But if in the development of the Scotist model reason gains the upper hand over God, then in the logic of the Eckhartian model it is difficult to understand how there can exist a world outside God; and so the mystical self-annihilation of the creature must change sooner or later into a renewed appropriation of the Divine Being, which after Scotus and Eckhart now appears mainly in the form of spirit and freedom. Even in the medieval mystical tradition which follows Eckhart, the glory of the Absolute is called into question by the fact that it has little or no remaining space in which and through which it can become manifest. Both models turn into one another—as two forms of a pan-theism of the spirit or of reason—and form in their dialectical reciprocity the structure of philosophy between the medieval and the modern periods.

The high points of this whole period, which guaranteed it world-wide influence, justify its designation as the Germanic age. There are three great movements; Scotus and Eckhart (with their descendents: Ockham on the one hand, Tauler and Nicolas of Cusa on the other) determine both the scientific and the religious self-understanding of Europe. The thought of Suarez will follow that of Scotus, while Ignatius of Loyola, and later the *Grand Siècle*, belong to the family of German mysticism, and the points of origin for those elements of the latter which return to Germany through Tersteegen and Poiret still remain Germany and Brabant. The second movement is Luther and his age (to which in the broader sense Erasmus and Shakespeare belong). Itself standing on the shoulders of mysticism, the Reformation offers its own shoulders to the third intellectual event, that which extends from Kant to Hegel and Marx. If the Reformation shapes the religious spirit of England and America, then it is here that the spirit of Russia and the 'scientific' age as such are given their shape.

We can see from this list of names that the philosophical history of the age was very strongly influenced by Christians. Even if, in what follows, we do not treat the biblical and theological problematic as a theme in itself, it is nevertheless impossible to ignore the contribution made by spiritual Christians, even and precisely when these employ the conceptual language of their day in order to make themselves heard and to ensure their comprehensibility. The dynamic interrelationship of classical theo-philosophy and the Christian theology of revelation is indissoluble, because the transcendental claim of reason and the universal claim of revelation will always sit uneasily together. Thomas Aquinas himself brought both together in a bold paradox when he declared that it belongs to the nobility of human nature that we can attain perfection in our *desiderium naturale* for the very

Highest only through a free self-disclosure by God.[7] No matter how the interpretations of later Christian theology may have reduced this principle, the nexus which it contains will preoccupy the philosophy of the modern period and will dictate its decisions: this double inheritance, which is both Platonic and Christian, will not cease to fascinate the human mind.[8] In the late middle ages, 'mysticism' (which flows almost without interruption into humanism) functions as a universalising medium: it drives the divisive dogmatic formulas to a point where they become transparent, as we can observe in the dialogue which Ramon Lull and Nicolas of Cusa conduct with Islam and later in Sebasian Franck's understanding of religion. In an age which sees the hardening of confessional positions, Catholic consciousness responds to Protestantism not only with a dogmatic counter-position, but quite consciously with a world culture (the 'Baroque') which wills and knows itself in terms of universality—in a sense of geographical catholicity which, though undergoing colonial expansion, is still Augustinian. Finally, the Enlightenment and Idealism stripped Christianity of dogma to such an extent that nothing more can prevent its total absorption into a transcendental philosophy. And if from the very beginning (Augustine and his theory of predestination) and with Calvin, Bañez and Jansen, Christianity seems to have been given severe, anti-universal contours, then it is Protestant orthodoxy (in the dogmatics of Karl Barth) which has significantly and prophetically stepped beyond these limits today and has set Christianity face to face on this basis with the transcendental claim of reason and of Idealism (Schleiermacher).[9] It is precisely in Barth's dogmatics that (despite all the protestations to the contrary) a feeling for 'glory' emerges in a new and elemental way.

[7] S. Th. II I, 5, 5 ad 2.

[8] Cf. my 'Geschichte und Integration', in: Das Ganze im Fragment (1963), pp. 201–215 (Eng. trans., Man in History, 1968).

[9] Cf. my Karl Barth (2nd edn. 1962), esp. pp. 181–259, also 'Christlicher Universalismus' (Origen and Karl Barth), in: Verbum Caro (1960), pp. 260–275.

b. Being as a Concept

SCOTUS, OCKHAM

The decision of DUNS SCOTUS to conceive of being as a concept springs from his concern for the formal object of philosophy in the face of Christian theology. If reason grasps Being alone as its first unlimited concept, then every anticipation of the self-revelation of the sovereign and free God is excluded. In this concept therefore reason transcends the distinction between finite and infinite Being, and thus becomes capable of attaining a natural knowledge of God and is not entirely unprepared for the Word which the free God utters. The concept has not only logical (expressive) universality, but also metaphysical universality, for it captures Being in its objective and all-comprehending ('catholic') generality, so that it can be univocally applied to infinite and to finite Being, that is to God and the world, to substance and accidents, to act and potentiality. That is its indistinction (*indifferential*),[1] which does not of course refer to the concrete reality of the oppositions which occur within it/them (where analogy holds), but to the objective content of the concept, to the 'essentiality' of Being, which as such pervades neutrally (*neuter*)[2] all its/their distinctions. 'Being' is therefore no longer reality, but the most comprehensive essentiality, 'ideality', the sole possibility of which is reality and which can on the one hand be infinite (God) and on the other finite (creature). 'Being' is therefore that which is wholly indeterminate, yet which can be determined by nothing other than itself. For Scotus, this paradox is the formal object of philosophy, which thus becomes capable from the very outset of achieving both too much and too little: too much, since in its concept of Being it raises itself above God and the world, comprehensively

---

[1] Works cited in the edition of Vivès, with the exception of the *Opus Oxoniense* which is quoted in the edition by Garcia (Quaracchi, 1912–14). *Qu. in Metaph.* 1.4 q 1 n. 6–7; *Op. Ox.* 1 d 3 1 3 a2 n. 14.

[2] *Op. Ox.* 1 d 3 q 2 a4 n. 6. That which exists is no longer neutral: *ibid.*, 1 d 8 q 3 a1 n. 11.

dominating the Absolute from the standpoint of a greater absolute, and too little, since reality, as insubstantiality, is silently eliminated in this realm of graded formalities and essences.[3] Even individuality is not determined by reality, but by a substantial 'this-ness' (*haecceitas*). Thus anything can be conceived of in this realm of essences with the removal of existence, and if existence is included in the concept of God, then this is so only as it were as the final consequence of his self-comprehending ideality. 'Who can fail to see that this position contains everything, in order through a form of speculation which is unmoderated by any *regula Fidei* (as in Hegel) to make the subsisting Spirit-God at the heart of the process of thinking (in contradiction to a *ratio* which univocally embraces Being ... and potentiality) into the ultimate determination of substance and finally, by Spirit's resolution, into "reality"?' (G. Siewerth).[4]

The assignment of Being as Being to the philosophers— apparently in accordance with their own wish and their tradition since Aristotle and Avicenna—is made by the Christian theologian, who hopes thereby to make space for the revelation of the living God. Scotus believes that he can derive from the non-Christian history of philosophy the fact that the *a posteriori* proofs of God from contingency and movement can lead the spirit only to a 'First Principle' (Avicenna preferred to call this the *Primus*) within the nature of the world (*physis*),[5] the personality and freedom of which remain just as uncertain as do the immortality of the human soul and its future destiny of eternal bliss. In order to give the

---

[3] *Existentia non est per se ratio objecti ut scibile est. Quodlibet.* 7, 8–9. On this, cf. Jean Gilson, *Jean Duns Scot* (the basic study today), 1952, pp. 451– 466.

[4] *Das Schicksal der Metaphysik von Thomas zu Heidegger* (1959), p. 97. On the self-determination of God to existence in the Scotist François de Mayronnes, cf. E. Gilson, *La philosophie au Moyen Age* (2nd edn. 1952), pp. 610–611, ET *History of Christian Philosophy in the Middle Ages* (1955), pp. 466–467.

[5] This drastic reduction of the scope of philosophic proofs of God, everywhere present in Scotus, is carried out in the *Theoremata* (Vivès edn., Vol. 3), whether this is by Scotus (Balic) or not (Gilson). This criticism of philosophy will soon be radicalised by Ockham.

philosopher access to metaphysical transcendentality, Scotus consigns to him the neutral essence, which encompasses God within itself, as the formal object of philosophy, and he does so knowing full well, of course, that even this will fail to overcome his uncertainties, while not suspecting that philosophy, on the basis of this newly acquired area of 'ideality' and its essential 'necessities', will once again (as with the Averroists) outstrip theology. For theology's object is God's most free salvific words and deeds, and faith in these is its foundation. For Scotus, it is an essentially practical science[6] which offers mankind the help we need in order, first, to be able to pursue our supernatural calling and, second, to assist our reason, scarred by original sin, in the acquisition of a knowledge of God which is also in philosophical terms more precise. In a reawakening of the Augustinian tradition,[7] the distinction between what the philosophers call 'God' (τὸ θεῖον, le Dieu des philosophes) and what Christians know through faith as the living God of the Bible, is perceived during the late Middle Ages as a yawning gulf, but with a new anti-philosophical emotion which opposes to the 'necessities' of the philosophical enquiry into existence the sovereign and arbitrary freedom of the living God, which entirely counters any deduction of Creation from God (through the Platonic ideas). Thus the following tragic situation develops: at the very same moment that the distinctively Christian glory of God would have been ready to emerge (freed from the religious aesthetics of antiquity), it is deprived of the medium by means of which it could have been manifested. Since on the one hand philosophy is assigned to an undifferentiated and neutral sphere of 'existence' and the vision of God through the medium of the Creation in its actuality (Rom 1.18f.) is obscured and cast into doubt and, since on the other hand, as a consequence of this, the contemplative component of theology is relinquished in favour of one which is wholly practical and *gnosis* yields

---

[6] This is set forth in detail by the Prologue to the *Op. Ox.*, also the Prologue to the newly-edited *Lectura in 1. Sent.*, critical edition Vol. 16 (1960), Pars 4 (pp. 45–62).

[7] Gilson, op. cit., pp. 617–620.

to pure *pistis*: therefore, although the 'sovereign' (*Herrschaftliche*)[8] dimension becomes manifest in the divine revelations for the theology of this time, a dimension that contains its own rationality within its sovereign and arbitrary will, because (as for Anselm) the *rectitudo* resides within the will of God, still the element of glory (*Herrliche*), the δό-ξα, does not truly become manifest; neither philosophical reason in its contemplation of existence nor theological faith in its practical, ethical and non-aesthetic orientation can any longer possess a sensorium for this. The philosopher, to whom the field of 'Being' is yielded, advances towards the ultimate principles—neutral to God and to the world—without ever glimpsing theological glory. He is empowered to approach them as reason, and they stand as 'intentions' before his eyes: and thus William of Alnwick (+1332) will be the first in his *Quaestiones de esse intelligibili*[9] to develop from every angle the question with regard to the mode of reality which pertains to the intentional.

WILLIAM OF OCKHAM, who was Scotus' confrère and compatriot as well as his most acute opponent, does no more than draw possible conclusions from the *esse univocum*. For if undifferentiated Being defines itself in its ultimate differentiations as *haecceitates*, why should we then not conceive of it from this pole as the utterly specific 'this' and view the determinative grades of the class and species as purely subjective schemes of classification, which point confusedly to what is individual and real? It is this alone which encounters sense experience, which—in the English empiricist tradition up to and including Locke and Hume[10]—constitutes the whole content of reality and presents it to thought. Thus it is the specific indivisible entity which is real, and in this 'specificity' there lies once again the univocity of Being, whose ground is only the possibility of being

---

[8] *Ibid.*, p. 599.

[9] Ed. A. Ledoux, Quaracchi 1937.

[10] Indeed, up to Berkeley, since God is powerful enough to permit the subjective immediate experience to persist even where its object had vanished: *ipsa re destructa potest poni ipsa notitia intuitiva* (quoted following Gilson, op. cit., p. 654).

posited specifically by the infinite power of God's freedom. This possibility of the specific individual entity which occurs directly through the freedom of God is an intensification of the divine sovereignty which goes beyond Scotus and which gives a theological basis to positivism, which refuses to ask questions that go beyond the mere givenness of what is. This formidable Franciscan creates space even more radically for the sole sovereignty of God when, sweeping away the entire Platonic and Aristotelian tradition, he directly opposes to the yawning abyss of absolute freedom a world which is fragmented into irrational points of reality. With this rupture within the tradition of a mediating or natural (philosophical) theology, every contemplative dimension of the *fides quaerens intellectum* is in principle removed. Theology, which now closes itself in upon itself, must become fideistic and can ultimately be only practical. And the Franciscan image of God—love beyond the limits of knowledge—must therefore degenerate into an image of fear (which is no longer even that of the Old Testament), since this God of pure freedom might always posit and demand what is contrary; for instance, that man should hate him (Robert Holkot), that the innocent should be damned and the guilty saved (Ockham), and why should he not be able to destroy the world in such a way that it would never have existed (Jean de Mirecourt)? And, of course, the late Augustinianism of double predestination makes its appearance here with renewed virulence (Gregory of Rimini); from here, it will be bequeathed to the Reformers.

We will ask in the following chapter how the central Christian experience could be represented in this philosophical atmosphere. Initially, it is evident only that this experience remains without the mediation to philosophy (in so far as radical empiricism can still be given this name), and to such a degree in fact that an entirely different logic is demanded for the mysteries of faith than for secular thinking (Holkot). The conceptual space between sensualism and formal logicism is the birth-place, devoid of metaphysics, of the modern 'natural sciences'. Following the removal of Aristotelian substance and of all causality, apart from that which relies upon immediate experience, and indeed explicitly of all hierarchies of values in the universe, which leads logically to a Democratic atomism, Nicolas of Autrecourt begins to investigate the laws of spatial movement, and is followed by John Buridan, Albert of Saxony, Nicolas of Oresme, from whom Copernicus and Galileo are directly descended. We cannot pursue these paths here, but should note how trenchantly positions are held only fifty years after the death of Thomas: how small the steps are, and how internally consistent, from an ontological formalism (Scotus) to empiricism (Ockham), and from pure theological voluntarism and 'positionism' to a positivism which possesses no values, and from there, quite consistently, to materialistic atomism. Along these pathways, nothing new has appeared down to the present time.

c. Being as Neutrality

SUAREZ

There is a direct line of descent from Scotus—despite the Renaissance—to Francesco Suarez, the father of Baroque- and Neo-scholasticism, for in this disciple of Ignatius Loyola the univocity of Being and thus the indistinction (*indifferentia*) of Being emerges anew. As it is here that the philosophical openness of the finite spirit to God is sought, and as indistinction is an Ignatian and indeed a basic Christian concept, this confrontation must prove illuminating.

What Ignatius will call *indiferencia* is nothing other than the 'detachment' of the German mystics and the *amici Dei*, which they themselves understood to be a serious commitment, involving the whole person, to the Franciscan ideal of poverty. Francis himself had seen 'wisdom, poverty and love' as one: the ascetic transcendence of all psycho-physical possession into a free receptivity to the love of God alone. We meet this too in Benedict as humility, in Augustine as the pure *desiderium* for the *caritas* of God, and in the early Church Fathers it bears the Stoic and Neoplatonic name of *apatheia*, which points back to pre-Christian forms of spiritual transcendence. Nor should we forget here that behind the constraining systematisations of the Stoa there stand Virgil and the Tragedians with their self-transcendence through suffering into their incomprehensible God-given fate, and behind these too, there is the Odyssey, whose hero conquers through his patience that bears everything.

Thus the pre-Christian *indifferentia* as the decisive proof of man's nature as spirit hovers between two poles: between blind faith in God, the courage of the heart, blind hope (chiefly in the poets) and a certain rationalised technique of withdrawal from all that is (in order not to be attached to anything), the self-projection into transcendence, the mastering of fate and ultimately even the mastering of the gods (chiefly in the philosophers). But in this indeterminacy we always find an exaltation of the heart, of the whole person, in the unity of thought and life. In the Christian world, this fundamental attitude is illumined by the love of God which breaks forth from the depths in the form of the πραῢς καὶ ταπεινός (Mt 11.29), who proclaims the 'poor in spirit' and the πραεῖς to be blessed (Mt 5.3, 5), always does the will of the Father and goes to his death into the incomprehensible darkness of God. Transcendence as a going beyond the self clearly becomes the yielding of the self (faith, hope, love) to the unfathomability of divine love. The technique of *apatheia* in antiquity for self-salvation from the world becomes, in the Christian age, the ascetic expansion of the heart and its preparation in order that it should flow into an unlimited readiness to love (*ecce ancilla*) and ultimately into God's ever greater glory of love in the Cross, which we encounter through grace: ad *majorem Dei Gloriam*. From Augustine *via* Benedict to Francis and Ignatius, this remains the primal truth which, though unchanging in its essence, is constantly illumined in new ways. Nor can it stand indifferently beside metaphysics with the latter's question as to the transcendence of reason; rather, it casts light on this very question and clarifies it from its own ultimate sublimity. But what is rejected in any case is the overpowering of God, either by a conceptual pre-apprehension of the mind or by mystical and ascetical technique. What is adopted in any case is the open acceptance of our fate, in daring and in trust, and this is so to such an extent that 'grace' does not destroy 'nature' here (only that *gnosis* which replaces daring trust with manipulative knowledge is destroyed: 1 Cor 13.9; 2 Cor 10.5); rather, the attitude of open acceptance is made both divine and eternal ('then there remain these three . . .': 1 Cor 13.13).

We must therefore ask in what ways the charisms of the founders of the great religious orders achieved philosophical expression. The charismatic *indifferentia* has rarely been immediately reflected in its philosophical counterpart, and so philosophical transcendence has rarely been the true initiation into the encounter with the glory of God. Not the least reason for this was the fact that intersubjectivity, upon which the ethics of the Gospel is based, failed to find an adequate philosophical foundation in the classical period, and even today has yet to become the principal theme of Christian philosophy. Accordingly, it is a largely Neoplatonic (and therefore undialogical) metaphysics which provides the conceptual underpinning for the Augustinian theology of *caritas*, to which the Benedictine theology of *caritas* (in Bernard and his school) also looks back. On the other hand, that which is originally Franciscan in Bonaventure is interpreted with reference to Augustine and Pseudo-Dionysius, the Dominican charism (which is difficult to grasp) is referred back to Aristotle and, in the case of Eckhart, to Parmenides, and what is originally Ignatian in Suarez turns back to Scotus, so that there is no inherent unity between his philosophy and his commentary on the Exercises. Thus in historical terms Christian thought is not commensurate with the forms of Christian inspiration, nor does it seek to keep pace with it, but is content rather to cut a paltry coat for it from the huge store of material of extant thought. Neoscholasticism, to which period the contribution of Ignatius belongs, was particularly burdened by the weight of prior thinking, of what was apparently already contained in the treasury of tradition, so that the original Ignatian vision of *Divina Majestas* and *Gloria* was no longer able to create any original mode of conceptual expression.

SUAREZ[1] has recourse to the Scotist notion of 'univocal being',

---

[1] *Disputationes Metaphysicae* (*Opera*, ed. Vivès 1866, 1866, Vols. 25–26).

the *ens ut sic,* which as the simplest and most universal concept
(*conceptus simplicissimus*)[2] is the precise object of metaphysical
enquiry. This concept *habet unam simplicem rationem formalem
adaequatam*[3] in itself, which, as 'abstracted' (*praecisa*) though
'real'[4] (*ratio quasi actualis*),[5] returns in all its logical *inferiora,*
to whose level we 'descend' (*descenditur*)[6] in order to be able
to conceive of individuality. If we wished to relinquish this
univocal, all-embracing notion for the sake of an unassailable
analogia entis, then all the clarity and the certainty of
metaphysics would be threatened, 'and so we ought not to
deny the unity of the concept in order to defend the analogy;
rather, if we had to relinquish one or other of them, then this
would be analogy, which is uncertain, and not the unity of
the concept, which is based on certain and demonstrable
grounds'.[7] This real concept 'must embrace God' (*debere
comprendere Deum*), as well as the angels and all material
substances and accidents.[8] A metaphysics which has
knowledge of Being as a whole 'includes God in the sphere
of its object' (*ut sub objecto suo Deum complectatur*),[9] and it can
develop *a priori* the dimensions of Being as such (unity, truth,
goodness) without direct reference to the *inferiora* (God and
the world),[10] between which, for the first time, analogy and
the principle of causality prevail. And yet God is the purest
realisation of 'real Being' and thus the precise (material) object
of metaphysics, its *objectum primarium ac principale,*[11] whereby
of course Scotus' endeavours to constrain metaphysics and to
set its limits with respect to theology, are lost sight of, and
the vigorous attempts of the nominalists to create room for
God's freedom are forgotten. Or rather: because the

---

[2] *Disp.* 2 sect. 2 nr. 9.
[3] *Ibid.* n. 11.
[4] I, I, 26.
[5] I, 2, 12.
[6] 2, I, 12.
[7] 2, 2, 36.
[8] I, I, 26; *cf.* I, I, 19.
[9] I, I, 19.
[10] I, I, 28; thus also *Disp.* 3.
[11] I, I, 19.

nominalistic reduction of reality to one plane, whether in terms of concepts (*conceptus*) or of sense experience (*experientia*), has abandoned the totality of actual reality between God and the world, Baroque Neoscholasticism can apparently recreate this by means of a constructive conceptualism. But once freed from the external theological discipline of faith and of the schools, what Suarez pursues with the complete naivety of the schoolman, becomes (as Gustav Siewerth has shown in his fierce analyses)[12] the direct foundation for modern metaphysics from Descartes, Spinoza and Leibniz to Kant and Hegel. At the same time, it will unchangingly dominate the clerical activity of philosophical and theological Neoscholasticism (that is to say, beyond Hegel and the collapse of constructive Idealism); this shows clearly that the *de facto* occurrence of the scholasticism of the schools continues to confirm Suarez's naive point of departure, whether or not the latter is formally taught.

The conjunction of the opening of the heart's most inward idea of God within the biblical sphere and Greek, metaphysical speculation on the Θεῖον and the Πᾶν, this conjunction in which speculation apparently gains the academic qualifications to know *about* God, his essence, his thinking and his acting within the Creation, salvation and perfection (in faith), to receive Being laid bare to its depths and to manipulate it in these depths by conceptual means, with the support of an immense body of tradition which is composed of what has been 'worked out' partly dogmatically and partly in the schools, and has been already objectively thought (and which therefore is not to be thought through afresh): this conjunction stands behind metaphysics as it exists in the modern period both in the Church and beyond. A symptomatic expression of this was the controversy over grace between the school of Bañez and the Molinists, the pitiful controversy *De Auxiliis*, in which the young Society of Jesus allowed itself to become entangled and the very problematic of which presupposes that the theological metaphysician can peer from above into the interaction of

[12] *Das Schicksal der Metaphysik von Thomas zu Heidegger* (1959).

the *Causa Prima* with the *causa secunda*, and that its precise, formal expressions and distinctions can be reduced to a single order of absolute validity. This is in essence the claim of the ancient Gnosis, and it is not so surprising therefore that at the outset of the Counter-Reformation the Augustinian General, Cardinal Giles of Viterbo, should have attempted in his 'Schechina' to renew the *Speculatio Majestatis* of the Kabbala and to transform it along Christian lines.[13] The Neoscholastic closed circle is virtually unbreakable: since the biblical revelation of God's depths, which the one who possesses the Spirit 'searches' together with the Holy Spirit (1 Cor 2.10–12), apparently invites us to bypass the philosophical mystery of Being, and since, with the disappearance of the sense of philosophical mystery, the sense of theological mystery also dissolves, and this, according to the axiom *gratia supponit, non destruit, elevat naturam*, ought to be an intensified and deepened feeling for the mystery of glory. But the clerical and Neoscholastic methods of instruction with their apologetic all-knowingness no longer convey any sense of this feeling, and they have a corresponding effect upon the preaching and the instruction of the Church, if not indeed on the prayer-life and contemplation even of those Christians to whose attitude this kind of enlightenment stands in stark and insurmountable contradiction. Whereas during the early Middle Ages, up to about the time of Bonaventure, theology and (objective) mysticism were indivisible—something to which Augustine and Dionysius, Gregory the Great and Erigena, the Cistercians and the Victorines, the Joachimites and the Spiritual Franciscans well attest—the 'mystic' is now identified increasingly in terms of his subjective experience of glory and is stamped as an exception, while the 'rule' is represented by the strictly logical and intellectualist metaphysics of the Church. Those who are concerned to restore the lost unity (Gerson, Nicolas of Cusa, Petavius, Gerbert, etc.) remain outsiders and often pursue paths which lead to speculative Idealism. What is characteristic here is that in Neoscholasticism, when the feeling for the glory of God was

[13] Ed. by F. Secret in: *Edizione Nazionale dei Classici del Pensiero Italiano* II 10–11, Rome 1959.

lost—that glory which pervades the Revelation as a whole but which is not perceived by conceptual rationalism, or concerning which it remains silent, or which it wholly removes by means of method—there perished also the sensorium for the glory of Creation (as 'aesthetics') which shone through the whole theology of the Fathers and of the Early and High Middle Ages. This sensorium passed pre-eminently to the poets and artists (from Dante to Petrarch, to Milton, Herder, Hölderlin, Keats . . .), but also to the great natural scientists (such as Kepler and Newton, the early Kant, Goethe, Carus, Fechner, Teilhard), whereby Neoscholasticism found itself doubly bereft and denuded.

The conceptualisation of Being in Scotus and Suarez annuls the experience of reality and encloses thought in a sphere which is characterised by bare, essential predications, by the play of the analysis and synthesis of concepts, and accordingly by the inner-subjective opposition of the act of thought (*noesis*) and the content of thought (*noema*). That bare, essential predication represents an irreducible contradiction, becomes clear once again in Suarez. Although Being as the highest category is the 'most perfect'[14] category, it is also the one which is most hollow, because it excludes its own determinations, which all nevertheless belong to and are Being, so that this category is filled only through contraction to the level of the singular.[15] Within this contradictory space, which Suarez—following Scotus[16]—calls 'real', reason plays its game of juxtaposing concepts in statements before resolving them again into other, homogeneous concepts. For Suarez, as for Scotus, the word 'real' denotes that which is compossible, realisable, not that which is actual, for which only the *positio extra causas* remains, though this can no longer be the object of thought, because the essence as the 'real' within comprehensive Being has already been thoroughly individualised. This is the case unless, of course, we conceive of comprehensive Being (as a concept!) as reality, which

[14] I, I, 30.

[15] From this point of view, all-embracing Being is *minus perfectum* than that which is specific: *ibid.*

[16] 2, 4, 14.

would mean, however, that all that is possible is actual. But it is evident that this cannot be said, and thus actuality remains excluded from 'reality' as something which has no place and which cannot be thought. Or if it is comprehensive Being which is reality, and existence as that which is possible is constituted by its 'being ordered to Being' (*ordo ad esse*), then it will be constituted beyond God (and thus *vis-à-vis* him) in the sphere of comprehensive Being,[17] whereby the formal precondition for 'Molinism' emerges, in which the creature attains an ultimate particularity and freedom which is independent of the will of God.

On the other hand, the concept of Being belongs to the subject; the latter stands in opposition to the former—and to all the concepts which inhere in the former—as to that which is conceived. For Suarez these do indeed 'represent' the so-called 'external world', but these concepts, which are 'abstracted' 'intentions', are understood to be objectified representations of 'things'. It is a short step from here to Descartes and Kant; less than that even, for here the Copernican revolution has already taken place, viz. the turning from Being to mental concepts, from things (and God) existing *in themselves* to things conceived as existing 'for me' and 'from me'. From now on, the subject can regard itself as legislative reason. In an original synthesis, it pronounces judgment *a priori* in its luminous space over the initial concept of Being, which it has been given and which lies open to its comprehension, to which judgment other *a priori* and *a posteriori* judgments attach themselves. And it can assure itself of the correctness of this judgment through reflection upon itself in its action (*cogito*), and then either seek the ultimate certainty in that kind of reason whose postulates are archetypal, in which it participates and which is God (Descartes), or understand this participation as an ultimate identity of the finite with the infinite subject and, in conjunction with it, project and creatively produce possible real essences (*concipere*): statically (as in Spinoza) or dynamically (as in Leibniz and Fichte), or both together (as

---

[17] 31, 4, 5. Siewerth, *op. cit.*, p. 179, and even more sharply on p. 186.

in Hegel). Beyond the realm of these projected essences, there remain at best those pure, irrational postulations *extra causas*, those positions which Ockhamism understood to be worthless atomic points of reality, and which in their lack of depth and their indivisibility already for Ockhamism are left over as pure matter: as matter which for Suarez is no longer (Aristotelian-Thomist) pure potency with respect to the act of form, but now appears—though colourless and actionless—to be constituted as actual Being. These are that 'passive mass', which appears in Descartes as *res extensa*, and which is the sole representative and last remnant of the external world and of the *Ding an sich*, the substratum of the 'classical physics', which in materialism (where the unreality of the conceptual realm which is constituted by the subject is perceived) must be raised to the level of the one sole reality which supports all things, even spirit and God. This *res extensa* is the pure quantitative element, the unlimited empire of numbers, and it is here that the metaphysical origins lie for the ideal of mastering the whole of the external world through numerical calculations. An ideal of this kind could never have arisen if the whole of reality had not already been stripped of its living depths and spontaneity, its own truth, goodness and beauty, and had thus been set in unmediated contradiction to the *res cogitans*. The foundations of our 'modern' materialism were laid long ago in the intellectual history of our Western, Christian tradition.

Besides the logical and conceptual apprehension of Being, there has existed since the death of Thomas another parallel strain, which achieved its greatest impact during the Germanic age: the position that Being is God. Having developed initially in independence from the logical and conceptual thread, it soon becomes intertwined with the latter, and thus possesses its own history in this limited form up to the time of Hegel.

d. Being as God

ECKHART

Eckhart, thanks to his disciples Suso and Tauler and their

innumerable successors, has become a father of modern
intellectual history and spirituality. He is further confirmation
of what the Origen-Evagrius case proved in the history of
the early Church: ecclesiastical condemnations of individual
extremist propositions from the writings of creative minds,
even their proscription for posterity, do not prevent them
bearing thousandfold fruit. They leave their mark on ideas
which, consciously or unconsciously, esoterically or openly,
have a determining influence on later thinkers in their most
fundamental stances. Eckhart's case has also perhaps a personal
resemblance to Origen's: an originally very pure Christian
piety clothes itself in an unsuitable garment that ill fits the
body. Origen expresses Christianity in Gnostic-Hellenistic
categories. Eckhart has to (and therefore wants to) translate a
very pure Christian experience of God in the technical
language of traditional and contemporary Scholastic
philosophy. No more than Origen is he an original
philosopher like his confrère Thomas. He treats the great mass
of philosophical speculation inherited from the past—
Platonic, Aristotelian, Arabic, Patristic, Thomistic—in the
way the Christians of Rome used the ruined temples of their
city: as quarries.

So we have to divest Eckhart's wholly limpid and
shadowless experience of God of its conceptual and verbal
attire. It is an experience that is authentically Christian, even
in its most daring conceptions, but it clothes itself in garments
of the past and, thus disguised, bequeaths to the future a
legacy with consequences almost beyond measure: Luther, but
also Nicolas of Cusa, Spinoza, Böhme, Kant, Fichte,
Schelling, and Hegel. Emphasising this in no way implies that
Eckhart was 'really' a pantheistic Idealist or a Protestant with
a forensic doctrine or justification. However, ideas have their
own historical dynamic; they are governed by and obey their
own laws, regardless of the meaning they had for their
originator. In calling God 'Being', Eckhart performed an act
of absolute religious devotion. He availed himself of a
language, rooted in antiquity, which Augustine and Boethius,
Erigena and Gilbert, had used with impunity. But he applied
it directly to God and the creature's immediate dependence

on God[1] in such a way that the derivation of a reality of being from God seemed to him like God's coming to being, as being's coming out of God. The assertion 'God is being' runs through virtually all his works, and the Thomistic mediation of the non-subsistent *actus essendi* is lost from sight. That loss has a spiritual cause. What Eckhart seeks is the total transference of all being, all unity, truth, goodness and glory to the one and only God, loved and worshipped above all things. Nothing that can be said and thought about God is too great, too bold, too unconditional: *id quo majus cogitari non potest*.[2]

The source is an experience of glory, which unfolds into four propositions and thus defines Eckhart's theological aesthetic:

1. God is beyond everything explicable by finality (the good) and propositions (the true). He is 'the Whyless'. The only thing worthy of God and appropriate to Him is what takes place 'whylessly' as a free act of homage. Shining through the face of things is an unquestionable and unfathomable mystery. 'The rose is without why; it blooms because it blooms'.[3] The words are those of Angelus Silesius, who had the profoundest understanding of Eckhart. He also expresses the other aspect of the truth: this 'whylessness' of the rose points to that first principle which is God:

[1] *Non enim ipsum esse et quae cum ipso convertibiliter idem sunt* [the transcendentals] *superveniunt rebus tamquam posteriora, sed sunt priora omnibus in rebus. Ipsum enim esse non accipit quot sit in aliquo nec ab aliquo nec per aliquid, nec advenit nec supervenit alicui, sed praevenit et prius est omnium. Propter quod esse omnium est immediate a causa prima* (Prol. gen. op. trip.; L I 153). Our citations are from the critical edition: Latin works = L, German works = G, then volume and page number; n = marginal numbers; S = Sermons; D = Instructive Discources; C = Book of Divine Consolation; N = Of the Nobleman. For supplementary material: Joseph Quint, *M. E. Deutsche Predigten und Traktate* (Hanser, Munich, 1955) = Q; F. Pfeiffer, *M. E.* (1957) = Pf.

[2] *Prol. gen.* (Amplon) L I 38, 41; *Tab. prol.* L I 129; *Prol. gen.* L I 156f.; *Prol. op. propos.* L I 166f., ibid., 181; *In Exod.* 3 n. 16, L II 21f.; *In Sap.* 5 n. 55, II 382; *Serm.* 6 n. 53: *Deus communis est: omne ens et omnium esse ipse est:* L IV 51. *In Exod.* 3 n. 21: *Omnis perfectio eget ipso, qui est ipsum esse . . . modus est ipsius esse, ipsi innititur, ipsi inhaeret:* L II 28; ibid., 15 n. 29: *Deus autem esse est et solus dat esse immediate omnibus:* L II 34; cf n. 177 152; S 3 G I 55–56.

[3] *Wandersmann* I 289.

> The rose which here thine outer eye doth see
> Hath bloomed in God eternally.[4]

Eckhart himself speaks thus: 'In the Beloved, Love contemplates not How and Why, but purely and simply the spotless essential form. Thus the Holy Spirit is the Love between Father and Son, a pure and generous outflow, beyond efficient and final cause.'[5] The ultimate whylessness of love, of freedom, but also of thought and form: this is the root of Eckhart's strange statements about the 'uncreatedness' of the latter in the creature.[6]

2. This whylessness is perceived in the wonder of eternal being, its being always now, its fontal character (*fontalitas*),[7] the fact that it is unceasingly occurring and disclosing itself. Eckhart identifies this with God's eternal birth from God, the perpetual now of the Son's generation from the Father: *semper nascitur*.[8] When that birth takes place for me and in me, when I am born with the Son from the Father, then God is born for me as well.

3. What this comes down to is that being a Christian means simply, unresistingly, letting God be born, letting God happen. Eckhart calls this pure *fiat* the *passivum*, which is the very heart of the glorification of God. *passivum generaliter est laus, honor, gloria sui essentialis activi . . ., passivum enim . . . clamat et testatur in omni et ex omni sui perfectione et bono suimet egestatem et miseriam, activi vero sui superioris praedicat divitias et misericordiam.* The glorifier must not, therefore, take up the Glorified into himself as if he were trying to keep and possess Him for himself. No, it all has to be *quasi in transitu*, an endurance, and not a permanent possession acquired by endurance. So it does not belong to the glorifier, but comes from the Other and is in the Other, to whom all honour and glory are due, for that is proper to Him. 'For example, an

---

[4] *Ibid.*, I 108.

[5] *In Eccli.* 24 n. 8, L II 237.

[6] *In Sap.* I n. 22, L II 343; Quaestio Utrum laus Dei etc. n. 11; *arca in mente non est creabilis* L V 60; *Serm.* 29 n. 301: *intelligere est increabile* L IV 268/.

[7] *In Sap.* I n. 38, L II 359.

[8] *In Joh.* I n. 8, L III 9.

expensive coat that servant wears when he attends his master does not give honour to the servant but to the master.'[9]

4. Man is meant, then, to be built up beyond himself in God. His course is a flowing stream, like the flowing essence of God and His grace: *Gnade enist niht ein blîbende dinc, si ist allez in eime gewerdenne.*[10] According to Paul, in the glorifying vision, we are transformed by the Spirit of the Lord into God's glory. Now 'it is said of the first of the just, of the Son of God, that He is the reflection of God's glory and bears the very stamp of His nature (Heb. 1.3), and this what we want to say: namely, that the virtues, justice and so on are unceasingly occurring assimilations rather than something with a fixed form, entrenched and rooted in the virtuous person. They are in a state of permanent becoming like gleams of light in ether and reflections in a mirror'.[11] Thus the whole of the life of faith is a movement towards divine sonship: *est ergo credere et fides quasi motus et fieri ad esse filium.*[12]

These four fundamental themes place Eckhart in a line with Benedict, Francis, and Ignatius: they signify a life of total disappearance, pure transparency to the ever greater glory of God. There can be no doubt that this and this alone is what Eckhart, as preacher, philosopher, theologian, and poet, with all the conceptual and linguistic means at his disposal, was trying to say. And since this was his one intent, he could treat all forms of expression with a sovereign freedom. He melted down the philosophy of every thinker and recast it into the central theological mystery of the divine birth. Appealing to Augustine's use of Scripture in the last three books of the *Confessions*, he was able to relate dynamically each and every Biblical text to the one mystery, from the same passage opening up very different perspectives on the one thing needful. In particular, he could and had to deepen

[9] *Lib. parab. Gen.* 1 n. 25, L I 495–496.

[10] *Sprüche* 6 (Pf 599).

[11] *In Sap.* 1 n. 45, L II 368. The major aesthetic text in Paul (2 Cor 3.18) is cited by Eckhart with predilection: *cf. In Joh.* n. 106, L III 91; *ibid.*, n. 119, L III 104; *ibid.*, n. 155, L III 128; B 2 G V 32.

[12] *In Joh.* 1 n. 158, L III 131.

his interpretation of the Genesis creation narrative by connecting it with the prologue of St John's gospel: the eternal generation of the Word is the ground and goal of all creation and gives it its form and measure. He was well aware that treating the Word of God in this way had something poetic about it. But everything that the infinite God wants to express about Himself is *sensus litteralis*; God, says Augustine, 'has made Scripture so fruitful that everything the mind can elicit from it He has seeded and sealed therein'. 'Plato himself and all the ancient poet-theologians (*sive theologizantes sive poematizantes*) used to teach about God, nature, and ethics by means of imagery, for the poets never wrote fables without meaning.'[13] But all philosophy becomes a parable, which, once detached from the context of a doctrinal system, points to the mystery.[14]

The mystery is the mystery of absolute love, the Love that created the world out of love[15] in order to shine resplendent in it. For the man who has received God into his innermost soul, 'all things taste of God, and God's image can be seen in all things; for him God is gleaming (*blinket*) all the time.[16] God shines (*liuhtet*) as brightly in worldly things as in the most divine.[17] At all times and in all circumstances God is aglow (*liuhtet*).[18] 'Man should grasp God in all things'.[19] He need not, therefore, flee the world; he has only to 'learn inner solitude . . . to break through things to reach his God *in them*'.[20] Just as the thirsty man has the constant thought of drink in mind, so the man who loves God constantly thinks of God. However, he must not make do with a 'thought

[13] *Lip. parab. Gen. Prol.* L I 450–451. Reference to the last books of the *Confessions: Prol. in opus Expos.* II, L II 321.

[14] *Cf.* Vladimir Lossky, *Théologie négative et connaissance de Dieu chez Maître Eckhart* (1968), p. 125. Lossky's great study is now the most accurate and unbiased analysis of Eckhart's thought.

[15] *Creaturae productae amore: Lib. parab. Gen.* n. 45, L I 125.

[16] D 6, G V 205.

[17] D 7, G V 210.

[18] D 21, G V 276.

[19] D 6, G V 203.

[20] D 6, G V 207.

God'.[21] Instead he must so humble and impoverish himself before God that the true and living God fills all the space within him.[22] God is nearest of all to us, but near through His loving will, and so it is only he who seeks and does God's will who dwells in God.[23] He is to seek 'only the most precious will of God and nothing else; whatever God then sends him, let him immediately accept and deem his best possession and be fully and completely contented with it'.[24] Transparent, pure obedience is 'being of one will with God, so that one wills all that God wills'.[25] Obedience is the 'virtue above all virtues' and the one perfect work that gives all other works their worth and fruitfulness.[26] It is 'the pure way to return to God'[27] and, at the same time, 'the true and best penance of all',[28] a perpetual attitude of confession before God, laying bare all that is one's own, offering it, handing it over.[29] It is the surrender of all finite images, exterior and interior, which as acquired and defended possessions can be played off against God and prevalent a total and transcendental opening up of the heart. The heart should be pure wax in the hands of God:[30] then the whole man, existentially and in free self-realisation, actually is what as spirit he potentially is: *quodammodo omnia*, and therein *capax Dei*.[31] But just as the 'intellect is "nothing at all" in order to understand all',[32] and just as the eye must be free of all colour

[21] D 6, G V 205.

[22] 'The soul is more closely united to God than soul and body, which make up *one* human being' (D 20, G V 269). 'Man must in no sense ever regard himself as distant from God' (D 17, G V 249).

[23] 'For the man who surrenders himself to God and seeks with all diligence only His will, the best is whatever God gives him' (S 4 G I 61).

[24] D 22, G V 285.

[25] C 2, G V 22.

[26] D 1, G V 185–186.

[27] C 1, G V 12.

[28] D 16, G V 244.

[29] D 21, G V 275; *cf.* S 11, G I 185–186: 'Nothing should be hidden within us that we are not prepared to expose completely and hand over entirely to God.'

[30] C 2, G V 55.

[31] *Expos. Gen.* 1 n. 155, L I 270–271.

[32] *In Joh.* 1 n. 100, L III 86.

if it is to perceive all colours,[33] so must the lover of God be
calm and serenely surrendered (*gelassen*) if he is to make full
room for God in himself.

Eckhart's *Gelassenheit* is one of the most beautiful
illustrations of that unchanging Christian challenge of the
saints which in the last chapter was described as the necessary
condition of a Christian transcendental aesthetic. 'Whoever
wants to receive all things must also give away all things:
that is equitable trade and fair exchange.'[34] For 'the more we
have of our own, the less we own of Him'. That is why
poverty of spirit is the first of the Beatitudes in the Gospel.[35]
'The nobler things are, the more inclusive and universal they
are; love is noble because it is all-inclusive'.[36] In the form of
Gelassenheit, it is the organ of universal receptivity. All finite
things are only truly known and received when they are
accepted as the gift of the infinite Giver, who wants to give
Himself in them; yet only the person who is serenely
surrendered (*gelassen*) is capable of that.[37] Although he does
make reference to Seneca and Stoic indifference, Eckhart's
interpretation of them is completely Christian.[38] Indifference
'in adversity and prosperity, in sorrow and in joy',[39] means
having the same love for all that God decrees, and thus, with
the same love, deeply and gladly loving all men, who are of
equal dignity with me.[40] Paul was prepared to get every one
of his brethren into heaven at the price of his own
damnation.[41] 'So long as you love just one person less than
yourself, you are not truly loving yourself . . . In one man all
men; and this man is God and man.'[42] Even though he is not
constantly affirming it, it is self-evident for Eckhart that this

[33] *Ibid.*; according to Aristotle, *De an.* II (418 b 26). The image constantly
recurs in Eckhart. C 2, G V 28.

[34] D 23, G V 295.

[35] D 23, G V 97.

[36] S 4, G I 67.

[37] D 21, G V 278.

[38] C 2, G V 20; C 3, G V 60; N, G V 111.

[39] S 5a, G I 81; S 6, G I 102; S 11, G I 200.

[40] S 5a, G I 79.

[41] D 10, G V 223–224; C 2, G V 21; *ibid.*, 26; *ibid.*, 40; S 12, D I 195; *In
Exod.* 32 n. 270, L II 217.

[42] S 12, G I 195.

great love is only mediated through Christ; it is the love He had for us, the love He gave us through His Passion.[43] True renunciation is based 'upon the precious Passion of our Lord Jesus Christ, the perfect work of expiation; the more a man is conformed to it, the more all sins and punishments for sin fall from him. Moreover, the man must accustom himself to conform himself always, in all his actions, to the life and work of our Lord Jesus Christ, in all he does and consents to, all he endures and experiences. And in doing this, let him keep [Christ] before His eyes, just as He had us before His eyes.'[44] Suso and Tauler will recall the Passion more frequently and penetratingly, but they will add nothing new to what their Master had said before them. The indifferent person has handed himself over to God in everything, and so God takes over care and responsibility for him. To be in contact with him is to be in contact with God; God takes over his suffering, which comes to him only by way of God and in that way is transfigured by God.[45] Transfigured, for one no longer knows whether this suffering is bliss with God precisely because it is love, and one 'would be glad to suffer incessantly for love of God and of the good'. Or is this suffering a 'super-suffering', given infinite dimensions in God?[46] 'Since the Son of God could not suffer in His divinity and in eternity, the heavenly Father sent Him into time so that He could become man and capable of suffering'.[47] However it is experienced, 'only the sorrow that is suffering in God's will and from God's will is perfect sorrow.'[48] Eckhart thus

[43] D 12, G v 232.

[44] D 16, G V 246; cf. D 17, G V 249; D 18, G V 259.

[45] 'And so it is that God suffers before I suffer, and if I suffer for the sake of God, all my suffering easily becomes for me consolation and joy' (C 2, G V 52). 'Everything that the good man suffers for the sake of God he suffers in God, and God is with him, suffering in his suffering'. And then 'my suffering loses its sorrow, and my sorrow is in God, and my sorrow is God' (ibid., 53–54; cf. S 2, G I 36–37); 'The man . . . entrusted to God does not suffer. Were he though to suffer, the heart of God would be struck' (S 13, G I 214).

[46] C 2, G V 39.

[47] C 2, G V 48.

[48] C 2, G V 22.

completely transforms Indian/Greek/Arab *apatheia*: it is the opposite of a technique of preserving oneself from sorrow; it is not a question of pain or pleasure but of the total gift of oneself to eternal love.

And now indifference is seen in a Marian light: 'remaining maidenly and free, without any obstacle to supreme truth'. 'For a human being to conceive God in himself is good, and in that conceiving he is a virgin. But for God to become fruitful in him is better, for the only gratitude for a gift is to be fruitful with the gift. The spirit is a wife, in its gratitude giving birth in return, when it gives birth to Jesus once more in God's fatherly heart.'[49] 'As soon as Mary gave up her will, she immediately became the true Mother of the eternal Word and straightway conceived God.'[50] The more masculine the man is in giving and the more feminine the woman in conceiving, so the more perfectly successful are generation and birth. The more naked the spirit makes itself for receiving God, the better it conceives Him. This can be expressed in a philosophical analogy: 'Anaxagoras says that the intellect must be separated, unmixed, and naked if it is to be able to distinguish. Aristotle himself says that the intellect must be like an empty, that is, naked tablet. The greater the nakedness, the deeper the union. Therefore, the absolutely first act, which is being or form, rightly befits *prima materia*, since among all the powers of receptivity and acceptance it alone is utterly naked and pure.'[51] It is the nakedness of Paradise, a nakedness of which the spirit is not ashamed for it is the state in greatest conformity to its nature.[52] Again there is a philosophical analogy: 'Just as the thing seen exists for seeing and, *vice versa*, the seeing for the thing to be seen, the two coinciding in the act of seeing', just as, as a general rule, 'desire and the desired, active and passive, seek each other out',[53] so God and the ready soul come together in the 'kiss of his mouth' (Cant. 1.1). If, on the other hand, in the act of spiritual conception, we place obstacles, 'we do violence to God and kill Him'.[54]

[49] S 2, G I 26f.
[50] D 11, G V 226.
[51] *Lib. Parab. Gen.* 1 n. 32, L I 501.
[52] *Ibid.*, n. 124, L I 589.
[53] *In Joh.* 1 n. 177, L III 146.
[54] S 4, G I 74.

The doctrine of *Gelassenheit* attains its Christian completion in a Trinitarian context. The Marian womb receives the seed of the Father, and since the Father is eternally, at every moment, begetting the Son, the eternal procession of the Son takes place in the pure medium of receptivity. 'Were God to find man as poor as *this*, God would do His own work, and man would suffer God',[55] 'and the Father gives birth to His only-begotten Son as truly as in Himself . . . and [man's] spirit with the Father gives birth to the same only-begotten Son and to itself as the same Son and is the same Son in this light and is the truth'.[56] The mention of man's spirit shows that Eckhart remains aware that here the creature is caught up by grace into the inner life of the Trinity. But for Eckhart creation takes place for the sake of grace, nature at its summit touches supernature, createdness has its deepest and most secret roots in Uncreatedness and in the eternal procession of the Son, which happens now and at every moment and for ever. 'Where the Father gives birth to His Son in the innermost ground, there this human nature is suspended.'[57]

In God's birth in man rests the freedom that makes man at home in the Immemorial, the Absolute, the Unfathomable, in a depth from which, according to Eckhart, God Himself originates. The divine birth is the root of all ethics, for the act of giving oneself up totally in order to receive is *the* work *par excellence*, an interior, spiritual work that gives value to all exterior works and in fact takes the place of all exterior works, for it contains all fruitfulness in itself: 'this work is to love God . . . whereby all that the man with a pure and perfect will wants and would like to do in all good works is already done'.[58] True, the exterior work gives testimony to the interior,[59] but—here Eckhart is at odds with Aquinas and anticipates Luther—it 'adds in no way whatever to the goodness of the interior work'.[60] In God's begetting of

[55] Q 307.
[56] S 2, G I 41.
[57] S 5b, G I 87.
[58] C 2, G V 38.
[59] *In Joh.* n. 169, L III 139.
[60] C 2, G V 40.

Himself in the soul is also to be found every commandment:
the self-imprinting form as such bestows, in a process which
happens now and at every moment and for ever, the natural
law on the creature: 'Just as fire, by producing and
communicating its fiery form in the sufferer, imparts to him
all that goes with fire . . . so God, who in His perfection is
Being and Goodness and Kindness, imprints what is good,
imparting it, commanding it, moving and promoting and
inspiring it.'[61] The content of such an ethic is the ever-
greaterness[62] of self-dispossession: the disowning of all
'owning' (the fetter of self)[63], ever deeper poverty—the word
now receives its comprehensive spiritual and interior meaning:
letting go of self,[64] or even inadequacy, 'which God imposes
on his friends so they lose every support . . . and find their
support in Him alone.'[65] And 'the more complete and naked
this poverty, the more one possesses this possession': God.[66]
But man must let go even of this possession; he must 'for
God's sake let go of God'.[67] This means going out into the
'wilderness', like Yahweh's leading of His people into the
wilderness to wed her there (Hosea 2.14),[68] the wilderness
where 'the spirit has no more why'.[69] But, in imitation of
Christ, this way is a way that leads below—a *homo* of the
humus, humilis:[70] 'Whoever would receive from above must
of necessity be below in true humility'.[71] He must abide 'in

[61] *Lib. Parab. Gen.* 2 n. 87–88, L I 549f.

[62] Eckhart continually insists on the infinitude and unendingness of the
striving for an ever greater love, devotion, purity, availability. 'In this life
a man never lets go of himself so totally that he finds himself in the position
of not having to let himself go further' (D 4, G V 196). 'You never get to
the end of progress' (D 22, G V 290).

[63] D 10, G V 218; S 6, G I 102.

[64] D 3, G V 194.

[65] D 19, G V 260–261.

[66] D 23, G V 299.

[67] S 12, G I 196.

[68] C 2, G V 46; *cf.* S 12, G I 193.

[69] Q 291.

[70] M, G V 115; *Serm.* 2 n. 17, L IV 19; *Serm.* 22 n. 206, L IV 191; *Exod.*
20 n. 240, L II 197 and passim.

[71] S 4, G I 73.

humble self-annihilation and abasement',[72] still better by bearing the inflicted shame,[73] even the inner shame of insuperable temptations.[74] He must renounce interior consolation and joys in prayer, when the needs of his fellow men demand it.[75] But he must also come to terms with the limitations of his path to God; if he is really poor, in the one 'way' he has all others.[75] The more expropriated he is of his own justice, the more penetrated he is by the justice of God; indeed, he becomes (in the divine birth) a 'Word of Justice' himself.[77] The sermons on the chief commandment give the key and conclusion to all this: the highest love 'with all one's heart' for the highest Beloved 'is the standard for every lover and beloved'. Self-love is measured by love for God, not for the sake of His rewards or His attributes, but solely because God is God, and accordingly one's neighbour. According to St Thomas, each member or part loves the whole more than itself. This transcendence is natural, but nature is rooted in grace, because God is love, and to share in God's inner life of love is beyond all claim and thus beyond all reward.[78]

But this is not enough for Eckhart. He collects together everything beautiful and sublime he has found in the wide realm of philosophy to give form and multiple expression to the mystery. He heightens philosophy's powers of expression and raises it above its own level of systematisation. He uses it in a paradoxical and hyperbolic way, approaching problems from a variety of angles, thereby proving he is unafraid of contradiction. His audacities are intended to arouse a sense of the mystery. The whole of tradition supplies him with his material, which, sharpened and intensified, he bequeathes to a distant future. That future will not think, as he does, with a worshipping heart, and so will misuse his words and insights for the purposes of its Titanic Idealism.

[72] S 5a, G I 82.
[73] D 17, G V 254.
[74] D 9, G V 214–215.
[75] D 10, G V 221.
[76] D 22, G V 285.
[77] In Joh. 1 n. 15, L III; ibid., n. 50, L III 50; n. 171, L III 140.
[78] Serm. 30 and 40, L IV 271f., 335f.

If God is Being, Not-God is Non-Being. 'All creatures are pure nothing. I am not saying that they are of little value or really something after all. They are pure nothing.' And here is the proof: 'Add the whole world to God, and you have no more than if you had God alone.'[79] 'Our whole being consists in nothing coming to nothing.'[80] 'God begins where the creature ends.'[81] If God (and the idea in Him of the creature) is light, the creature, as it is in itself, is darkness. The words of the Gospel about the light shining in the darkness, about John not being the light but bearing witness to the light, sum up the whole God/creature relation. 'The just man or the just thing in itself is dark and does not shine. But in justice itself, its principle, it does shine. Justice shines in the just man, but the just man, being inferior, does not comprehend it.'[82] This is Plotinian: the inferior can never adequately express the superior, which is why the idea in the artist's mind is always more perfect than its material realisation.[83] This suggests new analogies: the creature relates to God like pure matter to form.[84] Its supreme opportunity is supreme passivity. God fulfils it as light pervades pure air. However, though light absorbs heat and retains it after the sun goes down, 'light puts down no roots and does not remain in a medium once the luminous body has gone'.[85] The fact that the creature takes into itself (as air absorbs heat) the gift or rather 'loan'[86] of God's being is less important to Eckhart than God's preservation of the creature in being through the perpetual event-act of His presence. Thus to be creature is to be constantly drinking God and, in the drinking, constantly thirsting, 'so that it is constantly in a state of becoming, and the becoming is its being'.[87] 'He who feeds on me', says

[79] S 4, G I 69–70; cf. In Exod. 15 n. 40, L II 45.

[80] D 23, G V 294.

[81] P 5b, D I 92.

[82] In Joh. 1 n. 22, L III 18; Lib. Parab. Gen. n. 56.

[83] Cf. preceding volume, pp. 280ff. (Eng. tr.). The axiom frequently recurs in Eckhart: In Joh. n. 22; Lib. Parab. Gen. n. 43, n. 56, n. 61–62.

[84] Prol. in op. propos. n. 17, L I 176.

[85] Lib. Parab. Gen. n. 24, L I 494; In Joh. n. 182, L III 150.

[86] C 2, G V 36.

[87] Lib. Parab. Gen. n. 23, L I 493.

Wisdom, 'hungers more'. In his exegesis of this passage
Eckhart distinguishes 'eating', in the sense of taking being into
oneself, from 'drinking', in the sense of ever greater
dependence on the grace of being.[88] And the more active the
work of God, the more passive must the creature's disposition
be, for only thus do the two become one in the pure act-
event. This is a participation in the intra-divine act/unity of
begetting and being begotten.[89] Thus 'building is the same as
being built; either both are or neither is'.[90] True, in God the
persons are distinct, but the event of the Godhead is one.[91]
Because of this divine principle all natural events have a
threefold character: they always involve *generatio* (generation,
bringing forth), both active and passive, and the mutual love
breathing within it.[92]

If God is pure event, Being does not suffice Him as a name:
'Being is His forecourt', 'His Temple is Intellect',[93] pure *per
se* and *ad se*, spirit. The *quaestio* whether in God Being and
Intellect (*intelligere*) are identical, is first of all answered by
Eckhart in the affirmative, in keeping with tradition, but then
he explains that the *actus secundus* is nobler than the *actus
primus*; consequently, 'God does not know because He is, but
He is because He knows; knowledge is the foundation
(*fundamentum*) of His being'.[94] But in knowing—here is a
further philosophical elaboration—things have not real but
intentional being. For example, an image as an image has no
being in itself, 'and the more attention you pay its being, the
further you are led away from the thing whose image it is
... Thus what belongs to the intellect is as such non-existent
... and so all that is in God is beyond being and utterly
intellect'.[95] From this point Eckhart takes a few swift steps
forward: he sees the depths of God as absolute identity that
comes to be—in thought, Eckhart transposes it beyond the

[88] *Super Eccli.* 24 n. 42–61, L II 270–290.
[89] *Serm.* 2 n. 6, L IV 8.
[90] *Lib. Parab. Gen.* 1 n. 51, L I 519.
[91] *Ibid.*, n. 14, L I 484; *In Joh.* n. 24, L III 20.
[92] *In Sap.* 1 n. 28, L II 348.
[93] S 9, G I 150.
[94] *Quaest. Paris.* n. 4, L V 40.
[95] *Ibid.*, n. 7–8, L V 43–44.

Trinitarian process.[96] Now if this depth is spirit and freedom, something of the spiritual creature must be grounded in its ineffability. Eckhart calls this the 'spark' or 'little castle': 'the intellect as such is uncreatable.'[97] This is just like Plotinus: the innermost motive core of the intellect (νοῦς) is the One (ἕν) beyond all *discursus*. At this point Eckhart reorders the transcendentals: truth (according to Thomas) is more in the mind, goodness is more in things, the mind tends towards the good. And so, Eckhart concludes, the Good is deeper than the True,[98] since it presupposes that being is placed *extra causas*,[99] and that means a *casus, a descensus*,[100] a fall, a descent, exile in the external.[101] This necessitates a Plotinian 'reassembly', the return to 'where there is no opposition. When the soul comes into the light of reason, it knows of no opposition'.[102]

Here Eckhart's entire speculative edifice enters into crisis. The philosophical material threatens to overpower the content it expresses. Parmenides and Melissus are invoked,[103] all the Platonists, Origen, Denys must play their part, Eriugena's cosmology is at hand. The elevation of intellect above love; the argument that it is primarily the intellect and only secondarily the will that is free;[104] the interpretation of creaturely perfection as pure relation to God,[105] pure ecstasy, of virtue as something flowing, eternally becoming, without

[96] C 2, G V 41; S 10, G I 173.
[97] *Quaest. Paris.* n. 10–11, L V 60.
[98] Lib. Parab. Gen. 1 n. 36, L I 503; *ibid.*, n. 53–55, L I 521–524.
[99] S 8, G I 132; Q 295; *Lib Parab. Gen.* n. 11: *cadit in plura . . . cadit in numerum. Cf.* n. 13 and n. 16, which is expressed in a completely Plotinian way: *natura non facit saltum, sed . . . ordine progressivo deficit paulatim* n. 73: *casus ab uno et per consequens ab ente et a bono. Exp. in sap.* n. 38: *cadit ab uno et cadit in distinctionem* (L II 359).
[100] C 2, G V 41.
[101] *Descendit foris, extra esse producentis et extra ipsius vivere et intelligere, obumbratum umbra temporis, vel saltem factionis* (*Lib. Parab. Gen.* 1 n. 62, L I 529).
[102] S 8, G I 136.
[103] *Prol. op. propos.* n. 5, L I 168.
[104] *Quaest. Paris.* n. 14, L V 62; *cf. Lib. Parab. Gen.* n. 63: *Voluntas autem et amor descendunt ab intellectu et cognitione* (L I 530).
[105] *In Eccli.* 24 n. 4, L II 233.

root in the virtuous person, only like the reflection in a mirror, only like a gleam in the air:[106] all of this converges, against Eckhart's intention, towards the abolition of created natures and their proper operations, towards, in fact, an Indian kind of doctrine that everything is God.[107] Eckhart clothes Christian humility and poverty without qualification in the mantle of pagan antiquity's doctrine of departure and return. In so doing, against his most deep-seated intentions, he gives Christian accentuation and enhancement to the pre-Christian religious systems later inherited by the post-Christian Geistphilosophien. Thus the gory of Biblical revelation, which Eckhart had authentically glimpsed, is robbed of its expression. And though he knows and says that the innermost point within God is the infinite free 'I' of the God of Israel,[108] it is only a question of time before the move is made to construe all being in terms of that point of identity in the intellect where God and creature coincide. Looking forward from Eckhart to Luther, Hegel, and Heidegger, we can without difficulty discern the inner affinity between these great speculative systems.

Luther, in particular, needed only to change the emphasis of one or two points in Eckhart's thought. The creature, after all, is and remains of itself sin and darkness[109] and, when inserted into the justice of God mediated by Christ, is ecstatically outside of itself. To be good is adhaerere Deo, something already taught by Augustine. Eckhart calls this adherent trust hope, confidence, love.[110] Luther calls it faith. Of their very nature neither attitude can involve mistrust; both possess interior certainty of salvation;[111] both cover a multitude of sins. Eckhart too stresses that 'the greater and graver the sins, the greater the immense gladness with which

[106] In Sap. 1 n. 45, L II 368.

[107] Rud. Otto, Westöstliche Mystik (1926).

[108] Especially in the commentary on Exodus on the text 'I am who I am' (In Exod. 3 n. 14f.; cf. In Eccli. 24 n. 8–10).

[109] 'Man should consider that, in his natural being, of himself he is nothing but badness and misery. All that is good, all being good, has been lent him by God' (C 2, G V 36).

[110] D 14, G V 36.

[111] D 14, G V 239.

God forgives them.'[112] The exterior work has no value of its own; it is merely the outward radiation of the 'interior work', of 'faith'.[113] Any kind of 'trade with God', even in 'good Christians' is exposed as unbelief.[114] Looking at it in the light of Eckhart, one is hesitant about interpreting Luther's 'forensic' doctrine of justification as simply Nominalist; it may well also have Platonic features. Thus Eckhart can say: 'Being and every perfection . . . such as unity, truth, goodness, light, justice and so on are predicted of God and creatures analogically. Consequently, the good, the just and the like [in creatures] derive their goodness entirely from something outside of themselves, something above them to which they are raised up, namely God.'[115] Karl Barth's doctrine that the real subject of justice and faith in man is God Himself thus becomes unavoidable.[116]

The relation of finite to absolute Spirit will later cease to be seen as the adoration of pure loving abandonment. Eckhart prepares the way for this by interpreting that relation as a kind of speculation knowledge. For 'the secret way is inwards', while the exterior approach to God in the sense of a sacramental theophany (the cosmos and the Church) has almost entirely disappeared. Eckhart, so to speak, stares fascinated at the absolute point of identity with the divine in the subject. It is almost a challenge to speculation, and the distinctions between theism, pantheism, and atheism are immediately blurred. The relation between absolute and empirical subject, once placed at the centre of philosophy, moves inevitably from the atmosphere of prayer to that of concepts or intellectual speculation. And it is precisely through this that something crucial for us takes place: the waning of the category of glory.[117]

[112] D 13, G V 238.

[113] C 2, G V 40.

[114] S 1, G I 6–7.

[115] *In Eccli.* 24 n. 52, L II 281; cf. *In Sap.* 1 n. 41–42, L II 363–364.

[116] 'I say . . . that a good man, inasmuch as he is good, has a property of God'. God is not just the object of what he does but the subject too, 'for *what* he loves is God the Father unbegotten; *the one who loves* is God the Son begotten' (C 2, G V 44).

[117] Paths can be traced from Eckhart that lead not only to an admirer

This waning characterises the post-Christian philosophy of the modern era in contrast to pre-Christian philosophy (from the pre-Socratics through Plato to Plotinus), which had always preserved a glimmer of *doxa*. Scripture in both Old (Wisd. 13.1–5) and New Testaments (Rom. 1.18f.; Acts 17.22f.) speaks to Hellenistic man about this glimpse of glory. Now, though, history approaches a moment of decision: Christian man stands before the glory of the Christian God, which enables him to preserve something of the glory of creation; non-Christian man stands before the yawning abyss of reason and freedom, first opened up by Christians, and encounters there the self-glorifying Absolute. Faced with this destructive fissure, he once more invokes the aid and mediation of the glory of antiquity. That aid will sustain more than three centuries before being exhausted and leaving spirit to make its lonely and unavoidable decision. But since the darkening of the eyes of the spirit is the fate of a whole epoch, to which Christians also belong, this moment of truth compels them to make a specifically Christian decision of their own, a decision repeatedly postponed through the alliance with antiquity, one that even the Counter-Reformation did not completely make: self-surrender to the sign, in all its purity, of the glory of God's love revealed in Christ.

like Nicolas of Cusa (Herbert Wackerzapp, *Der Einfluss Meister Eckharts auf die ersten philos. Schriften des Nikolaus von Kues, BGPhThM* 39/3 (1962), but also, for example, to Böhme and Kant, and especially to Fichte, Schelling, Hegel, and Dilthey. Heinrich Maier Heimsoeth (*Die sechs grossen Themen der abendländischen Metaphysik*), Erich Seeberg, Ernst von Bracken in a comprehensive monograph (*Meister Eckhart und Fichte*, 1943), and Gustav Siewerth (*Das Schicksal der Metaphysik von Thomas zu Heidegger*, 1959) have indicated the fatal connecting lines.

2. THE METAPHYSICS OF THE SAINTS

a. *Christology and Tragedy*

Eckhart renounced the idea, to be found in antiquity and the Areopagite, of a relationship with God mediated through the cosmos. This desire for immediate contact with God was not only the first step towards idealistic speculation (already present, in rudimentary form, in the contemporary 'Brethren of the Free Spirit'), it was also a stimulus to critical reflection on the Christian's relation with God, reflection that was undertaken theoretically with hitherto unprecedented purity. This event left an indelible mark on the development of western metaphysics or transcendental philosophy and forms the antithesis to the ascendant speculation of modern philosophy. We must therefore give it the space it deserves in the course of this investigation, even though to some extent this will anticipate the later theological problematic. It is above all important to recognise that we are dealing here with an over-all turning-point in intellectual history, at which this distinctively Christian metaphysics (even though as yet incomplete) emerges for the first time.

This is the interim period when Aristotle's reputation is in the decline after the death of St Thomas and the condemnation of the Averroists, and the Neo-platonist upsurge of the early Renaissance has not yet taken place. Christians who do philosophy are intent above all on destroying misleading philosophical tenets. And yet the question of transcendentality continues to be posed. What is the open 'being' into which—according to Avicenna, Thomas, Scotus—the human spirit ascends? On the existential level it is experienced, during the sombre fourteenth century, as emptiness and darkness. Unprotected man is exposed to an uncertain destiny, the grounds for consolation derived by the Stoics and by Boethius from the surrounding divine cosmic order no longer apply, philosophical *apatheia* does not do justice to reality, since life is sorrow. In this interregnum between Aristotle and Plato a face emerges which both the great philosophers concealed: the face of ancient tragedy. Human existence, even when it attains authenticity and greatness, means suffering, physical suffering, of course, but above all spiritual. And it is this which distinguishes man. He finds himself exposed to a superhuman, divine destiny, the meaning of which remains indecipherable: is it wrath or benevolent providence? Suffering man can rebel against it, but at a deeper level he knows that he must place himself at the disposal of the divine disposition he cannot escape. He must give himself up in abandonment (*Gelassenheit*), which is not a technique for avoiding pain (*a-patheia*), but the patient perseverance (ὑπο-μονή) of Odysseus and Aeneas: patience, in the face of one's destiny, with the God and in the God. Tragedy existed before philosophy, and philosophy has not made it redundant. Christianity encountered philosophy, and not tragedy, and so its history of salvation always appeared just as an 'existent' in the background of existence: Christ with his redemptive suffering appeared above all as the 'way', the true method, leading to the truth (of the Father, of heaven, but also of gnosis): a way which led (as no other could do) through himself as man to himself as God. This 'way towards' was the realisation of what 'philosophical eros' (*desiderium*) could have as some kind of aim but could not attain without the descendant grace of God. Agape then appeared as an eros empowered by divine grace, expiated by the Passion of Christ and purified in the imitation of Christ. Augustine saw it as an insatiable longing, Thomas as *amor Dei* ('*naturalis*') *super omnia*. And it was all directed towards an experience of God, which could be expressed, with Aristotle and Denys, as 'a suffering of God' (θεῖα παθεῖν, *pati Deum*).

This suffering/experience of God was, however, in the main interpreted 'metaphysically'. Presupposed (as a way) was liberation from finite existence in the sense of an ascetical and practical, and then as a contemplative and theoretical, elevation of ἀπάθεια from images to pure, imageless being (the experience of light in Evagrius, Simeon, Palamas). But

Thomas had taught that the total 'indifference' of the *actus essendi* and the active, luminous 'indifference' of the *intellectus agens* should be understood as the objective/subjective openness of the creature as such. In Eckhart there was the increased tendency to conceive the being of God as spirit. The consequence of this for the doctrine of man was that Thomas's notion of the luminous openness of the act of being (which descends from God to every essence) would be based on the luminous open-endedness of the human spirit (which ascends from every essence to God). Eckhart thought of this empty open-endedness as freedom, but he explicitly, almost passionately, maintained that it was freedom, not of the will (that is, as inclination and eros) but of the *intellect*, face to face with the absolute free existence of the divine intellect. Eckhart came dangerously close to making an ultimate identification of the two freedoms; speculative Idealism will make the identification. And when that happens, the finite person is bound to be absorbed in the absolute person.

The other possibility was to interpret the transcendental locus of human freedom in relation to God in a Christological manner: to see indifference as 'tragic' patience in the face of the obscure destiny decreed by God, not only the active contempt of the world, *despicere mundum* (the Buddhist, Platonic and Stoic idea), but also the passive endurance of contempt by the world, *despici a mundo*. This goes beyond the *Supplices* situation, where the 'truth' of man is defined in terms of loss of the world, and takes account of the truth of original sin in general (the destiny of the sons of Atreus extended to the whole of humanity) emerging in the personal subject of destiny. But it also takes account of the truth of God's providence (a providence shrouded in obscurity) in the sense of grace, to which the sufferer can surrender himself. At the same time the barriers fall which in tragedy had obscured the ultimate metaphysical transparency of the situation: the barrier of thinking that God cannot suffer and must disappear when the one who suffers in his mission goes into the extremes of dereliction and death, for Christ is himself a divine person who suffers as man. The original barrier made the destiny decreed by God seem senseless and unjust and provoked man into Titanic defiance of God, and that made the sufferer seem greater than the one who inflicted the suffering upon him. In Christ suffering took on meaning because it was substitutionary; in the night, in which God hid himself, there was the darkness of an extreme love, which could still be affirmed even in non-vision and the naked faith of indifference. This theology was in a new way an elevation and fulfilment of metaphysics, because explicitly and for the first time it knew how to explain *ontologically* the *ontic* (historical) event of salvation. It was historical inasmuch as it revealed to concrete man (in his condition of guilt and death) where and how transcendence is to be found. It was personal inasmuch as only *one* concrete man (and not abstract neutral human nature) could be the subject of this self-abandonment and agony, in personal love for a personal God. At the same time it was universal inasmuch as his unique self-giving and suffering opened up for all access to concrete transcendence in the form of salvation. It is possible to measure the progress made in this period by this assertion in the *Theologia Germanica*, which takes up and expounds the Dionysian formula of *pati Deum*: 'Whoever wants to suffer God must suffer All in the One and not resist any suffering whatever. But this is Christ.'[1]

In the Eckhart school, with a clear choice of the Master's Christian life and rejection of his speculative extravagances, we have the foundation of the 'Metaphysics of the Saints',[2] which has left its mark on the whole of Christian thinking right up into the modern era, including Ignatius, Francis de Sales, Fénelon and Newman, and has drawn them all together into a single spiritual family. To see in all of this a phenomenon of mere 'spirituality', separate from so-called rigorous or scientific theology, would be foolish and quite

[1] *Eine deutsche Theologie*, ch. 46, translated by J. Bernhart (Insel, 1920), p. 177.

[2] The expression comes from Henri Bremond, who takes this 'metaphysics' into consideration (vols. 7 and 8 of his *Histoire littéraire du sentiment religieux en France*) in the major figures in the spirituality of the *Grand Siècle*. But classical French spirituality, as Bremond himself clearly sees and shows, descended from the late medieval spirituality of Germany and the Low Countries.

mistaken. On the contrary, theology or theological metaphysics is the central phenomenon, whether we consider it theoretically or in terms of its impact on intellectual history.[3] This impact is to be judged in terms of the concept, fundamental to this work, of a distinctively Christian glory, which we deal with thematically in the final volume. For the present, in the foreground must stand the transcendental aspect, and then it becomes clear that the brief sketches which now follow are on the pinnacle and at the axis of authentic metaphysical investigation. This Christian metaphysics goes back beyond Plato to Greek tragedy and enters into dialogue with the existential situation of real man. And dialogue with Asian metaphysical ways of redemption becomes possible, too, starting with the Christian Eckhart, indeed only with him. The 'abandonment' found in Christian Neoplatonism (in its most rigid form in Evagrius Ponticus) may introduce this dialogue but cannot conclude it. Only when *despicere* becomes *despici*, and gnosis therefore becomes love, does the West have something of its own, something to offer the East that surpasses it in the same line.[4] The different configurations of this metaphysics are innumerable; we must content ourselves with presenting a few in brief sketches.

b. Abandonment (Gelassenheit) and Imitation

TAULER, SUSO, THE AUTHOR OF THE *THEOLOGIA GERMANICA*

JOHN TAULER, both directly and through the Latin translation of the Carthusian Surius, was to have a very great influence on Europe. He vigorously opposes the Christian spirit to free-wheeling reason. 'Here they come now, the reasonable people with their natural light. Look how they turn inwards upon that natural light, their bare, empty, unspoilt "ground".

---

[3] See my essay 'Theologie und Heiligkeit', in *Verbum Caro. Skizzen zur Theologie* I (1960), p. 195f.; ET, 'Theology and Sanctity', *Word and Redemption. Essays in Theology* 2 (New York, 1965), pp. 49–86.

[4] Above all: Henri de Lubac, *Aspects du Bouddhisme* I (Seuil, 1950), *La Rencontre du Bouddhisme et de l'Occident* (Aubier, 1952), *Amida*, Aspects du Bouddhisme II (Seuil, 1955).

They possess their natural light there as if it were their own property, precisely as if it were God, and yet it is no more than mere nature. The pleasure they take in it is greater than all the pleasures of the senses.' False light and false freedom seduce them into extreme arrogance, while the just, in contrast, are distinguished by their 'humility, fear, abandonment, meekness';[5] they reckon themselves 'the smallest, the most contemptuous, the weakest, the most blind'.[6] But while the latter have springs of living water within them, the former have only 'cisterns, for all their lofty intellect'.[7] The criterion that distinguishes the two is the fact that the reasonable people see in Christ only a way which one passes through and out of. 'But I say: no, no one can get beyond the image of Our Lord Jesus Christ'.[8] 'You can be certain of this: a good man never thinks he has got beyond anything'.[9] Anyone who fails to remain on the way of Christ, who is always also the door, 'in the end goes astray'.[10] For this reason the metaphysics of indifference, as is the case already in Eckhart ('Discourses on Discernment') and will be true in the Baroque age (Ignatius: 'Rules for the Discernment of Spirits'), has to be essentially a doctrine of discernment: between abandonment to the personal decrees of the Holy Spirit and the empty impersonal transcendence of one's own spirit.

In true abandonment everything is directed towards the supreme activity of worship, which 'the Son of God offered on earth to His beloved Father', and which 'completely surpasses all reason'.[11] Everything else happens for the sake of worship; the mighty work of building a cathedral, for example, ultimately only has one purpose: to make it a house of prayer, a place for worship.[12] False abandonment is

[5] Tauler's Sermons in the translation of W. Lehmann (Diederichs, 1923), Bd. 1–2, Nr 40 I 176–177.
[6] Nr 19 I 82.
[7] Nr 60b II 92.
[8] Nr 15 I 74–75.
[9] Nr 54 II 53; cf. Nr 48 II 18.
[10] Nr 55 II 62.
[11] Nr 15 I 70.
[12] Nr 39 I 164.

prayer-less, whereas God wants to be prayed to.[13] It is above all love-less and stands merely 'in the light of its reason and in false interior freedom'.[14] While true abandonment is directed at an infinite liquidity of the heart, false abandonment leads to a petrification of the heart; its 'ground becomes as hard as a millstone', incapable of confession, blind and coarse.[15] In the Church there are well-informed people, spiritual persons especially, who inflict real martyrdom on the others, those who are genuinely indifferent.[16]

True abandonment means constantly giving back to God all He has given us and 'returning it all to the ground and source whence it sprang'.[17] 'The man who with gratitude returns all things to God is a reliable and genuine witness'.[18] Christ always performed this restitution, because he 'sought the Father's glory alone'.[19] It is the acknowledgement of our essential poverty with respect to every spiritual good: 'Children, all our holiness and righteousness is absolutely nothing, and our righteousness is unrighteousness'.[20] Thus our act of restitution is not the noble ascent into the darkness of God as maintained and described by Denys;[21] no, it is merely letting go of all that is one's own, and of the things which are not God, as a sign that one prefers God. 'For God is a lover of hearts, and what matters to Him is not what is exterior but an interior living benevolence, which involves a predisposition to be ready for anything . . .'[22] 'Benevolence', 'predisposition': the offering of the heart to God, 'the calm peace of the man who is ready for anything to which the

[13] Nr 50 II 25–26.
[14] Nr 54 II 53.
[15] Nr 60a II 85–86; Nr 60b II 90.
[16] Nr 56 II 69.
[17] Nr 8 8I 35.
[18] Nr 21 I 92.
[19] Nr 13 I 66.
[20] Nr 56 II 69.
[21] 'Yet, on account of his littleness, he must not think that he is approaching the noble darkness, of which a saint (Denys) writes: "God is a darkness despite all the light". He is approaching only the darkness of his unknowing, in which he may give himself to God in simplicity without asking or demanding anything' (Nr 56 II 67–68).
[22] Nr 55 II 57.

Lord might lead him and for what He wants to do with him, like a slave, who stands before his master's table, just looking at him, waiting in readiness to do what is wanted of him'.[23] The Christian understanding of indifference is to be seen in the two sets of three virtues: 'humility, meekness and patience; faith, confidence and love'.[24] Tauler underlines (against Eckhart) the creature's capacity for autonomous activity. God made the creature, in its nobility and likeness to God,[25] capable of activity, but even this activity actively transcends itself in abandonment to God: 'Now faith goes and robs and takes away all of reason's knowledge and makes it blind; it must renounce its knowledge. Then comes confidence and takes away security and possession. Finally comes love and robs the will of all self-awareness and all property'. And likewise with the other three virtues: 'Humility sinks totally into an abyss and loses its name . . . and knows nothing of humility. Meekness has robbed love of its own will, so all things are the same for it and it encounters no resistance. It is not therefore conscious of having virtue. The virtue has lost its name. The same is true of patience.'[26]

However, the point of all this expropriation of all possession of virtue is simply to make the soul ready for God, and this is where Tauler's great experience begins. God works in our not-working.[27] When we fall silent, God calls us and invites us back to our source. These 'calls' from God take a variety of forms: he calls us through admonition and punishment, through providence from within and without, through joy and sorrow, through calls both sweet and bitter.[28] When man seeks God, God is long before in search of man, and like the woman looking for her lost coin, God turns the house of man upside down.[29] Man may hunt for God like one pursuing a deer with bloodhounds through fire

[23] Nr 54 II 55.
[24] Nr 55 II 57.
[25] Nr 39 II 165.
[26] Nr 55 II 59–60.
[27] Nr 43 I 191.
[28] Nr 53 II 43.
[29] Nr 37 I 151.

and water, against lance and pike,[30] but God's hunt for man is even wilder. 'St Paul says: "I find within myself an eternal struggle. My inner nature contends with the eternal hunt of the spirit, and I do what I do not want, and I do not do what I do want." So these two hunt one another, and in between them comes God from above and hunts them both, and likewise grace, and where this hunt is truly understood, it is a very good thing, for "all those hunted by the Spirit of God are children of God"'.[31] He hunts the deer through its thirst for the water's source, but he acts like the huntsmen: 'When they are sure that they have the deer in the forest, they leave it to recover its breath for a little while, about an hour. In that way it regains its strength and can endure the hunt so much better for a second time'. So it is with the consolation and sweetness God gives man only to pursue him the more later on through desolation.[32] The emphasis is placed thus on darkness, on on 'trials and strange and peculiar ways which no one knows except the person who experiences them'.[33] No one 'can ward them off with wisdom', nor can they be 'avoided by force and natural adroitness', even if he does not want to stay there and what he longs for he cannot attain.[34] The stronger the previous feeling of consolation, the more intolerable is the present deprivation and bitterness.[35] It is 'winter', the same state Christ was in when He was abandoned by the Father,[36] in 'abandoned dereliction'.[37] It is 'the deepest misery', in which man understands the words of St Paul: *mihi absit gloria* . . .[38] It means being endlessly thrown up and down from the heights to the depths, from being in God to being in a situation where one no longer knows 'whether one still has a God',[39] where God acts as if he knew nothing

[30] Nr 20 I 86.
[31] Nr 9 I 41.
[32] Nr 11 I 52.
[33] Nr 3 I 14.
[34] Nr 41 I 181.
[35] Nr 39 I 170.
[36] Nr 13 I 63.
[37] *Ibid.*, 64.
[38] Nr 50 II 31.
[39] Nr 39 I 170.

of all our torment,[40] where he 'behaves as if he heard nothing'.[41] 'Thus man hangs suspended between heaven and earth: with his higher powers he is raised above himself and above all things and dwells in God; with his lower powers, on the other hand, he is darkened down below all things in the depths of humility and is like a man who starts at the very beginning—he can stay in the lowest exercise of all . . . And so he is an important witness to Our Lord, because He is the one who came down from heaven and went back to heaven'.[42] In these men 'the greatest and the least are one. God has in fact so ordained it in nature that the highest is coordinated with the lowest. Heaven is the highest and earth is the lowest. Now heaven works nowhere so fruitfully as in the depths of the earth. And so the height of God works nowhere so fruitfully nor so divinely as in the deepest abyss of man.'[43] Man tossed about in this way can in the final analysis only seek 'joy in sorrow, simplicity in multiplicity, consolation in bitterness',[44] and press on between knowing and unknowing in faith, between certainty and uncertainty in hope, between peace and un-peace in self-abandonment and humility.[45] And so, with all that he possesses, he is shipwrecked on God: 'God has respect for such men. They have steered their ship on to the high seas, they have cast their net and had a big catch. When the net too comes to the heights and into the depths in this way, the ship with its net sinks, and everything is smashed to pieces . . . Everything sinks. Created nothing sinks into uncreated nothing. But this is something one cannot understand and grasp in words'.[46] Such self-surrender to God and his 'tempests',[47] when 'God out of great fidelity often shatters man to pieces',[48] is the imitation of God in the imitation of Christ. 'Then man can

[40] Nr 40 I 178.
[41] Nr 9 I 42.
[42] Nr 21 I 93.
[43] Nr 54 II 55.
[44] Nr 21 I 90.
[45] Nr 47 II 12.
[46] Nr 41 I 185.
[47] Nr 23 I 98–99.
[48] Nr 21 I 91.

say: "Lord, who are you that I must follow you thus into the depths, into the wilderness, into solitude?" And then the Lord may reply in this way: "I am man and God and I am far more than God". Man then might answer him out of his essential, recognized ground: "I am nothing, therefore, and much more than nothing." Children, that would be a beautiful reply, because the only real place for the activity of God, whose name is above every name, is in the ground of deepest self-abnegation.'[49]

For Tauler, the man who has thus abandoned and surrendered himself to God is the pillar of the Church and of the world, for with Christ he performs the one work that conditions and sustains all others.[50] His prayer will always be heard.[51] In a wholly contemplative manner he exists in an inward movement towards God, and in a wholly apostolic manner he exists in an outward movement towards sinners and the holy souls in Purgatory, and this 'in and out' movement is the fruitfulness of love.[52] As in Eckhart, he is abandoned in another sense; he lets himself be sent from prayer to his suffering neighbour.[53] As in Eckhart, he performs the interior work of letting God have his way, of letting him be born, the work which transcends action and passion and includes them both.[54] It is a work which corresponds to the Eucharistic life of Jesus: to eat God and be eaten by God; God's will as food, oneself as food for God.[55]

HENRY SUSO[1] does not add many new stops to the mighty

---

[49] Nr 55 II 60.

[50] Nr 5 I 20; Nr 19 I 84 end.

[51] Nr 15 I 72; Nr 40 I 179: 'These are they upon whom Holy Church rests, and were they not to be found in holy Christendom, Christendom could not last another hour. For their mere existence, the simple fact that they are, is of greater worth and utility than all the world's activity.'

[52] Nr 25 I 107–108.

[53] Nr 56 II 68.

[54] Nr 54 II 49.

[55] Nr 60c II 98–99.

[1] *Deutsche Schriften*, ed. K. Bihlmeyer (1907). LS = *Leben Seuses*; BWe = *Büchlein der ewigen Weisheit*; BW = *Büchlein der Wahrheit*; BB = *Briefbüchlein*, with chapter and page numbers.

organ of Tauler. In his 'Little Book of Truth' he defends his master, Eckhart, and he too clearly distinguishes between true and false reason, true and false freedom. 'Inflated reason', when it 'begins in part to understand eternal and non-begotten reason', imagines itself to be 'full of God and that there is nothing that is not God'; the real nature of things vanishes from its sight; it despises heaven and hell, angels and devils, even the humanity of Christ, because all contours disappear from its view and are lost in God.[2] But 'God's essential light permits only order and distinction': the irreducible opposition of Creator and creature, and the 'magnificent light of nature' does not count against it.[3]

Suso pledges himself, as in marriage, to divine Wisdom, who (in a not entirely credible vision) appears to him in sensible form,[4] and whose 'radiant splendour' breaks forth as 'pure light' with 'powerful beauty' from his devoted heart.[5] Immoderate asceticism forms a long preparation for his final initiation into the 'higher school' of 'abandonment' (*Gelassenheit*).[6] This abandonment will immediately express itself as 'dereliction',[7] especially in the form of human calumny, contempt, torment, but it can also become an interior feeling of 'eternal damnation'.[8] God's will for man in general is quite clear from revelation, 'but no one can say with certainty what the best would be, according to his deserts, for any one person in particular'.[9] There is no rule for this except self-surrendering abandonment to God's inscrutable personal will. There is only the offer of and preference for suffering 'for the sake of conformity' to the suffering Christ, for 'love conforms itself and makes itself pleasing to love whenever it can and wants to'. However, the one who is ready for suffering is repelled by the distance between the 'unique sufferer' and the sinners who claim to

[2] LS 47; 158, 159.
[3] BW 6, 356.
[4] LS 3, 11–14.
[5] LS 4, 17.
[6] LS 19, 53.
[7] LS 20, 57.
[8] LS 21, 62.
[9] BB 9, 388.

imitate Him. There is no imitation on an equal footing. All we can do is place ourselves in a 'great wide circle', with the Crucified at the centre, 'and widen our thirsty veins, opening up ourselves to you with great longing, O gushing fountain so rich in grace!'[10] Christ's suffering belongs to God's side: it is the best, the most exact, most exhaustive revelation and representation of his most extreme, most exalted, most hidden love.[11] 'My unfathomable love showed itself in the great bitterness of my suffering, like the sun in its radiance, like the beautiful rose in its scent, and like the blazing fire in its fierce heat'.[12] Suso's most sublime idea is, therefore, the praise and glorification of Wisdom streaming forth and offering itself for worship.[13] And precisely because God's suffering is the manifestation of his glory, those who suffer have 'so much glory in the will of God that everything that God decrees for them fills them with so much joy that they neither want nor desire anything else'.[14] They offer themselves so that the unfathomable, obscure and hopeless pain of the world may, through oblation, be transformed into a hymn of praise to the glory of God. Yes, all the world's pain, 'the groans of all the sick, the sighs of all sorrowing souls, the insults heaped upon all the oppressed, the tears of all poor and needy widows and orphans, the breaking of the will of joyful youth when it is in full bloom, every deed that gives pain to the friends of God . . .'[15]

Suso perceives that the wisdom of God reveals itself fully in the folly and weakness of the cross. This great insight discloses to him the two great mysteries of suffering and self-sacrificial abandonment: the Eucharist[16] and, pre-eminently, the compassionate soul of the Mother of Christ. The place where metaphysical transcendence reaches its highest fulfilment, where God's Wisdom is manifested, has distinctly

[10] LS 31, 92.
[11] BWe 2–4, 206–19.
[12] BWe 1, 209.
[13] The whole of ch. 24 in BWe: 'How one must always praise God in an unfathomable way', 308–314.
[14] LS 32, 95.
[15] LS 31, 91.
[16] BWe 23, 290f.

Marian characteristics for Suso.[17] As in the liturgy, the texts about Wisdom take on this creaturely significance, which is only possible because the abandonment bestowed by grace ('Behold the handmaid of the Lord') becomes the chosen place and womb for the manifestation of the Son's giving up of himself to suffering.

The THEOLOGIA GERMANICA was written about 1370 by an anonymous member of the Teutonic Order from Frankfurt. It is an independent continuation of the Eckhart/Tauler tradition and was edited by Luther, first in 1516 and for a second time in 1518, with a preface that proves incontrovertibly, despite all later indications to the contrary, the reformer's dependence on the 'Friends of God'. It was translated into Latin by Castellio and Sebastian Franck, and then, in more than seventy editions, spread the spirit of German mysticism throughout Baroque Europe.

Its essential doctrine is one of differentiation: between self—sufficient reason and reason belonging to God. The greatest danger is 'where lofty natural reason is to be found, for it ascends so high in its own light and into itself that in the end it imagines itself to be the eternal true light'.[1] 'Now take heed how from the beginning it is deceived. It does not will and choose the good absolutely, for the sake of the good; no, it wills and chooses itself and what is its own as the best. This is false and is the first deception. Moreover, it imagines itself to be what it is not, for it imagines itself to be God, but in fact it is only nature . . . It likewise says and imagines that it has passed beyond Christ's bodily sufferings and that one is meant to be impassible and invulnerable (ἀπαθής) like Christ after the resurrection . . . In short, this false, deceived light flees everything that is arduous and repugnant to nature . . . It is of course true: he who can attain his best, that is the best. But that does not happen so long as man seeks and strives after his best. For if he is to find and attain his best, he must lose his best . . . and pursue, not his own will, but the

---

[17] LW 8, 26; 10, 29; 18, 49.

[1] Cited from the edition of Josef Bernhart in the Dombücherei (Insel, 1920). Numbers refer to chapters. —20.

commandments of God and of his superiors, and should in no way at all seek what is his own, neither in spirit nor in nature, but in all things only the praise and honour of God'.[2]

God is the 'being of all beings, the life of all the living, the wisdom of all the wise',[3] since he is the selfless Good, which 'loves itself not as itself but as the Good',[4] and he is only tripersonal in order to surmount the principle of self-hood in total self-giving prodigality.[5] Self-hood is the centring of freedom on a point which belongs to the self in its own right.[6] It is thus presumption. The essence of freedom in contrast, is to belong to no one, because it is absolute and universal.[7] Freedom and property is a contradiction: 'In heaven there is no property'.[8] Freedom is poverty with respect to coveting and the will to possess, since even the eternal freedom of God does not want itself but the Good, love. For this reason enlightened men give up 'all desire and choice, and commend and surrender themselves and all things to the eternal Good'.[9] 'The more "mine", "I", "me", i.e. self-hood and egotism, decrease in man, the more the "I" of God, i.e. God himself, increases in man.'[10] This growth of God in man is seen when man's love is 'pure and unalloyed', when he 'loves everyone and everything, when he wishes well of all men and all things and in purity favours and does the good.' It is the love of enemies that we see in Christ, who addressed his betrayer as friend, 'as if he wanted to say, "You hate me and you are my

[2] 40.

[3] 36.

[4] 43. *Cf.* 32: 'God loves himself not as himself, but as the Good'.

[5] The author expresses this, as does Eckhart, in such a way that he does not want to attribute either selfhood or self-identity to God 'except in so far as he requires them in order to be personal' (32, *cf.* 43).

[6] 3.

[7] 'To be free is to be nobody's property, and he who makes it his own property does wrong. Now among all that is free there is nothing more free or as free as the will, and he who makes that his property, and does not allow it to exist in its noble freedom, does wrong indeed ... But he who allows the will to exist in its own free manner has contentment, peace, repose and happiness both in time and in eternity' (51).

[8] *Ibid.*

[9] 10.

[10] 16.

enemy, so I have love for you and I am your friend"', and on the cross he prays for forgiveness for all.[11] In the life of Christ, therefore, there appears the pure essence of the goodness of God.[12] Christ's (anhypostatic) human nature is in an attitude of pure acceptance of the activity of the divine nature; God and man 'are one and the same', and in the pure acceptance by Christ's humanity God acquires a place in the world where he can be completely himself as love and at the same time experience, by suffering, the anti-godly, the sinful. That is the central doctrine of the *Theologia Germanica*.

The work can be defended against the charge of Theopanism, which would allow the creature no ontological reality of its own: 'This must be known, that no creature is in conflict with God, or causes him pain or woe, in so far as it exists or lives, knows, has skill or power, or whatever. None of this is in conflict with God'.[13] 'In truth: conflict with God is neither a creature nor a work of the creature, but only disobedience'.[14] Nonetheless, the absolute abandonment of Christ to the will of the Father remains the model for every authentic relationship with God,[15] even though the author of the *Theologia* knows that the mystery of Christ 'is inexpressible, and has never been, and never will be, fully fathomed'. In other words, he sees that the humanity of Christ 'did not arrogate to itself the divinity whose habitation it was', because in it 'there was neither presumption nor claim nor demand, but only the claim and demand that the divinity should have what it deserved'.[16] In this sense the humanity of Christ is the place of God's manifestation, 'for in God without creation there is nothing except being and source; there is no operation. But the One who is all of this (that is, will and love and justice and truth and every excellence) takes a creature to himself and makes it his own, and it obeys him. It seems good to him to reveal himself, in

[11] 33.
[12] 18.
[13] 36.
[14] 16.
[15] 45.
[16] 15.

all that is most proper to him, in that creature. And behold, since there is a single willing and loving, it is instructed by him himself in so far as it is light and understanding: it shall then will nothing except the One which it is itself'.[17] Eckhart had maintained that as long as the creature is in God, it does not have a God; it must be distant from God so that God may be God above it. Here it seems as if God needs the creature beneath him in order to reveal himself in that which is most proper to him. And so the speculative idea emerges of the diffusive goodness of God needing the world in order to prove itself as love. Ought that which is most divine about God 'remain idle: What would be the good of that? Thus it would be just as good, indeed better, for it not to exist at all ... If there were no doing or happening or the like, what then would God Himself be, or what ought he to be, or of whom would he be God?' The speculative temptation that continues right up to Schelling and Hegel is beaten off, though it is already almost too late: 'At this point you have to turn round and stop. For if you were to go on and investigate further, you would not know where you were and how to find your way out again.'[18] And yet: ideas cannot be revoked. He wants to incorporate the speculation he has pursued, following Eckhart, at least in his Christology. Since he emphasises the anhypostasia to the verge of Monothelitism, Christ's submissive human nature really becomes the place in which God suffers, though Christ's soul, transcendentally turned towards the Father, rests beatifically in the Father's will.[19] The place where Christ is abandoned is the place where the sin of the world dwells, and so God's dwelling in this place becomes suffering. 'God is grieved by man's sin. Since this cannot happen in God without the creature, it has to happen when God is man or when God is in a divinised man', for this man, for God's sake, suffers because of the offence done to God: 'And this is the source of Christ's secret

[17] 32.

[18] 31.

[19] This is especially noticeable in the formulations in ch. 51, where the absolute character of freedom, its belonging to no one as his own property, is emphasised.

suffering, of which none but Christ says or knows anything
. . . It is also a *state of God*, which he wants to have and which
pleases him in man, and is God's own'.[20] 'And the more the
will is free and unhindered so much the more painful is the
not-good to it . . . This can be seen in Christ',[21] where through
the mediation of the human nature the absolute Free and
Good comes into direct contact with sin. It is plain to see: the
sinner is a murderer of God.[22]

The abandonment of Christ means that he freely lets God's
freedom be free in him. In Christ, therefore, humanity
participates in the why-lessness of God. 'Were someone to
ask the sun, "Why do you shine?", it would say, "I have to
shine, I cannot do otherwise, for it is my characteristic and
. . . in this shining I am completely unencumbered and do
not arrogate it to myself. And the same is true of God and
Christ in everything . . . willing, working and desiring
nothing except the good precisely as the good and for the
sake of the good. Apart from that, there is no why."'[23] This
also applies to the Christian life: 'When man in this way
cannot reach any further nor achieve any advantage, what
else should he do? It is not practised for the sake of achieving
some advantage or of attaining something, but out of love
and for the sake of its nobility and because it is so dear and
precious to God . . . For the man who does not do it out of
love does not have it at all. He may imagine that he has it,
but he deceives himself. Christ lives his life not for reward
but out of love.'[24]

Here we are looking into the very heart of the theological
aesthetic. We are looking at a 'why-less' ray of light from the
sun of the good (as understood by Plato and Plotinus), which
is given a deeper Christian meaning when it is seen to be
absolute love. Eckhart thinks of it as a why-less freedom, and
so it is passed on to Luther (who does not want it to be given
a goal in works), to Francis de Sales and Fénelon (who speak

[20] 37.
[21] 51.
[22] 54.
[23] 26.
[24] 38.

of *amour pur*), and to Spee, Scheffler, Tersteegen, Zinzendorf
and Hölderlin. We can also see now why all of Christian
ethics depends upon this theological aesthetic of the saints:
because the imperfect (the ethic for sinners) derives its inner
form from the perfect, from the love of God in Christ, which
is its own (original) ground and its own reward and goal. It
is form alone which makes all emulation truly Christian.

The author of the *Theologia Germanica* knew how to
interpret the theological opinion that in his Passion Christ
enjoys beatitude in the highest powers of his soul, while in
his lower powers he is in the night of dereliction.[25] For him
the only happiness here below is to be found in resting in the
will of God, who himself in the Passion of Christ descends
into the night. When man makes no claim to anything,
'neither existence nor life, neither knowledge nor ability,
neither activity nor passivity, nor anything else' and instead
'becomes completely poor and makes himself nothing, and in
him and with him everything that is something, all created
things', it can also happen that 'God himself becomes man, so
that there is no longer anything which is not God or of
God'.[26] Then man is 'penetrated and shot through with the
eternal and divine light and enkindled and inflamed with
eternal and divine love'.[27] But this 'becoming nothing' means
descent into hell for the sinner (Christ, as our example, went
through the experience of that). If he is to understand himself,
the sinner must 'mark who and what he is: vile, wicked and
unworthy of all good and consolation'; he must 'bear in mind
that he deserves to be eternally lost and damned, which would
be right and just, it would in fact be too little in comparison
with his sins. And so he does not want or desire consolation,
nor redemption, and as long as man is in hell, no one can
console him, neither God nor creature'.[28] 'The soul of Christ
had to descend into hell before it went into heaven . . for
this hell passes, while heaven remains.'[29] Although hell is the

[25] *Cf.* 6.
[26] 53.
[27] 41.
[28] 11.
[29] *Ibid.*

awareness of selfhood, the experience of it takes place out of abandonment, and this is 'pure submission and obedience to eternal goodness',[30] which elects the sinner in grace.

c. In the Whirlpool of Glory

RUYSBROECK

The work of Ruysbroeck the Admirable, though partly influenced by Eckhart, is nonetheless original and stands on its own.[1] Through his own personal example (as prior of his foundation at Groenedal) and his instructions to Gert Groote, he gives the impetus to the Brethren and Sisters of the Common Life (who will help to shape the Renaissance), and he will make an impression on Tauler. Hendrik Mande, Rulman Merswin and Hendrik van Herp will draw upon his writings; Blosius, the reformer of the Benedictines, regards him as a supreme authority, and through Blosius he will have an influence on Francis de Sales. Like the Rhineland mystics, but more forcefully than they, he vigorously opposes the misuse of Eckhart in the sense of a 'liberty of the spirit':[2] 'Whosoever then would know and study what God is— which is not permitted—he would go mad'.[3] Everywhere the firmly-maintained background is Christological, [4] ecclesial,

[30] 10.

[1] Critical edition of the Ruysbroeck Society (Antwerp, 1931f.). [Tr-Balthasar quotes from German and French translations. For 'The Adornment of the Spiritual Marriage' (=A), 'The Sparkling Stone' (=S), and 'The Book of Supreme Truth' (=T), we shall make use, with occasional modifications, of the English translation of C. A. Wynschenk Dom (London, 1916).]

[2] Represented by the false mystic, Bloemardine, and her circle. He writes his first work against her, 'The Kingdom of Lovers'. He continues the struggle in his second book, the 'Adornment' (II, chs. 74–77) and takes it up once again in 'The Book of the Four Temptations', where the gravest temptation is idle speculation, 'dumb cowering in oneself, vain self-examination'. Then again in T 4:'(They) are turned in upon the bareness of their own being . . . the simplicity which they there possess they take to be God . . . But in fact they have lost God' (ET, p. 230).

[3] A I, 21;ET p. 35.

[4] On Christ's humanity and his Passion, see: S, II; A I, 21; II, 65, 77.

sacramental spirituality, and any suggestion of an essential deification of the creatures is energetically rejected.[5]

The situation in which Ruysbroeck's central experience of God takes place is different from that of the Rhineland mystics. It is not the abandoned poverty of the sufferer which becomes for him the key to the fathomless depths of God; no, instead, at the point of Christian indifference, which seeks to live only for God's honour and glory, the luminous glory of god itself erupts and overflows, burning with Old Testament vehemence.[6] Perhaps nowhere in the history of Christian spirituality is the experience of *kabod* and *shekinah* more direct and personal.

At first sight there is much in Ruysbroeck's work that seems backward-looking. The longest treatise, an allegory, worked out in minute detail on the tabernacle and its furnishings, belongs to the world of Hugh of St Victor, and the four degrees, stages and steps of self-purifying love are reminiscent of Richard. The eternal, insatiable hunger of the soul of God, its 'eternal craving and continual yearning in eternal insatiableness',[7] looks like a passionate Augustinianism. And yet the fundamental experience—a very personal, solitary experience (which is however expressed, as in John of the Cross, with a claim to universal validity)—is quite different. It is the experience of a super-rational contact with God, which not only gives meaning and fulfilment to spiritual nature, and is consequently the centre of metaphysics, but is also the supremely free bestowal of God's grace and thus the centre of theology. From man's point of view this synthesis presents itself thus: 'A threefold unity is found in all men by nature, and also in all good men according to a supernatural manner.' The first is the unity of man in God, on whom he depends for being, life and preservation. In God is our

[5] This forcefully reappears in the final, programmatic work, T, chs. 2–3, 8. 'The creature feels distinction and otherness between itself and God even in its most inward vision' (ch.II). 'Through his own power no man ascends into heaven, save the son of Man, Jesus Christ' (ch. 14; ET, p. 249f.) 'we are one with God, yet we must remain eternally distinct from God' (S 10).

[6] For example, the twelfth 'Book of the Beguines' and most forcefully of all in the 'Book of the Spiritual Tabernacle'.

[7] A II, 53; p. 121.

archetype, which belongs to the divine essence; there we are 'without selfhood' and possess our ultimate unity 'within us in our depths and yet at the same time high above us, as the ground and the preserver of our being and of our life'. The second unity is 'really the same', though now considered as the centre of our spiritual life with its faculties and acts. The third is the heart in the sense of the centre of the unity of embodied spirit. This threefold unity of man is now 'as one kingdom and one eternal dwelling place . . . adorned and taken into possession in a supernatural way' by God.[8] For Ruysbroeck, this supernatural life exists for the simple reason that the spiritual soul is grounded on the personal God and thus on an eternal Thou. In him alone it can realise itself, though the possibility of this realisation depends on its free opening up of itself.

This becomes evident when one looks, not in an ascendant manner from the soul up to God, but in a descendant manner from God down to the soul. In the eternal generation of the Son from the Father 'all creatures have come forth in eternity, before they were created in time. So God has seen and known them in himself, according to distinction as the living Cause, and in an otherness from himself . . . This eternal going out and this eternal life, which we have in God eternally, and in which we are without our self-hood, from the beginning, is the origin of our created being in time. And our created being abides in the Eternal Essence and is one with it in accordance with its essential existence.'[9] In this way the dialectical ethic of relationship with God is given: 'And therefore God wills that we shall go forth from ourselves in this divine light (of the idea of ourselves in God), and shall strive ourselves in a supernatural way after this image, which is our own life, and shall possess it with him in action (actively) and in fruition (passively), in eternal bliss.' This notion of the archetype in God can be called Platonic metaphysics, but it can also be interpreted in Biblical terms as election 'before the foundation of the world' (Eph. 1.3). Indeed, since this election is accomplished 'in Jesus Christ' (ibid.), it can be interpreted

[8] A II, 2; p. 52f.
[9] A III, 3; p. 173f.

theologically, with Bonaventure and Eckhart, as grounded
upon the generation of the Word in the inner life of the
Trinity. Ruysbroeck states this explicitly. Man's whole
philosophical   self-understanding   is   thus   inevitably
transformed into a theological, dialogal understanding. By
doing this Ruysbroeck succeeds, even more clearly than
Eckhart, in overcoming Fichte's fundamental premise, the
anchoring of the empirical in the absolute subject. Not only
does he take up Augustine's idea: 'Grace flows from within
. . . for God is more inward to us than we are ourselves',[10]
but he also sees that the reflection of the finite subject on and
in its own unity enables it to perceive that 'the foundation of
his being is without ground, and he possesses it only in this
manner'.[11] Looking into his own ground, he sees beyond it
into the eternal I, which for man is both the source of his
own I as well as his eternal Thou, and in the final analysis
this is because the eternal I is already in itself I and Thou in
the unity of the Holy Spirit. Therefore the finite subject finds
there also 'all creatures as yet without distinguishing selfhood
as one being in their eternal cause'.[12]

Using an image taken from the old cosmology,
Ruysbroeck writes thus: 'God has created the highest heaven,
a pure and simple radiance, which encloses all the heavens
and all bodily and material things that God has ever created
. . . The sphere which is nearest to this glowing heaven is
called the First Movement'. Similarly, 'the essence of the soul
is a spiritual kingdom of God, full of divine radiance,
transcending our powers . . . At a level lower than this essence
of the soul, where God reigns, the self-awareness of our spirit
is like the sphere of the First Movement; for, the spirit is
driven and moved from above in the power of God, both
naturally and supernaturally.'[13]But the sphere of movement
or reflection draws all its energy from the surrounding sphere,
of which we are not conscious, of the depth of God, which
discloses itself, to those who believe and love, as the place of

[10] A II, 3; p. 56.
[11] S 3; p. 184.
[12] T 10; p. 241.
[13] A II, 50; p. 116.

eternal beatitude. All the activity and teaching of Christ is meant to lead us into this depth, and 'whoever wishes to understand this must have died to himself, and must live in God, and must turn his gaze to the eternal light in the ground of his spirit, where the Hidden Truth reveals itself without intermediaries. For the Heavenly Father wills that we should see; for He is the Father of Light, and this is why he utters eternally, without intermediary and without interruption, into the hiddenness of our spirit, one unique and unfathomable word, and no other.'[14]

The originality of Ruysbroeck is that he experiences as an encounter, indeed as a 'nuptial encounter', the relation between the I that seeks its own ground and the God who discloses himself. His major work, 'The Adornment of the Spiritual Marriage', is an exposition, in three stages, of the verse, 'Behold, the bridegroom! Come out to meet him'. 'In this meeting lies all our bliss, the beginning and the end of all virtues; and without this meeting no virtue has ever been fulfilled.'[15] But 'every meeting is a coming together of two persons, who come from different directions . . . The coming of Christ to us is from within outwards, and we go towards him from without inwards'.[16] The virtues play a great role for Ruysbroeck, but they are developed purely out of the New Testament, without regard for the philosophical systems of antiquity, and all of them together revolve round loving indifference. Serial order has no importance. They are in 'seven steps': willing what God wills, voluntary poverty, purity of soul and body, humility (a river into which flow four tributaries—obedience, meekness, patience, the reincarnation of self-will), seeking God's honour in all things, finally the vision of the ground and the union beyond all knowing.[17] In the 'Adornment' humility is the foundation stone of all the virtues, then comes obedience (to the Church as well as to God), abandonment, patience, meekness and kindliness, compassion for those in need of any kind and

[14] A III, I; p. 168f.
[15] A I, 25; p. 43.
[16] A II, 56; p. 125.
[17] 'The Book of the Seven Steps', 95–149.

generosity in giving help, zeal, temperance and sobriety,
purity. Faith, hope and charity appear above all as a letting
go of everything that is one's own, as a bold entrusting of
oneself to God.[18] Because the nuptial meeting is experienced
above all as the shining forth of divine glory, the soul is
prepared for it by an abandonment which seeks and sees in all
things the glory of God. Ruysbroeck's formulations are a
direct anticipation of the fundamental principle of the *Spiritual
Exercises*. The recollection of the heart in interior unity leads
to a 'devotion to God and to his glory . . . Devotion impels a
man . . . towards the service of God . . . We should praise
God by means of everything that we accomplish. To praise
God means that all his life a man is devoted to, reverences
and venerates the Divine Omnipotence . . . in humble
service.'[19] This self-forgetful humanity is rooted in the
unbounded humility of Christ, whose 'soul with all its powers
bowed down in reverence and adoration before the most high
might of the Father' and for his sake also 'was humble and
subject to the old law, and to the commandments, and also
to customs of the country as necessary'.[20] It is rooted
ultimately in this consideration, that as 'God has served
[man] so humbly, so lovingly, and so faithfully', so it seems
to the Christian that 'his worship of God and his lowly service
are always falling short',[21] The awareness of this unceasing
'falling short', which can never be made up, is very typical of
Ruysbroeck. On the metaphysical level, it establishes the idea
that 'man remains constantly beneath himself',[22] an aspect
which will continue in the infinite dynamism of the Idealists
and Neo-Kantians. But the metaphysical level rests here on a
theology of dialogue, and so, in the final analysis, it is the

[18] S 6, 8.
[19] A II, 12–13; p. 64f. This is a very common theme. For example, S I,
A I, 20, I, 25: 'at all times and all places to recall God and his glory and
honour'; AII, 3; 'with all the other virtues to have in mind the praise and
honour of God and to submit ourselves to him beyond things, opinions
and ourselves'; A II, 65: 'to seek only the dear will of God and not ourselves,
but to seek at all times the honour of God', and so on.
[20] A I, 3; p. 13.
[21] A I, 12; p. 429.
[22] A II, 15.

humanity of the lover before the ever greater glory of the
beloved, which arouses this feeling of constantly falling short.
And then again it is a lover's humility (not a Gnostic light-
mysticism) which is the motive for the beloved God's coming
to meet man so much as overwhelming *kabod, doxa, gloria,*
majestic splendour.

God gives himself through the mediations of nature as well
as those of grace (as *gratia creata*), but he flashes forth through
all the veils of mediation and touches as the Unmediated, as
gratia increata. Ruysbroeck soars, swings, dances throughout
his life through the veils towards what is immediate and
glorious, that touches *him* and again and again eludes him.
This is the encounter with Christ, his advent and parousia,
'(His) inward touch or stirring . . . in his divine brightness'.[23]
'And above this touch, in the still being of the spirit, there
broods an incomprehensible brightness. And that is the most
high Trinity whence this touching proceeds'.[24] The soul's
reflection on this point and act of touch transcends itself: 'By
means of the enlightened reason the spirit . . . beholds and
observes the most inward part of itself, where this touch
occurs. Here reason and every earthly light fail and can go no
further. For the supernal brightness brooding over all, which
gives rise to this touch, blinds in its coming every earthly
sight; for it is unfathomable . . . Yet the spirit is continually
invited and urged anew by God and by itself to sound out
and to discover what is stirring these deeps, and who God is,
and what this touch is.'[25] In such an 'investigation', however,
in the face of so much glory, as Ruysbroeck says, the spirit
becomes 'impotent'.[26] 'That measureless splendour of God,
which is full of incomprehensible brightness, is the cause of

[23] A II, 51; p. 118.

[24] *Ibid.*

[25] A II, 52; p. 119f.

[26] Of the angels it is said: 'They lose the power to act and fall powerless
before the abysmal height of God' ('The Book of the Seven Steps', 12);
'Their flame is burnt out, they are liquefied and lost in their super-essence'
(*ibid.*, 14). They are consumed and swallowed up in the abyss of the infinity
of God, 'where all spirits lose the power to act and become impotent out
of enjoyment' ('The Book of the Four Temptations' (German translation
of F. M. Huebner, Dombücherei, 1924, p. 208).

all gifts and of all virtues, that same uncomprehended light transfigures and penetrates the fruitive (passive) self-giving of our spirit in love, with the non-form and incomprehensibility of its light. And in this light the spirit immerses itself in the enjoyment of rest, for this resting is without form and without limit . . . And the abyss of God calls into the abyss (of the self-giving creature) . . . and this inward call is an inundation of the essential brightness . . . (which) causes us to be lost to ourselves, and to flow forth from ourselves into the wild darkness of the Godhead.'[27] Ruysbroeck interprets this inundation by the glory of God, which 'renders us impotent', as the finite consciousness 'being taken in' to the idea in God (which is God himself). It is, however, only one aspect of the supreme experience of God; the other is a renewed sense of being sent by God into self-consciousness, so that the life of love is an eternal oscillation between resting in God and acting with God's help, between *systole* and *diastole*. This image is perpetually repeated with variations: 'The Spirit of God blows us outwards, so that we can cultivate love and the practice of the virtues, but He also sucks us inwards, so that we can give ourselves up to rest and enjoyment. And this is eternal life. It is the same as when we exhale the air that is in us and again inhale a new breath . . . To go inwards in an unrestrained enjoyment, to go outwards with good works, and in both at all times to remain united with the Spirit of God.'[28] The one is 'death to oneself' and an 'inward-drawing transformation', and the other is 'sending out by God' of the 'faithful servants', who are at once 'called inside as friends'.[29] 'In moving inwards we have to be completely empty', in order to belong only to God, 'yet in the steaming forth he wants to be completely ours'.[30] But the Father utters the eternal Word in those who have been drawn in to God: it is the 'inundation of his light and grace' into the single ground of the soul. Moved by this Light/Word, 'the higher powers flow out to

---

[27] A II, 54; p. 149.
[28] 'The Book of the Seven Steps', 14.
[29] S 9; pp. 201ff.
[30] S II, as also 12.

become active in all the virtues',[31] so that the two movements
are once again one. 'This streaming of God into us demands
of us a flowing out and a flowing back ... into the same
source from which that torrent has flowed.'[32] For 'God is a
sea that ebbs and flows, pouring without ceasing into all his
beloved according to the needs and merits of each, and ebbing
back again with all those who have been thus endowed both
in heaven and on earth, with all that they have and all that
they can.'[33]

Man, however, who in loving abandonment surrenders
himself completely to God and his glory, can, when he goes
out, 'no longer think of and seek himself, but the honour of
him, who has sent him out ... He has a rich, generous core,
rooted in the richness of God, and so he must uremittingly
flow outwards and spend himself on all who have need of
him ... And so his life is an all-embracing life';[34] he has
attained to the true Catholicity of love. 'He shall go out ...
with overflowing love towards heaven and earth ... towards
God and towards all saints ... towards sinners and towards
all perverted men, towards Purgatory.'[35] He puts his trust in
the immensity of the love of God: 'Now, since this man is at
home in such a universal love, he prays and beseeches God
that his love and mercy may flow forth towards pagans and
towards Jews and towards all unbelievers',[36] and for that
intention he offers himself to God, as well as all the interior
devotion of the saints and angels, of the Church and of
Christ.[37] He takes 'as a model Christ, who was, and is and
eternally shall remain, common to all ... [who] had
nothing of his own, but everything in common, body and
soul, mother and disciples, cloak and tunic. He ate and he
drank for our sake; he lived and he died for our sake ... And
the glory of his merits shall be common to all in eternity.'[38]

[31] A II, 3; p. 55.
[32] A II, 6; p. 58.
[33] A II, 40; p. 103.
[34] S 14; p. 220f.
[35] A II, 39; p. 102f.
[36] A II, 41; p. 105.
[37] A II, 63; p. 146.
[38] A II, 45; p. 109f.

Thus as Christ in His loving poverty is the common, Catholic outflow of God into the world and the world's flowing back into God, so the truly Catholic man 'gives himself away' 'in generous participation of love towards heaven and earth, and swells out and flows back . . . into the ground . . . from which all things proceed' with 'the fruits of his apostolate',[39] He is 'in constant activity and constant rest'.[40]

Considered speculatively, this rhythm of being swings round this narrow central point of indifference. Indifference, for the Christian, means Catholic love, which lets itself be robbed of form in the movement from the world to God and transformed in the movement from God to the world. Through being rooted in a personal ('mystical') experience of God, this Catholic love illuminates the rhythm of life common to all Christians—contemplation and action. Psychologically, it illuminates the oscillation of life between the three centres of man: super-ego, mind (consciousness)and heart (active potencies). Metaphysically, it illuminates the cosmological schema common in Indian philosophy, Plotinus, Erigena and Thomas Aquinas (the *egressus* of God to the world, the *regressus* of the world back to God), but it elevates it Christologically: the departure of the Son from the Father into the world and His return to the Father (John 16.28). But Ruysbroeck's understanding of Catholic love further elevates the cosmological schema by placing it in a Trinitarian context, since for Ruysbroeck God is not only rest (in his essence) but also activity (in the processions of the divine persons). This is not so much Eckhart's idea of the ultimate ground of the divine essence lying unattainable 'behind' the persons and the movement of their processions;[41] it is more the idea that the divine essence is the resting ground *in* the processions of the persons, the essential love which they are together.[42] Indifference, understood as Catholic love, holds everything

---

[39] A II, 50, p. 117.   [40] A II, 75.

[41] Though many expressions here show themselves to be influenced by Eckhart.

[42] T 9; p. 240: 'And there we may behold how the persons give place and pass away in essential love, that is, in their fruitive unity, and yet they dwell for ever, according to their personal modes, in the working of the

together, even the apparently pantheistic aspect (the dissolution of self-hood as it flows back into the idea in the divine mind and thus into God), by making it just one pole in an absolute disponibility. From the very beginning Ruybroeck repeatedly took energetic precautions against the absolutisation of this aspect. His final experiences and words lie more in the experience of the everlasting flow, which occasionally appears (here there is affinity with Tauler) as a hunt for God and through God.[43] In certain states it is 'a fierce hot flash of the divine rays', which makes the heart 'frantic with love' and torments it with the unattainable excess of glory'.[44] It can mean floating through, wandering through every level of the world-order.[45] It can be a 'whirlpool', a 'whirlwind', and finally a 'loving strife' in the 'storm of love', in which 'the two spirits . . . sparkle and shine one into the other, and each demands that the other give what it is' and the finite spirit 'is burnt up in the fire of love'.[46] And yet this happens in such a way that the sun (which is God) shines over the lover in a complete zodiac: as Spring—summoning and enticing, as Summer—burning, as Autumn and Winter—cooling, until finally the lover is left in forsakenness.[47] All this is so personal and so colourful that, through a much more substantial relation with God, it makes credible the rejection of all forms of Quietism and places man outwardly in a tension, between the world and God, home and abroad, combat and crown,[48] which in turn, most unexpectedly for

Trinity'. In the same work (ch. 10; p. 240f.) Ruysbroeck explains how the world is created out of the common contentment of love of the divine persons and how this bliss pours itself out over the natures as the lordship of grace. Cf. also ch. 12 and A II, 37, where the person's unity of essence and love becomes the object of mystical experience. The divine essence is often described as 'twilight' and 'night', but this is the traditional (Dionysian) expression for the superluminosity and invisibility of the divine unity.

[43] A II, 5, 8.
[44] A II, 25.
[45] A II, 41.
[46] A II, 54; p. 122f.
[47] This whole progress is described, with consummate poetical power, in A II, 16–33.
[48] A II, 73.

the philosopher, but most correctly for the Christian, places him inwardly *before* God *in* God.

d. Espousals in the Night

THE WOMEN

Ruysbroeck's experience remains personal. Once schematised, it will have a certain influence, but in this depersonalised form it cannot claim general validity, any more than John of the Cross's personal way can. Human abandonment is not a sufficient basis for systematically anticipating the different ways in which God will reveal himself. In Christian terms it is Tauler rather than Ruysbroeck who is the central figure, the one who points the way forward. Let us now look at some of his specifically Christian themes. These already existed, of course, in the Patristic period and the early Middle Ages, but only now, with the emergence of abandonment (*Gelassenheit*), do they attain a properly metaphysical status by illuminating the essence of spirit—as *quodammodo omnia*—in the analogy of finite and infinite spirit. For as long as spirit was interpreted by the standards of 'eros' as the divine wisdom, its own characteristically dynamic and orientating light dwelt within, where it 'suffered divine reality'. As already mentioned, the historical mysteries of Christianity appeared chiefly as indispensable means of finding and keeping to this way. But when finite spirit found itself confronted with the unimaginable revelation of the personal God, its ultimate attitude (with all the 'longing' that might and must inhabit it) became one of open and defenceless expectation. It became an attitude of *apatheia*, which is no longer a self-generated ethical or mystical transcendence of the finite forms of what is into the all-embracing formlessness of being, but a 'passive' readiness to accept every positive impression made by God. The element of 'glory' no longer consists in the ascent of eros, which gazes upon the eternal, but in the encounter of the spirit, disponible and humbly ready to serve, as the 'handmaid of the Lord' with the Son who descends.

These themes had been adumbrated in the commentaries on the Canticle,[1] where they revolved round the central mystery of Christian theology, Only now, however, do these themes attain their historical *kairos*.

1. First and foremost there is the *Passion of Christ*, the dimensions of which are amplified. From being a particular event in history (of universal validity because of the dignity of the God-Man who suffers) it is amplified to become the concrete, normative and defining attitude of the historical creature in general, the creature, that is, which is sinful and alienated from God. Christ's substitutionary death on the cross now displays openly in the openness of his experience on behalf of all what, at the point of transcendence, the sinner's remoteness from God truly means. It is *night*. But it is no longer the metaphysical night of the Areopagite, based upon the ever greater being of God and the dazzling glory of his essence. No, this is the night in which God in judgment turns away from the sinner. This night has a fourfold depth into which we may sink. First of all, there is the consciousness of the sinner, who has lost God within himself, and who, emerging from the obscurity of being, can only experience existence as sinister and destructive. Secondly, there is the growth in awareness of the paradoxical presence of God, who is present as the one who is absent, who abandons, forsakes and judges. Thirdly, there is the assumption of this experience of the night into Christ's sinless experience of suffering. This alone brings the real content of the 'night' to 'light', by transforming the 'infernal' difference between God and the sinner into a modality of the difference of love between the Father and the (incarnate) Son. Fourthly, there is the participation by the engraced member of Christ in the experience of the Head. This participated experience can rest primarily on any one of the three other levels of the night. The experience of night can begin by simply revealing the reality of the sinner's situation before God (and will normally

[1] Above all: H. Riedlinger, 'Die Makellosigkeit der Kirche in den lat. Hohelied-kommentaren des MA', *BGPhThMA* xxxviii/3 (1958); and F. Ohly, *Hohelied-Studien*. Grundzüge einer Geschichte der Hoheliedauslegung des Abendlandes bis um 1200 (1958).

do so), before the Christological dimension as a presupposition of grace enters in any way into the experience of faith. The pedagogical aspect of the night, which John of the Cross almost exclusively brings out (weaning away from the world, initiation into the nakedness of faith, which is as such pure surrender to God in the night), is hardly mentioned at all by name at this stage, but is there on the side, as an outcome of the night for those who suffer it. Transcendence thought of as night is primarily a Christian insight and was long experienced by Christians in the abyss before, in secularised form, it became a modern experience of existence. As a Christian experience it remains—in all the darkness and opacity that it is for the one who undergoes it—a function of the experience of the cross, where *passio* was extreme human *actio* and the supreme locus for the manifestation of the glory of divine love.

2. The attitude of abandonment (*Gelassenheit*) is feminine. On the purely creaturely level, it is handmaidenly, and on the level of the revelation of God's love, it is bridal. The entry of the idea of abandonment into the realm of transcendence becomes the occasion for women to express themselves in a Church that thinks of itself as womanly. The theological commentaries on the Canticle had all been written by men. From the Gothic period to the Baroque, *women* are prominent in spirituality. Of course, occasionally, the sensibility slips down from its metaphysical sublimity to the level of the private and erotic, but it is not the deviations that must be taken as the standard but the pure realisations. Loving, handmaidenly service is imprinted with the marks of the Lord: after Francis, almost all the stigmatics are women. And the hallmark for understanding and experiencing this suffering love is not (as it was in the mysticism of men in the twelfth and thirteenth centuries) the self-transcending mind but the defenceless and open heart. It is women above all who establish devotion to the pierced Heart of the Redeemer[2] and to the Mother of Sorrows. In its best representatives it becomes clear that this devotion is essentially ecclesial, that is

[2] K. Richtstätter, *Die Herz-Jesu-Verehrung des deutschen Mittelalters* (1924²); A. Hamon, *Histoire de la dévotion au Sacré-Coeur*, 5 vols. (1923–40).

to say, brings to our awareness the universally normative attitude of humanity before God.

3. A third aspect not only characterises the hidden heart of Christian piety, as do the first two, it also has a further effect, through its symbolic imagery, on general culture. All the spirituality of Christian antiquity and the early Middle Ages was a passionate quest for the Wisdom of God, a Wisdom that was hidden but revealed in Christ, and in this sense *philosophia*.[3] However, when, as in classical tragedy, the ultimate human attitude became one of abandonment and exposure to the night, then 'wisdom' assumed anew the traits of *folly*. And then this night of suffering transcendence reached a deeper level: it became the night of that folly which is sin and the night of God's Wisdom broken in folly on the cross. At that point the fool, the buffoon, became straightway the representative image of man. The fool is continually contradicted, as is obvious, by images of man preoccupied with wisdom, and this is more than ever true once antiquity's and Christianity's concept of the tragic is displaced and obscured by the Platonist Renaissance, the Enlightenment and classicist criteria of beauty. Nonetheless, the fool remains the 'classical' image of man in the West in the modern era: from Parzival to Prince Myshkin. The 'glory' that surrounds him is greater and more mysterious than the contours of the figure of the classicist ideal man. A special chapter must be devoted to the fool, because here a vital gleam of Christian faith becomes perceptible in the domain of art. It is precisely this mysterious and paradoxical flash of 'glory' which for the poets becomes a pure manifestation of man.

The history of spirituality from the Gothic age to the Baroque can only be outlined by means of certain representative figures. Important people such as Gertrude, Bridget, Joan of Arc and Teresa have to remain unmentioned; all that matters is that we bring out the common characteristics of this European spiritual family. The common factor is an interpretation of man based upon the

---

[3] Jean Leclercq, 'Pour l'histoire de l'expression "philosophie chrétienne"', *MelScRe* ix (1952), 221–226; E. Curtius, 'Zur Geschichte des Wortes Philosophie im Mittelalter', *Rom. Forsch.* lvii (1943), 290–309.

transcendence of abandonment in the sense of a loving disponibility for God, upon the primordial being and absolute elective will of love, whose glory (*major gloria*) appears *for* and *in* this indifference.

ANGELA OF FOLIGNO, who precedes the Rhineland mystics in time, is the direct daughter of the Poverello.[4] But through the particularity of her vision the understanding of poverty is expanded, in Angela, to metaphysical dimensions. She 'sees' God as the 'supreme being',[5] 'while everything else exists only to the extent that it derives its existence from Him Who Is'.[6] She sees God as 'the one who is being' and sees also 'in what manner he is the being of all creatures'.[7] But Angela sees this in an inexplicable non-seeing. Not only does the 'object' (of her vision) transcend all objectivity, so does the mode of experience which in its positive elevation arrives at the necessarily negative statement: 'In the end you attain the fulness of light and comprehend that you cannot comprehend'.[8] Having seen 'God in great clarity and fulness', she sees him later 'in total darkness, because he is a good greater than man's devising or understanding . . . And then the soul was given a most certain faith, a sure hope, an unshakeable trust'.[9] And were she to lose all perspicuous knowledge, all 'God's many and indescribable attestations of friendship', her constancy, says Angela, would not be shaken, that constancy produced in her by the 'All-Good who is seen in great darkness'.[10] For 'the soul receives more from what she does not have than from what she does have, more from what she does not feel than from what she does feel, and more from what she does not recognise than from what she

---

[4] In one of her visions Francis calls her 'the only daughter to whom he ever gave birth'. Angela's works cited from the edition of M. J. Ferré, *Le livre de l'expérience des Vrais Fidèles* (Paris, 1927). Numbers refer to those in Ferré.

[5] 200.

[6] 123.

[7] 121.

[8] 130.

[9] 105.

[10] 106.

does recognise.' The reason for this is that everything which even the most perfect soul, such as 'the soul of the holy Virgin, knows of this uncreated God, a God of such immeasurable governance, is nothing in comparison with that of which the soul *sees, perceives* and *recognises* that she cannot comprehend it, nor perceive it, nor see it, nor recognise it'.[11]

This recognition comes to her in the presence of Christ, for she 'sees and feels and recognises the lesser in the greater and the greater in the lesser; she finds the God who has not come into being in the God who has become man.'[12] 'And what shines (*resultat*) from these eyes and this face is precisely that of which I said I saw it in that darkness, breaking out from within'.[13] But what breaks out there is the incomprehensible identity of eternal, majestic 'fulness', charged with glory, and the eternal 'humility of God',[14] which shines forth with irrefutable clarity in the 'humility of Christ', in his poverty ('for poverty is the root and the mother of humility')[15] and humiliation for the sake of the 'miserable nothing' that is the sinner. Christ's humiliation, his infinite, 'indescribable, manifold and hidden' pain on the cross, is habitual, being rooted in the 'eternal saving decree which is ineffably conjoined with Christ from eternity and which evokes in him this supreme pain'. It is a 'pain which sprang from the ineffable divine light given to him'.[16] This 'incessant and immoderate pain', in the word from the cross about abandonment by God, bursts forth out of hiding so that it can be seen and heard by men.[17] But it began in the first moment of Christ's conception and lasts until his death.[18] 'For on the cross Christ began, on the cross Christ had his mid-point, and on the cross Christ had his end',[19] and so 'his

[11] 166. *Cf* the similar formula in Anselm: *comprehendit incomprehensibile esse*. See *The Glory of the Lord*, vol. II, p. 228 (Eng. tr.).

[12] 167.

[13] 107.

[14] 63.

[15] 95.

[16] 127.

[17] 129.

[18] 140.

[19] 194.

pain was ... without relief'.[20] It is the foundation of the
mode of his human existence, and this foundation is the mode
in which the humility of God is manifested.

In the face of the humiliation of God Christian love is
enkindled, and every kind of particular eros, about which
Angela issues harsh warnings, is transcended.[21] Not only will
the soul 'love every creature with all her powers, because in
every creature she sees, recognises and discerns God . . . who
humbled himself for this miserable nothing'.[22] Through
God's grace she will transform herself into the properties of
the humble love of God himself.[23] But in so doing she falls
into that terrible dialectic which is characteristic of Angela:
seeing herself in the humility of God, she will understand
that she is 'nothing but pride'.[24] In order to come to the
truth about herself, she will thirst for humiliation and reckon
herself unworthy of it.[25] All that she does and says seems
radically false to her.[26] She despairs of herself and feels and
knows herself to be damned.[27] She lives like a hanged man
dangling on the rope and unable fully to choke.[28] She is
'nothing but rage, despair, bitterness, arrogance and
torment'.[29] Angela did not by any means describe these states
simply as a participation in the cross of Christ, but chiefly as
the most just lot that could befall her. Only through a grace
that is incomprehensible to her are these experiences anchored
firmly in the deeper transcendental experience of the God-
Man. Then they coincide with the first experience that God
is and accomplishes all the good in the creature, 'while we
ourselves accomplish all the evil. And this is true annihilation:
to see in truth that we are not the authors of a single good.
Only those who acknowledge the aforesaid truth possess the

[20] 112.
[21] 130, 190, 199.
[22] 181.
[23] 187.
[24] 63.
[25] 44.
[26] p. 494f.
[27] p. 499.
[28] 97.
[29] 103.

spirit of truth'.[30] Then can the soul be shown the goodness of God's entire creation together with the sin contained therein.[31] Then she becomes capable of loving God, the all-inclusive being, for his own sake and all things for God's sake alone,[32] without expecting any reward.[33] Then the soul, beyond its total perversity, becomes in God 'completely little, dangerous to no one, troublesome to no one',[34] because she has been 'swallowed in the throat of humility',[35] but she is also 'completely true, completely just' and 'in possession of all the truth in heaven and hell and the whole world'.[36] However, because all is God and belongs to God, all this is real poverty and at the same time perfect Marian handmaidenliness.[37] And because love is the absolute principle of all action (whether acting with or without external works),[38] the soul that has thus gone beyond itself into God is at the same time both supremely free and supremely obedient.[39] She has gone 'beyond the abyss of her self-knowledge ... and sunk into the infinity of divine goodness'.[40] This is, accordingly, *duplex inabyssatio divinae immensitatis et cognitionis propriae vilitatis*, a double descent into the abyss, which for Angela bears the definitive name of humility.[41]

JULIAN OF NORWICH[1] is a connecting link between Angela and Catherine of Siena. For her, too, contemplation of Christ's suffering on the cross stands face to face with contemplation

---

[30] 203.

[31] 67.

[32] 197f.

[33] 'I do not desire to serve and to love for the sake of any reward; no, I would like to love and serve for the sake of the goodness of the incomprehensible God', 160.

[34] 157.   [37] Cf. 95, 131.

[35] p. 494.   [38] 202.

[36] 121.   [39] 165.

[40] *Ut in hac profunditate vestrae cognitionis profundemini . . . inabyssemini in immensitate divinae bonitatis*, 182.

[41] 182.

[1] Tr. Balthasar makes use of a German translation of the short text of *The Revelations of Divine Love*. In what follows we shall quote from the

of the absolutely universal goodness of God, which, as with
Catherine a few years later, is also seen chiefly as the sovereign
providence of grace. There is a complete absence of literary
tradition and dependence, yet nowhere do we see more
clearly the objective accord between the great metaphysical
tradition (as represented, for example, by Plotinus) and
Christian transcendentality. Julian sees everything in the
perspective of the bleeding crucifix: 'God is everything which
is good, and the goodness which everything has is God.'[2]
But this vision can only be attained if one recognises that 'he
has made everything which is made for love, and through
the same love is it preserved'. This is shown to Julian by the
'plentiful shedding of his precious blood' and by 'the virgin
who is his beloved mother',[3] and who is 'more worthy and
more fulfilled than everything else which God has created,
and which is inferior to her'—the universe.[4] Julian is initiated
into the Catholic love of Jesus and Mary by a perpetual
alternation between consolation and desolation, from which
she has to learn that 'he keeps us safe all the time, in joy and
in sorrow',[5] and that 'any man who voluntarily chooses God
in his lifetime may be sure that he too is chosen'.[6] In Christ
God loves all that he has created, and man, in faith elevated
above himself, attains the same indivisible unity of love. 'If
any man withdraws his love from any of his fellow Christians,
he does not love at all, because he has not love towards all.
And so in such times he is in danger, because he is not at
peace; and everyone who has general love for his fellow
Christians has love towards everything which is. For in
mankind which will be saved is comprehended all that is, all
that is made, and the maker of all; for God is in man, and so

modern English version of Edmund College OSA and James Walsh SJ,
Julian of Norwich: Showings (Classics of Western Spirituality, New York
1978). Numbers refer to Julian's chapters and the page references of the
translation.

[2] 5; p. 133.
[3] 5; p. 132.
[4] 4; p. 131.
[5] 9; p. 140.
[6] 20; p. 161.

in man is all'.[7] Julian clearly thinks of this 'Christian humanism' in transcendental and Christological terms. Only in this light do we understand why her anxious question about evil and sin can be answered so calmly by gazing at the cross and dereliction of Jesus.[8] 'Sin has its meaning'. It can be understood on the cross as initiation into the self-dispossession, into the love, of the forsaken Son, who is accused of no offence.[9] There is not the slightest question of *pecca fortiter*.[10]

Julian's vision is concerned with the universality of redemption. She does indeed say: 'I may not and cannot show the spiritual visions to you as plainly and fully as I should wish',[11] she distinguishes 'two portions': the first is 'clear and fair and bright and plentiful, for all men who are or will be of good will are comprehended in this portion'; this is, so to speak, the good thief aspect. The second is 'closed to us and hidden', for 'it is fitting to God's royal dominion to keep his privy counsel in peace', and even 'the saints in heaven wish to know nothing but what our Lord wishes to show them'.[12] But light shines through even this hidden portion in the vision of immense mercy when the Lord says: 'I will make all things well, I shall make all things well, I may make all things well, and I can make all things well; and you will see that yourself, that all things will be well',[13] namely, 'the union of all men who will be saved in the Blessed Trinity'. And in Christian simplicity Julian adds: 'It is God's will that we should know in general that all will be well, but it is not God's will that we should know it now except as it applies to us for the present, and that is the teaching of Holy Church.'[14] What was shown her in her visions she had always understood in a Catholic and universal way: she sees everything as the representative of all, in the name of all,[15] her visions belong

[7] 6; p. 134.
[8] 10; pp. 141ff.
[9] 13; pp. 146ff.
[10] 17; p. 154.
[11] 7; p. 135.
[12] 14; p. 150.
[13] 15; p. 151.
[14] 15; p. 152.
[15] 6; p. 133.

to˚all.[16] For this reason she has to surrender her anxiety about
the salvation of a particular person to God's universal
providential love: 'It is more honour to God to contemplate
him in all things than in any one special thing.'[17] Perfect
prayer unites the two: one prays not for something definite
but that God's will be done and his honour respected—and
one asks in faith, hope and charity for that definite thing,
of which one knows that it corresponds to God's will and
honour. 'So Our Lord wants us both to pray and to trust.'[18]
In our own time such a wide and generous attitude of
loving glorification of God has been seen perfectly in
Elisabeth de la Trinité.[19] Julian's insight into universal
redemption will be once again granted to Marie des Vallées,
with whom John Eudes, the theologian of the hearts of
Jesus and Mary, was closely associated.[20] But the insight will
be granted together with terrible experiences of (mystical)
night.

THE CLOUD OF UNKNOWING. The anonymous fourteenth
century treatise, *The Cloud of Unknowing*,[1] stands at a complex
point of intersection. Its source is the classical theology of
Denys, the school of Bernard and the Victorines, and it flows
into the world of the *Devotio Moderna*, but at the same time
it unintentionally offers a side-glance into late scholasticism's
understanding of spirituality. For the contemplative monk
who experienced it and described it as the principal
characteristic of the way to God, the 'cloud of unknowing' is
not the 'darkness of God' as he presents himself to the finite

[16] 7; p. 136.
[17] 16; p. 153.
[18] 19; p. 158.
[19] Hans Urs von Balthasar, *Elisabeth of Dijon*. An Interpretation of her
Spiritual Mission, ET (London, 1956).
[20] Emile Dermenghem, *La Vie admirable et les Révélations de Marie des
Vallées* (Roseau d'Or 9, 1926).
[1] Critical edition by Phyllis Hodgson, *Early English Text Society*, Original
Series, ccxviii (Oxford University Press, London, 1944). [Tr. We shall
make use of the modern version of Abbot Justin McCann, 6th and revised
edn. (The Golden Library, London, 1964). Numbers refers to the *Cloud's*
chapters and the page references of the modern version.]

intellect, nor is it the incapacity of the sense-bound intellect to comprehend God; no, the 'cloud of unknowing' means exposure, in an attitude of transcendent indifference, in the 'no-man's-land' between the world and God. 'Thou must, as this *cloud of unknowing* is above thee, betwixt thee and thy God, right so put a *cloud of forgetting* beneath thee, betwixt thee and all the creatures that ever be made.'[2] The context of this experience is the same as the passive night of John of the Cross, except for the latter's hell-like abandonment:[3] it is a love that ardently stretches upwards in naked faith, beyond all sensation, even of the spiritual senses.[4] 'Smite upon that thick cloud of unknowing with a sharp dart of longing love'.[5] 'And mean God that made thee, and bought thee, and that graciously hath called thee to this work (of contemplation)'.[6] On the other hand, every thought about 'what is', such as particular attributes of God, the angels, Mary, the saints in heaven,[7] or even the mysteries of Christ's passion and one's own earlier sinful life,[8] every such thought must be pushed aside as distracting. All clearly-defined concepts and judgments are (as in John of the Cross) quietly and calmly to be discarded[9] in favour of a 'blind beholding unto the naked being of God himself'.[10] We are required to 'look [at things] as it were over [our] shoulders, seeking another thing', and if they annoyingly besiege the imagination and intellect, 'cower then down under them as a caitiff and a

[2] 5; p. 13.

[3] *Cf.* the indication of place in ch. 21.

[4] Explicit mention is made of the incapacity of 'our ghostly wits' to lay hold of God, and precisely in this connection appeal is made to 'Saint Denis'. But it is clear from the context that by 'ghostly wits' all is meant is the reason, which cannot ascend to any 'unmade ghostly thing'. *Cf.* ch. 70; p. 95.

[5] 6; p. 15.

[6] 7; p. 16.

[7] 5; p. 14.

[8] 8; p. 17f.

[9] The 'sharp and clear beholdings of thy natural wit' (ch. 8; p. 18) are not rejected as bad in themselves, but because they impede contemplative transcendence. 'And therefore purpose thee to put down such clear beholdings, be they never so holy nor so liking' (ch. 9; p. 21).

[10] 8; p. 20.

coward overcome in battle',[11] passing under them if we
cannot pass over them. We are required, as it were, to 'hide
from God' and 'conceal'[12] even our passionate longing for
God. Now this perseverance in a state of emptiness before
God is, in the final analysis, to be understood in Christian
terms as the quintessence and supertemporal distillation of that
love of God with which man, through grace, responds to
God's temporal economy of salvation. This striving after the
'naked being of God' means, in fact, 'a naked intent directed
unto God for himself',[13] and thus a 'meek stirring of love'
for God the Creator, Redeemer and Sanctifier,[14] a stirring
which is itself pure grace. 'And yet there is no soul without
this grace, which is able to have this grace: none, whether it
be a sinner soul or an innocent soul'.[15] The passivity of the
'work' of contemplation—'Let it be the worker, and thou
but the sufferer'[16]—means in all seriousness that man cannot
arrive at contemplation by means of exercise and training of
the spirit. 'All good means hang upon it, and it on no means;
nor no means may lead thereto'.[17] For the Christian this
means 'humility' in view of one's own sinful weakness, and
especially in view of the 'overabundant love and the
worthiness of God in himself'.[18] The single thought of 'praise'
ought to characterise this state and so pervade it[19] that even
the thought of one's own sin gives way before it.[20]

It is possible to see in the 'cloud', in this no-man's land of
indifference between the world and God, a parallel to
contemplation in the Indian and Arabic traditions, with its
formless void that nonetheless hides within itself an

[11] 32; p. 48.
[12] 51; p. 71.
[13] 24; p. 40.
[14] 7; p. 15.
[15] 34; p. 50.
[16] Ibid.
[17] Ibid., p. 51.
[18] 13; p. 26.
[19] 7; p. 16f.
[20] 16; p. 29. There is an uninterrupted transition in the author's thought
from Mary Magdalene's being the 'sinner' to her being the pure
contemplative, Mary of Bethany. Cf. chs. 16–17.

inconceivable fulness. However, while it is true that the *Cloud* can accommodate this kind of non-Christian contemplation, the indifference it describes nonetheless remains also a function of humble Christian love, which preserves within itself the 'spirit' of Christ and his cross. Then again one might to want to find a parallel in the *Cloud* to the abstract 'univocal' concept of being to be found in Avicenna, Scotus and Suarez, which remains in suspense between absolute and finite being and represents the true state and content of transcendence or metaphysics. However, the *Cloud* explicitly forbids any kind of metaphysical reduction of its doctrine and consequently avoids, through its simple attitude of love, the contradictions of which a philosophy built upon the concept of being necessarily runs the risk.

It is true, however, that the *Cloud* presents that universality and Catholicity of love which is the real heart of the Christian doctrine of indifference, and which also enables it to incorporate at a higher level the entire positive content of the Buddhist ethic of compassion: 'And that in this work . . . charity unto thine even Christian is verily and perfectly fulfilled. For why, in this work a perfect worker hath no special regard unto any man by himself, whether he be kin or stranger, friend or foe. For all men seem alike kin unto him, and no man stranger. All men, he thinketh, be his friends, and none his foes. Insomuch, that he thinketh all those that pain him and do him hurt in this life, that they be his full and his special friends: and he thinketh that he is stirred to will them as much good as he would to the dearest friend that he hath.'[21]

CATHERINE OF SIENA. The 'metaphysics of the saints', in the sense of an aesthetic of Christian transcendental reason, attains perhaps its purest and most exhaustive form in the *Dialogue* of Catherine of Siena (1378), where it becomes evident that the 'mystical' in her Christian experience is simply an elucidation of what is contained in every genuinely evangelical vision. The 'dialogue' that takes place here is the

[21] 24; p. 41.

dialogue between infinite and finite reason, in Christian terms, between the triune God (whose voice resounds from the heights as the voice of God the Father) and the completely universalised soul, which has been broadened out to become the *anima ecclesiastica*. The attitude of this soul is at once both total indifference with respect to the will of the personal God of love and a totally urgent love, which identifies itself with this universal saving will. It is an attitude of self-offering and disponibility for the plan and work of all-embracing mercy, not out of presumptuous self-determination but out of pure obedience to the Word of God, which seeks people to imitate the Son's work on the cross. As an attitude of self-offering in obedience, it is at the same time an earnest supplication that God's will may be done in the world and that, accordingly, one may be made use of to that end. This prayer of passionate indifference is penetrated and imprinted by the expository, explanatory utterance of God the Father, who speaks in his Son and through the Son's words and deeds, and who with His Holy Spirit expounds the Son in men's hearts. It is, in fact, the utterance of a three-fold Father: 'of me, God, your Father, the eternal Trinity'.[1]

In those words resounds a voice that has never before been heard in Christian literature, a voice that will ring out again only in Péguy's *Mystères*. And yet it is a voice with a thoroughly credible ring, because it is nothing other than the echo of the Biblical Word in, as it were, the resonating chamber of the Holy Spirit and the ecclesial soul. Here the circumscribed Word of the Gospel is heard for what it is: the self-verbalisation of the depth of infinite being itself. In the process, the Biblical Word loses none of its precision or definition: it is a Word which clarifies, instructs, which relentlessly exposes things to the light and judges. Where need be, it is threatening, but equally it is a Word of comfort and promise, a strengthening and creative Word. It does not fail

---

[1] Italian text: *S. Caterina da Siena: Dialogo della divina Provvidenza*, a cura del P. Innocenzo Taurisano OP (Rome, 1947). [Tr. We shall quote from the English translation of Suzanne Noffke OP, *Catherine of Siena: The Dialogue* (Classics of Western Spirituality, London, 1980). Numbers refer to chapters and the page references of the translation.]—135; p. 278.

to accuse sinners, especially Christians, but without the slightest compromise of its absolute supremacy. Everything takes place in the atmosphere of familiarity made possible by the Christian revelation: the familiarity of the 'most beloved daughter' and the adored, truly 'idolised' Father, with the bridal relationship with the Son as the invisible presupposition. For Catherine, 'betrothal' and 'marriage' with the Word, the wedding ring that is visible to her alone, belong eleven years in the past, so do the 'crown of thorns' and the stigmata (which at her request remained invisible). As with Joan of Arc, her contemplative Passion was to be only the dim background for her active Passion in the world and the Church. By means of her life God the Father expounds his Son to the Church, an act that presupposes suffering and that can lead only to suffering. Catherine's church-political mission logically involves this exegetical aspect: in her very heart God—Father, Son and Holy Spirit—expounds himself, just as her life must become the exposition of God to men.

It is crucial that we appreciate that such exposition can take place only where there exists an attitude of total ecclesial indifference. This is constantly presupposed and inculcated. God's 'servants' (as consecrated souls, especially members of religious orders, are called) 'are stripped of their own will and clothed in mine';[2] they 'want nothing but what I will'.[3] 'Because [their will] is not their own and has in fact become one with me in love, they can neither will nor desire anything but what I will'.[4] They 'go by this way of the will immersed in and subjected to my gentle will',[5] 'bowing humbly to Yes or No, whichever pleases my divine goodness'.[6] Catherine has a predilection for describing this indifference as 'desire', 'longing', 'thirst', but this should not arouse the suspicion that we are dealing here with *desiderium*, in the Platonic and Augustinian sense of the ontological love of the creature for

[2] 48; p. 98.
[3] 84; p. 93.
[4] 84; p. 154.
[5] 104; p. 196.
[6] 91; p. 169.

the absolute God. What matters here is not attaining and possessing God, but the ardent desire to correspond with God's requirements and expectations. In the very first sentence of the *Dialogue* the object of desire is the manifestation of God's glory in his work of salvation.[7] Indeed, it is called *desiderio infinito*,[8] *fuoco del desiderio*,[9] *infinito affetto d'amore*,[10] *dolorosi desideri*,[11] even downright *spasimato desiderio*.[12] This longing is compared to tears of fire, 'and if you open your mind's eye you will see that the Holy Spirit weeps in the person of every one of my servants who offers me the fragrance of holy desire and constant humble prayer'.[13] But this longing is Catholic and universal: she longs for the salvation of all, for the coming of God for all. And if so many sinners escape the net cast by the soul, 'the net of desire had certainly been held out to all, because the soul who is hungry for my honour is never content with a fraction but wants them all. She asks the good to help her get the fishes into her net ... She would have the imperfect become perfect. She would have the bad become good. The darksome unbelievers she would turn to the light of holy baptism. She wants them all, whatever their condition, because she sees them all in me, created by my goodness in such burning love and redeemed by the blood of my only-begotten Son, Christ crucified'.[14] And so, like Peter, she casts her net in obedience to the Spirit and will of God.

While it seemed at first that her urgent petition must be directed at the 'renewal of the Church', now the soul 'stretched out her prayer, like one starved, to the whole world, and as if (God) himself were making her ask it'.[15] The bold venture of widening out her prayer in this most

[7] The first sentence begins: 'A soul rises up, restless with tremendous desire for God's honour and the salvation of souls' (1; p. 25).

[8] 3.

[9] 4.

[10] 11; *affetto di desiderio*, 66.

[11] 129.

[12] 167.

[13] 91; p. 169.

[14] 146; p. 308.

[15] 16; p. 55.

audacious manner is itself obedience and presupposes the revelation of God's boundless mercy, and God's self-revelation is essentially the self-disclosure of this boundlessness: 'Know that my mercy toward you is incomparably more than you can see, because your sight is imperfect and limited, and my mercy is perfect and without limit. So there can be no comparison except that of the finite to the infinite'.[16] 'My mercy, which you receive in the blood, is incomparably greater than all the sins that have ever been committed in the world'.[17] 'My mercy is incomparably greater than all the sins anyone could commit'.[18]

However, the finite as such cannot penetrate this infinity of love. Man's works, all that he has to offer, are of themselves finite. But 'I who am infinite insist upon infinite works'.[19] 'I ask you to love me with the same love with which I love you. But for me you cannot do this, for I loved you without being loved. Whatever love you have for me you owe me, so you love me not gratuitously but out of duty'.[20] Is there a solution? The solution is to be found in the God-Man, whom the Father has made the 'bridge' between heaven and earth.[21] He 'became our justice'[22] and has given us the capacity for infinite love when we imitate him. While our love for God is out of duty, to our brethren we can extend, in the God-Man, something of this 'infinite love'.[23] It happens in this manner: 'The soul cannot live without love. She always wants to love something because love is the stuff she is made out of, and through love I created her'.[24] And since the Creator made human beings as a race, in which no single member has everything or is or can be everything, he has given them 'reason—necessity, in fact—to practise

[16] 31; p. 72.
[17] 129; p. 260.
[18] 132; p. 268.
[19] 11; p. 42.
[20] 64; p. 121.
[21] 20ff.; pp. 57ff.
[22] 13; p. 50.
[23] 'You have nothing infinite except your soul's love and desire' (92; p. 170).
[24] 51; p. 103.

mutual charity'.[25] 'In this mortal life, so long as you are pilgrims, I have bound you with the chain of charity. Whether you want it or not, you are so bound'.[26] 'So the cleric and religious have need of the lay person, and the lay person of the religious; neither can get along without the other. And so with everything else . . . In my providence I wanted to make each of you dependent on the others, so that you would be forced to exercise charity in action and will at once'.[27] Now, however, only love for God is infinite and without measure, while love of neighbour, by nature, remains measured.[28] This order is, nonetheless, breached when God becomes man, for his 'longing for humankind was infinite'.[29] With God, in the crucified Son, it becomes possible for man to love his neighbour too infinitely, since he can place himself, infinitely and limitlessly, at the disposal of the work of God in Christ. This love is the heart of every fruit and every work that man can achieve. But because it is an imitation of Christ even unto the cross, it is also, therefore, essentially a humiliated love, a love exposed to insult, mockery, persecution.

Catherine is thinking here along simple, direct lines. The creature is nothing in two senses: created out of nothing, it is of itself nothing,[30] and through the nothingness of sin it is a reinforced nothing.[31] The root of all true love is necessarily in the self's acknowledgment of this nothingness and thus in self-humiliation. Out of love Christ humbled himself to our nothingness, for he did not distinguish between himself and the sinner. The imitation of Christ means, therefore, sitting down 'at the table of the cross' (or as Catherine also puts it, at the 'table of souls') in order to continue the work of love in a humiliation that does not make distinctions. 'When you think you discern vice in others, put it on your own back as well as theirs, acting always with true humility'.[32] 'If you

[25] 7; p. 38.
[26] 148; p. 311.
[27] 148; p. 311f.
[28] 11; pp. 42ff.
[29] 75; p. 138.
[30] 'I am she who is not' (134; p. 273 and frequently).
[31] 131; pp. 262ff.
[32] 102; p. 194.

reprove, in humility include yourself in the reproof. You should have compassion for one another and leave judgment to me'.[33] The one who loves 'prays to me for the sinner . . . saying with perfect humility, "Today it is your turn; tomorrow it will be mine unless divine grace holds me up"'.[34] At the 'table of the cross',[35] however, the one who loves enjoys the food of suffering reserved for sinners in the fundamental virtue of patience, which bears all things and is 'the mark of love' and the criterion for the truth of all the other virtues.[36] The high estimation of patience, that 'queen' who is always accompanied by her handmaids, fortitude and perseverance,[37] shows that what Catherine means by love is above all unconditional steadfastness and generous disponsibility.

It is, therefore, Christian love in the self-evident form of the evangelical counsels, at least in spirit, where possible in fact. The whole book culminates in praise of the counsels, for which Christ is the norm.[38] Poverty means choosing to await everything from God alone and to let ourselves be dispossessed of all that is our own.[39] Virginity, for Catherine, is profoundly rooted in the dignity of our flesh established by God becoming man, in exclusive attachment to Christ the bridegroom, in the eschatological incorporation of our body into his glorious flesh so that we can see the Father together with Christ.[40] Finally, obedience, with which the book concludes, is the incarnation of disponsibility for God in the Church, and in this connection Catherine constantly emphasises that the full measure of perfection does not consist in the counsels as such, but in love. But obedience, rightly and spiritually understood, quite certainly is this full measure.

[33] 104.
[34] 100; p. 190.
[35] chs. 76, 78, 95.
[36] 95; p. 177f.
[37] Ibid., p. 178, cf. 119; p. 227.
[38] 151; pp. 318ff.
[39] 149, 151; pp. 313ff., 318ff.
[40] On the estimation of the body: chs. 113, 126; p. 212f., pp. 244ff.; on bodily incorporation into Christ at the resurrection: chs. 41 (conclusion), 42, 62; p. 5, pp. 85ff., pp. 116ff.

'Each of you will be rewarded according to the measure of your love (of your obedience)'. 'There are many who hold this obedience so ready and have so incarnated it within their souls that they not only want to see the rightness of the intention of those who command them, but they scarcely wait for the words to come out of their mouths. By the light of faith they understand their superior's intention. Thus the truly obedient obey the intention more than the word, assuming that their superiors' will is within my will, and that they give their commands by my permission and will. They obey the word because they have first obeyed their superiors' will with their own'.[41] Without this mystery of divine-ecclesial obedience, the indifference of love would never be unconditionally realised. Ignatius of Loyola will add nothing new to Catherine's formulation.

For Catherine the concreteness of love has its culminating point in the 'blood'.[42] Whereas, for Mechthild, the Godhead is streaming light, for Catherine of Siena, in Christ, it is streaming blood. Blood—which is at the same time fire and spirit. Blood—which gushes out ever afresh from the wound in the Saviour's heart as an unceasing and living stream of eternal love. Why the wound in the side? 'The actual deed of bearing pain and torment was finite and could never show all the love I had, because it was infinite. This is why I wanted you to see my inmost heart'.[43] The blood cannot fail to renew even the most degenerate Church and clergy. The blood forbids even the one dying in mortal sin to doubt at all, for such doubt would itself be the real and utterly unnecessary sin against God's mercy.[44] The blood makes the glory of God in all creation visible to the believer. God the Father describes it thus from his lofty height: 'Whether the world wills it or no, it offers me glory. True, the people of the world do not offer me glory in the way they ought, by loving me above all things. But I for my part draw from them glory and praise for my name. For my mercy and the fulness of my charity

[41] 165; p. 357.
[42] 14; p. 50f.
[43] 75; p. 138.
[44] 132; pp. 266ff.

are reflected in them because I lend them time and do not order the earth to swallow them up for their sins. No, I . . . order the earth to give them a share of its fruits, and I command the sun to warm them and give them its light and heat . . . I give to sinners as I give to the just—and often more to sinners than to the just, because the just are ready to suffer, and I will deprive them of earthly goods in order to give them abundantly of the goods of heaven . . . By offering constant humble prayer my suffering servants turn (persecutions) into glory and praise for my name. So whether the wicked will it or not, they offer me glory in this',[45] for 'I always pluck the rose from your thorns'.[46]

CATHERINE OF GENOA *and the Path to Luther.* One hundred years after Catherine of Siena we have her namesake of Genoa (1447–1510).[1] She was born into the Fieschi family, which was soon after ruined in the Fiesco conspiracy. Her experience of God she described with the radical categories of Eckhart, the ancient categories of hylemorphism, which we have encountered repeatedly, in Erigena and in Chartres, in Grosseteste, Alexander, Angela and Eckhart himself. God is Being and the self-diffusive Good who gives form to all things. The creature, of itself, is nothing, indeed sin (just as in Plotinus it was matter that was objectionable).

'All the glory is God's, all the malice is man's.'[2] The tone is set in the very first assertion. 'I see clearly that all the good that is in me or in any other creature and even in the saints is God's alone'.[3] 'There was shown to me a living fountain of

[45] 80; p. 150.

[46] 143; p. 297.

[1] *Vita ed Opere di S. Caterina da Genova*, 13th edn. 1887. V = *Vita* (with the chapter numbers); P = *Trattato del Purgatorio* (with the chapter numbers); D = *Dialogo* (in great part inauthentic, though use is made of sayings of the saint. Even in the so-called authentic works or sayings it is difficult to determine the extent of the interpolations from other sources.) The major work on Catherine is F. von Hügel, *The Mystical Element of Religion*, 2 vols. (London, 1908). Cf. L. Sertorius, *K.v.G. Lebensbild und geistige Gestalt ihrer Werke* (Munich, 1939).

[2] V 40.

[3] V 9.

goodness in God, which was entirely in itself, without participation by any creature. Then I saw how he began to distribute himself to creatures . . .'[4] 'All along I have seen, and more and more clearly, that all that is good is in one place only, namely in God. All other good things below are only good by participation'.[5] This means that the sun, beauty, the sweetness of God become, 'through admixture with the creaturely, darkened, bitter, rotten'.[6] Hence we have the tendency in Catherine to turn back from all that is created to the absolute and original creative principle by means of self-negation and clothing with God,[7] by means of consumption from within and from without by the power and the goodness of God,[8] until the creature 'is led back to that pure Being from which she originated'.[9] Thus existence in the world becomes a torment for Catherine,[10] and the body is experienced by her as a prison.[11] This means, it must be admitted, that love appears in her works not so much as 'indifference' and more as the passionate transcendent impulse of eros: could there be a connection between Genoa and the Florence of Marsilio Ficino? It is a thrust into the absolute, and consequently it means going beyond all the powers of the soul together with its experiences, 'Because love climbs higher than the powers of the soul, these powers feel best under the influence of love . . . If someone were to ask me, 'What do you want? What are you striving for? What do you remember?' I would answer: 'Nothing except what love wants and strives for and remembers. For love has so filled me that I do not have to beg any more to nourish those powers. Rather it seems that if love did not exist, they would be bound to die of starvation and want'.[12] Because God is uncreated love, 'for that reason I say that I do not want

[4] V 13.
[5] V 14.
[6] V 9.
[7] V 9.
[8] V 14.
[9] P 9, likewise V 35.
[10] V 9.
[11] P 17.
[12] V 40.

created love ... I want no love that passes through the intellect, memory and will. Pure love goes through all this and goes beyond it'.[13] 'Man must become outwardly blind, deaf, dumb, without taste, without the action of the intellect, memory and will. He must be so lost that he no longer knows where he is. He must be deprived of himself and appear foolish to other people'.[14] However, in this pure ascent he encounters eternal love as a judgment of the utmost severity: love is jealous of her absolute purity and fiercely burns up whatever at any point still clings to the finite or to itself.[15]

In this perspective we can understand the emotional dialectic so fundamental to Catherine's thought, which she repeatedly describes in the *Vita*, and in the treatise on Purgatory projects into the hereafter:[16] the infinite attraction exercised over the soul by the absolute love of God, and at the same time the torment of seeing oneself unworthy in the light of this love and consequently of having to plunge oneself, of necessity, into a purifying fire of judgment. The simultaneity of satisfaction (in fact the beginnings of glory) and intolerable torment[17] is not imposed upon man from outside but expresses the state of his self-consciousness. If he realises the co-existence of God's glory in him and his own sinfulness, then he must reply: 'I do not want this glory with such an adjunct; no, rather send me into hell'.[18] For the way through hell seems to be the nearest, indeed the only, way to go out and meet God. The experience Catherine has of God's contact with her soul are 'blows' from God's glory. They are very like the *toques* of John of the Cross and at the same time refer back to Ruysbroeck: 'From the presence of God flare up the jets of flame and scorching lightning-flashes of divine love',[19] 'sparks of that glory to which the soul is already

[13] V 14.

[14] V 35.

[15] The whole of ch. 41 of the *Vita* depicts this remorselessness of the love of God, which brings to light the most hidden imperfections of the creature which it does not know itself.

[16] As she herself says at the beginning of chs. 1 and 17 of P.

[17] P 12 and the whole treatise, *passim*. Likewise in V, chs. 30, 39.

[18] V 39.

[19] V *ibid*. Likewise P 10.

near'.[20] They express the 'consuming' element in love, the fact that the soul, which rushes away from this fire in order to purify itself, in fact rushes straight into it, because there is only one flame, and only this one flame can purify it.

Catherine presents us with the simultaneity of worthiness and unworthiness, of love and judgment. Metaphysically, it is the simultaneity of the fullness of God's glory and creaturely poverty and shame, which Eckhart in particular had expressed in the philosophical language of form and matter. This two-sided experience, which is characteristic of the whole of late medieval spirituality, leads uninterruptedly to Luther's *simul justus et peccator*. If we add to creaturely poverty the fact that man of himself—according to Ockham—is incapable of thinking of God, while the omnipotent God, on the other hand, has every capacity, by a decree of his will, to declare man to be whatever seems good to him, then Luther's fundamental doctrine appears in its continuity with the way that leads, in western thought, from Eckhart to Fénelon. We shall have to investigate this later.

e. Ignatius of Loyola and 'Representation': Glory in the Age of Baroque

Like all the great founders of religious orders, Ignatius derives his vision directly from the Gospel. With Benedict he sees the love of Christ as reverence and humility, with Francis as a cleansing poverty, the giving up of all personal possessions for the sake of total receptivity to the mystery of the cross. Indifference (*indiferencia*),[1] the central concept in the 'Principle and Foundation' of the Spiritual Exercises, shows how much Ignatius stands in late medieval tradition. It is in direct continuity with the Christian *apatheia* of the Fathers and the *Gelassenheit* of the Rhineland mystics, and in the *grand siècle* it will appear in its final form as *abandon*. The basic structure of the Exercises shows their historical roots even more clearly.

[20] D 11.

[1] *Exercitia spiritualia* (Spanish-Latin text of Roothaan, Marietti, 1928) with the usual numbering of paragraphs; ET, J. Rickaby, second edition (London, 1936), p. 18f.; n. 23.

At every stage the principle of indifference means detachment from all created things for the sake of immediate union with God; it thereby places man in the transcendent 'neither God nor the world' situation of *The Cloud of Unknowing*. Similarly, the First Week of the Exercises involves the purgative and preparatory 'hell of self-knowledge' (*Theologia Germanica*), which strips the sinner, as he stands before the cross of Christ, of any consciousness of his own goodness. This enables him, dispossessed of any self-constructed pattern of life, to enter into the imitation of Christ, to which he is introduced in the Second, Third and Fourth Weeks of the Exercises by means of contemplation of the life of Jesus. Now this imitation is decided for the individual in a personal call from Christ himself. According to Ignatius, this call will ring out loud and clear during contemplation of the life of Jesus if that is being done in an attitude of 'indifference' and readiness for anything God may ask. It will imprint and bestow on each person a form of life which descends from above as a gift of grace. In that form of life the Christian, as matter totally receptive to being conformed to God, can conform to his will and so attain the perfection of the Christian life. There is a parallel here with Catherine of Siena. In the 'indifference' and readiness of her love, she was endowed with the stigmata of God's loving will and instituted in her mission. Similarly, the Jesuit receives his mission in that school of abandonment and contemplation which is the Exercises and is thereby enabled to fulfil a particular task without any mental reservations and from a disposition of transcendent universality, being basically ready for anything.

The continuity from German and Dutch spirituality to Ignatius is proved by his meditative reading of Ludolf of Saxony (who, in the introduction to his book, summarises the imaginative affective method of meditation in Pseudo-Bonaventure's *Meditationes*); he treasured that classic of the *Devotio Moderna*, the *Imitation of Christ*;[2] also the *Ejecitatorio de la vida espiritual* of the Benedictine, García de Cisneros,

[2] This is the most widely read book in Christendom after the Bible, and yet, for all its sobriety and forcefulness, there is something strangely opaque about it. It rejects and eliminates every speculative element not only of

Abbot of Montserrat (the book was printed there in 1500 and doubtless became familiar to Ignatius during his stay in the monastery).[3] (More will be said later of the influence of the knightly and crusader ideals mediated through his upbringing and reading.)

What is absolutely decisive, however, is that, though Ignatius continued the idea of abandonment in all its Christian radicalism, he did not adopt the metaphysical formulation given it by the German mystics, most notably Eckhart. Christian abandonment does not imply, even when conceptualised and lived in an uncompromising way, the ancient hylemorphic model whereby God is form and the creature is matter. The practice of indifference, as understood by Ignatius, does not therefore mean the inevitable annihilation of man's own being and will. That interpretation, which is to be found in varying degrees of strength in spirituality from Eckhart to Fénelon, is the symptom of a latent monothelitism, not to say eastern-style pantheism. No,

scholasticism but also of mysticism, and yet, at the same time, it abstracts from the colourful multiplicity of the Bible and—since it is written for those who have turned from the world—disregards the world, in all its richness, as a field for Christian activity. This really leaves only the personal-ethical order as a field for contemplation. The *Imitation* is a Christian Epictetus. In place of the openhearted readiness of a Catherine of Siena, a subdued and melancholy resignation runs through the book. Admittedly, there is love of the crucified love of Christ (II, 11–12), and desolation (II, 9; III, 50) and folly (I, 17, 5) are accepted for the sake of Christ. It is true that the idea of dispossession of all one's own good (I, 22; III, 40) and of total trust in the grace of Jesus is worked out thoroughly. But there is an excess of warnings about the world, the illusions of egoism, the dangers of speculation and of the active apostolate. In this way, even 'the idea of the imitation of Christ does not become the dominant perspective . . . There is no mention of the mediation of the God-Man, of access "through Christ, in the Holy Spirit, to the Father". The mystery of the Church, therefore, does not come into view either'. The individual 'is unaware that his love of God can only be fulfilled if it expands into love of neighbour and into the apostolate'. All the remains is a flight from the world, a world that has not been brought home in Christ' (E. Iserloh in *LThK* (1962) vii 764. *Cf.* by the same authork 'Die Kirchenfrömmigkeit in der Imitatio Christ', in *Sentire Ecclesiam* (1961), 251–267.

[3] For these sources, *cf.* J. de Guibert SJ, *La Spiritualité de la Compagnie de Jésus* (1953), 142–148.

the true mystery of Christian revelation is this: the perfection of the kingdom of God ('God all in all', 'it is no longer I who live, but Christ who lives in me') can be pursued as the universal operation of God in the active co-operation of the creature—in abandonment, surrender, service. This co-operation can no longer remain at the level of indifference in the sense of *merely* letting things happen; no, the particular will of God, which is to be actively grasped and carried out, must also be actively pursued. For the Rhineland mystics, abandonment came in at the end; Ignatius transfers it to the beginning. In the Second Week of the Exercises it moves to a higher level through the central process of 'election'. Election means that a person, in the analogy of freedom between God and the creature, chooses 'what God our Lord gives us to choose', spontaneously and voluntarily cooperating in that particular choice which, in the eternal freedom of God, has been chosen for us. Progress is clearly made here beyond the concept in Eckhart, Suso and Ruysbroeck of the creature's returning to its eternal idea in God. Man's self-surrender to God is thereby accepted by God; he is 'honoured' to participate, in grace and freedom, in the elective act of God himself.

It is, however, precisely in this way that Eckhart's vision of the groundlessness and 'why-lessness' of God and of his entire self-revelation in generation and creation is fulfilled. When man's responsive act of freedom is taken up into God's free and why-less self-giving, it transcends all simply teleological ethics and enters the pure sphere of disinterested adoration and love. The essential definition of man is that he is created for the adoration and praise, the veneration and worship, the selfless service, of God, and 'thus' (as if to say, 'it goes without saying' or 'by the way') he will 'save his soul', find his salvation. As with Ruysbroeck, to be a true Christian is to exist purely for the 'ever greater glory of God', to be immersed in that glory, to be at its disposal, to radiate it through grace. This is the innermost religious kernal of Baroque culture.

Ignatius lays aside the metaphysical (hylemorphic) shell and concentrates on its theological kernel. This enables the spirituality of the modern era to survive, when Fénelon is

discredited, the abrupt end of so-called 'mysticism' with more
than a banal and enlightened Stoic moralism. The process
demonstrated moreover how the fundamental evangelical
attitude of receptive contemplation could survive inwardly
and authentically, without involving strict monasticism, in an
active apostolate in the Church and the world. Models for
this had already been provided not only by Francis and
Dominic but also by such influential figures as Ramon Lull,
Catherine of Siena, Bridget, Angela Merici and Joan of Arc.
In these cases the contemplative act itself was regarded as a
work of the greatest fruitfulness, for both world and Church
(an idea which continues from the Rhineland mystics through
Teresa of Avila to Thérèse of Lisieux). But that is not all.
This fundamental act, this fundamental work, of
contemplation could also now be translated, without
compromising its Christian integrity, into specific deeds in an
active apostolate of service to neighbour.

Ignatius was the first person to justify and to propagate
boldly this understanding of contemplation; in the age of
Baroque it quite logically took the form of 'representation'.
The imitator of the Lord places himself, in total 'indifference',
at the disposal of his Master's will and command, without
ceasing, for all that, to be a spontaneous and free human
subject. For himself and for others he is still only the agent,
the representative, of his Lord, like a viceroy, who more
perfectly represents the king the more absolutely he places his
personal, intellectual and creative powers at the service of the
thought and will of his monarch. He remains a person, but
his own person becomes as it were completely transparent to
the person who sends him. Self-abnegation is no less radical
in Ignatius than in Francis or Eckhart, but he avails himself of
the Thomist metaphysical doctrines of secondary causality and
the *analogia entis*, which is now at last taken seriously. By so
doing, Ignatius achieves the inner synthesis of the two major
parallel currents of the middle ages—scholasticism and
mysticism. Baroque culture, in those aspects which from a
Christian point of view are the most positive, builds upon
the idea of representation. It underlies not only the apostolate
of a man like Francis Xavier and of the entire Jesuit mission,

including the experiment in Paraguay, but also the theatre, both secular and sacred, where a man—Calderon!—plays the 'role' entrusted to him in the 'costume' lent him and consequently makes present, re-presents, a fragment of eternal knowledge. The idea of representation thus brings about a new awareness of the manifestation of divine glory in the world. For now this glory finds a receptacle, in and by which it manifests itself, not, as with Eckhart, Ockham and Luther, a receptacle it has to smash to pieces in order to reveal itself in its uniqueness. No, this is a receptacle in which it can stand out clearly as the real glory of the Lord, the manifestation of absolute sovereignty. This deep level of Baroque consciousness deserves to be considered first of all in its own terms, independently of any connection with the Church's Counter-Reformation, on the one hand, or with political absolutism, on the other.

This living source of the idea of the 'ever greater glory of God' (*ad maiorem Dei gloriam*) is only a simple gaze directed, through Christ, at the Triune God;[4] in the loving and chivalrous service of this God Ignatius wants his life to be consumed. To the gaze of Ignatius God appears—as he does to the Fathers and to Anselm—as the one who is inexhaustibly 'ever greater'. The dynamic comparative conveys much more than any exclusive superlative, and yet he does not faithlessly regard it as impossible for God's grace and mission to find a form for expressing that glory in the Christian life. Luther's dialectic of law and grace, which never allows any kind of obedience to arise but constantly and consciously represses it, appears from this perspective as a defective faith.

[4] The Trinitarian dimension of Ignatian spirituality is firmly established from the time of Manresa, where the Trinity in the image of an organ's three keys resounds forth into his heart and soul 'for the whole of his life' (*The Autobiography of St Ignatius Loyola*, ET, J. F. O'Callaghan (New York, 1974), p. 38). It again comes clearly into view in the fragment that has been preserved of the *Spiritual Journal* dating from the years 1544–45 (ET, W. J. Young (Woodstock, Maryland, 1958)). He 'prayed daily to each of the Three Persons' as well as to the Trinity as a whole, and he asked himself 'why he said four prayers to the Trinity', but immediately dismissed the question as 'totally irrelevant'. And in all this one discerns a total lack of interest in Eckhart's speculations about the one essence beyond the Trinitarian processions. As in the version at La Storta (*Autobiography*, p. 89;

Even prescinding from the idea of serving the Church, the mutual relationship of God and the world has a cosmic comprehensiveness, which, in the concluding meditation of the Exercises, begins to sound thoroughly Dionysian.[5] Already at the time of his conversion 'the greatest consolation he received was to look at the sky and the stars, which he often did and for a long time',[6] and later on he went off as a pilgrim, barefoot in Franciscan style, 'jubilant and loudly singing across the fields'.[7] It is the same Ignatius who deepens this vision of the world to a fourfold contemplating of the immanence of God in all created things. First, he is in them as the Creator, the bountiful Giver who draws near and offers himself through all his gifts. Secondly, he is in them as the Indweller who is present in and governs all things—in being as the source of being, in life as the source of life, in sense as

Spiritual Journal, p. 16), mediation through Mary and Jesus to the Father is what matters most and is experienced with the utmost intensity (Journal, p. 1ff.). This is not contradicted by the fact that Ignatius also has visions which show 'very clearly the very Being or Essence of God under the figure of a sphere', or reveal 'from this Essence the Father [seeming] to go forth or derive' (ibid., p. 27). At other times he sees 'sometimes the Being of the Father, that is, first the Being and then the Father . . . sometimes [the Father] in another way' (p. 31), or 'a partial revelation of the Being of the Father, and likewise of the Being of the Most Holy Trinity' (p. 34), or the indwelling of the other two persons in the Father (p. 15). These changes of aspect have nothing to do with speculation; they simply enable Ignatius to vary the direction of his devotion (p. 31), until he reaches the point where 'I am united, beyond all measure, with the love, so bright and sweet, [of the Trinity]'. Very often Ignatius's visions are accompanied by phantasms of luminous splendour, of the Holy Spirit (p. 4) and the Trinity as a whole (p. 19) as well as of the humanity of Christ (p. 20) and of Mary, of the process of creation, of the Eucharistic miracle (ibid.), as if the mysteries of the faith were being presented to him as they exist in their supreme form in divine glory. The glory of God, as it breaks in upon Him, can, however, also manifest itself as an 'interior word' (pp. 16, 44) accompanied by a corresponding 'loss of exterior speech', and this 'interior speech' possesses an 'interior inexpressible harmony' and stands in an immediate relation to the 'heavenly language of music' (cf. p. 44).

[5] The parallel with Denys has been shown in detail by E. Przywara at the end of his commentary on the Exercises (Deus Semper Maior III (1940), 369–407).

[6] Autobiography, n. 11.

[7] Ibid., n. 79.

archetypal sense, in thinking and willing spirit as primordial Spirit. This indwelling of God exists at the natural level but takes a special form at the supernatural, where the creature is consecrated to be the temple and monstrance of God. Thirdly, he is in all things as 'the one who labours'. His tireless work in the world, at every level of reality and at every moment of history, supremely in the Passion of the God-Man, puts an end to any suggestion that God is uninterested in the world. Fourthly, as both James and Plotinus maintain, he is the good Father of lights, from whom every good thing comes down, so that in the end all spiritual subjects who harden their hearts against God are softened afresh so that they flow with the eternal fountain and shine with the eternal sun.[8] And so God is in all things; in everything the glory of Triune love shines and pours itself forth. In the concluding prayer, the creature who grasps this glory in faith offers itself up to God and asks to be made one of glory's rays: 'Take, O Lord, and receive all my liberty', the sum total of my existence, both as an individual and in relation to others, 'my memory, my understanding and all my will', the Augustinian *imago Trinitatis* in the created spirit is thus referred back to its archetype, 'all I have and possess', in love's freely-chosen poverty; 'you have given it me, Lord; to you, Lord, I return it', in the *epistrophê* of Plotinus here given the higher meaning, in the spirit of Old and New Testaments, of the return of all beings and all hearts to the God of love, 'all is yours, dispose of it entirely according to your will. Give me your love and grace, because that is enough for me'.[9]

Obedience only became prominent in the thinking of the founder and his first companions at a later stage, that is, when, with their new Christian disposition of being ready for anything, they began to offer themselves openly to the visible hierarchical Church as instruments at her disposal. The Pope became the administrator of this store of 'readiness', the real 'general' of the new society, which became the outstanding instrument of the Counter-Reformation. The universal

[8] Exercises, nn. 234–237; Rickaby, pp. 208–210.
[9] *Ibid.*, n. 234; Rickaby, p. 208.

'device'—'To find God in all things'[10]—is not denied, but
now these things become *par excellence* the things of the
Church Militant. The Exercises first of all centred round the
'discernment of spirits', which was intended to help me make
the right decision about what God's will was for my life; but
the final word of the Exercises is *alabar*, praising, affirming
and consenting to the things of the Church.[11] Ignatius
'praises' them just as Francis, in his 'Canticle of Brother Sun',
praised the elements of nature as transparent to God. Ignatius
praises them with perfect simplicity in an act of filial and
chivalrous fidelity to 'the true Spouse of Christ our Lord,
which is our holy Mother the Hierarchical Church'.[12] There
is a slight touch of humour, or, at any rate, of wise patience,
about Ignatius's love of the Church—in contrast to the
impatience of Luther's reformation with its violent attack on
dogmas, structures and images.

> Give me my good old religion,
> It's good enough for me . . .

Nevertheless, as was typical of the times, deductions came to
be made, in the style of the Counter-Reformation, that
Ignatius had not made, and the positive ecclesiastical structures
and institutions were made into the definitive form of
manifestation of divine glory. *Bellarmine* did this in
ecclesiology, and Baroque art, with its tendency towards
extravagant glorification, extended it to all the phenomenal
aspects of the Catholic Church. It is true that this theology
and art first of all inherit the forms of worldly beauty
recovered from antiquity during the Renaissance, forms
which are now *as such* reinvigorated and become forms of
divine glory. It is also true that theology and art accomplish
all this in a conscious act of faith and loyalty to mother
Church, in a conscious rejection of the Protestant rejection of
the idea that divine revelation can have any real visibility in

[10] Joseph Stierli, 'Das Ignatianische Gebet: Gott suchen in allen Dingen'
in *Ignatius von Loyola. Seine geistliche Gestalt und sein Vermächtnis 1556–
1956*, Echter Verlag (1956) 151–182.

[11] *Exercises*, nn. 352–370; Rickaby, pp. 220–225 (Rules 'for the true
sentiments which we ought to hold in the Church Militant').

[12] *Exercises*, n. 353; Rickaby, p. 220.

the time of the Church's history or in the charisms of sanctity, which the Holy Spirit so richly poured out on the Church in this very century, and which the art of Tintoretto, El Greco, Zurbaran, Rubens and many others tried to represent visibly as the splendour of grace.

And yet not everything has been said. However high the light of antiquity may have risen above the natural world and made it into a theophany, the crisis of the late middle ages could not be undone. The spirit of critical philosophy, of empiricism, of the positive natural sciences, spread itself out beneath the Baroque ceiling, and men realised the precariousness of trying to summon Plato or even just Denys back to life. Luther was a fact. And so, despite their radiant power, there was something contrived about triumphantly celebrating ecclesiastical forms as revelatory icons of the eschatological Jerusalem, as anticipatory glimpses of a gorgeous Pozzo and Tiepolo kind of heaven, full of saints and angels. Despite its radiance it was unbalanced, it did not correspond to the equilibrium of the Gospel, and whatever the subjective sincerity of those who made this profession of faith, there was something objectively untrue about it. Not only do all boundaries disappear between natural revelation and redemptive revelation as proclaimed in Bible and Church, but even the scandalous form of the cross and the humble form of the Church are treated as if they were, without qualification, forms of worldly beauty, with nothing to radiate but the eternal power and glory of God. Cosmic glory breaks out from the cross, and from Bernini's Chair of Peter there shines anew an immediate form of the glory of the Christ who is raised on high. But there is an even greater paradox. The Church and salvation history have been fitted into the framework of a cosmos that manifests God, and yet now the Church has to restore to the world the light of glory, the very thing the world was in danger of losing, and which ultimately the Church had borrowed from it; both Church and world are now reflections of a borrowed glory. This dialectic was not to be guaranteed by the concept of representation in the Ignatian sense, and so Ignatian spirituality could survive unharmed the downfall of Baroque.

The substitutions and hidden exchanges reach their climax when political absolutism is transfigured in the religious lustre of ecclesiastical Baroque; in fact, the concept of representation to a certain extent embraces both spheres. Even imperial and royal representation could be understood, with the utmost Christian seriousness, as a service of the Kingdom of God—as can be seen in the cases of Charles V and Philip II. Pomp, sacred and secular, could be justified on the same grounds. The Escorial could be half palace and seat of government and half church and monastery; St Peter's basilica and piazza were the two things in one: the homage of all man's worldly art to the Church and the brilliant display to the world, by means of art, of the Church's ideals. The centre of unity and gravity in this kind of monolithic Baroque culture is to be found, of necessity, chiefly in its theatrical aspect and in the role played more than in the realities of life which act it out. The part can only be played in an existentially valid and credible manner if it can be accepted and carried off with total Ignatian 'indifference' and in the analogical process of election. If there is any deviation from this, the role, the business of representation, will be confused with the essence of glory, and men will cease to persevere in pursuit of the greater glory of God (*AD maiorem Dei gloriam*). What makes the Baroque so ambivalent, what makes the 'discernment of spirits' (the starting-point for Ignatius and the Rhineland mystics) so indispensable, is that there can be countless gradations from genuine pursuit of the greater glory of God to pseudo-religious self-glorification.

The principle of an active indifference, as understood by Ignatius, was a steep summit and a constant challenge for his numerous spiritual successors to climb. However, it concealed in itself the danger of two kinds of spiritual deviation, quite distinct from the deviation, already mentioned, in Counter-Reformation ecclesiology.[13]

The idea of an 'indifferent' opening up of oneself to the God who elects could very easily be interpreted regressively

[13] And equally irrespective of the confusion of Christian indifference with metaphysical indifference, which creeps into Suarez, a confusion for which Ignatius himself never gives the slightest pretext.

in terms of the received 'mystical' tradition, which was very much alive everywhere. Ignatius had already had to struggle hard against this tendency in his own lifetime (P. Araoz and the Spanish contemplatives and Quietists), and later on it attained the height of subtlety in the teaching of P. *Balthazar Alvarez* (P. de Ponte was his biographer) and, dependent on him, in the *Doctrine spirituelle* of P. *Louis Lallemant* and his school. These teachers quite rightly stress the importance of truly hearkening to God's inspirations, to the impulses and gifts of the Holy Spirit. But the onesidedness of the approach is betrayed by an anxious preoccupation with personal contemplating and a withdrawal from active apostolic involvement. As in ancient monasticism and German mysticism, action and contemplation are once again dualistically split up, and the primacy of (passive) contemplation is defended in a literalist sense. Suspicions and condemnations, on the part of the order's authorities, of the 'mystical' tendency gave an impetus to the opposite extreme, which, with relative correctness, emphasised the spontaneity of human action in the analogy of freedom and election, and thereby brought active asceticism to the fore (represented by P. Rodriguez' *Manual of Perfection*); in consequence, unexpectedly but inevitably, Ignatian 'indifference' was mistakenly interpreted to mean 'achievement' in the Stoic or Buddhist sense. This distortion becomes recognisable in the studied aloofness of its attitude to the world as creation and in the pseudo-ethical superiority that follows from it, where one's fellow human beings are regarded as illusory, irrelevant, perhaps even dangerous, which compromises the authentic Christian idea of the encounter of I and Thou. These two possible deviations are both forms of flight from the steep and narrow charism given to Ignatius.

The dangers show how exposed a peak is Ignatian transcendence. It can be baptised with the name 'obedience' provided one preserves an unrestricted sense of all its paradoxical implications. It is first and foremost obedience to God, beyond passivity and activity: an act which completely purifies all the powers of intellect, will and emotion and stretches them to the limit in order to place them at the

disposal of God's eternal, free and loving will. Obedience, in
this form, is faithful adherence to the will of Christ, to his
obedience to the Father, and by the same token adherence to
the faithful obedience to Christ of the Church, his Bride,
who, in her spirit of faithful obedience, is our mother and
educator. It is an obedience that transcends the oppositions of
light and darkness, blindness and sight, for obedience, is
'blind' only in relation to what *I* can see;[14] in itself, as 'the
holocaust of private judgment', it enables me to see, with the
Church, what I do not see on my own.[15] This, then, is what
the adventure of transcendence really comes down to, this is
true metaphysical action: identification with the action of the
Church (concretised in the superior recognised by her) as a
Christlike obedience incarnate in the here and now.

f. The Final Systems

FRANCIS DE SALES. The spirituality originating in the Germanic
countries spreads through a wide variety of channels. It goes
as far as Spain and then reaches its climax in France during
the *Grand Siècle*. Here it affects everyone: Francis de Sales,
Jane Frances de Chantal and Camus; pious humanists like
Louis Richeome SJ; the Capuchin, Ives de Paris; the
Englishman, Benedict Canfeld, who passes on the radical
mysticism of abandonment; the blind organist, Jean de Saint-
Samson, who anticipates and propagates it; the 'French
School' of the Oratorians and the Jesuit school, already
mentioned, of Lallemant; the ardent spirituality of Vincent
de Paul and Pascal; the apostles of devotion to the Sacred
Heart; the great and untainted figure of the Ursuline, Marie
de l'Incarnation; finally, Bossuet and Fénelon. These are just a
few of the best-known names.[1] The tradition is of such an
overwhelming richness that the common factors are easily

[14] 'The white that I see I would believe to be black, if the Hierarchical
Church were so to rule it' (*Exercises*, n. 365; Rickaby, p. 223).

[15] Letter on obedience to his confrères in Portugal, in: *Ignatius von Loyola:
Geistliche Briefe*, with an introduction by H. Rahner (Benzinger, 1956),
p. 248.

[1] See above all Henri Bremond, *Histoire littéraire du sentiment religieux en
France*, 12 vols. (1916–1936), the fundamental work despite its idiosyncratic

lost sight of. And yet they are there: distinguishing characteristics, negative as well as positive, are at hand. The positive characteristic is that these are all systems of dialogue and transcendence: mind and heart are thoroughly purified and illumined to prepare them for a definitive and transcendent openness and readiness for God, which leads, through God's free and loving self-revelation, to loving union with Him. Abandonment or indifference, understood and practised as a humble love ready for suffering, is man's ultimate act in relation to God. God alone can lead man to union with Him: man does not really 'strive' for it (abandonment is not a religious form of *eros*); he just leaves it to God. The negative characteristic is the way the general religious fervour of the age expresses itself in a constant tendency to discursiveness, making comparisons and refinements, mutual observations, 'spiritual direction', and thus psychologising. This imperceptibly and very easily shifts the emphasis from a pure Godwardness (as in Ignatius) to reflections on transcendence. The devout mind is self-conscious and paradoxically takes self as its object in the very process of transcending and escaping from self. In still ardent faith the French write a critique of religious reason without noticing that they are anticipating the critique carried out by the Enlightenment in unfaith. The most fruitful impulses of the Reformation, which destroy this kind of introspection at its roots, did not come to anything, even in the spirituality of Port-Royal, which mostly remains at the moral and ascetical level. People automatically tend to look at themselves in a mirror. To justify herself, Teresa of Avila has to observe herself, consider herself, describe herself. Even a simple and straightforward person like Marie de l'Incarnation is compelled to write reports, in minute detail, about herself and her mystical experiences. This tendency to introspection rests upon the celebrated spirituality of the *Grand Siècle* like mildew (or should we say, like talcum powder?). In the case of Pascal there is the added factor of Jansenist brooding about predestination: 'Am I one of the

interpretations and choice of texts. *Cf* L. Cognet, *Crépuscule des Mystiques*, 1958.

elect?' The result of all this is that, in the midst of a great flowering, one has a sense of decline and fall, which pervades all the glory of the Baroque age, a glory which spreads out, legitimately enough, half aware, half unaware, of its own fragility.

The crowning masterpiece among the works of St Francis de Sales is the great *Treatise on the Love of God*.[2] The title itself poses a problem: is it God's love of us or our love of God that is meant, or are the two combined, univocally as it were, in a higher concept? This problem is immediately and unequivocally resolved by the fact that the central theme of the book is our love of God as a response to His supernatural providence and as the perfection of all the virtues, powers and potentialities of man. Beginning with a summary psychology (Book One), Francis describes the 'Progress and Perfection of Love' (Book Three), its decline (Four), its fundamental acts (gratifying love and benevolence, Five) and prayer (Six). Certain liminal situations (rapture in love and dying of love) are brought in (Seven), and only then does he deal with love as conformity to the will of God, His commandments, counsels and inspirations (VIII), as perfect indifference (Nine). Finally, he speaks of the chief commandment (Ten), the chief virtue (Eleven), and, as a kind of appendix, practical methods (Twelve). This leaves only Book Two to recount 'The History of the Generation and Heavenly Birth of Divine Love', though this is mainly concerned with 'supernatural providence', 'divine inspirations' and the three theological virtues. This means that the most important thing of all—the whole objective history of salvation, Incarnation, Redemption, Justification, the Church and Christian life in the world (obviously because it belongs to dogmatic theology)—is excluded, and so all that this 'spiritual theology' is left with is an anthropocentric point of view. This naively unintentional anthropocentrism of a spirituality that imagines itself to be totally theocentric, and indeed excessively presents itself as such, characterises many of the systems of the seventeenth century and at least infects

[2] *Traité de l'Amour de Dieu*. Cited from the *Oeuvres complètes de St François de Sales*, 4 vols., Paris, 1836.

several others. The spirituality that knows everything about love and perfection secretly presupposes a univocation which compromises the *analogia entis*. It alligns itself with Baroque scholasticism's speculative univocation of being and, in conjunction with it, gives birth in the next century to pietistic rationalism. The regular, unctuous grandeur of the Salesian style, with all its superlatives, is the unconscious expression of this univocation in contrast to, say, the Ignatian style, which is sobered down to the point of dryness by the comparatives of analogy (with the ever-greater God).

Within these limitations Francis de Sales can say very beautiful things about love—as, for example, in the famous parable of the deaf minstrel whom a prince appoints to sing before him. Some of the time he listens to him attentively, but occasionally he leaves him playing his lute and goes off to hunt. 'But the musician's desire to do his master's will made him continue his music as carefully as if his prince had been present, even though he had no pleasure in singing, since he was deaf and his prince absent'.[3] 'The human heart, the true chorister of the love of God, usually enjoys listening to itself and delights to hear the melody of its own song'. Those who do this 'are deceived without noticing it. Instead of loving God in order to please God, they begin to love Him for the pleasure they feel in exercising holy love ... for though this holy love is called the love of God, because God is its object, yet it is also ours, because we are the lovers ... and this deceives us: we love the love because it comes from us, the lovers'.[4] 'It is difficult, I admit, to enjoy looking at a beautiful mirror for very long without catching sight of ourselves in it, even when one does not feel any particular pleasure in seeing oneself ... Our aim ought to be to love God for His beauty, not to enjoy the beauty of loving Him. At prayer, if you notice that you are praying, you have not given yourself up completely to prayer'.[5] The person who prays for the pleasure of praying will abandon prayer in times of aridity.

[3] Book IX, ch. 9.
[4] *Ibid.*
[5] Book IX, ch. 10.

But in this instruction to love God solely 'because He is beautiful' is there not concealed the opposite danger? Does it not look as if the disinterestedness of Christian love has been now confused with aesthetic disinterestedness? Is the Christian contemplative act not identified, in a new kind of univocation, with this-worldly contemplation of the beautiful in general? Perhaps the very first sentence of the *Treatise* is relevant here: 'Introduce unity into diversity, and you create order; order yields harmony and proportion; harmony, where you have perfect integrity, begets beauty.' Beauty, not the glory of the Lord, is the dominant concept in this often very severe and ascetically demanding doctrine of love.

Another factor points in the same direction. It is more remote, but it strongly influences the spirituality of the *Grand Siècle*. The transcendence being strived for touches what Eckhart calls 'the spark of the soul', Ruysbroeck 'the deepest unity', the French *la cime et suprême pointe de l'esprit*[6] (or *la fine pointe*), which has all the appearances of a natural organ for contact with God, though, of course, it goes far beyond all sensory or categorical knowledge: you 'see without seeing, meet without recognising'. Bérulle will speak here of a 'state' beyond acts, of 'a zone of our soul unknown to us', which is 'the proper seat of grace'.[7] Here lies the danger of real transcendence being replaced by a kind of transcendental psychology, which, under another form of illumination, will be continued by German idealism.

Francis de Sales does not want to be tied down to the metapsychology of the *fine pointe*. What he is really getting at is the mystery of how the human will, by love and indifference, enters the divine will. One can speak of the will 'passing away' (the *trépas* of the will). 'Although the will cannot really die, sometimes it departs from the limits of ordinary life, to live entirely in the will of God.' 'The heart embarked on doing God's good pleasure (*embarqué dans le bon plaisir divin*) should have no other desire than to be carried along by God's will (*se laisser porter*).' 'The will that has died

[6] Book IX, ch. 12.

[7] Bremond, op. cit., vol. VII, ch. 3, points out the *identité foncière* between the Salesian philosophy and Bérullism.

to self in order to dwell in the will of God has no particular wishes of its own. It is utterly self-obliterated and transformed into God's will, like a little child still unable to exercise his will to want or love anything except the breast and the face of his beloved mother.'[8]

g. The Metaphysics of the Oratory

PIERRE DE BERULLE,[9] who founded the French Oratory in 1611, was also responsible for a spiritual synthesis of great significance, which developed in a variety of ways in his disciples, of whom only Charles de Condren can be discussed here. Our concern has to be with 'metaphysics'. Now in the Oratory all theological is rooted once more in the fundamental relation of the *analogia entis*, which, for the creature, is expressed by *religio*: the realisation of the infinite grandeur and majesty of God over and above the essential nothingness of the creature. In his beautiful introduction to Bérulle's works, the third General of the Oratory, Bourgoing, describes this fundamental attitude: 'To honour means to consider and esteem some perfection and excellence in another together with a respect and self-abasement proportionate to the degree of that excellence. Now since all excellences are divine and infinite in God, and are divinely human, and of an infinite dignity, in Jesus Christ Our Lord, by reason of His divine person, they are worthy of a like esteem, reverence and submission . . . Christ's pains and sufferings too deserve the same honour . . . So there is nothing in Him that does not deserve homage, honour, profound reverence . . . It is the essential act and exercise of religion, the creature's first obligation towards his God, the principal duty of the Christian towards Jesus Christ Our Lord.'[10] This primordial act does not originate in the creature's free deliberation and self-reflection, but is the response of homage to God's will for glorification. God 'wants to glorify Himself in us' and holds

[8] Book IX, ch. 13. *Cf.* Book V, ch. 2.
[9] Works in the edition of Migne (Paris, 1856). In the 1960 facsimile of the first edition of 1644 Migne's page numbers have been inserted.
[10] 86.

sway in us through His Holy Spirit in accordance with that will. He 'makes our soul adore the divine majesty, not only by its own thoughts and affections but also by the operation of His divine Spirit, who acts in our spirit, and makes it bear and feel the power and sovereignty of His being over all created beings by the experience of His grandeur applied (*appliquée*) to our littleness and by the experience of our littleness incapable of bearing His grandeur; for it is infinite and infinitely distant and disproportionate to all created being.' So 'this divine Being, adorable in all His attributes, has attributes that are apparently contradictory. He is infinitely present and infinitely distant, infinitely exalted and infinitely applied (*appliqué*) to created being, infinitely delightful and infinitely severe, infinitely desirable and infinitely insupportable'.[11]

Bérulle does not entrust the performance of this primordial metaphysical act to man's spontaneous deliberation; no, he makes it clear that it involves the co-operation and collaboration of God the Holy Spirit. In the analogy of being the analogy of the finite and infinite subjects is permanently in force. And in the concrete order of the world, as the supreme miracle of divine grace, the God-Man Jesus Christ is like the bridge between infinite and finite, between absolute glory and absolute adoration, the mediator of the religious act. Ontologically and psychologically, He is the full reality of analogy. One or two decades later, Pascal, in great turbulence, in a state of Jansenist shock at man's spatial and ontological disorientation (the Oratory has some influence here), will make this discovery for himself:[12] Christ is the definitive proportion between God and man, a proportion not found anywhere else. Bérulle had already established this truth by the simple contemplation of Christ and without prior consideration of man's sinfulness and incapacity for adoration. In Christ 'God incomprehensible makes Himself comprehended . . . God ineffable makes Himself heard in the voice of His Word incarnate, and God invisible makes Himself seen in the flesh that he has united with the essence

[11] 1417–1418.
[12]*Cf.* vol. III of this work, pp. 205–218 (Eng. tr.).

of eternity, and God terrible (*épouvantable*) in the magnificence of His *grandeur* makes Himself felt in His gentleness, in His kindness and in His humanity.'[13]

Both in His being and in His consciousness Jesus Christ is the point where glory is transformed into worship; indeed, since He is personally God in human nature, the transformation is total and perfect: 'You alone serve God as he deserves to be served, that is, with an infinite service, and you alone adore Him with an infinite adoration ... From all eternity there was an infinitely adorable God, but there was still not an infinite adorer ... O grandeur of Jesus, precisely in His state of abandonment and servitude ... since from now on we have a God served and adored without any kind of defect and a God adoring without a [selfish] interest in His divinity.'[14] This precision is not just ontological, because it is expressed by Christ's own act of adoration; and yet it is not just functional either, for the particular act totally corresponds to the ontological situation of the God-Man. To express the unity of the two aspects Bérulle invents the idea of 'state' (*état*). This denotes the psychological and existential dimension of Jesus' ontological reality; constantly and precisely, His actions reveal His being. Now man is historical and goes through various states of life—the state of being in his mother's womb, the state of childhood, of maturity, of joy and sorrow, of living and dying. In Jesus all the states of a truly human existence are experienced and shaped into a precise expression of His eternal adoration of God. According to Bérulle, all Jesus' particular states (*les états*) are integrated in His general state as God and man, which, in precisely *this* integration, is the place of man's true transcendence towards God. In fact, here finite being's perfect act of homage to God (the foundation of all authentic knowledge of God) is performed with divine validity.

The integration of the states of human life in the state of the God-Man is familiar to us today through Odo Casel's 'theology of the mysteries', which is concerned with the question of how what is essentially temporal in Jesus becomes

[13] 217.
[14] 183–184.

eternal. Bérulle provides a prudent and circumspect answer to this question. He sees that both the temporal acts and the temporal states of Jesus (e.g., His Infancy, Passion, pierced Heart, His Burial etc.) *emerge* primarily from His permanent and fundamental attitude as the 'perfect adorer' and are then contained again within that same attitude, not just as a permanent disposition of mind but as the harvest of all the real achievements of Christ in time. Like Eckhart, Bérulle especially emphasises the fact that the incarnate love of God is always Now, grounded in the eternal Now of the Trinitarian procession.[15] In this eternal Now of the God-Man 'the actual enjoyment, the living disposition, by which Jesus effected any given mystery [of His earthly life] is always living, actual, present for Jesus'; 'the interior condition of the exterior mystery, its efficacy and power, which make the mystery alive and effective in us', transcend time. If Jesus could take the scars on His body into glory, 'why can He not preserve something of his suffering in His soul, in the definitive state of His glory? . . . But what he takes with him in body and soul of his passion is itself life and glory . . . what remains in Him of these mysteries of his life forms on earth a kind of grace, which pertains to those souls chosen to share in it.'[16]

This 'kind of grace' is Bérulle's central preoccupation. He does not dispute the dogmatic fact that sanctifying grace as such cannot be directly experienced at the conscious level, but can only be grasped by faith. Nevertheless, because of his christological orientation, he is bound to think of the life of faith as a transcendent participation in the fundamental state, at once both ontological and psychological, of 'the perfect Adorer', whose entire state has been opened up to all mankind and above all to the believing members of His Mystical Body. For Christ as Mediator and Substitute possesses in Himself 'two wonderful capacities (*capacités*)': one for the fullness of God, 'the other for souls, whom He contains in Himself, and has in His authority, in His power . . . a capacity that contains, conserves and protects'. For those with faith and love it is a

[15] 921.
[16] 1052f.

capacity which 'in Christ gives them life and subsistence, strengthens them and makes them grow', a space which enables them to live more in Christ than in themselves.[17] One can see here how Bérulle gives a metaphysical foundation to the Pauline concept of the indwelling in Christ by faith and thus surpasses and removes the poison from the Platonism of Eckhart and Ruysbroeck, the Platonism which taught that the creature lives more in its divine idea than in its own existence outside of God. Existence in Christ, integrated by the integration of His human states in his fundamental state as the God-Man, is an existence which explains our spiritual capacity (*capacité* in the sense of the possibility of existing spiritually in another, the world or God) in terms of Christ's capacity for us.[18] 'For Jesus alone is our fulfilment, and we must bind ourselves to Jesus as to the one who is the ground (*fond*) of our being by His divinity, by His humanity what binds our being to God, the spirit of our spirit, the life of our life, the fullness of our capacity.'[19] At the same time, this potentiality of our faith is of necessity realised by our grace (always Christological in form) becoming conscious in a transcendent manner (according to Karl Rahner, 'non-categorically', to be precise). To partake of the divine life means to participate in the fundamental state and attitude of the 'perfect Adorer', Jesus, who in His freedom chooses us for a particular place within His states: one person shares with Him specially in being the Father's child, another shares in His contemplation in the wilderness, a third is incorporated into the agony in Gethsemane, a fourth in the dereliction of the cross.[20] The experience of one's own existence is the understanding of one's destiny; Christian experience of existence is the interpretation in faith of all that happens as a modality in the sphere of Christ's life, which therefore trains one in his perfect adoration of God's glory.

The perfect example of someone incorporated into Christ

[17] 968–970.
[18] 916.
[19] 1181.
[20] 940–941. This idea was used impressively by Bernanos. *Cf.* my book, *Bernanos* (Hegner, 1954), p. 433 and *passim*.

and His states is the life of Mary in her unlimited *fiat*. The Oratorian school unites Jesus and His Mother in the closest possible way (as does St Ignatius, who speaks of 'the mediators'). St John Eudes, with his devotion to the hearts of Jesus and Mary,[21] also depends on Bérulle, for Bérulle, for all his inclination towards integration, never neglects the sensible and historical formation of the interior sentiment; on the contrary, he lovingly emphasises it.[22] The fundamental mystery for him is abasement (*abaissement*), which he contemplates above all in the infancy of Jesus (this devotion too and the 'spirit of infancy' are revived and promoted by the Oratory), and more precisely still in the act of the Incarnation itself, when the Word sinks into the womb of the Virgin. Bérulle's work, entirely directed towards transcendence in the sense of the Christological act of adoration, delineates in clear, vertical style the foundation of Christian metaphysics, though not without neglect of the ethics of love of neighbour.[23]

CHARLES DE CONDREN, the second General of the Oratory, had, at the age of twelve, a totally Old Testament kind of experience of God, which radically and decisively affected his life and thought.[24] While at work, he suddenly found himself surrounded by a luminous splendour, in which 'the divine Majesty appeared to him so immense and so infinite that it seemed that nothing but this pure Being could subsist, and that the whole universe must be destroyed to His glory. He saw that God had no need of any creature, that even His own Son, on whom His entire good pleasure rests, had to offer Him His life; that only the disposition of offering, of

[21] Bremond, vol. III, pp. 629–671.

[22] Texts in Bremond, vol. III, pp. 57–59.

[23] *Ibid.*, pp. 511–582. This meditation represents the largest part of the Cardinal's unfinished major work, *Discours de l'Etat et des Grandeurs de Jésus.*

[24] Detailed biography and doctrinal exposition by Denis Amelote (1643). Among his own works the following stand out: *L'Idée du Sacerdoce et du Sacrifice de Jésus-Christ* (edited by Quesnel, 1677), and *Lettres* (first edition 1642, later enlarged, quoted here from the fourth edition of 1644). See also Bremond (III, pp. 283–418); and Molien in *Dict. Spir.* II, 1373–1388.

oneself and of all things, with Jesus the Victim, was worthy
of His grandeur; and that it was not enough to love Him, if
you were not willing to annihilate yourself, with His Son,
for love of Him. This light was so pure and so powerful that
it made an impression of death upon him, which was never
effaced. He gave himself with all his heart to God, in order
to be reduced to nothing in His honour and to live for ever
in that disposition. At that moment he knew that the whole
world was to go up in flames for the sins of men, to which
the divine purity, holiness and justice had an extreme
aversion, and that God looks with joy only on Christ and His
Spirit . . . And the force of this divine light had such a
powerful effect on him that he would have desired to be
immolated, that very hour, in the presence of the glory that
filled his spirit . . . He felt a special joy when he saw that the
Son of God was always His Father's Victim . . . He realised
that the sacrifice of Jesus Christ was the fulfilment of the zeal
of all those who wanted to be sacrificed themselves but knew
they were incapable of honouring God worthily by their
sacrifice.'[25]

Once again the root of this experience is a radical,
Eckhartian *analogia entis*. Though saturated by an Old
Testament image of God's *kabod* as a consuming fire, it is of
philosophical origin. God, in His being all, is so inexpressibly
glorious that beside Him everything else not only is as
nothing but, truly speaking, *wants* to be as nothing. 'God's
rights oblige us to accept that God is more in us than we
ourselves are . . . and to perform for Him not only the duties
of a slave'—obedience to His will and law—'but the duties of
a creature, namely, adoration and the sacrifice of ourselves.'[26]
As creatures we owe God not just individual actions but our
very being. The central idea of sacrifice has an ontological
foundation; it is not primarily soteriological. Condren refers
back to sacrifices in classical antiquity (such as that of
Iphigenia), to the Old Testament sacrifices; he could have

[25] Amelote I, 41f. Bremond observes correctly that the biographer has
projected into this experience of Condren's childhood the whole of his
later theology.
[26] Letter 25, p. 117.

quoted Philo and (even more so) Origen.[27] Franz von Baader
will develop his ideas.[28] In sacrifice he sees the will to
represent the truth (that God is all), but, of course, only in so
far as the action comes from the creature: being assumed and
transformed by God into God is something the creature no
longer has the power to represent. Man can throw himself,
for better or worse, into God's consuming fire; how the
sacrifice is consumed is the affair of God alone.

But in Christ we can see what God does with the victim
wholly consumed. 'Of Him, the perfect holocaust, nothing
remained that had not been consumed (*consommé*) in the
glowing furnace of the Godhead'. This annihilation (*exinanitio*)
was, however, His surrender to the Father; His intention was
to be 'consumed (or completed, consummated, *consommé*) into
us, that is to say, to be all in us'.[29] Here Condren's idea of
transcendence becomes clear: the total 'liquidation' of the
sacrificed Christ in us is the presupposition of our own
'liquefaction' or annihilation into Him, but because Christ is
God, His own burning up is also the creaturely mode of the
divine incandescence itself. This is how God 'consumes/fulfils
(*consommant*) His creatures into Himself, without being
anything other than Himself'.[30] So what is consumed/fulfilled
in us is the Christ who lives in us. Our effort must be to allow
Him to live in us as much as possible, to hand ourselves over
to Him, 'to the One who raises the dead to live in His divine
power'.[31] From our point of view, this passing over is death,
so it is not something we can become conscious of 'through
any interior experience';[32] no, it is the entry into 'divine,
incomprehensible life', to which pure faith alone is the
appropriate response. It is the *adhaerere Deo* of the Psalmist,
Augustine and John of the Cross, which voluntarily renounces
any kind of comfortably reassuring comprehension.

[27] *Cf.* my anthology, *Geist und Feuer*, second edition 1951, texts 814–
825.

[28] In *Vorlesungen über eine künftige Theorie des Opfers* (1836), *Fermenta
Cognitionis* (1825), *Vierzig Sätze aus einer religiösen Erotik* (1831).

[29] *Considérations sur les mystères de Jésus-Christ* (1882), p. 74f.

[30] Letter 21, p. 108.

[31] Letter 30, pp. 139–140.

[32] Letter 32, p. 235.

FÉNELON. After such radicalism we find it strange and certainly unexpected that the very words of Fénelon about 'pure love' (*amour pur*) scandalised Bossuet so much that he set in motion an ecclesiastical condemnation. The radicalism of the analogy formulas quoted above is not very far behind Eckhart at his strongest: for Bérulle, the creature had to become 'pure relation' to God or to relate to Christ in a way analogous to the relation of His anhypostatic human nature to His divine person. Condren's annihilation-formulas in a way went even further than that by comparing sacrificed man to the accidents of bread and wine in the Eucharist: 'So Christ must be our substance too.' This identification of God with being, inherited from the medieval German mystics via Benedict Canfeld, as an influence on the Oratorians Olier, Gibieuf and Bourgoing, on Renty and Bernières, and later on Madame Guyon,[33] through whom it reaches Fénelon. If one surveys the path taken by the 'Metaphysics of the Saints' since the late Middle Ages, one is struck by the fact that, though it was always primarily a theology of contemplation for contemplatives, at the same time it clearly perceived in its beginnings the active, soteriological and apostolic efficacy of the attitude of abandonment to God. For Eckhart and his disciples the 'essential work', the birth of God, was the origin and form of all external works that have as their goal the diffusion of Christian life on earth; the most perfect example of this quality is to be seen in Catherine of Siena. Ignatius strove to achieve a balance between contemplation and action, indeed, so far as was possible, the integration of the two: the Christian should be *in actione contemplativus* by dying to all earthly love and then 'loving the Creator in all His creatures and all them in Him'.[34] The French, though, seem so preoccupied with their personal encounter with God that Catholic openness to the world recedes into the background, or remains alongside contemplation as an isolated external factor.

[33] L. Cognet, *Crépuscule des mystiques* (1958) and 'La spiritualité de Mme Guyon', *Revue XVII siècle*, special number (11–14) devoted to Fénelon. Fénelon's works are quoted from the Paris edition of 1852 (10 volumes).

[34] *Constitutiones*, pars 3, c. 1, n. 26.

Thus, for Fénelon, who had, of course, studied in detail the poetry and philosophy of classical antiquity,[35] *indifférence* acquires certain autonomous and therefore pre-Christian and aestheticising features. When he and Mme Guyon refer, with all their historical knowledge, to the universal Christian tradition of *apatheia*/abandonment/indifference,[36] they see in it a kind of 'secret tradition' of true perfection.[37] For the majority of Christians, with their more modest pretensions, ordinary Church doctrine is sufficient; indeed, it would be imprudent to try to lead the imperfect by force any higher.[38] Fénelon's fundamental vision, concealed behind this doctrine of *apatheia*, is the necessary overcoming of Eros by Agape. Eros is the creature's love of God, in so far as the creature is a 'nature', which necessarily strives for its perfection. Eros is not egotistical in the sinful sense (though original sin tragically puts its seal on love's fall into egocentrism and for man makes that fall definitive), and yet, considered simply as a function of created nature, it is incapable of loving God purely for His own sake. Nevertheless, Fénelon demands that 'pure love' at all costs, the love that gives God absolute preponderance over

[35] The following were written for the Dauphin: the pedagogical Homeric novel, *Aventures de Télémaque*; the translation of part of the Odyssey (Books 5–10, and a summary of the other books); a 'Sketch of the Lives of the Ancient Philosophers with an Anthology of their Most Beautiful Sayings' (from the pre-Socratics to the Stoics), the amazing *Dialogue des Morts*, with characters both from the Iliad and from history from the Romans to modern times; a book of *Fables*.

[36] At the end of the three volumes of Madame Guyon's *Justifications* (Cologne, 1720) there is a 'Collection of Some Quotations from the Greek Fathers', the authors quoted covering the whole of Christian tradition. *Cf.* on this: Jeanne-Lydié Goré, *La notion d'indifférence chez Fénelon et ses sources* (Presses Universitaires de France, 1956), p. 75f. Fénelon was, typically enough, dependent on Clement of Alexandria and wrote a book about him (*Le Gnostique de S. Clément d'Alexandrie: opuscule inédit de Fénelon*. Publié avec une introduction par le R. P. Dudon SJ, Paris, Beauchesne, 1930). In fact, Clement was the first person to try to explain the transcendental dimension of Christian *agape* in terms of the ancient concept of *apatheia*. *Cf.* Theodor Rüther, *Die sittlichen Forderungen der Apatheia in den beiden ersten christlichen Jahrhunderten und bei Klemens von Alexandrien* (Herder, 1949).

[37] Dudon, 125f.

[38] *Instructions sur la morale et la perfection chrétienne* 20 (VI, 117a).

the loving 'I'. This preponderance is not based primarily on the supernatural grace of Christian Agape, but (as with the Oratorians, but with St Thomas Aquinas as well)[39] is ontological. It is the act of man, not in so far as he is a *nature*, but in so far as he is *spirit*. For as spirit man is open to the *analogia entis*; as spirit he is capable of realising God's absolute preponderance over the creature and thus the absolute necessity of His being preferred above all things. As spirit-love the act of love is a clear *choice*: it chooses the beloved without second thoughts or secret self-concern.

Now, since God as beloved is Himself absolute love and 'the glory of God', He can act only for Himself and His glory. He is necessarily jealous of this immediate glory; indeed, as He Himself says (Is. 42.8), He can give it to no one. On the other hand, the lowliness and dependence of the creature is such that—unless it wants to make itself an idol and infringe the inviolable law of creation—it can do nothing, say nothing, want nothing for itself and its own glorification.' As the absolute, however, God is not 'Something Else' outside and alongside us. If we really love, we do so only in virtue of His absolute love in us: 'You yourself love yourself in me . . . you are more present to me than I am to myself. This "I", on which I lavish so much care and attention, ought to be a stranger to me when compared with you. You have given it to me, without you it would be nothing, so it is your will that I love you more than it.'[40] Since God created all things for His own glory, 'to attain the essential goal of our creatureliness, we must prefer God to ourselves and strive for our happiness only for the sake of His glory, otherwise we would be turning his order upside down'. 'To the objection that God has given us a natural inclination to the happiness that He Himself is, perhaps we can say that He did so because He wanted our union with Him to be realised with greater

---

[39] On this see Pierre Rousselot's detailed work, *Pour l'histoire du problème de l'amour au moyen-âge.* BGPhMA VI, 6 (1908). But Rousselot shows clearly how St Thomas unites the two forms of love, the natural and the spiritual aspect, inseparably, whereas Fénelon unhappily and abstractly tears them apart.

[40] *Instructions* etc. 18 (VI, 101a, 101b–102a).

ease . . . the motive of our own beatitude is not forbidden, but it has to take second place to that other motive: we must want God's glory more than our own happiness.' 'We would have to love Him just as much, even if (we are supposing the impossible!) He did not want to be in us as our beatitude', even if—and this really is something God could do[41]—'He annihilated our soul at the moment of death.' 'If one accepts these presuppositions as real possibilities, there is no longer any promise for me, no reward, no happiness, no hope for the life to come . . . but could I therefore exempt myself in this ultimate moment from the love of God?' What is more, if God were compelled to promise me eternal life, in other words, Himself, without fail, on the grounds that I am His creature, then he would be dependent on His creature, 'He could no longer exist without it, it would become a necessary being.'[42]

So, then, an absolute love of God even without any promise of eternal life. Are we coming close here to the heroic love of the Old Testament, where eternal fidelity to God is sworn *ad tempus*, in the clear knowledge that 'in the underworld no one praises Him any more'? Or are we to see in this Old Testament fidelity the coming into play of a paradoxical Messianic hope, incomprehensible to the Old Testament itself? If we do, then perhaps we are coming close to the *amor intellectualis* of the Jew Spinoza, for whom this hope no longer exists. And does this not lead logically to Hegel, according to whom there is likewise no hope of eternity for the individual spirit, which is just one passing moment in the infinite ascendancy of Absolute Spirit? It is then a short step to materialism. Mysticism and atheism in a strange way look one another in the eye,[43] for common to both is disdain for human finitude in the interests of an all-embracing Whole in which the little 'I' disappears.

[41] A supposition which St Thomas Aquinas could never have made, presupposing as it does post-Thomist voluntarism. Once created immortal by God, the soul has immortality because of its nature and thus as the presupposition of all its spiritual acts in itself. God cannot, therefore, annihilate it without contradicting himself.

[42] *Instructions* 19 (VI, 109ab; 11b–112b).

[43] *Cf.* Karl Barth, *Kirchliche Dogmatik* I/2 (1939), 344–356.

Fénelon is an impatient educator; monotonously he demands 'emptying, annihilation of my own limited being' in order to enter God's infinitude,[44] 'external mortification ... for then God takes it upon himself to take hold of the ground of the soul ... and he does all that is necessary to detach man from himself, and though the coat is costlier than the shirt, you feel the loss of the shirt more than the loss of the coat. In the end all that is left is bitterness, nakedness, shame.' 'You realise you depend on something, only when it is taken away from you.'[45] One would like to be spiritual, great in virtue, but that means 'letting oneself become small' (*se laisser apetisser*).[46] Everything must serve the loss of self, which must not be content with resignation, but must press on to real self-abandonment (*abandon*). 'It is sufficient, when suffering, to be little and abandoned (*abandonné*). That does not mean courage, but something less and more: less in the mediocre eyes of virtuous people, more in the eyes of pure faith. It is a littleness in itself which transfers the soul into all the greatness of God.'[47] The philosophy of abandonment has its deep roots in Christ abandoned on the cross. For us this means: 'The night of pure faith, in which everything is agony ... Not only does God hide Himself from us, He also hides us from ourselves.'[48]

And yet Fénelon's doctrine lacks a Christological emphasis; instead it remains spiritually idiosyncratic with its abstract idea of indifference; abstract, because it comes from a dissociation of nature and spirit. It is a mysticism in the state of scholasticism and thus, as in the case of Francis de Sales, in constant danger, through sheer 'theopanism', of turning into a pantheist univocalism. The state becomes more important than the object, for if someone really does want to rise above hope, must he not also get beyond 'I and Thou'? Once again

---

[44] *Manuel de Piété* (VI, 54a).

[45] *Instructions* etc. 22 (VI, 121b).

[46] *Ibid.* (VI, 124b). Cf. *Correspondance* (VII, 266a): 'Laissez-vous donc apetisser par vos propres défauts ... Le grand point est de vous mettre de plein-pied avec tous les petits les plus imparfaits.'

[47] *Instructions 37* (VI, 151b).

[48] *Correspondance* (VII, 263a).

speculative idealism seems to have been anticipated by a pious idealism. Once again everything is to be worked out in terms of the glory of God, with direct reference to the total gratuitousness of God's love, the centre of an 'aesthetic theology'. And yet in Fénelon's work the glory of God fails to shine as it should: the search for selflessness is far too self-concerned.

True, Fénelon's tedious trial and final condemnation are muddied by an odious political background and by the conflict of personal ambitions.[49] True, it is not difficult to vindicate Fénelon[50] and to promote him to be a patron of the authentic spirituality of our century. Nevertheless, he brings something to a close, and the sentence against him— the last in a series of condemnations beginning in Spain against the *Alumbrados*, continuing in France against the 'mystical Jesuits' (B. Alvarez, Lallemant, Surin), the verdicts against Port-Royal and the beginnings of the Enlightenment coming out later—historically speaking represents an abrupt termination.

The 'Metaphysics of the Saints' was a procession of widely differing figures, presenting at every stage a penetrating insight into essential truths, but leaving out, in the historical period covered here, other attributes that must be taken into account if a complete theology of glory is to be achieved. The theopanist aspect from Eckhart to Fénelon offers an open flank to Idealist speculation. All in all, only Ignatius of Loyola had the balance right. And so it is one of his sons who gives us a final synthesis to draw this period to a close.

CAUSSADE. Forty years after Fénelon's condemnation, in the middle of the Enlightenment, in a commentary on Bossuet's treatise on prayer 'against the false mystics of our time', Caussade[51] succeeded in expounding, in intact form, the heart

[49] R. Schmittlein, *L'aspect politique du différend Bossuet-Fénelon* (Baden, 1954).

[50] Henri Bremond's *Apologie pour Fénelon* (1910), later frequently endorsed, for example, in the fine book by François Varillon SJ, *Fénelon* (Aubier, 1954).

[51] On Caussade, see *Dict. Spir.* II, 354–370. Works: *Instructions spirituelles . . . suivant la doctrine de M. Bossuet* (1714), new edition with an introduction

of Fénelon's doctrine. What is more, he summed up the entire 'Metaphysics of the Saints', from the Rhineland mystics to St John of the Cross and the French School, in a unity of persuasive simplicity.

Once again the main idea is indifference[52] or abandonment (*abandon*), understood as love—'L'art de l'abandon n'est que celui d'aimer',[53] and thus as unconditional self-surrender, being at God's disposal in transcendent openness to His provident will.[54] In every situation of life abandonment is a unique, sustained act, passive and universal in relation to God, to be terminated in every case by Him in active and finite conduct and behaviour.[55] The all-important thing is the 'inner work' (Tauler) of absolute openness, like the *fiat* of the Mother of God, and proves itself in the act of obedience. This *fiat* sums up 'the entire tradition of Old Testament spiritual theology'.[56] It means 'receiving everything and letting God act'.[57] The *fiat* is the pure, naked, undefiled faith which does not want to decide for itself and so does not want to know anything; it is thus 'faith in darkness'.[58] Or rather: this total faith (John of the Cross) is the indissoluble unity of faith, hope and love, which are together 'just one single

by H. Bremond (1931). P. Ramière composed the central work out of Caussade's letters: *L'Abandon à la Providence divine* (1861). The 5th edition (1867) includes numerous letters to the Convent of the Visitation in Nancy. We shall quote from the 20th edition (Gabalda, 1928) and use its page numbers. 'II' refers to the second volume. [Tr.—Kitty Muggeridge has published an English translation of Father Olphe-Galliard's 1966 reconstitution of the original text under the title *The Sacrament of the Present Moment* (London, 1981).]

[52] 72.

[53] 134.

[54] *L'être propre étant livré au bon plaisir de Dieu, ce transport fait par le pur amour s'étend à toute l'étendue des opérations de ce bon plaisir* (64–65).

[55] *Un même acte universel et général, [qui] n'est point du tout limité par le terme ou par l'ordre spécial.* The termination of the act is then no longer humanly limited, but derives from the will of God, 'who terminates Himself in it' (65). *Accomplissement actif de la volonté divine . . . et acceptation passive de tout* (79).

[56] 2.

[57] 49.

[58] 114.

virtue', though in an infinite variety of possible gradations, all making up the personal richness of Christian life.[59] 'One can just as well call it pure love (*pur amour*) as pure hope, pure faith', since 'the darkness and the shadows of the night are totally pure'. The Christian rests in this holistic act: God's 'mercy leaves me, instead of certainty, pure hope, which in value immeasurably outweighs certainty, without depriving me of the merit of my surrender . . . And on what is this firm hope founded? On the treasures of the infinite mercy and infinite merits of Jesus Christ.'[60]

By understanding the act of faith universally and transcendentally, Caussade rediscovered not only the content but also the act of Biblical revelation. He saw the importance of the (Kierkegaardian) category of the 'moment' (*le moment présent*, which contains the 'one thing needful'),[61] and thought of this as the Holy Spirit's exposition of the Word of God in our hearts, an exposition which always takes place in the here and now, indeed, as the continuation of the one revelation in Christ through all the ages: 'The Holy Spirit holds His pen in His hand, and holds His book open before Him, in order to continue the history of salvation, which is still not closed, and the content of which will be exhausted only at the end of the world.'[62] All the mediation of the Church comes in only at a secondary level: 'God still speaks today, as He spoke to our fathers, where there were no spiritual directors or methods. it is fidelity to God's order which constitutes the whole of spirituality.'[63] 'The beautiful book of the Holy Spirit is currently being written, is just being printed.'[64] With all the passion of the *Devotio Moderna*, Caussade warns against the decadence of a compartmentalising theology and invites his readers to follow God, as Abraham did, as Israel did, without knowing where the journey will end. 'If you have neither map nor path, neither wind nor tide, you are bound

[59] 59–62.
[60] II, 263.
[61] 43–44, 88ff.
[62] 133.
[63] I.
[64] 35.

to have a successful journey'.[65] 'Let us abandon ourselves to
God without thought of the vain and futile systems of sanctity.'[66]
'March off in the direction you are sent, and without knowing
the map, walk blindly on.'[67] 'The doctrine of pure love can
only be experienced through God's action, and through the
effort of reason.'[68] 'Come, I want to teach you a mystery, to
outwit all these clever minds . . . Come, not to know the map of
the land of spirituality, but to possess that land.'[69] Lucifer was an
enlightened and beautiful spirit (*le plus éclairé de tous les beaux
esprits*), 'but dissatisfied with God and with His order'.[70]

If man, abandoned man, sets sail 'on the vast ocean of the
will of God',[71] and if he accepts from Him, at every moment,
the bounds[72] and the order[73] established by Him, he must, if
he is to attain these standards, lose all standards of his own.
'Tear, like threads, all the soul's notions, all the soul's
standards! You must lose the very ground on which you
stand.'[74] The ability to do what at any given time is 'the
best', to do God's will in the present moment,[75] is an
unmysterious mystery, an artless art'.[76] For it is not the art of
man, but of the Holy Spirit, who inspires him. A good
musician, even in half-unconscious improvisation, plays
everything according to the laws of his art, 'which cramp the
spirit when followed too conscientiously.' So the person
trained in surrender is no longer able to preface his action
with cautious deliberations: 'All he can do is act at random (*à
l'aventure*), since only then is he able to give himself up to the
genius of grace, with whose guidance nothing fails.'[77] But it

[65] 69.
[66] 104–105.
[67] 90.
[68] 77.
[69] 51.
[70] 139.
[71] 29.
[72] 65.
[73] 78.
[74] 111.
[75] 85.
[76] 93.
[77] 124.

is precisely this initiation into the total docility of naked faith which demands (as John of the Cross showed) that God hide Himself: He dresses up in strange masks (*déguisé*),[78] appears (as Kierkegaard says) incognito. 'The life of faith is nothing other than an unceasing pursuit of God through all that disguises Him, disfigures and, as it were, destroys and annihilates Him'.[79] Then God no longer stands before the soul, but 'behind it and propels it in front of himself: since he is no longer the clearly-perceived object of its perception, he is the invisible ground of its activity.'[80] Thus Joseph 'deceived' Benjamin and 'allowed him to weep';[81] thus God plays a game of 'tricks' and 'impostures' (*tromperies*), and the soul glides 'dreamlike' through the veils.[82] A dream full of 'anxiety, despair, fear',[83] because the 'infallible means of darkness' demands it.[84] The soul really must learn to do without support both in and outside itself, to be 'sheer weakness'[85] precisely in the endurance of suffering,[86] to consider itself completely useless, humiliated[87] like a 'shattered jug, no longer of use to anyone',[88] to 'hold itself in such low esteem that it disappears before its own eyes'.[89] In short, 'the soul is as light as a feather, as fluid as water, as simple as a child, as mobile as a globe, in order to receive and obey every movement of grace.'[90] For 'God wants to dwell in us in a poor way (*pauvrement*) and without all the accessories of sanctity (*accessoires de sainteté*) which make souls a cause of wonder'.[91]

[78] 25, 123.
[79] 27.
[80] 120.
[81] 120.
[82] 119–120.
[83] 117.
[84] 114.
[85] 105.
[86] *Qu'il est avantageux de souffrir faiblement ... plutôt que grandement, fortement et courageusement!* (II, 264).
[87] 105f.
[88] 56.
[89] 158.
[90] 88. On being a child (56).
[91] 104.

In this night of faith, whenever God's will meets the readiness of the soul, at that moment the act of revelation, the act of nuptial union, the act of communion, can take place: 'O festin, ô fête perpétuelle! Un Dieu toujours donné et toujours reçu, dans tous ce qu'il y a sur la terre d'infirmité, de folie, de néant!'[92] This is the 'communion de tous les instants'[93] and the adoration through all things and situations of life. 'For things proceed from God's mouth like words. At each moment what God does is a divine idea, signified (signifiée)[94] by a created thing.' Everything is consequently a 'sacrament'.[95] God's 'water surrounds me. Everything becomes bread to feed me, soap to wash me, fire to purify me, a chisel to sculpt in me heaven's outlinc'.[96] 'Everything is God's hand. Everything is divine earth, air, waters. His action is more extensive, more present than the elements of the world. He penetrates you through all your senses, provided you use them in accordance with God's commandments ... All bodily states under His influence become effective mediations of grace.'[97] 'Everything is full of meaning, everything makes perfect sense. This line ends here, because it has to; no comma is too much, no full stop redundant.'[98]

What a strange aesthetics in the midst of the night of faith! It is like the back of a piece of embroidery, where only tangled threads can be seen, and yet everything is done, 'stitch by stitch', for the sake of the perfect sample, which will only be turned round and become visible in eternity.[99] Occasionally, as if by chance (when God wills it), rays break forth from this invisible beauty, revealing accidentally the hidden substantial glory: 'Everything extraordinary that we perceive in the saints—visions, revelations, interior

[92] 40.
[93] Ibid.
[94] 44.
[95] 46.
[96] 49.
[97] 50.
[98] 36.
[99] 37, 122.

locutions—is but a reflection of the sublimity of their state, which is guarded and concealed in the exercise of faith. For faith guards everything in itself, since it knows how to see and hear God in everything that occurs from moment to moment. When this is perceptibly and externally revealed, nothing is happening that faith does not already contain within itself; only the grandeur needs to be made visible and the soul stirred to exercise. Thus the glory of Tabor and the miracles of Christ were, not an increase of His grandeur, but lightning flashing out from time to time from the dark cloud of His humanity in order to make it venerable and lovable for others.'[100] So God makes His grace visible in some of His saints for the salvation of many. 'But there is a multitude of other saints in the Church who remain hidden; destined to shine only in heaven, they spread no sort of light in this life, but live and die in deep darkness'.[101]

Now this darkness is at the same time the light of the Word of God. 'God speaks. He speaks a mystery, so it is a death for my senses and for my reason, for it is proper to mysteries to sacrifice senses and reason. The mystery is life for the heart by means of faith; for the rest, only contradiction reigns. The divine action kills and quickens at the same time, and the more deeply aware you are of death, the more you believe that there is life; the darker the mystery, the more light it contains.'[102] Faith is the way to God; it always has been: 'Faith is the spirituality which sanctified the patriarchs and prophets, long before people made so much fuss about it (*avant qu'on y eut mis tant de façons*) and long before there were so many experts in it.'[103] Faith still sanctifies today, but 'not through studying books ... for what instructs is what happens from moment to moment: it educates us in the science of experience, which even Christ wanted to acquire before He began to teach'.[104] This experience of faith is the real presence of revelation, for the work of the Holy Spirit is

[100] 63.
[101] 64.
[102] 38–39.
[103] 8.
[104] 41.

'an inexhaustible source of ever new insights, new sufferings, new actions, new patriarchs, new prophets, new apostles, new saints, who do not need to copy the life or writings of their predecessors, but merely to persevere in constant surrender to your work'.[105] Caussade regards it as self-evident that this surrender should demand Fénelon's *amour pur*: 'Were we to love God a little for the sake of His gifts, He would be loved for His own sake when the gift was no longer noticed.'[106] And 'if the divine goodness does not require us to despise the happiness for which we are destined, it surely has the right to be loved for its own sake without any regard of our own interests'.[107] That is well said and corresponds to the metaphysics of the saints in every century.

One can see how Caussade, protected by the sound doctrine of his order's founder, avoids the snares of Quietism—indeed, he explicitly attacks it.[108] He does not express total surrender with the kind of ontological concepts that deny or paralyse the proper activity of the creature, and yet he does not abandon the radicalism of the tradition discussed in this chapter; he just reconnects it more closely with Biblical revelation. In this form Christian transcendentalism is unsurpassable and the proper partner in dialogue with every form of Asiatic or Sufi mysticism (Al Hallaj). Caussade clearly saw that every attempt to give created reason *more* than the surrender of the perfect fiat (*more* in the sense of a speculative or mystical idealism) would in reality deprive it of its noblest act and clearly turn it into something *less*.

Nevertheless, this Christian transcendentalism from Eckhart to Caussade cannot yet be proposed as the definitive form of Christian 'metaphysics' (there can be no such thing). However precise his comprehension of Christian transcendence as such, he remains within it—it is after all a spirituality predominantly of contemplatives—and does not exhaust the complementary act of *conversio ad phantasma*, of the Ignatian *hallar Dios en todas las cosas*. To reflect on this act without

[105] 42.
[106] 121.
[107] 176.
[108] 85.

throwing away the results of transcendental spirituality is reserved to our own times. Just as Eckhart said you should give up contemplation in order to take broth to a sick man,[109] so Caussade demands: *abandonner cet abandon même*.[110]

---

[109] Discourses of Instruction 10.
[110] II, 157.

3. FOLLY AND GLORY

*≠ human under-
standing
predicament*

a. Holy Fools

The classical art of antiquity took its canon of beauty for the human figure from the gods; our study began with this derivation of beauty from glory. What image of man should be canonical for Christian or post-Christian art, when the 'Metaphysics of the Saints' just described, intentionally or unintentionally, gains validity? This question must at least be posed, even though we cannot be expected to provide a detailed, art-historical answer to it. Poetic art offers the best outline of an answer. Antiquity's influence on architecture and music was much more neutral and inconspicuous; painting may well have been dominated by the cultic icon in its abstract and heavenly dignity: but literature is meant to reveal what the living man of flesh and blood is and the standard by which he is measured. There is a constantly recurring attempt to reassert antiquity's canon with or without its gods (or with its gods reduced to ideals), and there is a typically Germanic version of this: the man of chivalry's ideal of *mâze* (measure), of relative originality and susceptible of stylisation in a Christian direction as well as in a classical pagan one. And yet, astonishingly, very little by way of an image of the living human being has come down to us intact from this late classical and classicist art. Only the original myths themselves are intact—Antigone, Oedipus, Alcestis, stimulating new emulation in every generation. In addition, there is the small contribution of the Germanic myths—the achievement of Hebbel and Wagner in their Nibelungen, and possibly also Roland, Gudrun and others.

For a long time, in countless Latin and vernacular legends, the saints were the canonical image of man, but the heart of sanctity, abandonment in transcendence to the open will of God, cannot be put into epic or dramatic form; only the indirect, accidental effects—miracles, heroic achievements, strange behaviour—offered narrative material capable of gripping a reader. But the saint as hero was a mistaken interpretation, and the more clearly this was seen—the history of this kind of discernment lasts well into the last century, perhaps into our own—the more sharply were the genres distinguished.

But if the saint disappeared into intangibility (though no less dear to pious hearts), how was living art to measure man? The simple adventure story—from the Alexander novel to Amadis—is indeed entertaining, but does not answer the metaphysical question about the nature of man. And in the Christian world all the lustre of mighty deeds was always outshone by the unsurpassable deed of the Redeemer's Passion. The saints stood beside the emperors, restraining, guiding, directing: Athanasius beside Constantine, Ambrose beside Theodosius, Maximus beside Heraclius, Benedict face to face with Totila. The great encounters of worldly power and sanctity in medieval and modern times have been described by Reinhold Schneider:[1] dramatic situations exposing the rift between earth and heaven, a rift which in a Christian context deepens still further the rift between ethos and power (Plato and Dionysius of Syracuse, Aristotle and Alexander, Seneca and Nero). But a rift is still not a figure.

However, when literature from the Middle Ages to the present day is examined straightforwardly in terms of what has an immediate affinity with us, what concerns us, touches us, moves us, then one figure does stand out. In the world of chivalry it is Parzival, in the age of humanism it is *The Praise of Folly*, in the Baroque it is Don Quixote and Simplicissimus. And once this gallery of representative fools and buffoons has come to our attention, it is joined by an immense band of dubious characters from the wandering clerks and François

[1] *Cf.* my book, *Reinhold Schneider* (Hegner, 1953). Among others, the following pairs are considered: Anselm and William the Conqueror, Louis XI and Francis of Paola, Francis of Assisi and Innocent III, Celestine V and Boniface VIII, Charles V and Las Casas, Henry VIII and Thomas More, Pius VII and Bonaparte, etc.

Systematically: *Macht und Gnade* (1940), *Weltreich und Gottesreich* (1946), *Macht und Gewissen in Shakespeares Tragödien* (1947), *Herrscher und Heilige* (1953), and numerous other writings.

Villon through Brant's *Ship of Fools* to Quevedo and Goya, but also from Shakespeare's comic and tragic fools (Hamlet, Lear with Edmund) to Kapellmeister Kreisler and Dostoievsky's *Idiot* and to Rouault, to Hofmannsthal, Chesterton and Unamuno. What is the meaning of this *ostinato*?

The classical hero without his gods may still be 'beautiful', but he is no longer glorious and soon seems boring. But there is a gleam of unconscious, unintended sanctity about the real fool. He is the unprotected man, essentially transcendent, open to what is above him. In the post-Christian era 'classical man' in his beauty is always somewhat melancholy. The real fool never is. Since he is never quite 'in his right mind', never quite 'all there', he lacks the ponderousness that would tie him down to earth. He stands nearest to the saint, often nearer than the morally successful man preoccupied with his perfection. The Russians knew that the fool belongs to God, has his own guardian angel, and is worthy of veneration. And yet the fool is not the saint. He is not in any danger from purism or exclusiveness, which, especially during the final days of the 'Metaphysics of the Saints', separated candidates for sanctity from the existence of ordinary mortals. Thus even the pure fool, Parzival, is convicted of being a great sinner, Simplicius is self-evidently one, and Don Quixote never sees himself for a moment as anything else.

There is also a transition. The saints follow in the footsteps of Jesus, who was despised, abused, thought to be mad (Mk 3.21) and possessed (Mt 12.24; Jn 7.20; 8.48) and yearn, for the sake of Jesus, to be regarded as fools. In their abandonment to God's every command, the finger of their yearning points in this direction, and they know that, as the imitation of Christ, it could be pleasing to God. They may not strive after it, but they rejoice when the grace is given to them. The extreme gestures which they have to perform, such as when the Poverello strips himself naked, can be interpreted this way. 'The madman, *il pazzo*', children called after him. At the Portiuncula chapter, in the presence of the Cardinal of Ostia, he informed the friars that the Lord had told him he was to be 'a fool in this world', and that Christ wanted to lead them along no other path than that of *this* wisdom. Angela of Foligno shrieking outrageously at the church door, is regarded as insane although she does not will this; and many others shared the same fate. But it is not just a matter of the saints doing what is in human terms abnormal, and which leads to their being decried as foolish. In the self-surrender of the saints there are transcendental possibilities which they do not foresee. Some saints, who like Paul offer themselves to be accursed by God in place of their brethren (Rom 9.3), are plunged into the depths—not only of abandonment by God, but also of explicit experiences of Hell, even to the point of being handed over for a time to demons, whether in the form of physical torment or as a deep spiritual experience of what the anti-divine spirit is. These experiences lie in the realm of Christological (soteriological) *a priori* of Christian transcendence. As an example it is sufficient to mention the tribulations of Blessed Christine von Stommeln.[2] St Ignatius Loyola's words can count as definitively valid. In the first contemplation of the life of Jesus he at once emphasises that we must imitate the Lord 'in putting up with all injustice, all abuse, all poverty',[3] and at the climax of his introduction to the making of a truly indifferent choice of a state of life, he demands 'the most perfect subjection'. This consists in desiring 'to be poor along with Christ in poverty rather than rich, to be insulted along with Christ who was so grossly insulted, rather than to be well thought of: I would rather be thought a helpless fool for the sake of Christ who was so treated, rather than to be thought wise and clever in the world's eyes'.[4] Novices are to be examined to see whether they 'accept and desire with all possible energy whatever Christ Our Lord has loved and embraced. Just as the men of the world who follow the world love and seek with such great

[2] A detailed account can be found in Theod. Wollersheim, *Leben der ekstatischen und stigmatisierten Jungfrau Christine von Stommeln* (Cologne, 1859); *Acta SS Juni* IV (1707), 270–454. Many examples, nowadays forgotten, in J. Görres, *Christliche Mystik.*

[3] *The Spiritual Exercises of St Ignatius Loyola.* In a New Translation by Thomas Corbishley SJ (London, 1963), n. 98, p. 44.

[4] *Ibid.*, n. 167, p. 59f.

diligence honours, fame, and esteem for a great name on earth, as the world teaches them, so those who are progressing in the spiritual life and truly following Christ Our Lord love and intensely desire everything opposite. That is to say, they desire to clothe themselves with the same clothing and uniform of their Lord because of the love and reverence which He deserves, to such an extent that where there would be no offence to His Divine Majesty and no imputation of sin to the neighbour, they would wish to suffer injuries, false accusations and affronts, and to be held and esteemed as fools (but without their giving any occasion for this)'.[5] This final clause has not held true of all Christ's disciples, as will be shown, and yet it seems necessary to add it if the call to folly is to be accepted with complete indifference and not rashly anticipated.

Such naive anticipation is reported of the Byzantine saints.[6] *Simeon the Fool* makes his way from the world into the monastery, from the monastery into the desert, from the desert into the most extreme form of humiliation, with the intention at the same time of winning souls for Christ: from now on he will 'play the fool for Christ's sake', in the 'loneliest of struggles'. It really is a 'game' for Simeon—as it is for *Andrew the Fool* as well—and so they live a consistently double life: foolery by day so as to 'expose, by ever new forms of foolish provocation, the folly of the world, everything speaking and acting in a way that goes against the grain of the world';[7] by night an unexpected visitor witnesses the outbreak of glory from behind the carefully guarded mask: 'The fool appears to him in a radiant, regal form, his

[5] *Examen Generale* c. 4, n. 44; St Ignatius Loyola, *The Constitutions of the Society of Jesus*. Translated with an Introduction and a Commentary by G. E. Gans SJ (St Louis, 1970), p. 107f.

[6] St Symeon the Fool (PG 93. 1669f.) and St Andrew the Fool (PG 111.611f.). On the latter: Sara Murray, *A Study of the Life of Andreas the Fool for the Sake of Christ*, (Munich, 1910). On both: Ernst Benz, 'Heilige Narrheit' in *Kyrios* 3 (1938), 1–55. On Symeon: Water Nigg, *Der christliche Narr* (1956). On the fools' forerunners among the Desert Fathers, see Stephan Hilpisch, 'Die Torheit um Christi willen', *Zft f. Asz. u. Myst.* 6 (1931), 121–131.

[7] Benz, op. cit., p. 10.

face shining like the sun . . . the glory of the Lord gushes out of him.'[8] The incognito can be kept up only by annoying behaviour, and only in an utterly indirect way through symbolic gestures (as in the case of the prophets), through miracles, albeit still shrouded in madness, through preaching the Word of God in disjointed parables and scarcely intelligible hints. But under the protection of his folly's freedom, the Christian can approach people unreached by official churchmen or no longer moved by fossilised forms of piety. This form of life is explicitly described as lying beyond *apatheia*, indeed as a crossing of the frontier of the measure proper to human nature.[9]

The only true penitent fool in the West,—apart from the Russians, is JACOPONE DA TODI (+ 1303), doctor *utriusque iuris* and advocate, follower of the Poverello. Having discovered a hairshirt on the body of his dead wife, he decides spontaneously to live henceforth as a fool. His ecstatic leap beyond reason gave birth to his unprecedented poetic inspiration; songs to God's foolish love were given to him of a kind that had never been heard in dialect. He accomplished this before Dante, whose power on occasions he anticipates, and before Eckhart, whose understanding of the 'whylessness' of God he possesses because of his own folly:

> Goodness knoweth no why,
> Why doth outward fly.
> Seek not healing balm,
> In thy sickly sinful harm.[10]

The frailty of all that is earthly taken as far as the *danse macabre*; the glory of the love of God taken as far as the Franciscan embracing of all God's beloved creation; the plunge into the bottomless depths of the divine essence, and then, on the other hand, after his entry into the Franciscan order, the hard earthly struggle to maintain the purity of the order's original spirit taken as far as the horrendous five years of incarceration in the castle of the intensely hated Boniface

---

[8] *Ibid.*, p. 14.
[9] Texts cited in Nigg, pp. 38–41.
[10] Federmann, *Lauden des Jacopone da Todi*, 57.

VIII, whom he cursed in his songs and whom to the very end Jacopone resisted to his face; the desire to go to hell, when he dies, to take the place of all the damned and suffering: these are the hallmarks of the fool who, like Angela of Foligno, was hurled to the heights of heaven and into the depths of hell. Italian poetry owes its origin to him. Other names can be added: Giovanni Colombini (+ 1367), founder of the Jesuati, John of God, founder of the Hospitallers, and shortly afterwards Philip Neri; men famed for going to the limit and beyond. In fact, Philip Neri was the only saint to sneak into the heart of Goethe. And it was only thanks to his voluntary madness that John of God was able to gain Christian access to the inner world of the mentally ill, being exposed like these to horrific treatment with chains and blows.

b. Gallows-birds and Duellists with Death

The saints fly so high, soaring above even *apatheia* in their holy folly, that they discourage sinners. It is not surprising that the voice of Archilochus can be heard in the Middle Ages, but the way it sounds in a Christian age is remarkable. The indifference of the holy is an act of all-embracing love. For good or for ill, the indifference of the unholy, in fact of absolutely everyone, exists too: it is death. In the Christian world this death is not quite the same thing it was before. For every human being it is the brutal leveller, the ravager of all things, and yet death itself inescapably confronts one with a mystery: God's death, the death He died out of love. For the sinner expecting judgement this can make death doubly hateful and threatening: but it silently demands his love, for it reminds him of love, of everything in his wasted life that was intact, immaculate: this he will encounter anew. The songs about the fleetingness of life may sound cynical, even blasphemous: the tunes of the wandering scholars are travesties of sacred chants: hymns to Our Lady provide the elements of drinking songs and love songs. Yet behind all this stridency and bitterness, all the defiance and provocative arrogance, can be heard quite unmistakably the humble voice of the Prodigal Son, certain in his knowledge of grace. About the middle of the twelfth century it can be heard in the 'Archpoet'; a hundred years later in poor Rutebeuf, dissolute yet so tenderly devout; in the time of Dante in Cecco Angiolieri in Siena, drunkard author of a sacrilegious psalter; and finally in the most brilliant member of this clan, FRANÇOIS VILLON, baptised in 1431, Bachelor and Master of Arts, felon, recidivist, and jailbird, missing presumed dead at the age of thirty, author of the immortal 'Great Testament' and of a dozen poems, which, with perfect formal control, build up an extreme tension in much the same way as Jacopone does, but precisely from the criminal's point of view. For years in prison this man must have stood facing death. At the end he distributes the possessions left over from his life of mendicancy among his friends and among his enemies, for whom he wavers between bitter hatred and universal forgiveness. To his old mother he bequeaths, as a prayer for her to say, the most beautiful Marian hymn in French literature.[11] Alongside this are the crudest of brothel songs, as crude as they are because Villon is constantly measuring the distance in himself between Heaven and Hell, between baptism and sin:

> We love filth, filth pursues us;
> We flee from honour, it flees from us,
> In this brothel which is our home![12]

But he also writes about his own death, his long hanging on the gallows. From the vantage point of non-existence he surveys the great failure that was his life. He intensifies the contradictions of this situation in a 'Ballade of Contraries', in which he goes far beyond Qoheleth in experiencing and expressing the self-dissolution of finitude:

> I die of thirst beside the fountain,
> Hot as fire and trembling with chattering teeth;
> When in my home country, I am in a far land;
> When beside a fire, I tremble though quite warm;

[11] *The Works of François Villon. With Texts, Translation, Introduction and Notes.* Edited by Geoffrey Atkinson (London, 1930), pp. 126ff.
[12] *Ballade de la Grosse Margot*, p. 175.

Naked as a worm, I am dressed like a Peer;
I laugh when weeping and wait without hope;
I find comfort in sad despair;
I rejoin and find no pleasure;
I am mighty without strength or power;
Well received, I am rebuffed by everyone.
For me, nothing is sure but an uncertain thing;
 Nothing is obscure except what is clear;
I have no doubt in a certainty . . .[13]

In the 'Ballade of Unimportant Matters' is the refrain: 'I know all things except myself'. In the 'Ballade of Untruths' he sets out the complications and paradoxes that make impossible any tranquil knowledge of self and of existence: 'Only the coward is courageous, only the traitor is true'. In the 'Argument Between Villon's Heart and Body' the split runs right down the middle of man: when Heart tells him to remember, Body says he remembers well enough, but does not let it bother him. In the 'Epitaph' Villon addresses his *frères humains*: he asks them not to be hard of heart towards us (the hanged), but instead to beseech Lord to forgive us all. What is more, they should not despise the gallows-birds for daring to address them as brothers. They were justly condemned, and yet all men lack an accurate view of the good, so, as a precaution, the guilty should be pardoned. Hanging there, they are dried black and hard by the sun, chilled by the rain, tossed about by the wind as it pleases, and remain a strange kind of brotherhood:

Do not, therefore, join our confraternity,
But pray God that He may forgive us all![14]

At the beginning of the *Great Testament* there is a simple, honest confession of sin, based on what Scripture says about God not wanting the death of the sinner, but rather that he repent and live: 'Although I die in sin, God lives, and His mercy gives me pardon by His grace, if I repent in my conscience.'[15] And then, despite all the bitter complaints and curses:

[13] *Des Contraires*, p. 213.
[14] *Epitaphe*, p. 239.
[15] *Grand Testament*, p. 79.

> If, through my death, the public good
> Should be in any way advanced,
> I should judge myself fit to die as a pernicious man,
> So help me God![16]

For the salvation of others he is gladly willing to be hanged. We are all, every single one of us, 'deluded fools', *fous abusés, démis du sens, comblés de déraison*,[17] for, in oblivion of our birth, we all submit 'out of cowardice to a shameful death' instead of 'taking heart and placing our trust in God.'

One final challenger of death deserves to be mentioned here. He too calls death a fool, an imbecile, though he himself is not to be included among the especially 'unholy'. In 1400 JOHANNES VON TEPL held his vehement debate with death.[18] Death had robbed him of his young wife, loved by him above all things, and thus had confronted him with nothingness. True, Boethius is referred to,[19] Seneca, Aristotle, Plato are mentioned by name. But the situation is completely changed. Although mighty Lord Death approaches the wretched mortal with arguments similar to the ones Philosophy uses on the prisoner in the condemned cell, this is a book, not of 'consolation', but of bitter struggle and disputation. Not without compassionate irony, Death defends only *his* standpoint. Without him, the world would have been filled up long ago.[20] The 'workings of nature' demand that species constantly change and renew themselves.[21] It is part of being a mortal, finite creature that pain comes out of love,[22] for 'End is Beginning's sister'.[23] So wisdom consists in entrusting oneself to the great law of change: 'Break off, let go . . . he who will not drive past love from his heart must bear present pain all the time. Drive the memory of love from your heart, and you will soon be out of sorrow's reach.'[24] Nature herself advises such detachment: 'Love not too lovingly, sorrow not

---

[16] *Ibid.*, p. 79.

[17] *Ballade du Bon Conseil*, p. 201.

[18] *Der Ackermann aus Böhmen*. Edited by A. Hübner in *Altdeutsche Quellen*, edited by Ulrich Pretzel 1 (1954²). Cited by chapter numbers, 30.

[19] 29.   [20] 8.

[21] 10.   [22] 12.

[23] 20.   [24] 22.

too sorrily.'[25] Keep your distance from man, he is only frail flesh, 'a latrine, a rotten carcass; a greedy gullet, a whited sepulchre', 'if you could see through to his interior, it would horrify you. Let love flow past, let sorrow flow past, let the Rhine run like any other water . . .'.[26] All that is earthly is mere concupiscence of the flesh: lust; concupiscence of the eyes: avarice; the pride of life: honour. Sheer vanity. 'The earth and all it contains is built on transience.'[27]

But man has a countercharge. Death is not pure nature. It is first and foremost a vile and merciless enemy. It cannot destroy true love in its humble glory. It is the most hideous, the most unjust thing in God's creation.[28] It only mocks, it does not comfort; it only robs, does not repay. When asked for honest advice, it advises disloyalty. It annihilates, ill-treats, dishonours noble man, God's dearest creature, and thereby denigrates the Godhead. 'Now I know you are a liar and were not created in Paradise as you maintain.'[29] Man is capable of being faithful, and thus he gives the lie to death. He proves the contradiction: Death had said he would survive all mortal life, but once all life is dead, what can it mean to die? In the final analysis death is just a way of life; life is not a way of death. Life is eternal, death cannot be.[30] Man appeals against death to God.[31] And God as judge of both resolves the controversy: death is a mere servant of God, but that is all man is too; both have 'fought a good fight', but both have to restore what has only been lent them. 'So let the plaintiff have the honour; let death have the victory.' That looks like a decision against man, because what is the use of honour if death is victor? Nevertheless, the philosophy of death is no longer, as it was in Boethius, the philosophy of God. Death is the instrument of glory,[32] not an integral part of it. Glory towers high above created being and its passing, and to glory rises up the magnificent final prayer:

'Light sempiternal . . . founder of Hell's abyss . . . Creator of all the elements—of thunder and lightning, of mist, hail, snow, rain, rainbow, mildew, wind, hoarfrost, and of all their

[25] 24.
[26] 24.
[27] 30, 32.
[28] 15.
[29] 25.
[30] 31.
[31] 19.
[32] 16.

effects, the one and only Master Builder; Captain of all the heavenly hosts; Emperor whose fealty none can forswear; mildest, mightiest, most merciful Creator, have mercy upon me and hear my plea! . . . Well-spring whence all pure streams flow . . . of all beings, ephemeral, temporal and eternal, the almighty quickener, preserver and destroyer, whose nature, what thou art in thyself, none can fathom, fancy, see, or comprehend, Supreme Good above all goods, most noble, eternal Lord Jesus, graciously receive the spirit, in thy goodness receive the soul, of my dearly beloved wife. Rest eternal grant unto her, bathe her in the dew of thy grace, hide her in the shadow of thy wings. Take her, O Lord, into thy perfect contentment, that contentment which is for the least as for the greatest. Grant her, Lord, a dwelling-place in thine everlasting kingdom whence she came'.[33] As in Dante, the love of man and woman overcomes death and hides, praying, in the bosom of eternal life. In this masterpiece, for the first time, the New High German developed in the Bohemian Chancery of Charles IV entered German literature. It is 'a monument of the German language without equal before Luther'.[34]

c. The Transformations of the Fool

WOLFRAM

The theme of the fool, which receives its first metaphysical treatment in the poetry of Wolfram,[1] is not really a tragic

[33] 34.

[34] Wolfgang Golter, *Die deutsche Dichtung im Mittelalter* (1922[2]), 531–532. On the late medieval experience of death: Johan Huizinga, *Herbst des Mittelalters*, ch. 11, 'Das Bild des Todes' (8th ed., Kröner, 1961); W. Stammler, *Die Totenänze* (Leipzig, 1922); L. Spitzer, 'La danse macabre' in *Mél. A. Dauzat* (Paris, 1951).

[1] We are taking the Parzival material at the stage of evolution it has reached in Wolfram, although the fundamental conception of folly (*niceté*), which changes from rustic uncouthness into the recognised folly of sin in the elect, and even the individual episodes of the story, are to be found in the unfinished epic of Chrétien de Troyes, *Li Contes del Graal* (ed. W. Roachs 1956). Wolfram gives the material not only its exterior and interior rounding off but also, and chiefly, its theological depth and its touching human cordiality, even if at times the story's themes lose their sharpness of outline.

theme. Tragedy dominates the ancient world of Eros and its Christian continuation. In Wolfram and Grimmelshausen the fool emerges from the protection of the forest, the forest of Paradise, one might almost say. He makes his way into, but also through, guilt and pain, shielded by the angel wings of his folly. The Parzival theme ('Parzival' comes from *perce à val*, 'pierce through')[2] originated in the world of fairytale— the fool who, by means of a question, is supposed to set an enchanted king free and attain the object of his desire. Behind the fairytale there may well be an ancient myth of a pure saviour who delivers a kingdom from sorrow and decay. In the Christian world there is only one true saviour; all the myths and fairytales become transparent to Him and consequently lose their weight. It is no accident that, in Christian literature, comedy on the whole outweighs tragedy. In Shakespeare the two are finely balanced, but in the English novel, right up to Chesterton, it is humour which increasingly has the upper hand. Molière has more penetration than Racine, Goldoni more weight than Alfieri. In Austria, with Mozart, Raimund, Nestroy, Hofmannsthal, Christian light triumphs again over the bogus gravity of Germany, though there too Jean Paul had more readers than even Goethe. From the margin (Hebel, Reuter, Keller, Timmermans) humour penetrates and transfigures the Kantian realm. We are talking now about the light of humour, for irony presumes to take on the perspective of God, and satire exposes pharisaically (accusingly or leniently) the faults of one's neighbour. Moral faults, notice, not sins; when sin is involved, only God is competent to judge the foolish man. The Christian humorist, though, knows about the mysterious relationship between engraced wisdom and sinful folly and about the abyss, at once open and closed.

WOLFRAM creates an epic of chivalry, but the values that underlie its conventional ethos come from beyond the world

[2] 'Your name means "Pierce-through-the-heart"', Wolfram von Eschenbach, *Parzival* (ed. Lachmann), 140, 16; 81. [Tr. The number following the Lachmann references is the page number in the Penguin English translaton by A. T. Hatto (Harmondsworth, 1980)].

of chivalry: the lay Christian wisdom he calls *mâze*, which is almost the equivalent of Aristotle's *meson*,[3] the equilibrium between extremes, between body and soul, heaven and earth, with *staete* and *triuwe* as Germanic-Christian *constantia*, with *kiusche* as *temperantia* (discipline) and *schame* (sensitive appreciation of what is noble). Wolfram's epic is above all based on a transcendant folly (*tumpheit*), which, having been first a deficiency (the mother gives the boy a rustic upbringing in the forest), passes through full measure before becoming an excess (Parzival struggles to attain the symbolic Gral of the mythical tale and finally becomes King of the Gral). Chivalry, with its ideal centre in the round table of King Arthur, is the balance, hard won after much sacrifice, to 'an ethic and aesthetic of measure'[4] and, in this sense, the archetype of a beautiful world. This idea is indisputably valid for Parzival too (and behind him for Wolfram): it is the absolute unity of God's grace and the world's. Like Dante, Wolfram's hero strives to attain, as his ultimate goal (for him, it is a *conditio sine qua non*), faithful love of God and faithful love of his beloved lady. 'My desire has always been for both.'[5] The two loves are graded: 'great is my longing for the love of (Condwiramur), but greater still for the goal sublime.'[6] 'My greatest need is for the Gral, after that for my lady.'[7] But the loves are never separated: his 'great fidelity' to his lady is by his own will inseparable from fidelity to God. 'If I am to strive for the Gral, the thought of your chaste embraces must also drive me on'.[8] And so finally there appears on the Gral stone the inscription electing Parzival as king together with his wife and son, Lohengrin.[9] The knights of the Gral are religious men fighting an earthly battle

[3] For example, the way Gurnemanz introduces the young fool to knightly virtue, the right measure between meanness and generosity, poverty and riches, loquaciousness and taciturnity, between courage in battle and mercy for the conquered (171, 7–30; 95f.).

[4] E. Köhler, *Trobadorlyrik und höfischer Roman* (Berlin, 1962), p. 22f.

[5] 389, 12; 200.

[6] 441, 11; 226.

[7] 467, 26–27; 239.

[8] 732, 19–21; 364.

[9] 781, 13f.; 387.

for a sacred relic. They are all virgins, except for the king, who has a wife. Only 'lofty servitors' are chosen,[10] yet what is decisive is not 'stock' but pure grace. Thus the kingdom of the Gral is a symbolic and eschatological anticipation of the perfect unity of religious and secular, renunciation and fulfilment, pure availability (*diemuot*: willingness to serve—for the knights may be sent to rule over any land)[11] and earthly wealth.[12] From a modern Christian perspective, chivalry seems to be moulded and illuminated by one idea, which cannot *as such* be fully realised in time: as a reality at the end of the epic (though polarizing the entire action) it is 'fairytale' which, in so far as it is polarised, gives the whole chivalry a Utopian quality. Much later Cervantes will expose this Utopianism, but it also harks back in a way to the eschatology of Irenaeus, which was expounded in the second volume of *The Glory of the Lord*.[13]

Thus Wolfram's chivalric ideal is in a strange tension between the immanent (which has the transcendent in and above it as an 'ideal')—the Kingdom of Arthur—and the transcendent (which raises up the immanent along with itself as its inner form)—the Kingdom of Gral. The tension can be seen in the fact that the story has two main heroes, Gawan for the Kingdom of Arthur and Parzival for the Kingdom of the Gral. But Gawan too is in quest of the Gral (he finds instead a magic castle from the Thousand and One Nights: Schastelmarveile and the Duchess Orgeluse), and Parzival strives for acceptance at the Round Table and succeeds. The two kingdoms are intertwined by all manner of familial and social relations. The desire for a totality of religious and secular (Péguy's ideal of the *temporel-spirituel*)[14] does not stop at the borders of Christianity. The ideal of the 'aristocratic man' spans the divide between Christian and pagan. White Christians travel to pagan and Moorish lands, and there they marry black queens and have children, who then—like

[10] 493, 22; 251.
[11] 494, 7f.; 252.
[12] 796, 24–25; cf. 395.
[13] Volume II, pp. 92ff.
[14] Volume III, pp. 465ff.

Parzival's half-brother, Feirefiz, spotted black and white like a magpie—return to the Christian world and even find entry into the Kingdom of the Gral: a beautiful, humanist, ecumenical, lay world.

Behind this there is a corresponding awareness of the ambiguity of all that is earthly and human: God created 'the crooked and the straight', and he alone can divide them.[15] All things are inwardly double: 'Were one to place a love story on the scales and weigh it, one would never find anything but love *and* sorrow.'[16] 'With Adam's race there began both sorrow *and* joy.'[17] Thus Gramoflanz tells Gawan that he 'both gladdens *and* saddens' him.[18] Itonje cherishes 'both love *and* hate'.[19] And in a recognition scene: 'All who wanted to saw both joy *and* sorrow. Love drove them to it. Tears *and* laughter in one moved their mouths. It came from a greater love.'[20] And after Parzival has fought with his brother and the two have recognised each other, Feirefiz 'secretly laughed *and* wept'.[21]

And yet no picture of the world is as untragic as Wolfram's. However ambivalent the world and man and the kingdom may be, however easy it is for even the heart to become sinfully dual in *zwîfel* (ambiguity), there is still, at every level of human existence, the cohesive force of *einvalt*.[22] This key notion, which provides the foundation of Parzival's folly, is primeval in both the Bible and general human culture (antiquity). In human terms it is the heart's capacity manfully to withstand the world's contradictions, which is turned philosophically into the late Platonic ideal of uniformity, simplicity (ἐνιαίως). In Christian terms it is the 'simple eye' which finds light and vision in everything and leads, in the

[15] 264, 25–27; 139.
[16] 272, 15–18; *cf.* 143.
[17] 465, 1–2; 237.
[18] 609, 30; 306.
[19] 636, 5; 319.
[20] 672, 15f.
[21] 752, 23; 374.
[22] Just the term: 689, 27. In its content, the word *diemüete* covers the field of the concept. R. Gruenter, 'Parzivals "einvalt"', *Euphorion*, 52 (1958), 297–302.

poor and emptied-out heart, to the vision of God (Mt 11.26; 5.8; 6.22f.; 10.16). Thus, in the history of spirituality, simplicity is almost a synonym for *apatheia*, *Gelassenheit*, indifference; but whereas these are closer to the mind, simplicity is closer to the heart. As *sancta simplicitas*, holy simplicity, the concept dominates the Christian world from the Fathers to St Bernard.[24] In antiquity and the Middle Ages, while *mâze* (μέτρον μέσον) is the basis of beauty, simplicity is surrounded by glory. This simplicity may be interpreted more philosophically or more theologically, or more in the direction of 'wisdom' (beyond 'science') or more in the direction of 'folly' (beyond 'wisdom'). Folly itself may wear a great diversity of colours: from the proud philosophical folly of, say, the Cynics to the mystical folly of the (*docta*) *ignorantia* of Denys, a theme which continues through the whole Dionysian tradition of the Middle Ages as far as the learned *idiota* and *laicus* of Nicolas of Cusa and the, by contrast, more self-conscious folly of the non-clericals, the 'unlearned' (*illiterati*),[25] who in fact are well-educated knights and courtiers; Wolfram counts himself as one of these. However, all this is very far short of the real Biblical 'folly of the cross', which theologians, especially of the early Middle Ages, are only too glad to interpret in terms of a folly of the 'higher wisdom' kind mentioned above.[26]

Whatever the place of Wolfram's fool in this network, the whole poem is in any case immersed in an all-pervasive light.

[24] Jean Leclercq, *Sancta Simplicitas*, *Coll. Ord. Cist. Ref.* (1960), 138–178; P. Lehmann, 'Die heilige Einfalt' in *Erforschung des MA*, Bd III (1960), 213–224; further literature in Alois Haas, 'Parzivals tumpheit bei W. v. Eschenbach' in *Philol. Stud.u.Quellen Heft 21* (1964), 295f.

[25] H. Grundmann, '*Litteratus-illiteratus*. Der Wandel einer Bildungsnorm vom Altertum zum MA' in *Arch.f.Kulturgesch.*, 40 (1958), 1–65, and the admirably documented article of Fr. Ohly, 'Wolframs Gebet an den Heiligen Geist im Eingang des Willehalm', *ZfdA* 91 (1961), 1–37; A. Haas, l.c., 232–235.

[26] The texts, for example, which A. Haas (296f.) cites as instances of the folly of the cross theme in the circle of St Bernard (William of St Thierry especially), in so far as they are not just paraphrases of 1 Cor 1–2, show this very clearly. In the Victorines the preoccupation is with the 'follies' of ardent love and desire, a theme of classical and Augustinian origin, and not primarily with the imitation of Christ.

The courtly poets delight in colour and light, but Wolfram goes further: the words *lieht*, *liuhten*, *blanc*, *clâr* are omnipresent. It is not primarily nature that is *lieht*[27] but human beings; the beauty of the human beings is experienced as the radiance of light, as *schîn* and *glanz*. Arthur has luminous eyes.[28] After his cure the face of Anfortas has the lustre the Frenchman calls *fleur*.[29] We hear of 'bright sweet boys' (*clâren süezen knabn*).[30] The young fool meets a knight who is 'brighter than anything he had ever seen' (*ern hete so liehtes niht erkant*).[31] Gawan's eyes are *reht ein meien glast*.[32] Beakurs 'was of dazzling appearance' (*pflac varwe lieht*).[33] But it is above all the women who are described as *lieht* and *clâr*, pre-eminently, Parzival's wife, Condwiramurs. A 'blaze of light' (*ein liehter glast*) emanates from her;[34] her face has a 'lovely radiance' (*ein minneclîch antlützes schîn*);[35] she is a spouse of light (*diu lieht gemâl*).[36] But Orgeluse too is pure radiance.[37] Of her it is said that she is so *lieht* that, even if no candles had been furnished, there could have been no night around her because of the shining of her eyes.[38] Similar things are said of Itonje and of Repanse de Schoye, where it is stressed that there is a correspondence between purity of heart and bodily radiance: 'Great purity dwelt in her heart. The flesh without was a blossoming of all brightness.'[39]

But the divine world shines no less brightly. When Parzival as a boy asks his mother, Herzeloyde, what God is, she replies: 'brighter than the sun'.[40] And because she has told Parzival that what distinguishes God is light (*unterschiet den liehten*

[27] 516, 21.
[28] 661, 22; *cf.* 331.
[29] 796, 5–6; *cf.* 395.
[30] 74, 16; *cf.* 370.
[31] 122, 1; 73.
[32] 374, 24; *cf.* 186.
[33] 722, 9; 360; *cf.* 721, 21.
[34] 186, 20; 103.
[35] 186, 17; *ibid.*
[36] 619, 9; 742, 28.
[37] 612, 16; 624, 12 and passim.
[38] 638, 16f.; 320.
[39] 809, 13–14; 401.
[40] 119, 19; 72.

schîn), the boy thinks the brightly shining knight is God.[41]
Later Trevrizent teaches him that God is 'a light that shines
through all things' (*ein durchliuhtec lieht*)[42], because He 'shines
through' (*glestet durch*)[43] even the walled darkness of our
secret thoughts 'with an unseen leap', God as *durchliuhtec*, the
light that shines through all things, is 'serenity'; even a radiant
human being, like the dead Cidegast, can be given that
name.[44] Thus Wolfram's world is an infinitely illuminated
one (both naturally and supernaturally). Long before Claudel
he discovered the analogy of transparent water and the eyes
and light and baptism. On the occasion of the baptism of
Feirefiz, he says:

> Trees have their sap from water.
> Water fecundates all things made that are called
>   'creature'.
> We see by means of water.
> Water gives many souls a splendour
> Not to be outshone by the angels.[45] (Simrock)

One must not overlook the fact that these attributes together
constitute the beauty of this world seen as the glory of God
raining in upon this world. So that glory is not, first and
foremost, a hidden glory. It is significant that Parzival is
constantly and loudly praised for being beautiful, radiantly
beautiful, indeed as the most beautiful human being of all.[46]
'He bore the marks of God's handiwork' (God's *kunst* [or
gunst] *lac an im*).[47] He is like a wingless angel that has
blossomed out on earth.[48] He 'brings the vigour and beauty
of youth with him'.[49] He is 'the glorious hero'.[50] As such his
'*victory is innate to him*'.[51] Indeed, he is infallibly and

[41] 122, 24; cf. 73.

[42] 466, 2; 238.

[43] 466, 21; *ibid.*

[44] 613, 1–2.

[45] 817, 25–30; 406.

[46] 727, 21; 362. Cunneware laughs when she sees him, having made the
vow to laugh only when she saw the most splendid hero of all (151f.; 86).

[47] 123, 13; cf. 73.

[48] 308, 1–3; 160.

[49] 311, 16; cf. 162.

[50] 331, 24; cf. 173.   [51] 717, 22; cf. 358.

perpetually victorious, even against the Knight Templar, even against triumphant Gawan. He has supreme *werdekheit*,[52] which can mean dignity, reputation, as well as glory. This must be borne in mind in considering Parzival's Christian life, his 'humiliation'. The fact that when the accounts of God's grace and the world's guilt are drawn up, the books can be balanced, indeed—in the fairytale and in its eschatologically proleptic significance—they must balance, is a real problem for the existential formulation of the question. And yet Wolfram is able to set forth purely the kernel of his *maere*, free from all ambiguity.

The starting-point is the boy's simplicity. This simplicity is 'supernatural' in the sense that it is the unaffected openness to God of someone who later on will be called and has already been chosen for a purpose. His 'natural' simplicity has two forms: first, it is something inherited from his parents, the good knightly 'breeding' which is bound to assert itself; secondly, it is the ignorance, artificially produced by his mother, of all courtly things, of the upbringing befitting his station. After meeting the knights in the forest, the knightly part of him awakes, and he becomes desperately keen to go to King Arthur. His mother lets him go but makes him dress in fool's clothing, and after his departure dies of a broken heart. Next come a few scenes of stupidity: the naive embracing of Jeschute, who has to do bitter penance for it, and who will later be reconciled with her jealous husband by Parzival; the naive slaying of Ither with the little javelin and the stripping of his corpse in ignorance of the fact that he is related to the red knight. Gurnemanz instructs him in courtly manners and thereby removes his natural foolishness. Now Parzival can look back knowingly on his former folly as a thing of the past.[53] But this cessation of folly for the purposes of chivalry is not enough to rid him of his folly for God's

---

[52] 169, 2 and passim.

[53] 'I was a young fool—no man—not yet grown to years of discretion' (269, 24; 141). 'If ever I stripped a corpse, it was because I was dull of understanding' (475, 6; 242). '. . . as befitted his youthful folly' (744, 18; *cf.* 371).

sake. It is precisely his training in *mâze* (which means, *inter alia*, not talking too much) that makes him miss the opportunity to ask suffering Anfortas in the castle of the Gral the question that would have redeemed him. True, a typical fairytale situation, but a Christian one too: it would have meant showing a mercy that lay beyond the ethics of *mâze*. This inadvertent omission earns him Sigune's double curse of the world of chivalry[54] and Cundrie's curse of everything to do with the Gral,[55] which in its turn triggers off desolation in his relationship to God. The simplicity of that relationship disintegrates in *zwîfel* and discontentment with divine providence, the repercussions of which are such in his knightly spirit that he is prepared bravely and defiantly to bear the weight of God's hatred of him, which he thinks he feels.[56] On the other hand, with an unselfconscious sense of election, he strives for the Gral, even though it can only be found 'unsuspectingly'.[57] He wants to wring it out of God, but in this respect too he is rent asunder, for no one can force anything out of God through anger.[58] That is what he is taught by Trevrizent, who has to admit, though, at the end: 'A greater marvel never occurred, in that, after all, with your defiance you have wrung the concession from God that His everlasting Trinity has given you your wish.'[59] Even when defiant: 'God will appoint me [through the Gral inscription]',[60] he speaks as someone who is still an undoubted sinner but already called by God.

This subtle Christian situation—there is a parallel here with Dante[61]—must be resolved, not just by explanatory instruction, but, over and beyond that, by a Christian

[54] 249f.; 135f.
[55] 312f.; 164f.
[56] 332, 8; 172.
[57] 250, 29.
[58] 'You can gain nothing from Him by anger' (463, 1; 236).
[59] 798, 1–4; 396.
[60] 472, 9; 241.
[61] Gust, Ehrismann, 'Dantes Göttliche Komödie und Wolframs von Eschenbach Parzival' in *Idealistische Neuphilologie*, Festschrift K. Vossler (1922), p. 191: 'Parzival's confession in the presence of Trevrizent corresponds to Dante's *confessio* before Beatrice'.

confession. The central Good Friday scene (just as Dante goes through Hell on Good Friday) demonstrates Wolfram's supreme mastery. No human being can open himself up to God's grace by unconscious simplicity alone; there also has to be a conscious and free decision or choice. However, man affected by Original Sin, when he chooses God in this way, necessarily encounters his fallenness, which becomes evident to him in its depths in concrete actual sins. It is precisely this falling away from God which is his supernatural folly, his simplicity or stupidity in the bad sense. By disclosing to Parzival the absolute fidelity of God's grace, the Grail hermit, Trevrizent, Anfortas' brother, shows him at the same time that man's only response can be an equally unconditional fidelity to God (in the form of faith, hope, love, surrender), and that this is the only appropriate and wise attitude, the rebel against God being therefore simply stupid. Trevrizent's view of confession is what every modern *homme révolté* fails to see: the realisation which dawns on you only when you are at confession that the person who does not trust in God is 'out of his senses'[62] and 'sick in his wits' (*an den witzen kranc*).[63] 'God is named and is Truth', because 'God Himself is faithful and true'.[64] He who is not faithful and true falls from all truth. Originally the earth was created virginal in fidelity and truth (Wolfram takes over the Patristic theologoumenon of *terra/virgo/mater*), but through Adam and Cain's 'discontent and vainglorious greed' (*ungenuht, gîteclicher ruom*),[65] 'wrath' (*nît*)[66] has invaded mankind and still persists. Man has fallen away from God, but God becomes man, and 'His faithful humanity fought faithfully against unfaithfulness'.[67] 'In His divine love he that is highest of all released us in Hell'.[68]

Parzival's 'sins' certainly pose problems for moral theology

[62] 461, 27f.; *cf.* 236.
[63] 463, 3; *ibid.*
[64] 462, 25; 236.
[65] 463, 25, and again 782, 23, *gît* is greed, avarice.
[66] 464, 21.
[67] 465, 9–10; 237.
[68] 465, 28–29; *ibid.*

which do not need to be dwelt on in detail here.[69] (Individual) guilt, which the sinner is conscious of, is dovetailed with objective sin, which, through some kind of culpable ignorance (*ignorantia*), he remains unconscious of, and when he does become aware of it, he discovers the abyss of original guilt and, precisely in that, the lack of supernatural love for God and neighbour. This whole catastrophe Wolfram grasped and described with intuitive accuracy, and so all the glorious light of his poem streams from the convergence of humble confession with descendant grace in the hero's lay shriving.[70] This convergence constantly underlies everything that follows: Parzival's permanent awareness of his sin,[71] his humble and resolute fidelity to God, and following from that his view of human courtly love (*Minne*) as 'great fidelity'[72] and his distinguishing of love's true fidelity from the amorous insanity that grips the Arthurian heroes[73] and—even worse— Gottfried's Tristan. True, 'Frau Minne' makes every man 'a fool', and Parzival, when he falls in love, 'loses his reason' and is 'beside himself' when he sees the three drops of blood in the snow which remind him of his wife.[74] But, for Parzival, human falling in love is safely contained within fidelity; it is part of creaturely simplicity and does not endanger it. To absolutise this 'folly', as Gottfried does, is, to Wolfram's mind, the reversal of all truth, which consists for him solely in the ecstasy of fidelity. After confession Parzival is now only one who serves, so the second chance to ask Anfortas the saving question (this time consciously and for that very reason as one who has been humbled) is given to him out of pure grace. And so the all-pervasive quality of Wolfram's poem is joy. Towards the end it goes from celebration to celebration, from reconciliation to reconciliation. What in the beginning was 'care' melts away into the simplicity of joy:

[69] Alois Haas, following the careful study by Jul. Schwietering, 'Parzivals Schuld', *ZfdA*, 81 (1944), has produced sufficient evidence from contemporary Scholasticism to justify Wolfram's ethics (l.c., 247–276).

[70] 501, 17; 255.

[71] 783, 7; cf. 388.

[72] 732, 8; 364.

[73] 532, 17–21.

[74] The long episode, 281–305, 6; 147ff.

You raised a brood of cares in tender years:
But the happiness which is on its way to you
    has dashed their expectations.
You have won through to peace of soul
And outlived cares to have joy of your body.[75]

d. The Analogy of Folly

ERASMUS

Wolfram's poem, dating from about 1200, still just about belongs to a world of intact sacrality: the mutual symbolic reflection of sacred and secular is not regarded as Utopian caricature but as an adequate résumé of reality. A hundred years later we enter the age of Dante, Ockham and Eckhart, none of whom can develop the theme of folly, nor can their immediate successors. One more century and Villon is singing of the gallows and the Bohemian ploughman is quarrelling with Death. The theme of the *danse macabre*, already audible in Jacopone, places—with brutally constrained indifference—all existence under the sign of vanity, all idealism under suspicion of eccentricity. Only the artful humorists—Eulenspiegel, Reinke de Vos, the sturdy characters of Wittenweiler—seem to stand out against this gloomy background. Neither they nor the great band of fools assembled by Sebastian Brant, with bitter moral earnestness, in his 'Ship of Fools' of 1494, to attack them and even perhaps to reform them, have very much to do with our theme of 'the Glory of the Lord', still less 'The Exorcism of Fools' (1512) and 'The Guild of Knaves' (1512) written by the disputatious Franciscan Thomas Murner against the decadence of the Church and used later as confessional polemic.

Erasmus of Rotterdam's *Encomium Moriae* (1509),[1] in which Dame Folly boasts of being the all-governing cosmic principle, elevates the theme once again to metaphysical

[75] 782, 27–30; 388.
[1] In the translation by Clarence H. Miller (New Haven and London, 1979). References are to page numbers.

heights. The fixed point among all the shifts of Erasmus'
thinking about folly (he was everything but a philosopher),
the point from which an analogous unity can be seen is the
position of the 'wisdom' against which his polemic is
directed: the 'gloomy' wisdom of scholastic philosophy,[2] the
'gloomy worthiness of the male mind'[3] (by which doubtless
he means the earnest triviality and scientific bustle of the
humanists), and also the gloomy moralistic wisdom of 'the
frogs of the Stoic ilk',[4] who, for the sake of pure *apatheia*,
condemn all passions. The hallmark of reality, in contrast to
the dreary 'truth' of philosophers and moralists but also of
theologians, ascetics, ecclesiastics and monks, is everything
that goes by the name of 'folly': everything that lies beneath
the mind and in which it is rooted: all that is vital,
passionate, irrational about love's and friendship's choices,
the 'splendour of youth' in its perishability, even the self-
love and self-contentment of a life of isolation, for that
inevitably means some kind of illusion (when someone acts
as if he were the be-all and end-all), in a word all 'the
splendour of life'.[5] On the other hand, folly is also
everything that lies *above* the mind: all that is gratuitous,
unfathomable, playful, grace-ful; it is because of all this that
folly is a goddess and at home in the world of the gods.[6]
The deeper, Christian meaning of this supra-rational folly is
the incomprehensible making straight of the crooked and
ultimately the outplaying of sin by grace, the interpretation
of evil on the cross as 'not knowing what they do',
foreshadowed in Aaron's prayer for his sister, 'I beg you,
Lord, do not hold us responsible for this sin, which we have
committed in our folly', and in David's plea, 'I beg you,
Lord, to take away the inquity of your servant, because I
have acted in my folly.'[7]

[2] 22.
[3] 32.
[4] 57.
[5] All these themes are dealt with in close connection with one another
(31ff.).
[6] 18, 24f.
[7] 131.

Stretching the meaning of folly to include both the highest level of grace and the lowest level of animality gives Erasmus unlimited scope in the game of connections. On the one hand, there is no doubt that the realities of human life, including its noblest values, are rooted in the sub-spiritual realm, which usually cannot stand up before the bar of pure spirit. Examples of this are heroism in a reprehensible war,[8] determination in hazardous and horrifying competition, the theatrical excitement of life in its multifarious masks and disguises,[9] the cleverness of life based on silly 'aggression and grappling with things' and on an irresponsible forgetting of earlier situations of guilt, a general immersion in things of the moment, a rejection of that 'high standpoint', from which 'human life in all its immense misery can be seen'.[10] Needless to say, such directness has to accept the dialectic intrinsic to it: 'What appears "at first blush" . . . to be death, will, if you examine it more closely, turn out to be life; conversely, life will turn out to be death; beauty will become ugliness; riches will turn to poverty; notoriety will become fame; learning will be ignorance; strength, weakness . . . success, failure . . . what is helpful will seem harmful; in brief, you will find everything suddenly reversed.'[11] The wandering scholars of the Middle Ages knew that, as did Villon in his prison cell.

On the other hand, all these relativities tend to get taken seriously and to be sanctioned before the tribunal of reason. The result is that reason, in the presence of the higher 'folly' of grace, not only makes itself ridiculous but proves its guilt as well. And then, as in Brant's 'Ship of Fools', all the states of human life, secular and religious (especially the latter), are bitterly exposed: huntsmen and insatiable builders, diceplayers and miracle-seekers, merchants and pilgrims, lawyers and philosophers, theologians and monks, kings and princes of the Church. Where ecclesiastics are concerned, Erasmus uses the sound criterion of the *Devotio Moderna*, in whose spirit he

[8] 35.
[9] 42.
[10] 49.
[11] 43.

was brought up.[12] At this point, when the idea of 'simplicity' becomes central,[13] the great tradition—of classical antiquity and the Bible, of Bernard and Wolfram—is brought in. For does not Paul attribute 'a certain folly' to God himself when he says that 'the foolishness of God is wiser than men'?[14] In the critique of the Church the 'analogy of folly' shifts more and more to the divine pole, so that, through the playful tone, unambiguity breaks through with Christian seriousness: 'The life-style of princes has long since been diligently imitated ... by popes, cardinals, and bishops ... to teach the people is burdensome; to interpret Holy Scripture, academic; to pray, otiose ... poverty is embarrassing, obedience humiliating and unseemly ... and finally, dying is disagreeable, death on the cross, disreputable.'[15] Erasmus shines light into the depths when he exposes Christian existence as an 'evasion' of reality and thus a betrayal of, and flight from, the truth: 'If there is some responsibility, they prudently shift that on to someone else's shoulders and pass the buck down the line from one to another. In fact, just as lay princes parcel out the duties of ruling to deputies, and the deputies pass them on to subdeputies, so too [ecclesiastical office-bearers] leave the practice of piety, in their modesty, to the common people. The people foist it off on those whom they call ecclesiastics, for all the world as if they themselves had nothing to do with the Church, as if their baptismal vows had had no effect whatever. Then the priests who call themselves secular—as if they were united to the world rather than to Christ—pass on the burden to the canons regular, the canons to the monks, the laxer monks to the stricter ones, both groups to the mendicant orders, the mendicants to the Carthusians ...'[16]

[12] Albert Hyma, *Renaissance to Reformation* (Eerdmans, Michigan, 1951).

[13] 'The privilege of simplicity and of truthfulness is the striking attribute of folly' (195). 'The pious strive with all their hearts to reach God Himself, who is purest and simplest of all' (269).

[14] 128.

[15] 110–112.

[16] 115.

At this point Dame Folly breaks off and concludes with a kind of bibliography: a few quotations from classical authors, many texts from Sacred Scripture. They are chaotically thrown together—it is after all the 'lower folly' which they are also meant to corroborate—and yet the great evangelical folly of Jesus does not fail to rise resplendent: the folly of the Incarnation itself,[17] revelation communicated to the simple, the foolishness of the evangelical counsels, the proclamation of the folly of the cross 'by simple, rough and ready heralds', the ass as a mount (instead of the noble stallion), the dove (and not a hawk or eagle) as the bird of the Holy spirit. 'Consider also that he calls His own followers, destined for immortal life, sheep. No other animal is more stupid.'[18]

Equally great is the folly of the life and theology of St Paul. To sum up: 'It seems to me that the Christian religion taken all together has a certain affinity with some sort of folly.' This can be seen in the fact that 'children, old people, women, and retarded persons are more delighted than others with holy and religious matters', and finally that 'no fools seem more senseless than those people who have been completely taken up, once and for all, with a burning devotion to Christian piety: they throw away their possessions, ignore injuries, allow themselves to be deceived, make no distinction between friend and foe . . . In this light, it is not at all surprising that the apostles seemed to be intoxicated with new wine and that Paul seemed mad to the judge Festus.'[19] Here Erasmus shakes the hand of the knight of La Mancha.

Erasmus would not be Erasmus if he did not end— inexplicably!—by committing the folly of fleeing from the folly of world and Church in a Platonic flight into the realm of pure spirit. The ecstatic flight of spirit from body, of the mind from the world up to God—that is the illogical conclusion of his treatise, which in the end closes its eyes before the radiant glory of true folly.

[17] 130.
[18] 129.
[19] 132.

e. Ridiculousness and Grace

CERVANTES

Cervantes' ageless masterpiece,[1] turgid life in fable's brightest hues, cannot be reduced to any formula or theory. Many-layered like all genuine humour, the world that is *Don Quixote* is deliberately susceptible of a multitude of interpretations. On each storey the light falls differently, yet top floor and ground are clearly part of the same building: at one level unintentional absurdity and burlesque, at another the light of grace descending from the heights of the Christian revelation of love, eluding all the textbook interpretations, *even* the various philosophical ones, e.g. Don Quixote and Sancho Panza as the ideal and the real, the tragic unreality of the ideal woman (Dulcinea de Toboso), and thus the illusoriness of every great human life. In the first place, we have to come to terms with the author's constantly and clearly expressed aim: to ridicule the ideology of the heroic and gallant Christian knight. This Utopian, fairytale eschatology marked *Parzival* and a hundred other epics and romances, the idea being that the Christian knight in his armour was the living analogy of the saint in his supernatural struggle for the Kingdom of God. Cervantes regarded this analogy, in the sense of a seriously attempted form of existence, as pure folly, totally out-of-date, and yet at the same time he was fully aware that it would be precisely in his hero that this out-of-date existence would survive as immortal foolishness. A travelling companion says at one point to the knight: 'Heaven be praised, for that history of your noble and authentic chivalries, which your worship says is printed [Don Quixote in the second part knows about the publication of the first], will consign all the innumerable stories of imaginary knights

---

[1] [Tr.: von Balthasar uses the classical German translation of Ludwig Braunfels, *Der Sinnreiche Junker Don Quijote von der Mancha* (Büchergilde Gutenberg, Zürich o.J.). We shall follow, wherever possible, the English translation of J. M. Cohen, *The Adventures of Don Quixote* (Penguin Books, Harmondsworth, 1950). On occasions, a direct translation from the citations of Braunfels has been necessary in order to capture von Balthasar's sense. References will be given to part and chapter.] On the origins of the work

errant, of which the world is full, to oblivion, such harm they
do to good manners, and such damage and discredit to genuine
history.'[2] 'I'll bet', says Sancho, 'that before long there won't be
a wineshop or tavern, an inn or a barber's shop where the
history of our exploits won't be painted up.'[3] 'It is ... so
familiar to all sorts of people that whenever they see a lean horse
go by, they cry: "There goes Rocinante!" ... in fact, this story
is the most delightful and least harmful entertainment, ... for
nowhere in it is to be found anything ever resembling an
indelicate expression.'[4] If ever in the Christian era a myth was
created, this is it: the merry myth of the ridiculousness of the
Christian fighting as a knight for the Kingdom of God. In no
way should Quixote be taken as a symbol of Christ Himself.
However, by way of ingenious counterpoint, the novel provides
many other examples of madness of a purely human kind,
especially scorned erotic passion—crazy Cardenio,[5] Anselmo
in the table of stupid curiosity,[6] Eugenio and Leandra,[7] Basilio.[8]
This commonplace madness, provoked by particular incidents,
is far removed from Quixote's constitutional folly, which is not
'psychological' but purely ideological. His folly closes the gap
between the 'ideal' of God's redemptive grace in Christ and the
'reality' of the earthly, allegedly world-transforming actions of
Christians. In his 'simple' faith and his well-intentioned conduct
Quixote sees the gap bridged, but as he approaches his fate and
failure, it is laughably evident to everyone that it is yawning
wide open. Quixote thus becomes the true patron saint of
Catholic Action. He is a bit of dogmatics neglected by Catholic
theologians, a tract that can be written on the Catholic side only
with and by means of humour, whereas Luther tried to express

and the reasons for its composition: Menendez y Pelayo, *Cultura literia de
Cervantes y elaboración del Quijote* in *Estudios de critica literania*, 4th series,
Madrid 1905. Philosophical commentary by M. de Unamuno, *Das Leben
Don Quijotes und Sanchos*, German trans; no date, Phaidon-Verlag.

[2] II, 16.   [3] II, 71.   [4] II, 3.

[5] I, 23f. Cardenio has only moments of insanity in his interludes of
rationality.

[6] I, 33. 'I am ... inclined to abandon you to your folly', his friend
Lothario tells him.

[7] I, 51.

[8] II, 19.

it tragically in the contradictory dialectic of *sola fide* and *simul iustus et peccator*.

Quixote is simple. As Sancho says, 'He has a heart full of simplicity. He can do no harm to anyone, only good to everybody. There's no malice in him. A child might make him believe it's night at noonday. And for that simplicity I love him.'[9] He constantly preaches and practises love of enemies.[10] He scolds Sancho for being a bad Christian. because 'you never forget an injury once done to you, though you should know that a noble and generous heart sets no store by such trifles.'[11] He preaches love on every occasion, presumes the best in other people[12] and instructs Sancho, when he takes over the governorship, to be always gentle and kind, as a judge to show mercy to the accused and the tears of the poor,[13] and in all this to ascribe nothing to his own merits. He sees his chivalry as pure service of God[14] and as faith's answer to the call and mission of God.[15] For him, the last knight in the 'strict order'[16] of chivalry, this means 'protecting those who need protecting and coming to the aid of the afflicted',[17] 'stumbling here, falling there, flung down in one place and rising up in another . . . succouring widows, protecting maidens, and relieving wives, orphans and wards.'[18] And when they do this, 'it is no concern . . . of

[9] II, 13.

[10] *Cf.* the author's prologue [24], where 'love your enemies' is tackled thematically.

[11] I, 21. Sancho will later say to his master: 'There is no reason, sir, to take revenge on anyone, for it's not right for a good Christian to avenge his injuries' (II, 11).

[12] For example, I, 17.

[13] II, 42.

[14] *Ibid.*

[15] After the adventure with the flock of sheep: 'God, the provider of all things, cannot let us want, especially as we are engaged in His service' (I, 18). 'God who has put it into my heart to embark on this unparalleled adventure [which comes to nothing, because the sound is merely the swish of windmills] will take care to watch over my safety' (I, 20). Quixote is 'sent to earth' (I, 28).

[16] 13.   [17] II, 27.

[18] II, 16, and other very frequent descriptions of the mission: I, 1; I, 2; I, 14; I, 52 etc.

knights errant to investigate whether the distressed, chained
and oppressed persons they meet on the roads are brought to
that pass . . . for their crimes or their whims. Their only task
is to succour them because they are in distress, taking account
of their sufferings and not of their villainies.'[19] And if monks
'in all peace and quiet, pray Heaven for the well-being of the
world', then 'we soldiers and knights carry out what they
pray for, defending it with the strength of our arms and the
edge of our swords, beneath no roof but the open sky, exposed to the intolerable beams of the sun in summer and
the biting frosts in winter. We, therefore, are God's ministers
on earth, and the arms by which His justice is executed here.'[20]

Quixote goes on to say humbly that he does not mean that
the vocation of the knight errant is as virtuous and
meritorious as that of the monk: 'I only want to argue from my
own sufferings that it is most certainly a more painful and
belaboured one, hungrier and thirstier, more miserable,
ragged and lousy.'[21] Having taken his leave of the castle of
the Duke, where he had been so cruelly mocked, he comes
across some peasants transporting statues of the saints for an
altarpiece. Quixote looks upon them with reverence as his
unattainable models: St George ('one of the best errants in all
the heavenly Host') and the Dragon, St Martin, on horseback,
and the beggar ('he gives him half of his cloak. No doubt it
was winter at the time, otherwise he would have given him
the whole, since he was so charitable'), St James the Moor-
Killer, and St Paul, hurled from his horse. 'These saints and
knights professed, even as I do, the calling of arms. But the
difference between us is that they were saints and fought in
the heavenly fashion, and I am a sinner and fight in the human
way. They conquered Heaven by force of arms, because
Heaven suffers violence, but up till now I do not know what
I am conquering by the force of my labours.' In any case,
'the wise Christian should not pry too curiously into the
counsels of Heaven.'[22] So these four saints bridge externally

[19] I, 30.
[20] I, 13.
[21] I, 13.
[22] II, 58.

the gap between spiritual and worldly chivalry; all that is left
is the one between the holy and the sinful. In all sincerity
Sancho thinks that 'we should set about turning saints. Then
we shall get the good name we're aiming at rather sooner . . .
A couple of lashings have more effect with God than a couple
of thousand lance-thrusts, even against giants, or hobgoblins,
or dragons.' To this Quixote replies: 'All that is so, but we
cannot all be friars, and many are the ways by which God
bears His chosen to heaven. Chivalry too is a pious order,
and there are sainted knights in heavenly glory.'[23]

He thinks of himself as an 'establisher of peace' (and in this
role delivers an anti-militaristic speech),[24] the restorer, to the
best of his ability, of the Golden Age (as he explains in his
wonderful discourse to the goatherds), the last 'real knight' in
a world of flunkeys.[25] He was prepared to make war all
alone, against Islam[26] (very like Claudel's Marie de Sept
Epées),[27] just as, all alone, he went into combat against the
circus lions, though, admittedly, they were disdainful of battle
with him.[28] The result of his interference in most cases is that
things go from bad to worse. The whipped boy, Andrew, is
afterwards beaten even harder, ending up in hospital, and begs
Quixote not to defend him any more.[29] He causes havoc
among a flock of sheep.[30] The liberated galley-slaves show
their gratitude by pelting him with stones[31] and bring him
into conflict with the 'Holy Brotherhood'.[32] 'I was born a
very pattern for the unfortunate, and to be a target and mark

[23] II, 8.
[24] I, 37. Cf. his remarks against firearms, which make heroism impossible
(I, 38).
[25] I, 11, a theme to which he frequently returns (I, 20).
[26] II, 64. 'I was just going to say that I should have been delighted if
everything had turned out otherwise, for then I should have had to cross to
Barbary, where by the force of my arm I should have liberated not only
Don Gregorio but all the Christian captives in Barbary' (II, 65).
[27] The Satin Slipper, ET J. O'Connor (London 1932), 4th Day, 8th
scene.
[28] II, 17.
[29] I, 4.
[30] I, 18.
[31] I, 22
[32] I, 45.

for the arrows of adversity.'[33] 'Observe, Sancho, that virtue is persecuted wherever it exists to an outstanding degree.'[34] That was the way it was for Alexander and Caesar, for Hercules and Sir Galaor, brother of Amadis of Gaul. But for the Christian knight 'the path of virtue is narrow cramped and hard', [35] indeed, 'the narrowest path of all'.[36] Although Quixote himself is unaware of it, this superlative applies exactly to the ridicule which all his schemes, his incompetence, and the world's appetite for a joke conspire to produce.

St Ignatius Loyola in his early life filled his head with the romances of chivalry and his autobiography shows some strange affinities with Quixote. On a solitary journey from Genoa to Bologna he loses his way and only escapes death after much toil and tribulation, but then, as he enters the city across a narrow wooden bridge, he falls into a ditch full of mud and extricates himself amidst the great laughter of a crowd of onlookers.[37] This kind of thing happens constantly to Don Quixote. As he climbs from his horse in the presence of the Duke, he falls headlong, while Sancho hangs by one leg from the stirrup of his pack-saddle.[38] On his solemn entry into Barcelona, mischievous boys put furze under the tails of Dapple and Rocinante, with the results that horse and ass rear up and rid themselves of their riders.[39] At great moments it is always like this, without mentioning the many thrashings, bruisings, pinchings,[40] the herds of wild bulls[41] and dirty pigs[42] unexpectedly rampaging over them as they sleep on the ground. In fact, the knight clearly quoting St Theresa of Avila can say to his squire: 'I was born, Sancho, to live dying, and you to die eating.'[43] The first part of the book closes

[33] II, 10.
[34] II, 2.
[35] II, 6.
[36] II, 18.
[37] *The Diary of a Pilgrim*, n. 91.
[38] II, 30.
[39] II, 61.
[40] Cf. I, 4; II, 11; I, 24; II, 27: II, 48.
[41] II, 58.
[42] II, 68.   [43] II, 59.

with the knight in great humiliation, being imprisoned in a
cage and then hauled back on an oxcart into his native village.
The second part, on the whole the more subtle of the two, is
even more extreme with its story of the cruel happenings at
the Duke's court, where, beneath a façade of the highest
honours, Don Quixote and Sancho become the butt of foolish
quips and jokes, to the huge amusement of Duke, Duchess,
and courtiers. Called a fool by a priest, the knight gently
reproves him for it: Can it be right to censure me so harshly
in public and without knowledge of the sin, to proclaim the
sinner bluntly a blockhead? . . . I always direct my purposes
to virtuous ends . . . whether he who so acts deserves to be
called a fool, let your Highnesses decide.'[44] And so the author
is of the opinion that 'the mockers were as mad as their
victims, and the Duke and Duchess within a hair's breadth of
appearing fools themselves for taking such pains to play tricks
on a pair of fools'.[45] Don Antonio, who leads Quixote
through the streets of Barcelona without his knowing that he
has a placard on his back, exclaims: 'You have the knack of
turning everyone who has to do with you into madmen and
dolts.'[46]

But what is the point of these humiliations, which our hero
bears 'so silently and patiently',[47] so as to become 'the
example and model' for every knight 'in the centuries to
come'?[48] The answer is that he bears within him an ideal,
embodied in the beautiful virgin[49] and lady, Dulcinea. He
has never seen her, and yet he loves her and dedicates himself
to her, as is proper for a true knight. For him Dulcinea is the
'sum of all beauty',[50] 'superhuman,'[51] so much so that he can
pray to her.[52] He believes in her after he has pictured her in

[44] II, 32.
[45] II, 70.
[46] II, 62.
[47] I, 47.
[48] Ibid.
[49] II, 59.
[50] I, 43.
[51] I, 13.
[52] II, 22.

his mind ('in imagination I draw her as I would have her be'),[53] and for the sake of her greater glory he undertakes everything.[54] When people express their suspicion that she might be 'an imaginary mistress', the knight evasively replies: 'God knows whether Dulcinea exists on earth or no, or whether she is fantastic or not fantastic. These are not matters whose verification can be carried out to the full. I neither engendered nor bore my lady, though I contemplate her in her ideal form.'[55] Meanwhile she has been changed by a magic spell into an ugly and malodorous peasant woman, and only thus, in the form of her 'abasement', can Sancho make her visible to the knight.[56] But, in fact, Quixote serves her for her own sake with 'the kind of love', says Sancho, 'I've heard them preach about. They say we ought to love Our Lord for Himself alone, without being moved to it by hope of glory or fear of punishment':[57] the doctrine of *pur amour* on the lips of Sancho Panza and applied to the Knight of Sad Countenance. But Quixote still hopes for an eschatological dis-enchantment: 'when least we expect to, we shall see her in her proper shape'.[58] The foolery involves Sancho subjecting himself voluntarily to 3300 strokes of the lash on his 'wonder-working flesh', all for the sake of the dis-enchantment, though he only succeeds in whipping the trees.[59] At the end, when the knight has been defeated in a duel and compelled to return home, hope, because of the fatal blow, is slowly extinguished and vanishes into intangibility.[60] Only the watchword remains true: 'at every step to attempt the impossible',[61] and the conclusion has its own nobility. 'I did what I could.'[62]

[53] I, 25.
[54] '. . . since she will see that everything serves the extolling of her glory and her fame' (I, 31).
[55] II, 32.
[56] II, 16.
[57] I, 31.
[58] II, 33.
[59] II, 71, his power is *gratis data* (*ibid.*).
[60] II, 73.
[61] II, 17.
[62] II, 66.

The knight sees earthly things in the most exalted light; he alone knows them in their true worth.[63] He alone knows who the ladies and gentlemen here assembled 'really are'.[64] So he is aware of his own dignity: he knows the 'rules [of chivalry] better than any knights who have ever professed them in the world.'[65] Moreover, the ancient romances and epics 'do not paint or describe [their heroes] as they were, but as they should have been, to serve as examples of their virtues for future generations'.[66] However, if the historicity of these idealised figures is called into question, Quixote instantly rallies to their defence: he knows them, bears them all in himself,[67] so much so that 'I might almost say that I have seen Amadis of Gaul with my own eyes'.[68] In other words, Quixote is really the archetype, representative and successor of them all in this age so poor in the spirit of chivalry. It is almost as if his folly were the penance for all that was unconsciously foolish about the old chivalry, in his rationality demonstrating his superiority to it. In the first part the exterior foolish deeds predominate whereas in the second the author demonstrates more and more the interior supernatural rationality of his hero, so that at the end, after his final defeat, all his foolishness, like a light garment, falls unresistingly from him. Quixote's folly is 'systematic folly, if in folly system there can be,'[69] in a much deeper sense than Hamlet, who has method in his madness. One can even ask oneself 'which is the madder, the man who's mad because he can't help it, or the man who's mad by choice.'[70] This is why his associates are all reduced to 'amazement' (*thaumazein*), because his reason is so foolish, and yet his foolishness is so sensible.[71] The proportion of folly and rationality in him is

[63] Thus he recognises the cheap barber's bowl for what it is: Mambrino's helmet made of finest gold (I, 21), and 'since the people see only a shaving bowl, they are not interested in pursuing it' (I, 25).

[64] I, 37.

[65] I, 25.

[66] I, 25.

[67] II, 1. *Cf.* I, 49.

[68] II, 1.

[69] I, 50.

[70] II, 15.

[71] II, 16.

constantly under investigation. At all events he is a 'noble fool' 'a fool garnished with intelligence',[72] a finely-educated fool.[73] When he gives Sancho instruction in wisdom, he 'raises his sagacity as well as his folly to the highest level'.[74] If Quixote is all chivalry's representative, one of his obligations is also to take on, in his own madness, the madness of a 'raving Roland', to imitate his 'desperation' and his 'penitential exercises', or rather to make them real in his own time.[75] And all of this he does out of pure magnanimity: 'The real test is to be mad without cause, for then my beloved is bound to think, "If this happens in the green wood, what will become of the dry?" '[76]

Cervantes is the scourge not only of ancient chivalry but also of all the nonsense of the modern pastoral style and pastoral verse (a more harmless and yet often no less tragic madness). This runs through the whole novel, and Quixote constantly weaves it into his own adventure. The sickness that infects the whole of Europe from Renaissance to Revolution, with its own ideal of beauty, is handled here with a smiling indulgence, and yet also with savage and merciless medicines. Cervantes and Quixote are so far removed from these feeble imitations of the Alexandrines as Virgil was in the Georgics. The whole idyllic, erotic, tragic world of pastoral beauty is weighed and taken into account from a higher vantage point, but found to be too light in itself.

The main theme of the book is the virtue of Quixote (to which Sancho Panza is not really a dialectical counterweight but a positive complement, for his chief quality too is simplicity[77]. Quixote himself shows how the life of the

---

[72] II, 18.

[73] II, 59. Cf. II, 33; II, 34.

[74] II, 43. He leaves 'Don Juan and Don Jerónimo in great amazement at the mixture of intelligence and folly shown by the knight' (II, 59).

[75] I, 25.

[76] I, 25.

[77] 'Sancho was one of the solemnest blockheads of our age' (II, 7). He himself speaks of 'the broad cloak of my simplicity—which is always natural and never artificial' (II, 8). When his master scolds him as an ass: '. . . all I need to be a complete ass is a tail. If your worship would care to

knight is the integration of all the Christian virtues.[78] He lives a life of real and hard poverty (this is humiliatingly thrown in his face in the luxurious court of the Duke).[79] He lives a life of absolute chastity, which is attacked in a variety of ways, yet always in vain.[80] He lives in perfect obedience to his exacting, humiliating, all-consuming ideal. He preaches against litigiousness and the useless bearing of arms, and for the love of enemies which comes hard only to those 'who partake less of God than of the world, and more of the flesh than of the spirit'.[81] He knows magnanimity when he see it even in the roguish morality of the robber chief Roque, and does not fail to deliver a speech to his gang about the dangers for body and soul of their way of life.[82] On his death-bed he proclaims that 'God's mercy knows no bounds, nor can the sins of men ever limit or hinder it'.[83] In short, Don Quixote is so much better a Christian because subjectively he makes no claim to sanctity, and because objectively it is never possible, at any moment or in any respect, to count his ridiculous doings among the solemn deeds of God and Jesus

put one on me, I should reckon I had deserved it, and would serve you as an ass for all the remainder of my life' II, 28). The Duchess is surprised 'at the greatness of Sancho's simplicity. For he had now come to believe that Dulcinea's enchantment was the infallible truth, although he had himself been the enchanter and the trickster in that business' (II, 34). His simplicity resembles Quixote's: 'Sometimes his simplicities are so shrewd that it gives me no small pleasure to consider whether it is simplicity or shrewdness that prevails' (II, 32).

[78] II, 18.

[79] 'Here Benegeli [the author's supposed Moorish source] exclaims in his writing. 'Oh, poverty, poverty! . . . Moor though I am, I know very well by the commerce that I have had with Christians that holiness lies in charity, humility, faith, obedience, and poverty. But, for all that, I declare that anyone who grows content with poverty must have much of God in him, unless it is that kind of poverty of which one of His greatest saints says: 'Possess all things as if you possessed them not', and this they call poverty in spirit. But that other poverty . . .' the righteous poverty that makes the poor ridiculous, that is admirable (II, 44).

[80] Quixote's extreme modesty: II, 30; II, 48, the ball scene (II, 62), the final temptation scene with Altisidora (II, 70).

[81] II, 27.

[82] II, 60.

[83] II, 74.

Christ. He recognises the absolute distance between God and
man, between Christ and the Church (in so far as *he*, Quixote,
embodies it). In a truly Christian way it is the good and
nothing but the good that he wants, and yet, as he leaves this
world, he has to see all his Christian chivalry as foolishness: 'I
know my folly now . . . Now, by God's mercy, I have learnt
from my own bitter experience . . .'[84] It is precisely in this
way that Quixote's life becomes a permanemet monument of
Christian existence and a reflected ray of the glory of God.

f. The Fool as Rogue

GRIMMELSHAUSEN

Simplizissimus (1668–1669) is 'the only great literary
monument of the German Baroque to have retained its
vitality into our own times'.[1] Kosch considers it 'the most
important [German] literary monument between Wolfram's
Parzival and Goethe's *Faust*'. Once again, though differently
from Cervantes, the Christian fool is at the centre. While the
contemporary romances of heroism and gallantry continue to
spin out the ideology of chivalry, even after the horrors of
the Thirty Years War, Grimmelshausen laughs in the face of
this dusty old dream-world and does not even need his foolish
hero to play the part of that world's judge and gravedigger.
Like Parzival, he is brought up as a pure fool in the solitude
of the forest—first of all in 'the most ancient office of
shepherd . . . with all its glorious dignity',[2] 'perfect and
complete in ignorance'.[3] Then, after the robbers' raid on the
farm and the boy's flight, he is introduced by the hermit into
pure Christianity, when the holy man inscribes 'on the tablet
of [his] heart, soft and smooth as wax',[4] prayer, the love of

[84] *Ibid.*
[1] A. Kelletat, Epilogue in the Buchklub Exlibris Zürich edition, 628.
[2] I, 2. *Simplizissimus* is cited by book and chapter from *Die
Simplicianischen Schriften des Hans Jacob Christoffel von Grimmelshausen*, edited
by F. Riederer (F. M. Hendel-Verlag, Leipzig, 1939).
[3] I, 1.
[4] I, 9.

God, 'honest service'. After the hermit's death, this natural and supernatural fool is thrown out into the wild world of war, which is not only cruel and brutal, but full of unimaginable wickedness, such as the soldiers who 'first cruelly torture' [the country people] and then make them solemnly renounce God before killing them, because 'that is the best way of getting their revenge, ensuring their punishment both in time and eternity'.[5] The foolish boy first of all becomes a page; he has 'nothing more precious than a pure conscience and ... a noble innocence and simplicity'.[6] That is why he does not understand the first thing about the world that surrounds him and calls itself Christian: 'Christ says: "Love your enemies, bless those who curse you, do good to those who hate you ..." But I found not only did no one want to comply with this command of Christ, but that everyone did the exact opposite ... Things became blatantly clear to me, and I was forced to conclude that because of this public sinners, tax-collectors and prostitutes, who were vehemently hated for their wickedness and godlessness, were far superior to us modern Christians in their practice of fraternal charity.'[7] And when he hears sinners 'boasting of their sin and shame and vice' and begins to rebuke them, he is laughed at and written off as a fool. He decides to keep silent, but 'out of Christian charity he could not maintain it.' The pastor, when consulted, replies: 'Of course they are Christians, and I wouldn't advise you to call them anything else', though, mind you, if the apostles and the first devout Christians were to come back today, they too would be 'regarded as fools by everyone'.[8]

This question of the contradiction between God and the world (already the dominant theme in Grimmelshausen's first works, *Der satyrische Pilgram* (1666) and the *Histori vom keuschen Joseph* (1667)), as well as the gravity of the appalling chaos of war which Grimmelshausen experienced, makes the problem of the book's literary form seem of secondary

[5] I, 14.
[6] I, 24.
[7] I, 25.
[8] I, 25–26.

importance. It is certainly influenced by the Spanish picaresque novel. The translations of Lazarillo de Tormes and Guzman de Alfarache (artistically superior to the German comic novels and adventure stories such as *Herzog Ernst* and *Fortunatus*), and not Don Quixote (also available in translation), were the ones taken as a model and provide the literary form for the story of Simplicius' life and military adventures. At first, like Quixote, he is the fool, a butt for the amusement of the officers and soldiers; indeed, they even contrive to 'make a fool' of him.[9] Yet, even at this rascally stage, he is the one who holds the reins. He enjoys the fool's freedom to tell his superiors the truth, even Christian truth.[10] This old theme allows writers, especially in times of absolutism, to speak the truth to their princes and the powers that be (e.g. Shakespeare and Molière). Yet, unlike Quixote, who to the very end remains the pure ideal fool suspended above reality, Simplicius the fool gradually becomes Simplicius the wily rascal; the one 'who could not adapt himself to the world'[11] learns to adapt remarkably well. While still a lad, he becomes the 'famous huntsman of Soest', successful, ambitious, haughty, pampered, and yet lacking any spiritual admonition or direction, something he frequently regrets. Like Parzival he is very handsome, and so, led astray by novels of chivalry,[12] on a trip to Paris, he falls prey to women and becomes a kind of gigolo until 'eventually, in sheer exhaustion, he grows weary of foolish pranks'.[13] Robbed of his physical charms by an attack of measles, he becomes a quack and charlatan, regarded in a new sense now as a fool. Next he becomes a musketeer, 'a real savage who cared nothing for God or His Word.[14] No wickedness was too much for me, since all the graces and benefits I had ever received from God were completely forgotten, and so I didn't pray for anything, neither temporal nor eternal . . . I was

[9] II, 5ff.
[10] II, 7–14.
[11] II, 13.
[12] III, 3.
[13] IV, 5.
[14] IV, 8.

threatened with the gallows and the whip, but that made no difference. I carried on my godless way, and it began to look as if I was playing at despair and running on purpose towards hell.'[15] In all his ups and downs he is 'a ball of changeable luck, a model of mutability, and a mirror of human nature's inconstancy'.[16] And so in the religious sphere too he is tossed between remembrance of God and forgetfulness of God. When he is literally drowning, he prays fervently. Having been dragged to the bank, 'I should have just fallen to my knees and thanked the divine goodness for my rescue'. Once it is all 'behind him', everything is forgotten again, and yet not so forgotten that the memory of innocence, of the 'oath sworn',[17] of the 'natural law',[18] does not constantly break through. He remains suspended in the middle: in the company of the crafty villain Olivier,[19] he feels totally alien and strives by every means to escape. After this he joins up with the pious Brother of the Heart and accompanies him on pilgrimage to Einsiedeln, but cooks the peas in his shoes and follows the brother 'mournfully like someone being led to the gallows'.[20] At the shrine he is frightened by the devil as he comes out of the possessed person during an exorcism. He makes his confession and is converted to the Catholic faith, but the change does not last for long, 'because my conversion had its source, not in love of God, but in fear and dread of damnation, and so gradually I became quite half-hearted and lazy'.[21]

Grimmelshausen, with his unerring psychological perception, looks, not just at his hero's outward inconstancy, but at the inward quality of his virtue, which is again and again shown to be *calculation*. Simplicius 'has learnt' how to win people over to his side:[22] by playing the part of the

[15] IV, 11.
[16] VI, 15.
[17] III, 15.
[18] IV, 15: 'You may or may not be permitted to rob and steal. All the same I know that it is against the law of nature, which says that you should not do to someone else what you don't want done to yourself.'
[19] IV, 14–24.
[20] V, 1.
[21] V, 2.
[22] II, 31.

generous benefactor, distributing gifts,[23] overlooking insults, praising everyone but himself.[24] So 'everywhere I went, I took care to make friends with those who otherwise might have had cause to hate me'.[25] 'I saw clearly that my own arrogance might inflict masses of enemies on me, so I decided I had to pretend to be humble, whether or not I really was.'[26] And later on: 'I became at once again a fellow who looked like a brave soldier.'[27] In his final judgment about himself, when he is trying to practise the principle of *nosce te ipsum*: 'I took care of my honour, not for its own sake, but for my own advancement.'[28] In the *continuatio*, he does not persevere in his chosen hermitage; instead of praying he looks out at the countryside and gets himself given alms in abundance. In fact, one might almost call him 'a hypocrite or holy joker'.[29] Grimmelshausen himself, like his hero, converted to Catholicism, but both retain a deep-seated Protestant mistrust of virtue, especially their own: there is no guarantee of its stability, nor of the purity of its motivation. The great goddess of the picaresque novels, as earlier of the medieval vagabonds and gallows-birds, is Fortuna.[30] Grimmelshausen turns her into a new metamorphosis of 'old Proteus'[31] and gives her the name 'Baldanders',[32] her nature being demonstrated by the cosmic transformations of a piece of lavatory paper.[33] This goddess rules not only the external

[23] III, 13; III, 14; III, 16.

[24] III, 19.

[25] III, 8. Cf III, 11: 'I began to behave somewhat more reputably than before, since (!) I had such magnificent hope to have a little banner in the near future.'

[26] III, 14; cf. III, 19: 'I could behave so humbly it seemed I had never known arrogance.' In ch. III, 20 an old clergyman is taken for a ride.

[27] IV, 13.

[28] V, 28.

[29] VI, 1.

[30] The treacherous luck that is something like the Sirens (III, 16).

[31] VI, 9.

[32] VI, 9: 'I make you, more than other people, now big, now small, now rich, now poor, now high, now low, now happy, now bad, now good. In a word, now this way, now that.'

[33] VI, 11–12. At the end the paper says to Simplicius: 'The way you treat me now is exactly how death will deal with you.'

lower world, but also the spiritual and religious. That is why
no conversion of Simplicius' is absolutely definitive. After the
superb conclusion of Book 5—'Adieu, world!' (taken from
Guevaro)—a sixth book is added in which Grimmelshausen
writes the first great German equivalent of Robinson Crusoe,
transporting his hero off to an inaccessible South Sea island,
where by rights he should become the perfect pious hermit.
But then further Simplicius stories are added—*Courage*,
Springinsfeld, *Vogelnest*, and above all the calendar stories
spread round the country by Simplicius himself, which clearly
show that the author's final word is not a contemplation that
turns its back on the world but a wisdom that is hectically
active in this changing world; not a wisdom that induces
temporary madness as a prelude to the regaining of sanity in
heroic disillusionment, but a wisdom whose final garb is the
mantle of the fool.[34] Having become a calendar seller again,
Simplicius addresses his public thus: 'Dear sirs and present
good friends of mine![35] Not unjustly does that most scholarly
and excellent of men speak of the likes of me: *Saepe etiam sub
sordido palliolo latet sapientia*. A revolting mantle often hides a
splendid wisdom.'[36]

On his South Sea island the hermit fastens 'biblical texts
and other lovely quotations' on to the trees to spur himself to
devotion. The 'noblest' of these quotations, the only one
recorded, runs as follows:

> O highest and greatest Good! dwelling in a light so
> dark!
> That for very brightness we cannot see the greatness
> of the gleam.[37]

This quotation, which Grimmelshausen derived from a
polyhistorical source (Garzoni's *Piazza Universale*) and which
Vittoria Colonna placed at the beginning of a sonnet, simply

[34] As Paul Gutzwiller rightly argues in *Der Narr bei Grimmelshausen*, Diss.
(Basel, 1959), 70–81.
[35] Cicero.
[36] First *Continuatio*, *Simpl. Schriften* I, 554.
[37] VI, 24.

encapsulates the fundamental doctrine of Denys the Areopagite: Dazzling Darkness—which now appears to Simplicius as the foolishness, the roguishness, of divine glory.

There can be no doubt about the sincerity of the author's conversion to the Catholic faith; at the end even his hero ratifies his own conversion, compelled as it was in the first instance by the fear of Hell. Yet both of them are very pensive and reserved about the multiplicity of Christian denominations. The only real madman in the book, a man who thinks he is Jupiter and professes to govern and judge the world, is also the only one to consider a unification of the Christian Churches. He wants to dispatch a great German hero to restore universal peace to the world; he will abolish the 'exceedingly harmful divisions' and by 'his lofty reason' bring about unity.[38] Simplicius himself has a more modest vision. He admits he is 'neither Petrine nor Pauline' (Protestant); he just 'believes *simpliciter* what the twelve articles of the universal holy Christian faith contain', but he does not see why it should be 'unfitting for a Christian' to venerate the Mother of his Redeemer. In any case, are not all other religions of the opinion that they are the only true one? Faced with the mutual denunciations of the denominations, he must be allowed temporarily to postpone his decision until he can see things more clearly.[39] That is an almost Lessing-like point of view,[40] and was very common in the seventeenth and eighteenth centuries among those who could only see disobedience to the Gospel in the divisions of Christianity and consequently nothing of God's glory. Grimmelshausen manages to be a faithful Catholic and at the same time completely tolerant because of what he believes about God's unlimited mercy—at the time this was a rare achievement.

[38] III, 5.

[39] III, 20.

[40] 'One religion must be right, and the other two wrong. Were I to announce my allegiance to one of them without mature reflection, I might end up with the wrong one instead of the right one, and then I'd be regretting it for eternity. I would rather stay on the main road than get lost down a side-street. What's more, there are other religions besides the ones we have in Europe . . .' (III, 20).

So everything remains eschatologically open. The world is unbearably strife-torn, and man constantly has to look for the right way out of the labyrinth, but only God knows the door. Behind the vanity of the world the great struggle between Heaven and Hell is being played out. Hell, together with its strategy and tactics, is familiar territory, and in the final book it is again graphically described.[41] In the case of heaven there is nothing comparable, just a wide-eyed glimpse of the incomprehensible mercy of God embraced by faith. In the world the devil is glaringly visible everywhere, but God is not his opponent, but inconceivably transcends position and opposition. The meaning of the hermit's wonderful night song at the beginning of the story, 'Come, night's consoler, O Nightingale', is that, though we have to live in the dark, no night can prevent us from singing God's praises, and that it is not just beautiful sounds that harmonize in this praise:

> Even the owl, which cannot sing,
> Shows by its screeching
> That it too wants to praise God.

And this 'harmony' sounds so lovely to the boy that he wants to join in.[42] In the course of his life the owl's screech becomes the screech of all the dark powers of this world and of the abyss, and the harmony dies away into inaudibility. Just occasional snatches of the melody can be heard later and are carefully recorded. There is the sweet music of the universe as represented by the spirits of Mummelsee, who are endowed with reason and mortal, though sinless, and can serve as an example to men, who have been chosen for something so much higher.[43] Simplicius hurls himself into this cosmic centre like a new Empedocles leaping into the crater of Etna.[44] There are the pure communities of Hungarian Anabaptists, who, like the 'Jewish Essenes' in Josephus, thought they could achieve a 'lovely harmony' of the kingdom of this world and the Kingdom of God, 'so much

[41] VI, 2–8.
[42] I, 7.
[43] V, 12–17
[44] V, 12.

so that it seemed to me it surpassed even the monastic life'.[45]
At the novel's beginning and end there is the possibility of a
total detachment from the world in the eremitical life, and in
that perhaps a definitive anchoring of the heart in God,[46]
though here too it 'could be necessary to proceed with
caution, as if we were still living among people in the midst
of the world'.[47] Finally, there is perseverance in foolish and
roguish wisdom 'in the midst of the world' and in the
incomprehensible contradiction between the wisdom of
eternal love and the cleverness of the devil. The defenceless
heart is exposed to both. Like Homer long ago, but now
with a Christian intensity, man explains himself in terms of
the ascent to the God of mercy.

g. The Christian as Idiot

DOSTOIEVSKY

The period in which classical antiquity was transmitted, the
age of speculative theology, did not raise or develop the
theme of folly, at least not in the deeper, metaphysical sense.
Classicism confined itself undialectically to the beauty of the
finite natural and human form. It went in for the evolutionary
novel, in which the hero does indeed begin in relative folly
or naivety but is then educated into wisdom, usually by a
providence more human than divine (for example, by a
benevolent secret society as in Goethe's *Wilhelm Meister*).
Idealist romanticism, however, lives in the tension between
the finite and absolute subject. The Absolute can inspire the
man of genius to the point of foolish and farcical behaviour
(e.g. Kreisler, E. T. A. Hofmann's conductor), and yet in the
process he only proves his superior intelligence. On the other
hand, the Absolute Spirit can also use as its base a spirit-less
finitude or materiality—in other words, a non-ground of
non-sense (*cf.* Baader and Schelling). Again, for Jean Paul, the
hall of mirrors of the absolute 'I' can produce insane persons,

[45] V, 19.
[46] As the conclusion to Book 6 describes it.
[47] VI, 21.

but their insanity is merely a punishment for misunderstanding reality, not an expression of being exposed to it.
When Idealism, fatigued by thinking, falls back into its Indian
origins, as happens in the case of Schopenhauer, the whole
world of the intellect becomes madness, a madness which
aesthetics unmasks. This fatigue then teams up with the
absolutised Eros of Gottfried's Tristan to produce the hybrid
art of Wagner, who nowhere—neither in the revival of the
myths of the Nordic gods nor in *Tristan* or *Parzival*—
confronts real existence.

Then, quite unexpectedly, the folly motif reaches its climax
in a work that surpasses all previous forms—Dostoievsky's
Idiot (1868). With instinctive self-assurance the author discards
triviality and frustration and roots the world of beauty in the
sphere of glory. For here we have moved beyond the two
great attempts in the modern age to reduce glory to beauty,
to regard (classical) beauty as glory enough: Classicism and
Romanticism. Classicism provided the images, while idealist
Romanticism—the real creator of modern aesthetics—
constructed the theory. However, once Marx and
Tchernischevksy (1855) have left behind Hegel's philosophy
and aesthetics, once God and the spiritual have been banished
from the universe and its laws, the only choice left is between
materialistic and atheistic aesthetics. Dostoievsky[1] had
contacts with the early Communist circles and, along with
many others, was condemned to death. In the bitter cold he
was led out to the place of execution to be shot. He had
expected certain death and had anticipated it in his mind, but
instead he was sent off to the 'house of the dead', Siberia,
where he was humbled into naked Christianity. On his return
home appeared (after the Raskolnikov prelude) the three
novels with a universal vision: *The Idiot, The Brothers*

[1] [Tr. von Balthasar uses the German translation of *The Idiot* by E. K.
Rahsin (*Sämtliche Werke* I, 3–4). We shall use the Penguin translation by
David Magarshack (Harmondsworth, 1955). References will be to the page
numbers of this version]. A general interpretation of the work of
Dostoievsky can be found in my *Apokalypse der deutschen Seele*, Bd II (1939),
pp. 202–419. On the 'Idiot', cf. the study by Walter Nigg, *Der christliche
Narr*, pp. 349–403, with bibliography.

Karamazov, and *The Devils*. *The Idiot* the author's favourite book and his child of pain, contains all that follows in kernel.

'The fundamental idea is the portrayal of a truly perfect and beautiful human being. And that is a very difficult thing to do, especially these days. Every writer, not just our Russian ones but foreign writers too, every writer who has attempted to describe positive beauty has proved unequal to the task, because it is incredibly hard. What is beautiful is what is ideal, but the ideal, here just as much as in civilised Europe, has not been secure for some time now. There is really only one positively beautiful figure: Christ. This infinitely beautiful figure is without doubt an eternal miracle (St John's gospel is full of the idea: John sees the miracle in the Incarnation, in the appearance of the beautiful). I have gone too far in my explanations.'[2] Dostoievsky wanted to show, not the miracle itself, but the reflections of the miracle in a figure who can be called a Christian. The sphere of 'miracle' is superior to the sphere of worldly beauty. Prince Myshkin, last of his race, epileptic, spends his youth in the Valais Alps and is given a partial cure from a degree of self-alienating idiocy by a sensible doctor. In Switzerland he experiences the beauty of nature, which in the main causes him 'terrible depression'.[3] Later, after his return to Russia, fate places him between two very beautiful women. When he has to make a judgment about Aglaya, he says: 'It is difficult to pass judgment on beauty. I'm afriad I am not ready yet. Beauty is a riddle.'[4] For Dostoievsky, what that means is this: beauty is in no way a straightforward transparency for the divine: it can just as easily be a mask and sacrament of the devil. While the mountain landscape leaves Myshkin with the impression that he can 'hear some mysterious call to go somewhere',[5] the consumptive and mortally ill youth, Ippolit, is only irritated by it: 'What do I want with your nature, you Pavlovsk park, your sunrises and sunsets, your blue skies, and your smug faces, when all that festival, which has no end, has begun by

[2] *Raskolnikov's Diary*, ed., Fülop-Miller (1928), p. 168.
[3] 82.
[4] 105.
[5] 85.

refusing admission to me and me alone?'[6] Even if one accepts
that 'my worthless life, the life of an atom, may simply have
been needed for the completion of some universal harmony,
for some sort of plus or minus, for the sake of some contrast,
etc., just as the lives of creatures are daily required as a sacrifice
because without their deaths the world could not exist', I
Ippolit, must still confess that such cosmic harmony neither
interests nor concerns me. For 'how can man accept
responsibility for what he cannot understand', namely, that
the harmony of the universe is built on pain and death? And
so, as Ivan Karamazov will do later, Ippolit refuses to agree
with this cosmic harmony and gives back his 'entry ticket' to
eternal blessedness by means of the only action with which
he can disturb the harmony or at least protest against it—
suicide.[7] The great aesthetic argument from Plato to
Augustine and Boethius, from Erigena and Bonaventure to
Bruno, Hölderlin and Hegel, has lost its force. For the
nineteenth century hardly anything divine shines through the
beauty of this world.

But Myshkin is not a prince for nothing, a prince of ancient
lineage. He shows he is conscious of this in his last great speech
to the distinguished, partly grand-aristocratic gathering at the
Yepanchins (he speaks in the shadow once again of his illness,
which this time takes definitive hold of him): 'You think that
. . . I am . . . a democrat, an upholder of equality? . . . I am
afraid for you, for all of you, and for all of us. For I am a
prince of ancient lineage myself, and I am sitting among
princes. I am saying this to save you all, so as to prevent our
class from vanishing for nothing into utter darkness, without
realising   anything,   abusing   everything   and   losing
everything.'[8] He is one of Parzival's race, naive,[9] simple,[10]
though his simplicity is not of the natural primitive kind that
would need to be transformed slowly into Christian humility.
No, by virtue of a mysterious deficiency, conditioned by his

[6] 451.
[7] 455f.
[8] 595.
[9] 'Prince, you're so naive' (306).
[10] 571ff.

illness, he is, as it were, by nature inserted into humility. Like Don Quixote, he is a 'virgin knight errant'[11] and a ridiculous one at that, because in his naivety he lives by an ideal which contradicts all conventional experience of the world. Aglaya puts his letters into a copy of Cervantes' novel,[12] and recites to him, half jokingly, half in earnest, Pushkin's 'Ballade of the Poor Knight', in which the poet describes a medieval knight of Our Lady, who, in penitence, turns away from all earthly women and fights for Christendom. Finally he dies, 'ever silent, sad, and cheerless, of reason bereft', and is exalted by his Mistress to the paladin of the eternal Kingdom.[13] Cervantes/Pushkin now rises from the dead in the person of the prince, who listens to the ballade 'as embarrassed as a ten-year-old boy'. For Aglaya he is a person who has 'devoted his whole life to an ideal. This does not always happen in this age'.[14] In fact, in Christian times there was 'an idea stronger than any calamity ... Show me anything resembling that force in our age of liners and railways ... There is more wealth, but less strength; the binding idea is no more; everything has become soft, everything is flabby.'[15] Myshkin in the end is close to Simplicius in the sense that he moves, as it were naturally, in the world of sinners, and yet he is totally different from Simplicius, because he does not have the will to sin, but only the will not to distance himself in any way from the sinner, to be, simply and unreflectively, alongside him.

From several starting-points the author moves on to the mysterious point of *identification*, which is the point of absolute *reality*, though ordinary awareness never makes contact with it.[16] Dostoievsky draws on his own experience: those five minutes before the execution. What enormous

[11] 623.

[12] 219.

[13] The Ballade scene, 285f.; cf. 383.

[14] 282.

[15] 417. Cf. 563: 'In those days people seem to have been animated by one idea, but now they are much more nervous, more developed, more sensitive...'

[16] '... life [is] ... the continuous and everlasting process of discovering it—and not the discovery itself' (433).

intensity, pregnant with eternity, what fullness they had! Myshkin has seen an execution and thinks his way into the condemned man's awareness of the time.[17] The moment is intensified by the feeling of absolute dread, by the 'absolute certainty' of what is approaching: the very moment nothingness appears, being totally disappears. At this boundary, one realises what it means to say: 'There shall be time no longer'.[18] In a quite different way, the tremendous sense of light and elation which is the prelude to an epileptic attack takes one beyond the bounds of time. Dostoievsky realised that this experience was ambiguous and made literary and philosophical use of the ambiguity; indeed, it was only as work on the novel proceeded that the humble figure of Myshkin began to distinguish itself in the author's mind from the proud figure of Stavrogin (the character in *The Devils* who thinks he has experienced identity with God). Myshkin himself knows about this ambiguity. True, it means a massive increase in 'direct self-perception' and, as a consequence (!), an awareness of a 'higher being'; but ultimately, it is an 'interruption of normality', because it is 'just an illness'. But 'what if it is a disease and abnormal?' and 'what does it matter to me that it is normal or not normal?' The 'fact' remains, 'it awakes in me a feeling undivined till then, enables me to experience greatness, fullness and eternity . . .' The fact that the consequences are 'stupor, spiritual darkness, idiocy' does not invalidate the first truth.[19] And then there is a third, omnipresent motif: the Holbein picture in the Basel museum, which Myshkin and Ippolit encounter again as a reproduction in Rogozhin's hall—the cadaver of Christ, lying horizontally, putrid blue. This is the death of Him who is priceless. His real death, not His apparent death. It is the victory of nature, which 'as some huge engine of the

[17] 46–49, 86–93.
[18] 421f. *Cf.* also Lebedev's prayer for the Countess Du Barry, who in her fear of death screams beneath the guillotine: '"Wait one more moment, Mr [Executioner], just one little moment!' And for that little moment the Lord will perhaps pardon her, for a greater *misère* than that it is impossible to imagine for a human soul' (228).
[19] 259.

latest design ... has senselessly seized, cut to pieces, and swallowed up—impassively and unfeelingly—[this] great and priceless Being'; on the day when God Himself is dead, eternal life coincides with eternal death.[20] For Dostoievsky this picture is the symbolic diacritical point between faith and unbelief, between Christianity and atheism: twinned to the point of identification in the most extreme differentiation.

There are three improbable ways into the depths of reality: 'the more real it is, the more improbable it sometimes appears to be'.[21] These ways allow at the same time both an insight into human hearts and a communication with them. This insight has nothing in common with 'depth psychology', and the communion has just as little to do with *tout comprendre c'est tout pardonner*. Psychology 'establishes' things, whereas Myshkin understands by overlooking or forgetting or, if you like, forgiving. But he does not forgive because he 'understands', but because he loves. Everyone else 'understands' well enough the fault, the sin; it is clearly exposed, an objective reality. Myshkin forgives it by overlooking it, and thereby makes himself look ridiculous, an idiot. Indeed, the young nihilists subject him in a most offensive way to calumny and mockery in a pamphlet that is read out to him: 'The article ... never mind, let's forget it. I just think—it is totally untrue', so there is no point in talking about it.[22] The fact that Myshkin does not bear any grudges, that, in so far as it concerns him, he forgives everything, means that he is all the more shamelessly deceived. 'The prince will most certainly forgive him, if indeed he has not forgiven him already. He may even have thought of an excuse for him. Haven't you, prince?'[23] 'To know that you have been deceived and yet to trust! That was all we needed! But then, what else could we expect from you?'[24] It is 'naivety, blind trust, unsuspicious of derision or ridicule',[25] and

[20] 85, 93, 250ff., 446f.
[21] 414.
[22] Cf. 301.
[23] 326.
[24] Cf. 356.
[25] 372.

precisely that is the ultimate absurdity. That fact is not lost on the prince: 'You know, in my opinion, it's sometimes quite a good thing to be absurd. Indeed, it's much better, it makes it so much easier to forgive each other and to humble ourselves.'[26]

Myshkin's love is frequently given the name 'compassion', but basically only to distinguish it from any kind of erotic love: 'Compassion is the chief and perhaps the only law of all human existence.'[27] Only an ignorant person could raise the objection: 'Even compassion must have a limit. Why, an exaggeration like that is—is quite incredible!'[28] Myshkin himself explains that he loves the dubious character Nastasya Filippovna 'not out of love but out of compassion'.[29] That is why he can say of her straight out: 'No, I don't love her.'[30] And yet 'his heart is pierced through' by her.[31] Nastasya, abused by a wealthy rake while she was still a minor, feels—in Hölderlin's meaning of the word—to the deepest fibres of her being, that she has been 'insulted'. She has an 'insatiable need for contempt',[32] 'a conscious delight in her misfortune'.[33] She plays the part of the 'shameless woman', the 'reprobate', to which she has been reduced.[34] She enjoys giving the 'theatrical performance' of a 'fallen angel'.[35] The prince loves her with a non-erotic love and so can see through the tragic game she is playing to delude herself and the world,[36] with the result that she finds herself in the hopeless situation of returning the prince's love in all simplicity (and that she does) but in the process having to give up the game she is playing (and that she cannot do). And so, on the one hand: 'The prince . . . is the first man . . . in whom I can

[26] 595.
[27] 263.
[28] 624.
[29] 244.
[30] 472.
[31] 473, 615.
[32] 69.
[33] Cf. 74.
[34] Cf. 201f.
[35] 613.
[36] 147, 196, 173f.

believe as a true and loyal friend. He believed in me at first sight, and I believed in him.'[37] On the other hand: 'And when I offered to marry her, she told me that she did not want condescending sympathy or help from anyone, nor did she want anyone to "raise her up to his level".'[38] Rogozhin, who loves Nastasya erotically to the point of madness, is savagely humiliated by her. He draws his knife, first against Myshkin, and then against Nastasya, and has the last word. At the last moment, she flees from Myshkin into the arms and on to the knife of Rogozhin.[39] She flees from the honour in which the prince held her[40] to the dishonour which she so obstinately maintains: 'I am incapable of self-humiliation from purity of heart.'[41] She is right about one thing: Myshkin's nature, his love, cannot be kept within the limits proper to marriage, which he offers each time only under constraint.[42] Just as unjustifiable from the worldly point of view is his attitude to money. He lavishes it upon rogues, despite dire warnings; gives away his lawful inheritance to lawless creditors; consciously lets himself be deceived; purchases the old liar Ivolgin's release from the debtors' prison; gives money to his slanderers; in short, he commits every conceivable kind of folly. And he lives these evangelical counsels in a totally unconscious way, without any awareness or intention of doing anything connected with perfection; on the contrary, he gladly gives heed to every criticism of his stupidity, indeed, to every pronouncement of his guilt: 'Yes, yes!' the prince said again, in terrible distress, 'you're right. Yes, I'm to blame'.[43] 'Oh, I feel that it was all my fault.'[44] Although at the same time he knows that 'it isn't *that* at all—it's something quite, quite different!'[45] And so he says with unsurpassable

[37] 186.

[38] 473.

[39] 249, 498, 638.

[40] 624. Myshkin is not only willing to 'take [her] just as [she is]' (195), he also thinks that she will be doing him an honour, not he her (*cf.* 196).

[41] 495.

[42] 'And how can one love two persons at once? With two different kinds of love?' (627).

[43] 622.

[44] 625.

[45] *Ibid.*

precision: 'Oh yes, I'm to blame all right! Most likely it's all my fault! I don't quite know how—but it's all my fault . . .'[46] That is the only way identification becomes possible. During the last minutes before condemnation, when I am quite alone, I think to myself: 'There are ten thousand of them, and none of them is being executed, but I'm going to be executed!'[47] Similarly with Rogozhin, the man who wants to murder Myshkin: the prince exchanges crosses with him as a sign of fraternity; he knows that he is involved with Rogozhin in a common sin;[48] they are both in a similar situation (the erotic obsession of the murderer and the ecstasy of the epileptic).[49] In the end, after the murder of Nastasya, Myshkin catches up with Rogozhin, caresses him in his delirium as if he were a little child, shares a bed with him on the floor, and sinks with him into fever and final illness.[50] In a similar way he had caught up with Nastasya at the moment of crisis, 'stroking her head again and passing his hands tenderly over her cheeks, comforting and soothing her like a child'.[51] The same is true of his relationship with Ippolit: he praises his 'confession' (the expression of his revolt against God and the cosmic order), and defends it against the criticism of both Ippolit himself and other people. 'I'm sorry you repudiate that confession of yours, Ippolit. It is sincere and, you know, even the most absurd parts of it—and there are many of them—. . . are atoned for by suffering . . . That idea that inspired you had certainly an honourable basis.'[52] This resembles the way Alyosha in solidarity listens to and defends the revolutionary manifesto of his brother Ivan—the 'Grand Inquisitor'. Being called 'a democrat, who has gone crazy over the modern

---

[46] 627.

[47] 91.

[48] 'If you hadn't raised your hand against me then (which God averted), what would I have seemed to you *now*? For I did suspect you all the same. The fact is, we were both guilty!' (402).

[49] 258. 'Almost all' they talk about together is the epileptic experience, and Rogozhin says that at that time Myshkin was his brother.

[50] 640–657.

[51] 616.

[52] 562.

nihilism' is a matter of indifference of Myshkin.[53] To the very end his conversations with Ippolit are conducted in a spirit of serious communication. Execution, epilepsy, the Holy Saturday picture: the three states of absolute isolation in which he unselfconsciously lives (there is never a word, never a thought, about the 'perfection' of this habitual abandonment, this transcendence and indifference). Only rarely is he asked about the Christian character of this state;[54] it suffices that people feel there is something disconcertingly unique about it—'the first honourable man I've come across' (Ganya),[55] 'the first man . . . in whom I can believe as a true and loyal friend' (Nastasya),[56] 'You're more honest than any of them, better, kinder, cleverer than any of them' (Aglaya).[57] The others say the same. And yet the prince does not live this condition in an unconscious dream-world; on the contrary, he is highly conscious and can be very decisive, as his sudden vehement outburst against Catholicism and for Russian Christianity proves. Catholicism is 'worse than atheism', because its use of 'the sword of Caesar' makes nonsense of Myshkin's state of life. It thinks it has to prop up the Church with 'universal temporal power', which immediately opens the way to socialist atheism. Both Catholicism and socialism are 'begotten of despair'; both seek to 'quench the spiritual thirst of humanity' without that one 'word of Christ' on which everything depends,[58] the last word Myshkin utters, in extreme excitement, before his epileptic attack in the Yepanchins' salon: love.[59]

This word expresses 'the whole essence of Christianity', the 'whole conception of God', the 'fundamental idea of Christ',[60] if we understand love in its deepest sense: as

[53] 617.

[54] 420.

[55] 152.

[56] 186. Cf. 207: 'Rogozhin, come along! Goodbye, Prince. You're the first human being I've seen!' And 494: 'You alone are capable of loving not for yourself.'

[57] 378. Cf. 467: 'I think you're the most honest and truthful man I know.'

[58] Cf. 587f.

[59] 597.

[60] 253.

communication with the sinner, as communion with his guilt without the will to distinguish oneself from him and as the exchange crosses with him, as Holy Saturday, when Love died the death of sin with sin and for sin. The idiot knows for certain that no atheism, no revolutionary anti-Christian protest, ever touches the depths of this Holy Saturday mystery; it cannot, nor does it want to touch them. They will never talk about *that*.[61] Here all the rest is left behind. Here love always conquers in silence. But the person who dares to build his life on this scandal for all philosophy, theology and secular culture is destined to be ridiculed with such intensity that even Dostoievsky does not stand by his idiot, but takes flight in a naive, nationalistic chiliasm and puts impossible words into the mouth of Myshkin: 'Show [the Russian] the renaissance of the whole of mankind in the future and, perhaps, its resurrection by Russian thought alone, by the Russian God and Christ, and you will see into what a mighty, truthful, wise, and gentle giant he will grow before the eyes of the astonished world.'[62] So he is powerful, wise, a giant after all! It is true that 'humility is a terrible power',[63] but it cannot be used to drive the turbines of humanity. Myshkin's uncalculated destiny is to remain the ridiculous idiot. That is what everyone constantly calls him, whether *sotto voce* or unintentionally aloud; he is the man who is there, as it were by chance, to receive furious slaps in the face.[64] He is called, for want of a better word, a 'lamb'.[65] He is and remains 'a complete child',[66] and can be at his best with children.[67] He is practically incapable of loading a pistol,[68] and refuses a duel of honour ('There's nothing for us to fight about. I'll apologise to him, and that's all').[69] This

[61] 250, 253.
[62] 588.
[63] 434.
[64] 146.
[65] *Ibid.*
[66] 101.
[67] Myshkin's story of the children and poor Marie (94–104).
[68] *Cf.* 392.
[69] 398.

humility provokes ridicule everywhere, but, almost incidentally, it also proves that pride is no less ridiculous. Thus, in the case of Ippolit's pathetic suicide, which is treated in a very comical way ('. . . in your place I should . . . make a point of not shooting myself just to show them'),[70] and which, at the decisive moment, completely fails, because 'purely by chance' the firing-cap had been forgotten.[71] 'That is just like him', comments Aglaya. [72]

Myshkin's idiocy eludes all psychological explanations, precisely because part of it—though only a part—is caused by his illness. On no account can it be said that his illness is a psychological stroke of luck in the sense that it transfers him to a state in which he can understand the state of his fellow men better, since he can share their experience without the dividing wall of individuality. Moreover, even the sinners play at confession and revelation as a party game; each tells the worst thing they have ever done, the idea being that 'the game loses its point as soon as anyone deviates, even in the slightest, from the truth'.[73] It is not hard to imagine the fun Dostoievsky would have had with depth psychologists and Freudians had he encountered them in his own lifetime. The chief function of Myshkin's illness is as a veil; it veils the Christian mystery from himself and from others. It is the mystery of the glory of absolute love descending from above, the love whose magical power lies beyond both disclosure and concealment, memory and oblivion, objective and creative interpretation. It also lies beyond idiotic simplicity and the most penetrating clarity of mind. Aglaya tries to explain the force of this mystery in Myshkin by distinguishing higher from lower mind; though the latter may be faulty, 'the most essential part of your mind is much better than in any of them'.[75] That is true, for Myshkin quite obviously possesses the gift of discernment, a knowledge of hearts that is often little short of prophecy; he knows people's hearts

[70] 456.
[71] 459.
[72] 464.
[73] Cf. 175f.
[75] 467.

better than they do themselves. And yet this charismatic aspect is not the most important thing about Myshkin, not even the most conspicuous. No, the most important thing about him is without doubt that simple love which is not really at home, cannot settle down or be classified, here below—Aglaya describes it as 'medieval Platonic love'.[76] Certainly, it is clearly distinct from original transcendent Eros, for that is wise, but Christian love is foolish and, in its earthly form, ridiculous.

Dostoievsky was able to expound the Christian theme of the fool with such discretion and at the same time such precision that he remains its master. True, Gérard de Nerval in a unique way had handled the theme of a Spirit-impelled madness practically and with artistic skill, but in the sphere of medicine and human ethics. True, Bernanos in his *Diary of a Country Priest* (1936) will deepen it theologically and ecclesially. He paints a vivid picture of a priest closely conformed to the Christ of Gethsemane, a man exposed to humiliating ridicule, and suffering vicariously, as Myshkin does, from an inherited illness, though losing thereby something of the delicacy and lightness of the Russian figure. Graham Green's 'whisky priest' (the novel's very title lays claim to the word 'glory'—*The Power and the Glory*, 1940) continues more the line of Simplizissimus than that of Myshkin; if the author's claim is to show the same truths as Dostoievsky, in Christian terms he is wide of the mark.

h. Christ in the Clown

ROUAULT

One more name must be mentioned, though it is not the name of a writer: *Georges Rouault*. At first, he attempted to represent Christian things in the language of beauty—until 1903 he was painting angels and other religious subjects, but then the prophet Léon Bloy with his *Femme pauvre* opened his eyes, and in order to express the vision of glory that had

[76] 283.

burst in upon him, he smashed the canonical form. The inconceivable light breaks from the 'humiliated and offended' alone; the caricature of the bourgeois brings to light the truth about him, the truth hidden from him; prostitutes need to be depicted only as they appear to the straightforward Christian eye. But it is in the clown that the most open image of human existence is to be found: wanderer without a homeland, unarmed and exposed, in the very ridiculousness of his costume revealed in all simplicity.

In his pictures of clowns Rouault perfects a theme that made its first gentle appearance in Watteau's portraits of the italian comedians. In his enchanted Mozartian world, where music is in the air, Pierrot is at first only one charming character among many (the London 'Masquerade' and Italian 'Serenade', the Berlin 'Love at the Italian Theatre').[77] However, in the comedian picture of Althorp,[78] he is in melancholy isolation, and in the late 'Gilles'[79] he is totally dissociated from the hectic goings-on behind him and stands motionless before the beholder as a man of mystery. From Daumier and Baudelaire right up to Beckmann, Picasso, and Rilke (in the fifth *Duineser Elegie*), 'gypsies', the 'children of the ever-rolling wheel', 'knowing well all the routes to Heaven', 'far removed from the gurgle of lofty classicism or the last secret arms manufacture for world peace' (Rouault),[80] become an increasingly eloquent image, which receives its most powerful eloquence in the work of Rouault. The 'Tragic Clown' of 1903, whose features are scarcely distinguishable because of the sheerly disfiguring way in which they have been sketched, and the unfathomable 'Head Of A Tragic Clown' (1904), looking terribly through a veil of dark grey-blue, introduce the long series of portraits, in which it becomes almost irrelevant where the disfiguring element, the sinful element, wells up from: from this particular human being's cesspool or from other people's, those who deposit the ordure of their own ugliness on the

[77] H. Zimmermann, *Watteau* (1912), p. 24, cf. 183, 165, 35, 36.
[78] *Ibid.*, 57 and the copy 139.
[79] *Ibid.*, 96–97.
[80] *Le Cirque de l'Étoile filante* (Paris, 1938), p. 10.

person portrayed. In any case, what is comic and grotesque is tragic, and the artist's revolt against the disfiguring of men, like Dostoievsky's, increasingly becomes compassion. If the clown is the representative and summing up of all that is humanly grotesque, his portrait is bound, imperceptibly and in a continuous process, to turn into the image of Christ. The early 'Christ With The Crown of Thorns' (1905, New York), with His face streaked and contradicted by bright colour, is very close to the clowns; conversely, a picture like the 'Old Clown' (1917) has an affinity with many a portrayal of the face of Christ. It takes the eye of faith to see in Christ the humiliation and offending of eternal love and in one's disfigured fellow human beings the glimmer of the grace of Christ. Rouault's interest shifts more and more to producing this glimmer by means of hitherto unknown methods of painting. Colour, in the service of the eye of faith, receives a luminous power, indeed, a transparency and phosphorescence, which glows through even the late landscapes, making them holy ground. The effect is the same whether the scene is enlivened by a Christ with women or by ordinary poor people, whether it is called Galilee or some quite other place. And this is a poor, almost desolate world as far as its forms are concerned—the exact opposite of a classical landscape of Claude Lorrain or of one of the Impressionists. The glory that nevertheless fills it is not vegetative or atmospheric; it is more immanent and at the same time more transcendent; it is the same glory that streams from the face of despised and dying love. So the same interior style can hold sway over the two dark 'Miserere' series as well,[81] where the indictment of bourgeois society, sharpened by the horrors of war, changes into a profound fellowship in suffering with trampled, disfigured mankind. Only *one* clown, sorrowful unto death, still silently poses the question: *Qui ne se grime pas?*[82] Now identical gestures, by means of imperceptible modifications, express apparently contradictory things, in a kind of *coincidentia oppositorum*. 'The same throwing back of the head

[81] 58 etchings, printed 1927, published in Paris, 1948; a book edition in small format appeared at the same time.
[82] Plate 8.

conveys, in one case, a Virgilian sense of sadness' (the wonderful picture in question has the subscript: *Sunt lacrimae rerum*),[83] in another case, the hope of a man condemned to hard labour,[84] somewhere else the resignation of a dying man,[85] and then immediately afterwards the odious complacency of a conqueror,[86] finally the regal suffering of the Virgin of the Seven Swords,[87] and then again the fixed gaze of a blind man consoling and guiding one who can see.[88] Man can also appear, as in the late Middle Ages, as a skeleton; indeed, to the eyes of this visionary it matters little whether he is clothed with flesh or not, whether the human condition is expressed by a tender feeling for the presence of Christ ('Seigneur c'est vous, je vous reconnais')[89] or by a mouldy sepulchre with piles of skulls to left and right and the black cross in the middle ('Celui qui croit en moi, fut-il mort, vivra').[90]

Here the clown image and the whole metaphysics of that 'principal reason' (Myshkin), which in this chapter we have seen as honest, foolish, indeed idiotic reason, is superseded. The games of the fools from Parzival to Don Quixote and Simplicius were a merry prelude to the seriousness of the Idiot, but now the destiny of that lonely individual has become the destiny of mankind, a destiny which, at the point where human existence was proclaiming its senselessness and idiocy, has been taken up by the gentle divine Idiot on the cross. He silently contains everything in himself and imprints on everything His form, the form of the divine mercy, for which it is a matter of sublime indifference whether its glory is manifested invisibly in earthly beauty or in ugliness.

[83] Plate 27.
[84] Plate 6.
[85] Plate 47.
[86] Plate 49. From the introduction by Abbé Morel (p. 12).
[87] Plate 53.
[88] Plate 5.
[89] Plate 32.
[90] Plate 28.

4. THE KNOT. NICOLAS OF CUSA

a. The Remaining Themes and the New Beginning

After we have traced in rapid brush-strokes two lines which have their origin in the Middle Ages and reach out into the modèrn age—the 'metaphysic of holy reason' which begins with Eckhart, Ruysbroek and Tauler and continues without a break to Fénelon, and its reflection in the literary realm which as the 'metaphysic of foolish reason' reaches into the present, it is a matter of tracing both lines back to their source and—which is relevant to our problem—considering the whole intellectual scene at the beginning of the modern age. But first one thing is clear: neither the indifference of the saints nor the thrown-ness of the fool can raise any claim to conquer as a whole the world and existence therein. On either line human totality is not visible or only insufficiently so: the prevailing passivity before God (as the fashioning creator spirit) only with Ignatius of Loyola found an inner synthesis with active spontaneity; the fools on their side are only effective either as a stimulating contradiction (Jacopone), as a rebel (Villon), as a timeless and rootless utopian (Don Quixote), or they stride out over an incipient realm of folly (Parzival), often to become cunning rogues (Simplicius); seldom do they achieve a lasting memorial (even after they have sunk: Myshkin, close to whom one could place Kierkegaard and Bloy), or something both concealing and embracing at the point where all worldly reason comes to an end (Rouault). But to mock this worldly reason as folly, *a priori*, from a higher vantage-point, as Erasmus did for example, is to cut the knot before it has ever been tied; it means, expressed more deeply, precipitately to identify the analogy between created and uncreated reason with the contradiction between sinful-fallen and divine-redemptive reason.

Both the 'metaphysics of the saints' and the theme of the

fool attempted in their own way to short-circuit the problem: they skipped the reality of the world which was left as a nominalist-positivist scene of wreckage, and they sought the gleam of the divine glory in an immediate supernatural. A third line then needed to be drawn, that of the Reformation, which in its original impulse rejected the philosophical mediation just as much. Only its consequences can be mentioned here: the sundering of ecclesiastical unity, and all the theological and political consequences that flowed directly from it, contradicted the nature and the task of the Christian Church to such an extent that it—in so far as it was disunited—lost its credibility for the world and with it its role as mediatrix of divine glory. So the first great movement which originates at the end of the Middle Ages, the re-awakening of classical metaphysics (in all its breadth from myth through philosophy to religion), becomes not only an intrinsic philosophical necessity—as the sinking down again of a positivistically uprooted reason into the fruitful soil of origin and heritage—but even more, the vital necessity for the existence of a Christian culture, which has to secure an elemental enduring religious unity, beyond the destructive hostilities of the confessions. That thereby the great ecumenical outlines of the Middle Ages have to acquire a 'liberal', finally an 'enlightened' colouring, in the context of the modern age, belongs to the unavoidable consequences of the disunity of the Churches.[1]

The first major movement, which embraces humanism (fifteenth century), the Renaissance (sixteenth century) and further the baroque (seventeenth century), the Enlightenment and German Idealism from Winckelmann to Schiller and Goethe, and to Schelling and Hegel (eighteenth–nineteenth centuries), can therefore be recognised as a cry to the *mediation of antiquity* for help by the Christian community, threatened by the loss of the world. There is something paradoxical about that, in so far as the whole of Christian intellectual history from Origen and Augustine through Boethius and Erigena to High Scholasticism was a perpetual dwelling in

---

[1] As Friedrich Heer has again and again convincingly shown.

the thought-world of antiquity, and indeed with preference for the Platonic-Plotinian realm, which now once more—in the highest degree traditionally—was entered with rapture (after Dante and Petrarch) by the Florentine and the other Italian natural philosophers, and was made fruitful for metaphysics, art and religion. The darkening of human existence in the later Middle Ages, and also the darkening of the Christian realm of thought in late scholasticism, sufficed to give the impression to young eyes who beheld afresh the divine glory in the beauty of the cosmos, that they saw this for the first time since the Greeks. And because the Platonic-Plotinian view of the world understood itself as 'revelation'—an event in which the distinction of natural and supernatural becomes questionable, as the theology of the Fathers of the East and the West clearly indicates—it cannot be long before, for a further time in the long Christian tradition, the revelation of Christ is understood as the pinnacle, summation and synthesis of the whole divine revelation in the cosmos. Now more than ever are Plato and Plotinus 'baptised' as Christians before Christ, more than ever can the ancient gods be interpreted as partial aspects of God (as they seem to us in Homer) and be incorporated into Christian art and literature, more than ever the doctrine of the *Logos spermatikos* is seen to be valid not only in the case of the philosophies but in the religions inseparable from them, more than ever will the distinctively Christian be regarded as the highest example of the universal bridge between God and man.

But the wheel of history never turns backwards; on its spiral the point of the Renaissance lay higher than the point of antiquity, and so one or a few turns higher in either a Christian or a post-Christian realm in which no way lay open for a return to the naivety of the classical relationship to God. The passage of time becomes visible in the second major theme which will hold sway over the same period of the modern age and entwine itself with the classical theme, complementing it by a dialectic of contradiction: it is the theme, already familiar to us from Eckhart (where it had been broached, but was then abandoned), of the *speculative doctrine of God*, proceeding from the (Christian) experience of immediacy between the infinite and the finite I. A theme which was certainly already present in Plotinus and more strongly, because with a Christian edge, in Augustine, but which right up to Eckhart remained hidden under a double carapace: the theme of the classical 'shyness' before the divine and direct vision and utterance, and of the biblically deepened reverence before the unapproachable *Doxa: qui scrutator est Majestatis opprimetur a Gloria* (Prov. 25.27). And yet a friend of God like Eckhart was to tread the 'mysterious way inwards' which was reserved not for the slaves but for the friends, sons, heirs in Christ, immediately into the heart of the Father, indeed into the supra-trinitarian *Ungrund* of the still, dark Godhead. We heard the frightened cry of the 'Frankfurter' at the very edge of this abyss, his warning not to go further here, and saw at the same time how he succumbed to the fascinating temptation. For here too there was no way back, already the God of the Old Testament had been given up; Jewish Kabbalistic speculation invaded him, leading to Spinoza, to the Hasidim, to Salomon Maimon, to Hermann Cohen; it was rather the God of the New Testament that pointed the way from Boehme to Baader, from Fichte's speculation about the 'I' to the understanding of Christ in the young Hegel and to the pansophism of Rothe.

But decisive and characteristic of the age is the infinitely varied combination of both themes, something that constitutes both what is fascinating and kaleidoscopically ambiguous about the epoch and which finally, with Hegel, turns out to be a finished and done-with intermezzo. Where in antiquity the gods stood, there opens up now the realm of the relationship to the infinite I, a realm which will finally be controlled in different ways—ethically (Schiller), aesthetically (Schelling), erotically (Novalis), speculatively (Hegel), whereby, if not indeed the categories of the beautiful, yet certainly those of glory understood in either classical or biblical terms will pale.

Out of the combination of these two themes there finally emerges by itself the third principal theme of the modern age: that of evolution, which was entertained speculatively for a long time before experiment supported it. The world can come to lie nowhere else now than in the gap between the finite and the infinite I, and because, as long as pure materialism is avoided, the infinite I, even if simply as an idea, has the primacy, the world and man can in the end be nothing more than the goal of its Odyssean voyage of self-discovery. With the insertion of God into the world-process, however, his sovereign freedom over man is lost; speculatively, man emerges as an absolute standpoint, and consequently remains—in Feuerbach—the unique *divinum* in the landscape of thought.

At the point of departure of this double theme—classical mediation and speculation about God and Spirit—there stands, as almost an erratic block, NICOLAS OF CUSA,[2] who with a mighty hand ties together in a knot the threads of the great Western tradition—Hellenism and Christianity, past and future. Again, and with remorseless energy, fissiparous thought is plunged again into the primal philosophical act, as it achieved its finite and (as we said above) formally unsurpassable, classical form with Plotinus. This primal act, which enfolds all and can ever only posit itself and reflect itself, is the analogy of being: God is all *in* all, because he is inescapably all *over* all. So—as was noticed apropos

[2] The works fundamentally from the Paris ed. by Lefèvre d'Etaples (1514) cited (reprint 1962) by page (folio) *recto* and *verso*. The critical edn. of the Heidelberg Academy, so far as it has appeared, has been drawn on (in vol. XIII *De Non-Aliud*, ed. by L. Bauer, which is missing in the Paris edn.), similarly edn. by Petzelt (*Philos. Schriften*, vol. I, Kohlhammer 1949) and the translations with commentary of the *Philos. Bibliothek* in the Meinerverlag. The 'Cusanus-Texte' in the Sitzungsberichte of the Heidelberger Akademie der Wissenschaften will be cited *passim*, also the 19 *Predigten 1430–1441* (Kerle 1952) and the old translations by Scharpff (N. v. C., *Wichtigste Schriften* 1862).

Abbreviations: DI: *de docta ignorantia*, A: *apologia* DI, C: *de conjecturis*, DA: *de deo abscondito*, QD: *de quaerendo deo*, F: *de filiatione Dei*, DP: *de dato patris luminum*, G: *de genesi*, IS: *idiota de sapientia*, IM: *idiota de mente*, SE: *de staticis experimentis*, VD: *de visione dei*, PF: *de pace fidei*, CA: *cribratio alchoran*, LG: *de ludo globi*, Pr: *de principio*, B: *de beryllo*, P:*de possest*, NA: *de non-aliud*, V: *de venatione sapientia*, ATh: *de apice theoriae*, S: *sermones*.

Erigena—his scheme of thought returns again at the end of the Middle Ages: the world as explanation of the inexplicable, or as Nicolas puts it: as *explicatio* of *complicatio*. Philosophy is always simply the view through the unfolded into the enfolded, which is shown in the unfolded to be non-unfoldable. If Plotinus and still more Proclus and Erigena provide the classical foundation, then Eckhart offers the counter-theme that points to the future. With Plotinus the *nous* was already an image of the One, in its moved identity of thinking and thought, of its clear and yet dynamic transparency to itself, in its uniform integration of all that will be unfolded in the realm of the *psyche*: but it is only with Eckhart that the theme—in the solitary bringing together of the infinite (paternal-trinitarian) and 'created' (filial-begotten) spirit—contains a virulence, which with Nicolas will be used again in the problematic of *mens*: human spirit so much a reflection of divine spirit that, at the same time, as a reflection, it takes over the divine features as a 'second god' and genuinely becomes the creator of a reflected world (that of numbers), just as God is creator of the real world of things. Nicolas himself never consciously steps over the boundary of the analogy to an idealism of identity, but for those who are determined to make such a transition, everything is ready prepared.

Therefore, looked at as a whole, Eckhart is interpreted in accordance with Plotinus; the proof of this lies in the totally sovereign role of *desiderium* (as intellectual-ethical *eros* for God), while the theme of abandonment (*Gelassenheit*), which determined the 'metaphysics of the Saints', finds scarcely an echo. Thus Nicolas signifies a renewed, energetic replanting of all the fundamental truths of positive Christian theology in the total, cosmic and metaphysical revelation which seems to it. As examples there could stand: *De Dato Patris Luminum*, a verse of the epistle of James (1.17) which will be commented on (certainly with little strain) completely in accordance with Plotinus,[3] *De Genesi*, where the biblical account of creation is allegorised in a traditional manner (with reference to Basil,

[3] DP fol. 193r–196v.

Ambrose, Jerome, Augustine, and with echos of Chartres) and interpreted in the spirit of the *Timaeus* and Plotinus,[4] or *De Sapientia I*, where the simile of scent from the Song of Songs is interpreted neoplatonically in the manner of the Fathers (Gregory of Nyssa).[5]

If Nicholas, who was brought up by the Brethren of the Common Life, is happy to designate himself in their sense as *idiota*, this can only be justified objectively as a polemical thrust against the school philosophers, and his way of speech which often reaches the limits of presumptuousness has nothing to do with the ideal of folly, manifest from Parzival to Myshkin; at most, it reflects the Plotinian-Areopagitical reduction of the philosophical act to its 'simplicity': for the rest, Nicolas makes no secret either of his learning or of his will to gather together the whole of the Western tradition and as much as possible of the Eastern tradition (*The Sifting of the Koran*) in a synthesis with power to shape future thinking. Later Scholasticism has fallen from the spiritual to what is merely of the understanding; with it there is no longer any salvation. 'Because they hold wisdom to be nothing else than that which can be grasped by the understanding, and blessedness as nothing else than what they can attain, therefore they are far from the true, eternal and limitless wisdom and have devoted themselves to the finite.'[6] Where true authority and its chief emphasis lies, becomes recognisable when one hears the praises that he bestows on Denys the Areopagite: he is 'the greatest among theologians',[7] the 'great' and the 'divine',[8] the 'holy',[9] 'our Denys';[10] *florilegia* from his works support the main scaffolding of Cusan thought.

This means too that for the last time in the Catholic realm—perhaps until the new and differently-fashioned beginning found in Blondel's *Action*—the fundamental

[4] G fol. 69vff.
[5] IS 1, 76r.
[6] IS 1, 76v.
[7] NA c. 14. Baur 29.
[8] A fol. 36r.
[9] A 40r.
[10] A 38r.

articulations of the historical revelation remain enclosed within the parameters of the paradox of the *analogia entis*. This paradox is not simply the harmonious rhythm of 'contraries', but, as with John Erigena, the coincidence of opposites (*coincidentia oppositorum*), which lie side by side, unseparated, in the transcendent being of God. How else should the Incarnation of God, as the coincidence of God and the creature, of unlimited and limited, of election and reprobation; how else should the Church, as the coincidence of the historically particular and the humanly universal; how else should faith, as the coincidence of not-seeing and a transcendent seeing on the part of reason; how else should grace as the Absolute making itself accessible, without which no finite spirit could think; how else theology, as the emptying fulfilment of the philosophical act; how else even the Trinity, as an expression of the supremely living transcendent unity, not-otherness, almightiness of the Absolute, reserve here any fundamental surprises which are not already contained more hiddenly or more openly in the primal paradox? It must be noticed that Nicolas neither is not wants to be any kind of rationalist or liberal, that he wishes the *understanding* of faith (*intellectus fidei*) to be interpreted throughout in the Anselmian sense as *intellectus* fidei, and understands himself as a faithful son of the Church (in which as vicar-general of Rome he was the highest next to the Pope, his friend Pius II). But that is only so because he understood the act of faith itself in the classical sense as the pinnacle of the philosophical act, in an inner analogy (of philosophical and theological faith), which could endure no breach.[11] No breach, then, such as Luther will shortly maintain between the God of faith and the God of reason; but then is not Nicolas already prepared for that darkness, that paradox of the Lutheran God? Do these two Germans, the one starting from Denys, the other from Augustine, really stand so far apart? One can ask how far the Cusan analogical panorama of the utter otherness of the mystery of faith levels it down and renders it harmless–before all, the mystery of the cross, of

[11] K. Jaspers, *Nikolaus Cusanus* (Piper 1964), 58f.

the descent into hell and the resurrection, but also of the gracious leading of Israel and of the Christian people; one can ask how far Nicolas succumbs to the danger of sacrificing the distinctive glory of the living God once more to an aesthetic cosmic scheme; but one must on the other hand hold before one's eyes, what here once again, for the last time perhaps, makes possible a cosmic universal view of the glory of the living God as this is understood by the message and demand of St Paul. The God whom Nicolas encounters in all things is no *dieu des philosophes*, he is a God who combines the universal features of the Plotinian with the lights of Homer, the dark depths of Sophocles and the eternal longings of Virgil in the reconciling power of the biblical event. It is therefore right when Nicolas so often and in such prominent places goes back to Paul's utterances in Romans and the Acts of the Apostles about the hidden God being manifest in his creation, that he, transcendent over the world, is distant from no-one and wills to be sought longingly by all, always and through all things.[12] It can be said that here a German eye has been assimilated to that Greek vision which Paul appealed to in both places and pressed into service. That vision, for which the simplest was the most incomprehensible, as the *idiota* says: *qui mecum inteutur absolutam facilitatem coincidere cum absoluta incomprehensibilitate, non potest nisi idipsum mecum affirmare.*[13]

So one can expect from Cusa a vision of the unity of what in the context of the vision of reality found in Plotinus, Eckhart and the Bible may be manifest as 'glory'. We set forth this vision here, and we shall unfold it subsequently stage by stage.

b. Total Glory

It follows from what has been said that the Christian elevation

[12] Introduction of QD (197r) and the taking up again of the theme at the end (200r), the same broadly in the introduction to P (174v–175r) with reference to Acts 17.28: 176r (bottom), and once again reflecting on the beginning: 183v.

[13] IS 2, 79r. [he who beholds with me absolute facility coincide with absolute incomprehensibility cannot but affirm the same with me.]

of Plotinus' vision of God and the world formally implies the most favourable opportunity for an aesthetic theology. For Plotinus, Proclus and Erigena the world is the manifestation of the unmanifest God, which brings the fundamental aesthetic plan of form-light (harmony-idea of the spirit) into its highest use; but Christianly (= according to Eckhart) the unmanifest *(Un-)grund* of God is absolute freedom, which therefore, *when* manifest, implies the non-necessity, and therefore the sovereignty, of its manifestation. Both, taken together, imply: the 'shining forth' of the incomprehensible in the world-harmony (and its Heraclitean tension of contradictions reduced to unity: war as peace) is the shining forth of absolute sovereignty in a tension governed by law. But the self-glorification of God in his world rests upon his freedom, and therefore on his unfathomable love; so the relationship becomes bridal: the heart of the aesthetics of Nicolas is on the one hand the Trinity—Spirit-Love as glory between Father and Son—and on the other the wedding of God and the world in Christ in the mystery of the Spirit and the Church.

The words *resplendere, relucere,* are everywhere, as an expression of the hidden revelation of God in the world. To begin with, in a platonic way: 'As in every spoon only the one, most simple form of a spoon shines forth in different ways, in one more, in another less, in none exhaustively *(praecise)*',[14] 'thus the infinite form is only one, the absolutely simplest, and it shines forth in all things as the precise original of each and every individual thing that can be formed'.[15] And this divine 'original shines forth in the mind as the truth in the representation',[16] 'it shines forth in it as God, who is all', so that the mind can make use of itself to come to know everything.[17] And since the creative radiance of God can encounter nothing since nothing is outside him, 'the creature can be nothing else than this radiance *(resplendentia)* itself.'[18]

[14] IM 2, 82r.
[15] *Ibid.,* 2, 82v.
[16] *Ibid.,* 3, 84v.
[17] *Ibid.,* 3, 87r.
[18] DI 2.2, 14r.

In God as the not-other 'all other things shine forth
(*elucescunt*)',[19] as likenesses in the original: 'therefore the
original is the standard and ground of the image: and thus
God shines forth in the creatures as the truth in the image.'[20]
So far, this is Platonic. But the original is eternally-living
Person, and therefore his 'manifestation' is 'speech': the
sensible world is language, is a legible book (*libri mentis ejus
expressionem continentes*),[21] indeed precisely a 'voice, in which
God causes his spiritual Word to shine forth in a manifold
way, so that all sensible things may be a manifold speech of
God the Father through the Son as Word in the Spirit of all,
with the end result that through sensible signs the doctrine of
the highest teaching office is poured forth into the minds of
men . . . so that man is the ultimate purpose of the sensible
world and the glorious God the beginning, middle and end
of all his works.'[22] Particularly in the *Beryl* is this thought
strictly followed through and demonstrated with supreme
skill, viz. that the ancient philosophical quest for the essence
(*quidditas*) of things in their distinctiveness and uniqueness was
bound to founder so long as they could not be conceived of
as *intentions* (*intentiones*) of a God who communicates himself
in the creation freely and sovereignly. 'So I say with the wise
that there is no basis for any of the works of God in the
understanding, but to the question why the heaven is heaven
and the earth earth and man man, there is no other reason to
be given than that the creator wills it so. It is so, as Aristotle
. . . says: to investigate further would be a foolish and
arbitrary search for a proof of the first beginning, what it
was or was not . . . The will of the creator is the final reason,
and the creator God is simple Reason, which fashions out of
itself, so that the will is nothing else than reason or
intelligibility (*ratio*), indeed the ultimate source of any

[19] NA c. 9 concl., Baur 21.

[20] A 36v.

[21] FD 66r. The whole *Compendium* revolves round the problem of the
existent as the language and expression of Being. [books containing the
expression of his mind.]

[22] FD 67v.

intelligibility.'[23] The Presocratics, Plato and Aristotle 'attributed necessity to the first cause', in order thus to lend a necessity derived from thence to intelligible unities in the world, but in vain, for the contingent could not be absolutely explicated from the Absolute.[24]

There is therefore only 'one unique possible solution. For what does the creator *will*, when, through the revolution of the worlds and the instrumentality of nature, he draws forth from a thornbush such a beautiful and fragrant rose? What else can be the reply than that that astounding reason intends (*intendit*) to reveal in this its word, how deep is its wisdom and its intelligible motive and how great the riches of its glory, that it so lightly places such a wonderful and symmetrical beauty by means of such a slight thing in the apprehending sense, arousing joy and enhancing man's whole nature with sweet harmony.' And from the rose thought rises up to the higher revelations: in the whole life of living things, in intellectual apprehension holding sway beyond the relatively intransient forms (Aristotle!) and transient individuals. 'And so the teaching of the Gospel becomes ever more manifest, which gives to creation the purpose that the God of Gods is revealed in Zion in the majesty of his glory, which is the manifestation of the Father in whom is all delight.'[25] Because created things correspond to God's intention, they are good, as God himself says in the story of creation, 'so that the universe is a perfect revelation of the glory and wisdom of God.'[26] He himself remains beyond any worldly structure of beauty: 'above all multiplicity and number and harmonic proportion', and only 'to be seen without measure, number and weight',[27] to which vision the world points, as Trajan's column points to the 'knowledge of the glory' of this Caesar and to the indirect 'experience of his fame'; 'the column itself is not different from his will, even if the column is by no means will . . . but in the will wisdom and ordering sense are made known . . ., and the costliness of

[23] B 29, 189v–190r.
[24] B 36, 192r.
[25] B 36–37, 192r–v.
[26] NA c. 23, Baur 55.
[27] A 36r.

the work, which someone powerless could not have fashioned, is a reflection of the power of Trajan.'[28]

As a preparation for a sermon on the Song of Songs ('Behold, you are beautiful, my love') Nicholas excerpts freely from the treatise of Albert *de Pulchro et bono* and intersperses it with his own comments.[29] Albert's definition of beauty as 'the radiance of form beyond the proportionate parts of the matter' with the additional determinations, that the beautiful draws longing to itself and unites all things, could offer Nicolas a congenial starting-point: the double dimension—the material or horizontal one of *consonantia*, the formal or vertical one of *claritas* or *resplendentia*—could be applied in a transcendental manner to the relationship of God to the world, and render unnecessary for Nicolas any more than a merely formal separation between the beautiful and the good. More important for him (and going beyond Albert) is the relationship of the transcendental good-beautiful to the human mind: even if the higher senses pass an inchoate judgment on the beautiful, only the mind which is open to all being possesses it and can—from the transcendental idea of the beautiful which, as mind, it has and *is*—judge the degree of the concretely beautiful.[30] It *is* the simplified fullness of the beauty of the world: here Plotinus' concept of mind becomes decidedly more important than the *eros* of the *Symposium*, which strives after the beautiful because it does *not* possess it. Thus the *mens* for Cusa (Plotinus' νοῦς) is only a created copy of the divine primordial beauty, which—in contrast to Plotinus—has to know itself as beautiful, in order

[28] NA 9, Baur 20.

[29] *Excitationes, lib.* 8, vol. II fol. 139v–141r., in Jos. Koch, *Cusanus-Texte* I, Predigten 7. Untersuchungen (*Sitz. ber. Heid. Akad.* 1942), pp. 167–168 quoted as Predigt no. 240, without reference to Albert.

[30] *Natura . . . intellectualis . . . boni et pulchri naturam intellectualiter participat, quia haec est forma ejus . . . Nisi judex qui est intellectus in se haberet speciem pulchritudinis omnem sensibilem pulchritudinem complicantem, non posset judicium facere inter pulchra, dicendo hoc esse pulchrum, illud pulchrius, quare intellectus est quaedam universalis pulchritudo seu species specierum, cum species sint contractae pulchritudines . . . sic intellectus est vis complicativa omnium specierum intelligibilium, . . . antecedenter in se complicat omnes naturales pulchritudines, quae per species in universo implicantur.* fol. 140v.

(as the ultimate source of all self-conscious mind) to be spiritually beautiful: 'But when beauty beholds or understands itself, then it is impossible that infinite love should not be enkindled thereby. See here the trinity in a unity of the essence of beauty, where the source of the beautiful gives birth to an understanding of the beautiful from which love proceeds.' This self-mastered beauty is the intradivine glory whose authentic place is the Holy Spirit: '*omnipotens autem gloria procedit ex omnipotenti intellectu se intelligente,* . . . for without infinite glory the begetting almightiness cannot contemplate the almightiness begotten from it', and the glory therefore proceeds in order that the infinite understanding might become infinite 'goodness or love or delight or blessedness or joy'.[31]

Here there branch off important doctrines of Nicolas of Cusa: first, the general doctrine that the world could be created only for the sake of this intradivine glory, for the sake of its communication and knowledge,[32] and that, correspondingly, 'the science of praise (*scientia laudis*) is naturally born' in beings capable of knowledge, because the creaturely mind, reflecting on its nature, must think of itself as a ray of the glory of God, and therefore indeed is called to imitation of what is praiseworthy.[33] More important, and for Nicolas more characteristic, is the fact that the intradivine glory, even if it shines forth essentially in the creation, remains incomprehensible and unapproachable for the creature so long as God Himself in his freedom has not unlocked for the spiritual creature his inner mystery.[34] For the view from heaven to earth is one thing: this view sees only order, harmony and beauty; the heavenly Jerusalem is, so far as it

---

[31] *Excit. lib.* 6, vol. II, fol. 103v. (Koch no. 181).

[32] Apart from the two sermons just quoted, cf. also B c. 3, Letter to Albergati (*Cusanus-Texte* IV, Briefwechsel: 3. Sammlung, ed. by G. v. Bredow, p. 26): 'Nothing induced the Creator to raise up this universe, this most beautiful work, except his own praise and glory which he wished to show forth. So he who is its origin is also the goal of creation. And because no king is recognised without praise and glory, the creator of all things too willed to be recognised, so that he could show forth his glory.'

[33] Letter to Albergati, 377.

[34] *Excit.* fol. 104r–v.

extends, the region of love and therefore of beauty.[35] To the
view upwards from below, however, the eternal love must
make itself accessible by grace in order to be caught sight of
at all, and if it then needs the freedom of the creature to
respond to this love, it is once for all excluded by divine
love's nature as grace, that man should 'attribute to himself
the glory [the renown] of attaining blessedness', something
Nicolas, together with Augustine, powerfully establishes
against those philosophers who think to ascend to God by
their own strength. 'For they did not know that the
blessedness of God is grace', that only God's incarnate Word
and his Spirit breathed into our soul draws us into the
kingdom of his inner glory.[36] 'Thus Jesus Christ is the
medium without which God's glory cannot be communicated
. . . and the gift of Christ, the Spirit, folds into himself the
power of each gift.' But this means in the concrete order
subject to sin: 'there where the Father did not spare his most
beloved Son and his Son gave himself up to death, so that we
might acquire through the merit of his blood the purification
of our souls: there God revealed best the praise of his glory
(laudem gloriae suae), so that we might praise his infinite love
and see, beyond refutation, that he is the only one to whom
glory is due.' Where we 'acknowledge that we are in need of
the grace of redemption and implore it in all humility, there
we give God the glory, as is fitting, and the more greatly,
the more we acknowledge our depravity.' So it is glorification
by faith alone, for 'faith alone (fides sola) is able to strengthen
the weakness of our spirit by the Spirit of Jesus, who lives in
us by faith. For it is not in its own power that our spirit can
become speculator majestatis.'[37] So God draws his glory out of
everything: 'He made me man to prove by means of me his
great power, by raising me to fellowship with the angels. He
made me frail and weak to prove by means of me his power,
by accomplishing his mighty works in me. He allowed me to

[35] Excit. fol. 141r.

[36] Ibid. fol. 104v–105r. The gloria invisibilis is only perceived per auditum,
only by faith, not by vision. Therefore all 'knowledge of the kingdom of
God' is convicted of stultitia: Excit. lib. 6, fol. 109v (Koch no. 183).

[37] Ibid. 105v–106r.

sin, to show by means of me the power of his mercifulness and grace, when I am converted to him. He let me go astray to show by means of me the power of his wisdom in which he can raise me up again to knowledge of the true . . . life. He let all men sin, so that all might need grace, in order to prove the riches of his grace in Jesus Christ the Saviour of all.'[38]

And yet these intimately Christian sounds are inseparable from the universal concept that all being is a revelation of the 'beauty or glory of God': for both concepts apply to God identically, so that with Nicolas (as with the Victorines) philosophical longing and Christian love are of a single essence: *desiderium enim* sive *amor immutat continue amantem . . . attractione pulchritudinis* seu *gloriae dei. Nam non est gloria nisi in regia pulchritudine.*[39] But this *eros* is for Nicolas itself *caritas*, because the attraction exercised by God's beauty is the answer of grace to the revelation of grace: *pulchritudo de se amabilis caritas est, et ideo sine caritate nullus videbit absolutam pulchritudinem.*[40]

But a few years after this sermon (1456) there was founded in Florence the Platonic Academy (1462); and even Nicolas' knowledge of the beauty of God,[41] of the 'beauty of his countenance',[42] with which the beauty of the world 'bears no kind of comparison',[43] is essentially determined by a vision of the world. The light from above is refracted in the sweet harmony of the cosmic numbers, the knowledge and understanding of which is mankind's authentic heritage, and which form the visible ornament which, as is again and again emphasised, earns for the world the name of *cosmos* which at the same time expresses the fact that it has been 'adorned'

---

[38] *Ibid. lib.* 4, fol. 58v (Koch no. 56).

[39] *Ibid. lib.* 8, fol. 141r. [For desire *or* love continually changes the lover . . . by the attraction of beauty *or* of the glory of God. For there is no glory except in the royal beauty.]

[40] *Ibid.* 141r. [charity is beauty lovable by itself, and therefore without charity no-one will see absolute beauty.]

[41] *Cf.*, e.g., QD 198r–v.

[42] VD 101v.

[43] P 175v.

from elsewhere.[44] But this cosmos is so little something at rest that it is only comprehensible as the confluence and harmony of two contrary movements: as 'a kind of coincidence (*coincidentia*) of the descent of the identical to the non-identical, and of the ascent of the non-identical to the identical'; for the act of creation is the 'calling-out of the non-identical to the identical (*evocat Idem Nonidem in Idem*)',[45] the pyramids of light and darkness interpenetrating one another,[46] whence develops conflict (*oritur pugna*);[47] aesthetically speaking it is again the appeal of the beautiful (*kalos* from *kaleo*), now more believable because things are understood as 'words' of God. Thus it is possible to think that, from the point of view of ascent, the proportion of the material can become a condition for the radiance of form: 'Proportion is the place of form, for, without a proportion suited and measured to form, form cannot radiate forth ... Proportion is like the suitability of the surface of a mirror to the reflection of a picture; when that no longer offers itself, then the representation ceases. Correspondingly the infinite, original unity can shine back only when the appropriate relationship is at hand, and this lies in number. The eternal spirit is like a musician who wills to render perceptible his thoughts: he takes a multitude of sounds and brings them into a relationship corresponding to harmony, so that in the medium of proportion that music sounds forth gently and perfectly, when it comes across itself there as in its hereditary place.'[48]

But for Nicholas there stands between God and the world of the senses the created mind (*mens*, νοῦς), which, as God is the uncreated light and principle of everything, so after God and as his image and likeness is the created light and complicative principle of the materially unfolded world. In this mediation 'the mind is a kind of divine number, suitably proportioned in the best way to let the divine harmony

[44] P 183r–v; G 70v.
[45] G 70v.
[46] C 1.11, fol. 46r–v.
[47] G 70v.
[48] IM 6, 85v.

radiate forth and thus to gather together into singleness all sensible, understandable and rational harmony . . . in such a manner that each number and each relationship and each harmony which proceeds from our spirit itself lays hold of our spirit as little as our spirit lays hold of infinite spirit. For this is also a divine number, it is indeed so much number that it is one simple unity, which brings forth its (particular) number out of its power',[49] in other words: the unity of the created spirit remains derivative; even when it is itself a 'qualitative number' in God's creative intention, it is as a 'this', indeed already a real number, and therefore the substrate called upon for God's manifesting glory. Man is a 'creative' unity in his effect on matter, as mathematician, technician, artist, but for the uncreated unity he is the many, which holds itself open to the grace of the intradivine unity. Nicolas of Cusa therefore prepares the ground for the ethos of two-in-one of the developing Renaissance.

c. Training in Analogy

What we have just outlined needs depth if it is not to remain schematic. It will prove that Cusa certainly provides a provisional sketch for the structure of the period—from the Renaissance to Hegel—which is just opening up, but in the best elements of his foundation outlives its collapse. His renewal of antiquity is more than renaissance: it is a retraining in the lost primordial articulations of human thought; his sketch of a philosophy between spirit and God can (but need not) be judged transcendental in the modern sense. From the classical point of view (as philosophy of being) and from the modern point of view (as philosophy of mind and of freedom), Nicolas' effort of thought always serves the accomplishment of the *analogia entis*.

I. CLASSICAL POINT OF VIEW

It is renewal against a scholasticism blinded to the mystery of Being: 'Blind and without knowledge of their blindness they

[49] IM 7, 86v.

imagine they can see, and in their imagining they are
hardened in their doctrinal positions, just as the Jews, missing
the spirit, are in the letter.'[50] Renewal therefore of the
esoteric character of all theology: of the classical-'natural' and
a fortiori of the Christian theology. The true God is
encountered in rapture (*stupor*), in the suddenness that comes
upon one (*quasi via momentanei raptus*, Plato's 'ἐξαίφνης),[51]
'the true theology cannot be entrusted to books', 'it is
discourse about the kingdom of God, and this our master
Christ calls the hidden treasure', which is only found by the
poor in spirit: 'while today most of the professors, who
administer the field of Holy Scripture and have heard that
the treasure of the kingdom lies hidden in it, prize themselves
already as wealthy owners.'[52] There are writers who can lead
the way to true theology, such as Denys and his
commentators, Maximus, Erigena, Hugh of St Victor, Robert
of Lincoln, Thomas Gallus;[53] and others like Marius
Victorinus, Proclus, David of Dinant, who are not suitable
for everyone, as the unhappy attacks of Johannes Wenck on
Nicolas more than sufficiently demonstrate.[54] There is not a
twofold doctrine of God: a mystical and a so-called 'scientific'.
In the case of God, the scientific means understanding that all
creaturely knowing about the being of the origin remains a
'mirroring and a parable',[55] speech in riddling images
(*aenigmatice*)[56] and therefore in conjectural outlines
(*conjecturaliter*). Hence the titles of two of his early works: 'Of
learned (i.e., become conscious of this itself through thought)

[50] A 40r.
[51] A 36v.
[52] A 35r.
[53] A 38r.
[54] Edn. by E. Vansteenberghe: 'Le *de ignota litteratura* de Jean Wenck de
Herrenberg contre Nicolas de Cuse' in BGPhM VIII/6 (1910); Nicolas'
answer is the *Apologia doctae ignorantiae* fol. 34vff. Rud. Haubst, 'Studien zu
Nikolaus von Kues und Johannes Wenck', BGPhThM XXXVIII/1 (1955).
Cusa was defended by his friend, Bernhard von Waging: *Laudatorium doctae
ignorantiae* etc., in E. Vansteenberghe, 'Autour de la docte ignorance',
BGPhM XIV/2–4 (1915).
[55] P 183v.
[56] P 177v.

Ignorance', and 'Of Conjectures' (as the basic philosophical outlines). To make serious metaphysical conjectures one must have attained the *experience* of metaphysical thinking.[57] For this the 'learned ignorance' becomes 'sacred' (*sacra*),[58] indeed 'most sacred' (*sacratissima*) ignorance.[59]

Each concept is finite and cannot contain the infinite, which it intends, and which announces itself and conceals itself in it. According to the formula of Proclus, it 'participates in that which is imparticipable'.[60] Thus the expressions of Erigena come back again: wisdom 'is known in no other way than such that it is higher than all knowing and unknowable, inexpressible in every expression, incomprehensible by every understanding, immeasurable by every measure, concluded in no conclusion, unlimited by any limit, brought into no relationship by any relation, comparable by no comparison, unformable by any form, ... capable of being positioned in no positioning, undeniable by any denial, indubitable in any doubt, unsupposable in any supposition.'[61] Contrariwise that means that the nameless God can be called by many names, indeed by all names, for he is the object of all suppositions of naming: *hoc autem modo ineffabilis est effabilis, imparticipabilis participabilis*,[62] and there is 'the vision granted to us of the invisible God'.[63] 'Invisible are you, as you are; visible, as creation is, which it is in so far as it sees you.'[64] Thinking is the movement of this essential vision; so being created coincides with the *eros* that is drawn towards God, with the radical *desiderium* of the creature: *in idem coincidit esse et*

---

[57] *Qui per doctam ignorantiam de auditu* [by hearsay] *ad visum mentis* [to clear vision] *transferuntur, ii certiori experimento scientiam ignorantiae se gaudent attigisse.* A 34v, *cf.* IS 1, 77r. It is a matter then of tasting knowledge *experimentaliter. Scire multas amoris descriptiones, quas sancti nobis reliquerunt, sine amoris gustu vacuitas quaedam est.*

[58] A 38v.

[59] VD 107v.

[60] NA c. 10, Baur 21.

[61] IS 1, 76r.

[62] FD 68r. [in this way then the ineffable is expressible, and the imparticipable participable.]

[63] A 35v.

[64] VD 104v.

desiderare:[65] a movement like the *ephesis* of the Plotinian *nous* to the eternally transcendent One, which opens and lights up an intellectual space through an infinite longing after the spiritually infinite. 'Thus this holy unknowing of your greatness is the most longed-for nourishment of my understanding . . . How could desire not desire to be more? Whether our will desire being or non-being, the desire as such cannot rest, but reaches out ever further . . . Thus the more I conceive you, my God, as inconceivable, the closer I approach you.'[66] Thus Nicolas calls all his sermon-outlines *excitationes*: incentives, stimulants.[67] The eternal movement towards Being is philosophical (as Aristotle always demands to ask the question about Being), as a quest after *quidditas*, about which one 'knows', in order to be able to seek it, and which in endless approaching 'is seen from afar' (with Gregory the Great).[68] This indestructible stretching-forth is either fulfilled by God, and then is eternal blessedness, in which the spirit 'is ever moved in a most blessed longing, so that it may attain that of whose gracious closeness it never has enough';[69] or it is, if God does not fulfil it, 'eternal torture: to possess a rational nature and never to attain to reason'.[70] That is Gregory of Nyssa,[71] Augustine and his thirst 'as the hart desires the waterbrook';[72] it is universally Christian, without giving up the classical basis, because God, in revealing Himself, 'increases to fulfilment what nature denies us'[73] and thus does not give up the *analogia entis* (and therefore negative theology).

The explanation of the analogy of being proceeds inherently from the 'inconceivable' fact, that God is all (otherwise he would not be God), and yet the world exists,

[65] G 73r. [to be and to desire coincide in the same.]
[66] VD 107v.
[67] Cf. IS 1, 77r: *motus desideriosus in excitatione*.
[68] ATh 219r.
[69] IS 1, 77r.
[70] *Ibid.* 76v.
[71] Cf. my *Présence et Pensée* (1942), first part: La Philosophie du devenir et du désir.
[72] QD 200or.
[73] P 178v.

and this real world cannot be added to God's reality as an increment. God must be all the reality in the creature, and yet not be immersed (*immersibile*)[74] in it by this in-being, remaining unmingled (*nec immisceri*)[75] with it, he must indeed therefore be restlessly immanent in it[76] only because he is already in himself in simple totality everything that it is in its individuating unfolding. So the opposition between *explicatio* and *complicatio* becomes to begin with the 'best guide' to the intellectual ascent, especially when it is observed how already the resolutions in the world (of what is sensible and manifold in the Spirit) foreshadow the all-embracing mystery.[77] 'Just as what is sensible to sense is not sensible to the understanding, because it is not apprehended by the senses therein, but is intelligible and understanding itself, so [similarly] everything that is worldly in the world is unworldly in God, because here it is divine', or rather is the one God Himself.[78] For on the one hand 'If he were not truly himself the being of the totality and of every individual, how then could he bring it forth out of non-being?'[79] And on the other hand, he must 'really be all possible being', something possible only if he 'is everything in an enfolded way'.[80] If he is *really* the possible in the unity, then he does not *need* to be unfolded, in order to be really himself; not for a moment does Nicolas' intention run in the direction of Hegel. God as God cannot be unfolded or increased, he is 'simplicity before every root',[81] therefore attainable by no analysis or synthesis,[82] his unity has nothing to do with number (which would be capable of increase or division),[83] but if each thing in the world is a something in order to be able to be and be the image of God, then it is God and yet always an other over against the things that co-

[74] DI 3.1, 24r.
[75] DI 2.2, 13v.
[76] On the in-being of God in everything: *Possest*, German tr. n. 112.
[77] IM 9, 89r.
[78] P 183r.
[79] *Ibid.*
[80] P 175r.
[81] DA 2v.
[82] FD 67r.
[83] IS 1, 75v.

exist with it, something that cannot be said of God. With the discovery of this 'divine name': the not-other (*non-aliud*), Nicolas belives that he has taken a mighty step beyond Proclus and Eckhart. For this name is not only negative in the sense of a simple negation of the finite-creaturely, but is so negative that in any context he is so *pre*supposed (because anything is 'not-other' than what it is), and therefore simply supposed before anything, because in the context itself the 'other', the thing's particularity, commands attention.

Yet it could seem, in so far as the not-other is the cancelling of the other, that it is the coincidence of the worldly opposites—*coincidentia oppositorum*. But it is that only because it is more than that; otherwise God would be perceptible as the point of convergence of these opposites. Indeed this route is passable gnoseologically and methodologically: 'I look by means of the contradictions to the origin', but 'the origin lies *before* the contractions'.[84] Whoever therefore 'transcends every opposition, he alone beholds the infinite simple form'.[85] For 'as otherness is without otherness in unity, because it is then unity, so too the contradiction is without contradiction is infinity . . . In infinity there is the opposition of oppositions without opposition.' And the conclusion for the one contemplating God is: 'There is neither anything different from you or anything opposed to you . . . for if infinity did not include each being in itself, then there would be no infinity.'[86]

So Nicolas succeeds in expressing the relationship of God to the world through reduplications and therefore by way of Eckhart[87]—'God is Being'—passes beyond Eckhart: God is

---

[84] Pr, vol. II, fol. 10v; *cf.* A 37r: *super coincidentiam contradictoriorum Deum esse declaravi.*

[85] IS 1, 77v.

[86] VD 105v.

[87] In his *Apologia* he expressly supports Eckhart, of whom he says that 'the ordinary people are not fit to understand him, although the learned find much that is subtle and useful in his books' (A 39r). How much he owes to Eckhart has only recently become apparent through the researches of Herb. Wackerzapp: 'Der Einfluss Meister Eckharts auf die ersten philosophischen Schriften des Nikolaus von Kues', *BGPhThM* 39/3 (1962).

omnis formae formabilis forma,[88] he is 'not essence (*essentia*), but because he is the essence in essences, he is called *essentia essentiarum*'.[89] Therefore the transcendence of the Absolute should be expressed precisely in its immanence, he is *omne ens non entiter*,[90] as he is indeed in every other the (fundamental and therefore transcendental) not-other. With this reduplication Nicolas moves clearly beyond Eckhart and the immediate danger of pantheism and again back to Proclus and Denys, but in such a way that he cannot decisively transcend the classical, pre-Christian stand-point. He decisively wins back, through a firm anchoring in that very place, the analogical character not only of all worldly being, but of all worldly knowledge, and precisely metaphysical knowledge. For if God is the form of form and the essence of essence, then he establishes—as always—a creaturely form and a creaturely essence, and this is therefore not the pure 'nothing', which is ecstatically open to God-the-all (with the danger of a change into a man-the-all and God-the-nothing), rather is the fundamental experience the unlocalizable origination over against God of all world-being and world-thinking; while it is in God that the perfect reality and therefore exactness, precision (*praecisio*) consist, the derivatory thought can only be inexact, approximate, supposition, parabolic, and in the true sense of the word, 'reflective', speculative.

There is only one idea of everything, which is God,[91] and only in the idea have things their exactness, for any imitation could be other, infinitely more exact.[92] This thought, which is maintained from the beginning to the end of Cusa's work, is amplified and apparently modified only in so far as the mind, the reflected origin in the world, possesses an idea-character of its own, not however for the real, but for the unreality of numbers which unfold its simple essence. The

[88] G 70r. So frequently: A 36r: *forma omnis formae*; P 176r: *nec forma alicujus, sed omnibus forma quia causa efficiens, formalis seu examplaris et finalis*; P 182v: *formarum forma* (is God as *entitas*) . . . *ideo omnium formarum complicatio*; NA c. 10; Baur 23; *Natura naturarum omnium*: VD 7, 102r.

[89] NA c. 10, Baur 22; VD 103r.

[90] A 37v.

[91] P 177r.

[92] IS 2, 79v; Pr, II fol. 10v.

'exact science' therefore, which mind unfolds from itself, is unreal and only approximately applicable to reality; its knowledge of reality, whatever it conceptually pretends to be, is only conjectural, something that applies to the 'philosophical' doctrine of God, as much as to the 'theological', in so far as this too necessarily makes use of human thought. The concept remains according to its essence image and likeness, something that in a certain way points back to Plato's mythological thought, but even more strongly foreshadows the artistic element in the philosophical thinking of the Renaissance. Yet while the latter is inclined to rest in the symbolism of the image, the enigmatic in all thought remains for Nicolas an occasion of perpetual unrest. Certainly he knows the blessed touch of God who is present to and in all things: 'the eternal wisdom is tasted in everything that can be tasted; it is itself the pleasure in everything pleasurable; it is itself the beauty in everything beautiful; it is itself the desire in everything longed for', but at once there is again the question of its ineffable fragrance which we are only pursuing in all these forms.[93] It can mean for the art of thought: 'through reason the spiritual sweetness is tasted in the essence of things, as an image of the sweetness of the eternal wisdom, *quae est quidditatum quidditas*.'[94] And for the senses: 'he who sees a beautiful woman and is moved in his spirit, pays God the glory and turns to admiration of the infinite beauty, a most distant shadow of the light of which stands here before his eyes . . .'[95] But it is, as the examples bear out, a renaissance of the platonic longing, and not of a glutted worldliness. For Plotinus and Erigena, as for Ficino, the manifold things of the world remain '*apparitiones sive lumina . . . unius Dei*, who, although one, cannot be manifest otherwise than in manifoldness . . . These lights are called theophanies, and in all these lights he makes known the riches of the glory of his Light.'[96]

To this thought about analogy in the classical manner there

[93] IS 1, 76v.
[94] IS 1, 78r.
[95] *Excit. lib.* 7, II 119–120r.
[96] DP 4, 195rv, cf. 193v.

remains finally the insuperable problem of the establishment of the many out of the One. If pantheism is to be avoided—and Nicolas dismisses it as an indisputable vulgarisation of philosophy, for the real problems for thought only begin when one has passed beyond it[97]—then there remains for the unfolding of the unity of God in the world only the notion of a 'self-descent': not as if God could communicate less than himself (*communicat se indiminute*), but 'he cannot be so understood, as he is given, because the receiving of the gift takes place by way of descent (*descensive*).'[98] Yet what does it mean to say that no receptive 'matter' can be posited over against God, i.e. that no one is there beforehand to receive God's communication? Thus the final outcome can only be negative: for otherness there is not positive cause, it has as such no being,[99] the finitude of the creature emerges by change, *contingenter*.[100] But if no reason for the finite can be assigned within the *causalitas formalis*, then the question—why a world at all?—becomes insoluble by consideration of the *causa finalis* and *efficiens*. Plotinus had philosophised from its being and—by looking through to the mind and the One—had concluded that it had equal eternity with God: it is self-radiating goodness, beyond freedom and necessity. Since Nicolas of Cusa repeats the system in a Christian way in the *analogia entis*, he can experience and think the world only as contingency and an enigmatic likeness of God, and sees himself thus forced, without giving up the classically-attained analogy—to which belongs God-in-and-above-all and God's being not-other—to deepen it in a Christian manner.

2. CHRISTIAN POINT OF VIEW

While *De Non-Aliud* (1462) contains the last radicalisation of the classical point of view, there lies in *De Possest* (1460) and finally (in the year of his death, 1464) in *De Apice theoriae*—

[97] DP 2, 194r.
[98] DP 2, 194r.
[99] VD 14, 106r.
[100] DI 2.2, 13v; IM 6, 86r. This problematic is very clearly worked out by H. Wackerzapp, esp. 81ff.

after the Augustinian attempt of *De Visione Dei*—the Christian solution. Although it is close philosophically to Plotinus and further already prepared for by him, theologically it causes difficulties.

To the contingency of the finite there corresponds freedom as an answering concept in the Absolute. Plotinus sees it as the One's absolute being for itself, and somehow positively in the aesthetic dimension—as the purposelessness of the radiance of the Good. As a Christian, Cusa could have passed over from there immediately to the personality and love of God as the creator and revealer; but he considered that the philosophical form of analogy must be carefully introduced into the Christian context. The incomprehensibility of the God of negative theology is interpreted in the deeper incomprehensibility of the God of groundless Love: 'if anyone loves something because it is worthy of love, then he rejoices, if he discovers in the beloved infinite and inexpressible occasions of love. And the happiest realisation for the lover is when he grasps the inconceivable love-worthiness of the beloved. He would not rejoice so much if the beloved were comprehensible to him, as when it is clear to him that the love-worthiness of the beloved is completely incommensurable, indescribable, limitless and incomprehensible. That is the happiest comprehension of the incomprehensible and the tenderest learned ignorance, when he understands this in its way and yet does not understand it in exactness.'[101] Thereby, however, everything enters a new climate of thought: the negative incomprehensibility of the ever-greater God, whose essence glimmers behind all the veils of manifestation, turns into the positive incomprehensibility, that one who is utterly without need *wills* to have need of me, although he in no way *has* to.

Augustine once described blessedness as *videntem videre*;[102] Nicolas sets out from one of those images, the sight of which follows the beholder from all sides, and even seems to change along with the traveller. God's being is the utterly simplest being-with-himself and therefore infinite eye and universal

[101] IS 1, 76r (text as in Baur).
[102] *Sermo* 69.3; PL 38.441.

vision, so that he seems to accompany the moving, spatio-temporal creature and therefore continually to gaze just at me. The thought is biblical, the expression Plotinian, again in the form of reduplication: God is 'the countenance of countenances'.[103] It is a biblical thought too that God's seeing is characterised not only as his being, but also as his loving,[104] indeed as his being merciful;[105] and biblically grounded is the strange new consideration, that the absolute contraction of the divine Spirit into the power-centre of his eternally being eye makes him the infinite idea and original of every finite 'contracted' mode of being: 'everything that is finitely contracted together has its place in the Absolute, because the infinite beholding is the contraction of all contractions (*contractio contractionum*), it is thus an uncontractable contraction (*contractio enim est incontrahibilis*).'[106] God as a spirit-person is not *only* the infinite, but therefore *also* the transfinite. But then it is no longer an empty, pointless question—how multiplicity can develop out of unity—but the more perspicacious question of how the transfinite subject can be opposed to finite subjects. One sees (and much better than with Eckhart) that the analogy of being must in any event be also an analogy of freedom, that God's pure givenness can only be received, if man too has decided for God in a freely personal way, in a choice both of God and of himself. 'To that extent you compel my freedom, because you cannot be my own possession, unless I possess myself no longer; *but because* you have placed this in my freedom, you do not compel me, but wait, that I myself should choose to belong to myself,' and precisely 'because you do not restrict your limitless goodness, but pour it out freely to all who are receptive of it.'[107]

Nicolas does not want to let go of the first, Plotinian schematism: man's seeing of God is hidden in God's own vision, is a finite, creaturely participation in it, and because

103 VD 6, 101r.
104 VD 4, 100r.
105 VD 5, 100v.
106 VD 2, 99v.
107 VD 7, 102r.

God is the not-other, this can mean: 'each face that is able to look into yours sees therein nothing other, nothing different from itself, for it looks into its truth.'[108] But this truth is not man himself, but God; man's vision reaches that which lies unattainably above him, 'and so I am conscious that what I see is not known by me and could never be known'.[109] It is precisely here that Nicolas recalls the Pauline thought that perfection consists not primarily in seeing God, but in being seen by God.[110] 'If I saw, just as I am visible, I would not be a creature.'[111] Even the vision of the creature is, although it is a true vision, an analogical and enigmatic vision, as the beautiful formulation makes perfectly explicit: 'Lord, illuminator of hearts, my countenance is a true countenance, because you, the Truth, have given it to me. And it is an image, because it is not itself the truth, but a reflection of the unconditioned truth which in itself is. I therefore embrace with my concept the truth as what is mirrored in my face, and see therein such an agreement of the likeness with the truth beheld by it, that my countenance is true to the extent that it is an image.'[112] It is therefore consistent that precisely in this treatise the image of the 'wall' (of paradise) should appear, in order to express the shattering of all direct concepts of God in the *coincidentia oppositorum*, *behind* which the beholding God unattainably hides himself.[113] In consequence both the classical concepts appear again, that there can 'be nothing different or opposed to' God,[114] and that otherness remains without positive foundation and therefore without being.[115]

In *De Possest* the spiritual being of God takes on more relief. The ruling intention here is that no worldly being is its own capacity to be ('and this implies the knowledge of our

[108] VD 6, 101r.
[109] VD 13, 105r.
[110] Gal 4.9; 1 Cor 8.3; 2 Cor 5.11; Phil 3.12.
[111] VD 10, 103v.
[112] VD 15, 107r.
[113] VD cc. 9, 10, 12, 13, 17, 20 (also Jesus inside the wall).
[114] VD 13, 105v.
[115] VD 14, 106r.

creation'),[116] but that there must be a place where (beyond itself) its being and its capacity to be coincide: this place is God.[117] Here without any doubt there lies for Nicolas that experience of being which for Thomas is manifested as a 'real distinction' between being and essence,[118] only that now the image of God through the power of being which is identical with being as act (*cum esse sit actus*)[119] becomes simply obvious (as the power-centre of each *actio*), through that omnipotence by means of which alone does something become thinkable as nothing and as possibility and (based on that) as otherness.[120] But the thought is only rounded out in the final treatise, *De Apice theoriae*, because only here do the created essences appear not to be derivable by any process of diminution on the part of the Not-other, but are posited only by a positive 'intention'.[121] If in the *Not-other* it is asked, 'why the sun is sun, the moon moon, the earth earth and why anything is what it is', and thereupon the answer follows: 'if I knew that, then I would not be a creature and part of the universe, for my understanding would be the creative fashioner of all and therefore the creator of itself',[122] then the reason for the formation of essences is already imputed to the creator spirit. One may not undervalue the effort of this step for a thinker in the Plotinian tradition for whom it is a matter of saving the classical form of metaphysics and the *analogia*

---

[116] P 179r.   [117] P 175r.

[118] *Omnia autem quae post ipsum (Deum) sunt cum distinctione potentiae et actus. Ita quod solus Deus id sit quod esse potest*: P 175r. *Cf.* shortly before: God as *actualitas absoluta*.

[119] P. 180r. Cusa's critic, Gustav Siewerth (*Das Schicksal der Metaphysik von Thomas zu Heidegger*, 1959, 98–114) has paid too little attention to this transition when he says: 'In his thought there is no creation' (108). Of course, the mainlines of Nicolas' thought lie in the realm of 'essentialism'; a text like B 31–32 can convince one of that.

[120] P 182r. *Cf.* 177v: 'therefore because the not-being (of everything or of any particular thing) could exist through the Almighty, it is also thoroughly real, because in the Almighty unconditioned capacity is real.'

[121] As elsewhere already in *De Beryllo* (c. 23) it is said: 'So we see the whole creation as the intention (*intentio*) of the almighty will'; Baur 29. Similarly c. 9 and 31–32, and *De Ludo Globi* I, 154r–v; *mundus . . . perfectus est valde quia secundum Dei optimi liberrimam factus est voluntatem.*

[122] NA 9, Baur 19.

entis without loss in a biblical, Christian context. This effort forces us back to the thought-form of Aquinas: creation on the one hand as *emanatio* of God's fullness of being— *indiminute*, as Cusa says[123]—on the other, as *receptio* not by a nothing (something impossible), but by that which in the creature *corresponds* to the freely-apportioning *possest* of a possibility of receiving;[124] the first is the classical, the second is the Christian aspect of the analogy of being. *Possest* bespeaks much more than absolute simplicity of Being, even as the (easily misunderstood as 'neutral') not-otherness; it speaks of Being as an infinite *over*-mastering of itself and therein as the disclosure of the whole, infinite realm of Being in which God can be himself even outside himself. Without this dimension infinite Being would be restricted to itself. This intuition overwhelms the aging cardinal with renewed freshness: 'nothing is earlier, nothing stronger, nother surer, nothing more essential, nothing more glorious (*gloriosius*) than this capacity',[125] it is the ground of every ground, *'omnium quidditas et hypostasis*, by whose power necessarily what is and what is not is embraced', 'nothing is more luminous, nothing clearer, nothing more beautiful'.[126] As the light is revealed in the visible, so is capacity (*possest*) in Being. Cusa here draws on to a Christian plane the vision of Plato and Plotinus, who raised the Good above Being so as to understand this (Being) as a manifestation (of the Good); he draws in too Eckhart's vision that God is Being because he is Spirit and Freedom; it is the metaphysical dimension of glory which appears to him as *posse ipsum*: the beholding spirit perceives it without exercising power over it: *excellit posse comprehendere*. Again it is the formula of Anselm,[127] which expresses the final implications of analogy and is consciously experienced here as a new, extreme formula: 'this ability of mind to see beyond any comprehensible power and mightiness is the ultimate

---

[123] DP 2, 194r.
[124] Certainly there is found in Cusa no explicit doctrine of a real distinction, yet his thought ever more strongly converges towards this.
[125] ATh 219v.
[126] 219v.
[127] *Cf.* vol. II, 233, 236.

capacity of mind, in which Capacity itself (i.e., God) reveals itself in an ultimate measure, and, on this side of Capacity-itself, is unlimited. For this capacity for sight is so much ordered towards Capacity-itself, that the mind can foresee whither it is striving, and as the wanderer runs towards the goal of his wandering, . . . so [can the mind] towards Capacity-itself which it sees from afar, and is able to comprehend the incomprehensible in the best possible way. For it is Capacity-itself, when it is manifested in the glory of its majesty, that is alone powerful to still the longing of the mind.'[128]

While Nicolas in such a way raises the classical glory of God up to the glory of the almighty and sovereignly free[129] Christian God, and nevertheless causes the creature's intellectual capacity for sight to be transcendently established at the summit of his desire—beyond its capacity to comprehend—for this free glory, he necessarily finds himself in conflict with the positive theology. More consciously and more systematically than the Fathers of the Church he relates this creaturely longing and the free self-disclosure of the personal God to each other. Nicolas thinks within a sovereign and unbroken classical totality of philosophical theology in which the self-radiating light of the Good as it were automatically passes over to become the 'will to open up to each searcher on his quest and to reveal itself'.[130] On the one hand it remains, as far as man is concerned, within the classical dynamics of *eros*, for 'the dynamism (*vis*) of our reason is inexhaustible on this side of deification',[131] and with Nicolas this dynamism never for a moment yields to the 'indifference' which is at the heart of the 'metaphysics of the Saints'. On the other hand the dynamism of longing cannot attain its own inner target 'without the grace of the creator'[132] (just as a tree can flourish only in the warm light of the sun),[133] and

---

[128] ATh 220r.
[129] *Cf.* propositions 5 and 7 at the end of ATh, 221r.
[130] QD 199v.
[131] FD 65r.
[132] DP 1, 193r–v.
[133] *Ibid.* 193v.

for the created reason this grace is necessarily the personal self-disclosure of God, that is Jesus Christ as the word of revelation of the Father.[134] To this personal word there corresponds the attitude of faith which for Nicolas is likewise derived directly from the faith of classical philosophy, and, where God is manifest as free and personal, must necessarily so proceed.[135] The Plotinian ἐπιστροφή becomes just as immediately 'humility' in the reception of Christian doctrine,[136] just as the ontological doctrine of God over all things and in all things was already interpreted as God's majesty and humility.[137] So the revelation of creation passes over without a break into the biblical revelation: 'Plato had . . . with his mind conceived of the origin of things on the way of revelation in a way of which the apostle says to the Romans: God has revealed himself to them.'[138] Other than in this light the book of the world could hardly be deciphered or read, something that is however man's task, 'just as little as anyone could recognise a picture of Socrates, . . . if he did not know Socrates'.[139]

If in this way the relative separation between philosophy and theology characteristic of Thomism is again annulled for the sake of a total metaphysic (fashioned after the classical model), then if the believing Christian wants to draw dogmatics immediately into it, there looms up the immediate danger of a mystical rationalism. Under the Anselmian slogan of *intelligere*, indeed of *videre fidem*,[140] Christology especially must take up once again its Origenist form: Christ as the presence of absolute reason in the created reason, enkindling faith through the latter and leading to the understanding of the mystery of God, as the Sun of spirits. 'The word of God has it [the human reason] in itself, so that it does not need to search outside itself, for the mind will find the Word within

[134] VD 21, 110v.
[135] *Cf.* perhaps P 178v.
[136] P 178r.
[137] VD 13, 106r: 'How exalted you are, Lord over all, and equally how humble, because you are in all things!'
[138] NA 20, Baur 48.
[139] G 73r.
[140] VD 19, 109r.

itself and can approach it through faith';[141] a faith which Nicolas describes equally as choosing love (dilectio) and as prayer: but just as easily here will the transition be made to the transcendental reason of Hegel. God is already 'the Spirit of spirits',[142] rather like Leibniz's central monad, indeed he is already that one who is interpreted in the world by means of man: 'You, Lord, who work everything for your own sake alone, have created this whole world with a view to the rational, spiritual nature, as if you were like a painter, who mixes the different colours and blends them one with another in order finally to be able to paint himself.'[143]

d. Conjecture or Absolute Knowledge?

At one point Nicolas breaks through the Platonic schema: the human spirit does not appear as graded in an order hierarchically ascending towards the Absolute, it stands in a new proportion to the Absolute: as God (as originally simple unity) is related to the unfolded, real world, so the spirit (as reflected simply unity) is related to an unreal world, thought-out and sketched as a copy. The two relationships are related to reality as exact science and conjecture, because God has in himself the things he has created, while the spirit only looks up to them; but on the other hand, the spirit has its own exactness in so far as it develops the world of numbers out of its own unity, indeed beyond that unites complicatively the world of the senses in its world of spirit.

Here lies a momentous ambivalence. The created spirit, in so far as it is spirit, is incontractus; therefore it stands to God not in the relationship of subject and object, but—as De quarendo Deum shows—in that of the participation of a finite subject in the absolute subject that holds sway within it (in the speculatio or intuitio itself).[144] So Nicolas hesitates to class spirit (mens) with the rest of the finite (contracted) explications of the infinite God, rather the spirit is imago complicationis

[141] VD 24, 113r.
[142] VD 25, 113v.
[143] Ibid.
[144] QD 197v–198r.

divinae prima, in so far as both God and the spirit are *complicatio complicationum*; the spirit too has on the basis of its derived likeness to God 'the power to assimilate itself to any possible explication',[145] i.e., to use itself to make an idea of anything without recourse to (limiting) innate ideas, but simply through its openness to everything in virtue of its capacity for judgment.[146] In that, Protagoras was right: man is the measure of all things;[147] the sensible world is there for his sake and to be measured by him; 'man knows from the knowledge of the perceptive powers of his nature that the sensible is there on account of perception; so he measures the things of sense in order to be able to grasp in sensible form the glory (*gloria*) of the divine reason.'[148] So *mens* comes from *mensura*,[149] as 'a living measure which, measuring something else, displays its own ability; for the spirit does everything in order to measure itself, and yet it does not find its measure which it seeks in everything, except where all is one.'[150] 'As an image of eternal spirit it strives in this, like an image in the truth, to hunt out the measure of itself.'[151] And yet it is itself reflected all-exemplarity,[152] in which the truth 'radiates forth', and to this extent it is a 'second God',[153] representative of the divine countenance in the creation,[154] which is not only an explication of God, but of itself. For if man is complicative as spirit, as soul and body he is explicative.[155] This now almost means that man as spirit prescribes its laws for the world—in particular through his power of numbers—and so at least is a co-origin of the world-

[145] IM 4, 83v. K. H. Volkmann-Schluck (*Nicolaus Cusanus, Die Philosophie im Übergang vom Mittelalter zur Neuzeit*, 1957) places the *mens* at the centre of the speculative system, whence the opening up to the Renaissance and to Descartes becomes marked.

[146] *Ibid.*

[147] B 36, 192r.

[148] B 37, 192v.

[149] IM 1, 81v; 9, 88v.

[150] *Ibid.* 89v.

[151] IM 11, 90v.

[152] *imago exemplaris omnium.*

[153] So according to Trismegistus: B 6, 184v.

[154] IM 3, 83v.

[155] B 18, 186v.

harmony.[156] In *De Conjecturis* our spirit unravels its 'puzzle-world' out of itself, in order to look more clearly at itself in this world begotten from itself, so that more deeply stimulated by it it might understand itself more perfectly as an image of the eternal; for the more we deepen (*profundaverimus*) our spirit, the closer we come to attaining the vital centre, God.[157] It is the old way—prescribed particularly emphatically by Gregory of Nyssa[158]—of an ever-deepening, metaphysical self-knowledge in order to behold more clearly the archetype in the image which is actualised on all sides. Cusa only adds that this actualisation of the spirit through its explication of the world—whether it is prescriptive, or receptive—has to happen. If the human image (so the letter to Albergati puts it) 'recognises himself as a living image of his creator, then he beholds his creator while he looks at himself, for he is transported from the image to the original.'[159] But one wonders if such a method of coming to know God can be carried through practically in any other way than through human sketches of the world and therefore man's quests for self-knowledge ever again shattering and thus simply revealing their quality as unauthoritative and conjectural and so proving the proposition: *conjecturalis mundi humana mens forma existit, ut realis divina?*[160] What does it really mean to be the form of a conjectural world, to be a puzzle-world? To understand oneself as a bare 'image',[161] and 'to use a riddle to explain'?[162] It can indeed only mean that man in his self-questioning becomes himself the ultimate puzzle of all world-puzzles, that inexplicable archetypal cypher, which is the point from which all the rest of the world-cyphers derive. This thought is adumbrated but not carried through existentially in Cusa's expositions.

[156] *Cf.*, e.g., IM 7: *mens est ita numerus divinus . . . quod est unitas simplex ex sua vi numerum suum exercens*; 86v.

[157] C 1.2, 41v–42r.

[158] *Présence et Pensée* (1942): La Philosophie de l'image, 81–100.

[159] *Cusanus-Texte* IV/3, p. 28. *Cf. Compendium* 8, 172r.

[160] C 1.3, 41v. [The human mind is the form of the conjectural world, as the divine mind is of the real world.]

[161] VD 15, 107r.

[162] B 6, 184v.

Therefore finally the opposite way of thought gets the better of it: the philosophical longing—not simply Platonic as δαιμόνιον between God and the world, but quite really as a θεῖον—takes itself and its inner infinity as the vehicle for the knowlege of God, powerfully supported by the Christian revelation which seems to allow such an advance into the depths of the heart of God. The way in which Eckhart and in his own fashion too Ramon Lull (whom Cusa also had attentively followed) thought,[163] together with the impact of the renewed classical tradition, favoured the attempted construction of a total science fashioned out of philosophy and Christian theology together.[164]

What does the call to divine sonship mean, Nicolas was asked; the treatise de Filiatione Dei works this out in a way inspired by Origen and Eckhart: the sinking of the creature into the trinitarian process of begetting, the ascent of the yearning, conjectural knowledge into the mutual intuition of the Father and the eternal Son, through incorporation into Him, through actualisation of his potential presence (as divinum) in the finite reason.[165] So there takes place in all earnest a promotion through grace into the sphere of the eternal Logos, right to the participation in his omniscience,[166] a promotion from the dependence of the pupil to the maturity of the one who understands himself.[167] Because the beholding spirit promoted to the status of son is present in the Logos (where possibility and reality coincide), it lives the total life, 'as if only all that which is in it lives', indeed it is advanced to the place of the last coincidence, because in God every creature is God himself: 'and God will be for him not an other, not different and not distinct from precisely his spirit . . . Any otherness or any difference lies far behind the true childhood.' And in Plotinus' sense, in which Hegel must

[163] Eusebio Colomer: Nikolaus von Kues und Raimund Llull. Aus Handschriften der Kueser Bibliothek (Quellen und Studien zur Gesch. d. Philos.), ed. by Paul Wilpert, II (1961).

[164] Nihil ergo scitur, nisi omnia sciantur; IM 10, 89v.

[165] FD 65r. On incorporation into Christ, already: DI 3.12, 33v, on adoption within the Trinity: VD 18, 109r.

[166] FD 65v–66r.

[167] FD 65v, 69r, also IM 14, 93v.

recognise himself: 'The whole pure reason brings everything intelligible (νόημα) to intellection (νόησις), for each object of knowledge is in the mind the mind itself.' But then the mind *is* the truth, which has become eternity, because outside the living intellect which is present to itself nothing else can exist. 'Therefore sonship is the annulling (*ablatio*) of all otherness and difference and the resolution (*resolutio*) of all things in the One, something that is at the same time the transfusion (*transfusio*) of the One into everything, and precisely this is deification (*theôsis*).' This 'coincidence of the being of one in which all is, and of the being of all in which one is' is the perfect echo at the end of the Middle Ages of the theology of John Erigena, but unquestioningly foreshadows the coming Idealism; sonship is absolute knowledge, which is effected philosophically through progressive synthesis (as simplification) and theologically through being born together with the Logos. That the *conceptus absolutus*[168] of God is attainable from below, is indeed denied, since analogy and *docta ignorantia* hinder it; but the means of faith, of grace, of the God-man acquire what is sufficient for this. It is already striking how in the third, Christological book of *Learned Ignorance* the *a priori* construction of the Incarnation as the union between the absolutely greatest (God) and that which is greatest in the world (the humanity of Christ) seems to be worked out quite unquestionably where before it was always inculcated that the concept of a greatest-in-the-world was an internal contradiction because something greater would always be thinkable. So then there is suddenly available an exact proportion between God and the world which had seemed to be excluded by the imprecise character not only of finite thinking in images but also by the finite being of images, and indeed available for a knowledge which understands itself neither simply as theology (which never finally passes beyond faith into knowledge) nor simply as philosophy (because it will never seriously attain a rational deduction of the mysteries of the faith). The bitter reproaches that Nicolas heaped against the theological efforts of the

[168] P 179r.

Schools are not quite spared Nicolas himself; and that goes especially for the ever-continuing formal trinitarian speculations which only have meaning if they play around a mystery declared elsewhere, from afar, but which go astray as soon as they in all earnest think themselves capable of leading up to it from below. Christ is, as the absolute knower, ever again the 'way' to knowledge,[169] and to follow him is above all imitation of the teacher,[170] 'whose understanding is both truth as well as copy', this latter in the highest measure beyond all reaching.[171] Correspondingly faith is (in the sense of the early Augustine) wholly a means.[172] Here too belongs the tendency, which becomes stronger towards the end of his life, to pass beyond the Areopagitical negative theology to something positive:[173] for in the event of the speculative process, there comes the moment when thought is changed into true seeing and out of the 'difficulty' of dialectic is shown as something 'easy' (facilis),[174] incontrovertibly evident[175]— if it is once seen. So he can even speak against an exaggerated transcendence; if the finite is the negation, then the infinite is the negation of the negation, and therefore the pure assertion, as Nicolas, with Eckhart, affirms.[176]

[169] Via ad Seipsum qui est veritas: DI 3, 24r.

[170] Excit. 8, S. Crucifixus resurrexit, fol. 145, cf. also the whole, very intellectualist Christology in De Videndo Deo, c. 19–25.

[171] VD 20, 110r–v.

[172] DP 5, 196v; VD 24, 113r; similarly in the abruptly beginning theological intermezzo in De Possest, 178rv (where faith becomes 'seeing God', indeed 'seeing oneself'), and with a pedagogic turn in the letter to Albergati, no. 50f., Cusanus-Texte IV/7, 49f.

[173] Which at the beginning governed everything: DI 1.26; 12r.

[174] Facilis via: DP 1, 193v; breviter atque facile, facili compendio: G 69v, 70r; certe ista facilitas est maxima et stupenda ... quod Deus est ipsa infinita facilitas: IS 2, 78v; o miranda facilitas difficilium!: ibid. 80v; Ipso Posse nihil facilius: ATh 219v; Hanc nunc facilitatem tibi pandere propono: ibid. 220v etc.

[175] So above all the overwhelmingly clear simplicity of the concept of Posse as also that of the Non-aliud.

[176] Texts in the note on p. 171 by P. Wilpert to the German tr. of De Non-aliud (1952). Cf. G 70r: nec te moveat Platonicorum quamvis subtilis consideratio Primum imparticipabiliter superexaltatum. And P 177v, speaking of a humanum conceptum ducentem aenigmatice to a qualiscumque de Deo positiva assertio. Indeed in P 182v it is shown that every negation (e.g. non-being) already presupposes affirmation (Being) and can only cancel the finite mode

Such vision, where it is systematically interpreted and ordered, is theologically an anticipation of the eschatological essential vision of the Father in the Son, in the philosophical context of an intuition of the Absolute which comes to transcend the negative theology. Because this contradicts the whole enterprise of a doctrine of *analogia entis* and an enigmatics, Cusa does not let himself be tied down to it; it can only be maintained that he has not sufficiently considered the danger of the paths he takes and has not assumed responsibility for their misuse. This aprioristically understood Christology (in the last book of *Learned Ignorance*) was certainly meant in an Anselmian way, but it opened the way for Hegel, because the exact proportion between God and the world in the God-man—philosophically completely unmaintainable—finally is made accessible to reason. So then too the manifold philosophical and theological attempts at harmonisation of all partial truths into a complete system remain in an ambiguous light. There are the philosophical concordances, as in the 'wonderful teaching' of the *idiota*, 'which undertakes to reconcile all philosophies one with another',[177] sketched in the characteristic propositions of *De Possest* and the *Hunt for Wisdom*.[178] Already the *Learned Ignorance* has sought to understand the many gods as explications of the one true God and thus secured for the partial religious systems their share in the truth: the mistake would lie rather in the tendency of 'popular religion' to absolutise, from which the wise remain relatively free.[179] *De Filiatione Dei*, in a way corresponding to its gnostic character, underlines the unity of all philosophies to the point that even contradictory utterances about the absolute—God is all, God is nothing, God is, God is not—are reconciled thanks to the

of Being. 'In the way of negation you see indeed *simplici intuitu* that everything that is presupposed, which precedes non-being, is the *entitas* of each being to all eternity.' The *Compendium* too (169r) begins with the *intuitus* of Being above all conceptual knowledge, so as in this light to read every being as 'sign' and 'expression' (*expressio*): 171r.

[177] IM 3, 83r.

[178] P, after the Magdeburg Codex 166 tr. by E. Bohnenstädt (*Vom Können-Sein* 1947), p. 47f.; V 9, 204rv.

[179] DI 1.25, 11v.

coincidentia oppositorum and lead astray the wise not at all.[180] Even atheism—as a necessarily fragmentary utterance—is incorporated into the total system. The philosophical systematic passes over directly into the theological; begun ecclesiastically in Nicolas' great treatise for the Council of Basle (*De concordantia catholica*, 1433), it is continued in the heavenly council under the presidency of the Logos, which is to synthesise all world-religions without any loss to their own authentic features (*De pace fidei*, 1453–4).[181] It suffices to say about that, that the speculative background for both (as least as strongly as for Augustine's *City of God*) is Platonic: the earthly church as (ultimately, 'conjecturally')[182] a reflection of the heavenly Jerusalem must imitate it by concord (*concordantia*) as much as it can: both within and beyond the Church. There is one thing above all to be avoided: schism. But how the heavenly unity is represented within the Church—more in a conciliar or in a papal-monarchical way— is not from the Platonic perspective the main consideration. Jaspers has rightly pointed out that the concept of representation varies: between the universal-philosophical (everything transitory represents the eternal), the juridical-philosophical (the ordered forms of Church and State represent the abiding spirit of the community) and the constitutional (elected or appointed delegates represent the people).[183] Cusa endeavours as a Catholic to think universally and broadly within the Church; he wants to understand the Church, like the incarnate God in Christ, only against the cosmic background; even the ecclesiastically positive must be utterly transparent to the whole truth between God and man. The same thing is attempted on a higher plane by the treatise *On the Peace of Faith* which not only wants in all earnest to

[180] FD 68v: *Nihil itaque reperiet vere theologizans scholaris, quod ipsum perturbet in omne varietate conjecturarum. Nec minus apud ipsum hic dicit, qui ait nihil penitus esse [deum], quam ille qui ait omnia esse quae videntur. Nec verius hic dicit qui ait deum omnia esse, quam ille qui ait ipsum nihil esse aut non esse.*

[181] On the historical context of this treatise see the detailed introduction by Ludw. Mohler to the tr. (Meiner 1943).

[182] *Ecclesia conjecturalis: Epist. I ad Rodericum de Trevino* (in the second part of the second volume), fol. 3v.

[183] Jaspers, l.c. 173f.

exhibit the share of truth each religion has in the whole
Logos, but in the heavenly council of all religions requires
and outlines the indispensably necessary reconciliation
between the absoluteness and the relativity of the Catholic
Church. The individual steps, which need not be convincing,
will not be pursued here, only the undertaking as a whole is
important now: because with the greatest courage it demands
not only practical tolerance—to fight with the sword for the
peace of Christ is pure contradiction and can convince no-
one[184]—but theoretical agreement. It envisages the same point
as the present book: to behold the glory of what is Christian
without any reduction of its absoluteness in the context of
the total glorification of God in his revelation in the world.
Yet Cusa's attempt seems to be essentially hindered in its
working-out by the fact that he projects the world-religions on
to the background of the (Platonic-)philosophical and thus, as
has been shown, sees in Christ above all the Logos, the perfect
teacher of Wisdom who has appeared. Here lies that limit
which will bring the next steps after Cusa (for instance
Thomas More's *Utopia*) very close to liberalism. In the Logos
as Wisdom the 'religious element in mankind' becomes
available for this; thus the decisive glory of the God of Jesus
Christ is emptied out. In order to discover it both embedded
in and lifted from the background of myth, philosophy and
religion, it must be depicted otherwise. That Cusa knew
about this 'other Christianity' is not to be doubted and
emerges clearly from the wealth of his sermon-outlines and
notes.[185] That his will for universality is pure, is equally clear;
but the synthesis betrays—more distinctly than with
Aquinas—that the traditional structure of biblical revelation and
of its glory in the Platonic-Plotinian context with its own
conception of glory could not fully do justice to the biblical
concept of glory. The modern age will unveil the
consequences.

[184] Letter to John of Segovia, *Akademie-Ausgabe* VII (1959), 97.

[185] *Cf.* especially the 19 great sermons from the early period, tr. by
Sikora and Bohnenstädt with an introduction by the latter (*Predigten 1430–
1441*, Kerle 1952); and also the many extracts from the *Excitationes* in
Scharpff, l.c.

5. CLASSICAL MEDIATION

a. Refuge with the Past

It is unnecessary to depict the relationship between metaphysics and glory in the modern period from the Renaissance to the present in detail: it is well enough known, and, in the goal towards which it strives, is manifest to the eyes of all. It is best understood from a bird's eye view which reveals to us why certain prominences, which from beneath seem to be great mountains, could not disturb the flow of an inexorably advancing stream. Even such sublime heights as Ficino or Leibniz or Spinoza, or Kant or Goethe or Hegel, must not now be wondered at in isolation, but must be seen as waves in the stream. It is one of the most glorious periods of human history—add to the thinkers and the poets, Italian and German music, French painting, English and Spanish theatre—but stirred up by the inner contradiction of entrusting itself to two mutually cancelling spiritual fields of force, beside the Christian, which have been already characterised at the beginning of the last chapter[1] and the opposition between which is already palpable in the work of Cusa. On the one hand, there is a cry for help to classical piety to be rooted afresh in the primordial tradition, when in the late Middle Ages the Assize Courts of Being are beginning to quake; and, on the other, a bold storming ahead on the ways of thought which Christianity had certainly opened up, but only to those who would tread them in faith and in love: something that amounts to a reduction of revelation through logic to a speculative doctrine of God. The same thinkers will be ground down between these two opposing tendencies—one could mention the tragedy of Spinoza, or of Schelling, or of Scheler—and in the end, as a matter of history, classical antiquity, fighting on foreign soil, has to lose the battle; but

[1] B 4a.

also speculation about God, decking itself out with foreign, that is Christian, feathers achieves its inner end, to reveal itself as that which it was in secret from the beginning: a Titanic, Promethean human construct.[2] Does that mean then that Western history from the Renaissance to the present has been a false trail that can be disposed of and forgotten with impunity or even with profit? By no means. But the history, the lesson of which is so comprehensible that the feeblest schoolboy must be able to follow it, has in this period led up to an unavoidable decision. As far as classical antiquity is concerned, Christianity, as its fulfilment, possesses the key to it, and anyone who tries to bypass Christianity and reach back behind it, necessarily misses its mysteriously radiating glory. Michangelo and Hölderlin understood that. And in what concerns the knowledge of the heart of God's mysteries: here too Christianity offers the only approach. Whoever violently breaks through the doors, finds the treasuries bare: the experience of Hegel and Feuerbach proves that. The development speaks neither against the re-rooting in the primordial tradition nor against a bold progress into the future of thought. The seventeenth century falsely located the fundamental decision in this Either-Or and unloosed an embittered 100-year war, 'la querelle des anciens et des modernes'. What for thought can be 'developed' (and therefore must be), avoids error only when it thinks within the horizon of the primordial tradition, where archetypally the depth of Being as a whole has been opened out. There Heidegger is right. But for the perception of the world it holds good that no Titanic over-powering of the forms of nature makes up for, and still less surpasses, the Goethean vision of things; this most ancient, Greek view of the world and mankind must remain a guide to all scientific and sociological-cybernetic advance; and even the ideologies of evolution (often in transcendentalist clothing), which seek finally to do away with the idea of a primordial tradition, could not disturb the vision of the 'primordial phenomena' in

[2] On this unmasking, *cf.* my account of German Idealism under the *Leitmotiv* of Prometheus (*Apokalypse des deutschen Seele*, vol. I (1939), newly reprinted under the title *Prometheus*, 1947).

the Goethean sense. Did not the same Goethe, who perceived the uniqueness of forms, also know how to see the metamorphoses of plants and animals? Did not Aristotle, who here stands behind him, understand how to combine the finality of μορφή with the unforeseeable generation and decay of forms in matter, so that the idea of an evolution of forms, could it only have been scientifically proved, would not have shocked him at all? It becomes apparent from this that the 'battle between the ancients and the moderns' is a mock-battle, which obscures the real intellectual and historical points of engagement. The decision falls uniquely—and the history of the modern period has no clearer result—for or against the Glory of Being, and history has fashioned the Either—Or so simply that it has become a decision between Christianity and nihilism. The 'gods', the 'divine', hold sway still only where God's personal love in the Son of God is recognised and acknowledged, and the storming-ahead of metaphysical speculation is bridled only where thought—in the same epiphany—confronts the not-to-be-mastered majestic freedom of the God of love. That this simple result has always been obscured, both in the past and the present and certainly will be, too, in the future, by thousands of hypotheses, which are just so many attempts at evasion, needs no longer to be wondered at after this sketch of Christian history which proved itself to be just as full of such attempts. Over against all these stands the fact of the present's enormous loss of glory, which, itself played about by the most contrary hypotheses, of itself forms a quiet utterance not to be overheard, if there is anyone, like a Max Picard, with an ear for it.

The appeal of the humanist movement to classical antiquity for a renewed, more inward presence than had existed in the course of the Middle Ages was an event which perhaps first, on reflection, points to the depths of anxious need to which the Christian consciousness had fallen prey. The movement of these 'humanist' laymen, who, concerned for the *studia humanitatis*, for grammar, rhetoric, poetry, ethics, pursued a predominantly literary programme, stood neither in the service of ecclesiastical (clerical) theology nor in conflict with it (except where it had degenerated into a decadent scholasticism); it was, and understood itself to be, 'religious' precisely where, in the service of truth, the primordial sources of Western culture were, through the power of philology in its pure form and in the whole fulness which it had received, to be laid open as the living ground of all that was to come later. The Greek classics, and the no less studied Greek Church Fathers, both came, recovered in their original form, from Byzantium to Italy at the same period. How such access to the 'most ancient documents of the human race' was understood ideologically is indicated by the attempt of Gemistos Plethon (c.1355–1450) to follow Proclus' example in interpreting the Greek gods allegorically and to set beside Plato, as more ancient sources, Orpheus and Pythagoras, Hermes Trismegistus and Zoroaster (the 'Chaldean Oracles'), all witnesses to a universal-theistic revelation, the mainstream of which flowed into the Bible.

Long before, soon after Dante, Albertinus Mussato had in Latin epistles celebrated the value of mythic poetry, which in enigmatic form expressed the same thing as the Holy scriptures openly said: poetry is a second theology or an *ars divina*, and it should be linked to the tradition reaching from Lactantius and Augustine through Isidore to Thomas Aquinas: the most ancient 'theologians'—Orpheus, Musaeus, Linus— had been poets.[3] Among the many reasons Mussato brings forward for his comparison, he emphasises this original historical unity, but also that the poet is a *vates*, that poetry contains in itself an eternal fame and that Holy scripture itself often makes use of poetic forms.[4] It throws up again the problem of the veiling of the truth in images that had been a concern of scholasticism, and was now to be discussed in detail by Petrarch.[5] Against the scholastic ranking of poetry as the

[3] E. R. Curtius, 'Theologische Poetik im italienischen Trecento' in ZRPH 60 (1940), 1–15; *Europäische Literatur und lateinisches Mittlealter* (1948[2]), 220–226 (Eng. tr. (1953), 215–221). Karl Vossler, *Poetische Theorien der italienischen Frührenaissance* (Literarhistor. Forschungen, Heft 12, Berlin, 1900).

[4] Mussato, *Opera* (Venice, 1636).

[5] *Invective contra medicum*, ed. P. G. Ricci (Ed. Storia e Letteratura, Rome, 1950).

'lowest science',[6] Petrarch raises it above the liberal arts
(among which it is not mentioned); this sets it by itself in
relationship with theology: 'I would almost say that theology
is God's poetry.'[7] Salutati drops the hesitation in this utterance
and openly explains: *nullum . . . dicendi genus majus habet cum
divinis eloquiis et ipsa Divinitate commercium quam eloquium
poetarum.*[8] *Maxime cum certum* [*sit*], *ipsam divinam
Scripturam nihil aliud esse quam poeticam.*[9] Boccaccio has
given in books 14 and 15 of his *de Genealogiis Deorum
Gentilium* a justification for his wearisome compilation that
comes to the same thing: the poetic myths of the ancients are
true theology—*il nostro Dante* can interpret the ways of
theological utterance in images, *la onde è da chiamare Theologo
sacro.*[10] Earlier he had compared the 'fables' of the poet with
that which 'our theologians have called *figura*'[11] and in the
Life of Dante the formula of Salutati is already used: 'that
theology is nothing more than a divine poetry. What is it if
not poetry, when it is said in Holy Scripture that Christ is
now a lion, now a lamb . . .? How else can the words of the
Redeemer in the Gospel be heard than as a speech with a
hidden meaning, which manner of speech we are accustomed
to call allegory? So then it is clearly shown that poetry is not
only theology, but also that theology is poetry.'[12] If the
prophets speak in images and Jesus in parables, then for
Boccaccio these forms of utterance fall univocally under the
general concept of *favola*, which then lets itself shade off into

[6] Curtius, *Europ. Lit.*, l.c., 230, 473–476 (Eng. tr., 226f., 478–482).

[7] *Ep.fam.* X. 4.

[8] *Epistolario*, ed. Novati (1891–1905), III (XII.20), 540–542. [No way of
speaking has more to do with divine utterances and the divinity itself than
the speech of poets.]

[9] *Ibid.*, IV.I.233. [Since it is most certain that the divine Scripture itself is
nothing else than poetical.]

[10] Ital. edition (Venice, 1588), 258. [Wherefore he is to be called a sacred
Theologian.]

[11] Leben Dantes (deutsch von Otto Frh. v. Taub, 1909), 49. Eng. tr. by
P. H. Wickseed, *The Early Lives of Dante* (London, 1907), pp. 1–11. *Cf.*
Rolf Bachem, 'Dichtung als verborgene Theologie, ein
dichtungstheoretischer Topos vom Barock bis zur Goethezeit und seine
Vorbilder' in *Abh. zur Phil., Psychol. und Päd.* 5 (Bouvier, Bonn, 1956).

[12] 14th Book, 236. (Eng. tr. I. 72).

different forms. The picture develops when the typical existence of the poets comes to be described as one of poverty and solitude—with examples from Homer and Euripides, Ennius, Plautus and Virgil up to Dante and Petrarch; unnoticed, the poet takes over the place of the *poverello* and becomes—one needs only to leaf through Walter Musch's *Tragische Literaturgeschichte*—the modern type of the saint.

Boccaccio in the end saves himself from becoming in the least injurious to Christianity with his allegories of the gods. But what he and the others mentioned here were striving for is a back-projection of the isolated biblical revelation on to a primarily general, historical revealedness of God: in other words, on to a total poetic-theological symbolism, which, eighty years later when learned humanism has achieved its philosophical amplification and deepening in Cusa, Ficino, Pico and Leone, broadens to form a general cosmic horizon.

MARSILIO FICINO's lofty and long-influential philosophical vision is disarming in that it is intended as both sincerely Christian and sincerely 'Platonic' (or rather Plotinian). Both the treatise *de Christiana religione* and the commentary on the Epistle to the Romans[13] bear witness to an attachment, taken for granted, to the Church's faith. Yet when he asserts that 'his intention in the re-awakening of the ancients has been above all to serve divine providence',[14] much more is meant by that than an apologetic or paedagogical service,[15] rather the projection of what is Christian into a theology of humanity (brought to its highest development by Plato). Both are equally true: Ficino reads Plato with Christian eyes, and the Bible with Platonic eyes. That both are coextensive without remainder, that all differences are dissolved in a final presupposed identity beyond all analogies, is for him not at all problematic.[16]

---

[13] *Opera omnia* (Basle, 1576; repr. 1959), 1–77, 427–472.

[14] I 871, 3.

[15] As Raymond Marcel (*Marsile Ficin* (1958), 583–602) too onesidedly emphasises.

[16] P. O. Kristeller (*The Philosophy of Marsilio Ficino* (Columbia University Press, 1943, p. 36) carefully notes that Ficino deals with Being

The already frequently-mentioned identification of Eros and Agape (with which belongs Platonic friendship) has here reached perfection, but certainly not in such a way (as from Nygren's[17] perspective one would like to conclude) that Eros has overpowered and annihilated Agape. Already with Plato and Plotinus it has been shown that in its highest manifestation eros is thought of as self-less, because it loves the Good for the sake of the Good, so that it can become a reflection of the highest Good, radiating like the sun freely and gratuitously. This vision overwhelms the Christian Ficino and makes him interpret all being as beauty, for he sees in it the gracious self-radiation of the Good, deepened in a Christian sense as eternal love.

God as the centre of all things is the Good; the four circles which radiate from this centre—*mens* (= *nous*), *anima*, *natura*, *materia*—are the beautiful.[18] In place of *pulchrum* there can also stand *splendor*, *claritas*, *fulgor*. In the biblical-personal enhancement of the Platonic, the world-being can therefore directly be seen as *splendor divini vultus*, which reflected and refracted in the mechanism of the world appears as *gratia*: attractiveness and grace in one.[19] It is to be noticed that in this view *glory and beauty are simply identical*: as the beautiful is the radiant manifestation of the Good, so is the world the manifestation and streaming-forth of God. The intellectual creature has been created to perceive the wonder and grace of the eternal Good in the wonder of the Beautiful. Thus the authentic intellectual act is contemplation and love in one. 'The avidity (*aviditatem*), which unceasingly cleaves to the countenance of God, that I call love. O that such would fall to our lot!' The world in its beauty is therefore God's bait, hooked (so Plato's *Symposium*) to each individual beautiful form, which at the same time fascinates and disappoints us, because it promises more than it can keep and points to more in practice as the highest genus of all universals, and that he never mentions the analogy of being, although on the other hand he never excludes it either in his cautious formulation—as later a Giordano Bruno and Spinoza will do.

[17] *Agape and Eros* (tr. by P. S. Watson, rev. ed. 1953).
[18] *De Amore* (= commentary on Plato's *Symposium*), or. 2, c. 3; 1324.
[19] *Ibid.*, or. 5, c. 4; 1336.

than it has within itself: 'Men strive after God's form and their striving is implanted in them by God. Our longing for God too is enkindled by him when the bodily instinct is enticed by anything that encounters the senses. And so much the more, so much the most powerfully, can the highest God attract than the slightest good things. For in fact . . .: the luminous brightness of the highest Good flashes within each individual being, and where it shines with greater affinity, there above all it attracts the beholder to itself . . . and compels him to honour this radiating being as a higher nature (*numen*), indeed to strive towards nothing else than to lay aside its old nature and to be changed itself into the radiance. In this it becomes evident that he cannot be satisfied with the sight or touch of the Beloved, but often calls out: this person has something in himself that sets me on fire and I myself no longer understand what I am striving after. So, by the radiance that breaks forth from a beautiful human being, . . . the soul is drawn up by God, as with a bait, to become itself God. But God would be, as it were, a wicked tyrant, if he kindled in us a longing that remained eternally unquenchable.'[20] The longings of Plato and Plotinus are here provided, as it were, with a Christian stimulus: 'The lovers do not know what they want to thirst for, for they do not think of God himself who yet has mixed in with each creature a secret taste of himself like a sweet fragrance.'[21] Love is—as Franciscan mysticism had radicalised it—the drawing of the heart to God beyond all knowing and understanding, and this drawing in man (which at the same time constitutes his spiritual being) is his being ontically an answer to the creator's outpouring of love. Creation is first of all the discharging of chaos or matter from God, which secondly however is immediately called back by him to obtain God's form in return (ἐπιστροφή) and homecoming to the Light.[22] So the ancient poet-theologians said that eros came into being immediately after chaos and in its answering primordial

[20] *Theologia Platonica*, 1.13, C. 1; 306.
[21] *De amore*, or. 2, c. 6; 1326.
[22] *Ibid.*, or. 1, c. 2; 1321.

movement has become cosmos.[23] Thus there rules the circular movement: 'Insofar as it rises in God and attracts to him, it is called beauty; insofar as it proceeds into the world and brings enchantment to it, love; insofar as, flowing back to the author, it unites his work with him, holy delight (*voluptas*).'[24] For Ficino there can be no other love than religious love, even love between human beings, whether sexual or between friends, if it is love at all and not egoistic impulse, has its realisation uniquely in God. Doubtless Dante and the poets of the *dolce stil nuovo* have powerfully prepared the way here, as has Petrarch; yet what Ficino for the first time calls 'Socratic' or 'Platonic' love has been a fresh discovery for him by means of the *Symposium* and the *Phaedrus*. But Augustine's longing for God too and what Ficino made of *caritas* in the epistle to the Romans, makes its influence felt.

If then the eros of the creature is always first of all an answer to the divine beckoning back of grace, so that, on account of the eternal prevenience of grace it can be called 'divine' or even *'daemonic'*,[25] then this eros can, without further ado, be explained as agape, if only it is considered that the beckoning of grace to the chaotic sinner is accomplished in the incarnate love of Jesus Christ. The *caritas diffusa per Spiritum Sanctum in cordibus nostris* proceeds from the *bonum diffusivum sui*, which graciously provokes (*provocat*) us to an answering love.[26] God has died for us in Christ, but all true love essentially means such a death to oneself so as to live only in the beloved, it is 'bitter' as this 'voluntary death', and anyone is a murderer who will not love a lover in return and thus not give him the opportunity to rise again in the beloved.[27] Ficino has no difficulty, therefore, in elucidating God's act of love in Christ by Plotinus and Denys.

[23] *Ibid.* Cf. Hesiod, Vol. IV of this work, p. 80 (Eng. tr.), and as a final form of this *philosophoumenon* its depicition by Soloviev, (Vol. III of this work, pp. 279ff.). It is the concept of creation in Teilhard de Chardin also.

[24] *Ibid.*, or. 2, c. 2; 1324.

[25] or. 6, c. 2; 1341–2: *quoniam a Deo descendit, deus, quoniam a daemonibus* [i.e., from the angels and the spirits of the cosmic spheres] *confirmatur, daemon est appellandus* (1343).

[26] *In Pauli Ep. Comm.* 471.

[27] *De Amore*, or. 2, c. 8; 1327.

Is he not here silently passing over whatever does not come into his identity system of *eros* and *caritas*? All true love is mediated by beauty, all real love is mutual gift of self, indeed 'return',[28] something that only holds when both lovers, at least implicitly, love God and each other in God and for God's sake. But how is Christ's love for the sinner in his ugliness and unlovingness to be brought under the rubric of this general mystical death in love? At least it belongs on the side of God who loves a world which is not yet; and as a human gesture it is that which expresses God's love as comparable with none other. Pico della Mirandola sensed something of this and sharply attacked to his teacher and friend: *quanti errori . . . commetta el nostro Marsilio confundendo in tutto* (that is, God's love for the world and the world's love for Him, then love as *desiderio di bellezza* and the love of friends, which is something else)[29]—but then again went on himself to define love as longing for beauty and leave Christian love quite on one side.

Ficino's teaching had given the courtly, troubadour cult of the late Middle Ages its theological and philosophical justification even more than Dante had. Ficino creates the literary form of the *epistola amatoria* (according to which love is understood in its Platonic sense and as the pinnacle of a cultivated style of life), he initiated the countless *trattati d'amore*[30] of the fifteenth and sixteenth centuries. Among these the tightly-packed synthesis of LEONE EBREO in his *Dialoghi d'Amore*[31] had the widest success, even outstripping that of Ficino. This doctor (like Ficino), son of the last great biblical commentator of the Jewish Middle Ages, Yitshaq Abrabanel, like his father a restless wanderer, came with Pico

[28] Ep. to Ermalao Barbaro, 777–778.

[29] *Commento sopra una canzona de amore*, II.1, in *Scritti vari a cura di Eugenio Garin* (Ed.nat. dei Classici del pensiero italiano I, 1942), 488. [How many errors . . . our Marsilio commits by confounding everything.]

[30] L. Tonelli, *L'Amore nella poesia e nel pensiero del Rinascimento* (Florence, 1933). John C. Nelson shows in his *Renaissance Theory of Love* (NY, 1958) that Giordano Bruno too belongs here.

[31] Ed. with an account of the life and work of Leone (etc.) by Carl Gebhart, (curis societatis Spinozanae, 1929).

into touch with with the Platonic Academy and created for the Renaissance that identification of a personal intensity of love characteristic of the Old Testament with a world-view, explained and fully fashioned after the pattern of antiquity, as had once already been accomplished by Philo, and in the Middle Ages by Ibn Gebirol and Maimonides, and would again emerge in the Baroque period with Spinoza, in Idealism with Cohen, and finally in Bergson and the Jewish disciples of George: always in such a way that the intensity, with which beauty was declared to be the ground of being of all things, was nourished, apart from the much more exposed and sober utterances of the ancients, by an unknown or unavowed loan from the glory of the biblical God.

Again, therefore, it is a monism of religious love, for which in the act of *theoria* all is transparent to God: an erotic monism working with an analogy of God and the world, portrayed throughout in accordance with the ancient understanding, which however with Bruno and with Spinoza, who was deeply influenced by Leone, will become a theoretical and systematic monism. The erotic monism unites—as, fundamentally, do Plato in the *Phaedrus* and Ficino— spiritualism (as the dynamic transcendence of each individual form through longing) with symbolism (as a lasting gaze at the beauty of the individual form, in which the infinite beauty shines forth).[32] The spiritual and religious dynamic towards the highest beauty gives the moral measure to the relationship with individual beauty; it is itself one with the world-being, which, as with Ficino, is finally (as 'soul' of the world) *appetitus, desiderium*.[33] World-being is already chaos or matter turned back to the primordial love, which ascending from form to form and relinquishing the lower for the sake of the higher ('thus called by many a prostitute') pursues love of itself through to God.[34]

Now (in Plotinian fashion) God as *bello bellificante* is raised above the cosmos as *bello bellificato*, which stands in relation

---

[32] *Dialogue* III.113a, 129b–130a.
[33] Kristeller, *Ficino*, l.c., ch. 10 (*appetitus naturalis*), 171–199.
[34] *Dialogue* II. 10b–11a.

to him as a son to a father;[35] thus God can be designated as 'highest artist',[36] indeed as 'master builder'[37] of a perfect work; for Leone is not only an heir to the Old Testament, he is also the contemporary of Bramante and Leonardo. But then the relationship of God to the world is, as with Eriugena, Cusa and Ficino, one of centre to the periphery, of implication to explication, of the Good manifesting itself as the Beautiful, a relationship that for Plotinus possesses the highest exaltation (of the One over the many); the beauty is therefore understood, in opposition to the Renaissance artists' 'vulgar' aesthetics of proportion (especially, Leone Battista Alberti), in the Plotinian sense of the 'form' of the 'idea that shines through', which awakens the *eros* for the infinite.[38] As with Ficino, who in imitation of the classical and medieval metaphysics of light composed several treatises on light and the sun, light takes on with Leone a more than merely metaphorical meaning: it is the first manifestation—as simple beauty—of the primordial spiritual light, the single-formed mother of the differentiated beauty of colour and form:[39] already the way is clear for Goethe's doctrine of colour.

Of Leone's aesthetic metaphysics, Menendez y Pelayo[40] has said that nowhere before Hegel had such an idealist aesthetics been more comprehensively developed. It is important as mediating and inspiring the great subsequent systems. The Plotinian rungs of Being are rungs, objectively of beauty, subjectively of love: world-soul and the intellectual realm of ideas mediate to the glowing centre of Being, which streams forth into the many in order through longing 'to draw all things to itself'. In the homecoming to God the acts of *intellectio*, of *amor* and of *fruitio* (Ficino: *voluptas*) are one: as that *amore intellettuale*,[41] which, dying to individual being, surrenders itself to the One—Spinoza's highest philosophical act. The descent of God becomes ascent to God, and the

[35] III. 124b.
[36] III.100a.
[37] II.72b, III.106b.
[38] III.101a, b; III.37a.
[39] III.102b–104b.
[40] *Historia de las ideas estéticas en España*, III.60 (cit. in Gebhart, l.c., 63).
[41] III.99a; *amore intellettivo*: III.141b.

cosmic *circolo amoroso* is closed:[42] descending, it is beauty enticing attraction; ascending, it is that *eros* which, a Platonic mixture of fullness and need, charm and want, presses towards eternity.[43]

Here gapes that *aporia* which Pico discovered in Marsilio but had not been able to resolve. If creaturely love is essentially longing, how can it be quenched? How can it attain the form of divine love, which cannot be longing? Leone builds a bridge from both banks: God as infinite blessedness cannot grow through the blessedness of the creature, yet the communication of His love to the creature effects a glorification of God, as it were a super-fulfilling of his love, just as each lover is fulfilled in the beloved.[44] 'The upright man,' say the ancients [the Jews], *fa perfetto il splendore de la divinità.*[45] On the other hand, the lack of God in the creature burns the more fiercely, the more spiritual and loving it is; thus one sees that this 'need' cannot finally be something negative, but is a form of participation in the eternal love.[46] Here again we see the hidden biblical *a priori* of this theology. For while Plato and Plotinus view *eros* completely from the world's perspective, and depict the One, as the sun of the Good, only as a self-radiance at rest in itself (even in Aristotle's 'thinking of thinking' there is no trace of eternal love), God now becomes the archetype of *eros*: 'the first lover is God, insofar as he knows and wills; the first beloved is the same God, insofar as he is beautiful. Thus the primordial love is God's love of Himself . . . this inner relatedness fashions His most perfect and most simple unity . . . Just as the one who understands, the thing understood and understanding itself are only divided, so far as they are in possibility, so too the beloved, the lover and love itself are three and divided insofar as they are in possibility, but insofar as they are one and the same, undivided thing, thus far are they in reality.'[47]

[42] III.143b–146b.
[43] References collected in Gebhart, 85.
[44] III.43a, b.
[45] III.35b. [makes perfect the splendour of the divinity.]
[46] III. 68a, b.
[47] III.55b–57a.

Thus *eros* wells out of a love which is more than erotic and is again transcended in this love.

After the liberal Jew, the renegade Dominican: in GIORDANO BRUNO there occurs one of Fate's turning-points; he becomes secretly father of the modern religion of the cosmos, Spinoza and Leibniz are decisively indebted to him, on him Schelling will build further, and when Herder and Goethe say 'Spinoza', they really mean Bruno. His authority is Cusa in almost everything that he thought or sought to think, but if Bruno still takes along with him the form of Platonic-Cusan analogy—as a thin shell—the triumphant content is now plain identity. The theses on God's unsearchability and on negative theology that he expresses in the *Torch of the Thirty Statues* betray the ancient form: God as the infinite sphere with its centre everywhere (Alan of Lille; with a reference to Parmenides), as the identity of essence and existence (Thomas), as more inward than one's self (Augustine), as above, in and beneath all things (Gregory the Great), as 'essence of essence', 'nature of nature', 'centre of all things' (Erigena), as the identity of being, power and action (Cusa), as the unity by which everything is one (Plotinus), as transcendent over every contradiction, every agreement, every difference (Cusa), as the invisible whose sole visible reaction is the world (Ficino).[1] It is only necessary however to ascertain in what context these theses of the *Lampas* stand, to discern that the principal accent lies elsewhere. For the construction of the cosmos begins here—quite as in Hesiod— with the three 'unformable' entities: Chaos, arising from that Orcus or the Abyss, and its child, the Night: 'the begetting Chaos lacks all things, the granddaughter Night however seeks after all things, the son Orcus, in between, is avidity for all things.[2] 'Chaos means emptiness, Orcus passive potentiality, Night matter.'[3] Set over against this lower trinity of darkness

[1] Bruno, *Opera latine conscripta* I–IV, ed. Fiorentino and others (1880–91), *Dialoghi italiani*, ed. Gentile-Aquilecchia, in *Classici della Filosofia* VIII (Sansoni, 1958³). German trans. by L. Kuhlenbeck, Giordano Bruno, *Gesammelte Werke*, 6 vols. (Diederichs, 1904–9). Op. lat. III. 38–43.

[2] *Ibid.*, III. 19.

[3] *Ibid.*, III. 9.

is the higher one as *pater* (*pleroma*), *primus intellectus* (= *nous*) and light, the spirit of the universe. On the balance between the two trinities everything depends. 'For with evil it is thus: it is an evil, if there is not evil, for it contributes to the necessity of the good; if one takes evil away, then there is no longing for the good, the good is no longer that strived for, glorious and highly to be praised.' Therefore the three are necessary: 'the formless Chaos, the unformable Orcus, and Night which ever absorbs all forms and never itself takes shape.'[4] After the manner of Heraclitus, cosmology arises in the unfathomable mystery of the unity of opposites: a form of negative theology that is no longer 'Platonic' at all. The unfathomable ground of all things, which manifests itself in nature, the fathomable ground, corresponds, for Bruno, to nothing else than the intoxicating experience of the bottomless height, depth and glory of Being. Of this there is only one—but a penetrating—proof: for Bruno (in contrast to Cusa, Ficino, Leone) prayer exists no longer, it is radically excluded by what he says. In the place of prayer there steps the elevated feeling of the 'hero' who attains haughtily to union with the universe, even if the *coincidentia oppositorum* tears him apart. *Eros* as a trembling, unquenchable longing for God has turned into the titanic power of the hero in his ardour which flares up from absolute fire itself: *Eroici Furori*. He is himself the contradiction of God, which, insofar as it strives towards God, strains upwards not directly, in Platonic fashion, from the imperfect to the perfect, but 'in circular motion' strives towards the centre which is beyond every form.[5] This circling corresponds to the infinity of the world which is Bruno's great revelation: 'hundreds of thousands of stars and tides! . . . only *one* heaven, one infinite region of the aether, in which these glorious lights keep their determined distances from one another and share in the eternal life. These flaming bodies are the heralds, which celebrate the Sovereign majesty and glory of God! So we recognise the infinite influence of the infinite cause, the true and real reflection of

[4] *Ibid.*, III. 21.
[5] *Eroici Furori* I. 4; 1012.

infinite power, and need no longer seek divinity in the remote
...'[6] Circling in the infinity of the cosmos, the spirit is at the
heart of God's glory; there is no further ascent. That is the
message of the mystery of Diana and Actaeon, twice given
detailed exposition in *Eroici Furori*: by a transposition back of
the Cusan *venatio sapientiae* into the realm of pagan
mythology the human spirit (as a hero who is capable of the
philosophical, enthusiastic ascent) becomes a hunter in the
great forest, who perceives unawares (*exaiphnês*) the naked
goddess bathing and, changed into a stag, himself becomes
the prey, for at the command of the goddess his own dogs
tear his heart to pieces 'with pitiless, mutinous bites'.[7] In both
expositions it is a matter first of all of the transference: the
hunter becomes the prey; he who hunted the divine and
wanted to assimilate it to himself, is hunted by it and is
defeated, in the 'ecstasy brought about by so great a beauty'.[8]
It is true, Diana is the divine glory manifest, *splendor di specie
intelligibili*.[9] 'For no-one can see the sun itself, the universal
Apollo and the absolute light in its highest and most
withdrawn form, but one can see his shadow, his Diana, the
world, the universe, nature, which is in things, the Light
which is reflected in the darkness of matter, that which shines
in the darkness.'[10] But when the dogs have torn the hunter
to pieces, he no longer needs to behold his goddess 'through
lattice and window' (as Bruno says, recalling the Song of
Songs), but can 'without a dividing wall, himself become
wholly eye, see her immediately', her who 'is the true essence
of the being of all things', the 'comprehensible nature, in
which the sun and the radiant glory of the highest nature is
refracted', for 'from the monad of the godhead there proceeds
the monad of the universe'.[11]

Diana is Beatrice transferred back into the myth. Since

[6] *La Cena de le Ceneri* I; 34.
[7] Interpretation of poem 18, *Er. Fur. I. 4; 1005f.; of poem 54, ibid.*, II. 2;
1112f.
[8] 1008.
[9] 1113.
[10] 1123.
[11] 1125.

Dante and the *stil nuovo* the idea of the divine made manifest is feminine (with Plato it was masculine here below and in heaven sexless). But in truth Beatrice was the one who gave form, Dante the one who received it. Bruno-Actaeon however, the hunter torn to pieces, is utterly masculine, and the destruction of the *furioso* is in truth the ecstasy of sexual passion. In the speech for the Helmstadt Academy on the death of Prince Julius von Braunschweig he depicted himself complacently as belonging to the face of 'obscene fauns, gods of the forest and satyrs',[12] and in this consciousness the epilogue of his chief Latin work of natural philosophy *de Immenso et Innumerabilibus* mocks at the Ganymedes who are poured out like a shower in Platonic fashion, while he penetrates his object *durus, villosus, rusticus, asper, callosus, rigidus*, in short with an erect member—*memet ingero rigidum, membrisque viriliter acrem, infrenem, invictum, sementoseque sonantem*—and so the muses will have to love him.[13] Shortly before he had finally abandoned the Platonic ideas of things: God—or as one might call him: *mens, deus, eros, unum, verum, fatum, ratio, ordo*—is internal to all things, *motor ab interius*, and to be found nowhere else than in the cosmos, that is immediately in hearts overcome with enthusiasm.[14] Bruno cannot jeer enough at a Platonic *furor*, and just as much at a biblical *furor*—an inspiration that comes from above and catches one up into rapture. Such prophets are like the donkey who carries the sacrament. The true *furor* bursts forth from the innermost part of the heroic soul, it is not a 'neglecting of one's own self', but rather its elevation and realisation.[15] The dialectic of this *eros* will be dealt with below. But one can already see that attitude emerging here, which will be christened by the young Goethe under the name of Prometheus and of Faust, with an express and contemptuous refusal of prayer ('I to praise you: why?'): a masculine, creative attitude to Being and a conquering advance into the sphere of the 'macrocosmos' or the 'earth-spirit'. Diana will

[12] *Oratio consolatoria*, Op. lat. I/1, 36.
[13] Op. lat. I/2, 318.
[14] *Ibid.*, 313f.
[15] *Er. Fur. I. 3*, 986f.

then be called Helen, and Faust will have to be content to be courteous and polite towards her, indeed he will not be able to do without the Ganymedean, just as throughout Bruno stands in need of the Platonic. The philosophical act again demonstrates its complete ambivalence, which had been manifest in it since Promenades, Heraclitus and Plato: extremely masculine, form-bestowing with Kant and Fichte, the natural philosopher, and with Jean Paul, and finally masculine with Hegel.

Yet another conclusion remains to be drawn, and Bruno has towards the end even more shamelessly drawn it: his advance to the presocratics causes him to forget his Neoplatonic starting-point—Heraclitus and Parmenides step into the limelight (*de la causa*), but finally there emerges an atomism inspired by Democritus, Epicurus and Lucretius (*de minimo, de monade*).[16] It is an atomism that answers to the *Eroici furori*: yet it is, knowingly or not, the immediate expression of an infinite totality: in the 'Ganymedean' aspect the Eleatics are right, but in the 'Promethean' the atomists. It is basically, without the mediation of any analogy, Leibniz's system of monads; but both, Bruno and Leibniz (who knew him), seen as a whole, become steps towards a modern materialism. Why should the dark trinity, Chaos-Orcus-Night (as potency-laden matter), not in fact give birth out of itself as a superstructure to the trinity of light, which cannot exist without it, and thus contain within itself the whole mystery which the old metaphysics and negative theology vainly sought in imaginary heavens?

b. Eros: *The Glory of Melancholy*

The equation of Platonic *eros*—as the upward-attracting transparence of the beloved form to the divine—and biblical *caritas* was no arbitrary act of Ficino's: it only gave (as has been said) an expressly philosophical justification for the poets of the *dolce stilnuovo* and the Petrarcans. From the Middle Ages up to the present century there has held sway an image

[16] Felice Tocco, *Le opere latine di G. B. esposte e confrontate con le italiane* (Florence, 1889).

of *eros* which consciously or unconsciously was exalted, transfigured and divinized by the rays of *agape*. With Dante this Christianization of *eros* found expression for the first time and unsurpassably, yet with the imposition of a journey through hell, and a fully Christian penitence and confession before Beatrice. The step beyond classical antiquity is here taken with the utmost Christian conciousness. With Homer the highest love was the faithfulness of a couple; with Virgil religion and political duty inexorably limit and contain *eros*; with the tragedians exalted love is made manifest in austere sacrifice; Sappho alone can provide a faint anticipation of what in the Christian period would be made of *eros*. Yet even her cosmic feeling of love remained a matter of pious hope and painful supression. There is nothing in Plato to suggest that love for a boy accompanied the ascending *eros* of the *Symposium* through all the stages to the Godhead, still less (as with Beatrice) that it should illuminate the way ahead: the love of 'one beautiful body' is already extinguished on the next step of love of 'all beautiful bodies'. So the Platonism of the Middle Ages, of the Renaissance and of Idealism, where the beloved form as an incarnate Idea can attract upwards to reach God, is coloured and conditioned as a whole by Christianity: christologically, for only in Jesus Christ does a single human form make the Godhead present with complete validity and effectiveness (sacramentally); and in a trinitarian manner, because only the God of Jesus Christ is in himself freely and personally eternal love.

What then if this true infinity of *agape* meets the infinity of longing of *eros*? There was the possibility that *agape*, providing a limit and a measure of *eros*, would subjugate it to itself and take it into service: such would be aspired to and celebrated in the service of courtly love. There was no possibility of forgetting the being of *agape* and letting *eros* hold sway as formerly: *eros* was disturbed, challenged and judged by *agape*. So there was only left the last possibility that *eros* itself should attribute to itself the dimensions of *agape* and raise itself to the absolute in a new way, far surpassing Plato. A beginning had already been made in post-Christian paganism, for with Iamblichus, Porphyry and Proclus *eros* had been elevated as a cosmic principle, which—in opposition to the utterances of Diotima and Socrates—only within an all-embracing divinity *identity* was shaded off in analogical stages (God — gods — daemons — heroes — world-soul — individual soul). This hidden Christian *a priori*, which is naturally strengthened in the modern period and effectively gives form, can alone explain the unselfconsciousness with which the Christian cultures from the late Middle Ages to the nineteenth century deal with the gods of antiquity: not at all using them only as playful decoration and external allegory, yet without equating them with the genuinely confessed mediator, Jesus Christ. They exist and rule with a not-properly-established reality in the space granted them by *eros*, itself robbed of infinity by *agape*. One recalls too with what ease the otherwise so curt Augustine in exchange with Porphyry could equate the ('created') gods with the biblical angels,[1] angels which, after all, for a long time—*cf.* Dante—were held to be movers of the spheres and therefore spirits. Thus one can better grasp the equally easy exchange between gods, spirits and angels, between biblical and mythological figures, in the art of the Renaissance and the Baroque, for example in the figures which animate a landscape by Poussin or Claude Lorrain.

The direct equation of *eros* and *agape* lends to *eros* new colours and new properties. First there falls on it a ray of biblical glory: its *charis* receives traits of Christian grace, its charm (*pietà*) shimmers with the New Testament mercy of God, its transfiguring power becomes the power to forgive guilt and transform the world. But further, its being possessed, its rapture, its ecstasy and foolhardiness, that *mania* which Plato dealt with ironically in the *Ion*, which Socrates handled at least dialectically in the *Phaedrus* (for he delivers one speech against and one for the *mania* or *eros*), is now evaluated positively in the spirit of the New Testament decision of faith to the point of martyrdom and raised to a *furor* which from Petrarch through Ficino to Bruno, to Byron

[1] *De Civ. Dei* IX.23. The historical correctness of such a comparison, as far as the 'hosts' of Yahweh, the seraphs and cherubs, etc., are concerned, is known today. *Cf.* also Paul Vuillard, *De la Conception idéologique et esthétique des dieux à l'époque de la Renaissance* (Paris, 1907).

and beyond, will find its defenders. Finally (and this is the decisive point) the post-Christian *eros*, set up as an absolute, can only be melancholy. Its hidden Christological structure makes it an immediate unity of the finite and the infinite, of the beloved man and God; the dynamic symbolism of Platonic provenance certainly softens this immediacy, but it cannot cancel it. In the 'sacrament' of beauty of this worldly form—woman, boy, landscape or whatever—is the gracious presence of the totality of the divine beauty; the 'moment' has to last and then be exhausted. It is the starting-point for Faust, who only formulates what the whole Christian culture of *eros* from the Middle Ages to the modern period characterizes—in complete contrast to the classical and pre-Christian—as something melancholy. One can say with Kierkegaard that only in the post-Christian period could the 'aesthetic' emerge into such a mortal opposition to the 'ethical-religious', because only now has the latent melancholy and anxiety of Christian existence come to light in its irreducible contradiction. But in saying that, one is not to let out of one's sight the fact that marriage is in Christian terms a sacrament, that, with the whole man, his *eros* too is capable of redemption, that God's covenant with man in Christ (and the Church) bears a form inspired by *eros*, that the Platonic-Plotinian longing for God as the eternal beauty must and can, too, find a Christian justification. The relationship of *eros* and *agape* remains for the west a veritable place of decision, as Titian's picture of earthly and heavenly love recalls—though at the same time in a veiled way, because the two women hardly represent anything other than earthly (symbolic) and heavenly (symbolized) *eros*, or as Wagner's Tannhäuser recalls—though his Tristan at the same time says the opposite.

Tristan. Nothing shows more clearly that the *eros*-problematic only emerges apropos a Christian Platonism, than—in ultimate intensity—GOTTFRIED OF STRASSBURG's Tristan poem, which consciously undertakes to set the *eros* of man and woman absolutely face to face with St Bernard's Christ-mysticism based on the Song of Songs.[2] There had been earlier attempts to translate the 'drama' of the Song of Songs

[2] Julius Schwietering, 'Der Tristan Gottfrieds von Strassburg und die

into the courtly style,[3] but even in this context Gottfried's undertaking stands solitary and unique. *Eros* as the content of life, utterly self-purposed, without a goal outside itself, as both the highest suffering and the highest bliss, above all as utter exclusiveness: for any other human relationship, any other fidelity or honour or one-time virtue is transcended and denied in the closed-off interaction of Tristan and Isolde, and this as the highest, most difficult achievement, declaimed in esoteric doctrine for a small chosen circle of noble hearts—this had hitherto not been heard of. Final passion equated with absolute suffering; *passio* understood consciously in the instinctive and Christian double meaning—with which Claudel will delight in playing—and this suffering as self-glorification of love, as its 'resurrection' and its 'eternal life' in its own enjoyment of its absoluteness: all this, as Schwietering has rightly said and also demonstrated, can be represented only in counterpart to the mysticism of love and passion in the traditional interpretation of the Song of Songs, which attained its highpoint in Bernard's commentary on the Song and amongst his friends, continuators and imitators. As later Petrarch composed his spiritual-secular *Canzoniere* from the sources of Augustine's *Confessions*, as Hölderlin and German Idealism drew from the stores of Swabian mystical pietism, so Gottfried creates—but in what a mighty inversion!—from the treasures of cloistered contemplation. The wild forest and the cell, in which the lovers pass the time, are borrowed from the life of the hermit; the grotto of love with the crystal couch as the sacred centre is the *cubiculum* of the Song of Songs or also the transposition of Christian sacred space with the altar; the mutual nourishment of the lovers in their gazing at each other repeats the mystery and miracle of the Eucharist. Everything profane is sacred, for everything Christian has been taken up without remainder into the mystery of *eros*.

But it was not this work alone, but the 'Roman de la Rose' of Guillaume de Lorris, begun shortly afterwards (c. 1250), to

Bernhardische Mystik' (1943), printed in *Mysik und höfische Dichtung im Hochmittelalter* (Niemeyer, 1960), 1–35.

[3] *Ibid.*, 22–23.

which Jean de Meung contributed a long, unsuitable continuation, that determined the next three centuries. Begun in the purely courtly spirit of transfigured *Frauenminne*, it ended as something polyhistoric, or rather misogynist; in the first part, in many allegorical forms, the God *Amor* rules personally, but in the second, the goddess *Natura*, known from the Chartrians, rules, here too accompanied by a companion spirit. The early Renaissance will quarrel about the importance of this learned world of *eros*: Christiane of Pisa and Gerson reject it, while the first humanists defend it.

The future indeed belonged not to the gentle and learned allegory, but to the metaphysical symbolism of the heritage of Dante: Petrarch's book of songs coins the form of the modern lyric, in the whole tension between religious sublimation (for Laura does not return his love, and after her death floats up to the heavenly ideal) and self-consumption in a lonely fantasy, which the poet recognises as sinful and yet in which he wallows. What in Dante is purified into tall, pure flame, smoulders here dialectically in uncertainty: it is not the beloved who is the ultimate object of desire, but the gloriously melancholy state of the lover. It is the hour of birth of the erotic-poetic *furor*, which one can pursue from Petrarch to Leonardo Bruni, Ficino and Landino and which from there invades France with Ronsard and *la Pléiade*,[4] late to triumph in Bruno. The long, weighty tradition of the love treatise—from Dante's early works through Guido Cavalcanti's interpretations of the *Canzone d'amore* to the Neoplatonists whom we have already discussed, to Bembo's *Asolani*, to Castiglione and up to Tasso's love treatises[5]—does not teach as much as one glance at the struggles of the greatest: of Michelangelo and Shakespeare.

With MICHELANGELO,[6] the symbol-schema, taken over from

[4] Raymond Marcel, 'La fureur poétique et l'humanisme florentin' in *Mélanges Jamati. Editions du Centre nationale de la Recherche Scientifique* (Paris, 1956), 178–193.

[5] John Charles Nelson, *Renaissance Theory of Love. The context of Giordano Bruno's* Eroici Furori (Columbia University Press, 1958), 15–162.

[6] *Die Dichtungen des Michelangelo Buonarotti*, ed. with a critical apparatus by Carl Frey (Berlin, 1897). *Complete Poems and Selected Letters of Michelangelo*, tr. by C. Gilbert, ed. by R. N. Linscott (NY, 1963).

Dante and Petrarch, ..ands as a kind of framework to which he clings, but out of which he also creates.[7] But the content overflows the form—both in his passion for Tommaso Cavalieri and in his humble devotion to Vittoria Colonna— the melancholy has Christian depths and is broken through by a purely Christian confession of guilt, a deeply moving prayer ('So near to death and so far from God!'),[8] the conviction that only grace can help him (*Ne proprie forze o, c'al bisognio sieno/Per cangiar vita, amor, costume o sorte,/Senza le tue divine e chiare scorte,/D'ogni fallace corso guida e freno*).[9] Platonism indeed in form, but in weary and deeply humbled letting-go of the beloved 'symbol' in order to surrender it, and himself with it, to God. In SHAKESPEARE'S sonnets—love for a young man, with whom then the beloved woman (herself married) deceives him—all modish Petrarchism is shattered, till in the last collection (127–154) love is accused of wild, mad devastation (129). It is indissolubly tied up with hatred and with virtue:

> Love is my sin, and thy dear virtue hate,
> Hate of my sin, grounded on sinful loving . . . (142)

until the Platonic thought[10] unwillingly breaks out from one completely worn down, and the 'poor soul', the 'centre of my sinful earth', 'fool'd by these rebel powers' that assail it, is called upon, not to die any more of hunger in its body, 'painting thy outward walls so costly gay', but to live 'upon thy servant's loss' and to let it starve, so that its—the soul's— treasure may increase in heaven:

> So shalt thou feed on Death, that feeds on men.
> And Death once dead, there's no more dying then. (146)

[7] Erwin Panofsky, *The Neoplatonic Movement and Michelangelo. Studies in Iconology* (New York, 1939).

[8] No. XLVIII, p. 36.

[9] No. CLV (Carico d'anni . . .), p. 242. [It is not one's own powers, however necessary these may be, that can change life, love, custom or fate, without your divine and clear assistance, to act as guide and restraint from every erroneous course.]

[10] On this theme *cf.* Vyvyan, *Shakespeare and Platonic Beauty* (London, 1961).

Where Michelangelo weeps, Shakespeare is 'as a fever', 'past cure' and 'frantic-mad', his love longing 'for that which longer nurseth the disease', and the black-eyed and dark-haired beloved shows herself to him finally 'as black as hell, as dark as night' (147). If we had the verse confessions of Botticelli, Tintoretto and so many others, who created the inconceivably beautiful, who knows whether they would not sound the same, and with what melancholy the glories were purchased that should bear witness to the power of bodies to utter the eternal and to shelter the divine! Beside the dangerous heroic feats of *eros* there walks along, making all things gentle, a veiled, forming, playful, allegedly and to a large extent genuinely Christian culture in society, passing without interruption from the time of the Troubadours and Minnesingers to the *cortegiano* of the Renaissance and the *gentilhomme* of Baroque and Rococo. Arthur and his courtly circle still celebrate resurrection in the gigantic plan of Spenser's 'Fairy Queen' after the model of Ariosto and Tasso, and Amadis' triumphal procession we have already looked at—through the window of Don Quixote.

With Ariosto likewise, the Platonic-heroic *furor* of love is rendered harmless as the occasion for a lively social conversation, while the ambitious plan of the sick TORQUATO TASSO finally to create a valid Christian epic—and one knows how much it was admired and imitated a hundred times over[11]—regarded from the height of a Western perspective must seem a tragi-comic misunderstanding. As with Aeneas, a 'commander', and his 'pious arms' (*arme pietose*)[12] are sung, which 'liberate the great grave of Christ'; the 'knight of

[11] 'The influence of 'Liberated Jerusalem' on the [epic] poems published between 1582 and 1698—almost a hundred of them—will be all-powerful and unlimited': Wiese-Pèscopo, *Geschichte der italienischen Literatur* (2nd edn. 1910), 385. The whole of Christian history is gone through from the 'destruction of Jerusalem' under Titus to 'Constantine' and the 'discovery of the Cross' under Heraclius, to the 'converted Bulgaria', the Gothic wars, further episodes of the crusades, to the 'conquest of Granada', the French wars of religion, naturally Italian history, the discovery of America, but *Mondo creato*) and the 'Earthly Paradise' to 'Esther', to Marino's 'Massacre of the infants of Behlehem' and to various Marian epics . . .

[12] *Gerusalemme Liberata*, with notes by Pio Spagnotti and preface by

Jesus'[13] will 'in the Holy Land create a new kingdom', to make peaceful devotion possible for pilgrims to the Holy Sepulchre.[14] The world-historical commission of Aeneas-Augustus has shrunk to this undertaking, which, although intended in a Christian spirit, and also justifiable in a political perspective, is not at all to be recommended in the perspective of the Gospel. And while with Virgil the transcending of the limiting passion of love for the sake of the religious and political mission remains an episode, with Tasso *eros* becomes the all-pervading atmosphere. As a youth Tasso had written in close dependence on Ficino a first compendium of Renaissance love, *Conclusioni amorose* (1570), where he defined 'beauty as the reflection of the Godhead throughout the universe', equated beauty and goodness, described beauty as goodness causing attraction to itself through longing, whence 'the miracles of love are true', although he also conceded that 'each joy of love is accompanied by pain'. In a later treatise on love (1580), Platonism yields the place to a more realistic definition: 'Direi che l'amor fosse desiderio d'abbracciamento', and in yet another (1583) love (under the influence of Aquinas) is graded, that directed to God is called *caritas*, and all virtue is only the order of love.[15] This uncertain wavering between Platonism, realism and Christianity, makes the lyrical, erotic aether, which is condensed in the principal episode of *Gerusalemme*, appear as an ultimately *univocal*, all-sustaining reality despite its division into a good and bad love-enchantment.

Certainly there stands behind the strategic events, answering to the 'apparatus of the gods' in Homer and Virgil, a Christian apparatus too. God the Father looks with pity on his heroes;[16] he calles them and sends them;[17] he communicates to them through angels in dreams;[18] instead

Michele Scherillo (Hoepli, Milan, 1923,[6] cited according to Canto and Stanze. I.1.

[13] VII.56.
[14] I.23.
[15] Nelson, l.c., 150–157.
[16] I.7.
[17] I.9f.
[18] XIV.1f.

of gods he has his heavenly hosts who (as in the Homeric battle of the gods) engage in the decisive fighting;[19] prayer is made to him often and piously, there are miraculous answers to prayer (as in Homer the wounds of the gods are quickly healed, so an angel heals the wounded Tancredi with a healing herb).[20] Still more: a decisive episode, the liberation by Rinaldo of the heroes who have been turned into beasts in Armida's Magic Castle owes its success completely to gracious heavenly guidance. The Devil's kingdom and its machinations are painted with a psychology so much more colourful and humanly sensitive than in Dante, that Milton found here his model and with him all later (and increasingly sympathetic) psychologists of the Devil. Despite that all these are only obligatory accessories (instead of which Camões unhesitatingly retained the ancient gods): the real moving force is the bewitching *eros*, and the *follia d'amore* of even the most magnanimous heroes,[21] since Tancredi loves the pagan Amazon, Clorinda, in the 'drunkenness and fury' of his accursed heart;[22] Erminia loves Tancredi without requital of her love; above all the wicked magic of Armida, who, sent out by the hellish forces of opposition to seduce the heroes, finally carries off Rinaldo, whom she really loves and who really loves her, to her Magic Castle at the Antipodes. These three pairs of lovers carry the action, or rather kindle its lyrical pathos; that Tancredi without knowing it in a decisive duel kills his beloved who, dying, demands of him baptism and later appears to him as a transfigured Platonic spirit to comfort him, when, in a frenzy of love, he tears the bandages from his wounds and almost dies[23]—that is the 'sublime'. That Erminia in love-stricken grief goes to lead the life of a shepherdess on the bank of the Jordan and finally discovers Tancredi whom she had believed dead—that is the 'pathetic'. But that Armida is changed from an evil enchantress into a helpless, abandoned woman who pursues Rinaldo with

[19] XVIII.92.
[20] XI.72f.
[21] I.45
[22] XIX.104
[23] XII.70f., 83–86.

revenge, finally to perish of her own love, to be reconciled with him and humbly to speak to the hero a 'See, I am your maid, let it be according to your will',[24] is at the same time 'heroic' and 'human'. But when Rinaldo—and here the distance from Dante becomes clear—taking heart refuses the lovecharm of Armida, finds her love 'exaggerated' and obliterates his memory of her,[25] and when afterwards he, himself disenchanted, is able to banish the magic forest: this shows how much for Tasso love remains *eros*, its *mania*, the same as in Ariosto's 'Raving Roland'—a cosmic power, whose focal point lies not in God, but in the human heart.

This *eros*, that Sappho was the first to call bitter-sweet, smoulders throughout the 'classical' literature of the modern period: always both redeeming, making one taste sweetness in bitterness, eternity in the moment, and at the same time unredeemed, because it gathers up the contradictions in its own glory, beyond which it knows nothing higher. If with Cusa God was beyond the *coincidentia oppositorum*, and the longing of love, enkindled by this, streams out beyond it, then with GIORDANO BRUNO *eros* itself is the divine *coincidentia oppositorum*, where self-glorification and self-destruction must coincide. 'Who does not see that the principle of decay and of begetting are the same? Is not the final point of dissolution the origin of the one begotten? If we consider aright . . . love is hatred and hatred is finally love. The hatred of what is opposed is the love of what is related, in love for the one lies hatred of the other. In essence and root hatred and love are the same thing, friendship and enmity are all the same. Where then will the doctor seek a better means of healing than in poison? . . . And why? Because the ground of being of the one as of the other is single, as is the ground of their knowing.'[26] This absolute unity of opposites (absolute in the sense of being established on the ground of the world itself) the hero is able to attain in erotic *furor*; the metaphysics of the *Eroici furori* engenders the modern *eros*-poem, which is

[24] XX.136.

[25] XVI 53–55.

[26] Giordano Bruno, *De la Causa, Principio e Uno*, dial. 5, in *Dialoghi Italiani* (ed. Gentile-Aquilecchia, 1958³), 338–339.

based on uniting the 'heroic heart' with the life of the universal cosmos, so that mortality is united with immortality, defeat with victorious triumph, in a manner at once glorious and tragic. This hero has his muses and his Castalian spring within himself, he is 'through the grace of his own heart . . . no less favoured than others by the grace of kings'. But 'out of one and the same feeling of the heart there spring forth the two opposites: hatred and love',[27] as in the heroically heightened *eros* destiny (*sorte*) is nothing else than the *disposizion fatale* and the ordering of life's circumstances to which destiny subjects him.[28] 'For what are you, my destiny, other than my love, and you, jealousy, other than a part of my being? So then let love remain and consume my life . . . what it tears from me mortally, gives me wings, quickens me and lifts me up.'[29] For the beloved form 'and its power over me is indeed nothing else than the power of love, the norm of my love and my own norm.'[30] There is also the hatred of the 'cunning beasts of the priestly power of the Tiber', there are the 'slanders of hissing serpents, the network of frothing boars, for the highest necessity of fate encompassed me,'[31] which will soon still more horribly encompass Bruno in the dungeons of Venice and the Roman Inquisition, and carry him to the stake. But thus it is with the destiny of the *furioso eroico*. If all things consist of opposites, then the hero is marked out by the fact that he does not balance the opposites in himself feebly, but 'suffers under the excess of the opposites', he does not only endure the most extreme tensions, but he strives for them:[32] as he sinks down to hell and wings his way up to heaven, he has to oscillate 'eternally between the opposites', and thus is bound to Ixion's wheel.[33] And this on the basis of his own audacity: as he was Actaeon so now he is Icarus: very likely he senses in his ascent

[27] *De gli Eroici Furori*, dial. I.1:962.

[28] *Ibid.* 965. *Cf.* 1003: *Necessità, fato, natura, consiglio, voluntà nelle cose giustamente . . . ordinate tutti concorrono in uno.*

[29] *Ibid.*, 971.

[30] 972.

[31] *Oratio Consolatoria, Op. lat.* I/1, 43.

[32] *Er. Fur.* I.2; 978

[33] *Ibid.*, 979.

that he will crash down, 'but what life could be compared with such a death?'[34] One of Bruno's devices is the moth, which hurls itself into the flame; and to appreciate this interpretation, one has to keep before one's eyes, the fact that for him the consuming symbol of eternal beauty is always the erotic love for a woman: 'It delights him not less to perish in the flame of the ardour of love, than to be caught up in rapture in the rare vision of the beauty of her face; naturally drawn towards it, in a free decision and through the authority of fate, he submits and dies, joyful, resolved, serene.'[35] And because both, the necessity of fate as well as free virtue, are insolubly one in the heart of the hero, and this unity is participation in the divine all-unity, the great moment already, as with Goethe, conceals eternity, according to the device *amor instat ut instans* and its interpretation: *che l'instante sia tutto il tempo*.[36] The fullness of these emblems is truly baroque; but the baroque quality in them is precisely that in the mystery of an extreme contraction they permit one to grasp the whole, deep meaning of infinite truth: they are Reason's game with its own sacramental form. Everything constantly balances on a drawn-out reciprocity—*mutuo fulcimur*[37]—oscillating in a precarious balance between angel and beast: the level of being of 'daemons or heroes'.[38] But always this *eros* is exposed to the teeth of the hunting dogs which Diana sets on to him, and rightly Bruno draws on Lucretius' interpretation, which depicts the madness of lovers:

> They press closely to themselves the object of their
>   desire and cause pain
> to the body; with their lips they drive their teeth into
>   each other.
> They afflict one another with kisses, because there is
>   no pure pleasure.
> There lurk impulses that goad them on to wounding
>   whatever

[34] *Er. Fur.* I.3; 999.
[35] I.5; 1037–1038.
[36] I.5; 1066–1067. [that the instant be the whole time]
[37] I.5; 1034. [we support one another reciprocally]
[38] I.4; 1023.

They touch, and a madness from which such urges arise.[39]

'Through such an attraction the art-ful mastery of nature is effective, that one is melted away in a delight which at the same time annihilates, and in the midst of every torture senses satisfaction, and remains tortured in the midst of every satisfaction.' There is only a unity of opposites and the continual preponderance of one or the other pole.[40]

Certainly KLEIST did not think of Bruno, when he wrote his *Penthesilea*; rather, it was classical tragedies that had their influence, like the tearing in pieces of Pentheus and Lycurgus, or the demonic love of Phaedra or Medea. Yet his drama is not at all classical, but precisely presupposes the post-Christian, absolutized *eros*, with its *coincidentia* of greatest tenderness and utter cruelty, of divinisation (in the *Rosenfest*) and annihilation; for the queen of the Amazons lets loose her hunting hound on the defenceless Achilles and herself buries her teeth in his flesh. Why does she do this? Because she wanted to surrender herself to him only out of the sublime heroic feeling of having vanquished him, but he has defeated her and has concealed this from her. *Eros* as a haughty feeling of triumph here has achieved its extreme opposite to Christian, serving *agape*. In the whole piece Penthesilea is called time and again 'the raving'; she is smitten 'by the most poisoned dart of *amor*';[41] she speaks the word of the Gospel: 'Ah, my soul is weak, even to death'.[42] When Achilles once more calls her out to battle to let himself be defeated by her, it is too late, she has, in her love, let frenzy get the upper hand:

It is before the countenance of the gods—
I call down the furies!—that he should strike me![43]

'Amazons with packs of hounds in pairs, following them

[39] *De Rerum Natura* IV. 1079-1083.
[40] *Dial.* II.1; 1079–1080.
[41] *Penthesilea*, Scene 7.
[42] Scene 9.
[43] Scene 20.

elephants, firebrands, chariots with blades': these Kleist has
follow her on to the stage. 'Half-Fury, half-grace, she loves
me . . . she will do nothing to me,' says Achilles, and dares to
meet her in battle. Finally she is simply 'the dreadful', 'the
gruesome', the 'most monstrous'. But she says,

> I am so blessed, Sister! More than blessed!
> I feel myself, O Diana, to be utterly ready for
>   death.[44]

And throughout it belongs to this *eros* and again corresponds
exactly to the *Eroici Furori*, that Penthesilea, to kill herself,
needs no outward weapon—she willingly surrenders it—but
descends into her own heart and therein unearths an
annihilating feeling, as cold as steel, with which she stabs
herself.

Kleist's famous piece, rejected by GOETHE, with a half-
hearted, mute voice, far outstripped the latter's planned
Achilleis, in which Achilles, conscious of the approach of
death, falls in love with Polyxena and during the wedding is
killed by Zeus' lightning. Here Goethe wanted to transfer the
ancient myth from the religious to the private, erotic sphere,
just like the immense chain of courtly baroque operas from
the sixteenth to the end of the eighteenth century, which
never manage without such an eroticizing of the classical
material: a witness to the poverty of this whole period of
Christian culture! Goethe finally accepted honestly the
remoteness of his sketch from the Iliad: '. . . further, the object
holds a merely personal and private interest, whereas in
contrast the *Iliad* embraces the interest of nations, of
continents, of the earth and of heaven'.[45] To lend to *eros* this
cosmic dimension was only allotted to Claudel in his *Satin
Slipper*: a unique success. In *Faust* this cosmic form is not
successful, for the real love of Faust for Gretchen is a 'merely
private interest' and not even something ideal, whereas his
love for Helen, with its universal and cultural overtones,
remains unreal and therefore, too, cannot be ideal, but merely
allegorical. To elevate Gretchen finally in Christian fashion

[44] Scene 24.
[45] 'To Schiller, 16 May, 1798.

into a kind of little Beatrice is romantically and humanly touching,[46] but poetically and from a cosmic perspective irrelevant.

To the genuine stock of Penthesilea belong Racine's *Phèdre* and Grillparzer's *Medea* and many of Byron's characters: for here *eros* is presented in its self-glory and autonomy, as with Gottfried, but with a keener Christian edge. It is *eros* that forms the intelligible mean between heaven and hell, God and demon, eternal life and death; Kleist struggles and pleads for the 'understanding' of this self-glorified mean, even when it is to be seen as 'raving, gruesome, most monstrous'.

In his mighty *Nibelungentrilogie* (1862),[47] crafted with iron weightiness and subdued power, HEBBEL can resurrect the German heroic song in no other way than by making it throughout also a double tragedy of *eros*: the *eros* of the Valkyrie Brunhild who will surrender herself only to the one who can master her in the mightiest struggle: that Siegfried does it in darkness in place of Gunther is such a humiliation for her that Siegfried must die at Hagen's hand. And the *eros* of the bride of Siegfried, Kriemhild, who vows her life to vengeance and does not rest till, as queen of the Huns, she had murdered the Nibelungs all together in the burning hall of Etzel. The figures and the sequence of events are of superhuman greatness, Aeschylean: against what metaphysical background will Hebbel set them? Just where they belong; at the turning-point between the old German myth and Christianity. The Valkyrie is baptized only with difficulty, and her Norn-like prophetic power, her feeling for the Father of the gods forces its way violently back into her consciousness from beneath.[48] In Worms it is not much better. For there too the cross is honoured by 'letting it stand beside an oak of Wodan, because no-one can know whether any magic indwells it.'[49] The heroes are in a Christian

[46] And recalls the way in which in Tasso the tragically-killed Clorinda appears to the grief-stricken hero in the dream, transfigured as the 'eternal-feminine', etc.

[47] Historical-critical ed. by R. M. Werner (I. Abt., Dramen IV).

[48] II.Act 1, Scene 2.

[49] II.2.5.

context: at Etzel's house they go to early mass, 'and we are good Christians, as you know,' says Hagen grimly.[50] Hebbel nowhere characterizes so truly and deeply what is Christian than in the chaplain's speech to Kriemhild who thinks only of revenge:

> You seek revenge, yet revenge has
> Been reserved for the Lord, he alone
> Sees what is hidden, he alone repays . . .
> Perhaps you bear it hard, and want to cry to heaven,
> Yet look on Him, who yet bore much more hardly!
> Having come down to us in the form of a servant,
> He took the guilt of the world on himself
> And having experienced thoroughly every anguish,
>   made atonement . . .
> Even your anguish, and more deeply than you
>   yourself! . . .
> He was obedient to death on the cross.
> This sacrifice he offered for you in his love,
> In his unfathomable mercy;
> Do you want now to refuse him yours?[51]

Still more: Hebbel frames the event with two mottos: 'Consider him who forgave on the cross' (spoken to Kriemhild)[52] and 'In the name of him who died on the cross' (Dietrich von Bern's final word to the whole tragedy), words which are spoken not out of the psychology of the heroes but out of the great historical vision of the poet. And yet *this* tragedy can take place only in the twilight and in the transition from myth to revelation, it shows what happens to the reality of myth when it stands in the sphere of revelation. But whence can Hebbel, in the middle of the nineteenth century, give back to the myth true power (something that neither Goethe nor Schiller nor Wagner could do)? Only from the elemental powers of *eros*, which here again is made into a titanic, cosmic power, but quite without that looking up to the divine typical of the devout classical texts, the divine which is always right, even in Aeschylus' *Prometheus*.

[50] III.4.11.
[51] II.5.9.
[52] II.5.9

Michelangelo had already raised the human form to this superhuman, titanic format; within it, Henry Fuseli gathered together all the great Western poetry from Homer, Aeschylus and Sophocles through Dante to Shakespeare and Milton (even Wieland's *Oberon* is included); Wagner will—alongside various ambiguities in his world-view from *The Flying Dutchman* and *Tannhäuser* to *Parsifal*—compose in Tristan the apotheosis of post-Christian *eros* set up as an absolute: *eroici furori* as the unity of erotic passion and death. What is here preserved in a disintegrating (decadent) harmony, is agonizingly broken in pieces by Strindberg—quite in the spirit of Bruno's law—for each new attempt at love infallibly conceals within itself the seed of deathly hatred and dissension, finally to crystallise in new forms of *eros*. As in Tristan, the West here passes over, cancelling itself, into Buddhism.

The absolute self-glory of *eros*, which grasps eternity in a moment, if taken seriously, eliminates any accompanying thought of an individual immortality after death. The Greeks stood, when they surrounded the hero with the prestige of mythical glory (κῦδος), *before* this thought and already in part advanced towards it (Pindar); the classicising modern period clings to it ever more onesidedly (with Ficino the whole 'Platonic philosophy' is absorbed into proofs of immortality), ever more uncertainly and anxiously (Pomponazzi, Descartes, Herder, Kant, Jean Paul, Tennyson's 'In Memoriam'), ever more contradicted by pantheisms and empiricisms. Heroic *eros* sucks the radiance of the idea into itself; here man is timelessly raised beyond death. He can, as in Goethe's *Faust*, project himself into what lies beyond death, and thus the classical idea of the 'eternal feminine' (in Helen) changes into the 'virgin, mother, queen, goddess', 'highest sovereign lady of the world' (Mary). But this projection can only be understood as a bare 'postulate', perhaps only as a mere fugitive ray of the tragic self-glory of *eros*. Then everything classical becomes, together with what is Christian, a 'myth' of the loving heart.

A final, solitary success and thus something like a synthesizing retrospective of the whole tradition is that world drama that its author PAUL CLAUDEL has characterised as an *opus mirandum*, *The Satin Slipper*.[53] What Goethe had been incapable of—giving a universal meaning to the *eros* of two lovers—Claudel has fashioned out of a personal experience of existence (love and, as calling, exile), which is aware of being mysteriously related to that of Dante.[54] The tragic glory of the absolute love between Rodrigue and Prouèze, at once hell and paradise,[55] complete impossibility of fulfilment, pure longing and nevertheless presence of eternal blessedness[56]—this tragic love is 'used' by the king of Spain (Charles V, sovereign of the Old and New World) as a monstrous potential by which he can give form to the newly-discovered, chaotic continent. A lover like Rodrigue can be seduced by no earthly *gloire*, and a lover like Prouèze will hold in Africa the royal attributes right to the most extreme humiliation. When they meet again after ten years, because it is in earthly terms finally 'too late', Rodrigue addresses that speech to his officers on the tragic *eros*, in which he places himself beside Caesar and Mark Antony, while the poet of these *Eroici Furori* puts himself beside Dante and Shakespeare: as if he understood his mission here to be to utter the word of farewell to Western Platonism, his wayward Muse takes it back once for all into the service of Christian grace. At night, by passing through a purgatory of flames, Prouèze is purified by the guardian angel from a longing *eros* to an *agape* of renunciation, which wills nothing more than what God wills. So she withdraws from clinging to her beloved, leads the way, now without any wishes, into death, and becomes for him the guiding star. His earthly path continues a little longer. The drama is, so to

[53] *Le Soulier de Satin*, in *Théatre II* (Pléiade, 1948), 563–849. (Eng. tr. by J. O'Connor; London, 1931).

[54] 'Ode jubilaire pour le six-centième anniversaire de la mort de Dante'(1921), in *Feuilles de Saints, Oeuvres Poétiques* (Pléiade, 1957), 667–681.

[55] 'Each of your kisses gives me a paradise, which I know is forbidden to me. Where you are, there will be for me the impossibility of escaping from this paradise of torture, which ... penetrates me and from which I remain excluded ... You open paradise to me and prevent me from staying there ...': Second Day, Scene 14.

[56] Fourth Day, last scene.

speak, geographically laid out: Europe spreads (in Columbus and then in the pair of lovers) to America and Africa, but it discovers too (as Renaissance) its classical origins; at the same time it is divided in itself (in the Reformation) and struggles for its reunion (in the episode with Doña Musique and Don Juan d'Austria); China is from the beginning given a part, Japan becomes the final goal of conquest from America. But while the globe of the earth is covered, the whole earthly imperial glory (under Philip II) becomes fantastic and unreal and is smashed (in the defeat of the Armada), while at the same time the hero's earthly glory of *eros* crumbles away and what becomes visible beneath it is a simple Christian sinner—untrue to his own love (with the 'actress'), parleying with Christian love (Doña Sept Epées), and failing before her, Rodrigue degenerates into an aesthete, who paints 'folk' art, and finally becomes a traitor out of sheer blind presumptuousness, and so, ending up on a dunghill, is ready for confession in the face of the stars, to be picked up by a rag-picking Carmelite nun to be a servant of the monastery. Claudel therefore manages to associate with the *Eroici Furori* an element which, historically, remained almost completely foreign to it (if we make the exception of Ariosto and his imitators): humour, in which the univocal glory of *eros* is again resolved in the all-embracing *analogia gloriae*, to which *agape* says the last encompassing word. This fading and decay of baroque splendour in the 'Fourth Day', when every form of kingdom and art is dissolved into the glory of the all-bearing sea, would be immanently pure tragedy, but the poet knows how to undergird it with humour and to make it reflect existentially that higher harmony that rules everything, the Platonic-Christian symbol of which is the character of Doña Musique. So the poet is at the level of love and yet simultaneously quite transcends it: be it with the sceptical humour of the Chinese servant in the face of his raving lord, or with the guardian angel's love, drawing close with understanding, for the madness of Prouèze and the love of the great patron saint (in the church of Prague), which can, quite Platonically, be heavenly constellations too (like Sant Jago). Claudel's final word stands, like all the greatest poetry, in an historical *kairos*, from which it cannot be displaced and out of which it streams forth effectively. It is a word which, once again and quite personally experienced, gathers together and sets its seal on a long Western tradition—and one knows what Aeschylus, Pindar, Virgil and Dante meant to Claudel. It shapes them into a secular, historical form, which the world that follows will perhaps no longer understand, or only from the outside, just as, on a smaller scale, Hofmannsthal's *Schwieriger* brought a cultural form to an end that twenty years later would no longer exist and that can no longer be reconstructed by any actor.

What becomes of the 'heroic' *eros*, once this is no longer mediated in the post-Christian period, deserves no further notice, because self-consumption in absolute contradiction robs it of any glory: Penthesilea, Kriemhild and Isolde become a prey for psychiatry. And with Sartre the heart's most extreme contradictions grow cold as the pendulum-strokes of a lonely existence devoid of *eros*.

c. Retreat to the Human Person as Centre

The battle of the modern period about God's glory in the world was justified. It was no tactical error to call for help on intact powers of classical antiquity from humanism and the Renaissance onwards, for antiquity was intended and perceived as that which was valid for all human persons; but it proved to be strategically wrong. Seen as a whole, the battle has to be considered as lost. History brings a parenthesis to a close and distances it from the highest intellectual creations: Poussin and Watteau, Hölderlin and Goethe ... So it is a matter of exercising the most attentive discretion of spirits over the next step of the tradition: if its concerns are now ours, why are its instruments not ours?

The mediation of antiquity for the sake of the salvation of a total Christian culture has been seen so far from two points of view: the embedding of the biblical revelation in a theophanous cosmos, and the embedding of *agape* in the basic human orientation interpreted as *eros* (*desiderio di bellezza*). Both movements broke down at the point of the overwhelming of 'supernature' by 'nature'. The decisive battle is however fought only where the two great inroads on the hitherto tolerably intact world-view are made:

1. With the Reformation, the visible unity of Western Christendom, the sacramental expression of its nature as the unity of the love of Christ, was torn to pieces: a fearful incursion into the credibility of its form, the inner unity of which should bear witness to the world of the truth of the Incarnation. It is open to misunderstanding, and finally futile, when the baroque period exalts the outward ecclesial forms, both in theology and in art, as the 'representation' of the Christian divine glory. The retreat from the smashed form of the revelation to the still sound piety of men and women becomes inevitable: under English leadership, which operated on a European scale in the Enlightenment, the new attitude is established.

2. From the advance of natural science from Copernicus to Galileo and then to Newton, which initially suggested to man a changed attitude only to matter, radical metaphysical consequences were precipitately drawn: atomism, materialism, atheism come into sight almost simultaneously. The natural religion of mankind, which gave itself out as 'progressive' as opposed to the fragmented Church, was 'traditional' in its reaction to these these radicalisms; it could certainly admit the altered attitude of mankind to the cosmos, but did not need to draw the atheistic consequences because man as the embodiment of the world was for it a religious being. In this second stance, what we earlier characterised as the 'anthropological reduction'[1] is still clearer than the first stance: for here the theophanous character of the cosmos *can* already be given up, while the religious phenomenon in man is allegedly still intact. But in the first (anti-Church) aspect too, an inner logic compels the displacement of the religious dimension from all heteronomy and its relocation in the spontaneity of the heart and the autonomy of reason, and therefore essentially in ethics. This will become the criterion of the relationship to God in Shaftesbury's *Moralists*.

[1] *Love Alone: the Way of Revelation* (1968: German original 1963), 25–42.

This anthropologising of metaphysics, too, is still accomplished in close dependence on antiquity, even though cosmology retreats into the background. Plato's Republic, in which man has a world-structure, Plotinus' plan, which sets the intellect between God and the world, but above all the Stoics, for whom man stands as the steward of cosmic reason and the master of destiny, orchestrate an accompaniment to this turning-point. It is on man that the flood-light concentrates from all directions ever more clearly: he becomes the *focus of glory*, where the cosmos lightens up to the mind and the darkness of God steps into openness.

Cusa had already granted to man the position of a reflected implication of the cosmos and, correspondingly, of a reflected creativeness (as *secundus deus*) and designated him with Protagoras—in spite of Plato—as the 'measure of all things'. He had moreover proclaimed in a heavenly council the unity of the religions of mankind in the One Logos. In his programmatic (even if much over-valued) treatise, Pico della Mirandola develops the dignity of man who in his free self-determination surpasses the laws of the cosmos, is 'sculptor and poet of himself', 'and if he, dissatisfied with the lot of a creature, withdraws into the centre of his totality, then he becomes one spirit with God and in the lonely darkness of the Father, transcendent over all things, will likewise have precedence over all things'.[2] Around the centre of this man, Pico gathers together all arts and sciences, philosophy, mysticism and magic, and finally also Christian theology. The ideal of the *uomo universale* seeks for a time to realise in life this great man who will be equal to every intellectual exercise, like Leonardo da Vinci or even Erasmus, Paracelsus, Milton, Goethe. In order to probe his metaphysical being and at the same time his fitness for achievement, he is—like a chemical—isolated in strange retorts; on the island Utopia (Thomas More), in the kingdom of the Sun (Campanella), in New Atlantis (Francis Bacon), he is to prove how far he can create a society out of his own powers. In the later innumerable Robinson-stories, the experiment is sharpened,

[2] *De hominis dignitate*, ed. Garin (1942), 104–6.

for this experiment of abstraction is expected of the individual. From Hobbes to Rousseau, man—in a new abstraction—will be constructed out of his original, historical situation. In Rabelais, and more impressively still in Montaigne, he becomes the true point of reference for all classical (and especially Stoic-anthropological) and Christian 'benefits of culture': the scepticism of the *Essais* signifies nothing else than that man remains the measure of his historical and social constructions. The French moralists and tellers of fables (under the patronage of Theophrastus and Aesop) encircle him and pursue him with their aphorisms and parables, just as today the reporter pursues a star with his snap-shots: the surprise unmasks.

These positions are very consciously marked out, and defended very firmly: the philosopher, withdrawing from cosmology and leaving the field free for the natural scientist, and the theologian, withdrawing from church dogmatics, meet one another in a single person: he is the advocate of the man of autonomous religion. In 1593 Jean Bodin writes his religious dialogue called *Heptaplomeres* between a Catholic, a Lutheran, a Calvinist, a Jew, a Muslim, an upholder of natural religion and an agnostic.[3] The climatic differences between the different peoples and races—noticed by Aristotle, taken up by Shaftesbury and developed on a grand scale by Herder in his *Ideen*—are held here to explain the religious differences too; the Jew already stands close to Lessing's Nathan; the basis for understanding is natural religion and the decalogue. Castellio transcends the individual Christian points of view and their narrow ecclesiastical dogmatisms and persecutions of heretics; Sebastian Franck distances himself by his *Paradoxa* from the Church denominations, by making in gnostic fashion the biblical texts a 'manifestation' of an event of universal history, beyond time: of an 'invisible Christ' in whom the world as a whole is given grace *a priori*. Origen's Logos, interior to man, Augustine's *magister interior*, is already interpreted here as the intelligible element in man, in a way that foreshadows Kant.

[3] Ed. L. Noack (1857).

The sovereign autonomy of man is also the inner light that inspires the three great aggressive ideologies that are fought by the liberal theisms. *Niccolo Machiavelli's* leading idea in his *Discorsi* and *Il Principe* is—after his study of Livy and Polybius—the Roman state, in which man understood how to give himself firm boundaries imposed by an objective intelligence which could tame his subjective and ineradicable tendencies towards decadence. Man, as he is found in the idea of his own greatness and 'form', has here the power thoroughly to fashion the empirically always unstable man as 'matter'. Strangely enough, it is always a classical, purely anthropological blueprint that leads to the later scientific ideologies. The gloomy figure of *Francis Bacon*, the reckless, ambitious and faithless upstart who was accused of corruption and was soon once more ending his life in loneliness, transfers Machiavelli's political, manipulative harshness to man's relationship to nature. He must win back his lost paradisal sovereignty over it, something possible only by inexorably taming it: it is matter for the power of the mind, and this power increases with every partial victory. Knowledge is power: *scientia et potentia humana in idem coincidunt.* But considered like that, the whole of classical metaphysics – which was contemplation of the truth—is good for nothing; in place of its half-religious conceptual compositions the inductive methods must be introduced. 'The corruption of philosophy by . . . an admixture of theology is far more widely spread . . . from this unwholesome mixture of things human and divine there arises not only a fantastic philosophy but also an heretical religion'.[4] 'It were better to have no Opinion of *God* at all; than such an Opinion, as is unworthy of him'[5]—so in the *Essays*, behind which stands a Plutarch read through Montaigne's eyes. The third, *Thomas Hobbes*, fashions a strangely exact synthesis of them both. The classical author he started out from was, significantly, Thucydides[6] and his (sophistical) doctrine of the rightness of might; he

---

[4] *Novum Organon* I § 65 (Eng. tr. by R. Ellis and J. Spedding, pp. 86f.).

[5] *Of Superstition*, in *Essays* XVII (ed. W. A. Wright, London, 1879; p. 68).

[6] But one should not be silent about the fact that in his old age Hobbes

first became known by translating Thucydides: a demythologised classicism of the pure conflict of power. The philosophy has two themes: the bodies and the state, but only one method: subjugation under one imposed form. Extreme nominalism and sensualism united with mathematical method—to think is to reckon, to add and subtract—leaves a space free where abstraction of the most general geometrical forms can be understood as structures produced *a priori* and can be cast over the sense perceptions to subdue them. Correspondingly the material substrate must be conceived of hypothetically as something purely mechanical and atomistic. From all this it is clear that this hypothesis is derived, not from experience, but from the methodical presupposition (that knowledge is power and therefore a matter of reckoning). The theory of the state cannot be understood without Protestant presuppositions. The primordial bases of man, according to his experience, are the egoistical *cupiditas* of the individual for power, and the natural instinct to avoid violent death: a personal 'chaos' (like the former atomic chaos), which is subdued only by an absolute social form of power from above, required by the universal necessity of escaping the war of everyone against everyone else. In this form lies every value: what it includes is good, what it excludes (forbids) is bad, and this holds, too, for the conscience of the subjects. This form of power—it is a matter of indifference whether it is realised in a monarchical or a democratic manner—is therefore humanity, collectively rising above the condition of instincts, structuring itself by its own rational power. There is left for religion, revelation, theology—outside any relationship with strict philosophy, which knows nothing of God—a place in an empty vacuum.

In Holland and France, Hobbes was in intensive exchange with the circle of Descartes; the stark mind-matter dualism of the latter was one of his starting-points, as it will also be for mind-matter speculation. And remarkably enough it was from

translated the whole of Homer into rhyming verse. On the classical bases of Hobbes: F. Tönnies, *Thomas Hobbes, der Mann und der Denker* (1922); W. Dilthey, *Weltanschauung und Analyse des Menschen seit Renaissance und Reformation* in *Ges. Werke* II (1923³), 292f.

Descartes that the great English opponent of Hobbes, the leader of the Cambridge Platonists[7] *Ralph Cudworth*, initiated his return to Plato, or better to that classical-Christian, ethical and aesthetic view of the world as a whole, which had nowhere in Europe been more deeply and more convincingly maintained, even up to the present, than in Anglican England.[8] Cudworth, who originally wanted his *True Intellectual System of the Universe* (1678) to oppose all forms of determinism—mechanistic atomism, Stoic-pantheist fatalism and Calvinist predestinarianism[9]—in fact covered only the first position in the form given it by Hobbes. Elementary propositions lay the foundation: truth is greater than man; the concept of God underlies all religions in such a way that man must mount up above himself to God; faith—which cannot be derived from the natural concept of God—is necessarily rooted in the fact that even the Divine Trinity, once revealed, shows itself, as with Cusa, to be present everywhere in vestigial form in natural religion. Christianity is here—and in an unbroken tradition from Cudworth and Butler (*The Analogy of Religion: Natural and Revealed*, 1736), through the Oxford Movement (and its recourse to the Platonism of the Church Fathers), to the present with Farrer and Mascall—essentially the revealedness of the Glory of God: archetypally in the heavenly, eternal world, in the earthly, mortal, sinful world in a veiled mirror and likeness, mediated by Christian death which therefore takes on a central significance (*cf.* the great English poetry of meditation).[10]

And yet it is not this tradition that is historically dominant, but the other, which will engage the anti-materialistic battle over God on a purely anthropological front. With Herbert of Cherbury, the principal contents of Christian thinking are

[7] F. J. Powicke, *The Cambridge Platonists, a Study* (1926).

[8] J. H. Muirhead, *The Platonic Tradition in Anglo-Saxon Philosophy* (1931). E. Cassirer, *Die platonische Renaissance in England und die Schule von Cambridge* (1932). K. Schmitz, *Cudworth und der Platonismus* (Diss. Giessen, 1919). *Cf. The Glory of the Lord*, vol. III, pp. 354–355 (Eng. tr.).

[9] Lydia Gysi, *Platonism and Cartesianism in the philosophy of Ralph Cudworth* (Diss, 1950; H. Lang, Bern, 1962), 1.

[10] Louis L. Martz, *The Poetry of Meditation, a Study in English Religious Literature of the Seventeenth Century* (Yale University Press, 1954).

entrusted to purely religious reason which is given responsibility for them. Later with John Locke (*The Reasonableness of Christianity*, 1695), John Toland (*Christianity not Mysterious*, 1696), and Matthew Tindal (*Christianity as Old as the Creation*, 1730), man is ethically obliged to measure any revelation that is revealed to him against his free, autonomous reason (Locke), to strip down the Christian religion, disguised in dogmas, to the simple, universal-human truth in the preaching of Jesus (Toland), to base Christian teaching simply on man's universal piety (Tindal), in a decided secularisation of the Augustinian *civitas Dei ab Abel*.[11] But this whole movement is important for the history of the concept of glory only as the presupposition of a new synthesis into which it leads, and which again is itself the fundamental presupposition for the next phase.

ANTHONY, EARL OF SHAFTESBURY, creates this strange synthesis of Enlightenment (with its anthropological reduction) and antiquity (with its aesthetic, cosmological dimension), that was to be one of the starting-points for the classicising, humanist-cosmic religion of the period of Goethe.[12] Thus his creation must be briefly set out.

Shaftesbury[13] fought a battle on two fronts: with Cudworth against the materialism of Hobbes, and with the freethinkers against the dark, humourless dogmatism of the guild of theologians and, in the background, against the similarly humourless image of God in the Old Testament that is unworthy of a free man.[14] Our own black melancholy

---

[11] On the whole subject: Emmanuel Hirsch, *Geschichte der neueren evangelischen Theologie im Zusammenhang mit den allgemeinen Bewegungen des europäischen Denkens*, vol. 1 (1949), 244–344.

[12] C. F. Weiser, *Shaftesbury und das deutsche Geistesleben* (Teubner, 1916).

[13] Shaftesbury's *Characteristics* (his own collection of his most important works, especially: 'A Letter concerning Enthusiasm' (E), 'Soliloquy or Advice to an Author' (S), 'An Inquiry concerning Virtue or Merit' (M), 'The Moralists, a Philosophical Rhapsody' (R)), cited in the annotated ed. by John M. Robertson (2 vols. London, 1900). Newly discovered works collected as *Second Characters* by B. Rand (Cambridge University Press, 1914).

[14] There is polemic against the followers of 'some religions', who

makes us fashion both: a mindless, materialistic universe and
a God, on whom we project 'wrath, and fury, and revenge,
and terrors'.[15] So it is a matter of finding a position,
independent of atheism and revealed theology and
invulnerable to attack by either, which contains sufficient
absolute criteria on which to judge the two hostile
standpoints: for Shaftesbury, this is ethics, modern and
humanist, but understood with the breadth of classical
cosmology. And within this ethic it is a matter of finding
that subjective 'situation of mind'[16] which best answers to
the dignity of man's freedom, and which therefore best brings
him into contact with absolute reality, with divinity present
in universal nature: Shaftesbury calls it 'good humour'[17] not
only in the classical sense of ἁρμονία of the powers of the
soul and the humours and their agreement with the universe,
nor only with the Platonic supplement of the philosophical
irony of the 'man of the world', but in a specific way
characteristic of the Enlightenment as the inner, serenely
superior self-possession of the free, self-determining spirit. The
reduction of the two antinomian 'religious' positions to a
religiously neutral ethics corresponds to Descartes' theoretical
reduction to the *cogito*, yet with this difference—indicative of
the passage of time—that ethics is seen as an irreducible
minimum, based on freedom as autonomy, and at the same
time as a self-sufficient maximum, because the fundamental
moral phenomenon can generate from itself the whole world
of ethics even as conduct in relation to the universe and to
God (cosmology and theology) and can thus become the
judge of any externally-announced doctrine of the world or
of God.[18] It then becomes clear, for example, that atheism
has a fairly neutral stance to the ethical phenomenon, neither

'expressly give no other idea of God than of than of a being arbitrary,
violent, causing ill and ordaining to misery; which in effect is the same as
to substitute a daemon or devil in his room': M I.242. On the Jews, their
'surliness' and consequent intolerance: E III.23.

[15] E IV.24.

[16] R II.31.

[17] E I.17, I.39. And the whole essay on the Freedom of Wit and Humour:
I.43–99.

[18] M I, II.243, 255; M I, III.260–1.

essentially furthering it nor essentially threatening it,[19] while positive religion, in accordance with its purposes,[20] *can* certainly inwardly exalt and perfect the ethical,[21] but in general tends to endanger it. This is because the free man essentially loves the good for its own sake and correspondingly does the good too, and only from this, his most sublime perspective, can see the true nature of absolute spirit: God is either pure selfless good and self-radiance[22]— and in this selflessness pure beatitude—or he is simply nothing. The act of looking to God takes place in an ethical, aesthetic intuition of the whole, which lets itself be split up for the ratiocinating reason, when the implications of the primordial ethical phenomenon are discovered:[23] Platonically, because the order in the self on the higher spiritual plane reflects the order of the universe, and the natural social disposition of the beasts must be realised spiritually through ethical self-renunciation for the sake of the common good.[24] The world-harmony is stamped with ascetic 'temperance',[25] 'decency',[26] and in so far as the universe is orientated to self-preservation, the individual too will strive for it and thereby also know the 'self-enjoyment'[27] of virtue, which all the same rests principally on triumph over self for the sake of the generality. If beauty and goodness are characterised as 'still one and the same',[28] if the ideal of εὐδαιμονία is realised

---

[19] M 1, III.275.

[20] '. . . the end of religion is to render us more perfect and accomplished in all moral duties and performances': M 2, I.287.

[21] 'So . . . nothing can more highly contribute to the fixing of right apprehension, and a sound judgment or sense of right and wrong, than to believe a God who is ever and on all accounts represented such as to be actually a true model and example of the most exact justice and highest goodness and worth': M 1, III.264–5.

[22] R III.110.

[23] R III.140–1.

[24] Virtue is largely defined by the notion of a public interest: M 1, II.252, III.258, 279; M 2, I.280.

[25] R II.41f.

[26] R III.137.

[27] M 2, I.292; 1, II.248.

[28] R III.128.

already on earth[29] in a quite classical way through ethical renunciation, expressly through a preference of choice,[30] through the distinguishing of deep joy from superficial pleasure,[31] then here we find a link with Plato and Aristotle *via* Kant's separations to Herder, Schiller, Goethe, Hölderlin and Jean Paul. Yet even Kant will be included in the synthesis insofar as the moral good may be sought and posited solely for its own sake, and any thought of merit (which religion had a partiality for including) is to be excluded from it; for the moral good is primarily its own reward.[32] In order to elucidate this, Shaftesbury calls on the non-functional character of beauty, which the admirer must let be. The beautiful ocean: 'The bridegroom-Doge, who in his stately Bucentaur floats on the bosom of his Thetis, has less possession than the poor shepherd, who from a hanging rock ... stretched at his ease, forgets his feeding flocks, while he admires her beauty.'[33] Not for nothing does Shaftesbury look across to 'the mystics of the ancient church, whom these of latter days have followed',[34] to the advocates of *amour pur* who wish to love the eternal Good for its own sake alone. Thus he clearly draws out the principal line of the Western metaphysics of glory: from Homer and Heraclitus, Plato and the Stoics to the Christian lovers of God, but also to Leone, Spinoza and their adherents. It is not personal immortality that stands in the foreground here, but that glory of the intrinsically-worthy good, which in Shaftesbury's opinion is the only legitimate starting-point for any hope of immortality on the part of the individual: 'if by the hope of reward be understood the love and desire of virtuous enjoyment, or of the very practice and exercise of virtue in another life, the expectation or hope of this kind is so far from being derogatory to virtue, that it is an evidence of our loving it the more sincerely and for its own sake.'[35] Shaftesbury, who

[29] R II.58, 67.
[30] R III.130–1.
[31] R II.29f.
[32] R II.37–8.
[33] R III.127.
[34] R II.55.
[35] M I, III.273.

was so displeased with the Jewish religion because of its notion of reward, had not noticed that without any primary perspective of immortality it demanded the loyalty of faith and caused the (eschatological) reflection to shine forth from the divine covenant which was an end in itself.

But the ethical starting-point which methodically brackets off the religious, both against atheism and Christianity,[36] in order to be its measure, establishes a relationship to the Godhead immanent in the world, which in the end is necessarily one of identity. Negative theology completely vanishes. Prayer has assumed the form of 'enthusiasm' which sings those great hymns to the harmony of the universe which have had such a mighty impact on posterity. Sharply marked off from all its ethically rejected forms, the true enthusiasm means being filled by the spirit of the pure divine love,[37] which is simultaneously (as selflessness) our pure being-outside-ourselves and (as the essence of our morality) our pure self-realisation—or even the pure immanence of God in us. Here lies the knot: the glory of God, which, if we have eyes and heart, manifests itself to us everywhere in the cosmos, shines for us primarily in the glory of our own love. In it we feel that God is present and that we are inspired by him.[38] This is a God, who has decided to travel incognito, like a prince, through his world,[39] who even (in a deeper image) exists in his world-nature in a condition of pure unconscious self-distribution, although all the children of this nature consider this to be so obvious that it is not at all striking: 'Who then understands for ever [i.e., Nature], or is interested or concerned in her behalf? No-one; not a soul.'[40] The eternal God-nature kenotically among men: Hölderlin, Rilke and Heidegger will take this thought further.

[36] R II.52–3.
[37] R II.54: '. . . whether there be anything in divinity (= theology) which you think has more the air of enthusiasm than that notion of divine love such as separates from everything worldly, sensual, or meanly interested? A love which is simple, pure, and unmixed, which has no other object than merely the excellency of that being itself . . .'
[38] R II.97.
[39] R III.102.
[40] R III.104.

The all-embracing, unexpressed identity, the replacement
of prayer by enthusiasm, indicate that Shaftesbury was deeply
influenced by Giordano Bruno.[41] Even if his basic accent is
quite other, much more measured and more gentlemanly, still
it is Shaftesbury who, picking up from the titanic behaviour
of Bruno and his *Eroici Furori*, places the *symbol of Prometheus*
in the foreground of the creative artist.[42] One thinks back to
Cusa, for whom the created mind as a *secundus deus* produces
from itself an unreal world after the model of the creator;
one can mention the famous *Poetica* of Julius Caesar Scaliger
(1561), who seizes man's position of pre-eminence for the true
poet: while the rest of the arts only imitate and, like an actor,
bring to expression what has already been composed, the true
poet is creative like a second God (*velut alter deus condere*).[43]
But there is still need of Bruno's and Shaftesbury's new
metaphysical presupposition, to raise man up to a true Titan
who administers the divine fire: 'such a poet is indeed a second
Maker', 'a just Prometheus under Jove': the one who from
the inner apprehension and experience of the divine, creative,
universal nature and from the fullness of his ethical personality
becomes himself a creator—and now we hear the Plotinian
word—from 'inward form'.[44] In the transition to the Germans,
the use of the expression 'Schöpfer' (creator) for the poet at
first causes offence.[45] It makes its way with Klopstock and
the Swiss; in the Sturm-und-Drang circle the 'under Jove' is
simply abandoned. With Herder all 'gods, heroes and
goddesses' become the *disjecti membra poetae*,[46] that is, of man
as inner meaning of the world, who is extended through and

[41] This has been proved above all by Dilthey: *Werke*, vol. II, 335f., 342f.,
and the comments by G. Misch, p. 521. Frischeisen-Köhler follows him in
his introduction to the *Moralists (Ein Brief über den Enthusiasmus, Die
Moralisten*, trans. and introduced by Max Frischeisen-Köhler, *Phil. Bibl. 111*,
1909); according to him, it was Toland, not the Dutch philosophical circle,
that was the decisive mediator: pp. XIIf.

[42] Oskar Walzel, 'Das Prometheussymbol von Shaftesbury zu Goethe',
in *Neue Jahrbücher für das klassische Altertum etc.* XIII (1910), 40–71, 133–65.

[43] *Poetica* (1561), 3a.

[44] S I.136.

[45] Walzel, l.c., 56–8.

[46] *Ibid.*, 52.

by means of nature, and whom the Promethean poet gathers together from his inner, divinatory power.[47] With Goethe (*Zum Schäkespears Tag*, 1771; *Von Deutscher Baukunst*, 1772), Shakespeare (and in him Goethe himself) is at first the rival of Prometheus: he 'copied his men from him stroke by stroke, only in colossal size . . . and then breathed life into them all by the breath of his spirit'; then Erwin von Steinbach becomes the 'godlike Genius': 'more than Prometheus he leads the blessedness of the gods on to the earth'. In the Prometheus Ode and the *Dramenfragment* (1773) the 'under Jove' (which governed Aeschylus' trilogy) is finally converted into its opposite; in the latter, the Titan becomes the absolute poet, beside whom Minerva stands as 'my goddess', as the inspiration of his own genius: 'And you are for my spirit, What it is itself; From the beginning your words have been to me the light of heaven! Always, as if my soul spoke to itself and opened itself to itself, And inborn harmonies echoed in it from out of itself. Those were your words. So I myself was not myself, And a divinity spoke, when I supposed I spoke; And if I supposed a divinity spoke, it was I myself who spoke. And thus with you and me so united, my love for you so inward, so eternal!' Minerva: 'And I am eternally present with you.'[48] The relationship to genius (again, as in Shaftesbury, called god) cannot be depicted more clearly: the absolute, divine 'I' inspires what is Titanic, already in the sense of the saying of Heraclitus/Hölderlin: ἓν διαφέρον ἑαυτῷ. So Minerva can give life to Prometheus' clay creatures; so she can accompany him upwards, too, to the 'source of life', whether this is called 'fate' or 'Zeus', with whom too Goethe finally wanted to reconcile his Titan. Even though the poet later in *Pandora* distances himself from the principle of Prometheus, it has nevertheless grown far beyond him into the realm of world-history: in Fichte's I-philosophy, Schelling's concept of freedom, Hegel's dialectic: The vigorous force at work in this growth is quite different from the process whereby Plato's philosophy of *daimonion* has grown beyond the relationship between Odysseus and his

[47] *Ibid.*, 52–3.
[48] *Artemis-Gedenkausgabe* IV.188–9.

(true) goddess, Athene. For the Greeks thought in terms of analogy, but Bruno and Shaftesbury in terms of identity.

This hidden identity makes the man-Titan, and also the harmless citizen of the Enlightenment, essentially good. Only with this presupposition can his enthusiasm, that is his god-inwardness, suffice as prayer. His transcendence into the divinely-animated universe is always God's immanence in himself as well: as a gesture of self-emptying love, it is always reconciliation too, or better, the seizing of the state of being reconciled. The young Goethe is not lacking in piety, but he sharply resists a God who could hear prayer (Lavater and Jung-Stilling present him with a caricature of such a God). The word 'Gefühl' (feeling) which the whole Goethe-period—from Shaftesbury and Rousseau's confession of faith in *Emile*, to F. H. Jacobi and Schleiermacher, and to Faust's confession of faith before Gretchen—reserved for the relationship to God, could well characterise the 'feeling after him and finding him' of the Areopagus speech (Acts 17.27) and thus legitimately continue the *sentire* of the *sensus spiratales*[49] (from Origen to Bernard and Bonaventure), if only it did not function with the hidden presupposition of a final, encompassing identity. This identity characterises even the most sublime attempt of the succeeding period once more to make Christian glory coterminous with classical beauty, against all the overshadowing nights of the present: the poetry of Friedrich Hölderlin.

d. Hölderlin

1. 'GLORIOUS, HOLY, DIVINE'

In modern times, none has championed the cause of 'glory' as urgently and tragically as did Friedrich Hölderlin.[1] His need to express his experience of reality in terms of a general

---

[49] *Cf.* Vol. I of this work, pp. 368–371 (Eng. tr.).

[1] The text of the Complete Works follows the larger Stuttgart edition; the volumes are indicated by Roman numerals. Modern orthography is used. *Hyperion* = H, the 'Fragment of Hyperion' = FH, the metrical

validity led him to combine the three historically definitive intellectual forms—Christianity, the ancient world and German Idealism—by means of a two-fold reduction; subjectively the ancient world was to emerge as the predominant form, yet objectively Idealism properly became the higher centre. Hölderlin, after all, taking his lead from Schiller's progress (in his *Aesthetic Letters* and programmatic didactic poetry) beyond Kant, is certainly the inspiration behind 'German Idealism's oldest system in programmatic form',[2] a text formulated, presumably, by Schelling and preserved in Hegel's script; here the highest act performed by reason, that which embraces all ideas, is seen as 'an aesthetic act' postulating 'sisterhood of truth and goodness in beauty alone', and demanding 'a new mythology', a 'mythology of reason'. And yet, the further he went the more resolutely did Hölderlin turn his back on the Idealistic philosophy[3] and its destruction, through cold reflection and speculation, of the experience of theophanous reality; but while he took up his definitive philosophical stand-point beside Parmenides-Heraclitus and made this the basis for his interpretation of Homer, Pindar, Sophocles and Plato, the fundamental assumption remained identity (and not analogy), which implies at least essential agreement with Leibniz-Shaftesbury, Schelling-Hegel, Heidegger-W. F. Otto. At the same time, if the splendour of the ancient world and its gods was to enjoy such supremacy, all the forces and motifs that had belonged to Christian revelatory glory had to be transferred to the ancient glory, seen as a theophanous Nature-cosmos. This Hölderlin did yet more thoroughly and exhaustively than had the naiver Ficino, so exhaustively, indeed, that by the time

version = MH, 'Hyperion's Youth' = YH, the penultimate version = PH, and the order of reference is: Volume, Book, Letter; thus H 1/2, 4 = *Hyperion*, Volume 1, Book 2, fourth Letter. References to Empedocles give the version (1E, 2E or 3E), act, scene, and line. All other references are according to the volume (or half-volume) and page of the Beißner edition. The *Hölderlin Yearbook* for 1944 and 1947ff. = HYb.

[2] IV/1, 297–299.

[3] Thus the justified reaction of Johannes Hoffmeister (*Hölderlin und die Philosophie*, Meiner, 1942) against Wilhelm Böhm's one-sided philosophisation of Hölderlin.

Christ's prerogatives had all been made over to the priestess of love, Diotima, and to the true pantheistic mediator Empedocles, whose death reconciles the world, when at the last there came a more conscious return to Christ no more was left of him than a tree stripped bare of leaves, an empty treasure-chest, a brother to Heracles and Dionysus,[4] one who, even if called by the poet with the other gods to the 'Feast of Peace' at the evening of ages, nevertheless ultimately (in the final version) cannot suffice to perform in and through himself the eschatological *anakephalaiôsis* of heaven and earth (Eph. 1.10), and must leave this office to the 'First of the Feast',[5] the cosmic, world-historical, Germanic, spirit.[6]

It is with an amazement close to worship that Hölderlin contemplates the wonder of the ancient world, which succeeded in spiritualising, whole and unimpaired, in art a total experience of God in the cosmos; he contemplates this glory with Christian eyes, and a Christian heart which unquestionably sees and understands it as the glory of love. In an early apostrophe of the genius of Greece he says (1790): 'In the sight of the gods/ Thy mouth determined/ To found thy kingdom on love./ Then were amazed all the heavenly ones .../ On love dost thou found thy kingdom./ Thou comest, and Orpheus' love/ Soars up to the eye of the world/ And Orpheus' love/ Wells downwards to Acheron./ ... Maeonides![7] like thou!/ None loved like thou;/ Thy heart did embrace/ The earth and ocean/ And giant spirits, the heroes of Earth!/ And the heavens and all the heavenly ones/ Thy

---

[4] 'The only One' (1st vers.), ll. 5of. (II, 154), (2nd vers.) ll. 5of. (II, 158), (3rd vers.) l. 54 (II, 162).

[5] 'The Feast of Peace', ll. 15 and 112 (III, 533, 536).

[6] It must be acknowledged that Beißner is right in this interpretation, despite the many Christian interpreters who would still like to identify the prince of the feast (in the final version) with Christ, on the basis of his role in the three preliminary poems (beginning 'O Peacemaker thou who beyond all hope ...'). And that is a conclusion not derived merely from this isolated text, but wholly supported by its context, the late odes and prose texts. The Christian truth, to which Hölderlin remains faithful from beginning to end, has long since poured out over the entire garden of the ancient world, like a liquid, making everything bloom, while the old container ran dry.

[7] Homer.

heart did embrace!/ And the flowers too, the bee on the flower/ Loving thy heart did embrace!'[8] Five years later, in 'Hyperion's Youth', the strains of the Pauline hymn of praise (1 Cor 13) are transposed into a classical-Idealistic cosmos-hymn far outdoing the chords Shaftesbury had sounded: 'She [Love] bears with her the painful sense of lackingness, and fills heaven with her abundance, . . . unsuspecting that the holy half-light coming towards her proceeds from herself alone. In her is nothing, and outside, everything . . . She does but hope and trust; does but sorrow, that still she is there to feel her nothingness, for rather were she part of the holiness that hazily appears before her. The abundance of the Divine is too boundless, that in her insufficiency she should comprehend it. Marvellous! from her own glory doth she start back. Let the Invisible become visible to her! appear before her clothed as Spring! smile at her from a human visage!'[9] Here Hölderlin means nothing but that same love which in the early, Christian-Pietistic 'Hymn to Love' (1790), 'everywhere in lovely glory' fills the world: 'Love doth bring down rocks in ruins,/ Conjures paradises up,/ Anew creating Earth and Heaven—/ Godly, as in the beginning',[10] and which, shortly afterwards in a new version (1792), is already enlisting as an image of expression the *hieros gamos*: 'See! how with the Earth doth pair/ Itself Heaven's holy delight,/ How, o'ershadowed by the storms/ The Mother's breast enraptured quakes.'[11] And yet in the meantime, as, indeed, the most convincing expression of the loving All-and-One, the Idea of identity has come to the fore, as Heraclitus' 'divine Ἕν διαφέρον ἑαμτῷ',[12] the One that within itself parts itself, and sets itself opposite itself, called by Hyperion the 'essence of beauty' and *fons et origo* of all philosophy.[13] This means discovery too of the new god's new name: 'Know ye his name? the name of him who is One and All? His name is beauty.'[14]

---

[8] ll. 28–51 (I, 126).
[9] III, 203, ll. 7–20.
[10] 2nd vers., ll. 16 and 37–40 (I, 112–113).
[11] 'Hymn to Love', ll. 29–32 (I, 167).
[12] Frag. 51 Diels = Plato, *Symposium*, 187a (Beißner, II, 427; III, 465).
[13] H 1/2, 19 (III, 81, 83).   [14] H 1/2, 3 (III, 52–53).

Nevertheless, only as διαφέρον is the divine One-and-All 'beautiful'; as Έν it is 'holy', and as the holy appearing 'in beauty' it is 'glorious'. For Hölderlin, glory is the unity of the holy and the beautiful. But because the classical difference between gods and men dissolves into the Idealistic difference between (absolute) spirit and (thereto opposed through itself) Nature, the glorious is equally holy and equally divine when it is Έν (spirit) as when it is διαφέρον (Nature), when 'a god' as when 'man'; indeed, as is essential to its innermost divinity, holiness and glory, in becoming Nature and Man it strips itself of itself, descends from plenitude into poverty, changes from self-sufficiency into love: and because with Hölderlin this *kenosis* of the One-and-All is *the* poetic theme, executed with the intensity of Christian prayer and the world-commitment of a Christian mission, the unheard-of takes place: the Christian depletion of God depletes itself, becoming God's cosmic-pantheistic depletion. In the process, however, it is left undecided whether the Greek-Idealistic categorical schematism is not all the time—and the more so the deeper the work grows—a language to express an elementary Christian experience of faith: the immanence and nearness, the glory, present in concealment (absence), through suffering of the divine love, as being the water-mark of the cosmos; or whether, in the end, the language does not overpower its object, the 'tragic as such' and its 'calculable law'[15] becoming the inner form of the Cross. What is, in 'Tears', that 'Heavenly Love, tender' which, on shores of 'nigh-distorted' Greek islands, 'for her idolatry doth penance': 'Thus must be overreached,/ Too-trusting yet overall must be love'?[16] When the other 'intransigent genius powers' are frigid with winter, what is the single one left to man: '. . . yet Love doth love'?[17] And when the Titans rage, the world-forces, God looks on smiling, so long as 'the bonds of love' be not spoiled.[18] What is that love which in the pouring of the rain and the split

[15] 'Notes on the *Antigone*', V, 265.
[16] 'Tears', l. 15 (II, 58); *cf.* 'The Poetic Calling', ll. 38f. (II, 47): 'The Spirit . . . the simple one/ Deniest, heartless'.
[17] 'Vulcan', l. 28 (II, 61).
[18] 'The Rhein', l. 97 (II, 145).

blood alike proclaims itself as the single, flowing, world-substance?

> Then should I sing 'With rain doth quench thy thirst
> The cloud, thou Mother-ground! but man with blood.
> Thus rests and cools itself that love which
> Findeth no equal above or below.'[19]

A glance at Hölderlin's use of the great words is instinctive, showing, however, less the demarcation of the semantic spheres than their mutual interpenetration.

'Glorious' is used extravagantly in the early and middle periods, but in the late period more sparingly, the words 'pure' and 'clear' (to make clear) coming to the fore instead. Above all, Nature is glorious, in so far as she reveals God: 'O, if a Father's daughter glorious Nature be, is not the daughter's heart his own? Her innermost being, isn't not he?'[20] The sun is glorious,[21] and the spring 'in all the splendour of youth',[22] the landscape of the Alps[23] (the 'hook of dreadful glory'),[24] the flames of Etna,[25] and, most of all, the 'genial powres of Nature',[26] among whom Hölderlin numbers aether (the sky), light and earth, often water too. The Teck is 'of royal glory', 'God's most glorious work',[27] and in the youthful poems heroes are addressed as men of glory[28]—the phrase is recognisably drawn from Klopstock—and later the 'goddess of harmony'[29] too is at once of 'unbounded majesty', 'stately', 'of divine beauty'; here and in the cycle of poems to the Ideals the formulations for sublimity swell like a flood. In the hymn to the Muse we read 'Worship what is fair and glorious!',[30] an anticipation of Hyperion's

[19] 'To Edward' (1st vers.), ll. 13–16 (II, 39).

[20] H 1/1, 3 (III, 12).

[21] 'At Morn', l. 14 (I, 302); 'Go down, fair Sun . . .', l. 6 (I, 314).

[22] FH III, 166.

[23] 'The Canton of Switzerland', l. 7 (I, 143).

[24] Ibid., l. 27 (I, 144).

[25] H 2/2, 10 (III, 151).

[26] 1E 1/4, l. 411 (IV, 18); 2E 1/3, l. 435 (IV, 107).

[27] L.27, l. 53 (I, 55, 56).

[28] 'Keppler', l. 19 (I, 81); 'Gustav Adolf', l. 54 (I, 86); Rousseau in 'To Quietude', l. 25 (I, 93).

[29] L1.12,26,50(I,130,131).   [30] L. 116(I,138).

'Religion is love of beauty'.[31] With the 'Genius of Courage',[32] greeted as 'Glorious one!', we turn our gaze to man, whose calling, as 'King of the finite realm', is 'wonderfully and gloriously to heal';[33] his body even is glorious,[34] but his spirit is 'devouring glory'.[35] While in the Hymn to Humanity this glorification is still primarily seen in Christian-eschatological terms—'E'en now in greater glory from our tombs/ The splendour of the finite realm goes forth'[36]—in 'Hyperion' this glory gains immediacy through events; after the 'glorious voyage to Chios' we read 'Thus did we receive glory from the powers of Earth and Heaven'.[37] The sunset flows about Diotima 'like a gloria, such as the saints have',[38] and in the poems too Diotima is the 'glorious one',[39] the 'too glorious one';[40] for her too Hyperion is 'the glorious one',[41] and the two share 'the endless faith with which we gave ourselves glory'.[42] The expression can explain the words from the ode to Princess Auguste of Homburg: 'But glory hath from thy name my song'.[43] The Greeks are glorious: 'We in our poverty are annihilated by such glory';[44] Homer is glorious,[45] and

[31] H 1/2, 19 (III, 79).   [32] L.3 (I, 176).

[33] L.67 (I, 159).

[34] 'Sömmering's "The Organ of the Soul" and the Public' (I, 227).

[35] H 1/1, 4 (III, 12).

[36] L1.45–46 (I, 147).

[37] H 1/1, 7 (III, 30).

[38] YH 5 (III, 218, l. 5); Melete has already said this in FH (III, 168).

[39] L.26 (I, 212); l. 18 (I, 216).

[40] L.59 (I, 221).

[41] H 2/1, 13 (III, 109).

[42] H 1/2, 18 (III, 75). There is an echo of this in Letter 123, to Neuffer: 'How could I have become as I now am ... if this, this one and only being, had not come before me and with a light as of spring brought youth, strength, good cheer and glory to a life which I had come to think worthless?' (VI, 213).

[43] L.25 (I, 312).

[44] FH III, 169; YH 3 (III, 208–209): 'Who can endure that? whom doth not hurl down the dreadful glory of the past?' H 1/1, 5 (III, 18). Today, Hellas is clothed 'like a beggar-woman, with the rags of thy old glory': H 2/1, 11 (III, 107). Athens and its areopagus are glorious: 'The Archipelago', l. 196 (II, 109).

[45] FH III, 168; Sophocles: 1E 1/1, l. 114 (IV, 7).

Achilles is a 'glorious son of the gods,'[46] 'But nor is there aught more glorious on earth' than the proud pairs of Greek friendship.[47] Thus the friend Alabanda too, the young Titan, is glorious,[48] and as he goes to his death Hyperion calls after him: 'Die! Thy heart hath sufficient glory'.[49] Again, Empedocles is called 'the glorious one',[50] and as a thinker he is 'the glorious pilot'.[51] And in his spirit and Hyperion's alike the most comprehensive experience of glory is compressed into the words: 'That only in suffering do we first feel the true freedom of the soul—that is glorious'.[52] The use, often too extravagant, of the word glory becomes in the later period more sparing, for the sake of the thing itself. It disappears inside the language, which is made so compressed, so burdened, pregnant and costly as to become in each and every part a reliquary of glory. In familiar speech the word 'bright', which always for Hölderlin also means the holy quintessence, suffices: Father Αἰξθήρ = 'Father bright!'[53]

Things and beings are '*holy*'[54] in so far as they point to the presence of the eternal Spirit and intimate his infinite worth. Such, again, is Nature as a whole,[55] light,[56] aether,[57] and the sun, 'whom I never name without joy and thanks';[58] the stars

---

[46] 'Achilles', l. 1 (I, 271).

[47] H 1/2, 15 (III, 63).

[48] H 1/1, 7 (III, 24).

[49] H 2/2, 5 (III, 140).

[50] 1E 1/1, l. 49 (IV, 4); 1E 2/5, l. 1827 (IV, 76); 2E 1/3, l. 374 (IV, 105).

[51] 1E 1/1, l. 90 (IV, 6); 1E 2/4, l. 1738 (IV, 72): 'and glorious are thy thoughts'.

[52] Letter 162 (VI, 278, ll. 33–34).

[53] 'Bread and Wine', ll. 65 and 69 (II, 92).

[54] On the tradition, see Isabella Papmehl-Rüttenauer: *Das Wort 'heilig' in der deutschen Dichtersprache* (Weimar, 1937); August E. Hohler: *Das Heilige in der Dichtung. Klopstock | Der junge Goethe* (Zürcher Beiträge zur deutschen Literatur- und Geistesgeschichte, ed. Emil Staiger, Vol. 10 (1954)).

[55] 'Vanini', l. 10 (I, 262); 'Her Recovery', l. 13 (I, 253; II, 23). With emphasis, in Letter 229: 'To look upon holy Nature with true eyes' (VI, 416, l. 38).

[56] 'The Voice of the People' (2nd vers.), ll. 43–44 (II, 52).

[57] *Ibid.*, l. 67.

[58] H 2/1, 1 (III, 93).

are 'holy in their freedom',[59] the earth is holy,[60] the plant-world,[61] a mountain-valley,[62] the vine,[63] the wine of Bacchus.[64] The joy of living can be called holy,[65] as can suffering sent by the gods,[66] 'life's holy aberration',[67] and, since love came to it, the heart;[68] to Hyperion the names of the seasons have also become holy,[69] but the friends too become 'ever holier'[70] to one another in their suffering. Diotima is a 'Holy Being',[71] the poem, as it lies in the poet's heart, seeking form,[72] is holy, and the Muse is holy.[73] Empedocles is the holy man,[74] and his end is holy.[75] Nemesis too is holy,[76] as is the heretic Vanini, who dies for 'holy Nature'.[77] The poet begs his mother not to lose faith in the holy within him.[78] And then back—the holy spring,[79] the holy green[80]—but also forward to the end of times: pressing

[59] 'Peace', l. 56 (II, 8).

[60] 'What I do own', l. 28 (I, 307), and often elsewhere.

[61] H 2/2, 3 (III, 126).

[62] H 2/2, 4 (III, 133).

[63] 'Man', l. 16 (I, 263); 'The Spirit of Time', l. 13 (I, 300).

[64] 'The Poetic Calling', ll. 3–4 (II, 46).

[65] 'Her Recovery', l. 9 (I, 253, II, 23).

[66] 'The Land of Home', l. 22 (II, 19); so Neuffer's dying bride Rosine is 'the suffering saint', Letter 87 (VI, 134), 'the saint', Letter 100 (VI, 171).

[67] 1E 1/4, l. 403 (IV, 18); the fatherland is 'holy in endurance': 'On Returning to his Homeland', ll. 11–12 (II, 29).

[68] 'The Applause of Men', ll. 1–2 (I, 250).

[69] H 2/1, 13 (III, 109).

[70] H 1/1, 7 (III, 29).

[71] 'An Apology', l. 1 (I, 244).

[72] 'To the Fates', ll. 7–8 (I, 241). The art of poetry is early called 'The holy Path' (I, 79).

[73] 'Peace', l. 41 (II, 7; the Greeks can quite generally be described as 'the holy ones' ('Tränen', l. 9 (II, 58)).

[74] 1E 1/9, l. 1039 (IV, 45); 1E 2/4, ll. 1808–1809 (IV, 75).

[75] 1E 2/4, l. 178a (IV, 74); said of the death of the towns that pine for death in 'The Voice of the People' (2nd vers., l.22 (II, 51)).

[76] 'To the Genius of Courage', l. 64 (I, 178).

[77] 'Vanini', ll. 4 and 10 (I, 262).

[78] Letter 170 (VI, 297, l.65).

[79] 'To Spring', l. 9 (I, 202).

[80] 'The Wanderer', l. 4 (I, 207).

closer, the holy host of god-like men in the blue heavens;[81] and the 'holy, the universal Love'.[82]

Under holiness comes *majesty*, since Klopstock a well-loved word, but now acquiring a new and special ring: there is 'the majesty of the undestined soul',[83] and Diotima's wide, inspired eye, 'enthroned with the majesty of a god',[84] and poetry, by which 'a veil is woven about the majesty of the Invisible';[85] and then there are the unusual and yet so characteristic combinations of words: 'sweet majesty',[86] 'serene majesty',[87] even 'light majesty'.[88] Other key words, each from a different sphere, point the way into the mystery in its totality: the bright and brightening, the silent, the pure, the devout, also the much-used words from spheres of magic and enchantment—love, poetry, reality itself—are among the most crucial expressions.

All is comprehended by the generously-used word of exaltation 'divine', which bears superficial resemblance to the Homeric usage;[89] this would mean that not only the sphere of the gods is divine, but also everything earthly and human, in so far as it rises above itself and into the light of the gods. However, the Homeric tradition (and therewith also that of Pindar and the tragedians) is here interpreted conceptually within the all-enclosing identity, Nature herself,[90] and in particular man, being in the innermost spiritual core divine: 'But man is a god, so soon as he is a man.'[91] 'The god that is in man' may not be 'denied'.[92] And yet this statement

---

[81] 'Germania', ll. 31–32 (II, 150).
[82] Letter 231 (VI, 419, l. 26).
[83] H 2/1, 22 (III, 122).
[84] FH III, 166.
[85] 'To the Genius of Bravery', ll. 31–32 (I, 117).
[86] 'A Hymn to the Genius of Youth', l. 16 (I, 168).
[87] 'Diotima', later vers., l. 74 (I, 222).
[88] H 1/2, 5 (III, 55).
[89] above, p. 51.
[90] The limiting of the *Hen kai Pan* by opposition to the concept of identity (in 'Judgment and Being', IV, 216) is irrelevant in this context; both concepts are alien to Greco-Christian analogy.
[91] H 1/2, 19 (III, 79).
[92] Letter 171 (VI, 300, ll. 31f.).

(impossible in Greek literature) can be replaced and clarified by the Platonic θεῖον—Not to lose faith 'in ourselves, in our θεῖον, or however you wish to call it'[93]—providing a key to statements such as: 'In the Divine believe/ Those alone who themselves are',[94] 'Ah! little know we ourselves,/ For within us a god holds sway';[95] 'You shall remain among men and be a man, but a godly man'.[96] The word acquires a new density where the subject is the higher mystery at work between those who love one another ('So from time to time the deity that binds you and me must also receive an offering'),[97] but only in the conception of the holy (communal) spirit, which we shall deal with last, is it revealed in its entirety. But if we seek an indication with which to conclude for the time being, there is still that elucidation (it comes in the letter to Schütz, the editor of Aeschylus) according to which Greek tragedy 'was never permitted to make men into gods or gods into men, and commit impure idolatry, but only to bring gods and men alike nearer to one another', thus 'at the end leaving behind on the one side worship of the heavenly ones, and on the other, as the possession of man, a purified mind'.[98]

Time and history in human experience are therefore by no means divine as such. In particular, the present is a dreadful and godless time, 'brimming with cold unspeaking dissension'; 'as the instinct for slavery increases, so with it does a coarse sense of daring, as cares increase, so does intoxication, and hunger grows with luxury'; 'there is nothing holy that is not desecrated, denigrated into a miserable expedient',[99] so much so, indeed, 'that now the dead walk above on the earth and the living, the godly men, are below'.[100] Only to one looking back, with longing, and

[93] Letter 163 (VI, 278, l. 20).
[94] 'The Applause of Men', ll. 7–8 (I, 250).
[95] 'The Lovers', ll. 3–4 (I, 249); cf. the last lines of 'The Blind Singer' (II, 55).
[96] Letter 87 (VI, 133, ll. 14–15).
[97] Letter 169 (VI, 293, ll. 8f.; cf. Letter 231 (VI, 420, ll. 70f.).
[98] Letter 203 (VI, 382, ll. 34–37).
[99] H 2/2, 11 (III, 156, 154).
[100] H 2/2, 4 (III, 130).

forward, with presentiment, can the divine, the holy and
glorious, be present; it can also break in upon such longing
with momentary fulfilment when, in its (child-like) naivety
or elegiac brokenness, a soul is capable of the act and the
mood which Hölderlin calls *intensity*, and which he values
ever higher until, in the 'Basis to Empedocles', it becomes, as
'the deepest intensity', the all-supporting category[101]—in
such a way, however, that 'through excess of intensity' there
comes about 'a rift', and it must needs pass through a
purifying night of division, thereupon 'returning, more stable,
to the tone with which it began'. Now if 'intensity' is
understood simply, and ignoring the late dialectic of the
'Basis', then it is that state of surrender to the wonder and
mystery of Being which contains the experience of being
touched by 'God'. 'Could I but restore to thee this silent feast,
this holy peace within, when can be heard even the softest of
sounds that cometh from the depths of the spirit, and the
softest touch from without, from the heavens, from the
branches and flowers—then is he, the Invisible, so near to
us!'.[102] And, in yet more urgent tone and already at the stage
of 'withdrawal from all living things': 'I heard a reproach
from the heart of the grove, and a cry from the depths of
Earth and Sea: where is thy love for *me*?'[103] Thus to be
touched and called upon conceals in itself—beyond the reach
of all thought—a promise without end, confronting one who
knows it with that absolute demand which can be discharged
only by payment of life itself. This demand is that, despite
the detachment required by sober daily life, by action, by,
above all, the attitude of speculative philosophy, that deeper
intensity binding the single heart to the heart of the All should
never be abandoned. 'Inspiration' is a state demanding critical
limitation such as before him Shaftesbury had said should be
accorded it. 'Where moderation has left you, there is the limit
to your inspiration'.[104] But intensity, even if in its unrestraint
it must learn measure through pain and self-denial, can never

[101] IV, 149–162, esp. 150.
[102] FH III, 175.
[103] FH III, 183.
[104] 'Reflection', IV, 233, ll. 16–17.

turn back, not even when, as in Empedocles' case, this means the sacrifice of life.

This raises the question of *prayer*, which in Bruno and Shaftesbury, but also in Herder and Jean Paul, has run dry and passed into enthusiasm, and which is so grievously lacking in German Idealism generally from Kant to Hegel, in Schiller, Goethe, and Humboldt: for how could the 'I' adopt an attitude of prayer towards its own intelligible inner being, or towards a divine nature whose awareness depends upon man, a view maintained by Hölderlin too, even in his late period?[105] Surely in the end (as in Novalis's fairy-tales of love) this Eros in prayer will eventually be revealed in the light of identity: '. . . as t'were I could feel him, the Spirit of the World; but, awakening, I think t'was my own fingers I had held'.[106] Of love, we read: 'Marvellous! from her own glory doth she start back . . . Her whole being strives to bring forth, in all intensity, the divinity that is so near her, and, as her very own, fully to know it. All unsuspecting is she that, in the moment of her embrace, it will disappear'.[107] And yet all this remains theory, paling before what is truly Hölderlin's attitude of prayer—and which refines, as it grows beyond the enthusiasm of the youthful hymns and 'Hyperion', into ever more boundless reverence and worship. As for the theory, it can be interpreted equally well in terms of Plotinus (the One eternally impalpable beyond the conscious spirit in its longing), of the Christian theology of God's eschatological perception by God, or of Fichte's religion of the intelligible 'I'; it does not really matter.

[105] Letter 231, to his brother (1801): 'All is infinite unity, but in this all there is that which is supremely unified and unifying, which is not, in itself, an I, and between us let this be God!' (VI, 419, ll. 41f.). The idea occurs in 'The Archipelago': 'Truly, as heroes need their wreaths, alone in the hearts of/ Feeling men do enjoy the sacred elements glory' (ll. 60–61), 'For in the feeling heart and heavenly ones do rest gladly' (l. 235, II, 104, 108), and, with the utmost clarity, in the hymn 'The Rhein': '. . . if gods in/ The heavens have any need/ Then 'tis the heroes and men and/ All mortal things. For because/ In bliss complete nought feel they alone,/ Must haply, if 'tis permitted/ To speak thus, of the gods' fate/ Partaking, feel another,/ In their name. Him they need . . .' (ll. 106–114 (II, 145)).

[106] H 1/1, 3 (III, 12).

[107] YH 1 (III, 203, ll. 17ff.).

But what Hölderlin experiences, what he risks his whole existence for, is the presence, indeed, the urgency of an infinite love in the mystery of the world's being. Instead of the preacher's office, he chooses the life of a poet, poor and futile in the eyes of the world, in order to have a profounder influence as a priest';[108] outwardly, and yet more so spiritually, the poet must make his way 'defencelessly through life',[109] step 'bare into life',[110] that he may 'in humility' preserve the 'inner purity'[111] he needs above all things,[112] if he is to pursue this 'most innocent of occupations',[113] 'unharming . . . like the peaceful swans',[114] in 'virginity of the spirit'.[115] To begin with, 'inspiration' is that youthful state through which the 'needy' landscape is transfigured, appearing now 'like a bride';[116] which becomes 'a grave of bliss'[117] for the lovers, for it is the 'omnipotence of undivided inspiration',[118] but which, according with Nature, also pales with the sun and with spring, fading away to leave behind the darkness of perplexity. 'In the Arm of the gods grew I';[119] that is already the past, and when such abundance has

---

[108] Cf. e.g. Letter 193 (VI, 361); Letter 204 (VI, 384, ll. 50f.); Walter Rehm, Orpheus (1949).

[109] 'The Poet's Courage' (1st and 2nd vers.), ll. 3–4 (II, 62, 64).

[110] 'Foolishness', ll. 3–4 (II, 66).

[111] Letter 173 (VI, 308, ll. 22 and 29).

[112] Letter 235: 'Forgive me, that there may be purity between us' (VI, 425, l. 23).

[113] Letter 173 (VI, 311, l. 122); Letter 130 (VI, 225, 1.41) also speaks of poetry as 'these happy, at the least innocent, occupations'; they lift the poet into 'the innocent life of Nature' (Letter 141, VI, 245, ll. 25f.), as, in 'guiltless moments' (Letter 174, VI, 316, l. 67), he gives himself up to the landscape: 'to have felt the beauty of the earth with so pure a heart . . . is as good as having been in church' (ll. 69f.). Especially in Hauptwil he feels the 'innocence of life here beneath the silvery Alps' (Letter 231, VI, 420, ll. 74f.), a feeling which is preserved in 'A Song sung under the Alps' (II, 44), with its opening 'Innocence holy . . .'.

[114] 'Elegie', l. 41 (II, 72).

[115] Letter 144 (VI, 249, l. 7). Compare the early, naive, expression of this 'virginity' in Letter 4 (VI, 7, ll. 28f.), also Letter 193 (VI, 362, ll. 55–65).

[116] H 1/1, 6 (III, 21).

[117] 'Diotima' (second vers.), ll. 113–114 (I, 219).

[118] H 1/1, 4 (III, 14).

[119] 'When I was a boy . . .', l. 32 (I, 267).

been lost it can only be awaited till the end of days;[120] meantime nothing is left to man but complete self-devotion to the departed being hovering, perhaps, about him, intangible as a ghost. It is here that the poet's great experience of aether, air and wind belongs. If heaven (light, aether) and earth and the air which joins them are the cosmic trinity— 'ye three in Unity',[121] the great— And joyful forms of this our world',[122] 'Life's great genii'[123]—so the wind's breath is like the spirital 'murmuring descent' of the longed-for heavenly father,[124] soothing the heart. In the final version of 'Hyperion', after many preliminary attempts, Hölderlin achieves this extraordinary intimation of Diotima: 'The motherly Air came to all, even into their hearts, lifting and drawing them to herself. And the people went out of their doors, and felt the spiritual Breath in wondrous wise, . . . and, loosening their garments in welcome, received it to their breasts'.[125] Here the 'holy air' is called 'sister of the Spirit', and the poet never tires of praising her touch,[126] of longing

---

[120] 'But now, 'tis Day! . . . From the Aether aloft . . . / Anew the Creator of all/ Doth feel itself, Inspiration' ('As on a holiday . . .', ll. 19f., II, 118). But such inspiration is also man's achievement, bringing the parusia nearer: 'O Heaven's rain! o Inspiration! Thou wilt restore to us the spring of the peoples' (H 1/1, 7 (III, 32)).

[121] 'The Wanderer', l. 99 (II, 83).

[122] 3E 1/3, ll. 410–411 (IV, 137).

[123] 2E 1/3, l. 402 (IV, 106).

[124] 'To the Aether', l. 50 (I, 205).

[125] H 1/2, 2 (III, 50).

[126] 'When for the first time within/ Felt I godly stirrings, round me/ Whispering thy Spirit was', the poet says to 'Diotima' (fragments of an earlier version, ll. 37f., I, 213) (cf. the later version, ll. 22f., I, 220). Similarly in 'What I do own', ll. 13f. (I, 306), 'Palinode', l. 2 ('Why now, o Breezes, breathe ye on me as then?' (I, 308)), 'Encouragement' (1st vers.), ll. 10f. ('And Nature's breath doth, quietly forming, wash/ About us, as about bare fields,/ Cheer to all bringing, in soulfulness . . .', II, 33), 'The Blind Singer', ll. 7–8 (II, 54), 'Elegy', l. 100 (II, 74), 'Stuttgart', l. 31 (II, 87), 'Bread and Wine', l. 13 (II, 90), 'The Fettered Stream', ll. 5–6 ('The messengers of love that the Father sends,/ Canst know them not, the Zephyrs, their breath of life?' (II, 67), 'The Rhein', l. 190 (II, 148), 'Patmos', l. 129 (of the pentecostal spirit: 'the locks catching hold of, presently' (II, 169), and cf. 'Heimkunft', l. 35: 'The Spirit cometh in presence' (II, 97).

for the return of that pentecostal moment as 'the Soul of the world, the holy air everywhere surrounded him with her embrace'.[127] Thus Empedocles strives to reach the summit of Etna, where the gods are present: 'A! then will come to us the all-moving/ Spirit, the Aether with his tender touch'.[128] As the hour of death approaches, 'Now cometh, bearing tidings of my night,/ The evening Wind, true messenger of love. The time is nigh!'.[129]

Yet the touch of divine breath is merely a particularly convincing and joyful experience which confirms all the other experiences of the world, but is not separate from them. Light, too, 'softly rouses' (that is, touches),[130] 'the spirit/ Of the Sun touches',[131] and 'dark Earth's flowers' breathe 'on us with love';[132] from evening and morning, from trees and mountains, from autumn[133] no less than from spring comes the breath, and even the night, in its 'sad and majestic ascent' (in 'Brot und Wein'), brings 'a breath', its incomprehensibility for all wise men being a message of love.[134] The further the poet goes and bares his heart, the more the dark forces in their intangibility become instruments and vessels, until finally storm and lightening become the very heart of revelation,[135] 'the storm not just in its highest manifestation, but . . . as

---

[127] H 2/1, 15 (III, 112).

[128] 1E 2/3, l. 1207 (IV, 53). Empedocles is returning into the all, but in the whispering spirit he will draw near to those he is leaving behind: 'Then haply in the song will breathe my note,/ As, veiled in the fair world's choir of love,/ Once more your friend's word lovingly ye hear' (1E 2/4, ll. 1799–1800 (IV, 74)). We read of the godly powers ('As on a holiday . . .', ll. 36–37, II, 119) that '. . . in song doth their spirit breathe'.

[129] 1E 2/6, ll. 1912–1914 (IV, 80). Cf. 'The Fragment of Hyperion': 'My whole being falls silent, listening, when the soft and mysterious breath of evening blows upon me' (III, 184). In contrast, there is 'not a whisper of wind in the branches' on the occasion of the 'wake of my youth' (Waltershäusen paralipomenon, III, 577, ll. 10–11).

[130] 'The Journey', l. 15 (II, 138).

[131] 'For when from the grape a juice . . .', ll. 9–10 (II, 207).

[132] 'Go down, fair Sun . . .', ll. 13–14 (I, 314).

[133] [Autumn] 'lies closer to my hear than any other period in Nature's life' (Letter 145 (VI, 251, ll. 9–10)).

[134] 'Bread and Wine', ll. 18, 13 (II, 90).

[135] In an early form in 'Diotima' (I, 210), and wherever Hölderlin depicts the storm as a purification enabling Nature's brighter rays to follow.

might and form'.[136] The spirit in 'storms, those in the sky, and others,/ That in the depths of time were longer prepared,/ With meaning more pregnant . . .'.[137] But it behoves the poet 'To stand, bare-headed, beneath/ God's storms, and in his grasp the rays, ay of the Father, His own/ To clasp, and veiled, and of milder might,/ In Song to mortal men, that we do love, the heav-/ enly gift to give'.[138] All this finding highest expression in a single mythological image:

> Thus on Semele's house, so poets say, as
> She wished the visible God to see, did his lightening
>   fall
> And divinely-struck, she brought forth
> The fruit of the Storm, him, Bacchus the holy.[139]

In the lightning of the late poetry the entire cosmic theophany, which in the early and middle period has its centre in the whispering aethereal spirit, becomes compressed into the Platonic-apocalyptic moment of discharge (ἐξαίφνης). It is a road leading from the immediacy of an inspiration with its pulse in Nature's rhythm (with which it must therefore always die and be reborn),[140] passing through the endurance of divine distance 'when 'tis over, and the Day extinguished',[141] even to the experience of God in this selfsame darkness, as lightning. Certainly at first this road is made possible by Kant and Fichte, by the soaring flight (Hyper-ion!) over existence in servant form, Nature, by an 'I' that knows itself to be eternal, and even uncreated: 'I can feel in myself a life created by no god, begotten by no mortal. I believe 'tis through ourselves that we are, and only in the freedom of pleasure are we joined so intensely with the All';[142] soaring in flight as though 'to leave a city of plague

[136] Letter 240 (VI, 433, ll. 38–39); cf. also 'Homecoming', ll. 15f. (II, 96).

[137] 'As on a holiday . . .', ll. 39–41 (II, 119).

[138] Ibid., variants, II, 669.

[139] Ibid., ll. 50–54 (II, 119).

[140] The returning spring evokes these words: 'Mourn ye not, when your heart's melody doth fall silent! ere long a hand will there be to tune it' (H 1/2, 2 (III, 51)).

[141] 'Germania', l. 20 (II, 149).

[142] H 2/2, 5 (III, 141).

and flee to the mountains, where there is purer air',[143] and looking out from 'the proud heights ... the better to know ... the lovely and glorious things we can see from up on high'.[144] But eventually this philosophical flight must deny the intensity which for Hölderlin was primary, and kill prayer; and so, even before hearing Fichte, he has soon left Kant, and Schiller, still the all too faithful disciple, behind again. For Plato too can teach him that the 'I', being elevated above Nature, is eternal'[145] and his great love for Susette Gontard serves as proof positive that the descent of the spirit into the 'servant-form' of defenceless need is the ultimate truth and glory of all being. 'When thou art most hapless, dost thou perceive it [thy glory]'.[146] And even when love has long since turned to renunciation[147] this is still the one place where he can be struck by 'lightning', wounded by Apollo.[148] Even if the unsolved philosophical conflict (Idealism against ancient philosophy) reaches to the very centre of the poetic tragedy and is a contributing cause of it,[149] the poet cannot abandon either of the two poles, because in secret it always has been and always will be the third, Christian position that determines the way he feels and lives, and can alone enable his work to be what it is: prayer.

The young Hölderlin prays.[150] When a Spinozism (seen through Jacobi's eyes, and therefore taken to be atheistic) 'of reason, of the *cold* reason that has been deserted by the heart' seems unavoidable, he finds refuge with Christ, who 'shows through miracles that he is what he says he is, that he is God. He teaches us existence of the deity and love and wisdom and omnipotence of the deity so plainly. And he must know that God is, and what God is, for he is in closest union with the

[143] Letter 170 (VI, 297, ll. 55–56).
[144] Letter 83 (VI, 124, ll. 22f.).
[145] Upon whom he is now planning to write a commentary (Letter 88, VI, 137, ll. 89–99).
[146] YH I (III, 204, l. 5).
[147] The Diotima letters 182, 198 (VI, 336, 370).
[148] Letter 240 (VI, 432, l. 10).
[149] *Cf.* the next two chapters.
[150] Letter 15 (VI, 24, ll. 110–112).

deity'.[151] Christ wished to lead us 'to the feeling of the living
deity in which we live and are, to the feeling truest to Christ,
that we and the Father are one';[152] Christian theologians and
ritualists have committed an infamous betrayal of his
intention, turning 'him, the Living, into an empty idol',[153]
'gone to waste all heavenly powers, used up the kindly
ones'[154]—thus, in 'Empedocles', the tones of a Last Judgement
pour down wrath upon the 'god-forsaken'[155] 'wretches'[156]
who bind men, so that they know nothing of divine
presence,[157] and who deal in 'holy things as though in
trade'.[158] Only by leaving all these shameless ones behind
and entering into the pre-Christian divine intimacy can
Christianity too in its original meaning be saved for the
eschatological 'Feast of Peace'.

The poet assumes this holy office. 'Such are the cares that
whether he will or not, in his soul doth/ Bear a Singer, and
oft must, but unheeding the rest.'[159] His words are praise in
the Pindaric sense,[160] celebration, calling to the feast,[161] but
above all they are 'thanks', for through him man is to learn
to give thanks for everything,[162] 'to give heartfelt thanks for
that which is there'.[163] To do this, the poet's heart must rise
to that utmost chievement and, even while being spiritual,
also be worldly;[164] like the 'Blind Singer', he must follow
through darkness the 'voice of the Thunderer/ At noon-

[151] Letter 41 (VI, 64, ll. 43–47).
[152] Letter 151 (VI, 261, ll. 14–16).
[153] Letter 173 (VI, 309, l. 65).
[154] 'The Poetic Calling', ll. 46–47 (II, 47).
[155] 1E 2/4, l. 1319 (IV, 57) and l. 1364 (IV, 59).
[156] Ibid., l. 1295 (IV, 56).
[157] 2E 1/1, ll. 13–14 (IV, 91).
[158] 1E 1/5, l. 535 (IV, 23).
[159] 'Homecoming', ll. 107–108 (II, 99).
[160] For his early estimation of Pindar: 'A History of the Fine Arts . . .' (IV, 203, ll. 1f.).
[161] These two words passim. See Heinrich Knittermeyer, Fest und Feier: Ein Beitrag zum Wortgebrauch Hölderlins, HJb, 1950, 47–71.
[162] 'The Course of Life' (2nd vers.), l. 14 II, 22).
[163] Letter 228 (VI, 414, ll. 34–35); extensive discussion in Paul Böckmann, Hölderlin und seine Götter (1935), of which see index.
[164] 'The only One' (1st vers.), ll. 104–105 (II, 156).

day',[165] 'so sure on his wand'ring path'.[166] If it is the poet's office both evermore to sing of 'the Highest' to whom he is devoted and also, inspired by the 'unlooked-for Genius', prophetically to proclaim the 'days of destiny' of history, he cannot perform this second office unless he stands, protected only by his innocence, unarmed and guileless, 'alone before God', 'till that God's lack helpeth'.[167] In such an exposure of the heart, facing death itself with unflinching readiness, even in night and absence there is 'worship', 'prayer', 'devotion',[168] and the poet is prepared for the hope he invokes to 'affright the heart'[169] with its unfamiliar form. In this posture he is an intercessor who through his word, his silence (where holy names are lacking),[170] through his very being calls down blessings upon the world: 'Ye bless so kindly over our mortal heads,/ Ye Powers of heaven! that which to each is his,/ O do but bless mine own . . .';[171] 'bless for me rather then/ My mortal work . . .'.[172] In 'Palinodie' the plea that the gods may spare him is taken back.[173]

True, this prayer may sometimes be threatened by the Fichtean 'I'-identity and in theory demoted to a preliminary stage—when we read that the oriental god hurls men 'to the ground with his might and brilliance, and even ere man has learned to walk must he kneel, ere he has learned to speak must he pray; ere his heart knoweth equilibrium must he bow down'[174]—but Péguy too will contrast the prayer of the free, upright-standing Christian before God with oriental prostrations.[175] And through love Hyperion learns again

---

[165] 'The Blind Singer', ll. 25–26 (II, 55).

[166] *Ibid.*, l. 36 (II, 55).

[167] 'The Poetic Calling' (II, 46–48).

[168] The Frankfurt 'Empedocles' plan (IV, 146, l. 2, l. 5, 147, l. 6).

[169] 'To Hope', ll. 17–20 (II, 59).

[170] 'Homecoming', l. 101 (II, 99).

[171] 'What I do own', ll. 49–51 (I, 307).

[172] 'At Morn', ll. 18–19 (I, 302); *cf* the plea for a blessing in 'The Return to his Homeland', l. 23 (II, 29), and the blessing brought by the inclining aether in 'Go down, fair Sun . . .' (l. 16, I, 314).

[173] 'Palinode' (I, 308).

[174] H 1/2, 19 (III, 82).

[175] 'The Mystery of the Holy Innocents' (ed. Pléiade, 354–358).

humility and devotion; Hölderlin once more demands that man 'in all his arts and activity bow down, humble and devout, before the Spirit of Nature whom he carries within him, whom he has around him, and who gives him material and powers'.[176] There is not one among Hölderlin's poems which could be described as prayer-less, that is, in which his faith does not say in advance[177] an all-embracing 'yes' to reality: 'Let whate'er there befall always a blessing be,/ Be it turned into joy!'[178] The rush and tumult of human life, the desire of the human mind for progress, always remains no more than 'service to Nature', and returns, borne by her embrace, back 'into the Grave of Nature', 'and ultimately all is good'.[179] That is also Hyperion's final thought. Fichte's eternal asymptotic progress never becomes as strong as the Greek 'circulation' that, here with Christian meaning, is the hope that the spirit may return, and that God may be 'all in all'. Thus even Menon too, at the end of his lament for Diotima, can give glad consent to the death that could scarcely be overcome: 'Now would I too, ye heavenly ones, give thanks, and at last is/ Lightened my breast, and once more praying the Singer doth breathe.'[180]

With Hölderlin, nothing is rhetorical dressing-up or tradition appropriated without existential content (unlike, for example, Schiller's constant talk of gods). It is homage that is being proclaimed 'in poesy of prayer',[181] homage which he, like Empedocles, is prepared to reinforce with the sacrifice of his life. It is by virtue of this very unity of word and death that, towards the end, the figure of Christ makes its powerful resurrection. His grandmother's birthday poem, filled with piety towards Christ ('His breast in its love all the World's suff'ring did bear./ E'en with Death did he friendship tie, in

---

[176] Letter 179 (VI, 329, l. 128f.).

[177] 'Faith' is a fundamental word, not just in the letters to his mother (Letters 173, 175), in which he deliberately uses Christian language, but in general; thus in the letters to his brother (Letter 231), his relations (Letter 223), and Sinclair (Letter 171).

[178] 'The Poet's Courage' (1st vers., ll. 5–6 (II, 62)).

[179] Letter 179 (VI, 328, ll. 83–84).

[180] 'Menon's Laments for Diotima', 9, ll. 109–110 (II, 78).

[181] 3E 1/3, l. 417 (IV, 137).

the name of the others/ Vanquishing pains and toil did to his Father return')[182] threw the poet into such turmoil, making him feel so acutely how far and near his youth was, that later he 'could find no sleep'.[183] At the same time he is working on 'Empedocles', whose situation becomes closer and closer to that of Christ, a probable reason why the drama is left uncompleted. Christ joins the line of cosmic deities as the last theophany, being the 'quiet genius' who leaves behind humble gifts, 'bread and wine', because 'greater' gifts 'became too great',[184] yet also 'fulfilling' and concluding the 'heavenly feast', being 'the most loving' envoy that the Father had, so burning that men will be capable only of misuse and each 'unto himself sufficed, o'erweening Heaven forgot . . .', but even thus, by his death, bringing apocalyptic 'fulfilment of the times'.[185] That the poet then, in the final version, restores Christ to the series of earlier theophanies,[186] that in the very song, 'The One and Only', written to the glory of Christ he declares himself hindered, when to 'thee I would liken/ Those men of the world . . .' (Heracles and Dionysus), by a kind of shame, yet still, and despite the outburst of prayer 'My Master and Lord! O thou, my Teacher!',[187] calls him their brother,[188] that he once again, in a variant of the Johannine hymn 'Patmos', describes him as a 'demi-god',[189] that he can speak of a 'clover-leaf' (of the three demi-gods),[190] all this is a sign of the deadly earnest in which the poet conceives the mission he has undertaken, to sacrifice nothing of the cosmic

[182] 'To my revered Grandmother', ll. 16–18 (I, 272). The celebration was on 30 December, 1798. It had been at the beginning of the same year that Christ was mentioned in a letter (151, VI, 261, l. 15) for the first time since the beginning of 1791 (Letter 41).

[183] Letter 172 (VI, 306, ll. 151f.).

[184] 'Bread and Wine', 8, ll. 129–134 (II, 94); cf. 6, ll. 107–108; 9, ll. 155–156. The Christian title replaces the original 'The Wine-god' with its reference to Bacchus.

[185] 'The Feast of Peace' (1st draft), ll. 63–71 (II, 132).

[186] For a discussion of the newly-discovered final version, and bibliography, see HJb, 1955/6.

[187] 'The only One' (1st vers.), ll. 36f. (II, 154–155).

[188] Ibid., ll. 48f.

[189] 'Patmos' (preliminary stage of a later version), l. 146 (II, 177).

[190] 'The only One' (3rd vers.), l. 76 (II, 163).

theophany for the sake of the Christ-revelation. And when but 'Since converse we do have/ And can from one another hear . . .',[191] since the peoples can show each other the divinity each has, and at the 'evening of time' the sum of history must be assembled, to form 'One Speech',[192] indeed, one song,[193] one spirit?[194]

2. POOR LOVE

Hölderlin's Christology will not be found where those who squeeze the text look for it; perceivable only as a water-mark, it is dissolved throughout the existential statement as a whole, and can be most powerfully felt when directly contradicted by the framework inside which it is stretched. But the very frame-work itself holds contradictions: the absolute spirit is without consciousness, and so to be themselves the 'blessed gods' need 'destiny', the suffering heart of men: only if the One-and-All be thus drawn asunder ('Εν καὶ πᾶν as 'Εν διαφέρον ἑαυτῷ) can god be god and man be man. That, beyond intellect and reason, is both the central concept of philosophy[1] and the essence of beauty: Homer's 'analogy' (God-world) is interpreted in terms of Heraclitean and Parmenidean 'identity', and, equally, vice-versa; here, then, we have Hölderlin not just leaving Kant and Schiller behind and arriving at an objective idealism similar to Schelling's, but referring this idealism back to the Greek sphere as a whole. For even the spirit, however 'eternal' it may be—

---

[191] 'The Feast of Peace' (3rd draft), ll. 50–51 (II, 137).

[192] *Ibid.* (final vers.), l. 84 (III, 535).

[193] *Ibid.*, l. 93 (III, 536).

[194] This 'sublime Spirit' (l. 77), with the active participation of mankind (ll. 85–86), brings about and is—in a Christian rather than Hegelian sense—the eschatological revelation of God (and, in him, of all the gods), and as such is the 'Prince of the Feast' (ll. 15 and 113). Certainly he is 'blessed Peace' (III, 224, l. 27), but peace as such is not the same as the spirit it is created by; the late Hölderlin does not glorify abstractions. The ultimate object of 'our homage name we not'; it is at once the brightness that bursts in from above (the concealed master stepping out of his work-shop) and, rounding off its sum, the inner history of the world.

[1] H 1/2, 19 (III, 83).

indeed, as the individual spirit, eternal in the Platonic and Leibnizian sense[2]—is one element in the whole inasmuch as it has to acknowledge the poverty of its descent into love; both in and free from poverty it is tragic,[3] and as well in this very descent into 'servant form' as in its ascent into divine form it is 'glorious'. But this means nothing other than a transformation of Christology into (classical-Idealistic) ontology, or in theological terms: an equation of the economic with the absolute doctine of the Trinity.

By virtue of this latent Christological element the kenotic element, the humility in all worldly love and form receives a divine radiance, but at the price that the shadow of transitoriness and melancholy falls upon the godly. If man can bloom divinely, so too the godly in human form can 'wither'; this nexus is indissoluble. 'Nothing can . . . in real life appear as it originally is . . . but only in its weakness, so that in true reality the light of life and appearance constitute the weakness of every whole.'[4] For the poet and his infinitely vulnerable soul this means: 'Purity can only express itself in impurity, and if you try to depict a nobility free of all baseness it will look utterly unnatural and foolish, and that is because nobility itself, when it comes to be expressed, carries the colour of the destiny under which it originated, and because beauty, when it takes shape in reality, necessarily receives, from the circumstances under which it comes forth, a form that is not natural to it. . . .'[5] Thus beauty, as transcendental category of being, emphatically becomes the synthesis of the beautiful and unbeautiful (within the world).[6] Now, according to the perspective, and with it the modality,

---

[2] H 2/2, 12 (III, 159, l. 14).

[3] Such thinking is characteristic of the entire period, as Walter Rehm has shown, in 'The Silence and the sorrow of the Gods' (1949).

[4] 'The Significance of the Tragedies' (IV, 274).

[5] Letter 167 (VI, 290, 11.75f.). *Cf.* Letter 183 (VI, 340, l. 67) on 'delicate forbearance from the accidental', also the sentence from Letter 185: '. . . thus, in poetry, truth and harmony emerge from falsehood, error and suffering all the more beautiful and delightful' (VI, 344, ll. 25f.).

[6] Thus there is no season nor time of life which is 'altogether beautiful' the truth is 'that beauty consists in all the times of life together, as they follow one another, rather than in any particular one' (Letter 188 (VI, 351, ll. 29–31)).

chosen—tragic inolvement of the eternal in the transitory world, or heroic, ideal elevation of the transitory into eternity—within the all-comprehensive identity, there arises that 'alternation of tones'[7] which for Hölderlin is so decisively important; and the historical significance of which extends far beyond Hölderlin's own scale, for soon this same structure of identity will be met by the cold breath of atheism.[8] Nevertheless, all attempts to transpose Hölderlin forward and into *that* tone are unjust and absurd.[9] The focal point is 'the eternal heart': heart conceived as middle, between the loving man and suffering god:

> Deep-shaken, with a god doth suffer too the Eternal
> heart, but still it remaineth firm.[10]

Whether it be described as divine (heavenly), as human (earthly), as half-godly (Titanic) or as divinely-human, the place of the heart, mediator of heaven and earth, is all-important. The heart is the source of the truth that 'the divine, when it goes forth, can never be without a certain sorrow and humility',[11] and that 'the greatest joy' speaks not in joy, but 'at the last . . . in sorrow'.[12] Hölderlin's interpretation of this middle is emphatically in terms of the classical Eros (albeit in the light of Fichte): love unites the will to infinity and the

---

[7] 'On the various methods of Poetry' (IV, 228–232), 'The Alternation of the Tones' (IV, 238–240), 'On the Procedure of the poetic Spirit' (IV, 241–265), 'On the differences of the poetic genres' (IV, 266–273). See Meta Corssen, 'Der Wechsel der Töne in Hölderlins Lyrik', HJb, 1951, 19–49.

[8] Thus already in Jean Paul's 'The Alternation of the Tones', on which see Walter Rehm, *Experimentum suae medietatis: Eine Studie zur dichterischen Gestaltung des Unglaubens bei Jean Paul und Dostojewski*, Jb. des Freien Deutschen Hochstifts, 1940, 237–336.

[9] In particular by Beda Allemann, *Hölderlin und Heidegger* (1954). This interpretation needs intolerable force if it is to fit Hölderlin but proves itself to be correct as an interpretation of the subsequent development in historical logic.

[10] 'As on a holiday . . ' (Hellingrath, IV, 153; Beißner, II, 676). On the variant, see Herm. Pongs, 'Das ewige Herz in Hölderlins Dichtung', in *Worte und Werte, Markwardt-Festschrift* (19610, 292–314; and Ulrich Häussermann, 'Herz', HJb, 1958–60, 190–205.

[11] Letter 169 (VI, 294, 11.25–26).

[12] 'Sophocles' (I, 305).

desire for limitation, 'for the father is Abundance, yet doth she not deny her mother, Poverty'.[13] Only, the loving heart must bear an infinitely greater burden than in Plato's day, for it is a sacrifice, consecrated in the middle of mutual hate:

> Ay! I knew it ere this. Hatred hath taken root,
>   All hath sundered, and long parted the gods and
>   men.
>   Now, with blood to appease them,
>   Now must perish the lovers' heart.[14]

With Hölderlin's progress from 'Hyperion' to 'Empedocles' and then to the last songs, this insight matures.

'Hyperion' comes about in stages. In the 'Waltershausen version' (published through the 'Thalia' fragment), heavily influenced by Schiller, Hölderlin describes a path from natural 'simplicity' to spiritual 'culture'[15] as necessary, but all the more dangerous,[16] an 'excentric course'[17] without which, however, there could be no centre. Thus an absolute love is demanded,[18] while at the same time the self-sufficiency of the beloved glory is feared.[19] The fragment will, then, have achieved its ultimate goal when its hero is content to leave the beloved object of beauty as it is; when the lover is so

---

[13] MH (prose outline), III, 194, ll. 13–15.

[14] 'The Parting' (1st vers.), ll. 13–16 (II, 24).

[15] FH III, 163, 180.

[16] FH III, 165.

[17] FH III, 163. The concept remains central. There is an underlying element of doubt (YH 4, III, 211, l. 1), but: 'we must all travel an excentric path, and no other way is possible, from youth to fulfilment' (Hyperion (preliminary stage [henceforth pH]), III, 236, ll. 13f.). In the 'Oedipus' the rhythm develops the velocity of 'excentric rapidity', tearing with it, in the end, 'into the eccentric sphere of the dead' (V, 196–197). See W. Schadewaldt, 'Das Bild der exzentrischen Bahn bei Hölderlin', HJb, 1952, 3f.; and for a comprehensive examination in terms of the history of ideas, cf. Eudo C. Mason, 'Eczentrische Bahnen: Studien zum Dichterbewußtsein der Neuzeit' (1963).

[18] 'For me, that which is not All, and eternally All, is nothing' (FH III, 164, l. 8).

[19] 'This desperate sentiment—that the glorious object of my love was so glorious that it had no need of me' (FH III, 170). 'Why had I to demand that the glorious being should be mine, when it had no need of me?' (III, 577, ll. 27–28).

purified as to be absolutely free from self. Yet at the same time 'unfathomable Nature' is to appear (idealistically) as the 'veiled beloved';[20] and forthwith, under Fichte's influence, this now unfolds.

The author of the 'metrical version' knows of the elevation of the spirit above Nature, but in the very first sentence speaks of the guilt of one who has become tyrannical against Nature; a guilt that the sage (the old Hyperion who narrates his youth) is to help overcome. This he does by interpreting Fichte in the light of Plato, and the contradiction in Eros (the will to unlimitedness, the will to limitation) as 'beauty', and this in turn as 'appearance of the holy'.[21]

In 'Hyperion's Youth', with its highly compressed style, he is feeling his way beyond Plato and Fichte and into a third country. Only in the pain of poverty is the 'nobility' of the 'I' revealed; starting back before its own glory, it contemplates itself 'in the land of the senses . . . as in a mirror'; but when 'to thy lonely thought the forms of Nature would sisterly companionship afford, do thou rejoice, and love, but ne'er thyself forget'.[22] Such love must remain longing, for were the ideal attained, consciousness would end and 'the Divine would . . . be nothing'.[23] Thus man's glory is to endure the long wait[24] of 'unending progress',[25] eternally dissatisfied, hoping and striving, between self-sufficient poles, Nature and idea. When the hero encounters the 'superhuman' Diotima, round whom flows 'the gloria of the saints', and who venerates the 'Panagia' (Mary),[26] the tragic element comes to appear almost psychological: Hyperion drags his beloved down, we read of 'murder',[27] and the lover, torn by

[20] YH III, 184.
[21] MH III, 191–195.
[22] YH 1(III, 203–205).
[23] Ibid., 203, ll. 23–26.
[24] Ibid., 206.
[25] YH 4 (III, 214, l. 32).
[26] YH 5 (III, 218); veneration of Mary already occurs in MH l. 207f. (III, 197); the Christian and biblical echoes, which in the penultimate version are still strong, are in the final version eliminated.
[27] YH 6 (III, 230, 1.29). Cf. pH III, 249: 'Men killed, so the fable tells us, the living deity . . . The fable is true.'

conflicting emotions, 'inwardly rages against the heavenly creature',[28] having 'cursed . . . her most divine possession, that peace, that heavenly sufficiency';[29] and the end of the fragment moves towards the same solution, to 'leave be'. But the predominance of the idealistic philosophy of the spirit in this fragment, written before Hölderlin met Susette, really leaves no room for love: 'abundance' is sufficiency, and 'poverty' self-preoccupation; the one is beyond love, the other falls short.

In the prologue to the 'penultimate version', the whole question reverts to a presocratic context; 'Being' is the 'blissful unity' which has been lost and can 'only' be recovered through action 'in infinite approximation', but 'nonetheless' is always already present, in the sovereign form of 'beauty'.[30]

In the final version, all the metaphysical rocks and contradictions are smoothed, in order to express the marvellous paradoxes of love. That famous key sentence is truly at the centre: 'The Heart's wave, that foameth upward and becometh Spirit, ne'er would be so fair, did not the Rock of destiny stand, dumb and old, in its path.'[31] Radiant in the background, there is the 'consuming glory of the Spirit' that must conceal itself in Nature,[32] yet still retaining 'that monstrous striving to be All';[33] a spirit that burns up all resistance ('naught remaineth but ashes'),[34] returning as fire 'from straitened captivity . . . to the halls of the Sun, in triumph'.[35] But now the spirit has another, contrasting, image. She, Diotima, is, in the naturally spiritual simplicity of beautiful beings, an 'ideal', and becomes a 'Muse',[36] sending her lover into the world of events and political action,[37] which then being war, she turns pale and falls silent;

[28] Ibid., 232, ll. 33–34.
[29] Ibid., 233, ll. 33–34.
[30] pH III, 236–237.
[31] H I/I, 8 (III, 41).
[32] H I/I, 4 (III, 12).
[33] H I/I, 5 (III, 18).
[34] H I/I, 8 (III, 41).
[35] H I/2, 2 (III, 52).
[36] H 2/2, 4 (III, 130).
[37] H I/2, 19 (III, 87f.).

Hyperion, following the realistic logic of action, tears her away and on to a path among things which turn her to a 'sorrowing divine image',[38] and she withers, is consumed; he implores her to leave him, for he 'is no longer aught',[39] has failed the ideal as which he had always wanted to leave her: 'Nay, nay, need shalt thou never know! Thou shalt not behold in thyself the poverty of love.'[40] But when he wishes to go and see her again, she passes from him into death. Thus the conclusion has the form of a contradiction in the nature of being, in that, though needing the suffering poverty of love to feel itself, in death it must yet find its way back to the 'spirit'; a contradiction that glorifies itself within the 'injured heart'[41] whose only 'solace' can be 'among gods'.[42] This experience of the glory of love lives on in spiritualised form, and that is the elegiac mode, which also characterises in its entirety the rebirth of the ancient world in the German present. 'Beauty fleeth out of the Life of men and up into the Spirit; what Nature was doth become Ideal, and if below the tree hath decayed and been worn down, yet hath he put forth on high fresh branches, verdant in the shining sun. . . .'[43] The revival in German Idealism of the ancient world must always be this biologically impossible phenomenon: the green crest of a decayed root. About this contradiction Hölderlin, for whom elegiac feeling can never become the last word, casts the great mantle of universal Nature: 'Men fall from thee like rotten fruit, o let them perish, for thus do they return to thy roots, and I, o Tree of Life, that I once more with thee grow green, about thy topmost branches there to breathe. . . .' [44] Death—not only of bodies, but also of hearts—is Nature's dung; 'palingenesis' becomes the reconciling idea: 'The veins in the heart do part and return and All is one eternal glowing Life.'[45] The idea that, in this merging-back into the universal

[38] H 2/1, 4 (III, 98).
[39] H 2/1, 21 (III, 119).
[40] H 1/2, 16 (III, 65).
[41] H 2/2, 4 (III, 131).
[42] *Ibid.*, III, 129.
[43] H 1/2, 15 (III, 63).
[44] H 2/2, 12 (III, 159).
[45] *Ibid., III, 160.*

heart, earthly sublimity might confer a right to personal immortality[46] is only a fleeting thought, designed to keep faith with, express the everlastingness in, love; the comprehensive conception is Nature's eternal return, the image of the tree being a clear reminder of Herder.[47]

In the course of the drafts to 'The Death of Empedocles', the author tunnels his way deeper and deeper into the cul-de-sac of the identity of the contradiction, and here it is from Christology that the interpretation of the world and of man draws its innermost core; the profound philosophical interpretation appended by the poet ('The basis to "Empedocles"') is always in a state of reconciliation with the contradiction, which, indeed, provides the basis for his argument. Here, rather than love for a woman, as in 'Hyperion', is love for the All; Empedocles is (as a philosopher) spirit, 'manly', self-sufficient, 'Nay! all his own is he, the Living one,/ Alone his spirit on him law doth impose',[48] 'He free from want doth wander/ Within a world his own',[49] 'Himself to be that is/ To live; and we, the dream thereof we others are';[50] he is 'born free',[51] 'proud in sufficiency'.[52] As such, he opens himself to the all in absolute intensity, a feminine role, and has surrendered himself in 'inspiration'[53] to the holy genial powers: aether, air, sun, earth. . . .[54] But, in a terrible fall, this 'harmony' has been lost, 'chastised with desolation boundless he', 'For all his strength the Gods have from him stripped'.[55]

[46] Thus, in 'Elegy' (II, 71), those whose lives have been unfulfilled on earth sink into the depths of Hades, and only lovers find salvation; in the final version, 'Menon's Laments for Diotima', this fall into Hades is replaced by 'the power of a miracle' (ll. 76f., II, 77) at which 'from deep in their grave/ Must they return'; but underlying the Christian image of resurrection is the idea of naturally-occurring palingenesis.

[47] Letter 83 (VI, 124–125, ll. 31–36).

[48] 2E 2, ll. 567–568 (IV, 112).

[49] 1E 1/1, ll. 73–74 (IV, 5).

[50] 1E 1/1, ll. 101–102 (IV, 6).

[51] 1E 1/3, 1.313 (IV, 15).

[52] 1E 2/8, 1.2015 (IV, 84). Cf. Hyperion 1/2, 10: 'Ne'er have I known aught so free of need, so self-sufficient' (III, 58).

[53] 1E 1/1, 1.78 (IV, 5).

[54] 1E 1/3, 1.280f. (IV, 14–15).   [55] 1E 1/2, ll. 185–186 (IV, 10).

Where does the guilt lie? In the first version, it has the twofold countenance of reflection—'when the genial spirits of this World/ From love themselves in thee forgot, thy thought did/ To thee turn, fancying, meagre fool, to thee/ Their kind had them sold . . .'[56]—and of self-deification, 'when of himself/ A god he made'.[57] If the second aspect of his Titanism causes strife between Empedocles and the priests, who curse and exile him from the *polis*—a situation in which he can beg, in the true classical tradition, for one request,[58] and become 'sacer'[59]—so too he for his part can curse the hypocrites, as Christ did the Pharisees. But that aspect is purely superficial; how to appease a deity profaned, injured, by the Fichtean elevation of the sprit above Nature, that is the question. Through death alone: which, transforming the initial inspiration (with its unreflected-upon reflection) into the resolution to surrender existence, regains – on a higher, ethical-ideal level where the reflection upon reflection dissolves into an intense immediacy—the grace of renewed union, the reconciliation of heaven and earth.

The author's groping uncertainty as to how to motivate the guilt must not be allowed to obscure the paradox that the 'guilt' of the spirit in distancing itself from Nature is at the same time its very nature, and therefore guiltless. Accordingly, in the second version a different motif appears: Empedocles has betrayed a mystery, the experience of oneness (of being a god), to the people, degradingly allowing it into the public sphere of state and church.[60] In his 'daring' he has tried to utter 'what uttered ne'er may be',[61] thereby revealing himself as god and causing himself to be worshipped. But in the course of the versions the antagonists too are taken increasingly seriously. Instead of the ruthless priests there appears Strato, lord of the city and Empedocles' brother; and the 'institutionalisation' of the mystical has (like the 'political'

---

[56] 1E 1/3, l. 338 (IV, 15).
[57] 1E 1/2, ll. 251f. (IV, 12).
[58] qE 1/5, ll. 676f. (IV, 29).
[59] 1E 2/2, l. 1136 (IV, 49).
[60] 2E 1/1, ll. 29f. (IV, 92).
[61] 2E 1/1, ll. 175–176 (IV, 97).

sphere in 'Hyperion') its own necessity, even to the extent that it is no longer merely profanation for the feeling to become language.[62] Is not the truth, as in the first version, simply that a vessel so filled with divine substance must needs be shattered, 'that it to other purpose may not serve'? 'Through whom/ The Spirit hath been heard, soon be he gone.'[63] For in the second version, which gives Promethean affirmation to Fichte's elevation of the spirit, seeing therein the task of man,[64] Empedocles wishes through his sacrifice to call out from Nature the spirit; such a path Hölderlin could not tread, and so the fragment breaks off.

In the attempt at a third version, the whole question is transferred from the natural to the historical sphere, and here the 'Basis' will carry the thought further. Expelled by his royal brother, the hero acknowledges as guilt his self-sufficiency: 'For, since my youth, my sins have many been,/ I loved men, but ne'er as a man . . .';[65] it is this exclusive devotion to 'Nature, all-enduring' that impels him to his death, leading him to repel his loving disciple Pausanias with determination, and even greater harshness than in the earlier versions; universal love ultimately demands that all other bonds be cut, every personal and individual love sacrificed, notwithstanding all assurances of eternal faithfulness.[66] Here an 'all-sacrificing heart' is met with relinquishment of existence as an 'I' ('I am not who I am, Pausanias').[67] Then there is the temptation of the encounter with the Egyptian, Manes, who asks him: 'Art thou the man?'; for in the passing of an age none but an 'only one' can be 'the new saviour', 'One only may thy sin so black ennoble', something, then, that would be black sin for anyone who happened not to be the only one.[68] Empedocles' answer is yes, and then follow

[62] As he says in an earlier letter: 'Our silent bliss will always die if it is put into words' (Letter 136, VI, 236, ll. 48–49).

[63] 1E 2/4, ll. 1754–1755, ll. 1747–1748 (IV, 73).

[64] 2E 1/3, ll. 501f., 535f. (IV, 109–110). In the 'Basis' he writes: 'He had to strive for identity with her [Nature]' (IV, 159, ll. 5–6).

[65] 3E 1/1, ll. 35–36 (IV, 122).

[66] 3E, the entire second scene (IV, 101f.).

[67] 3E 1/2, 1.253 (IV, 130).

[68] 3E 1/3, ll. 369ff. (IV, 135–136).

his credentials; both the intensity of his relationship with Nature and the straying of the 'poor people'—'wearied with life, with life, with their own hands their own house they did break/ The temples too, displeasing now, forsaken'/have made clear to him his errand; he recognised the parting god of his people, 'and, to appease Him, went I forth'.[69] So the freely-chosen death of the 'only One', with its epochal significance, is now confirmed (as expounded in the 'Basis to Empedocles') and enabled to represent the age in which he lives, by resolving 'the problem of destiny' in it, thereby synthesising that age (of Greece) in a 'premature' model so that it can be handed down, as a promise, to the coming (German) aeon in which his sacrifice will bear fruit: 'and there remains behind a riper true pure universal intensity'.[70]

Hölderlin has broached the innermost treasures of Christ, and is placing them at the disposal of a messiah of identity. Proceeding from an unconditional intensity of existence with the divine All, whence his divinity ('I and the Father are one'), Empedocles falls into kenosis and, after recognising this (in the third version) as mankind's errant alienation from itself, thereupon devotes himself resolutely to death for the sake of love and atonement, the death which achieves a representative reconciliation of time with eternity and opens the prospect of an eschatological promise. While in the first two versions the drama was still essentially concerned with enacting the dialectics of a personal experience within the metaphysics of identity, so that, despite many biblical echoes, the parallel with Christ was still looser, that parallel now, as the historical *kairos* of this death gains a social and eschatological dimension, finally becomes evident. Here is the Johannine Christianity emerging, as in the late Fichte, the old Schelling, and the young Hegel, as the alpha and omega of Idealistic thinking. The eternal Logos, in the world in the form of poverty and humility, glorifying himself through suffering and death, then to ascend back whence he came; declaring his mission and all-embracing love in great parting speeches, consoling even as

---

[69] 3E 1/3, ll. 410ff. (IV, 137).
[70] 'The Basis to Empedocles' (IV, 157, ll. 12–13).

he withdraws, promising the Spirit and a second coming—there is correspondence everywhere. That, furthermore, the redeemer is to be proclaimed king, that the priests form an opposition to him, that he withdraws, that he asks the disciples whom they take him for and forbids their taking revenge, that Pausanias follows him like a John, and Panthea like a Mary; but above all, that every single one of the master's words carries the weight of the death he has seen in advance and chosen, aims at it, recalls it, and is justified by it: that completes the circle. But what divides the two figures? That Christ comes, acts, speaks and dies not in his own name, but in his Father's. That therefore the ultimate testimony is not his religious experience, but his mission. That his kenosis, so great that even God forsakes him, was not dialectical guilt, not fate, nor yet usurpation, but, again, a mission accepted out of obedience. All this presupposes, not cosmic identity, but the relationship of analogy between God and the world, freedom in the divine sending, and, in God himself, the Trinity; this is the insuperable obstacle for any intellectual construction of a figure of redemption parallel to the Christ. Thus 'Empedocles' remains uncompleted, and the epithet 'only One' returns to Christ: 'There yet a shame is, and doth hinder/From likening the men of the world unto thee. . . .'[71]

While resisting all such crystallisation into an actual figure, the Christological is nevertheless a fluidly pervasive element. Stripped of a metaphysical formulation dependent upon Fichte and Parmenides, the ultimate horizon of experience is: that all being is born of the abundance of eternal love, but that this love, out of love, enters the realm of poverty. This is already a conviction in the early ode 'To Nature' (1794/5): 'E'er the dearest love must pauper be',[72] while the ode 'Destiny' turns it round: 'From Need hath every pleasure sprung,/ And pain alone doth make to thrive/ The Dearest . . .'.[73] This might have encouraged a classical interpretation:

[71] 'The only One' (1st vers.), ll. 60–63 (II, 155).
[72] l. 57 (I, 192).
[73] ll. 25f. (I, 184f.).

that the 'undestined' 'unchanging Gods'[74] in their 'eternal youth'[75] 'o'erhead in Light'[76] gaze down on 'suffering' men as they are cast 'Through the years down Uncertainty's maw',[77] so that even to look up at them would be much, for who 'knoweth ye not is poor'. 'Thou, my Preserver fair/ Whene'er hath pain my soul', he says to the aether.[78] But for the riddle which in Euripides had no solution, how painful love can prevail over painless love, there is now a Christian clue: the divine itself penetrates suffering. So overpowering is the light of this truth that it is raised to become an overall necessity. 'Who then can say his feet are firm . . . if even the divine must humble itself, and share mortality with all mortal things!'[79] That 'must' could have remained tied to the world and its experience; instead it gains the profundity of a theological law/'O, well I know it . . . In her richness Love doth play a godly game; Need doth she fabricate for herself, that she may give of her abundance!'[80]—and, finally, a metaphysical expression: 'For it is an eternal law that the Whole, so rich in content, cannot, because of its unity, feel itself with the distinctiveness and vitality . . . of its parts, which also constitute a whole, albeit looser, so that it may be said, if the vitality, distinctiveness, singularity, of the parts, when their totality can feel itself, should exceed the limit set *for these*, and become suffering, and the *completest possible* separateness and isolation, then, and only then, can the Whole feel itself *in these parts* . . . vitally and distinctly.'[81] In that too much is asked of the parts, which are to become a vessel of the whole in order that in them the whole may feel itself, they too experience the 'arbitrary necessity of Zeus'.[82] But any such metaphysical expression of the law immediately implies its Titanic con-comitant, the spirit, which, knowing

[74] 'Palinode', ll. 8, 20 (I, 308); cf. 'Hyperion's Song of Destiny', l. 7 (I, 265).

[75] 'The Gods', l. 9 (II. 16).

[76] 'Hyperion's Song of Destiny', l. 1 (I, 265).

[77] *Ibid.*, ll. 19, 24 (I, 265).

[78] 'The Gods', ll. 1–2 (II, 16).

[79] H 2/1, 1 (III, 94).   [80] H 2/2, 5 (III, 136).

[81] 'On the differences of the poetic genres' (IV, 268, ll. 19–27).

[82] *Ibid.*, 269, l. 24.

of its infinity, rages in the confines of its cell; and so long as the law of love is not harmed, Hölderlin grants him his roaring till the last (see the fragments 'The Titans'). On the other hand, the heart, sharing 'the wounds that they inflict on Nature the divine',[83] is so deeply 'wounded', 'insulted',[84] by the world and its coarseness that it becomes a part of which too much is asked, which breaks, and thus it too feels something of the suffering of the whole, and learns how deep is the eternal love.

Between these two forms of suffering is the apocalyptic post of the poet's heart; he who creates beauty even as he is passing, lonely, strange and astray, beyond beauty, ultimately beyond words themselves, and into the opacity of 'converse' with God.

> Now cometh Spring. And each, in its own way, doth
> Bloom. He though far is gone; no longer there.
> Astray went he; for all too good are
> Genii; heavenly converse hath he now.[85]

3. THE APOCALYPSE OF THE SPIRIT

In Christian belief, it is from the Spirit sent by him that the ascending Redeemer receives glory in the history of the world; and it is good that the earthly form vanishes, or else the Spirit could not come. So too Hölderlin, despite his monistic philosophy of Nature with its pre-Socratic cyclical foundation, is totally and increasingly prophetic-eschatological in thought and feeling; the kingdom of the spirit must and will come. We may let the harsh words in 'Patmos' stand: 'An excess yet/ Of love, where is adoration,/ Bringeth danger, striketh the hardest. They though to depart from/ The countenance of the Lord/ Wished not, and from their homeland. Deep implanted/ Like fire was it in iron then, and there at/ Their side, *as 'twere a plague*, went walking the shade of their dear one.'[86] 'And harming the countenance

---

[83] H 2/2, 11 (III, 156).
[84] H 2/2, 4 (III, 129).
[85] 'Ganymede', ll. 21–24 (II, 68).
[86] 'Patmos' (fragments of the later version), ll. 185–191 (II, 182–183).

divine in verity/ Did walk as 'twere a plague beside them the shade of their dear one./ So them did send he/ The Spirit'.[87] Of the three Tübingen friends Hegel, Schelling and Hölderlin, who parted with the motto 'The Kingdom of God!', only the last kept a burning eschatological faith, with ringing utopian notes: 'It must change to its very foundations!'[88] 'All must rejuvenate itself, must change to its foundations!'[89] It is 'the holy glory of love' that must come in this way, before which 'egoism in all its shapes will bow';[90] for Hölderlin a hope concerning above all, and with ever more awareness, the fatherland. On the 'Day of the Fatherland', each casts his own into the festive flame of the offering, where, like pearls in wine, it dissolves.[91] Already in 'Hyperion's Youth' he is hoping for the 'harmony of our spirits'[92], a 'community in God',[93] and in 'Hyperion' this is called 'Time's fairest Daughter, the new church',[94] similarly, in a letter, 'the aesthetic church';[95] already it is time for it to assemble, 'so that out of this unification, this invisible, fighting church, may be born the great child of time, the day of days, which the man of my soul [Paul] . . . calls the coming of the Lord'.[96] In the late hymns, it is the 'holiday' at the end of time, the 'feast of peace'. The poet constantly rejects any conception of the parusia (as of the Christian faith in general) according to which 'the giver of a revelation does everything by himself, and the one who receives the revaluation may not even rise up to take it';[97] rather, with the help of the spirit humanity will in the course of history come to own the

---

[87] 'Patmos' (drafts for the final version), ll. 190–193 (II, 187).

[88] H 1/2, 19 (III, 89).

[89] H 2/1, 14 (III, 111).

[90] Letter 222 (VI, 407, ll. 27–28).

[91] 'Stuttgart', ll. 29–32 (II, 87).

[92] YH 5 (III, 224, l. 31).

[93] *Ibid.* (III, 224, ll. 3–4).

[94] H 1/1, 7 (III, 32).

[95] Letter 179 (VI, 330, l. 150).

[96] Letter 106 (VI, 185, ll. 51–54), and Beißner's commentary, citing contemporary parallels (VI, 761–763).

[97] Letter 171 (VI, 301, ll. 58–60).

gift from within, even if at first its excess leads yet further astray.

> The kindness of men is followed by thanks,
> But not so a godly gift, and for years
> Come toils first and straying,
> Till truly owned it hath become and well-earned
> And his so too a man may call,
> Divine and human, the gift now.[98]

In the next lines, the poet is aware of 'a danger vict'ry holds, when drunken and o'erweaning', for at first the sense of power induced by the gift of the spirit will lead to the mastering of Nature, the technologisation of the world, while the 'humble' prize, the 'nearest' [that which lies closest] and 'dearest' [love], will not be won till the end. So strong is the emphasis on the immanence of the eternal in the human spirit that there is a genuinely naive conception of the gods and their numerous forms as 'children' of man in his union with the divine;[99] he imparts to them the special 'qualities of his nation', makes them 'descend to earth, for the sake of beauty', 'in this way the myths were born'.[100] 'Since converse we do have' the spirit has been collecting up these images, drawing 'together the beauties of Earth', from 'abroad', from 'colonies',[101] from the 'sea' (where 'beginneth the wealth');[102] and the 'holy powers' have 'To love's true token a witness', for they still have their place in the assembly at the end of days, and are represented in the 'number holy', which is the sum of the world, the 'Feast of Peace'.[103] From early days, Hölderlin's life is devoted towards the end of time,[104] and it

[98] 'The Feast of Peace' (2nd draft), ll. 63–68 (II, 135); cf. the final version, ll. 85–86: 'But where the Spirit worketh, we too are, disputing/ What might the best thing be' (III, 535).

[99] H 1/2, 19 (III, 80).

[100] 'A History of the Fine Arts . . .', IV, 190, ll. 13, 16f.

[101] Variant to 'Bread and Wine', II, 608; Beißner's comment, 621.

[102] 'Remembrance', ll. 40–41 (II, 189).

[103] 'The Feast of Peace', ll. 100–108 (III, 536).

[104] 'Courage proud the son of Earth imbibeth/ From the Future's cup, of magic full' ('Hymn to Immortality', ll. 83–84 (I, 118)); 'While torches ye funereal yet hold. . . ./ E'en now doth dawn the newer better world' ('To the wise advisers', ll. 54, 56 (I, 224)).

is this that finally becomes the object of 'the high and pure delighting of songs of the Fatherland';[105] hence also his expectation of 'the peace of peace, that is higher than all reason'.[106] If 'our joy' is already 'well-nigh too small' to grasp a god,[107] if for now we are being spared by the heavenly ones, 'for not always the strength hath them to contain a weak vessel',[108] because they come with 'too bright', 'too dazzling', a happiness,[109] 'even that oft/ The light of the eye by the gifts of the gods was extinguished';[110] thus does that which the poets 'e'er divine',[111] the fulfilment of the *Hen kai Pan*, remain ineffable.

The darker his path and the firmer the grip of night, the more resolutely does Hölderlin maintain his attitude of prayer and total affirmation, even in the face of the abysses, the objects of dread, the chaos. Already in 'The Books of the Ages', a quite early hymn in Klopstockian tones, the poet, confronted by the books of the world's history thrown apocalyptically open with their merciless record of the most terrible miseries, nevertheless wins through to 'celebrating, trembling adoration/ About the shrine of the Unnameable'.[112] The metaphysics of beauty, at once classical and Idealistic, prove a sleep-walker's path back to this apocalyptic vision of the end; thus the plunge, 'the shortest path back into the All',[113] the delight in death with which Empedocles seeks life—'there doth well and flash/ A godly fire up from the depths to thee', and down he casts himself 'in shuddering desire'[114]—increasingly (in the tragedy) turns to an affirmation of the 'wild discord' that strives up 'from below'[115] and in which yet 'mindful of/ The Unity of old

[105] Letter 243 (1804), VI, 436, l. 19.
[106] pH III, 236, ll. 25–26.
[107] 'Homecoming', l. 100 (II, 99).
[108] 'Bread and Wine', 7, ll. 112–113 (II, 93).
[109] *ib.*, 5, l. 74 (II, 92).
[110] 'At the Danube's Source', ll. 62–63 (II, 127).
[111] 'As on a holiday . . .', l. 17 (II, 118).
[112] 'The Books of the Ages', I, 69–74.
[113] 'The Voice of the People' (1st vers.), l. 13 (II, 49).
[114] 'Empedocles', ll. 1f. (I, 240).
[115] 3E I/3, l. 382 (IV, 136).

the Mother dark [Earth]/ Doth stretch her arms of fire out to
the Aether';[116]; it is 'the old forming chaos',[117] the 'ancient
confusion',[118] celebrated (in the first strophe of 'Heimkunft')
as the awful and holy landscape where all things originated,
('The joyfully shuddering Chaos')[119] while in 'The
Archipelagus' it is a subterranean quaking by which even the
glorious islands are threatened, as when

> from the abyss set
> Free, at times did the flame of Night, the underground
>   tempest
> Seize upon one of the angels, and dying she sank in
>   thy bosom,[120]

and by which, equally, the life that has dissolved into chaos is
cast up anew in resurrection, as by a volcano

> When there is rumbling below, for Night with her
>   treasures doth toll pay,
>   And, in the beds of the streams, gold, for long
>   buried, doth glean.[121]

Thus do almost all the late poems[122] strive to return from
the formed land of Greece to the chaotic mother Asia, the
origin of love and of great prayers;[123] the Rhein flows
towards her at first and the Danube till the end, while as the
'Ister' the latter seems to the poet 'almost backwards to go',
that is, to flow from the East to the West.[124] The West is by

[116] 3E 1/3, ll. 476–477 (IV, 139).
[117] Letter 229 (VI, 416, ll. 26–27).
[118] 'The Rhein', l. 221 (II, 148).
[119] 'Homecoming', l. 5 (II, 96).
[120] 'The Archipelago', ll. 20–22 (II, 103).
[121] 'Menon's Laments for Diotima', 6, ll. 81–82 (II, 77).
[122] 'At the Danube's Source', 'The Journey', 'The Rhein', 'Germania',
'The only One', 'Patmos', 'Remembrance', 'The Ister'.
[123] There 'the Strong' have their place, they who 'Did fearless face the
signs of the world/ And the sky and all fate on their shoulders laden/ For
days on mountains implanted/ Had none done as they did/ Alone when
spake they/ With God' ('At the Danube's Source', ll. 8of., II, 128); whether
here he means the Indian worshippers, Moses on Mount Sinai, or the
Christian monks and stylites.
[124] 'The Ister', ll. 41–42 (II, 191).

its origins an open land, and perhaps it and the East might be joined in a marriage that would, as it were, pass over Hellas.[125]

Yet this ardent reaching-out far and ever further into the distance also signifies a twilight that is fading into an implacably destructive spiritual darkness; the tremendous intensity with which he thought to do justice to the glory of all being was, despite all the humility of its thanksgiving and praise, objectively hubristic; it reduced the freedom that is God's in his mystery of suffering to a law defining the nature of the One-and-All, a law open to be experienced. The Christ, having been dissolved into the cosmos, can therefore ultimately never be brought back. And immediately after Hölderlin the cold winds of nothingness come bursting into his glory, as already in Jean Paul; a nothingness whose approach Hyperion too can already sense: 'O ye poor people, ye who . . . are so utterly possessed by the nothingness that rules over us, who perceive so clearly that we are born for nothing, that we love a nothing, believe in a nothing, wear ourselves away for nothing, thus slowly to pass into nothingness—if your knees give way when ye contemplate that, how am I to help you?' And the next words could have been Zarathustra's: 'Remain below, ye children of the moment! strive ye not to scale these heights; nought is there up here'.[126] This darkest of shadows is inseparable from any kind of thinking based on identity; to interpret it as an 'absence of God' that will in the end be helpful is therefore over-confident.[127] But when, amid this aberration, the post 'would gladly beg a drop of oil, to shine yet a while through the night'[128]—as he writes to Diotima—then he has been absorbed into a movement which transcends his own moment, leaving him, as he remains, without weapons or guile, 'alone before God',[129] with shelter only in the utmost exposure. 'And mightily light doth flicker in/ The wildness of the Abyss'.[130]

---

[125] 'The Journey', ll. 40ff. (II, 139).
[126] H 1/2, 11 (III, 46).
[127] 'The Poetic Calling', l. 64 (II, 48).
[128] Letter 182 (VI, 337, ll. 6–7).
[129] 'The Poetic Calling', ll. 62–64 (II, 48).
[130] 'The Titans', ll. 72–73 (II, 219).

e. Goethe

I. THE MEAN AS A FORM OF RESISTANCE
THE CURVE

Such a dominant influence not only on the 'Age of Goethe' but also on the nineteenth century, Goethe[1] lived in the calm but often fearful awareness that, like a rock, he stood against a mighty racing current. All his religious experiences and their manifold expressions, despite their ring of affirmation, sprang from, were carved out by, a primal No. When he set out, the young man left behind two companions, a feeble Pietistic Protestantism and the flat materialism offered by France and the European Enlightenment: 'How hollow and empty the world had become in that gloomy atheistic twilight.'[2] And now, in powerful contrast, there arises a cosmic experience of Being which brings to our minds the names of Bruno, Spinoza, Shaftesbury, Herder. After Strasburg and Frankfurt came Weimar; was the pantheistic 'I' to fit comfortably into court life? to accept limitations which seemed at once an unbearable distortion and a beneficial necessity? This conflict (played out in Torquato Tasso) was not resolved until Goethe fled to Italy and found refuge in the classical world, where Nature and form are always in harmony. His next encounter was with the 'philosophy of the spirit' which Schiller and Fichte had developed from the Critiques. The resulting intense

---

[1] We shall quote from the Artemis Gedenkausgabe (24 vols. + 2 supplementary vols.). Abbreviations: P = Poems; D = West-eastern Divan: F = Faust; MA = William Master's Apprenticeship; MW = William Master's Years of Wandering; MV = William Master's Theatrical Vocation; EA = Electoral Affinities; IPH = Iphigenia; T = Tasso; IJ = The Italian Journey; TF = Truth and Fancy; A = The Annals; TC = The Theory of Colours; C = Conversations with Eckermann; L = Letters. The volume number is indicated in Roman numerals; e.g. MA 4, 16 (VII, 279) = Apprenticeship, Book 4, Chapter 16, in Volume VII, page 279. Sometimes fragmentary writings on natural science are quoted from the Insel Dünndruckausgabe (ed. G. Ipsen = Ipsen).

[2] TF 3, 11 (X, 538).

dialogue was highly productive, but drew from Goethe that primal No, indeed, only made him the more aware that something he had found in his cosmic experience was missing in the Idealistic version represented by Kant and Fichte, by Schiller, finally by Hegel. 'Schiller showed too little gratitude to our great Mother'.[3] 'All Schiller's works are pervaded by the idea of freedom ... What use to us is an excuse of a freedom we cannot use! ... Freedom lies not in refusing to acknowledge anything above us, but, on the contrary, in revering something that is above us.'[4] Even as he reacted against Idealism, Goethe's God-Nature religion became more profound, a religion of awe (in programmatic form in *Years of Wandering*). So too the primal No to the French Revolution can explain the greater profundity of the ethos typified by Eugenia and Ottilia, a noble heart with its renunciation; so too his determination to stand by the western tradition and its classical roots became, thanks to his rejection of Romanticism and the ensuing painful isolation, firm and unshakeable; finally, when from his essentially pious theory of Nature Goethe developed, and obstinately defended, an organic morphology and (Plotinian) theory of colours, the impetus is really his No to an increasingly technological natural science and its catastrophic consequences, man's (atheistic) departure from Nature.

Hölderlin we might compare to a fine and tapering flame; Goethe too, whose life and work have such a mighty compass, unquestionably represents a last secular manifestation of the heritage of 'glory' which the history of western metaphysics has bequeathed to us. His adherence to the tradition of Bruno and Shaftesbury (and their antecedents Cusa, Plotinus, Homer) was far from leading him into the temptations of Idealism; for out of his youthful religion of the One-and-All there arose an adoration of the mystery of Being characterised by distance and awe. And a paradoxical situation comes about; this 'child of the world' who never prays, unlike Hölderlin, who does, can truly be said to live within the *analogia entis*, rather than the mysticism of identity.

[3] 'My first acquaintance with Schiller' (XII, 621).
[4] C 18.1.1827 (XXIV, 216).

Never, not even in his youth, did Goethe feel any compulsion 'to take refuge in the doctrine of absolute unity; for therein gain but equals loss, and what is left at the end? the consolation of a disconsolate zero'.[5] Meanwhile, God's presence in the world, in every element and form, is a fundamental experience that only an ultimately irreligious Christian or Enlightenment deism can deny. The Ancient Persians became Goethe's friends because they based their worship 'on contemplation of Nature', turning, 'when they prayed to the Creator, towards the rising sun, since that was by far the most glorious thing they knew'. But 'nor was fire the only representative' of the deity, for 'their religion was intrinsically based on reverence for all the elements, inasmuch as these proclaimed the presence and power of God', reverence 'for God's universal presence in the works of his sensual world'.[6] Such a 'faculty of vision', that 'penetrates life in all its manifold forms', occurs, of course, 'only in a few divinely-favoured men'; for most, religious experience emerges 'only as a fiery feeling of inspiration which lasts a moment and departs, whereupon the subject, restored to himself, dissatisfied, unoccupied, at once relapses into a most endless emptiness', which the national religions with their pious ceremonies are then an attempt to fill.[7]

Goethe was never prey to doubts of an atheistic nature; and if he preferred to 'observe a profound silence' where 'God and things divine' were concerned,[8] nevertheless he could not but hear the Universal Being and his 'open secret,'[9] his 'holy public secret'[10]: that 'Nature doth in all her forms/But a single

[5] 5. D III, 452.
[6] D III, 423–425.
[7] D III, 424.
[8] A 1794 (XI, 637).
[9] D III, 304.
[10] P I, 519; playfully echoed in a conversation with Ulrike von Lewetzow (no. 1635, XXIII, 290), when Goethe tried in vain to keep his birthday a secret, and then called it 'the day of the open secret'. Cf. also Years of Wandering 2, 8: the 'happy rose of life' 'from secret life awaketh/ A meaning plain' (VIII, 277). The truths of the Theory of Colours are entrusted to the future as an 'ingenuous mystery' (Ipsen, Vol. 2, 680).

God reveal'.[11] And this God, far from being a mere unknown X, is the unattainable source of all ordered beauty. 'I do not ask', Goethe said, 'whether this highest Being is able to think and reason, for I feel that it itself is none other than thought and reason. All creatures are pervaded by it, and as for man, he has so much thereof as to recognise even some parts of the Highest.'[12] Such a religion 'really needs no faith . . . some such conviction imposes itself on everyone.'[13]

Yet God is so much the universal essence that, like Plotinus, Erigena and Ficino before him, Goethe is not prepared to attribute to him a private will, to burden him with prayers as such. We find prayers proper only in the early Weimar period, two poems reviving the strict ancient distinction between gods and men: 'The Limitations of Man' ('For with gods/ No man soever/ Should seek to vie . . ./ What is it divides/ Gods, and men? . . .'), 'The Divine' (which has man fulfilling his existence 'by brazen/ Great Laws bound', yet still playing a positive role, exercising choice, conferring perpetuity on the individual moment).[14] Then we have, with a conscious return to Homer and the tragedians, the prayers of *Iphigenia*; the rebellious, titanic 'Song of the Fates' is not the heroine's—for her it only represents a burgeoning temptation—but her nurse's.[15] To understand her own prayer we must remember how she was miraculously transported away from death by Diana;[16] she is a 'miraculée', and therefore a virgin and priestess:

Sole right unto my consecrated life
Hath not the goddess, who my life did save?[17]

In this mind she prays to the goddess to whom she owes her existence, and has towards her an intense relationship, listening, with an inner ear, for the divine voice:

[11] MW 2, 8 (VIII, 277).

[12] C 23.2.1831 (XXIV, 462–463).

[13] TF 1, 4 (X, 154), where the structure of the natural order is distinguished from revealed religion.

[14] P I, 323–325.

[15] Iph 4, 5 (VI, 198–199).

[16] Iph 3, 1 (VI, 183); 5, 3 (VI, 202).

[17] Iph 1, 3 (VI, 160).

This is no god that speaks, but thine own heart.
'Tis only through our hearts they speak to us.
And have I then no rights, myself to hear.
The storm doth overwhelm the frail voice.[18]

Later we read:

Thoas: Rough Scythians,
          Barbarians, hear not that voice, you think?
Iphigenia: All may hear it,
          Born under any heaven, if
          Through the bosom unhindered and pure
          The Spring of Life doth flow.[19]

Pylades too knows this:

Upon the will of those above must heedfully wait
All human wisdom, or 'tis nought.[20]

Thus Iphigenia's are true prayers, founded on that ancient cornerstone, the 'limitations of man' and the miraculous grace of the gods.[21] The first great step from enthusiasm to a distant reverence we may safely relate to Goethe's love for Frau von Stein, to whom he wrote in March 1781: 'The Jews have laces for wrapping around their arms when they pray: in the same way I wrap your beloved ribbon round my arm when I send my prayer to you, and wish to partake of your goodness, wisdom, moderation and patience.'[22] Later this dialogic element pales into a mere gesture of awe which, in the *Years of Wandering*, is elevated to become the very essence of the religious act. Thus *Iphigenia*, from the religious point of view, is like an exposed gash between the early and late periods; perhaps the breach of the mean goes deeper than the conventional picture of Goethe, for which the poet bears not

[18] Iph 1, 3 (VI, 162).
[19] Iph 5, 3 (VI, 205).
[20] Iph 2, 1 (VI, 169).
[21] Esp. Iph 1, 4 (VI, 163–164), 3, 3 (VI, 186–187), and the prayer of thanksgiving and entreaty for 'fulfilment' in Iph 3, 1 (VI, 179–180): the 'abundance' of the gift identifies the gods as the givers.
[22] L 510 (XVIII, 578).

a little responsibility, allows us to see. For could Goethe, that devotee of finished classical form, be asked what single essential image he planted in the history of the human spirit during the sixty years of his life's work, then would be revealed his tragic uncertainty.

A BREAK THROUGH THE MIDDLE

For the young Goethe, poetic creation was the act that joins heaven and earth, God and the world; the ecstatic discovery that creativity in Nature and in the heart of the genius has a single common source. 'Who, if you will, has formed gods, raised us up to them, brought them down to us, other than the poet?' 'If others dream ... why, he waking lives the dream of life ... Destiny has elevated him, god-like, above all such things.'[23] But in Weimar the titanic visions, confronted by the hard, limited and objective reality of things, lose conviction, as Jarno's words show: 'Man is only happy when his uncompromising aspirations put a limit on themselves.'[24] In 'Ilmenau' (1783) we find a first, implacable, self-judgment:

> The fire I lit hath not a flame so pure.
> The glow, the danger, are by storm increased,
> I falter not as I condemn myself.[25]

In *Theatrical Vocation*, two feminine figures—the muse of tragic poetry and the personification of commerce—compete for the young poet; William tears up his note-books and is about to throw them into the fire; Werner stops him, and he collapses in tears on the table, all covered with jumbled papers.[26] When he fled to Italy, Goethe won through to the positive side of the crisis: for this was in every respect the supreme and happy time, the heart of Goethe's existence. But the healing of the person meant the laming of his work. Shortly before leaving Italy, Goethe wrote: 'In Rome, for

[23] MV 2, 3 (VIII, 598–599), reappearing in MA 2, 2 (VII, 88).
[24] MA 8, 5 (VII, 593).
[25] P I, 362.
[26] MV 2, 3 (VIII, 604).

the first time, I have found myself; at last I have found an inner harmony, I am happy and reasonable.'[27] But that was not his initial emotion: 'I am like an architect who, having in mind to build a tower, has laid a poor foundation; at least he sees soon enough his mistake, and brings down without ado what he has brought up from the earth, seeking to broaden, to ennoble, his plan ...'[28] He is now sure of 'two of my prime errors': 'If I wanted or needed to throw myself into something, I was never prepared to learn the appropriate craft, which is why, despite great natural potential, I have done and achieved so little. My second is a closely related error: I have never been prepared to devote to a task or matter as much time as it needed.'[29] A dilettante, then, an unwitting one at that; and nearing forty. 'It seems, I fear, that I have wasted the best time of one's life.'[30] 'My titanic ideas were just phantoms of air.'[31] And, reflecting on the shamefully meagre harvest of his collected works: 'How can an existence leave so little trace?'[32] Thus, again, his William speaks for him when he says: 'Supremely happy is he ... who needs not to cast away all the life he has lived, to be in accord with destiny!'[33]

The significance of this break emerges from consideration of those three life-works which, in surviving the crisis of the middle years, bind youth and old age together: the *Faust* poem (begun in 1772, completed in 1831), the *Master* novel (in its three parts, *Theatrical Vocation*, *The Apprenticeship* and *The Years of Wandering*; begun in 1777 and though not completed, broken off in 1829), and, finally—if one goes by size—the major work: Goethe's autobiography, in which *The Italian Journey* (edited between 1815 and 1829) and *Truth and Fancy* (1808–1829), supplemented by an abundance of travel reports, annals, diaries, letters and conversation, constitute the

27 IJ 3, March 1788 (XI, 583).
28 IJ 1, 20.12.1786 (XI, 163).
29 IJ 3, 20.7.1787 (XI, 407).
30 IJ 3, 2.10.1787 (XI, 453).
31 IJ 3, 10.1.1788 (VI, 526).
32 IJ 3, 1.2.1788 (XI, 568).
33 MA 7, 6 (VII 494).

central parts. All three life-works were completed by the eighty-year-old. An individual work, *Tasso*, is the document proper of the break; it was begun shortly before leaving Germany, then towed around Italy ('I shall have to revise Tasso; as it is, it is useless'),[34] and not finished until the poet was back in Weimar.

Tasso embodies the poet's completeness, an ideal of the young Goethe seen, quite correctly, as continuing the spiritual tradition of the Florentine Academy; Ficino, Ariosto, the historical Tasso himself. And if for the young Goethe Eros was the clear and dominant medium of inspiration, in this too there is an unmistakable continuity with the classical-Platonic metaphysics of the Renaissance; indeed, we are inevitably reminded of the historical Tasso: fanciful ideas floating around *à la* Petrarch, and, in tense but unified contrast, a realistic sexuality.[35] *Tasso* portrays the poet's completeness; but the cost is an absolute exposure of the defenceless heart. The poet possesses

> That which only Nature can confer,
> And ever lies beyond the will of man,
> Beyond his every effort, and which gold
> Cannot force forth, nor sword, nor wit, nor long
> Endeavour.[36]

And if Iphigenia listens to the voice of the god in her heart, of Tasso we read:

> His ear discerns the harmony of Nature.[37]

But, to soar aloft in this harmony, his cosmic Aeolian harp needs the touch of Eros' breath, both as a longing for the unattainable ('for that unto this goal/ My life a wandering eternal is')[38] and as a passion for an exalted lady; the Princess, however, will always be beyond Tasso's reach (she is always herself a 'disciple of Plato')[39] and thus the two forms merge,

[34] IJ 3, 1.2.1788 (XI, 568).
[35] Above, p. 272.
[36] T 4, 2 (VI, 281).
[37] T 1, 1 (VI, 218).
[38] T 1, 3 (VI, 228), also T 4, 4 (VI, 289).
[39] T 1, 1 (VI, 219).

like the figures in 'Jerusalem Freed'.[40] Just as Iphigenia cannot, even to save herself, besmear her lips with a lie, Tasso's exposed heart senses every tarnishing of the moral order, every impurity, betrayal. Right to the end his penetrating insight never fails him. Antonio, the courtier and man of the world, insults him, the Duke punishes him; like Hyperion's, his 'wounded heart but slowly heals',[41] yet remains unswerving. Were the conflict that of the poet Goethe, confronted by the court and business world of Weimar, it would not in itself be so totally and tragically insoluble. But the web of lies spun by Leonore San Vitale—her 'love', a guise for selfishness, is exposed by Tasso in a magnificent scene (4.2)—snaps his wings, while the Princess' feeble and evasive Platonism (giving the light of 'scanty moonshine', but no warmth)[42] completely disrupts his precarious balance; bodily he embraces one who is bodiless, and, more tragic than the Faust who will clasp the garments of the withdrawing Helen, collapses in utter failure. The drama is by no means a pathological study of a single unfortunate person, but an ontology of poetic existence. In the foreground we have the tension between the ideal and real worlds (Tasso and Antonio); but in the background is the incurable tension between the pre-Italy Charlotte and the Charlotte who greeted the returning lover, the man who had fled from her without a word of farewell, with a coldness hardened into hatred; and yet further in the background, the whole problem of Eros classical and modern, a problem concentrated, for Goethe-Tasso, in the question of 'the moment' which gives that timeless (and therefore *unreal*) glimpse of the Absolute without which the poet could never create anything *real*.[43] Herein lies the true reason why Goethe, who even in the penultimate act champions his hero undauntedly against all the other characters, goes over to the side of the opposition in the fifth act; now, and only now, do the scales sink. The

[40] T 2, 1 (VI, 245).

[41] T 4, 4 (VI, 288).

[42] T 3, 3 (VI, 270).

[43] Strikingly, the word 'moment' recurs five times in lines 2129–2147, likewise in ll. 2674–2708.

crack running through *Tasso* betrays the hidden rift in Goethe's own heart.—The three life-works, once broken down, are easier to grasp.

Faust, determined to win the whole, rejects the piece-meal knowledge of the four Faculties and resorts to magic (not unfamiliar; we recall the magical path, in their case theological, of Porphyry and Iamblichus). He finds in his book two 'signs' for the All-and-One. The first is that of the 'Macrocosm'; of 'living Nature' wherein 'all things interwoven are,/ Each in another doing, being!/ Heavenly powers mounting and descending/ The golden buckets one to other passing!'[44] It is the hierarchical, dynamic, analogical universe envisioned by Plotinus or Denys the Areopagite; a magnificent 'show, but ah! a show and nothing more' for Faust. He wants, not classification, but immediate identification. So he decides he will not invoke this universal spirit: instead, turning the page over 'resentfully', he catches sight of the sign of 'the Earth Spirit': quite 'different', 'nearer' to him, and enticing him 'the woe and the delight of Earth to bear'. Rays of red light flash and a breath of chill air wafts down from the ceiling, as Faust invokes the spirit, who appears before him (according to the original version) 'in hideous shape'. Describing itself as 'A sea eternal/ A ceaseless weaving/ A glowing Living', billowing up and down 'in floods of life, in storm of deeds', it points Faust away from itself to the spirit he understands—Mephisto, as we shall see. Henceforth the cosmos is the realm of the earth-spirit, viewed, that is, from Bruno's chthonic perspective, with Heraclitus in the background: the billowing *coincidentia oppositorum*, not analogy but an identity, which man soars up into, a cosmos not 'divine' but 'daemonic'. Here is not that contemplation which, in its sublime longing for the One, sees the laws of the universe soften (a motif which runs from Plato and Plotinus via Boethius and Bonaventura to Cusa); here is action ('In the beginning was the Deed'; 'He who acts has no conscience; only the observer has a conscience').[45] Action,

[44] F, ll. 441, 446ff. (V, 157–158).

[45] *Maxims*, IX, 522. On the whole subject, see the decisively important essay by Eudo C. Mason, 'Goethes Erdgeist und das Pathos des Irdischen',

however, consists in single steps, and therefore always needs an opposing complement and creative negation. This constant companion is Mephistopheles, and together, in their ceaseless striving and endeavour to be, or rather seem to be, the whole. Thus everything, even the highest deeds, performed through and with Mephistopheles retains a sense of illusion and deception. Properly, the absolute act should have been suicide ('The time is come, that deeds should finish proof/ A man may worthy be to scale the heights divine'),[46] the way of Werther, more precisely of Ippolit (in *the Idiot*) and of Existentialism. But a half-Christian, half-pagan Easter changes Faust's mood, and provides a transition to the 'pact' that, being a contract with contradiction, can itself only be contradictory: Faust *wants* the moment of divine-daemonic identity and, at the same time, curses it in advance. His path, seen from its starting-point, cannot be that of Eros, of the desired object, the 'restless heart' (Goethe's later insertions try to create that impression);[47] it is, rather, a path whose traces are never free of deceptiveness. All is appearance trickery— the eroticism of the Witches' Kitchen (leading to the Gretchen tragedy), the devilish goings-on of the first Walpurgis Night, the paper money at the Emperor's court, the phantasmagoric Helen and Euphorion—and the final trick is the great cultural achievement by the sea-shore, compromised by murder. In the end Faust, as he faces death, understands how ruinous was his initial decision in favour of the sphere of the earth-spirit and its concomitant spirit of negation:

> Could I but free from magic now my path,
> Put spells behind me once and for all,
> Before thee, Nature, stand a man alone,
> Then, 'twere not labour lost, to be alive![48]

This thread is clearly visible; it originates precisely in the

in *Exzentrische Bahnen: Studien zum Ditcherbewußtsein der Neuzeit* (1963), pp. 24–59.

[46] F, ll. 712f. (V, 165).

[47] In the glorious lines of Easter-eve (1064–1099), with the setting sun pursued by the yearning crane.

[48] F, ll. 11404–11407 (V, 503).

Bruno-like pathos of contradiction we found in Faust's opening programme:

> You giddy whirling world, excruciating pleasure,
> Love's hate and ennui's thrill, yours shall I be . . .
> That lot accorded the whole race of men
> I mean to feast on in my inner Self . . .
> My Self enlarge to be the equal of mankind
> And, like mankind, I'll shatter in the end![49]

The style, even the vocabulary, recall *Eroici Furori*. But this is the very style the classical Goethe sickened of; the Faustian in Faust therefore had to be dismantled in mid-stream. Faust's prayer, in which the 'Earth Spirit' is elevated and identified with the spirit of the macrocosm, with the Plotinian-Christian God in-and-above Nature, was composed in Italy:

> Spirit Sublime, thou gavest, gavest everything to me
> For which I prayed. And not in vain didst thou
> In fire turn thy countenance to me . . .[50]

This is a classical execution of the same apostrophe in a very early scene that was never used: 'Great and glorious Spirit, that hast designed to appear to me, that knowest me heart and soul, why chain me to this shameful companion? . . .'.[51] And really this elevation of Faust's is, within the context of the western tradition, not so difficult. The unity of opposites (Heraclitus, Bruno) is ultimately no more than the immanent variation upon the theme of the transcendent Platonic cosmos; if in the former case the poles are set out independently so that the pendulum swings *within* the conflict, here, brought together in a single perspective, they are the object of contemplation. The 'Prologue in Heaven' (1797), with its 'Song of the Three Archangels', now determines the new perspective from the beginning; the angels contemplate from above the wildly-foaming world of the earth-spirit, in which the brightness of Paradise alternates with a deep and dreadful darkness, storms roar in a raging chain, and ravaging

[49] F, ll. 1766–1775 (V, 196).
[50] F, ll. 3217–3219 (V, 244).
[51] F, 'A gloomy day. Field' (V, 281).

lightning flickers before the thunder. The sight 'gives the Angels strength', for they perceive in all this not only the ancient 'singing-match of the brother spheres', but God's *kabod*:

> And all thy works sublime
> Still know the first day's glory.[52]

This permits eros, the motif of desire, to come to the fore ('A good man, 'midst the darkness of his urge,/ Yet knows full well which is the righter way').[53] The pact can be passed over and finally treated simply as superseded (dirty work, on which Mephisto puts a bright face); the dreadful murders in the first part and the conclusion of the second are forgotten; and, lastly, the instrument of transcendence, eros, is transfigured, to become the Marian agape of Dante as descending grace. As we surface from the magical intoxication of the giant poem, we may ask which of the spheres is its true home, whence it derives the principle of its form; but the only answer lies in the movement itself—from the one to the other sphere—ultimately the movement of Goethe's existence. For Faust is Goethe, in him he has his justification, his living figure.

William Master begins with the belief in a theatrical 'vocation'; what follows is a retraction, this supposed vocation turning out a mistake. If Faust renounced his world-spirit because it remained 'a show, no more', for the young Master the theatre is to become an image, indeed a kind of symbol, for the world. After the successes of *Clavigo* and *Götz*, Goethe's sense of vocation and vision—not just of a national literature but of an actual German culture based on the stage—were of a grandeur that can scarcely be overestimated.[54] The artist builds the ecclesiastical and

[52] F, ll. 243–266 (V, 149–150).

[53] F, ll. 328–329 (V, 151).

[54] He states that he 'thought unceasingly on the German theatre' (TF, 3, 13 (X, 619)): a national poetry would have to be based on the great events in the destinies of nations and kings, for these 'become much more interesting than the gods themselves; the gods have no sooner determined a destiny than they withdraw from it' (TF 2, 7 (X, 308)). After *Götz*, he continues, he became secretly preoccupied with the idea, using the Thirty

spiritual house in which the nation is to dwell.[55] His is a self-sacrifice seen as a vocation, in that he projects the best he has on to the stage, which becomes like a secular pulpit; and this slow, progressive objectivising of his own existence for the benefit of the public was the 'theatrical vocation' of William-Goethe. As Goethe made clear to himself in the splendidly acrimonious essay 'Literary Sans-culottism', the beginnings had to be basic, indeed, almost from nothing.[56] From puppet-plays at fairs and in garrets, passing through all the stages of an actor's career with its misery and self-doubt, to the popular and amateur theatre, the court, and finally the regular town-theatre; such is the rise of Master, as writer and player. *Hamlet* provides the training-ground, an exercise in the meaning of real poetry, true theatre; all the accidents of Fortune's coat-of-many-colours prove to be linked by the inner necessity of the vocation[57] with its 'presentiment of the whole world',[58] so that the only question is whether the hero's inner core is strong enough for chance to crystallise into destiny. This is the question *Hamlet* raises, for here 'a soul is burdened with a deed too great for it';[59] at this point the focus shifts from the subjective to the objective sphere. 'Here, the hero does not have a plan, but the play does . . . All the circumstances unite and seek vengeance, but in vain! neither on earth nor below has any the power to execute what Destiny has reserved for itself.'[60] Shakespeare, not

Years War as a basis, of 'moving forwards and backwards, and treating the principal events in the same vein' (TF 3, 13 (X, 629)).

[55] It is the young architect of *Electoral Affinities* who puts this most beautifully: An artist's 'works leave him as do birds the nest in which they have hatched and grown . . . To him the royal halls owe their splendour, a splendour whose greatest effect he cannot share in. In the temples, he sets a boundary between himself and the Holy of Holies . . . just as a goldsmith will worship from afar the monstrance he has created with its glaze and pearls . . . Truly, since it was assigned to her to care above all for public works, for things that belong to everyone and so to the artist as well. Art has perforce become her own only strength' (EA 2, 3 IX, 151–152)).

[56] XIV, 179–185.
[57] MV 6, 14 (VIII, 877).
[58] MV 6, 11 (VIII, 859).
[59] MV 6, 8 (VIII, 846).
[60] MV 6, 10 (VIII, 856).

Hamlet, controls the course of the drama; so too Master's inner vocation is not the highest instance, for he too has a role, in a destiny greater than himself.

At this point the novel of vocation was broken off, in anticipation of the rupture again to come in Italy. Goethe 'abandoned the venture; and when he returned to it the "vocation" was no more. Into its place came a *Bildungsroman* (story of a young man's progress to maturity) called *The Apprenticeship*; those theatrical aspirations had now become a mistake, hardly even a "fruitful" mistake, of Master's youth ... Disillusioned with the idea of a German national theatre, Goethe now felt that the stage was not after all able to create a "people", in the truest sense of the word.'[61] Thus he who had a vocation now becomes, like Faust, a searcher: 'The story of his life is an eternal searching and never finding.'[62] Destiny has its core no longer in him, nor in a personal providence, but in the Masonic secret society in the background, which, in pulling the strings of a 'destiny' seen as pure 'chance' by William, turns the hero's wayward existence to good.[63] Here, once again, Goethe is condemning the first half of his life: ' "I have, I fear, nothing to relate but mistake upon mistake, aberration upon aberration," William replied';[64] but the Masonic abbé takes the view that 'error can only be cured through errancy'.[65] Thus such error and the failed vocation became, as with Faust, integrated into a meaningful process, to be called *Bildung* (formative education); 'Alas ... what endless operations Nature and Art must do, before there stands before them a fully-formed human being.'[66] Later still, in *The Years of Wandering*, Goethe imitates Plato as he bans the theatre altogether from the sphere of education: 'It has an ambiguous origin which it will never, neither as art nor craft nor simple pleasure, be able to shake off.' Goethe steps on to the platform and, as the 'editor of these papers', speaks to the

[61] Emil Staiger, *Goethe I*, (1952), 472–474.
[62] MA 8, 4 (VII, 571).
[63] MA 7, 9 (VII, 531–532).
[64] MA 7, 6 (VII, 480).
[65] MA 8, 5 (VII, 590).
[66] MA 7, 2 (VII, 459).

reading public: 'Has not he too, in many ways, expended more life and strength on the theatre than was right?'[67] It is pardonable because it has found a place in the unified whole of his striving existence. In *Vocation* and *Apprenticeship*, the idea of the 'role' provides the transition from the actor playing a part to the man who is the plaything of a universal 'world theatre'; Goethe praises the nobility, so favoured from the start in worldly goods, and at the same time criticises: to make up for his disadvantages, the humbler citizen has to 'sacrifice his entire self'. Unable to live by 'representation', he has to draw on 'loyalty', the 'prime resource of all our wealth'.[68] 'If through the portrayal of his person the nobleman gives his all, the ordinary citizen through his personality gives nothing, nor should he. The former can, indeed should, seem to be; the latter should only be, and what he tries to seem is absurd and tasteless. The former should do and act; the latter should achieve and create . . ., and it is an initial premise that in his being there is and can be no harmony, for in order to serve a useful purpose he has to neglect everything else.' Nor does Master-Goethe stop there: 'Now it so happens that I have an irresistible inclination towards that harmonious development of my nature my birth has denied me.' He would like to be both a 'public person' and a poet; and here too the theatre provides the bridge: 'On the boards, the cultivated man can appear in all his personal distinction, no less than in the upper classes.'[69] A profound dialectic; while the nobleman represents rather than really is, the ordinary citizen actually is, but cannot represent; in the theatre, however, he could do both at once, and in this way catch up and overtake the nobleman. This is undoubtedly a dream of Goethe's own, in that it envisages a middle way that neither Tasso nor Faust is able to achieve. Both Master and Goethe see their dream collapse; but if we ask what Master has learnt, *The Apprenticeship* provides no further answer, and we must look, paradoxically enough, to *The Years of Wandering*, or, *Paths of Renunciation*.

[67] MW 2, 9 (VIII, 278–280).
[68] MV 5, 13 (VIII, 811–812).
[69] MA 5, 3 (VII, 312–314).

But no structural cohesion shall we find here; for once again a painful fracture runs through the middle, distorting the original idea out of all recognition. Master has scarcely brought Natalia home—the transfigured Amazon of *Vocation*[70] who reappeared 'in a radiant halo' in *Apprenticeship*, where she was named the 'Saint'[71]—than he leaves her for a life of wandering, a way of renunciation which does no more than skirt human spheres and destines. In such detachment the world becomes objective and a true sympathy possible; but William strives afresh to escape from this distance. He becomes a surgeon. However, the problem of 'wandering' (in the 1821 version) is transformed into that of emigration to America (in the final, 1829 version). With the novel now disintegrating into a collection of loose bundles, the centre-stage is taken over by the question of education, that is, of character formation' once again, now on a comprehensive and systematic basis, extending from the religious sphere to art and craft. Even where Christianity appears as the third, highest and ultimate religion,[72] the ideal is really the classical *paideia*; for 'awe' (before the impenetrable), rather than love (for Him who has revealed himself), has the final word. The second element is a classical-stoic renunciation in favour of citizenship of the world; this is the inspiration behind Leonardo's speech on the endless fluidity of all human callings, classes and persons. A 'world-wide bond', so that 'everywhere is home',[73] that is the ideal, crowned quite logically by the figure of Macaria, in whom the mysticism of ancient astrology makes an unexpected resurrection of profound significance. This 'oldest of sibyls'[74] has the preternatural gift of clairvoyance: 'it was as though she could see through the mask that each of us wears to the inner nature behind'.[75] She lives in mysterious communion with the solar system, which she knows, by heart

[70] MV 6, 14 (VIII, 879).
[71] MA 4, 6 (VII, 244); MA 8, 7 (VII, 609).
[72] MW 2, 2 (VIII, 179).
[73] MW 3, 9 (VIII, 412–420).
[74] MW 1, 6 (VIII, 74).
[75] MW 1, 10 (VIII, 127).

and intuitively, according to its constellations; in Plotinian-Leibnizian terms[76] a cosmic entelechy or potency, and a soul whose consciousness is not separate from the material system indwelt by her. In a dream, William sees her transformed into a star (here the poet uses the words 'glorious' and 'glory' five times),[77] and the Astronomer has calculated that she, who since her childhood wandered always around our sun, in so doing 'departing, in a spiral, even further from the centre', is circling towards the outer regions; this represents, no doubt, a Dantesque progress towards the hyper-cosmic and truly divine spheres, such as Pater Seraphicus, in Christian language, commands the blessed boys at the end of *Faust*:

> Onward mount to higher circles,
> Ne'er perceived your constant growth,
> Thus, in pure eternal wise,
> Strength God through his presence grants.
> For such is the spirits' nurture
> Copious in freest aether;
> Love eternal's revelation,
> Unto bliss itself unfolding.[78]

Macaria lives 'like an angel of God on earth, for her spiritual entity, though orbiting around the sun, was moving outwards, in ever-increasing circles, towards the ultramundane'.[79] Such is the wide arc bringing Goethe back to Faust's starting-point, to the macrocosm; yet it is no magician who returns, but a human being wholly devoted to renunciation, indeed, free of self: ' 'Tis not the spirit-world is locked ...'.[80] Nevertheless, Macaria merely represents an already extrapolated, extreme piece of the world of William Master; as a whole, there is simply no centre, unless it were purely the movement of a life. For Master too is a shadow of Goethe's existence, a part of his *autobiography*, which, then, holds the true key to all his work.

[76] 'What we designate with the term 'entelechy' he [Leibniz] called monads.' C 7.3.1830 (XXIX, 399).

[77] MW 1, 10 (VIII, 134–155).

[78] F, ll. 11918–11925 (V, 520).

[79] MW 3, 15 (VIII, 482).

[80] F, l. 443 (V, 157).

Everything that delighted or tormented him Goethe felt the need 'to change into an image, a poem . . . whatever came to be known of me in this way represents mere fragments of a greater confession, and this book [*Truth and Fancy*] is the bold attempt to execute that task.'[81] Goethe indicates the nature of his annals in the heading 'Completing all I have told of myself'. All the myths he used or invented ultimately refer to himself; he himself is the 'Prometheus', his 'Mohammed' and his 'Ganymede', he drives in the coach of 'Postillion Chronos' (that is, Time), he is 'Faust' and 'Master', 'Werther', 'Clavigo', 'Tasso', Edward and the Major, the 'Man of fifty years' and 'Hatem', and it is he who, in the loneliness of the last years, sings the 'Elegy' of Marienbad. He had to construct a national literature out of practically nothing; *Truth and Fancy* describes the sparse material available. Beyond Klopstock, Lavater and Herder there was almost nothing worth while, and certainly there was no myth, so that one course only remained for Goethe: to give the essence of his own self as the point of crystallisation for an entire age; to make of himself a kind of substitute myth, in hand, at times unjust *résistance* (*Xenien*), and with one-sided aye and no, nevertheless of such universal breadth as to shelter an age which, after all, is not called the Age of Kant, or of Schiller, or of Hegel, since it can only be Age of Goethe. That is why at the beginning, and again at the end, Goethe identified himself so closely with Nature; we must consider 'with reverence a personality in which the seed of a great destiny has been shown, and which must now await the development of this conception and may not, cannot, accelerate either the good or the bad, either the happy or the unhappy times to come'.[82] And the further this destiny unfolds, the more does its bearer deem worthy to be borne, everything, even the most stray products of chance, becoming as Goethe would say mysteriously 'significant'. Unlike William Master, there is above him no 'society of the tower', and in chance he can see destiny, but in destiny the appearing glory of the guiding god himself. 'What men in their

[81] TF 2, 7 (X, 312).
[82] EA 2, 3 (IX, 148).

undertakings do not and cannot take into account, and whose power is most strikingly revealed just when their greatness should most appear in glory—afterwards they call it "chance"—that is none other than God, appearing directly in his omnipotence and glorifying himself through some utterly insignificant thing.'[83]

In *Master* and elsewhere, character-formation is admittedly seen primarily as a bringing-out of innate capacities;[84] 'every capacity is important and must be developed'.[85] Indeed, 'Our wishes are presentiments of abilities latent within us, signs of what we will some time be able to do'.[86] True, this view is contradicted by Natalia;[87] but while she allows her actions to be governed by the situation rather than by disposition and inclination, still the two possibilities unite perpetually in Goethe's conception that his destiny (being that of a 'great entelechy'), is determined at once from within and from above, at once in a micro- and in a macrocosmic context.

Determined 'from within', in the sense that the fundamental experience of his youth was the ever-flowing miracle of his creative powers, which he saw well up from the same centre as the springs of Nature themselves. 'Thou dwellst with me, thou source of Nature' the Artist says in 'The Artists spring wells up from Earth',[88] while the Poet of 'The Eternal Jew' says 'For 'tis an urge, and so a duty';[89] looking back on these two, Goethe said: 'I have become accustomed to regard my innate poetic talent entirely as Nature'.[90] In Italy the same statement, now reflecting his new-found classical objectivity, is applied to all great art: the 'great works of art were at the same time sublime works of Nature, produced by men in accordance with true and natural laws. Everything arbitrary and fanciful collapses; but here

[83] To Riemer, 25.11.1807 (XXII, 478).

[84] 'Nothing is possible without an innate gift' is the view of the Abbé in particular (MA 8, 3 (VII, 558)).

[85] MA 8, 5 (VII, 592).

[86] TF 2, 9 (X, 424).

[87] MA 8, 3 (VII, 566).

[88] IV, 227.

[89] IV, 233.

[90] TF 4, 16 (X, 735).

necessity, God, is at work'.[91] Such is the *raison d'être* of Prometheus; dispensing with individual gods, even Zeus, he works in harmony with his divine Muse and destiny, creating his figures: 'The mythological point where Prometheus steps on to the stage was something I was always aware of; it had become a living *idée fixe*.'[92] Hence also that vital concept 'the moment' (expressing consummated time and intimated eternity), at first much less a philosophical theory than a direct experience, the spring ever welling up afresh in the innermost centre. It runs through all the youthful poems, through *Master*, *Faust* and the *Divan*; and even in the later years there are lines such as:

> look . . .
> The moment in the eye! And no postponement!
> Go swift and meet him, eager and warm-hearted,
> Be it in action, joy unto your friend.
> E'er childlike, let where thou art be all,
> Thus art thou all, and shalt not be o'ercome.[93]

We should not forget Goethe's inherent ability to forget and begin again, his power of constant regeneration ('Ilmenau', the beginning of *Faust* II after the Gretchen tragedy, etc.). He rejects the very concept of memory; 'when we have encountered something great, beautiful or momentous, it must not wait to be re-called, re-collected, so to speak, from outside; rather it must from the outset weave itself in with, become one with, our inmost being . . . in this way it will live on in us, ever forming and creating. The past we long to bring back does not exist; there is only an eternal newness'.[94] We have here the *actus purus* in the origin of existence, the same that inspired Faust's translation 'In the beginning was the Act', and his creator to derive the immortality of the 'entelechian monad' from a 'restless activity.[95] This act is

[91] IJ 3, 6.9.1787 (XI, 434).
[92] A 1807 (XI, 821).
[93] P I, 478. And in a last addition to *Years of Wandering*: 'Now that they had accepted renunciation' it was among 'their strange duties . . . that when they met they might speak neither of the past nor of the future; only the present might concern them' (MW 1, 4 (VIII, 44)).
[94] To Chancellor v. Müller, 4.11.1823 (XXIII, 315).
[95] To Zelter, 19.3.1827 (XXI, 728).

purely procreative, in the *coincidentia oppositorum*, beyond good and evil ('what we call evil is but the other side of good',[96] a saying repeated many times in a watered-down form); it became for Goethe a constantly new and overpowering reality, in Eros.

Goethe's poetry draws from the quintessential vigour of Eros, and his 'May Song' testifies to his archetypal procreation. ('How splendidly doth/ Nature shine to me!/ The gleaming sun,/ The laughing meadows! . . ./ O Love, o Love!/ So golden fair,/ Like morning clouds/ On yonder heights!/ Thy blessing crowns/ The fields fresh,/ In blossom mist/ The world so rich./ O maiden, maiden/ My love for thee!/ Thy glance, thy eye!/ Thy love for me!')[97] There is, in *Years of Wandering*, a magical recreation of an earliest boyhood memory: William and a friend, a fisherman's son, are tumbling about by the river on a fine Pentecost day; the boys undress, bathe, and then stand there, 'dazzled by a triple sun': the sun in the sky and in the water, and the sun of the glorious human shape, 'of which I had had no conception'; 'amid fiery kisses, we swore an eternal friendship.' William-Goethe adds: 'In later life that first blossoming of the outside world came to represent pristine Nature as she truly is; thereafter, everything our senses apprehend seems no more than so many copies, lacking, however close the resemblance, the original spirit and meaning.' Without a pause he continues: 'What despair ours would be, to see the outer world so cold, so lifeless, were it not that something evolves within us to render Nature glorious in quite a different way, a creative power by virtue of which it is we who become beautiful in her'.[98] In their origin Nature and creative-transfiguring love arise inseparably: 'Amor, the landscape-painter'.[99] For Goethe, a word transfigured by love is 'glorious':

Today, all's glorious to me; if 'twould but last!
Today I see through Love's eye-glass.[100]

[96] 'On Shakespeare's day' (IV, 125).
[97] I, 52.
[98] MW 2, 11 (VIII, 292–297). Soon afterwards the beloved boy drowns.
[99] P I, 387–389.
[100] 'The Book of Suleika', D III, 369.

Out of love comes the art of poetry; rhyme, which Faust teaches Helen, is love's dialogic game,[101] invented by Behramgur for Dilaram: 'For sure 'tis Love's resplendent All.'[102] The quintessence of love the *Divan* calls 'spirit', and love itself is the quintessence of life:

For Life is Love,
And Life's life, Spirit.[103]

In the *Roman Elegies* the poet prays the god to grant him and everyone this alpha and omega of all the world's goods.[104] Eros is not just enjoyment; after every amorous disappointment love is still the same vital medium for experiencing the *kalon* and *agathon* of existence. Reflecting on Gretchen, on his love in Frankfurt, Goethe says: 'It seems to be Nature's will that each sex should find a tangible form of goodness and beauty in the other. Thus did the sight of this girl and my feeling for her open up a new world of beauty and excellence.'[105] The unbroken continuity between *eros* and *agape* appears in the deliberately shocking 'The God and the Dancing-girl',[106] while a letter looking back on the experience at Marienbad says: 'Meantime I have . . . enjoyed much; and according to Holy Scripture much must be forgiven me, for I have loved much'.[107] And just as Dante peopled his Venus' Heaven with women doing homage to *eros* while purifying themselves for *agape*, Goethe's Faustian heaven is filled with Magdalenes in the biblical and early Christian tradition, joined now by the Gretchen who once killed a child. It is they who lay before Mary the plea on Faust's behalf. Goethe knows and accepts that there is a price, that passion 'also means suffering' and imposes upon the

---

[101] F, ll. 9377ff. (V, 437–481).

[102] D III, 360. Not only rhyme but all poetry springs from eros. 'The words are like fans! Between the slats/ A pair of lovely eyes peeps out' (D III, 305).

[103] D III, 356; see the notes in *Divan* III, 456.

[104] P I, 178.

[105] TF I, 5 (X, 189).

[106] P I, 158.

[107] To L. F. Schultz, 8.9.1828 (XXI, 563).

coerced lover an experience of renunciation: 'To love is to suffer. Only under constraint can one enter upon it, that is, one must, one does not want to'.[108] We shall return to the question of renuncation later.

If the great figures we have here encountered bear but fragmentary witness to the continuity governing the Goethean 'formation' of the genius—whose essence is, since *eros* blossoms ever anew, a gaining and a generation of form—nevertheless this idea of formation is not just exposed to the winds; it remains embedded in an all-embracing Nature whence 'stream floods of heightened figures'.[109] 'Heightened' does not mean 'random' or 'arbitrary'; it refers to a process which constitutes the second fundamental law, as Goethe saw it, of Nature's activity. '*Tuchê*, Chance', may 'dally' her way through life, '*Eros*', Love from heaven, cascade down on the 'graven form', '*Anankê*, Necessity', '*Elpis*, Hope' stretch it; the 'law by which thou entered first' remains intact. In 'Utterances. Orphic' are most profound statements on both man and Nature;[110] Goethe, heedless of all Idealists and Romantics, draws back into their all-embracing framework; only by virtue of God's revelation in Nature can he be a human being, and only by virtue of the formed figure, he, as a human being, has received through God-Nature can he be lord of creation and, in his own way, pious. For Goethe, Nature is the proper site of glory; glory to him consists precisely in the truth that the 'graven form' displays from *within* itself the infinitely mysterious Idea, which idea—being the one and only[111]—always, however, remains the divine *beyond* all appearing phenomena. His research into Nature produced what Goethe saw as his most important work, the *Theory of Colours*; but there is all his other research as well— mineralogical, botanical, zoological, anatomical, meteorological—all fragments of a monstrous morphology the outlines of which he worked so stubbornly to draw. It is here

[108] To Riemer, 11.7.1810 (XXI, 563).

[109] P I, 522.

[110] P I, 523.

[111] 'The Idea is eternal and unique; to use the plural is inappropriate' (XVII, 701).

that he once again stands alone, and never more lonely, against his age, experiencing not without bitterness their lack of understanding. His aim was to combine the cool precision of scientific research with a constant awareness of the totality apparent only to the eye of reverence, the poetic-religious eye, the ancient sense for the cosmos. But the scientists had gone over to his arch-enemy Newton, the Idealists preferred to deduce Nature as an *a priori* system, or, if they were Romantics, to feel a vague irrational feeling of the whole. Goethe was just as much a lone fighter in his age as Thomas Aquinas had been when he sought to combine exact research and intellectual work with a reverentially pious perception of the divine presence in the cosmos. For without uniting the two, there can be no attitude objective enough to do justice to existence.

2. THE FORM OF NATURE AND GLORY
GOD AND NATURE

Like the ancients, Goethe neither could nor would separate God's immanence from his transcendence, not least because— with the exception of poetic licence—he refused to explain the convergence of all Nature's individual entelechies in terms of a universal soul distinct from and subordinated to God. At the same time he rejected a flat pantheistic interpretation of the mystery, and so was left with the hyphenated formula 'God-Nature',[1] which, however, he expanded in careful periphrases; he could speak of the 'purity and beauty of the universe in which God reveals himself',[2] could describe Nature as an 'organ of the Divine',[3] and warn against dividing 'what God in his Nature brought forth united'.[4] Thus none can afford to reject the conception that 'at the root of the entire structure that is the world' 'there lies an Idea, whereby God may work and create in Nature, and Nature in God, in all eternity'. To this he added his lines on

[1] P I, 522, and often.
[2] 'Aphorisms on Light and Colour' (Ipsen 2, 649).
[3] XVII, 708: cf. P I, 521.
[4] XVI, 884.

'the eternal Weaver and her masterpiece'; how busily she lays the warf, 'That the eternal Master can/ So carefreely his weft cast in'.[5] Goethe, like Plato, could not be content with a plethora of ideas, no more than his Mohammed (in the first fragment of the planned drama) with a polytheistic heaven. The stars ascend in glory, and each time the glowing heart would gladly consecrate itself to the glowing object of its longing. To the sun: 'Be my lord thou my God! Allseeing, lead me. Thou too o glorious one descendest'; the heart lifts itself up to the 'Creator', the 'all-loving Thou' present in all things as love: 'Seest thou Him not? By each quiet spring, each blossoming tree, he cometh to find me in the warmth of his love. How I do thank him, for that he hath opened my breast, and taken away the hard shell that did encase my heart; now can I know of his approach.'[6] This Mohammed of his youth looks forward to the aged Goethe's *Divan*, in which Islam and, with yet greater sincerity, the ancient Persian creed are evoked; the religious form represented by the individual myth is superseded, for the poet, borne by the wings of Eros, looks beyond the marvel of the appearing phenomenon to the single mystery within.

It is here that Goethe likes to speak of *glory*; although without the ecstatic mystical ring, the sense of apotheosis, we found in Hölderlin, his lofty and solemn utterances often attain to the same sphere. In the *Italian Journey* the word, at least in its isolated sentence, makes a superficial if not pallid impression on the lower and middle levels; however, the dense overall usage conveys a general state of mind which the phenomena somehow through their heightened theophanous potential satisfy. So many things are 'glorious' in Italy: the climate,[7] the weather,[8] the morning,[9] the sunset,[10] the night of the full moon,[11] the clear sky,[12] a great

[5] XVI, 872–873; 'To cherish and be cherished by Nature' (P I, 509).
[6] 'Mohammed,' IV, 181–182.
[7] IJ XI, 121.
[8] *Ibid.* 185, 464.
[9] 126, 303, 404.
[10] 237, 345.
[11] 209, 251.
[12] 390.

stream in the gloaming,[13] an oak forest,[14] the sight of spring,[15] the sea,[16] the area of Campagna;[17] and Rome,[18] especially the historical city,[19] St Peter's[20] and its liturgy,[21] St Paul-outside-the-Walls,[22] Caserta,[23] Naples (time and again),[24] Capri,[25] (with great feeling) Paestum,[26] Pompeii,[27] Girgenti,[28] the view from Etna,[29] one of Raphael's pictures,[30] Michelangelo[31]—and much besides. Later, Goethe spoke of Italy as the 'glorious element of art',[32] and described how he lived there 'amid the most glorious phenomena'.[33] Often the word by itself seems not enough; while walking in Girgenti, for example, he reaches a vantage-point 'where the view ... was still more glorious';[34] or the full moon 'lends to the evening an indescribable glory'.[35] Goethe is 'comfortably at ease in all this glory'.[36] In the difficult time that followed Italy, the word fossilised somewhat into an ornamental epithet, with the role, for example, of investing the petty-bourgeois world of *Hermann and Dorothea* with a

[13] 492.
[14] 205.
[15] 298.
[16] 215.
[17] 200.
[18] 141.
[19] 167.
[20] 389.
[21] 170.
[22] 498.
[23] 225.
[24] 207, 241–242, 350, 385.
[25] 246.
[26] 238, later: 'Paestum is the last and, dare I say, most glorious Idea I now take north with me, intact' (352).
[27] 223.
[28] 298–299, 303.
[29] 321.
[30] 500.
[31] 158.
[32] XVI, 932.
[33] XI, 168.
[34] 299.
[35] 251.
[36] 167.

little mild shimmer. Here we find the German soil 'glorious',[37] and the wide landscape,[38] the rich acres,[39] the fields,[40] the rococo grotto where coffee is served,[41] the horses,[42] the men,[43] the maiden Dorothea,[44] Hermann's weighty words,[45] the naming of Paris as capital of the world,[46] the early days of the Revolution,[47] the two lovers,[48] their future together[49] and their hopes.[50] As for the *Achilleis*, in which the word occurs some twenty times, only the generally elevated tone makes it sound so sublime; it is a mechanical epithet used to lift the proceedings on to an heroic level.

How different, how much more from the heart, is its glow when it is used in the writings on natural science, or in the summary of these theories in the two programmatic poems on metamorphosis. In 'The Metamorphosis of Plants' it gains a new density through juxtaposition with the word 'holy'. His beloved need not be confused by the multitude of shapes among garden plants, behind which there lies 'a secret Law,/ A holy Riddle'. Let her consider how a plant unfolds its seed and breaks through the earth:

> Thus to delectable Light, holy and ever unresting,
>   Straightway entrusting the frame so frail of
>   burgeoning leaves.

The principle of height induces growth, such that often it 'arouses astonishment'; but then Nature slows the seed, thus to unfold 'the wonder' of the flowering on its rejuvenated

[37] 4, l. 100 (III, 192).
[38] 4, l. 77 (III, 191).
[39] 4, l. 186 (III, 195).
[40] 4, l. 195 (III, 195).
[41] 3, l. 90 (III, 187).
[42] 4, l. 5 (III, 188).
[43] 5, l. 99 (III, 201).
[44] 5, l. 192 (III, 205); 8, l. 96 (III, 231).
[45] 5, l. 222 (III, 206).
[46] 6, l. 16 (III, 208).
[47] 6, l. 36 (III, 208).
[48] 9, l. 55 (III, 233).
[49] 6, l. 156 (III, 213).
[50] 9, l. 293 (III, 242).

stalk. 'Thus doth Nature display her finery noble and rich
. . ./ Ever a marvel new . . . Yet the glory becomes the Herald
of new creation,/ Aye, the colourful leaf feeleth the hand
divine.' Goethe is referring to the mystery of fructification;
first the necessary organs evolve, then the pairs take their
places about the consecrated altar, 'and glorious scents stream
forth/ Mightily fragrances sweet, and up life springs all
around'. 'The letters the goddess doth print today' are
everywhere there for the beloved to decipher; then she will
understand the poet's invitation: 'upward doth holy Love/
Strive to the highest fruit: two that are of one mind.'[51]

In contrast, 'The Metamorphosis of Animals' is completely
dedicated to the immanent natural order; it is concerned not
with the εἶδος but with the μορφή, with how life takes
shape under necessary and wonderful limitations. Thus we
read of 'harmony', of the 'beautiful concept of power and its
limits, of arbitrariness and law, freedom and restraint, and
flowing order'; of 'the beauty of form' and the 'holy circle of
living formulation' whose boundaries no god can extend. All
these are classical concepts explicitly embracing sub-human
Nature and human moral nature alike:

> No higher concept will e'er be found in the realm of
> ethics,
>   Nor by the man of action, the artist, or the great
> ruler.

And it is man's prerogative to scale the heights of this 'highest
thought' of universal Nature.[52] Here the word 'glorious' is
absent, but it returns all the more insistently in the same
collection 'God and the World'; in the appended verses
containing the poet's reflections on Schiller's skull. With great
emotion Goethe considers the law dictating that the spirit be
introduced into this 'arid shell' that nobody could love,
'however glorious the essence it preserved'; but Goethe, so
adept at reading the forms of life, can decipher the writing of
this skull. 'The holy meaning did not speak to all'; he,
however, was able to pick out among the common crowd of

51 P I, 203–206.
52 P I, 519–521.

skulls 'a figure priceless, glorious'.[53] But this 'noble essence' and 'holy meaning' can never seek to exist outside the circle of 'Nature', as Goethe understands this; 'Is not Nature's essence/ In the hearts of men?'[54] Haller is called a philistine for maintaining that 'no created spirit/ In Nature's heart can see';[55] for who would be interested in the mere shell if the essence remained beyond all reach? For it is Goethe's 'ancient belief' 'that Nature has no secret she does not somewhere bring naked before the eyes of the alert observer'.[56] This is the truth without which one will never reach 'that glorious period' of life in which 'everything within our understanding comes to seem unworthy and foolish'; 'glorious' because it represents 'a point half-way between desperation and deification', as Montan says in *Years of Wandering*.[57] His explanation: 'Letters are no doubt a fine thing, but in vain do we seek in them the notes; notes we need, but from them we shall never hear the true meaning ... Nature has but one script, and all the scrawl we meet is so much useless lumber.'[58] Plotinus would agree; the mystery is plain and open because it is a true mystery.

A COSMIC ALPHABET

Schiller, when he first met Goethe, made a comment that left him perplexed and also annoyed; his 'original plant' was 'not real but ideal'. To which Goethe replied: 'That is what I like to hear; I not only have ideal forms in my head without knowing it, I can actually see them.'[59] He had to struggle hard to win this power of seeing, through unremitting observation, experimentation, induction, and provisional 'empirical laws' serving as hypotheses; and if a case contradicted the law, the whole perspective would have to be

[53] P I, 522.
[54] P I, 529.
[55] P I, 529.
[56] A XI, 626.
[57] M W I, 3 (VIII, 38–39).
[58] *Ibid.* 40.
[59] XII, 622.

shifted on to a higher level.[60] Goethe saw clearly that such a method took him into a sphere beyond empiricism and Kantian idealism, and Heinroth's comment that his thinking was 'totally engaged in the realm of objects' found a grateful ear ('A single intelligent sentence can be so much help').[61] Tongue slightly in cheek, he enlisted the authority of Kant's *intellectus archetypus*: 'We, through the observation of an ever creating Nature, made ourselves worthy of spiritual participation in her products'.[62] Goethe cannot be seen as a naive objectivist; 'Nature' is implicitly understood as the mutual reciprocity and indwelling of subject and object: 'All that is in the subject is in the object, and something more besides; all that is in the object is in the subject, and something more besides.'[63] That holds particularly true in the aesthetic theory: 'The Law that comes before our eyes, in complete freedom, under its own unique conditions, brings forth the beauty of objects; there must then be found worthy subjects, able to apprehend it'.[64] A similar structure of identity-in-tension is postulated for the relationship between the sensual and the spiritual spheres; Goethe had no time for 'lower and higher powers of the soul'. 'In the human spirit as in the cosmos nothing is higher or lower, for everything demands equal rights from a common mid-point that itself can only manifest its secret existence through the harmony existing between the parts and itself.'[65] Both dualisms are already implied for him in the concept of (appearing) reality (the appearance of God in his world), in the essential Pythagorean-Plotinian tradition; and here we meet a whole list of dualities with echoes in the history of ideas: 'We and the objects [Aristotle], light and darkness [Mani], body and soul [Plato], two souls [Paul, Faust], spirit and matter [Descartes], God and the world [Plotinus, Goethe], thought and extension [Spinoza], ideal and

[60] 'Experience and Science', XVI, 859–871.
[61] XVI, 879f.
[62] 'Perception and the faculty of Judgment', XVI, 877–879.
[63] XVII, 774.
[64] XVII, 703–704.
[65] XVI, 884.

real   [Schelling],   sense   and   reason   [Kant],
imagination   and   intellect   [Jean   Paul],   existence   and
yearning [Fichte]'.[66] To sum up: 'Reality and division
are synonymous.'[67] This fundamental structure, which
Goethe terms 'polarity', for once permits him to venture into
the Idealistic camp; he was able, much to the philosopher's
astonishment, to make a precise summary of Fichte's system[68]
and to translate his own ideas on to that plane (after all,
Fichte's 'I' with its various destinies is not far removed from
Faust).

The theory of colours is absolutely within the Plotinian
tradition. The premise here is the identity-in-tension of
objective and subjective light (the receiving organ is the 'sun-
like' eye). 'Thus the eye evolves by virtue and on behalf of
light, that the inner light may meet the outer.' In support he
quotes the Ancient Greek saying: 'Like is known only by
like.'[69] Thus colour is 'an elementary natural phenomenon'
that, operating within the analogical area of tension holding
object and subject, is characterised by continual transitions; in
the   three   fields—subjective,   subjective-objective   and
objective—it behaves respectively as 'physiological', 'physical'
and 'chemical' colour. Here it is decisive, firstly that this
analogical context provides the arena for everything that
happens in the world around us (any sweeping statement that
the senses are deceptive is therefore nonsense: 'So in the senses
put your trust,/ And never shalt thou see awry,/ If awake thy
mind thee keep').[70] Secondly, this complete openness is due
as much to the highest objective natural phenomenon, light,
as to the eye, and Goethe even accords priority to the
objective phenomenon. (Admonishing Schopenhauer: 'What!
Light is only there inasmuch as you see it? No! You would
not be there if the light did not see you!')[71] Light, being thus

[66] 'Polarity', XVI, 863.
[67] XVII, 700.
[68] Cf. also the scheme XVI, 917f., and comment by A. Speiser, ibid.
937–938.
[69] TC, Introduction, XVI, 20.
[70] P I, 515.
[71] XXII, 741.

identified with the manifestness of existence, represents the highest thing in Nature; this implies, in its proper sphere beside horizontal polarity, the dimensionally complementary second principle of all reality: the principle of height. Colour as such arises out of the primary polarity of light and darkness; light on a dark background (the sun-lit air before the darkness of space) produces blue, and darkness before light produces yellow (the sunset). Yellow and blue in horizontal polarity produce green, but when each is in its heightened form (as orange and violet respectively) they converge into the highest phenomenon in the spectrum, 'which, on account of its high worth, we have often called purple.[72] The resulting closed ring of colours is a most welcome confirmation of the classical theory of the world and of art, that finitude and perfection belong together; it is, in fact, three-dimensional, being at once qualitatively structured, horizontal and vertical. And this upward progression (to red) is in itself highly mysterious, for 'in its light state the colour is also a dark one [because it only originates through the 'sombre' medium]; if it is made denser it will become darker, at the same time acquiring a shimmer we designate with the word "reddish"'.[73] Thus to darken is to intensify and must, in a new sense, become illuminating.

The Newtonian theory of colours, whose bitter adversary Goethe was, cannot cope with such ideas. Instead, colour is treated as a random 'phenomenon' scientifically demonstrable in, i.e. reducible to, numbers. But 'measurements, numbers and signs do not constitute a phenomenon'.[74] 'Mechanical formulae . . . have an element of crudeness. They transform the living into the dead', even if 'in many cases they can be conveniently and successfully applied'.[75] They cannot express the qualitative distinction between the whole and its parts, in a word, the 'shape' (which is the key factor). Mechanistic thinkers are consequently also quite blind to the fact that the eye, in contemplating a secondary or tertiary colour, never loses the totality of the relevant colour, itself supplying the

[72] TC 703 (XVI, 189).
[73] TC 699 (XVI, 189).
[74] Ipsen II, 678.
[75] TC 732 (XVI, 203–204).

complementary components; this explains, makes possible, the art of painting in its own realm beyond Nature.[76] Goethe appreciates and indeed shows great interest in the methodical exactness of physiology;[77] he can see, and think of, an organism in terms of its functions as well as its shape, precisely in the unfolding of the original plant, that 'ideal form'. A function cannot, however, be isolated from its totality, and an awareness of the whole, the overall unity—that is, a philosophical or artistic awareness—is needed for the ('exact') comprehension of the object as it really is. Only by using such integration can so-called scientific exactitude really be anything like exact. Complete exactitude is impossible, since no original phenomenon can as such be explained; why is yellow yellow, or blue blue? whence this original 'decision' ('The evolution of a colour is its original decision')?[78] Hence Goethe's consistent liking for the word 'decisive' (colours, for example, in combination 'produce a partially harmonious, partially characteristic, often discordant, but always decisive and powerful effect').[79] Natural beings and objective forms are always taking objective decisions. And even accepting the plant kingdom as an unforeseeable series of variations upon an original ideal form, this would never ultimately be mechanical. Instead, it would consist of monitored 'dictums' to all of which, by virtue of analogy, the 'Utterances. Orphic' correspond.

Consequently all language, not least the conceptual language of philosophy, remains 'in fact purely symbolic'.[80]

[76] TC Intro., XVI, 20.

[77] 'It is absorbing to speculate whether one might gain insight into that organic-chemical operation in life whereby the metamorphosis of plants takes place subject to a single law, but in all kinds of ways', Goethe wrote, shortly before his death, to the chemist W. F. Wakkenroder, 21.1.1832 (XXI, 1029). Astonishment at the wonders of life and acknowledgment of the 'Unfathomable' are marvellously balanced with the necessity of scientific research throughout this letter; for 'if he is truly determined man cannot desist from his attempts to corner the Unfathomable, not until he is finally satisfied and admits defeat'.

[78] TC 695 (XVI, 188).

[79] Ibid. 758 (XVI, 206).

[80] TC 751 (XVI, 203).

And even philosophy is a secondary phenomenon in comparison with poetry (for poetry is the original language of mankind, 'until finally that one and only true poetry, of the very beginning, disappears almost completely. At the beginning the philosopher is always a kind of poet').[81] He who seeks to understand the world should begin not by constructing, but by observing.[82] In so far as science adopts a mathematical exactitude, however, it becomes 'dependent upon quantitative factors . . . and so, to a certain extent, upon the external features of the world. But if we consider the world with all the spirit and powers at our command, we see that the two poles of reality as we know it must be quantity and quality. This fact leads the mathematician to drive his formulaic language to its extremest limits, to see if he can grasp the unmeasurable element in his measureable and calculable world. He can now see everything as tangible, comprehensible and mechanical, and in this he comes under the suspicion of a secret atheism. For he now believes he can also understand that most unmeasurable of all things, which we call God, and whose particular or pre-eminent nature he appears willing to abandon.'[83] Such a position thus involves not only a complete reduction of the principle (equivalent to 'height' or 'analogy') of quality within the world; the relationship between the world and God, the analogical foundation of all being, is also reduced to nothing. In this fight-back against the despotic tendencies of scientific method, Goethe was also fighting for the true cosmos and for God; for these stand or fall together.

Such is the quantitive-qualitative nature of the world of colour. But there is a further, or rather higher,[84] realm of a similar structure, that of music. While the two cannot directly be compared, they can 'be seen in terms of a higher

[81] 'The Epochs of the Sciences' (draft for TC), XVII, 762.
[82] XVI, 878.
[83] XVII, 769.
[84] 'The effects of sound must almost be placed above all else. Were not language indisputably the highest form we have, I would place . . . music even higher.' He goes on to justify the priority of notes over colours (XVI, 862).

formula'.[85] If it were not for the highly formalised and
subjectivised nature of modern music,[86] Goethe's conception
of a subjective-objective musical totality would not be far
removed from the ancient and mediaeval conception: a
cosmic harmony of human dimensions uniting spirit and
senses. In the story *Novelle* the myth of Orpheus is in the
background: one of the characters, Honorio, is passionately
in love. When there is a fire at the local circus and a tiger
escapes, he can only think of shooting it; meanwhile the
showman's boy is leading the lion home, entranced as it is by
his flute. 'In the Lion's Den Daniel had no fear; he remained
firm and undismayed, and the wild roaring could not
interrupt his pious singing.'[87] The 'child in its transfiguration'
was 'like a mighty conqueror in the hour of his victory'; but
Honorio is told 'First overcome yourself'. But in the peace of
the song that follows the discord, the strains of Orpheus pass
into Christian tones:

> The Eternal rules on earth . . .
> Faith and hope, they are fulfilled;
> Wondrous power hath the love
> That in prayer is unveiled.[88]

CLASSICISM

If in his natural philosophy proper the forms of nature have
been freely associated with the religious mystery, we find that
the humanistic approach of Goethe's theory of art tends rather
to confine all such elements within a definite compartment;
this is especially so in the middle, high classical period. In
formal structure, this theory of art remains completely within
the context familiar since the Renaissance, but with an
unmistakable tendency to stress man's independence; he is the
middle and apex to which Nature relates. 'The highest
purpose of art is to show the human form in all the sensual

[85] TC 748 (XVI, 202).
[86] TC 750 (XVI, 203).
[87] IX, 451.
[88] IX, 452.

grandeur and beauty it can.'[89] 'We know of no world save in relation to man; we want no art save that which reproduces this relation.'[90] As far as their depiction of the gods is concerned, Goethe treats the Greeks, normally so canonical in respect to art, as though their religion itself were merely aesthetic, its setting purely immanent.[91] In the essay 'Elementary Imitation of Nature, Manner, Style' these three artistic forms are presented as a hierarchy: 'elementary imitation' presupposes an initial insight into the essence of the object to be reproduced, 'manner' (as the personal 'handwriting') requires a deeper insight, while 'style' is based on 'the deepest fundaments of perception, indeed, on the very essence of things, in so far as we may perceive it in visible and tangible shapes'.[92] This 'essence' is clearly the entelechy, in other words, the Aristotelian *morphê* at the world's heart.

When Goethe occasionally speaks of the 'ideal form', partly identifying and partly contrasting it with Nature, he is assuming the linguistic garb of the Renaissance, Baroque and Enlightenment as well as Idealism; but what he means is simply the entelechy, invisible as such, but present in shapes and movements. Beginning with the Renaissance, a struggle had raged over the 'Idea'; there had been the Aristotelian interpretation, in favour of an activity of the artist's mind, a process of selection seeking out the most beautiful features (so Leonardo, Alberti); and the Platonic interpretation: sparks of inspiration from the divinity irradiating the artist's spirit. This was the view of Ficino,[93] whom within the space of a

[89] *Writings on Art*, XIII, 71.

[90] XIII, 332.

[91] 'Winckelmann and his century': While the moderns went vainly off at tangents into the infinite, 'the Ancients had an intuitive sense for, felt uniquely at ease in, the physical limitations of their fair world' (on the ancient world). They had an 'admiration for the gods merely as works of art, as it were' (on the pagans), XIII, 417, 419.

[92] XIII, 66–71.

[93] Ficino had spoken of 'innate *formulae idearum*' that flash suddenly like sparks in the spirit, awakening the memory of when the gods were visible; this conception gained ground in the aesthetic philosophy of the Baroque, with its Platonic influences. The Renaissance artists thought primarily in psychological-empirical terms; the Idea preceding creative activity, or plan (*disegno interno*), being related to the role of the eye, its search for an object's

hundred years the Manneristic era had elevated into the leading theoretician, indeed the metaphysician, of art, and we find similar variations in Zuccari, Lomazzo, Ripa, Scannelli and Bellori, some of whom feature in *Italian Journey*.[94] There have been (in ancient thought as well) many positions compromising between the objective and subjective Idea. We have seen how Goethe locates the colours in the area of tension between the poles. Similarly, the subjective Idea can be innate or a god-given inspiration, or it can be won from the intuitively grasped 'true' intention of Nature. The formulation we may call classical, or at least canonical for Classicism, is that of GIAN PIETRO BELLORI, from his programmatic speech to the Academy (1664), 'The Idea of the Painter . . . a refinement of natural beauties superior to Nature'. In the starry world God's ideas find a pure realisation; in the earthly world—and especially in mankind—often, because the material is not sufficiently well ordered, the reflection is turbid. The artist must seek to imitate the highest Artist; he must always bear in himself an image of the highest beauty, which will guide him in his search to restore to Nature her true and pure essence, her Idea.[95] Thus Nature and art were conceived of as mutually dependent in the recreation of the Idea; never have Aristotle and Plato co-operated better. Also, the religious, almost priestly and prophetic, status adhering to the artist since the times of Petrarch and Boccaccio was reaffirmed; his role, according to Zuccari, was to bring to light man's true likeness to God and unveil the paradisiac nature of the world. No doubt Rubens, Poussin, Claude Lorrain and the other great artists Goethe loved had just such a programme.

Poussin had very close contact with Bellori and adopted the latter's theory of beauty, but added a strong neo-Platonic essence (the Idea is therefore present in the object). This is Raphael's view in the letter to Castiglione (1516), and also that of Vasari (who identifies the Idea with the artist's power of visualisation). The later classical-baroque aesthetic philosophy unites the two directions. Erwin Panofsky, *Idea: Ein Beitrag zur Begriffsgeschichte der ältern Kunsttheorie* (Teubner, 1924).

[94] IJ 3, Nov. 1787; Lomazzo and Bellori (*admiranda Romae*) are mentioned (XI, 483).

[95] Panofsky 59; text of Bellori's speech, 130–138.

accent. Bellori, the antiquarian and art theorist, became the decisive influence on Winckelmann, who enlists his authority; but the German too is more exposed to the light of neo-Platonism.[96]

On a theoretical level WINCKELMANN, that canonical figure of the Age of Goethe, was responsible for very little that was new, even 'Noble Simplicity and Quiet Greatness' being an old topic.[97] He speaks freely of imitation of Nature ('naturalism') as distinct from the higher stage of 'ideal beauty', but envisaging a perfect synthesis, such as the Greeks were able to achieve partly through a unique natural gift, but partly by their own efforts. Greece represents the very marriage of ideal and reality, and the swiftest way to true imitation of Nature is by imitation of the Greeks. 'The sensual beauty provided the fairness of Nature, and the ideal beauty those sublime features; from the former the artist took the human, and from the latter the divine, aspect of his depiction.'[98] When this synthesis is called a 'noble simplicity', 'simplicity' means, in the Plotinian sense, uni-formity (the 'state of unity'),[99] indicating 'the soul's true [namely, metaphysical] character', which is expressed physically in the 'state of rest'; while 'noble' means that the soul's natural-ethical state corresponds to its 'uni-form' essence, 'quiet' (like 'rest') expresing the external correspondence to this nobility. Consequently Winckelmann, like Plotinus, insisted that 'beauty, properly speaking, is not a matter of numbers and measurements'; you might know these, but if Heaven has given you no feeling for it you will never perceive the beauty in them. For 'beauty consists in multiplicity within simplicity; this is the wise men's stone which the artists must seek, and which few find.'[100] Winckelmann, however, went on to find the signs of this 'simplicity' in constant new examples of significant posture, gestures and situations (as Goethe later put

[96] References, ibid. 117f.

[97] Wolfgang Stammler, Edle Einfalt: Zur Geschichte eines kunsttheoretischen Topos. In Worte und Werte: Festschrift für Bruno Markwardt (Berlin, 1961).

[98] Joh. Winckelmanns sämtliche Werke, ed. J. Eiselein (1825), I, 19.

[99] I, 33.

[100] I, 207.

it), and demanded an ultimate catalogue of *sujets*, spoke of 'allegories' and 'independent thinking'. The Weimar art-lovers did indeed expend much effort in finding such *sujets*, some of which became subjects for essay competitions. All labour lost, of course; in fact, it was not long before all Goethe's plans in this regard collapsed into complete failure. But the pure humanism of his programme did come from Winckelmann; for the latter had already been convinced that 'the highest object of art for thinking men is man'.[101]

And yet, in his conversations with KARL PHILIPP MORITZ in Rome, Goethe had envisaged a broader metaphysical horizon for art; the subsequent piece by Moritz, 'On the formative Imitation of beauty' (1788), is discussed by Goethe,[102] and large extracts appear at the end of *Italian Journey*. The essay begins with a grand principle: 'the horizon of creative power in the forming genius must be as wide as Nature herself; that is, the organisation must be so finely woven, must offer the copious floods of Nature so infinitely many points of contact, that the uttermost ends, as it were, of all the elements of Nature find space within this miniature vessel, and need not jostle one another'.[103] In other words, the microcosm of the genius must, so far as possible, be co-extensive with the macrocosm; that is potentially Plotinian, but also accords with Bruno, Shaftesbury, Herder and the young Goethe himself (*Faust*, 'Prometheus'). Such an horizon is beyond the reach of thought, imagination, the senses; the genius depends on 'creative power' to capture the totality in a single focal point, to choose an object 'to which he may impart a reflection of that highest Beauty whose mirror his powers are', 'and for which this smaller scale is rejuvenation'.[104] Then comes the strict Plotinian doctrine also, however, prevalent in the cult of the genius: 'The living concept of the formative imitation of Beauty can only be found in the feeling of creative power as the work is being produced, in the first moment of its

[101] I, 207; *cf. Italian Journey*: 'The Alpha and Omega of all the things we know: the human figure' (IJ 3 (XI, 425)).

[102] XIII, 71–75.

[103] IJ 3 (XI, 588).

[104] XIII, 73 (XI, 589).

genesis'. Only in the moment of birth, when the chaos *becomes* shape, is beauty genuinely there; the process over, only a shadow remains. Thought, imagination (taste) and the senses by their nature seek always the beauty above them, but can never capture it; hence it appears as the abysmal, glorious and sublime. 'Confronted by Beauty, the power of thought can no longer ask why it is so; but that is the sign of beauty . . . There are no terms in which to speak of true Beauty, save as the very essence of all the harmonious elements comprising Nature's great Whole, which no power of thought can capture. Each of the myriad fragments of beauty we find in Nature is only beautiful in so far as it partakes, to whatever extent, of this essence of all the elements comprising that great Whole.' Thus beauty is something not to be understood, but to be produced. There is also the possibility of an empathy, taste, for the original totality by virtue of which the pleasure of creation can be compensated for by that of contemplation. However, Moritz and Goethe sound a double warning. Taste is not the same as creative power, so let there be no confusion or deception over this; and the genius who works with pleasure in mind will surely fail, for 'the slightest trace of self-interest must be erased'.[105] Beauty has no purpose; 'its sure reward is in itself'. Beyond this, the creative microcosm is not identical with the macrocosm; the greater whole is only interwoven with our being, and constantly searching 'to spread back out in all directions', as it must, by a law that governs the entire natural hierarchy. Thus plants, being amid matter, seek to draw it up into themselves, and so do animals; as for man, he 'develops, grows, enjoys, in the process transforming flora and fauna alike into his inner being. In fact, everything subordinate to his own organisation he absorbs . . . into his existence . . . and then returns it, but with a new beauty, to the outside world'.[106] Such transcendental aesthetic conceptions, despite their impression of modernity, are thoroughly classical. Two sentences form the climax: 'The organisation of Nature in her entirety would be our highest Beauty, could we for one moment (ἐξαίφνης) comprehend

[105] XI, 590–593.
[106] XI, 596.

it. Each fair work of art is in its unity a miniature copy of that highest Beauty in the entirety of Nature.'[107]

This synthesis, never in fact attained, was to be the summit, the *non plus ultra*, of Goethe's speculation; and towards the end of his life he became decidedly antipathetic towards such intellectual paths: 'I find nothing more hollow and fatal than aesthetic theories.'[108] Yet the synthesis represents a daring combination of the classical with the modern-Promethean outlook, of Plotinus with Bruno, of true transcendental glory with immanent sublimity (or, to use Moritz's word, 'majesty'). We cannot quite see how it is stitched together: how macro- and microcosm relate to one another. The genius is not the totality, yet creates from within it. Their relationship is like a brotherly intimacy; there is no place in it for an act of worship. Thus Goethe's aesthetic philosophy, even after the Italian rupture, is still clearly anthropocentric, in contrast to that of Hölderlin and indeed to the much less inhibited piety of the writings on natural science. An important reason for his dislike of Romanticism was the Romantic Belief that artistic ability could be replaced or at least invigorated, by religious feeling.[109] According to Bellori's theory, the glory of art resided in its power to assemble the supreme but transitory moments of existence, and confer upon them a kind of eternity. Winckelmann's essay has a similar conception: 'The ultimate product of the ascent of Nature is the beauty of man. Now it is indeed a rare achievement of hers; too many conditions obstruct her Ideas [!], and even she, omnipotent [!] as she is, cannot remain long on this level of perfection, nor bestow lastingness on the Beauty she has brought forth. For, to be truthful, human beauty has but a moment's life. But here Art makes her entrance; for even as man finds himself on the summit of

[107] XIII, 73.

[108] To v. Müller, 1.5.1826 (XXIII, 429).

[109] 'Final Exhibition of Art', 1805: 'Such an artist relies on moral value, which is supposed to compensate for artistic weakness. They seek to express an intuition of the highest moral value through art, ignoring that such a value has only one possible incarnation: in the highest form of sensuality' (XIII, 456).

Nature, he sees that he has now become himself an entirety of Nature, bound to bring forth just such a summit within itself.' Thereupon bringing 'selection, order, harmony and meaning' into the cosmos, he 'finally rises to the production of a work of art' into which 'passes all that is glorious, admirable, and delightful; such that, as life is breathed into the human form, man is lifted above himself, the circle of his life and deeds is sealed off [!], and he is deified for a present that contains past and future ... The god [i.e. Pheidias's Zeus] had become man that man might be raised to his godhead'.[110] In the face of this Weimar gospel, any questions as to the nature of the Idea become secondary. It may be said that his contemplation of ancient sculpture led Winckelmann to a perception of 'glory in fulfilment, the Idea';[111] thus, in the essay 'Myron's Cow', it is demanded that the highest truth be sought not through slavish imitation, but through a constant awareness of the Idea.[112] We are left with a dialectical conception of experience that embraces elements ranging from empiricism through Aristotle to Plato. 'When artists speak of Nature they always, without fully knowing it, mean the Idea. It is the same with all who extol experience alone, not reflecting that experience is but the half of experience.'[113] 'Nature and Idea may not be divided without destroying both art and life.'[114]

3. GLORY AS REFLECTION
BEING AND CELEBRATION

Thus far we have considered Goethe's view of the world in terms of its 'essence', and as a manifesto addressed to his own age in favour of the classical age, in its post-Christian resurrected form. Let us finally attempt to describe its inner

[110] XIII, 421–422. Cf. 'Myron's Cow': 'The Greek conception and endeavour is to deify man, not to humanise the deity. Here is no theomorphism, no anthropomorphism!'
[111] XIII, 441.
[112] XIII, 645.
[113] XIII, 332.
[114] XIII, 331.

dimensions, its private character; for here our historical account may find its most conclusive and revealing material.

Even the vitality that characterised the ancient world is not to be compared with the Renaissance and Baroque experience. Existence then was a celebration, and this uplifted mood found expression in the *trionfo*;[1] indeed, in every great work a triumphal element was sought and celebrated.[2] Admittedly, in the Baroque culture this emotive potential was channelled into specific forms, partly mythological or mystical, partly appertaining to court life. In Goethe, however, it does not so much reappear as erupt, with a new and stark power. In later years we find him absorbed in study of 'The Triumph of Julius Caesar', a painting by Mantegna known to many through Andreani's sequence of wood-cuts. A fascinating account of his reactions begins like this: 'Trumpets and horns, a declaration of war, musicians with puffed-out cheeks. Next, throngs of soldiers, their legionary ensigns, standards, lucky signs held aloft on poles. The busts of Roma in the van; then Juno, bestower of victory, her peacock in relief, goddesses of plenty with cornucopia and baskets of flowers, swaying over streaming pennants and floating banners. In their midst, torch-pans, flaming and smoking in the air, in honour of the elements, to stir all the senses ....'[3] Thus begins the 'extravagant triumphal procession'; then follow the captured gods, the booty, elephants, arms, captive women and children, mockers, musicians, Caesar himself in the tumult, and last of all, the academics, among whom Goethe is amused to discover Gottsched, and, he thinks, a certain professor of dialectical philosophy. He is impressed above all by the all-but impossible unification of classical greatness and realistic characterisation achieved by Mantegna's art; on the one hand, the 'noble spirit', but informed by 'Nature in all her primal force'. It is true Goethean festivity.

Such *trionfi* are high-points in Goethe's life and work. It all began with the jolly, crazy hubbub of the humble fairs at

[1] W. Weisbach, *Trionfi* (Berlin, 1969).
[2] André Chastel, Art et Humanisme à Florence (1959), 485–521.
[3] XIII, 924.

Frankfurt; here were born both *Faust* (out of the puppet-play) and the Master's *Theatrical Vocation*, in initial sketches rough as wood-carvings. 'A Fair at Plundersweilern',[4] 'Shrove-tide Carnival, also to be acted after Easter',[5] 'Merry Andrew's Marriage, or, The Way of the World';[6] here, everything is much and yet nothing; just so the 'eternal Jew' would see the history of mankind. In another plan of 1801, for a 'far-reaching project' provisionally entitled 'A Stay in Pyrmont' (a spa),[7] the revels were not to obscure the essential idea; set in the sixteenth century, the novel was to present 'the hustle and bustle' of throngs of people ravaged by infirmities of body and soul; 'the Inscrutable and Holy' would 'contrast attractively' with the atmosphere of the fair. 'Thus arises, amid the tumult of the world, a City of God, about whose invisible walls the rabble, as rabbles must, roars and rages'; a strange fresco which, though never executed, tells us, even from its outlines, much about Goethe.

But now let us move on to the great festivals of real life. After the 'unbelievable chaos'[8] of the busy market-days, we come to the grand celebration marking the coronation, in Frankfurt in 1765, of Emperor Joseph II. For the youthful Goethe it was a grand delight, and later, how the old gentleman enjoyed conjuring up that scene again; 'a never-ending procession of glory'[9] (but ending on an uncanny note, with the youth overtaken by a disastrous episode). What is unusual for Goethe is that this festival becomes a metaphysical experience, of which he provides an exact account: 'Ceremonies of political and religious import exercise an infinite fascination. We see before our eyes the earthly majesty, surrounded by all the symbols of its might; but then it bows before the might of Heaven, and we realise that the two exist together. For the individual too can sense his closeness to the Divine only in abject worship.'[10]

[4] IV, 160f.
[5] IV, 171f.
[6] IV, 247f.
[7] XII, 627–629.
[8] TF I, 1 (X, 28).
[9] TF I, 5 (X, 220).
[10] TF I, 5 (X, 222).

The elevating contributions Goethe made to court occasions received something akin to this religious gleam, if rather paler. There were presentation speeches to dignitaries (often highly rhetorical, in the Baroque style),[11] pageants for the stage,[12] and masked processions[13] (a genre which then passes directly into *Faust*). In contrast to the court occasion, the monstrous parade of the 'Roman Carnival' seemed like a kind of cosmic 'saturnalia'; and rarely did Goethe's heart beat so in time as to this mighty piece of prose.[14] The Carnival is a festival 'the people gives itself': hectic, ecstatic, breathless, dangerous, proceeding only along the long, narrow, overcrowded Corso, which 'reminds us of the roads of Life itself, where everyone, actor or onlooker, masked or unmasked, from balcony or platform, can see but little space before and beside him, and in coach or on foot advances only little by little, not so much walking as being pushed, and held up rather than stopping'. And thus 'the intensest and highest pleasures, like fleeting horses, are there for a moment, touch us, and are gone, leaving scarce a trace in the soul; thus freedom and equality can be enjoyed only in the giddy swirl of madness; and the highest pleasure becomes its most alluring only when it draws very close to danger, and gives itself up lasciviously to sweetly-fearful feelings.'[15]

In the summer of 1814, Goethe, now sixty-five, witnessed a Catholic festival, the Feast of St Roch[16] in the church above Bingen, a pilgrimage laid waste in the war and recently rebuilt. We share in the joyful anticipation at Rüdesheim; the cannonades resound, and the night is clear under a 'heaven burning with stars' as they start the ascent. 'And now the

---

[11] Thus 'To a noble Lady on a journey', (P I, 367), and the poems to Empress Maria Ludowika of Austria (in Carlsbad, 1810): P II, 257, 259, 260, 263.

[12] III, 569f. The open-air 'Celebrations in honour of Louisa' should also be mentioned; Goethe's description, XII, 610–617.

[13] III, 681f.

[14] XI, 533–567 (from 1789 onwards, often published separately, but later added to *Italian Journey*).

[15] XI, 566–567.

[16] 'By the Rhine, Main and Neckar', XII, 469–497.

tumult seizes us!'—a confusion of spiritual and worldly, a divine service and stalls selling rolls, muffins, ginger-nuts; and onward draw the faithful holding their statues, standards, canopies, all of a sudden a brief and cruel fox-hunt shoots through the middle, then there is the welcome smell of freshly-fried sausages, and more than ten thousand people are there feasting and drinking, and quarrelling about which is the village with the best wine; between times there is the pretty legend of St Roch, and a beautiful sermon on him to conclude. In this last the words tremor with the emotion and and agreement of the aged Goethe; they speak of a limitless surrender to God's will, easing a neighbour's burden, even when this is dangerous, without looking for earthly reward, for 'the span of Time is too short for boundless reward'.[17] All is embedded in a wonderful, radiant landscape, with ample time to look around during te sermon in the open; he already had the geologist's hammer out as they all went up the hill. A communal celebration in a Christian landscape.

All these festivals find their climax in *Faust*, in which the hero is led through three grand celebrations (or four, counting his marriage with Helen), each very different. First come the demonic revels of the 'First Walpurgis Night', then the celebrations at the Imperial Court, and last the classical-cosmic universal feast, 'The Classical Walpurgis Night'. The devils' revelry (written in 1800–1801) is built on the massive foundations of a grandiose landscape, rugged, chaotic. On they go up the Blocksberg, and the looming mountain plays host to the witches and their grotesque goings-on. But just as we see the bloody phantom of Gretchen, and a climax seems imminent, the action breaks off, and we finish with something quite out of place: the elf-play 'The Golden Wedding of Oberon and Titania' (explicitly called an 'intermezzo'). In contrast, the 'Emperor's Masked Ball', which closely resembles a blown-up Weimar masquerade, dallies and trifles its way through over nine hundred lines[18] of masked allegory. Faust's 'Boy Guide', symbolising poetry, only has to snap his fingers, and little flames dart all over the place; but suddenly

[17] XII, 495.
[18] Over 900 lines (5065–5986), V, 304–331.

the Emperor's false beard catches fire, and his disguise—Great Pan—goes up in flames. But the Emperor is fascinated by this harmless show, while the more serious magic involving the paper-money fails to satisfy him. He now wants to see Helen and Paris. Faust, having duly conjured them up, falls in love with the ghost: 'liking, love, worship, madness'.[19] Thereupon, in the next act, he is led into the vast phantasmagoria of 'The Classical Walpurgis Night', throughout which he seeks for Helen. We lose him from sight in the illusive twists and turns that become increasingly independent, reaching a climax in a universal feast of the elements, and issuing forth into a song of praise to cosmic Eros, a kind of symphonic orchestration of Pausanias's speech in the *Symposium*: 'And everywhere Fire doth overrun,/ So let Eros reign, by whom all was begun!'[20] It is as though the conclusions of the second, third and fifth acts of *Faust* II were in competition to see which can enact the highest celebration of Being. It we may call the solutions of the second and fifth acts Eros and Agape respectively, that of the third act is Dionysus. For after Faust's marriage with Helen and Euphorion's death fall, followed by his mother's return to the depths whence she came, the classical Chorus, singing a bacchic hymn, dissolves back into the elements; fluttering away into the breezes, running away into the streams, passing into the vines, where they too will be plundered when the wine-harvest comes, and offered up to the drunken, riotous god.

SEMI–REALITY

These three conclusions from *Faust* show with particular force that whenever Goethe most elevates the value of beauty, a shading of reality becomes necessary. Now Goethe was none the less convinced that the world's highest truth is its revealed beauty; indeed, in Italy the contemplation of beauty became the path to personal truth. 'I am now living here in a peace and clarity which I had forgotten were possible. My attempt

[19] F, l. 6500 (V, 347).
[20] F, ll. 8478f. (V, 409).

to train myself in seeing and understanding things just as they are, my determination to keep a lucid eye, my complete rejection of all pretention ...; I am quietly becoming extremely happy.'²¹ In the Sistine: 'I could only look and marvel.'²² So sublime is his experience that it seems even to demand theological language: 'The gleam of the greatest works of art no longer dazzles me; now I can wander in contemplation, in true critical understanding ... I have no words to express the quiet and wakeful bliss with which I am now beginning to look at works of art.'²³ It is a 'rebirth',²⁴ a 'self-construction from within':²⁵ 'I am growing from within.'²⁶ And this is also an encounter with God, and therefore certain truth. The 'great works of art were at the same time sublime works of Nature, produced by men in accordance with true and natural laws. Everything arbitrary and fanciful collapses; but here Necessity, God, is at work'.²⁷ Nor is this power something to be comprehended, for it is an 'infinite, inscrutable Presence'; however we may 'separate, distinguish, order', 'in the end we return to contemplation, enjoyment, admiration'.²⁸ 'How infinite the world can become; we need only abide by finite things.'²⁹ It is, once again, the 'holy-open mystery', that of the form which 'ultimately comprehends all'.³⁰ Nevertheless, what Goethe so admires is only an immanent transcendence which has been alienated from its true transcendent origin and use. Long before, Goethe had entered the 'sanctuary' of the Dresden Art Gallery, as one 'enters the house of God'; but 'the ornaments of the entire temple, objects of so much worship ... seemed only set out for holy artistic purposes'.³¹ But that

---

²¹ IJ, 1, 10.11.1786 (XI, 146).
²² IJ, 1, 22.11.1786 (XI, 152).
²³ IJ 3, 25.12.1787 (XI, 492–493).
²⁴ IJ 1, 20.12.1786 (XI, 163).
²⁵ IJ 2, 15.3.1787 (XI, 226).
²⁶ IJ 3, 16.6.1787 (XI, 386).
²⁷ IJ 3, 6.9.1787 (XI, 436).
²⁸ IJ 3, entry for April (XI, 600–601); cf. XIII, 180.
²⁹ IJ 3, 22.9.1787 (XI, 440).
³⁰ IJ 3, 11.4.1787 (XI, 598).
³¹ TF 2, 8 (X, 352).

is why the truest beauty gives the dreamy impression of a semi-reality, an impression so perfectly conveyed by the Helen act.

Faust receives the magic key to admit him to the realm of the 'Mothers'; there he will find Helen and bring her back up. The 'Mothers' can be reached only 'through wilderness and desert ways', through 'ever empty distance' beyond all forms; by fleeing the entire sphere of existence and disappearing into the 'unfettered realms of images'. The Mothers 'see thee not; designs alone they see'.[32] And these germs of reality are neither wholly ideal nor wholly real; they live, not in the eternal Mind, but in the undefined potentiality of Nature or matter. There, past and future manifestations can communicate outside time, Faust can enter into communication with Helen, and a marriage between Germania and Hellas can be born. The aura of ghostly unreality surrounding Helen and her attendants, as they enter the Palace of Menelaus, is an achievement unprecedented in the poetic imagination. Even Hölderlin's 'holy islands' are more real.

The same semi-reality occupies the central position in Goethe's theory of colours; it produces a half-light which, in weaving to and fro between light and darkness, is solely responsible for the phenomenon of colour, the only medium suitable for human sight and existence. But because the colours produced by this half-light have an objective-subjective validity, their appearance is not less a reality, even though they derive only from a screening of actual light itself. Goethe returns to this theme so often that it must have deep-seated existential roots. The most powerful expression of all comes in *Faust*; a tremendous roaring sound intimates the approach of the sun; and then it rises, and the human being is dazzled:

> A sea of Fire devours us, and what fire!
> The glow of this embrace, 'tis love or hate?
> Delight and pain in alternation dire,
> We look perforce to Earth, before too late . . .

[32] F, ll. 338–341.

Then he catches sight of the water-fall and the rainbow:

Ah, but what glory, springing from the storm,
O'erarching bow of many hues, so fixed in change . . .
By colourful reflection know we life.[33]

Thus the sun—God—is a devouring *coincidentia oppositorum*;
only the 'colourful reflection' is called glorious. This
shrouding factor Goethe even projected back into the
characteristic Italian clarity he had loved so much. 'The most
beautiful aspect is that even at a short distance the vivid
colours are softened by the tone of the air . . . It is a lustre,
and at the same time an overall harmony, a scaling, such as
we in the north have no conception of . . . It is the same as
with happiness and wisdom; their archetypal images hover
before us, and we scarcely touch the hem of their dress.'[34]
We are all familiar with Goethe's favourite Nature-symbols:
the mist (especially in the youthful lyric poetry) and the
cloud, depicted in its insubstantial changefulness in 'Howard's
Revered Memory';[35] the poet 'from airy worlds doth receive/
O'erpassing matter mild/ That he may clasp it, feel and form
it'.[36] In 'Entoptical Colours', optical experiments generating
a 'most lovely play of colours' are applied to man's
intermediate existence, and here too, in the weight of the
final line, the word 'glorious' occurs:

Mirror here and mirror there
Double setting, finely chosen;
In between and in the twilight
Crystalline the earth-dweller . . .
Let the Macrocosm in his
Eerie habitants rejoice!
'Tis the little worlds so dear
Hold the really glorious things.[37]

We find the same idea in the *Divan* ('The Reunion'): God's

---

[33] F V, 294.
[34] IJ 2, 24.11.1787 (XI, 478–479).
[35] P I, 524f.
[36] 'Nota bene', P I, 526.
[37] P I, 527.

creation divides initially into the pure duality of Light and Darkness, and then dawn 'unfolds from the gloom a ringing scale of colours', here symbolising the unifying power of eros.[38] Another variation (in 'A lofty Image') has the rainbow as a connecting bridge between Helios and Iris (the weeping rain-cloud); Iris brightens, but the god still cannot reach her.[39] The flight of the human spirit cannot bear the glare of the absolute; man 'Hath in likeness and image enough'.[40] He should 'perceive Life's colours bountiful/ As through fine crape, in pale yet pleasing guise', as the worldly-wise Princess puts it in *Tasso*.[41]

Within the context of 'The Gospel of Beauty'[42] this modifying process becomes particulary important in dealing with 'every sort of ugliness', which, since it 'cannot simply be driven from the world, has in the realm of art to be banished to the lowly sphere of the ridiculous'.[43] Significantly, the Nibelungen, which both fascinated and exasperated Goethe, represented, in a pejorative sense, something 'truly heathen', 'even if they did conform with church ritual; for Homer was always in contact with the Divine, but in these people there is not the slightest reflection of Heaven'.[44] This is confirmed in the Diaries: 'What is so terrible about the *Song of the Nibelungen* is that it does not reflect a further dimension; the heroes just exist through and for themselves, like so many beings of bronze.'[45] The profound words in the letter to Riemer have the same meaning: 'The Idea is closely connected with illusion; this is its image, so to speak, its painter. It is, indeed, none other than the Idea itself, clothed in a minimum of concrete form.'[46] Such radiant illusion both provides a transition to the finite world and invests finite things with their religious

[38] D III, 364–365.
[39] D III, 362–363.
[40] P I, 509.
[41] T 2, 1 (VI, 238).
[42] TF 2, 8 (X, 346).
[43] *Ibid.* 348.
[44] Conversation 837 (XXII, 521).
[45] Supplementary Vol. 2, 293.
[46] 20.2.1809 (XXII, 538).

aura. Clearly glory is no more for Goethe than a facet of beauty itself, namely its power to illuminate, and is therefore less independent than in ancient thought, to say nothing of Christianity. Glory attends the visible form while it lasts, and attends eros likewise. For both have their twilight, as Goethe knew too well.

FRAGMENT AND RENUNCIATION

But the boundary we have fixed is in fact crossed by all the great works and figures of the old poet. According to the experience and philosophy of the young Goethe, 'the moment' represents contact with, attainment of, eternity, whereas in the middle period the fulfilment given by beauty is a semi-reality. With the passage of time, with the fading of beauty, the nothingness and fragmentary nature of existence come to the fore, and so too the need for renunciation. We recall, at the very beginning, the violent crisis of *Werther*, the hero's 'disgust at life'.[47] 'The principal reason, however, for this nausea is the return of love'; the diasappointment that something which ought, by virtue of its inner meaning, to be unique can really be repeated. Add to this 'that our only prospect is to prolong our lives in a sluggish bourgeois existence devoid of spirituality',[48] and why not simply put an end to it all? Among the reminiscences of Strassburg we read: 'Real life often becomes so lack-lustre that it takes the varnish of fiction to restore its shine'.[49] But varnish cannot deceive for ever; Goethe had a mordant sense for the transitoriness and eventual disappointment of even the greatest experiences. At the end of his tour of Sicily comes a surprising retrospect: 'We had really seen nothing but utterly futile attempts by the human race to preserve itself against the violence of Nature, the spiteful malice of Time, and the wrath of her own internecine conflicts.'[50] In Girgenti he stood before 'ruins wearing away inexorably to nothing.'[51] In

[47] TF 3, 17 (X, 631).
[48] *Ibid.* 632, 637.
[49] TF 2, 9 (X, 402).
[50] IJ 2 (XI, 343).   [51] *Ibid.* 304.

Rome, even quite recent apartment buildings were disintegrating, like the families living in them; 'indeed, even that which had been kept fresh and alive seemed to be sickening, as though gnawed at in secret by some worm. For how could any earthly thing hope to remain standing without actual physical strength, relying only on moral and religious props?'[52] In *Electoral Affinities* the author considers whether human memory can provide a kind of perpetuity, but concludes that 'even this image, this second existence, sooner or later flickers and goes out'.[53] In the same novel, the lord has maintained his estates on behalf of a son 'who takes no interest . . . Who is there now to enjoy my buildings, my park, my gardens?' Ottilie, reflecting on what she herself has done, is aghast; it seems as though everything 'is really quite useless'.[54] The poet of the Marienbad 'Elegy' knows that even the memory of love fades; that the beloved keeps an eternal place in the heart is an idea now forgotten.[55] In such moments we sense all the conviction of Goethe's experience of life, and a change for the better, any progress, seems absurd. 'The more I see of the world, the less I can hope that mankind will ever become a wise, sensible and happy conglomeration.'[56] Witness the teaching of *Hermann and Dorothea*:

> Yet then too set thou but lightly thy fleeting foot on
>   the ground,
> For double the pain that doth lurk awaiting misfortune
>   new.
> The Day be holy to thee; but life shouldst thou not
>   esteem higher
> Than any other good, and all goods treacherous are.[57]

So too Wilhelm Meister finds that ill fortune and sickness 'have robbed him of the pure feeling of youth, and given him in return a sense for the transitoriness, the fragmentariness

---

[52] IJ 3, entry for Dec. (XI, 505).
[53] EA 2, 2 (IX, 146).
[54] EA 2, 10 (IX, 212–213).
[55] P I, 478.
[56] IJ 2, 17.5.1787 (XI, 352).
[57] III, 242.

of our existence'.[58] The logical ending to his life will be the way of 'renunciation'; so too for the Major in *Electorial Affinities*, Eugenia in *The Natural Daughter*, Nausicäa in the planned tragedy,[59] Epimetheus in *Pandora*; already in *Tasso* the hero is told that many things 'but through restraint/ And through renunciation may be ours',[60] and compare Faust's 'Thou must forego! Forego must thou!'[61] It is a lesson Goethe sought to inculcate into himself when still young, in 'Ilmenau': 'He who would truly lead others must be able to forego much.'[62] In his old age, he summed up his life in the same terms: 'Our physical and social life alike, our customs, habits, worldly wisdom, philosophy, religion, and indeed so many chance events, all cry out to us: we should renounce. So much of our most intimate nature we are unwilling to develop for the sake of the outside world; what we need from outside, to complete our inner selves, we are denied, while we have imposed on us so much that is alien and irksome.' We 'find ourselves forced gradually and then totally to abandon our personality. And ... the more bitter the cup, the sweeter our face must be, for the slightest grimace on our part might offend the casual observer ... We try everything out, and in the end we cry that all is useless ... Few indeed are those who, seeing the inevitability of this unbearable feeling, and seeking to avoid any partial resignation, resign themselves once and for all, for ever'[63]—or who, like St Roch, are capable of a 'limitless surrender to God's holy will', a 'complete submission'.[64] While the word 'resignation' has a classical-Stoic ring, 'surrender' recalls a Christian theme; between the two comes Spinoza's *amor dei*, so important to Goethe presumably precisely because of this mediating role. In the end, neither the Stoic nor the Christian solution could suffice by itself, and thus the last images of this search all

---

[58] MA 4, 17 (VII, 286).
[59] IJ 2, 8.5.1787 (XI, 325–328).
[60] T 2, 1 (VI, 245).
[61] F, l.1549 (V, 189).
[62] P I, 364.
[63] TF 4, 16 (X, 731–732).
[64] XII, 493.

cluster round that middle Goethe designated symbolically with the name of Spinoza, representing, like Leone Ebreo and Philo, a pre-Christian Jewish tradition in a classical context. Let us look at three such final images—*Pandora, Electoral Affinities* and *Years of Wandering*—and conclude with a few words on Goethe and the Bible.

Pandora, a fragment of a festival drama whose full title— certainly intended as a parallel to 'The Return of Christ'— was to have been 'The Return of Pandora', is a draft, of eschatological (and thereby unclassical) conception, whose theme is the possible integration of man. Pan-dora ('All-Gifts' of the gods), who should have brought healing to a humanity sunk in dichotomy and polarity, has, at least on her first visit, brought nothing but airy illusions, 'ideals' of integration: 'Shapes godly flitting to and fro, a charming company'.[65] Here Prometheus is no longer the youthful ideal; demoted to that half of the human person interested only in action and technological acheivements, he has no use for Pandora's eschatological ideas. It is Epimetheus, the 'Spirit of deep reflection' and his brother's counterpole, who adopts and indeed marries the 'god-sent image of bliss'; and the wonderful fullness of love grants him 'the moment that eternally life's fable sweet will be'.[66] There are twin daughters; and when Pandora departs she takes with her to heaven Elpore, Hope, who appears only in dreams, promising not earthly goods (they are for everyone to seize for himself), but the eternal aspect of love; meanwhile Epimeleia—'she who needs love'—her anxious and remorseful sister, remains behind with her father Epimetheus. Prometheus's son Phileros, who represents Passion (in every form: as Eros, as the sting of longing, as jealousy, wrath, revenge, desperation), falls in love with Epimeleia, then pursues her for what he thinks is infidelity; like Werther, he hurls himself to his death in the water, and Epimeleia ends herself in fire. The four Titans symbolise the four parts of man's divided soul, and the fathers represent the rent between action and contemplation,

[65] VI, 410.
[66] VI, 411.

while the earthly children are the dichotomy of passion and longing (in analogy to the horses in the *Phaedrus*). While these latter are overtaken by wild tragedy, Pandora—the possibility of integration—remains tragically unattainable, in a distant realm beyond the fathers. Prometheus and Epimetheus join in a hymn of praise to her which forms the centre-piece and includes those famous elegiac verses 'The fullness of bliss I have known!' and 'He who to part from his beauty condemned'. Here Epimetheus-Goethe has become the spokesman for the whole of unwhole mankind, expressing eros as longing for the once physically present and now unattainable ideal. We may compare Faust's love for the ultimately remote and ghostly figure of Helen; this more unappeasable eros is of tragic dimensions far exceeding its platonic-classical counterpart. Pandora cannot be Beatrice, for she lacks every Christian trait; she is the personified absence of the wholeness sought with such erotic desperation. This is not far from the tragic pathos of the Michelangelo and Shakespeare sonnets, but more hopeless still. While Goethe could not seriously attempt to bring Pandora back to the world, he does offer the glimpse of a solution in Eos, goddess of the 'dawn' and the iridiscent half-light. For she

Strong doth gently make the eyes infirm of mortal
    men,
That by the shaft of Helios my race be blinded not,
For it was born illuminated things to see, not Light.[67]

Through her miracles she brings back Phileros and Epimeleia to the world, but she herself represents a mere promise, and at the end does no more than open a prospect, full of signs of miraculous grace from above. Here, unusually, the name of the gods is given its due weight:

Ye nether dwellers feel what should be wished;
But what might given be know they above.
Ye Titans, mighty are your deeds; yet
Beauty and eternal Goodness can be reached
By guidance of the gods alone; this let them grant.[68]

[67] VI, 439.
[68] VI, 443.

Pandora is followed immediately by *Electoral Affinities* (1808); in the one case we have a metaphysical and in the other an ethical anthropology. Thus the novel is concerned with a rule for life, essentially based on renunciation in love, by which man may be purified and achieve the degree of integration possible on earth. There are two pairs—Edward and Ottilia, and Charlotte and the Major—but three stages of development. The lowest is that of Edward, who in his heart cannot renounce and is forced to do so, in a tragic and brutal fashion, by destiny; in the middle come the figures of renunciation, the Major and Charlotte; and the highest stage is represented by Ottilia, who does not need to think in terms of renunciation at all. Renunciation is already present in the selflessness of her nature and her love.

The marriage between Edward and Charlotte is characterised by the ethical attitudes we are shown at the beginning. 'Edward was not wont to deny himself anything',[69] whereas Charlotte 'was always anxious to be aware of herself, to rule herself';[70] when both are exposed to a violent temptation their reactions are, accordingly, in complete contrast. Edward, an 'extreme version of Werther' who in the end kills not himself but the woman he loves, cannot 'overcome himself'.[71] He simply 'cannot completely renounce [happiness with Ottilia]',[72] and soon 'knows no measure. The awareness of being in love, of being loved, drives him into the Infinite'.[73] 'He did not resist, for he could not.'[74] He does leave the house and seek his death in war; but is still accompanied wherever he goes by his unconquerable passion, and remains 'self-centered', just as 'pre-occupied with himself' as ever.[75] He proposes to his friend that they exchange women: 'I know you love Charlotte, and she deserves it . . . take her from my hand!

[69] I, 2 (IX, 16).
[70] I, 12 (IX, 9).
[71] I, 16 (IX, 117).
[72] 2, 12 (IX, 228).
[73] I, 13 (IX, 101).
[74] 2, 16 (IX, 254).
[75] I, 14 (IX, 106); 2, 6 (IX, 177).

bring me Ottilia!'[76] But there is an insuperable obstacle, the institution of marriage, seen as the 'foundation of any moral society', the 'alpha and omega of all culture'. 'This bond may never be dissolved, for it brings so much happiness that all individual unhappiness counts for nothing beside it . . . But from time to time people are assailed by impatience, and fancy themselves unhappy. This moment once safely past, they will be grateful for their happiness again . . . Are we not also wedded to our conscience?'[77] Let the *moment* of eros go past—here Goethe is admonishing himself, renouncing his own nature; this injunction is in fact put in the mouth of Middler, but the course of events shows that he meant it seriously. And that applies also to the Sermon on the Mount, with its insistence that adultery takes place primarily in the heart; Charlotte's child, conceived while both husband and wife bore within them the image of their pasion, has to die.[78] By virtue of the self-denial she and the Major have accepted, the selflessness she has achieved, Charlotte feels she can agree to the divorce Edward desires;[79] however, it is not for these three to unravel destiny, but for Ottilia, 'the glorious child'.[80]

Her love for Edward is as human and total as his; after his departure 'she felt an infinite emptiness',[81] and she 'had not renounced Edward'.[82] She does not need to; nevertheless, she feels 'that to become complete her love must become completely selfless . . . She wished only for the welfare of her friend, believing herself capable of renouncing him, even of never seeing him again, if she only knew that he was happy. Yet she was quite resolved in her mind never to belong to another'.[83] As Edward sees the entire meaning of love in the passion and direct experience of the moment, which cannot bring such fulfilment, Ottilia, because she is the one who does

[76] 2, 12 (IX, 231).
[77] 1, 9 (IX, 78).
[78] 1, 11 (IX, 94); 2, 13 (IX, 239).
[79] 2, 14 (IX, 243).
[80] 2, 14 (IX, 244).
[81] 1, 17 (IX, 126).
[82] 1, 17 (IX, 126).
[83] 2, 9 (IX, 205).

not renounce, is forced to sacrifice herself. She becomes, in the original sense, *sacer*, 'a consecrated person who, with a terrible evil threatening herself and others, has only one recourse: to devote herself to the Holy Presence that with its invisible arms can alone protect us against the dreadful and relentless powers'.[84] 'I am resolved . . . I will atone for it.'[85] She vows complete silence and almost unbroken fasting.[86] Thus, like Beatrice, she transcends, and eros is integrated into a perspective which incorporates death as a necessary but superseded element. This leads to the graveyard, and how it may accord with the deeper meaning implicit in the transcendence of death. The point is not a 'self-willed obstinate perpetuation of our personality, attachments and circumstances',[87] a narrow attitude Charlotte too had refused to accept; it is rather the mystery of yielding the self to an all-embracing and incomprehensible grace, and finding, in and through this abandonment of the self, total refuge in eternity. Here, for Goethe, is the meeting-point of Spinoza and Christianity, in all their true power; and the pagan element— Homer and the pre-Platonic philosophers, the search for goodness for its own sake and without selfish concern for the 'I'—is also satisfied.

From this, and not from a flat pantheistic interpretation, derives Goethe's fascination for Spinoza, as is made very clear by his own statements.[88] We find the same, in light-hearted vein, at the end of *The West-Eastern Divan*, in the image of the paradisiac harem; one member resembles Suleika 'to a hair', but 'Our self-love disappeared'.[89] In 'Higher and

[84] 2, 15 (IX, 251).

[85] 2, 14 (IX, 246).

[86] 2, 17 (IX, 259–261).

[87] 2, 1 (IX, 239).

[88] TF, 4, 16; after the great passage on renunciation, the need to relinquish our personality and embrace a permanent and total resignation, he goes on to speak of Spinoza, and adds: 'But one must not think that I could have subscribed altogether to his writings or been a blind disciple' (X, 731–733). *Cf.* TF 3, 14: 'What particularly fascinated me about him [Spinoza] was the boundless selflessness which shines out in every sentence' (X, 684).

[89] D III, 394.

Highest', 'man in his complacency/ His self would gladly rescued see/ Up above as here below'; instead, his scattered five senses are brought together, in Plotinian fashion, to exist as one (ἐνιαίως), and thus enabled to penetrate 'more easily the eternal circles' themselves interpenetrated 'by Word of God in pure and vital wise'; until, finally, 'Mid contemplation of eternal love/ We float away, we pass away'.[90] This 'selflessness' is one of the essential elements of Goethe's religion (the other is reverence), and can result in a refined version of the Christian tradition, as when the young architect's painting depicts Ottilia as a saint,[91] with a 'trace of life in heaven',[92] and when in the living picture of the Christmas crib she 'becomes like the very Mother of God',[93] her 'form, gestures, manner and expression surpassing anything a painter has ever depicted'. The scene appears first in nocturnal illumination, the only light being that from the child, a 'picture of night and lowliness'; and then in full illumination, a 'picture of day and splendour'.[94] In Ottilia's final destiny the two pictures merge; after the accident with the boat, her earthly light diminishes constantly, for suffering love has become her life; but once she is dead, miracles occur at her coffin,[95] and soon Edward, the man who has failed, is called to come through purifying fire and share her death and transfiguration. We are reminded of 'una poenitentium, once called Gretchen', and her Faust. Edward's last words express humility: 'To imitate the inimitable is a fearful task. Well I feel, dear friend, how everything, even martyrdom, requires genius.'[96]

Years of Wandering never reached a final form, and instead there are isolated peaks: the idea of wandering and renunciation, the cosmic mysticism of Aunt Macaria, but

[90] D III, 397–398.
[91] EA 2, 3 (IX, 148–149).
[92] EA 2, 2 (IX, 144).
[93] EA 2, 6 (IX, 181).
[94] EA 2, 6 (IX, 181–182).
[95] EA 2, 18 (IX, 270).
[96] EA 2, 18 (IX, 274).

above all the religious climax of the doctrine of *paideia*: the idea of threefold reverence. 'My temperament inclined by nature to reverence', the author says at the beginning of his autobiography.[97] The concluding fresco describing the threefold reverence reflects great artistic ability. Reverence is in the first place not something innate: 'It is with reluctance that man adopts reverence, or rather he never in fact adopts it; it is a higher faculty that has to be implanted in his nature, and which evolves only in particularly favoured people, who have for this reason always been considered saints, indeed, gods'[98] (saints, indeed, but not gods; it is gods one has reverence for). Religion begins where fear ends, in reverence: 1. reverence for that which is above us, which is 'ethnic religion' ('pagan', and 'one such is the Israelite religion as well');[99] 2. reverence 'for that which is like us', which is 'philosophical' religion ('for the philosopher whose position is in the middle has to bring down to himself everything higher, and bring up everything lower; only in this middle situation does he earn the name of a sage' and 'live, in the cosmic sense, in pure truth');[100] 3. reverence for that which is below us, in 'the Christian religion', which is 'an ultimate achievement in human potential and destiny. It would have been possible simply to abandon the earth below on the grounds of a higher birth-place; instead to accept lowliness and humility, scorn and contempt, disgrace and misery, suffering and death, as divine, learning to respect even sin and crime, to love them, because they do not hinder but help the Holy—here was an achievement beyond our imagination. True, traces thereof appear throughout history, but a trace is not a destination; and once such a destination is reached mankind can never return to its previous state, and we may well think that, having once appeared, the Christian religion can never disappear'. Every word of this statement merits deep consideration: the unity of all religions and the exceptional status of Christianity, in that its essential

[97] TF 1, 2 (X, 56).
[98] MW 2, 1 (VIII, 170–171).
[99] *Ibid.* 174.
[100] *Ibid.* 171.

movement is downwards, out of reverence for suffering and by virtue of the selflessness of *agape*; the definitiveness, supreme significance, of this movement, in which the first two religions become subordinated elements. The final fruit of all three is 'reverence before oneself', an idea which goes beyond Pascal's 'self-hatred' and even Spinozistic self-forgetting; it expresses a new, reverential attitude towards oneself 'without being dragged down to an unworthy state by arrogance and self-centredness'. The three religions are ordered in terms of the Creed and the Trinity: 'The first Article (Father) is ethnic', 'the second (Son) is Christian', and the third (Spirit) teaches the community of the saints, 'of those who are in the highest degree good and wise', thus completing the philosophical religion.[101]

Here Varro's three religions provide no more than the spring-board for a far richer conception.[102] The first (mythical) and third (political) merge to form Goethe's ethnic religion; the second, philosophical ('physical') religion—the one Varro clearly favoured, according to Augustine—is, with great insight, criticised for its levelling tendency; while Goethe's third religion, which has no place in Varro's work, represents a height of achievement that must be maintained, an 'ultimate religion'.[103] Nevertheless, Goethe did in the end reject the deification of the earthly Jesus; he is numbered among the wise men and prophets, no more than 'a true philosopher',[104] and only in this (classical) sense a 'godly man'. His Passion is revered too highly to permit images of crucifixion, which, so Goethe, are a 'degrading and tasteless insult to the Sublime'; the 'shrine of pain' remains veiled. That is a specious idea, but leaves the human dimensions of the cross equally obscured; in this light it counts for little that Goethe excludes the Jews from his 'sphere of education', for having opposed the founder of the highest religion.[105]

---

[101] *Ibid.* 171 172.
[102] See Vol. IV, pp. 216–219 (Eng. tr.).
[103] MW 2, 1 (VIII, 179).
[104] *Ibid.* 176–178.
[105] MW 3, 11 (VIII, 434).

Goethe's attitude to the *Bible* displays all the advantages and disadvantages of liberalism. God resolved to become man; 'we must therefore at all costs avoid making him into God again'.[106] Through his descent God showed himself as love, proved his glory; what need then for a reascent? 'In this knowledge I look to die, that I possess no happiness and may hope for no bliss, save that vouchsafed to me by God's eternal love, which shared in the misery of the world and itself became miserable, that the misery of the world might share in its glory.'[107] All the sayings of the Bible, and especially all the dogmas later made from them by the various Christian sects, the Pastor of ★★★ measures against this descending love. Love is the eternal content, and human symbols (such as the sacraments) are its vessels and means of communication, but only so long as they continue to speak to human 'feelings' and thus remain effective; for 'to require someone to feel what he cannot feel is tyrannical nonsense'.[108] 'We believe that the eternal Love became man that we might be granted our heart's desire':[109] the freedom of love, proclaimed, by the 'beloved John', as the essence of all.

These early utterances (1773) contain the seeds of almost all the later statements. First there is a tendency to interpret the 'positive' elements of the revelation of Scripture in 'natural' terms,[110] rejecting more and more sharply orthodox Protestant supernaturalism[111] and legalistic moralism.[112]

---

[106] 'The Pastor's Letter', etc., IV, 129.

[107] *Ibid.* 128.

[108] *Ibid.* 135.

[109] *Ibid.* 137.

[110] TF 2, 8 (X, 367).

[111] Thus he rejects a doctrine of original sin, since thereby man may no longer try to achieve (or contribute to) his own salvation; hence Goethe's leanings towards 'Pelagianism' (TF 3, 15 (X, 694–695, 698)); *cf.* the 'key words' of Faust: 'The man who strives in right endeavour,/ Him can we redeem!/ And if the Love that dwells above/ Hath entered into him . . .' (V, 520), and the observation to Eckermann, 21.12.1831 (XXIV, 504). Similarly, he condemns any education that seeks to instil Christian suffering without encouraging the child to learn a healthy self-defence (TF 1, 2 (X, 76–79)); and disapproves of the numerous motifs involving suffering to be found in Christian art (IJ 1, 19.10.1786; XI, 113f.).

[112] TF 1, 1 (X, 50).

Goethe would like a restoration of the sacramental cosmos in the Catholic sense, and explains why at length;[113] he regrets the demise of the monasteries under the Protestants,[114] and dislikes the churches' naked interiors.[115] And after all, the Reformation was soon back where it started:

> The Reformation had its feast,
> The priests they lost their grand estates,
> And priests became the new inmates.[116]

When, in 1817, there was a plan to celebrate the Reformation, Goethe thought it a very bad idea; he would have preferred a commemoration of the great Battle of Leipzig, to be celebrated by all the Germans together, and not again each other. It would be 'a pure celebration of humanity'; everyone, 'not just Christians, but Mohammedans and pagans' 'would come to church in unity' and share their spiritual experience' 'at the same divine service'.[117]

But the Catholicism he found in Italy proved equally far from the ideal. Rome—even if her liturgies have some merit[118]—is a Babel;[119] all that business has nothing to do with Christ. Christ would be as certain to be crucified in the Christian world of today as he was in Israel; that is a view Goethe persistently maintains.[120] For 'With Cross and Christ

---

[113] TF 2, 7 (X, 318–24): 'The sacraments are the highest features of religion, the tangible symbol of an extraordinary divine favour and grace.' Goethe would not part with any of the seven, not even the Confession, which had been so spoiled for him as a boy.

[114] EA 2, 15 (IX, 249).

[115] EA 2, 2 (IX, 142).

[116] 'The Eternal Jew', IV, 240–241.

[117] XIV, 263.

[118] 'I enjoyed ... everything enjoyable about the ritual [in St Peter's], and the rest I have quietly reflected on. Nothing made what people call an "impact" on me or really impressed me, but I did admire everything', for it all unfolds 'with great taste and perfect dignity' (IJ 3, 22.3.1788 (XI, 584)).

[119] XI, 427.

[120] When Marie Antoinette rode through Strassburg, all the sick and lame were kept well out of view; and Goethe composed 'a little French poem, comparing the coming of Christ, who seemed to walk the earth especially for the sick and lame, with the arrival of the Queen, who shunned these unfortunates' (TF 2, 9 (X, 400–401)). And in 'The Eternal Jew' he

there's such a fuss/ They've got no time for him and his cross'.[121]

As a boy, Goethe already loved the Bible and would never part with it; he paraphrased large portions of the Old Testament according to his ideas, making many shrewd and open-minded observations.[122] The Bible was and remained for him a mighty testimony to human belief; and only from such belief could any culturally fruitful and edifying experience spring. A much-quoted Goethean saying is that 'the real, single and profoundest issue in the history of the world and mankind, overriding all others, is and will always be the conflict between unbelief and belief'. Less often do we find the vital sequel: 'All epochs in which belief in whatever form reigns shine forth, uplift the heart, and bear fruit for their own and later times. All those, however, in which unbelief in whatever form claims its wretched victory may swagger in a

depicts Christ wandering through the modern Germany, both Catholic and Protestant, and 'recognised by no one'; in a planned sequel to the epic there was to have been a second crucifixion, an idea that came to Goethe in Italy, for 'my soul was overcome by the feeling that every trace of the original Christianity has vanished', leaving merely 'a distorted baroque paganism' (IJ 1, XI, 133–134). And when Goethe saw the Pope celebrating mass and 'gesticulating and mumbling like a common priest', he was struck by the thought: 'What would he [Christ] say . . . if he walked in and found his image on earth humming and swaying to and fro?' (139). In Sicily: 'For eighteen hundred years now Christianity has based its possessions, splendour and solemn festivities on the misery of its initial founders and most fervent believers' (IJ 2 (XI, 260)). 'If he came, they would crucify him a second time', the old man still says, to Eckermann (12.3.1828 (XXIV, 690)), for, as the Pastor's early letter says: 'Nowhere was Christ's teaching more suppressed than in the Christian Church' (IV, 136).

[121] IV, 238.

[122] TF 1, 4 (X, 143–158: the earliest history of mankind, the original polytheism of the Patriarchal age with its wealth of material available for fiction, the conflict between natural and revealed religion, his wish to turn the Joseph story into a novel). TF 2, 7 (X, 303–304, on the struggles between orthodox and liberal exegetes at the University of Leipzig: 'I was in the enlightened camp . . . although I could not conceal to myself that this admirably rational way of interpreting those scriptures would in the end mean the loss of their poetic as well as prophetic content'). In the 'Notes' on the *Divan* there is a lengthy essay on Israel in the desert (III, 504–523).

brief illusion of brilliance, but vanish from posterity. For who cares to toil away investigating something unfruitful?'[123] This is expressed with particular force in the *Theory of Colours*, even superstition being preferred to unbelief: 'Superstition occurs in energetic, great-hearted and positive natures; it is part of their inheritance. Unbelief, on the other hand, characterises weak, small-minded and unadventurous races that seem closed in on themselves. The former delight in marvels . . . but the sublime only destroys a generation that is important.'[124]

Goethe's best endeavours went into achieving a 'universal piety' (in contrast to the limitations of a domestic piety);[125] what this would mean for a Christian is made clear in the charming sketches devoted to St Philip Neri. Here the essence is that during the days of Luther someone in Rome conceived a great ideal: 'That the spiritual, indeed, the holy domain be united with the worldly; that the heavenly be brought into the secular, and in this way a different reformation become possible. For here and nowhere else is the key that will open the cells of Papacy, and restore to a free world its god.'[126] This idea, taken up again in an extended draft,[127] is accompanied by another: that Neri sought 'to conquer' the imperious traits of a natural leader, 'to disguise the shining brilliance of his being through self-denial, abstention, philanthropy, humility and abasement. The thought that by appearing a fool in the eyes of the world he might truly gain insight into God and things divine, and train himself in this knowledge, this became the inspiration of all his endeavours . . . St. Bernard's maxim *spernere mundum, spernere . . . se sperni* seems quite to have taken hold of him'.[128] It is the same motif that later becomes associated with Ottilia: the veiling of the image of glory in that of lowliness. Such selflessness represents a considerable advance upon the opaque mysticism

[123] D III, 504–505.
[124] TC XVI, 362.
[125] MW 2, 8 (VIII, 264).
[126] IJ 2, 26.5.1787 (XI, 357).
[127] XI, 509–523.
[128] XI, 513–514.

of 'The Thoughts of a Fair Soul', with its neo-Platonic conception (also important in Bruno and Shaftesbury) that the soul must purify itself, and then it will see 'the eternal sun reflected' in its pure mirror.[129] Such thinking distorts the simple and direct relationship to God.

To conclude: what does *glory* mean to Goethe? In 1805 he translated extracts from Plotinus and embodied them in Macaria's archive,[130] their theme being the beauty of the Spirit and the Idea in sensual form, the search for the One above through the ideal realm. But Goethe goes on to warn against escapism into a world of ideas, if this means losing touch with the true sense of the outer and inner experience. Only in the form of polarity can the mystery of the world appear. Thus eros is not primarily a soaring-up to God; its impulse is to seek the opposite pole, within the world and between the sexes. We are close to Feuerbach, and the vision of divine light in human relationships. We should also remember that in the theory of colours, for example, 'polarity' and limitation are related to the concept of 'decision', and thus have a positive meaning we do not find in Plotinus. In an ethical context, a decision in favour of one thing can certainly mean the rejection of another; indeed, this is for Goethe a condition of any total affirmation.

> In the end there is no choice,
> A poet many things must hate;
> All that's ugly, all that's gross,
> May not of its beauty prate.[131]

Yet such hatred is always—in Goethe's cosmos as in Bruno's—balanced within an overall polarity:

> Within the confines of his narrow being
> Man needeth twofold feeling, love and hate;
> Doth need not day alone, but also night.[132]

And so the end does end thus: 'Be it as it may, life is good';[133] 'Howe'er it may be,/ It was so fair!'.[134]

---

[129] MA 6 (VII, 388).
[130] VIII, 495–497 (marked by inverted commas).
[131] 'Elements', D III, 292.
[132] T 4, 2 (VI, 281).
[133] P II, 50.   [134] F V, 500.

Since its author is Goethe, this statement cannot be purely contemplative; it presupposes action, involvement, and is, indeed, an act of decision and choice. 'One can tell who really loves the truth: he who will always find and value what is good.'[135] Reflecting on Plato's maxim that beauty is hardest, he writes: 'Art is concerned with what is hard and good. When something difficult appears easy, we catch a glimpse of the impossible.'[136] Thus the ethical dimension affords a bridge to a philosophy summed up in the *Divan*: 'For all is glorious before God; is he not the Best?'[137] Such glory founded on goodness is reflected in Nature, man's universal home; here Goethe's experience of Being is that of the ancients and Hölderlin. The famous poem describing the 'event' of the rose contrasts a miracle of Nature with the prosaic restlessness of science:

> They say thou art the fairest thing of all,
> The flower-realm hath named thee as its queen;
> Should aught gainsay, in confidence serene
> The miracle of thy event to witness call.
> For seeing and believing meet in thee,
> No fancy art thou, but art wholly true;
> Yet tirelessly men toil for knowledge new,
> The law and cause, the why and how to see.[138]

Thus the antecedent Presence of highest excellence is a condition of human activity, determining the paths it will take. Man's role is to enact the lot that befalls him; otherwise he will bring neither himself nor the world to fruition:

> Whate'er thou dost in her, the world's already made,
> The Lord of Creation his plan hath laid.
> Thy die is cast, thou must follow the strains,
> The way is begun, but the journey remains.
> For cares and grief will change it no whit,
> From the saddle they'll shake thee where thou dost
>   sit.[139]

[135] MW VIII, 315.
[136] EA 2, 5 (IX, 176).
[137] D III, 379.
[138] P II, 54.
[139] MW VIII, 8. They become caught up in the 'velociferous' force (MW VIII, 312).

You Goethe's communication with the 'Lord of Creation' is not through prayer,[140] but only through reverence and the consciousness that the All is ultimately good. In this way the name 'Nature' (behind which is God) can be replaced by the word 'Being', expressing an all-embracing totality: 'In Being let thee rest rejoiced! Eternal is Being . . . .'[141] Thus prayer, all-pervasive in Hölderlin's Christian vision of the ancient world, gives way to Goethean reverence; to a sense of existence in which dependence is not the unquestioned experience of a created being, but the function of a cosmic polarity. The yearning of eros and *ephesis* is not for the *hen*, but for the derivative *physis* (Plotinus's *Nous-Psyche*); the shining images of the world remain ciphers whose meaning ends in themselves. The great conclusions to *Faust* are successive final hieroglyphs. Glory passes from God to the cosmos, to what Heidegger will call Being.

f. The Final Period

1. THE LEGACY OF GOETHE

To the extent that the overweening character of the Hegelian *Geist* (spirit) and its left-wing off-shoots fail to determine the nineteenth and twentieth centuries, these latter are influenced by the classical and the Goethean view of nature. These two paths remain clearly distinct even today. In the philosophy of spirit, the spirit comprehends nature as the object which serves it and which stands over against it, which it commands with exact scientific and technical means, applying it to its own ends. In the philosophy of Nature, on the other hand, the universe, in whatever way it is understood, is wholly comprehensive and is the landscape in which the Absolute encounters the spirit, and which makes it high-spirited, reverent and creative, setting a limit to its lust for technological supremacy. But in accordance with Goethe's

[140] *Cf.* the poem prefacing *Years of Wandering, ibid.*
[141] 'Legacy', P I, 514.

final lack of certainty, this universe retains its ambiguity even after him. It does not point to a transcendent unity beyond itself, as we find in Plotinus, for Christianity now occupies this space, which metaphysics accordingly avoids. It possesses its own unity, and thus its own glory, in itself, and the eros, which does not seek to penetrate beyond it, remains an anti-Christian 'cosmogonic eros'. But while man's gaze, stripped of its transfiguring longing, turns realistically to 'the world as it is', he is greeted by the fearful 'ruminating horror' into whose abysmal depths the young Goethe, following Bruno and Böhme, had peered. It is to this world that, if he can summon the strength, he must sing his *Song of Yes and Amen* with Zarathustra. Whatever he later feels in his 'old heart' of the 'seafarer's desire' for 'new shores' must be bent back into the 'nuptial ring of rings—the ring of (eternal) recurrence'.[1]

Because the classical substance increasingly recedes, both metaphysical projects—the philosophies of Nature and of spirit—must increasingly live from Christian material, despite their contradiction and rejection of it. Thus the concealed theological *a priori* element, which was characteristic of the late-classical and early medieval metaphysics of glory, now becomes manifestly Christian. In the philosophy of spirit, this takes the form of an adapted Augustinianism in Descartes, Malebranche, Rosmini; an adapted Paulinism in Kant; an adapted Johanninism in Hegel, Schelling and the later Fichte. In this way Christianity is positively reabsorbed. In the philosophy of Nature, on the other hand, there now occurs a *spoliato Aegyptiorum* in reverse: in the clear denial of Christian transcendence, the raiment of glory, which it reserves for the God of love and of the Cross, is removed from these and cast upon the members of the universe, or of that *physis* which Heidegger calls Being. But a universal philosophy which, precisely because it is anti-Christian, cannot and will not eschew religious pathos, must necessarily return via the path of 'metaphysics' to the mythic origins. The young Nietzsche in his *Birth of Tragedy* quite consciously completes a process begun by Creuzer, Görres and Lasaulx, and Heidegger will

---

[1] Nietzsche: *Zarathustra* 3, *Die sieben Siegel*, ed. Schlechta 2, 475.

bracket off the whole 'metaphysical' tradition from Hegel to
Aristotle and Plato in order to arrive at the Presocratics:
'Heraclitus and Parmenides were not yet "philosophers" '.[2]

In the wake of this renewal of myth we first find the broad,
dense seam which is the innerworldly humanism of *Bildung*
(educational development), almost wholly devoid of religion,
for which Goethe in his *Wilhelm Meister* and in many of his
short stories, even partly in *Faust*, provides the model. This
begins to celebrate its 'scientific' triumphs in the incipient
study of psychology, of sociology and evolutionary history,
while it overruns the field of art with its novel of bourgeois
realism: from Scott to Dickens, Thackeray, Galsworthy,
Freytag and Keller to Fontane and Thomas Mann, from
Balzac *via* Stendhal and Flaubert to Zola, from Pushkin to
Tolstoy and Hamsun, in all of whom we see man within a
milieu, an environment, nature, world, and how he grows
into or out of these, both involving and extricating himself.
Neither that heaven-directed gaze of foolishness prevails here,
nor the thrust of a transcendent eros. The former is
submerged in a kind of human wisdom, the wisdom of
Bildung, while the latter becomes an interpersonal problem of
love. Even the demonic and heroic grandeur of the
metaphysical eros (from Shakespeare's sonnets and Kleist's
Penthesilea) is taken captive by psycho-(patho)logical analysis,
as it develops from Kierkegaard *via* Dostoievsky to Freud.
What is initiated by Stendhal in his *Tentation de Saint Antoine*,
continued by Rimbaud and Lautréamont and taken to excess
by Thomas Mann and more recent writers, is the dissolution
of an immanent anthropology which in its enclosed dialectic
must increasingly have recourse to forms of perversity in
order to awaken any kind of tension.

Beyond this level there comes a more ambitious one, viz.
the attempt to resuscitate authentic myth through a power
that is analogous to the prophetic inspiration of Classicism or
of the Bible. Schelling and Görres yield to myth as such a
newly secure place within the domain of speculative thought.
In *Faust*, Goethe retrieved a certain mythic dimension for
'modern man', as did Mozart and Byron in *Don Juan* and

  [2] 'Was ist das—die Philosophie?', 1955, p. 24.

Nietzsche in *Thus spoke Zarathustra*. By employing the resources of all the arts, Wagner creates a phantasmagoria which (in *The Twilight of the Gods*) occupies the existential position where myth, although still exercising a certain fascination, has by now degenerated to the extent of being merely symbolic of the human. This was the lesson Wagner learnt from Berlioz, and which Richard Strauss and Hoffmansthal (himself deeply influenced by Freud), not to mention Thomas Mann, were in their turn to learn from him. The entire Homeric world of the gods is resurrected in Spitteler's marvellous *Olympian Spring*, which however is in truth an Olympian Autumn, because all the glory of the gods is played out against the sombre backdrop of a heartless, materialistic *anankê* as the ultimate authority of the world. Despite all the distance that pathos lends, it is the same attempt to heighten the glory of beauty of form against a barren background that we find in Schopenhauer, who coloured so decisively the universal feeling of his century, particularly among the bourgeois levels of society, and who has influenced even the heroic pessimism of the twentieth century via E. von Hartmann and Wagner. Wagner provides the stage scenery for the brief myth of the Third Reich, while Hartmann celebrates his resurrection first in the early and then in the later Scheler. But nowhere does the material of the classical myths attain more than a purely psychological penetration (Giraudoux, Hofmannsthal, Anouilh). Rilke's 'angel' and his 'Orpheus' (to which we shall later return) evoke something of the mythic, whereas George's new God, incarnate in Maximin, had a merely comic effect upon the majority of his contemporaries. And what should one say about Mombert's attempt to raise humanity as a whole to the level of a mythic figure in a comprehensive universe whose divine powers become man? Or what of Klage's contradictory attempt to proclaim simultaneously the kingdom of myth ('soul') and its refutation ('spirit')? Challenging cries resound on all sides (Ernst Michel: *Der Weg zum Mythos. Zur Wiedergeburt der Kunst aus dem Geiste der Religion*, 1919),[3] but in exterior terms the closed culture is

[3] Michel's book, which repays attention even today, situates the modern

lacking that which is essential for its realisation, and inwardly the pre-Christian religion is irretrievable. Of course, many classical myths retain symbolic expressivity, indeed take on a greater expressivity where the fate of modern mankind takes on a more tragic form—the myths of Prometheus and Dionysius,[4] for instance—but the titanic or divine figures themselves are not thereby reanimated. They remain at best 'names' with which we designate our universal fate, well aware all the while that this in its occurrence transcends all names. But we remain unsure how far such names are mere labels for that which proclaims itself, or how far we ourselves are responsible for falsifying by our defective mode of reception what presents itself. It is on account of this uncertainty (unknown to the Ancients) that the myths are rendered ambiguous by their transformation into 'cyphers'. Jasper's 'cyphers' correspond exactly to the place at which Goethe drew an invisible dividing line between Nature and God, which denies entrance to the eros.

The final stage of the metaphysics of the 'classical tradition', which began with Nicolas of Cusa and Ficino and reached its apogee with Bruno, Hölderlin and Goethe, can be resolved into three distinct strands. The comprehensive universe can, according to Goethe in his writings on natural science, appear to be wholly a 'biological universe'. This seems to erect a bridge between the classical theophanous world-view and the modern scientific world-view. Or the comprehensive universe succumbs to the universal experience and creative power of the artist in the manner of Prometheus or Ganymede as *Weltinnenraum* ('world-inner-space') by virtue of the identity between the microcosm and the macrocosm. Or, finally, the comprehensive principle is no longer conceived as universe (since this classical concept is no longer possible after the advent of Christianity and of the philosophy of spirit), nor is it seen as absolute inwardness and subjectivity (since this loses

period from the middle ages onwards in its relationship to myth. Mombert appears to him as a promise of the return of myth's creative power.

[4] I have used these as the guidelines to explain the modern course of history in my *Apokalypse der deutschen Seele* (1937–39).

its location within the comprehensive principle), but becomes in Heidegger the phenomenon of Being, which, only masked by the *logos* metaphysics of subjectivity, always was contained in the classical notion of *physis*. Thus Heidegger becomes the executor of that epoch-making enterprise which we have dubbed here 'the classical tradition'.

2. THE PHILOSOPHY OF LIFE AND *WELTINNENRAUM*

The first two ways of grasping the comprehensive principle, which are interrelated, transport one 'to that sea whose flood engenders intensified forms', but which however gives them shape only as sea, that is to say causes them to solidify from flux, only to dissolve them into movement again. These forms were 'intensified' for Goethe in the double sense that, being of a spiritual nature, they were themselves an intensification of life and second that each form, the mental and the submental, possessed not only a horizontal but also a vertical polarity—such as colour, for example—as their formal principle. This principle of intensification will have a parallel effect in extreme Idealism too, but will find unexpected confirmation in the philosophy of Nature through the evolution theory of empirical biology. When this appeared, there already existed a well-established, religious view of nature, such as we find in Goethean form in the work of Oken and Carus, according to which the Macrocosm of 'Divine Being'[5] divides 'harmoniously' into a dimension of rationality and one of nature, and man as Microcosm strives on the basis both of empiricism and of speculation towards a participation in the act of the Divine World-Thought within nature through ideas, types and homologies. Even as Evolutionism took on an all-dominating aspect in the second half of the century, it left its mark on the existing model of the world, which in Fechner's work (*Zend-Avesta*, 1851: *Die Tagesansicht gegenüber der Nachtansicht*, 1879) is a mystical

[5] C. G. Carus, 'Welches sind die Anforderungen an eine künftige Bearbeitung der Naturwissenschaften?', 1822, in: *Biologie der Goethezeit*, ed. Ad. Meyer-Abich, 1949, p. 209; *cf.* p. 210; 'Nature and one's own ego, as equal emanations of the highest essence'.

God-Nature organism of Christian inspiration, closer to the stoic-neoplatonic kind than to that of Leibniz and Spinoza, and which in the anti-Christian monist melée of the close of the century still offered the basis of a naive, enthusiastic and religious aesthetics of the world (Bruno Wille, Wilhelm Bölsche).

With Bergson, universal Biologism first seriously enters the field of metaphysics: the tension between living being in its actual duration (*durée réelle*) and intellectual conceptual thinking becomes central. From the directly aesthetic, marvelling and participatory beholding of the leaping fountain of life (*Évolution Créatrice*), thought deepens to that reflexion which runs counter to the stream of life (again we sense the proximity of Plotinus' ἐπιστροφή), to that exertion of thought which precisely guarantees its own authenticity and which was to influence so deeply Péguy[6] and finally take the form of the mysticism of the *Deux Sources* with its Christian emphasis.

For Georg Simmel, the religious philosopher of life and theoretician of art, Being is likewise life which in an inner transcendence overflows its own boundaries and confronts that which is objective and form-like, significant and of valid worth, whereby however, it encounters its own limits. The retreating sea leaves the rejected images stranded on the beach, that which was objectified loses its vitality and validity, and a new educational process begins. Objectification originally signifies, as in Bergson, the stream of life in reflex upon itself, that 'first miracle of the spirit' which, 'while remaining in its own unity, opposes itself to itself'.[7] But in Simmel we find buoyant hope: 'Perhaps the next step for philosophy will be the conquest of a new concept of life, with which the latter is removed from those contraries, raised to a perspective from which the flow of the real and of the ideal, and the constancy of both, extinguish the absolute character of their opposition and are glimpsed as the revelatory modes of an as yet inexpressible unity of metaphysical life.'[8]

[6] *Cf.* Vol. III of this work, pp. 415ff., 465ff. (Eng. tr.).
[7] 'Philosophische Kultur', 1911, p. 211.
[8] 'Zur Philosophie der Kunst', 1922, p. 145.

But how sad such promises sound, how forced the Monists' fever of inspiration, how thin even the young Bergson's harmonious voice, and how defenceless all this is against the ever-possible, indeed already actual, transformation of this 'day-side' (*Tagseite*) into the 'night-side' (*Nachtseite*) of unadulterated mechanism and materialism! Their inspirations are no less illusory and forced; this merely proves that mankind needs some kind of Absolute, no matter which, which he can worship and in the service of which he can expend himself. NIETZSCHE shows this most clearly when he dissolves all objective truth in favour of the 'lies' of which life has need, and then proceeds to sing the praises of this annihilated Being as the 'eternal affirmation of Being . . ., untarnished by any negation', consecrating himself to its 'voiceless beauty': 'I shall be your affirmation for all eternity, for I love you, O Eternity!'[9] This 'Eternity' is the 'eternal recurrence of the identical'; it is the sea 'whose flood engenders intensified forms' in a sense which goes far beyond that intended by Goethe. It becomes the intensification of life beyond man to the 'superman', to the new, untrodden shores.[10] In his earliest work, Nietzsche drew attention to the insuperable and fatal contradiction by pointing to Dionysian music, which in concrete terms is that of the Schopenhauerian-Wagnerian kind: for Dionysian Greek tragedy too had proscribed 'the myths of the Homeric world which dance ahead of us' for the sake of its 'deeper scrutiny of the world' and laid an embargo on them: Zeus now trembles at the threatening rebellion of the Titan, and the latter himself is now pressed by the Dionysian artist into the service of the new deity. 'The Dionysian truth appropriates the whole realm of myth as the symbolism of its own occurrences'. When they are bathed in music, the myths, which were near to extinction, blossom once again in all their colour.[11] Nietzsche later had no more need of the pessimistic

[9] 'Ruhm und Ewigkeit', Schlechta, II, pp. 1262–1263; cf. *Zarathustra* 3, 'Der Genesende': 'The ring of Being remains eternally true to itself' (II, p. 463).

[10] Conclusion of the 'Morgenröte', I, p. 1279.

[11] 'Die Geburt der Tragödie', I, pp. 62–63.

music of intoxication, and the mercilessly Mediterranean *Carmen* sufficed. The principle of Dionysius, as Zagreus torn to pieces, even as 'the crucified one' ('against the crucified one') was music enough for him to harmonise out every contradiction. It was finally the contradiction of a man who wants to break out of the suffocating atmosphere of Platonic-Christian metaphysics into what is greater than that which has ever been thought,[12] and who thus finds himself in the circles of Being from which there is no escape: 'The eternal recurrence even of the very least detail! That was my weariness and disgust at all existence!'[13] But where are the most extreme happiness and the most extreme disgust held together, if not in that 'ego' of Nietzsche-Zarathustra, which has become his *fatum*? He portrays himself as the 'man of fate' in the manic *Ecce Homo*, whose true form has finally been presented to us by Erich F. Podach.[14] 'God or a buffoon—that is what I cannot choose, that is what I am'.[15]

Goethe's polarity was erotic—almost still in the great classical sense. The glory of the world became visible to him in the beloved ('Is it possible? Star of stars, do I press you again to my heart!') Nietzsche's polarity between God and the buffoon is wholly solipsistic; women are worth nothing and men only in so far as they are potential disciples. In Goethe the Plotinian *Hen* remains untouched, but Nietzsche replaces it with his monstrous Subject which extends from the universe in its entirety to nothingness. It is wholly self-sufficient; Zarathustra knows of no possible fidelity other than that to himself, to his own highest idea. If he shudders, then it is at the sight of his own abysmal depths.

RILKE's experience of the world is not so different from that of Nietzsche. He knows the same early, life-long and

---

[12] On this, *cf.* the excellent analyses of Eugen Biser, *'Gott ist tot'*, *Nietzsches Destruktion des christlichen Bewusstseins*, 1962, esp. pp. 49ff., where he speaks of the Anselmian 'concept' of God (as the 'boundary value of all conceivable contents of thought') with reference to Nietzsche.

[13] II, p. 465.

[14] *Friedrich Nietzsches Werke des Zusammenbruchs*, Rothe 1961, p. 321.

[15] *Ibid.*

passionate rejection of Christianity, this time of Catholicism, the same time-conditioned, biologistic-evolutionistic foundation (later strengthened for Rilke by his involvement with psychoanalysis), the same fundamental imperative to remain faithful to the earth, the same searching (nevertheless) for an overcoming of the current world condition along utopian, eschatologically productive lines—in Rilke's case to the extent of demanding of God (who does not as yet exist) the attempt to create productively 'Him who will finally hear us'[16]—the same comprehensive unity of all contradictions on the basis of a prophetic soul's creative powers of transformation. Orpheus stands beside Zarathustra. The successive attachments of Lou Andreas-Salomé, who was first Nietzsche's lover and then, from 1897, partner to the twenty-two-year-old Rilke, and who was later also to be the friend of Freud, form a highly significant garland that weaves its way through time. Innumerable women will follow Lou and his wife Clara, but they are no more than occasions for awakening anew that 'intransitive' love which has no 'Thou', for which Rilke strives, which he demands from others and which in all his works is the object of his teaching. This is no longer the eros of Goethe, who grasped the glory of the world each time in a real Thou, nor is it Nietzsche's 'love at a distance' which lacks virtually all eros. This is, rather, a Platonic Love, transcendent in its inner structure, which comes alight at a Thou who is physically present, but immediately transcends this and expends itself in the Infinite (and therefore comes most easily to those who suffer abandonment, compelling them to infidelity). And yet it does not reach towards a Platonic Sun of the Good, and still less towards a Christian God, but aims into the emptiness of space which perhaps ultimately, in the last days, warmed and animated by this love, will give birth to a deity. In the early *Tuscan Diary*, a vision of the convergence of the absolute artist with the new God is hinted at in an almost speculative

---

[16] R. M. Rilke, *Sämtliche Werke* (Insel Verlag, 1955f.), I, p. 767. More detailed analyses in: *Apokalypse der deutschen Seele*, Vol. 3 (1939), pp. 193–315.

manner.[17] But what is rigorously excluded, both in the human domain and in the relationship with God, is the element of dialogue, the sense of community which takes lovers captive, the fidelity. It is from within a monological love that Rilke enquires into the human capacity for being whole.

The first reply is harmony: the harmonisation of the world with the poet's soul. His work begins with a flood of highly atmospheric poems among which, after the journeys to Russia with Lou, the *Book of Hours* appears as the first genuine fruit. These prayers are inspired by the Russia of an instinctive, mystical piety, though one which can turn instantly into atheism (*The Letter of the Young Worker*); they are a monologue in dialogical form, and they cover a post-Christian core with classical and Christian clothing. The God who is addressed in prayer is the God of the future who inherits the world and above all the great tradition of art, and who yet already has a covert presence in the form of poverty, in the extraordinary final poems on poverty. 'For poverty is a great radiance from within': this line focuses the full meaning that 'glory' can possess for Rilke in the *Book of Hours*. The poor man, the man without resources, the cast-out leper is the place where kenotically the divine dwells, in irreconcilable opposition to the 'great cities' which parade and 'glitter like whores', to the kingdom of wealth, of technology and of progress ('and call their snail's tracks progress'). But the poor, who are 'laden with all the dirt and abused like things going rotten in the sun',[18] are not in Rilke's view something that can be bypassed, but are the painful, real indication of that 'poverty in spirit' which the poet needs in order to achieve his cosmic work. Thus the book closes with the praise of Saint Francis, who was poor in body and in spirit. But although Rilke brushes very closely against the mystery that lies at the heart of Christianity, his attempt at

[17] 'Tagebücher der Frühzeit' (Insel 1942). 'Nothing will exist apart from him [the artist-God] . . . When he makes a gesture, he will create and hurl into infinity many millions of worlds . . . I do not know how other distant worlds will mature to become gods. But for us, art is the way . . . Thus I feel that we are the ancestors of a god' (pp. 139–140).

[18] I, p. 364.

poverty does not set him free for his fellow man, but invariably only for himself in his work, which surrounds his narcissistic centre like a hall of mirrors and to which he sacrifices all his amorous relationships when they have out-lived their use. It is in his work that the intransitive and object-less eros for which Rilke strives and which he forever glorifies, finds its purpose and its limit. What Rilke really intends and can conceive and achieve, though not without contradiction, could be solved only in Christianity's Trinitarian love, though this can no longer be viewed as a variant of eros.

The poet transforms the crude world into a permanent, eternal form, and it is Rilke's middle period, culminating in the *New Poems*, which delivers this transformation. It is a Platonism from below, as by the power of the human heart the poet distils the idea from the most sensuous forms of experience. The idea is both the substance and the poet himself. It becomes visible where the emotional content and resonances coincide fully with the form. It is striking to what extent Rilke, the atheist and anti-Christian, persistently transforms Christian themes in this way, incorporating them into his artistic universe. They are a decisive part of the experience of mankind, and as a reality which people experience in depth, they are material that he must use. He feels them, examines them, from within: precisely where faith is demanded of the Christian, Rilke applies feeling and through feeling experiences the entire, transcendent, other-worldly dimension of mystery: the Cross, Death and Resurrection. The early *Visions of Christ*[19] claims to participate in the whole transcendent existence of Christ through sharing Christ's feelings (revealing, of course, his despairing failure), the *Life of Mary* and numerous other Marian poems express empathy—through the medium of a tender human eroticism—with her mysterious radiance, and even the most mature cycles make use of themes from the Old and New Testaments and from church history.[20] Almost everywhere it is a question of gingerly exploring the Christian

---

[19] III, pp. 129–169; also 'Glaubensbekenntnis' and 'Christus am Kreuz', III, pp. 489–493.

[20] Especially emphatic: in the 'Buch der Bilder': 'Das Abendmahl'

mystery, which pervades life and death, in its entirety, but not in a manner substantially different from the exploration of the transcendent myths of antiquity, those three great myths, for instance, at the end of *New Poems*: 'Orpheus, Euridice, Hermes', 'Alcestes' and the 'Birth of Venus'. The many 'kenotic' poems of the middle period also attain a mythic force; these derive from experiences of poverty of every kind: infancy, madness, loneliness, autumn, the poverty of beggers, of the blind, drunkards, suicides, widows, orphans, idiots, dwarves, lepers (all these in the cycle *The Voices* and *Going Blind, The Blind Man, The Leper King*), the poverty of corpses in the *Morgue* and in the *Washing of Corpses*. These and other images form a fluid motif that runs through all else, even the radiant and blissful pieces. Even here praise and lament are everywhere inseparable, more than in the highest achievements of antiquity (because there the plain and ordinary was not the object of praise), and in a manner which, albeit concealed, is thoroughly Christian.

Rilke's work ends with the two mythical cycles of the *Duino Elegies* (1912–22), which embrace the angel myth, and *Sonnets to Orpheus* (1922). In the former it is the note of lament, in the latter that of praise, which predominates. Both explore the potential for wholeness of temporal, finite existence. The *Elegies* envisage a domain of angels as totalities enclosed within themselves and as containing a world. These are the ὅλα of Neoplatonism, the intelligences of Dionysius and Dante, and angels as Thomas Aquinas understood them

(p. 388), in the 'Neue Gedichte': 'Der Ölbaum-Garten' (I, p. 492), the erotic poem about Magdalen, 'pietà' (I, p. 494), 'Gott im Mittelalter' (I, p. 502), in a grotesque manner the 'Auferstehung' (I, p. 524; also, in the 'Buch der Bilder', 'Das jüngste Gericht', which appears to the monk at prayer as an extreme disaster that must be warded off at all costs: I, pp. 415f.; and the later 'Jüngste Gericht', I, p. 575); in 'Der neuen Gedichte anderer Teil' once again a number of Old Testament themes (I, pp. 562–571) and a crude 'Kreuzigung' (I, p. 581), while 'Der Auferstandene' (I, p. 582) carries through the theme of the intransitive eros. Further Christian scenes are to be found in the 'Späte Gedichte': 'Himmelfahrt Mariä' (II, p. 46), 'Auferweckung des Lazarus' (II, p. 49), 'Emmaus' (II, p. 55), 'Christi Höllenfahrt' (II, p. 57), 'Worte des Herrn an Johannes auf Patmos' (II, p. 108), etc.

to be, that is beings endowed by God with such intuition that they have no need of external experience and only figuratively hold converse among themselves and with men, and finally they are the windowless monads of Leibniz. The 'narcissism' of Rilke's angels therefore can be exactly located in the Western tradition but, in contrast to that tradition, we do not find here the golden chain of emanations, hierarchies, and sendings-forth which, despite all, their domain discloses to the world of men, allowing them to partake in the heavenly totality.

> Who, if I cried, would hear me among the angelic
> orders? And even if one of them suddenly
> pressed me against his heart, I should fade in the
> strength of his
> stronger existence. For Beauty's nothing
> but beginning of Terror we're still just able to bear,
> and why we admire it so, is because it serenely
> disdains to destroy us. Each single angel is terrible.
> And so I keep down my heart, and swallow the
> callnote
> of depth-dark sobbing . . .[21]

Because the descending chain is broken, longing as eros can no longer reach upwards. Therefore there is no longer any continuity between the beautiful and the glorious, which can now appear only as the terrifying. Man's sobbing heart possesses the measure of the beautiful, which is that which the heart in its own transcendence can attain by feeling; the 'terrifying' dwells in a place beyond beauty which is not to be mastered. This is the same divide which already Goethe draws, softly but surely, between God and Nature. The angels represent God and, being unattainable, they are also unreal. They are only an X which in the appearance of dialogue serve to delimit the other innerworldly totality which remains. The summoning call of the First Elegy has become a warding-off gesture in the Seventh:

> Don't think that I'm wooing!
> Angel, even if I were, you'd never come! For my call

[21] 1. Elegie, I, p. 685.

is always full of 'Away'! Against such a powerful
current you cannot advance.[22]

The *eros* from below has won a decisive advantage over the
agape from above: *it* now becomes the Absolute against which
a revelation from beyond the divide cannot prevail. So there
only remains the innerworldly information: 'the flowing', 'the
night filled with world-space', 'the uninterrupted message
which forms itself from the silence', which also sounds forth
from 'the youthful dead' and contains the 'task' to be
'accomplished'.[23] When with regard to this 'accomplishment'
the poet immediately points to the lovers, whose 'framed
feeling' is far from being 'immortal enough', then he thinks
at once of those who have been forsaken, who 'lovingly free
themselves from the beloved', because otherwise the lovers
merely conceal 'with each other their fate'. The Second Elegy
therefore urges upon them the 'circumspection of human
gestures', because the experience of 'pure duration' in mutual
love happens only once and in the case of its repetition obeys
the universal law of 'evanescence' ('like the heat from hot
food . . . that which is ours rises from us'). But the end of the
Elegy fixes our gaze on the 'strip of fruit-land between river
and stone' for, although our heart outstrips us as with the
Greeks, we can no longer form from our transcendence
'calming images', 'divine bodies' in which 'it achieves a
greater moderation'. Our self-transcendence is open-ended,
and we must cling to 'our contained human reality'. The
Third Elegy shows how questionable even this is in view of
the (biological-psychoanalytical) depths and complexities of
the blood: the youth sinks, not to be protected by a woman's
love, 'into the crevasses . . . where the terror lay', and if he
cannot love the 'terrifying' angels, then he loves this deeper
'horror', which 'smiles' at him.[24] With such an underground
the performance on the earth's stage—in the Fourth Elegy—
can only become semi-radiant, semi-annulled. Once again our
gaze is led beyond what is offered in the present, and 'angels

[22] 7. Elegie, I, p. 713.
[23] I, pp. 686–687.
[24] I, p. 695.

and puppets' (Kleist's puppet play), the superhuman, must
appear on the scene to pull the strings of its unresistant toy
and thus to create a whole. A dying child who *prior* to life
contained within itself death's entirety, yet without being
'angry', would be an image of the same kind of unity. The
Fifth Elegy (the last to be written), 'Les Saltimbanques',
introduces a second image: the skilled gymnastic figures of
voyagers, which now even point to an eschatological image
of hope, in which not only the forsaken ones, those estranged
from interpersonal love, 'correspond' to the summoning call,
but human love—contrary to Rilke's general thesis—could
also find its fulfilment:

> Angel!: suppose there's a place we know nothing
>   about, and there,
> on some indescribable carpet, lovers showed all that
>   here
> they're for ever unable to manage—their daring
> lofty figures of heart-flight,
> their towers of pleasure, their ladders,
> long since, where ground never was, just quiveringly
> propped by each other,—suppose they *could* manage it
>   there,
> before the spectators ringed round, the countless
>   unmurmuring dead.[25]

And—in the Sixth Elegy—the hero similarly 'can'; for him,
the mystery of his provenance, previously so threatening,
displays itself as his election from afar to the company of the
saved on the grounds that he avoids the seductive temptation
towards reflexion, towards self-reflected achievement, and is
'in advance of his own smile',[26] 'a raging flood' (like
Hölderlin's Titan river, the Rhine). And now, in the Seventh
Elegy, there is the poet who, following the child, the
voyagers, the lovers and the hero, 'launches himself' like the
lark 'into the serene sky', who is 'the nature of his cry' and is
the 'summons-steps up to the dreamed temple of the
future':[27] he in the power of his assent dares to praise the

[25] I, p. 705.
[26] I, p. 706.
[27] I, p. 709.

world as glorious: 'Being here is glorious'. In this act of praise
he gathers also 'the nights', all the shameful, indeed all the
terribly 'suppurative' forms of love, and gathers them by
transforming them into an 'inner' reality. At this point of
culmination the poet dares even to thrown down the gauntlet
to the technological world and to analyse in his own way its
destruction of the valid and 'prayed' images of the past and
its transformation into 'imageless activity' and mere 'tensive
propulsion':

> Though this
> shall not confuse *us*, shall rather confirm us in keeping
> still recognisable form . . .
> Angel,
> I'll show it to *you* as well—*there!* Angel, in your gaze
> it shall stand redeemed at last,[28]

Here Rilke is praising human achievement—'pillars, pylons,
the Sphinx', the cathedrals—in the same way that Hölderlin
praised Hellas, salvaging it in his poetry. Indeed, Rilke wants
to know that these achievements are preserved in the angel's
vision, although he is uncertain as to whether this vision
actually exists. He flees for a moment to the angels from the
menacing, iconoclastic, modern world. But what an inner
menace there is in the seemingly insignificant 'not yet': 'the
form not yet known'! The Ninth Elegy fleshes out the
achievement of the Seventh in an almost prescriptive manner:
'being here is a great deal' and yet it is only that which is
eternally unique, evanescent. And yet, the transient, if it is to
endure, has need of 'us who are most transient', in the trusting
belief that 'we, the most fleeting of beings, possess something
salvific' and this once again in the face of the rise of a
technology which suppresses 'things that can be experienced',
substituting for them 'an imageless activity'. 'Familiar death'
as 'the secret stratagem of this silent earth' heightens to an
infinite degree the intensity of the moment: for the lovers,
but even more for the poet, who can 'transform' the
intensified moment 'in the invisible heart'.[29] Between these

[28] I, p. 712.
[29] I, pp. 718–719.

two, the Eighth Elegy, written in the spirit of Bergson and of the philosophy of life, casts again a shadow over the human manner of existence which, instead of going with the stream of life and existence unreflectingly and open 'to the Open' as do animals and embryos, turns in upon itself and thus becomes spirit at the price of its own alienation. What Thomas describes as *reflexio* in *conversio ad phantasma* in a way that both limits and sets free, becomes for Rilke the tragedy of existence, and yet is not thought through deeply enough, for being distinct from something is the prerequisite for proximity to it. Secretly, however, he does not intend something philosophical here, but something that is of a theological nature: even the animals have 'remembrance, as if that for which one strives, was once closer to hand',[30] as if the creature had sunk from some primal state, forced into a place of hopelessness, and now, in its futility, trustingly believes in some salvific force in the possession of man. This is the great hope of Creation as we find it in Romans 8. The Orpheus Sonnets also note the discordance of the cries of children within the harmony of the whole ('order the cries, singing god!'). They will ask in gnostic language when the 'Demiurge' will 'ravish' the heart 'that belongs eternally to the gods'; they will lament that we are 'blades' that continually wound the 'serene and divided' God, that we 'have a grievance' and are 'parasitical teachers' for those uncertain beings who 'achieve eternal childhood'. The Tenth Elegy completes the whole by raising the lament first to the ontic level and then to the mythic; it is only in suffering that man and the world attain their glory:

> May a new-found splendour appear
> in my streaming face! May inconspicuous Weeping
> flower![31]

when the lover 'gave himself more freely' into the 'loosened hair' of the night, for his sufferings are 'place, habitation, encampment, ground, dwelling'. Bypassing the mendacious marketplace of the modern world, we can, by following a

---

[30] I, p. 715.
[31] I, p. 721.

lament 'of glorious origin', attain to the mythic landscape of lament of actual being in which indeed 'the spring of joy' flows. Finally there is a moonlike landscape beyond life and death, static and soundless, in some way comparable to the mothers' landscape in *Faust* and, as backdrop to the world, infinitely disenchanting.

Rilke conceived the plan for the Elegies in 1912 and moulded the fragments later (until 1922) in keeping with the initial project. Even by the year 1918 he had grown beyond their world and had begun to devote himself to his last poems of Orphic vision and form,[32] in which existence, with all its depths, becomes glory for him through the power of his art. The words of the dying man are intended as a testament: 'Do not forget, my love: life is glory'.[33] But in the last instance it becomes glory only for the one who possesses the creative power to make it such: 'When I was inspired, then it was by the glorious spirit which does not permit itself to be summoned, not even to be pleaded with. My art possesses a glory which is beyond that of David's house . . . How must God had been with me that I can say such a thing!'[34]

In the *Sonnets to Orpheus*, the lament can move only 'in the sphere of praise',[35] but this space, which is the 'world–inner–space',[36] the 'double domain' between life and death, between soul and world—as that wonderful poem of breath in the spirit of Goethe's systole and diastole[37] expresses it[38]—now receives a mythic definition which is prior to all that occurs within it:

> For this is Orpheus. His metamorphosis
> in this one and in that. We should not take
> thought about other names. Once and for all,

[32] Eudo C. Masson, *R. M. Rilke. Sein Leben und sein Werk* (1946), pp. 96f., 100–103.

[33] J. R. von Salis, *Rilkes Schweizer Jahre* (1936), p. 202.

[34] Letter to Magda von Hattingberg, 18.2.1914: *Briefwechsel mit Benvenuta* (1954), p. 105.

[35] 1st part. 8th sonnet, I, p. 735.

[36] 'Es winkt zu Fühlung', II, p. 93.

[37] 'Im Atemholen sind zweierlei Gnaden: / Die Luft einziehen, sich ihrer entladen . . .', III, p. 290.

[38] 2,1.

it's Orpheus when there's song.[39]

'Song is existence', 'a floating in God',[40] but in a God scattered and poured out through all the world who, divided among lions and cliffs, trees and birds, sings on, and whose transcendental harmony precisely in this state of fragmentation drowns out the hatred of destruction:

> You that could sound until the end, though, immortal
>   accorder,
> seized by the scorn-maddened Maenads' intemperate
>   throng,
> wholly outsounded their cries when in musical order
> soared from the swarm of deformers your formative
>   song.

Indeed, man hears the harmony of the world and gives utterance to it poetically only because of the prior mystery of the fragmented God.

> O you god that has vanished! You infinite track!
> Only because dismembering hatred dispersed you
> are we hearers today and a mouth which else Nature
>   would lack.[41]

It is Heidegger who will soon explain how this *a priori* element, this comprehensive principle is to be conceived. Rilke asks in his own way 'What surges up from grounds, serene and sacred?'[42] The Christ-mystery—as the *a priori* of Creation precisely in its kenotic aspect—will have lent him colour, without his wishing it, as it does in the *Book of Hours*,[43] but he will experience it only as an innerworldly secret in the diametrical mirror relationship of world and soul, which is fulfilled when 'clear, easeful Narcissus penetrated'[44] the mirrors. In Heidegger's language this is the bifurcation of Being (*Sein*) and (human) existence (*Dasein*). The first ten pieces of the second series develop this interdependence almost

[39] 1,5.
[40] 1,3.
[41] 1,26.
[42] II, p. 162.
[43] Mason, op. cit., p. 126.
[44] 2,3.

didactically, using both real and mythic images: the breathing in and out of world-space, the mirror and the losses of the earth captured in it, mirrors as vessels which select and dissipate, the imaginary unicorn, realised in the actuality of being loved, the muscle of a flower's calyx as successful pure openness to the light, the rose 'enfolding with layer upon layer a body that is nothing but radiance', i.e. an essential form which reveals only the 'glory' of Being which is beyond all form, the cut flowers in their 'relation' to the girl's hands which broke them off, the children in play who together become real beneath the 'glorious arcs' of the balls' flight, and finally (in 2,9 and 2,10) the contrast between modern tolerance and the God of 'real clemency' whose coming is wholly different, the contrast of the all-threatening machine which is everywhere manifest 'so that the more beautiful hesitation of the glorious hand is no longer resplendent' and which yet cannot destroy the true glory of Being:

> Even today, though, existence is magical, pouring
> freshly from hundreds of well-springs,—a playing of purest
> forces, which none can surprise unless he humbly adores.[45]

Everywhere where single forms are portrayed with the art of the *New Poems*, in the flowers and fruit, fountains and sarcophagi, the horse-rider, the dancer, the beggar, the gardens, the fallow earth in early Spring, in all these their clear contours are wholly transparent to the singing secret of Being whose fullness, wholly permeated by nothingness, is present in them and reveals itself there. This is the reason for the didactic sonnet which praises metamorphosis, though not as a general dissolution, but which interprets the form from the point of its transformation:

> Choose to be changed. With the flame, with the flame be enraptured,
> where from within you a thing changefully-splendid escapes:
> nothing whereby that earth-mastering artist is captured

[45] 2,10.

more than the turning-point touched by his soaring
shapes.[46]

This is the reason also for the advice to remain aware of
abundance in the midst of renunciation, and to anticipate all
departure:

For through some winter you feel such wintriness bind
you,
your then out-wintering heart will always outlast.[47]

The instruction of the *Book of Hours* on poverty,[48] the allusion
in the *Book of Images* to the blind and to beggars with their
'hand eternally open',[49] even the teaching on renouncing the
present God in order to help engender and to build the God
of the future,[50] are drawn together into the final synthesis.
That which is ours is precisely that which we let go and do
not wish to hold on to: this convinces us of the 'mistaken
idea that there is privation'; provided that we are woven into
the whole as 'silk threads . . . into the fabric' and, with
whichever of the single images we are united, still feel 'that
the whole, the glorious carpet is intended'.[51] 'We, who are
only just when we praise'.[52] 'Praise: that's it!'.[53]

3. HEIDEGGER
THE WAY BACK

Heidegger[1] brings the period of the 'classical tradition' to a
close. Like all the poets and thinkers of this intellectual family,
he seeks salvation—from the fate of the world which is the
product both of Christianity and of modern technology—by
a return to the classicism of antiquity which need only be
pursued more thoroughly than it was by the German classical

[46] 2,12. [47] 2,13.
[48] 2,17. [49] 2,19.
[50] 2,24. [51] 2,21.
[52] 2,23. [53] 1,7.

[1] We quote from Heidegger's work: *Sein und Zeit*, 1927 (SZ), *Vom Wesen
des Grundes*, 1929 (WG), *Kant und das Problem der Metaphysik*, 1929 (K, 2nd.
edn. 1951), *Die Selbstbehauptung der deutschen Universität*, 1933 (U), *Was ist
Metaphysik?*, 5th edn. 1949 (M), *Vom Wesen der Wahrheit*, 4th edn. 1949

movement and even by Hölderlin and Nietzsche. What was falsely construed by these as 'Nature' is in fact the φύσις of the Presocratics and has to be seen simply as all-comprehending Being. This philosophy of Being of Heidegger, a Catholic and briefly a Jesuit, is permeated with Christian theological motifs in changed form, just as is the case with Nietzsche, who was a pastor's son, and with Rilke, who came from a narrow Catholic background. In virtue of the fact simply that Heidegger endeavours with all his strength to leave behind the western metaphysical tradition in its entirety (from Plato to Hegel), he is brought face to face of necessity with the Presocratic myth, which however has been historically subsumed into the Christian revelation.[2] The return to primordial Greekness[3] is not historical, intended as a 'renaissance of presocratic thought', for 'such a purpose would be futile and contradictory', but as a 'retrieval of the origins of our historico-spiritual being'.[4] Thus even the 'destruction' of the Western ontological tradition in *Being and Time*[5] serves only the 'disclosure of a yet more fundamental, more universal horizon which could yield the answer to the question: what is Being?'.[6] The 'overcoming of metaphysics' means 'neither an elimination nor even only a repudiation of metaphysics' but its 'fundamental appropriation'.[7] And this is achieved by the disintegration of all forms of unconscious

---

(WW), *Erläuterungen zu Hölderlins Dichtung*, 2nd edn. 1951 (H), *Platons Lehre von der Wahrheit, mit einem Brief über den Humanismus*, 1947 (P, 2nd edn. 1954), *Holzwege*, 1950 (HW), *Einführung in die Metaphysik*, 1953 (E), *Vorträge und Aufsätze*, 1954 (V), *Identität und Differenz*, 1957 (Id), *Gelassenheit*. 1959 (G), *Unterwegs zur Sprache*, 1959 (S), *Was ist das—die Philosophie?*, 1956 (Ph), *Hebel—der Hausfreund* (HH, 2nd edn. 1958), *Der Satz vom Grund*, 1957 (SG), *Nietzsche*, I/II, 1961 (N).

[2] *Cf.* above, p. 000.

[3] M, p. 10; the same rejection at pp. 133–135: that which is thought in Greek terms ought to be thought 'in still more Greek terms'.

[4] E, p. 29.

[5] SZ, pp. 19–27.

[6] *Ibid.*, p. 26.

[7] S, p. 109. 'As that which is greatest, the beginning has already advanced proleptically beyond everything that is to come and thus beyond us too': U, p. 11.

dogmatism by 'rethinking' the tradition 'in the form of a dialogue.'[8] Metaphysics, which is concerned with the very question of Being, can be neither one academic 'subject'[9] among others nor even a science, something it first became in the hands of Plato.[10] Being, which has been reduced to the status of a concept, must be 'experienced fundamentally anew'.[11] In the many forms of Idealism (Greek, Christian, modern), thought itself has 'ascended improperly into subjectivism', and the descent to 'the proximity of the closest reality' is 'more difficult and dangerous than the ascent' away from it.[12] This explains Heidegger's rejection of Kant and of all that derives from him (a rejection which is particularly fierce in the case of the philosophy of values: to proclaim God as 'the highest value' is 'the greatest blasphemy'),[13] of Hegel (for whom Being is no more than the content of thought,[14] though 'reason, glorified for centuries, is the most obstinate adversary of thought'),[15] of Phenomenology, which has bracketed out the very thing which for Heidegger is of sole interest,[16] of Descartes' *cogito*, of Scholasticism and its thinking on being distorted by the theology of the schools, and, together with Nietzsche, of Plato for whom the *logos* of Being 'has already been covered over and lost'[17]: 'the

---

[8] S, p. 124.

[9] M, p. 37.

[10] P, pp. 55–56; E, p. 33. Where philosophy becomes ἐπιστήμη, and this in turn is made into a matter of schools, 'thought is abandoned': P, p. 106.

[11] E, p. 155.

[12] P, p. 103.

[13] P, p. 99. Heidegger's only attempt to come further than idealism by using categories of idealism ('synthesis') was his book on Kant, but he disavowed this as 'mistaken' and incorrigible in the preface to the second edition.

[14] Id, pp. 38–39.

[15] HW, p. 247. This does not prevent Heidegger from following and explaining Hegel's thinking with the utmost reverence and competence: HW, pp. 105–192; on the onto-theo-logical constitution of metaphysics: Id, pp. 35–73.

[16] P, p. 87; S, p. 95.

[17] P, p. 98

ἀλήθειὰ is subservient to the ἰδέα'[18] and 'the original reality of the world, the φύσις, has been reduced to the status of a blueprint for reproductions and imitations'.[19] The entire philosophy of Spirit from Plato to Kant, Fichte and Hegel is made responsible for the decline into materialism and technicism: 'The essence of materialism does not consist in the assertion that everything is only matter, but rather in a metaphysical resolution according to which all that is serves as material for work', and this is so because of the 'objectification of the real by man in his self-experience as subjectivity.'[20]

The elemental experience of the mystery of reality is expressed by the Greek 'wonder' (θαυμάξειν),[21] in the face of the form of existent things, their order and radiant beauty. Behind the question concerning their appearance (εἶδος), there is the much more bewildering one as to why anything should exist rather than simply nothing at all.[22] His first work, Being and Time (Sein und Zeit), begins by locating the Da-Sein ('Being-there', 'existence': man conscious of his own existence) in the extreme perplexity, the anxiety in which all existence slips away, in order to open up access to the question of Being. It is certain that, since in this early period it is the truth of Dasein which is the central issue for Heidegger and which he interprets as finitude structured towards death and as temporality, he does not as yet fix his gaze on Being and that his later interpretations of this period (as a methodical laying-bare that permits him to address the question of Being) are not wholly convincing; although this is relatively unimportant.[23] For very soon his gaze seeks out the decisive issue: the emergence of Being. Let us say beforehand that this

[18] P, p. 41.

[19] E, p. 48.

[20] P, pp. 87–88.

[21] Heidegger does not deny this, but intends rather that 'astonishment' as ἀρχή should govern 'every step of philosophy': Ph, p. 39.

[22] M, p. 38.

[23] Karl Löwith, in Heidegger, Denker in dürftiger Zeit (1953), has clearly set out the contradictions and incompatibilities of the two periods and thus also the essence of the 'turning' from 'Dasein' to 'Sein', esp. pp. 21–42.

emergent existence is not adequately expressed in the distinction between essence and existence of Thomist scholasticism (which Heidegger opposes),[24] since as this scholasticism understands essence (in the Greek manner) in terms of a being that is intelligible in itself, to which existence can ally itself or not, at will (or at God's will). But we will still have to ask whether Heidegger's way, which is to remove the φύσις of the Greeks from the realm of essence to a more comprehensive realm, is adequate. Φύσις means for him Being which emerges into phenomenal existence from its primal ground (*Urgrund*) or depths (*Abgrund*) and which is prior to all subjectivity.[25] This emergence lends phenomenal existence (φυ is cognate with φα[ίνεσθαι]) its ontological dignity.[26] It removes time and history, which were previously rooted in human existence, to the domain of Being itself, which emerges 'cosmically' (*weltend*) as world and, in a primal and critical struggle (the πόλεμος of Heraclitus would then be identical to the *logos* which is realized in this emergence),[27] as that 'dominating and undominated becoming-present (*An-wesen*) to thought'. Resting within this primordial event and remaining radically open to it (in ecstasy: standing 'outside' himself), man possesses true (co-creating) history.

If one asks which figures in the western metaphysical tradition Heidegger can spare in his all-destroying return to the primal question, then besides Nietzsche and his own radically destructive enquiry[28] we should mention the ontological poetry of Rilke[29] and 'of Trakl[30] and, more significant than either of these, Hölderlin. In his work the cognate origins of poetic creativity and thinking (*Dichten* and

[24] P, pp. 68f.

[25] Interpretation of Hölderlin's 'nature' in the direction of φύσις: H, pp. 54f.; systematically in E, pp. 11f.; *cf.* SG, p. 102.

[26] E, p. 47.

[27] E, p. 47.

[28] But Löwith has correctly shown that Heidegger's interpretation of Nietzsche is questionable and, if one looks to the final form taken by Nietzsche as a whole, mistaken: *op. cit.*, pp. 73–110.

[29] 'Wozu Dichter', H, pp. 248–295.

[30] 'Die Sprache', S, pp. 11–33, 'Die Sprache im Gedicht', S, pp. 37–82.

Denken) are highlighted; this is always of central concern for Heidegger,[31] as is the connection between primal language and prophecy, the essence of 'in-sistence' ('standing-in') as the penetration of Being into man and of man into Being,[32] the idea of man's 'home-coming' to Being and of his essential 'recollection' of Being,[33] the interconnection, equally significant for both, between thinking and thanking (*Denken* and *Danken*),[34] the existence of man as a self-offering to Being (as in Hölderlin's *Empedocles*),[35] and finally a christology and a theory of *kenosis* which in both are fully exploited in the service of an all-comprehending metaphysics. Goethe, too, is in harmony with Heidegger when the radical openness of man to the reality which is comprehensive and self-revealing is at issue,[36] or the mistrust of any form of Idealism, or the attitude of awe[37]—which in Heidegger too is eliminated as the condition of 'Angst'—or the knowledge of the 'meaning' of all essential forms in their orientation towards Being. But more than anyone else, Thomas Aquinas is in harmony with Heidegger, with whom he shares the insight into the transcendence of Being[38] and into the fundamental distinction between Being and existent,[39] which is fundamental for all thought, even though their respective understandings of the nature of this distinction diverge from the first point on. For both, the act of Being, which comprehends within it all that is, is illumination (and thus the original locus of truth),[40] is origin, the greatest proximity (*intimum*) in the greatest distance ('more existent than all that exists'),[41] and at the same

---

[31] 'The poet's act of giving names comes from the same provenance' as 'the utterance of the thinker . . . the thinker utters Being. The poet names that which is holy': M, p. 46, *Cf.* Ph, p. 45; E, p. 20; P, pp. 112, 117.

[32] M, p. 42.

[33] P, p. 86, H, pp. 75–143.

[34] M, p. 44; G, pp. 66–67.

[35] M, pp. 44–45.

[36] This is the quintessence of the 'Letter on Humanism': truth is in Being, not primarily in man.

[37] M, p. 45.

[38] SZ, p. 38.

[39] WW, p. 11.

[40] WW, pp. 6–7; WG, p. 6

[41] P, p. 113.

time it is nothingness (the non-subsisting),[42] the unity beyond all number.[43] Behind Heidegger, and behind Thomas, there stands not Aristotle, but that Plotinus for whom Being remains a superconceptual mystery (beyond 'metaphysics', which is 'located' in the *Nous*).[44] This family tree shows to what extent Heidegger's thought is and seeks to be fundamentally western. Even his dialogue with the Far East is that of a Westerner rooted in the ontology of German mysticism and the 'metaphysics of the saints'. So the question arises: how far can Heidegger's philosophy give a place to the fundamental principles of classical-mythic and Christian-theological thought, together with its 'glory', which appeared to him to be so under threat in all the various metaphysics of spirit (we shall discuss this first), and how far does his thought fail to do justice to precisely the object which is the orientation of his thinking; Being itself (we shall discuss this later)?

THE MYSTERY OF BEING

Heidegger eschews metaphysics and ontology in the traditional sense in order to penetrate beyond them to the 'recollection of Being itself'.[45] And he permits the everyday Greek *ousia* of Being as *par-ousia*, as being-present, to be radically shaken and held up to question in the state of anxiety in order that the 'ground for the decision for the existent rather than for nothingness' may emerge 'as the ground for the vacillation of the existent that bears us and releases us, half being, half non-being, from which it follows that we can never wholly belong to any thing . . .'.[46] 'The participation of human existence in nothingness on the grounds of concealed anxiety is the transcending of the existent in its

[42] SG, p. 93: 'Only *Seiendes* "is" the "is" itself, the "*Sein*" "is" not.'

[43] M, p. 44.

[44] Because Plotinus is usually assigned a place within the Platonic tradition, and this counts as 'forgetful of Being' for Heidegger—something that is in reality not the case for Plotinus—Heidegger prefers to begin first with the Pre-Socratics.

[45] M, pp. 8–9; P, pp. 65, 76; E, p. 31; S, pp. 109, 116; G, p. 39.

[46] E, p. 22.

entirety: it is transcendence'.[47] In the evanescence of the existent, in its loss of essence the wholly Otherness of Being is intimated, which locates all existents in Being, 'mysteriously', as the 'simple proximity of an unassuming power',[48] as the 'inviolable',[49] 'the most singular reality that there is' and which 'cannot bear comparison with anything else at all'.[50] It is dominant in all forms of essence, making them possible, and yet goes far beyond them. Only by the presence and indwelling of Being is there such a thing as existence or essence. In his celebrated analysis of the essence of a jug, Heidegger shows what is meant by the 'jugness of a jug': 'The receiving of inpouring and the containing of what is poured in', 'the pouring out' (*Aus-schenken*), which in its turn presupposes the act of giving (*Schenken*) and the gift (*das Ge-schenk*). In the water which has been given, there remains the spring which is nourished by Heaven and Earth, which is to be drunk by mortals and yet which also, as libation (χέ-ειν = to sacrifice), is a gift for immortals. Thus 'in the gift which is a drink poured out, the divine beings are present in their own way, and to them the gift of donation is returned as the gift of offering'. Taken together, Earth and Heaven, mortal and immortal, form 'a single quadrilateral' which, as the openness of Being and as a 'multifold yet unified consort', makes possible the 'essence of the jug'.[51] And so *ousia* is comprehensible only in the presence of Being (*parousia*) which, however, as an open space, is always an absence, an un-presence and a distance. Since Being is that which is non-essential in its distinction from the existent (essence), it attracts the kind of definitions which negative theology reserves for God. 'Being is not an existing quality of the existent ... This, which is wholly Other to all Being, is Non-Being'.[52] We cannot say that 'there is' Being, but only that Being 'is',

[47] M, p. 33.

[48] P, p. 78.

[49] S, p. 148.

[50] E, p. 60.

[51] VA, pp. 170–172, with reference here to G, p. 54, S, pp. 22–23, HH, p. 18.

[52] M, p. 41.

in the sense that all that is, is.[53] This is the case, because the existent is an indication of and towards Being,[54] a kind of 'word' or 'legend', which breaks forth from the silence.[55] The giving of Being is the 'productive appropriation . . . the event', and this is 'more creative than all functioning, acting and grounding. That which happens is the event itself—and nothing other than that.' It is not the result of something else (*Ergebnis*), but the self-giving (*Er-gebnis*) whose generous giving alone guarantees the possibility of a 'there is'.[56] Thus words appear such as the 'graciousness' or *Huld* ('kindness' in Hölderlin's translation of χάρις) of Being,[57] the 'favour of Being'[58] which 'preserves things in the radiance of the world', 'the world offers its favour to things'.[59] They have their origin in the place of the dispensing abundance, which 'reveals' itself in things and 'has always offered itself'[60] prior to all thought and comprehension and thus permanently enjoys the value of a 'homeland'[61] for all that exists. Language possesses the same primordial character as the emergence of φύσις, which derives directly from Being and from its history,[62] which speaks from out of Being itself and is prior to all human utterance, which speaks authentically only when it 'speaks-in-accordance-with' (*ent-spricht*),[63] responds (*ant-wortet*), echoes (*nach-spricht*).[64] 'This speech-in-accordance-with (*Ent-sprechen*) is a form of speech. It stands in the service of *language*'.[65] This is the 'house of Being',[66] in

[53] P, p. 80.
[54] S, pp. 114–117.
[55] S, p. 255.
[56] S, p. 258.
[57] VA, p. 204.
[58] M, p. 44.
[59] S, p. 24.
[60] S, p. 135.
[61] P, p. 84.
[62] P, p. 79; E, pp. 62–63.
[63] 'In reality it is speech that speaks, not man. Man speaks only to the extent that he corresponds (*ent-spricht*) to speech (*Sprache*) on each occasion': HH, p. 34; S, pp. 12f. and 20.
[64] S, p. 70.
[65] Ph, p. 44.
[66] P, p. 79.

which it dwells, as man for Hölderlin lives 'poetically on this earth', i.e. when he co-responds.[67] The difference therefore between Being and existent (whose essence will be explicated later) is the locus and the possibility of language,[68] which can truly speak and bear weight only as a word that comes from silence and returns to silence, as the 'sound of silence',[69] and can therefore hardly take itself as its own object.[70] It is evocation.[71]

The greatest effect of such a delineation of all-comprehending Being is upon the way in which we interpret *Da-Sein* (human kind). This is no way follows the leitmotif of eros (as it otherwise does in the whole regeneration of classical culture since the Renaissance, and still in Goethe), but follows that of serenity (*Gelassenheit*: indifference, impassiveness, detachment), which is the title of one of Heidegger's works, which is to say as that 'essence' which can allow Being to be itself, as a 'stepping back from the existent so that this can reveal itself in what it is and in the way that it is, and the assimilative representation can take its measure from it'.[72] This stepping back creates the possibility of unconcealedness as 'truth' (ἀ-λήθεια); this standing-out (ex-istence) is human freedom as harmonisation with the comprehensive whole.[73] Will is rooted in 'determination', and the latter is rooted in 'the disclosure of human existence with a view to the illumination of Being, and not at all in the gathering of strength which is associated with "action". But the link with Being is letting be. That all willing should be grounded in the act of letting be is the cause of bewilderment for the rational mind'[74]—but not for the mind which knows the intellectual inheritance of Christianity. For

[67] HH, p. 32; VA, pp. 187f.

[68] Heidegger relates that his first questioning concerned speech: S, pp. 92–93.

[69] S, p. 262.

[70] S, p. 149.

[71] 'The act of naming does not distribute titles, nor does it employ words, but calls to the word': S, p. 21.

[72] WW, pp. 14–15.

[73] WW, pp. 16–18.

[74] E, p. 16.

Origen and for Scholasticism, the essence of freedom was *indifferentia*, which in the period from Eckhart and Tauler to Ignatius appeared as 'submissiveness',[75] as 'indifference',[76] as 'serenity'[77] and in this as 'attentiveness to the voice of Being',[78] and as 'obedience to the voice of Being'.[79] Thus a 'solitude'[80] is demanded of us or, as the medieval mystics called it, a 'detachment'[81] which first makes possible that 'insistence' (in the sense of 'standing in') towards Being,[82] and is attuned to the gifts of Being. Heidegger, who avoids the word 'spiritual' (*geistig*: 'of the mind, intellect or spirit') in one sense, does however make use of 'spiritual' in another sense (*geistlich*: here in the sense of the Spirit which breathes forth from Being as a fearful flame,[83] and which 'drives the soul to journeying ... and to remote places'). He speaks of 'poverty',[84] of 'the nobility of poverty',[85] viz. of the 'essential poverty of the shepherd',[86] for man is the 'shepherd of Being',[87] to him is entrusted the 'custodianship of Being'[88] which he must exercise with 'care'[89] and 'patience'.[90] His thinking must be a thanking which 'does not first offer thanks for something but is only grateful that it may give thanks'.[91] It is an 'act of praise'.[92]

The relationship of self-revealing Being to the passive

[75] S, p. 70, will render 'pious' as 'submissive'.

[76] M, p. 45.

[77] G, p. 34 (with a reference to Eckhart, 'from whom however much good can be learned'), p. 51.

[78] M, p. 42.

[79] M, p. 46.

[80] M, p. 265.

[81] S, pp. 52, 58.

[82] G, p. 62.

[83] S, pp. 58f.

[84] S, p. 66.

[85] M, p. 45.

[86] P, p. 90.

[87] P, p. 75.

[88] M, p. 44.

[89] M, p. 46.

[90] S, p. 73.

[91] G, pp. 66–67.

[92] S, p. 69.

human creature who receives it is seen here in primal biblical categories, so much so in fact that the Old and New Testament category of 'glory' is also present. Thus man, as the locus and 'organ' of the reception of this revelation, becomes fundamentally the 'one who can hear',[93] whose responsibility it is to listen to the language[94] or the word or the 'silent voice'[95] of Being in order himself to master the language.[96] He is the one for whom Being is present, and present in its individual occurrence, as God is present to Moses as the 'I am present on each occasion as the one that I am'.[97] Being and man are 'bound over one to the other'[98] as in the biblical covenant, and this 'belonging in hearing' (das hörende Ge-hören) is very close to biblical faith. 'Truth' (Wahrheit) can be not only the Greek 'un-hiddenness' but also (as Löwith justifiably notes) the English 'truth' (cognate with the German Trauen and Treue, which mean 'trust' and 'fidelity'); wherever Being 'entrusts' itself, we are 'betrothed' to it.[99] This is that biblical cycle of fidelity as a precondition of truth and of revelation, which is reflected systematically in the inescapable but fruitful 'hermeneutical cycle'.[100] In the cycle of grace and homage to grace, everything is structured towards a dominant, if discreetly reserved, love (Möglichkeit [possibility] derives ultimately from mögen meaning 'to like', just as the neutral 'there is' conceals a 'there is on offer', or the neutral 'principle of sufficient reason' [Satz vom Grund] presupposes a principle which proceeds as a leap [Satz] from the ground of one thing to the ground of another). This dominant love is groundless self-giving, self-expending: 'Thought . . . exhausts itself in Being for the truth of being in so far as man entrusts his historical being to the simplicity of the one thing necessary, which . . . creates the need that is fulfilled in the freedom of sacrifice . . . Sacrifice is

[93] S, p. 241.
[94] S, pp. 254–255.
[95] M, pp. 42, 44.
[96] G, p. 49.
[97] On the time of Being; M, p. 16.
[98] Id, p. 23.
[99] S, p. 127.
[100] SZ §63f., 310f.; S, pp. 150f.

the pouring forth of human essence in maintenance of the truth of Being for the existent and is raised above all compulsion because it emerges from the depths of freedom. In sacrifice there occurs a concealed act of giving thanks.'[101] 'Therefore sacrifice can tolerate no calculation, by which it can be judged only in terms of usefulness or uselessness, whether its aims are noble or base.'[102] In contrast to the usefulness of all the sciences, philosophy therefore remains essentially useless,[103] without result or effect,[104] just as the self-giving of Being unquestionably has no justification but that alone which it derives from itself. Eckhart, too, said this of God, as Being, and of all that derives from Him, and Angelus Silesius, quoted by Heidegger with regard to the 'principle of sufficient reason', repeats it:

The rose has no why and wherefore:
it blooms because it blooms,
And has no regard for itself, and does not ask
if it is being looked at.[105]

The 'because' here does not contradict the 'without why or wherefore'; its blooming is self-justifying. The death of philosophy is critical transcendentalism and the nuclear age, which have obscured the 'why-lessness' of Being by turning it in every case into an object and subordinating it to an end, although this 'why-lessness' still persists in the background throughout all ends.[106] But this would mean the extinguishing of all forms of transcendental aesthetics in the classical and medieval sense, for 'What is beautiful appears sacred in itself' (Mörike).[107] Thus Heidegger demands a renewal of aesthetics by the philosophy of the Ontological Difference between Being (*Sein*) and being-there (*Dasein*: human existence), which is the emergent manifestation (φαί-νεσθαι) of Being (φύσις from φύω) in the ecstatic space of

[101] M, p. 44.
[102] M, p. 45.
[103] E, p. 7.
[104] P, p. 111.
[105] SG, p. 68.
[106] SG, pp. 100–101.
[107] 'An eine Lampe', quoted SG, p. 102.

Dasein, and he comments on this distinction in his dialogue with the Japanese, a dialogue which ultimately in the encounter between Western and Eastern discourse and thought allows the occurrence of Being and its expression to draw near only in 'aesthetic' categories: as 'that which takes gracious form' (*das Anmutende*, though not in the sense of Schiller's *Anmut*, grace, but) as 'the breath of the stillness of radiant rapture' and 'luminous veiling'. 'Thus all presence has its origin in grace in the sense of the pure rapture of a summoning silence' in which 'however that which causes rapture itself . . . is always manifested in the unrepeatable moment with the plenitude of its grace'.[108] In this definition the Greek 'χάρις' and the German *Huld* ('grace' as 'favour') are married. The *Huld* of Being itself 'is poetic, that which truly makes reality poetic', and the poet (and thinker) merely correspond again to the language of Being, which 'addresses' us and 'is radiant for us'.[109] The mystery of Being, unrevealable even in its revelation, as the open space in which all things are gathered and exist, is 'like a region by whose magic all that belongs to it returns to the place where it rests'. Such a 'return' to the 'free expanses' of this region causes the transformation of 'objective reality' (*das Gegenständliche*) into an easeful resting beside the 'hearth': all these expressions recall Plotinus and Eckhart, as does man's 'waiting' which 'has no object', and which thus gives itself access to the 'open spaces' and awaits the 'arrival' which derives from the metaphysics of detachment.[110]

Here the biblical concept of δόξα is retrieved and taken into the service of Being, together with the inner tension which comes to it from its Greek usage. Ἀόξα means regard, namely the regard in which one stands. In the event that that regard is an excellent one in accordance with what it reveals, then δόξα means fame and renown. In Hellenistic theology and in the New Testament δόξα Θεοῦ, *gloria Dei*, is the glory of the Lord. The act of extolling, of bestowing esteem on and showing esteem towards, has in Greek the

[108] S, pp. 140–142.
[109] S, pp. 152–153.
[110] G, pp. 40–46.

meaning of putting in the light, and thus creating duration and Being. Renown for the Greeks is not something additional which one might or might not attain: it is the manner of the highest being'. There is a reference to Pindar here in support of this. But the concept undergoes an inner development. Δόξα is regarded in a broader sense too as 'that which every existent conceals and reveals in its appearance (εἶδος, ἰδέα). A town is a wonderful sight ... Depending on the different standpoints, the view will change'. Thus there is a shift from the objective sight to the subjective view, opinion, mere supposition, and correspondingly from manifestation to seeming appearance. 'Where there is the unconcealedness of Being, there is also the possibility of seeming appearance'.[111] The enchantment and the glory of Being in its revelation always contain seeming appearance and concealment as their counterpart; the 'essence' of truth always brings with it its own inessentiality as 'non-unconcealedness'. 'The concealment of the existent within the whole, as actual 'untruth', is prior to the openness of this or that existent. It is prior even to the "letting be" itself'. Beneath all thing there lies the abyss, the 'mystery',[112] the irredeemably mysterious character of Being. But the openness of Being in its emergence into manifestation casts so great a light that this overwhelms its nature as mystery, and concealment is itself concealed. The recognising individual rests content with what is manifest, though 'his rootedness in the transient is in itself the failure to allow the concealment to prevail of the concealed'. 'The forgotten mystery of human existence' (in the section entitled 'Man' from *Being and Time*) effects however its 'own presence'; it causes man to err and to make misjudgements when he takes 'the measure' of himself in accordance with his new intents and plans,[113] not just as the practical *homo faber* but no less so as the theoretical *homo sapiens*. Thus 'evil and 'ire' (Böhme, Goethe, Schelling)[114] are rooted in the ontic-ontological (non-)essence

[111] E, pp. 78–79.
[112] WW, p. 19.
[113] WW, pp. 20–21.
[114] P, p. 112.

of truth as freedom so that 'error is the essential counter-essence to the initial essence of truth' and it 'thoroughly dominates man'[115] from the point of the primal historical occurrence of Being, without the necessity of postulating an historical 'Fall'.[116] Being, as something imposed, is not only graciousness but also fate. In its own nature, in its concealed unconcealedness which is eternally occurrent in the now, it is something which is self-directional (*epoché*), which is selfgiving and fate-forming, as destiny.[117]

Theologumena, which prevail throughout the entire Western tradition of thought but have been forgotten, emerge here:[118] the idea that God conceals Himself precisely when he reveals Himself is not only Presocratic but also Plotinian and patristic. Maximus the Confessor extensively glosses Gregory of Nazianzen's φαινόμενος κρύπτεται,[119] and this also constitutes the pathos of both the Pseudo-Areopagite and Scotus Erigena (*dum silet clamat, et dum clamat silet, et dum videtur invisibilis est . . .,)*[120] as it does in the work of Nicolas of Cusa and Ficino. But together with this there also arises the doctrine of kenosis, familiar to us from Pascal and Hamann,[121] from Tauler, Condren and Hölderlin. The openness of Being in the duality[122] of the Ontological Difference is in itself 'pain',[123] and as ec-static sense (*Sinn*) is 'madness' (*Wahnsinn*, which does not mean lunacy or *Irrsinn*),[124] 'downfall' and 'death'.[125] In the loss of selfgiving Being which holds to itself and withdraws, we discover its preciousness: because 'it is only in the most extreme withdrawal of Being that we glimpse the essence of Being',

[115] WW, p. 22.
[116] P, p. 78.
[117] Ph, p. 65.
[118] P, p. 81; G, p. 59; Ph, p. 18.
[119] See my *Kosmische Liturgie* (2nd edn. 1961), pp. 292f., 523, 530, Migne, Patr. Gr. 91, 1048–1049A.
[120] See above, p. 000.
[121] See Vol. III of this work, pp. 247–273 (Eng. tr.).
[122] S, pp. 118, 126.
[123] s, pp. 62f.
[124] S, p. 71.
[125] S, pp. 42. 46.

because 'we only recognise what belongs to us in the loss of what has been lost'.[126] In 'the alienness (*Unheimlichkeit*) of angst, we understand what home (*Heimat*) is; in alienation and estrangement, we know intimacy.[127] This all belongs indissolubly to the comprehensive glory of Being: the Δόξα of 'the undominated dominating coming-into-presence'[128] and of mere 'opinion' in irretrievable absence. The Greeks did not know this second aspect, only the Christians. But did Heidegger really succeed in incorporating the Christian dimension into his ontology?

THE LOSS OF GAIN

The attempt to incorporate all aspects of the Christian inheritance within an ontology stands or falls with the interpretation of the Ontological Difference between the existent and Being. For Heidegger there can be only one distinction, which displays many aspects: first the dual aspect of the ('objective') 'illumination' ('*Lichtung*') of Being in existent beings and its ('subjective') 'illumination' ('*Lichtung*') in the ec-static locus of freedom which is *Dasein* (i.e. human existence); these two aspects constitute in a complementary manner a single event. A further dual aspect is best illustrated by historical delimitation. In regard to this distinction classical, Greek metaphysics remains bound to the 'existent' and thus to a thinking in terms of essences (which is 'oblivious of Being'): ὂν ᾗ ὄν, the object of metaphysics, is for Aristotle existence *qua* existence (and not *qua* Being). Although the individual existent is construed here within the context of 'existence as such', and thus with an orientation towards Being, nevertheless Being itself remains occluded,[129] and appears only as 'the general', which it cannot be because, co-differentiated, it predominates in all distinctions. And yet if we construe Being as 'God' (which marks the beginnings of the early Middle Ages and which will lead *via* Eckhart and

[126] SG, p. 101.
[127] M, pp. 29–30.
[128] E, p. 47.
[129] M, p. 11.

Nicolas of Cusa to Spinoza and the modern forms of Monism), then we get the true mystery wrong and leap over it, this time by shooting too high, for this mystery inhabits the opposition between the existent and Being, the latter of which is both the abundance of all existence and yet non-substance—in such a way that existents assist Being towards its illumination objectively while man does so subjectively, although it is from Being that they receive the light in the first place. This is a mystery which cannot prevail between God and the world. There remains therefore for the genuine difference between them only that space which to some extent opens up in Plotinus (and Dionysius) and is uniquely grasped by Thomas Aquinas: the *actus essendi* as non-subsiting abundance which attains a state of rest and self-realisation from and within finite essences, and *essentiae*, which attain to reality by act, without however reducing or subdividing the infinite act. This mode of thought does not, as Heidegger says, reduce the difference 'to a mere distinction, to the potency of our intellects'[130]—that only happens when a pedantic scholasticism turns the mystery into a 'real distinction' etc. But for Thomas this structure remains *the* sign of the indeterminate non-absoluteness, speaking in Christian terms, of creatureliness: for how can a non-subsisting act of Being generate subsisting Beings from itself alone, and how are the essences to acquire a closed and meaningful form? Both these questions therefore point to a subsisting and absolute Being, God, who both offers a share in His abundance of Being (in the *actus essendi illimitatus*) and also from His absolute power and freedom (which as such presupposes nothingness as the locus of the ability to create) devises the forms of essences as the recipients of this participation in Being. Plotinus, working from a pre-Christian viewpoint, went some way towards this understanding of the difference when he construed the One, which transcends everything (even the Nous), as the mystery of Being which, for him, was transparent to the Divine-Absolute, to the extent of identification. The non-subsisting

---

[130] Id, p. 60.

character of the act of Being fused for him with the transcendence of the One beyond ontological comprehension. Heidegger, on the other hand, who belongs to the post-Christian age, revokes the Christian distinction between limitless non-subsisting and limitless subsisting Being. He creates the notion of a superconceptual *actus essendi* which renders itself temporal within essences, by attributing to it the properties of the subsisting (divine) act. And because the former must be radically annihilated in order to attain temporal expression, this nothingness, which makes the subjective-objective 'illumination' (*Lichtung*) possible, becomes an attribute of absolute Being. In other words: *Heidegger identifies the negations of the classical, Christian doctrine of God (as 'Negative Theology') with the nothingness of the act of Being which constitutes world.* The consequence of this is that once again (as with Erigena, Eckhart and Nicolas of Cusa) God has need of the world if He wishes to make explicit His own implications, so that no *analogia entis* prevails in the distinction between Being and existent, but rather an *identitas* which both generates the distinction and embraces it at the same time.

Heidegger initially denied that Being stands in 'need' of the existent in order to become itself, although later he affirmed it in ever clearer terms.[131] 'Human essence is given over to truth, because truth needs man'.[132] It is the 'message which needs us as messengers'.[133] If world is to come into being historically, then man as agent of choice and as legislator is indispensable.[134] The ultimate reality therefore becomes 'the event' as the 'independent region through which man and Being attain to each other in their essence', a 'self-supporting construct'.[135] The difference between Being and the existent, which is the primary characteristic of createdness, in thereby raised to the status of the absolute, of God. Accordingly man cannot perform the classical act of wonder

[131] On a silent alteration of the text in this sense between the fourth and the fifth editions of *Was ist Metaphysik?*, cf. Löwith, *op. cit.*, pp. 39–40.

[132] G, p. 65, cf. p. 66.

[133] S, p. 155; cf. S, p. 256: 'Speech needs human speaking'.

[134] E, pp. 47–48.

[135] Id, p. 30.

in the face of the miraculous ordering of the world, nor the Christian act of a yet deeper wonder at the incomprehensibility of his own and of all earthly existence. Now he is himself a co-essential part of the mystery of Being which prevails necessarily as such. Within this identical framework, it makes no sense to distinguish men from gods; where the comprehensive principle remains impersonal (because non-subsisting), personal beings cannot be distinguished by any thoroughgoing analogy. For this reason, the borrowing of biblical categories for the purposes of a transcendental aesthetic also fails to convince; for *Kabôd-Doxa* in the Old and New Testaments refers to the sovereign and majestic freedom of the God of gracious covenant and absolute love. But Heidegger wishes to banish all that has to do with the will (which decides, elects, judges) from the realm of being.[136] Thus the primal act of man, despite all ec-stasy, remains a pure act of 'thinking',[137] which is to be the primal ground of existence on this side of theory and practice.

In the work of Heidegger, the true wonder at the fact that something exists rather than nothing does not run its full course, for it points to a freedom which he does not wish to perceive. However strange this may seem, his emergent and fate-like φύσις remains within the horizon of Greek, essentialist, even naturalistic, thinking. Although he grasps, beyond Aristotle, the Thomist distinction between Being and the existent as a mystery impenetrable to reason, and can from this position accuse both the Greek and the moderns of forgetting Being itself, yet he does not construe this difference in Thomist terms, viz. in the Christian way as a sign of creatureliness, and therefore he falls back from this distinction into a (non-Greek, only apparently Presocratic) identity. The two points of departure of the Christian *analogia entis* are divided in Heidegger's thought between the early texts (*Being and Time* and its dependent works) and the later texts, which are separated from the earlier ones by the 'turning-point'; and yet these two halves do not form a whole. In the one we find the 'thrownness' (*Geworfenheit*) of human existence, but

[136] G, p. 60.
[137] M, p. 12.

without a throwing agent, and in such a way that the temporal structure of man leads to a finitude of Being and truth; the illumining *ec-stasis* generates itself into nothingness. But in the other, Being appears as the origin of the 'throw',[138] though 'thrownness' has now vanished and there remains only the principle of sufficient reason (*Satz* ['principle' and 'leap'] *vom Grund*) as the leap (*Sprung*) from and into the origin (*Ursprung*). The 'turn' merely displays the same thing from the other side.[139] Where the immanent analogy of Being which pertains between the *actus essendi* and *essentia* does not deepen to a transcendental analogy of Being between God and the world, it annuls itself by becoming identity and pays the price that it now needs to reconcile within itself the most contradictory elements—as is the case with Giordano Bruno. Here too Hölderlin's Ἐν διαφέρον ἑαυτῷ is the final word.

This does not change the fact that in the modern period Heidegger's project is the most fertile one from the point of view of a potential philosophy of glory. In the face of all unmediated forms of theism, he keeps the process of his thought firmly fixed on the main issue, which is the mystery of the immanent distinction between Being and the existent, with his question ('How does God enter philosophy?').[140] Christian theology as a science loses its entire basis if it thinks that it can develop the revelation of the living God while bypassing the mystery of this distinction, and it sinks accordingly to the status of being a science of existent things amongst others, and will properly be subject to the jurisdiction of philosophical thought. This is more true today than ever before, where theology thinks that without a pholsophical mediation, indeed renouncing even the medium of the human sciences, it can enter into dialogue with the exact and technological (natural) sciences, a dialogue in which it is clearly fated to draw the shorter straw. Heidegger's

[138] P, pp. 71, 84.

[139] As 'Sein *des Seienden*' or as 'Seiendes *des Seins*': Id, p. 59.

[140] Id, pp. 52f. The decisive answer to the question is given by Gustav Siewerth, *Das Schicksal der Metaphysik von Thomas zu Heidegger* (1959), ch. 21: 'Wie kommt Gott in die Philosophie', pp. 463–508.

powerful warnings against technocracy and the ever more terrible philosophical nihilism which is emergent within it are justified, even if no one heeds them any more. They are heeded all the less, of course, because Heidegger has no adequate answer to the question of existence which he raises. A philosophy which will not firmly answer the question of God one way or the other[141] lacks intellectual courage, and a pragmatic and realistic humanity will pass it by and get on with daily living.

If Christianity, failing to preserve a theology of glory, does not itself wish to fall victim to the new naturalism (of which there are terrible signs in the triumph of Teilhard de Chardin), then it must make Heidegger's inheritance its own and thus apprehend the true intent of the whole period which we have outlined here as 'the classical tradition' and which, as Heidegger has always correctly stressed, makes the past present, not for the reason that it has historical value, but because it is essential for the philosophical task of modernity.

[141] P, p. 101; WG, p. 28: 'Questioning itself becomes the highest form of knowledge', U, p. 12.

6. THE METAPHYSICS OF SPIRIT

a. *The Other Possibility*

The return to classical antiquity, in order to find a way out of the confusion of the late Middle Ages, would have been successful in the long run only if antiquity had been understood as an Advent-like openness looking to Christianity, not as a comprehensive ('cosmic-religious') form in which Christianity was embedded as a potentiality (perhaps the greatest one of all), nor indeed as a base for an anti-Christian reaction. It also proved impossible to invest fundamentally pre-Christian forms with Christian substance in order thus to salvage them. Eckhart was the first (in a radicalisation of Augustine) to point to a second way: that of making everything dependent on the personal relationship (which the biblical revelation had opened up) between the infinite and the finite spirit, and to interpret the spirit, free and self-possessing Being, as the quintessence, the meaning and the reason for all forms of non- or sub-spiritual Being. Now it was the Christian 'stage of consciousness' which produced its own metaphysics from within itself, but without holding any longer to the pre-Christian metaphysics of Nature as a prior and grounding stage. We have already made the acquaintance of this kind of metaphysics of the spirit, still wholly within the Christian theological sphere, as 'the metaphysics of the saints', which however dwelt so much on the highest religious act of *indifferentia* (of the finite spirit in orientation towards the infinite one) that the philosophically grounding substructure remained largely undeveloped, thus causing their 'mysticism', which lacked a metaphysical foundation, to perish on account of its unreality. Nicolas of Cusa was the first to take Eckhart's project further by erecting a (classically construed) analogy between the primary Creator-spontaneity of God and the secondary creativity of man, both being an essential exposition of the respective unities of spirit. This seed would soon germinate, but not without absorbing into itself one further late medieval motif.

The shift of emphasis to the spiritual and personal relationship between man and God was, from the point of view of the history of ideas, not only a step forward (from 'Nature' to 'Spirit'), but also a step back. During the Nominalist period the universe lost its theophanic radiance—the devout no longer encounter God outside but only within themselves. At the same time, the universe loses its hierarchic gradation and collapses into 'matter' which, itself without essence, becomes that which is merely mathematically calculable and which is present only to be exploited by man. This is where the source of the materialist mentality lies, which was and still is both the effect and again the cause of the retreat of the (devout) spirit from the world. Thus the philosophy of spirit—in which the immediacy of relationship between the divine and the human spirit is no longer mediated by the universe—is on the one hand the fruit of Christianity and, on the other, its greatest threat, because the material conception of the world tends, of itself, towards materialism. The exact natural sciences are the progeny of positivistic Nominalism and are the dialectical counterpoint to the *Devotio Moderna*; they will strengthen the philosophy of the spirit with their technical triumphs and, since the latter lacks any mediating understanding of Being, will drive it of necessity into a Monism of spirit. The stages reached and the paths taken can be drawn up virtually *a priori*.

I. Descartes picks up the gauntlet of the natural sciences: he leaves the external world as mere matter ('extension' and thus 'automation') to the exact sciences and removes the focus of metaphysics to the 'I think', from which he extracts the existence of both finite and infinite spirit. Augustine and Christianity, even religious interiority (including that of Luther), are salvaged, and at the same time the way forward is prepared for modern research. The universe is retrieved again—in a classical universalism—by the analogy of spirit: if we are raised with Spinoza and Leibniz to God's point of view, then we can now restore the interrupted communication between God and matter occasionalistically (*via* God), or read matter as a mode of spirit (Leibniz) or drop it as mere appearance (Berkeley).

2. Metaphysics gains by the fact that the natural sciences are given a free hand; just as, with Nicolas of Cusa, man is established as the analogous and 'enigmatic' co-creator with God, even if only in the unreal domain of numbers. But if the external world is nothing other than extension (i.e. matter *as* infinite divisibility), where does the distinction lie in the long run between God's exemplary creation and man's technical calculation? The confinement of philosophy to the domain of spirit is particularly inclined to lead to an inescapable identity: 'I think—I am' is not a 'conclusion' but an immediate intuition, if not in a psychological sense, then certainly in a speculative one. The Eckhartian position of the 'spark of the soul' as a point of identity beyond all analogy is reached in Descartes by a fundamentally philosophical method and is developed in Kant's 'original and synthetic unity of apperception', in Fichte's *Ich*, in Schelling's point of indifference and in Hegel's process of the spirit. On account of the diversity of its forms, it is difficult to discern any possibility of halting this process. If it is to be understood, all thought-content must be incorporated into the form of 'I think—I am', which is formally unsurpassable and thus absolute (divine). Accordingly, the question must be asked: what can 'glory' possibly still mean within the philosophy of spirit? From the point of view of the unity of apperception or of the logical subject, there can be only *one* spirit, only *one* Lord; in the event that 'glory' is fitting for it, over against the material world which it 'glorifies', then this can only be a 'self-glory'.

3. The second alternative, which is that of Eckhart and Nicholas of Cusa, comes to the fore. This is the co-creative aspect of the finite subject, not only in the sense of a *causa secunda*, but of an immediate involvement in the *Causa Prima*, whose inner form it already possesses. The point at issue here can only be the distinction between the absolute character of the spirit in terms of its form and its content, a distinction which the 'world-process' must serve to eliminate, interpreted in such a way that in its 'real' aspect it is construed as the

'evolution' of Nature into 'spirit' and in its comprehensive 'ideal' aspect as that which is projected *a priori* from the (formal) absolute spirit itself and that through which the spirit attains its totality of content and existence. A fully-developed philosophy of spirit, whether Christian, non-Christian or anti-Christian, will always have to accept this circle as inevitable, and it does so all the more willingly when the old cosmology too seems thereby to be surpassed and to be assumed into the final synthesis: 'Nature' (which somehow comprehends the finite spirit) is not intelligible without the prior projection of an (absolute) spirit, but the source of that projection is now at the same time the human spirit, which thus also grasps its own process of becoming within the universe (in the evolutionary sciences) and thus possesses the latter definitively as its own 'material' 'beneath itself'.

There are of course many different variations of a philosophy of this kind, although it does have an ultimate destination in historical terms, viz. the ever more consistent representation of the identity which is concealed within it. In the initial period, the influence of the classical, Christian analogy is still so strong that the renewal of the philosophy of spirit has the appearance precisely of a revaluation of the most magnificent visions of the past, and this without doubt in the best faith, in subjective terms, of the philosophising Christian (or Jew). These are the great systems of the Baroque, which understands itself to be the highest dynamicisation of the Western tradition, and thus to be a 'glory as never before'. Meanwhile the primary shock of the analogy diminishes, and this alone can distinguish in absolute terms the glory of representation from represented glory. There is no possibility of coming to a halt on the path from Leibniz to Hegel. The world is philosophically constituted from the divine grounds, and the Christian thinker feels himself empowered to achieve this, indeed challenged to do so, by the biblical self-revelation of those same divine grounds. In essence this is a titanism of piety which perceives only later what it has conjured forth and which, as Heidegger remarks, will find climbing out of its pit of error more difficult than falling into it.

b. The Immediacy of the Man-God Relation

I. DESCARTES

Descartes' spare speculative system,[1] which must be viewed as the beginning of the modern philosophy of spirit, appears as a retreat from all that is subject to doubt to the last rampart of the indubitable. All that presents itself as external world might be as unreal as our dreams; all that we have are mental representations ('ideas'), which include the involuntary sense-impressions. This retreat in doubt is on the one hand the declaration of our freedom and ascetic power: 'detachment from the senses' (se détacher[2]), 'turning away' (se détourner[3]), and is portrayed as a unique and grave conversion of life (entreprendre sérieusement une fois en ma vie de me défaire ..., commencer tout de nouveau dès les fondements[4]). We should 'pull everything down and start again',[5] and 'close our eyes and ears, turn away from all the senses and banish all the images of corporal things from the spirit'[6] in order to become free for the 'contemplation of truth'.[7] The process requires not only a period of training of 'several months or at least several weeks,'[8] but also each time afresh particulière attention,[9] grande application d'esprit,[10] soigneusement recherché,[11] circonspection[12] and 'seriousness of mind'.[13] 'Intuition' does not take place by

[1] Descartes, Oeuvres et Lettres, ed. André Bridoux (Pléiade, Gallimard 1952). Règles pour la direction de l'esprit = RE; Discours de la Méthode = D; Méditations = M; the appended Réponses = 1 Rp, 2Rp, etc.; Principes de la philosophie = P; Traité de l'homme = T; Recherche de la Vérité (fragment) = RV; Lettres = L.

[2] M, Abrégé 262.

[3] 2 Rp 370.

[4] 1 M 267; cf. P 1, 571.

[5] RV 888.

[6] 3 M 284.

[7] P 571.

[8] 2 Rp 367.

[9] Ibid. The concept recurs immediately.

[10] 5 M 315.

[11] 1 Rp 355, 357.

[12] P 576.

[13] 2 Rp 371 and frequently.

itself, but requires *un esprit pur et attentif.*[14] This endeavour displays the other side: our truth is not something which is fundamentally certain; that we *can* doubt is not only an advantage of our freedom,[15] but proves the uncertainty of our entire existential situation. What the senses offer us as external world, even as human community, may be sufficient for a practical form of knowledge, for biological conservation, self-advancement and self-defence,[16] but the reality which corresponds to this in terms of theory remains uncertain. Disillusionment when we thought we were certain makes us extremely suspicious,[17] and even the intuitions of mathematical regularity lack ultimate inner clarity and transparence:[18] when they are before our eyes, they appear indubitable, but when we look away, we are not so sure. While proximity to intuition is a criterion of truth,[19] for the most part Descartes speaks prudently here in nuanced terms of 'sufficiently clear and distinct' and so forth, which does not wholly exclude the possibility of subjective delusion. Behind this there is only the apparently indivisible point where consciousness (*pensée* embraces for Descartes all the acts of consciousness, including will, endeavour, mood, imagination etc.)[20] and being coincide.[21] Of course this is possible only so long as I think,[22] but since thinking is the form of my self-possession, in which I do not perceive myself to be dependent upon any any mediating thing, therefore I think continuously, as light is always radiant.[23] In comparison with this kind of evidence for self-possession, the outer world,

[14] RE 43.
[15] P 1, 6; 573.
[16] 6 M 328.
[17] 4 D 142.
[18] P 1, 5; 572.
[19] 'Ideas that are clear and distinct cannot be other than true': D 152 and very often.
[20] 2 M 278.
[21] 4 D 147; 2 M 275.
[22] 2 M 277.
[23] L (19.1.1642) 1142; 4 M 148: 'une substance dont toute l'essence ou la nature n'est que de penser' (a substance the whole essence or nature of which consists only in thinking).

even one's own body, emerges only as a likelihood, and, in the event that it has extra-mental existence, it could only be the 'Wholly Other' of the spirit (Non-Self), viz. instead of pure indivisibility pure divisibility, pure materiality, pure automatism, which is true also for our own body and for the animal kingdom.[24] The classical and scholastic 'famed *arbor Porphyriana*' (of the degrees of Being: Existence, Life, Feeling, Consciousness) is thus 'disdained' and dropped in favour of a bald opposition.[25]

And yet Descartes retrieves in another form what has been discarded. Self-possessing consciousness has the truth directly: in the *intuitus*,[26] which is prior to every logical conclusion,[27] 'I have never doubted truth, it always seemed to me *une notion si transcendentalement claire* that it is unmistakable',[38] it is *expérience, témoignage intérieur*.[29] Here for Descartes there presides that original *clarté*, which inherits and develops the classical and scholastic *claritas*. Nevertheless, this luminous quasi-Absolute of the unity of being and consciousness cannot ground itself. Why not? On the one hand, because I had to call everything into question in order to reach this point, and was able to do so: 'Consequently my being was not perfect, for I clearly saw that knowing is a higher perfection than doubting, and so I came upon the idea of investigating where I had learned to conceive of something more perfect than myself'.[30] Here it becomes evident that doubt is not only capacity but also incapacity (to ground the being-in-itself of the phenomenal world), that it is in no way merely a trick of method in order to isolate a phenomenon by blacking it out, but is an existential intermediate position between God and nothingness.[31] This experience necessarily contributes to the manner in which I know myself to be identical with being-

---

[24] L (3.1638) 1003–1004; RV 896.

[25] RV 892.

[26] RE 43f.; *intuitus mentis*: L 1060.

[27] 'Aucun syllogisme': 2 Rp 375 and frequently.

[28] L (16.10.1639) 1059.

[29] RV 899.

[30] 4 D 148.

[31] 'Je suis comme un être entre Dieu et le néant' (I am like a being between God and nothingness): 4 M 302.

consciousness, so that time enters this circle and I cannot vouch for my subsequent being, nor, therefore, can I create myself.[32] Now these deficiences are known to me and thus the idea exists in me 'of certain perfections which I do not myself possess'. I therefore recognise myself to be 'dependent' upon an absolute consciousness of Being the idea (*idée*) of which is 'inborn' within me, both in my being (existentially) and in my consciousness ('objectively'), which at their root are one. The way in which we explicate Descartes' 'proof for the existence of God', whether we see it as an apparently 'ontological' proof or as a proof based upon the contingency of Being, is therefore of little consequence, for both are for him two sides of the same coin.[33] The notion that 'the concept of a most perfect being implies its existence' is always deduced from the fact that this 'concept' is present in a being whose existence is imperfect and which can draw this conclusion only because it experiences within itself through its own existence the distinction between *Dasein* and perfect (or necessary) Being. Only on these grounds can Descartes express the 'different degrees of reality or entity', not only of the existing substances but also of ideas and their objective content.[34] He calls for 'serious attention and consideration' in order to understand just this point: 'It is an [intuitive] *première notion* that all reality or perfection, which only exists objectively in ideas, must exist formally and eminently in their causes' so that if we possess the concept of a being which grounds both itself and us, then this being must also exist.[35] This idea is greater than I am[36]—it is evidently greater even

[32] 3 M 297–298. 'Were I alone and independent of everyone else, i.e. in such a way that I would have been able out of my own power to possess the little measure of perfect Being that I might have possessed, then should I also have been to give myself everything else that I was aware of lacking, and I should thus myself have been infinite, eternal, immovable, all-knowing and all-powerful.' 4 D 149; in a similar manner, 3 M 296.

[33] *Cf.* for example, 2 Rp 372, P 1, 13–18.

[34] 'There is more objective reality in the idea of the substance than in the idea of the accident, and more in the idea of the infinite substance than in the finite substance.' 2 Rp 394–395; *cf.* 3 M 290.

[35] 2 Rp 371.

[36] 3 M 290–291, 294.

than what I could ever become (for it is contradictory to suggest that I could ever be a God in the state of becoming),[37] and it is greater than my fellow men. But I know too that ideas can be merely the products of a consciousness, and thus the idea of God in me is like 'the artist's personal mark in his work'.[38] For Descartes this is wholly central in the identity of being and consciousness in so far as the occurrence of the latter is the last refuge from the unreality and dream-reality of earthly existence which presses in on all sides, which fact however recalls the quality of this being–consciousness: in the ideas of things there is much that is 'confused and obscure, since they participate in nothingness, that is, they are so confused in us only because we ourselves are imperfect'.[39] Therefore I not only know my striving for something more, but also the fact of my being radically and incontrovertibly surpassed by something that is absolutely More, something that is eternally greater than I can ever be.[40]

Henceforth the absolute ascendency can be given to God in the *cogito-sum* precisely because He makes Himself present within it only through His 'personal mark' ('which does not need to differ from the work itself'), the mark, that is, of createdness. He 'created me in a sense in His own image and likeness, and I understand this likeness (which contains the idea of God) with the same faculty with which I understand myself. For when I reflect upon myself, then I not only recognise that I am imperfect, incomplete and dependent upon Another, always striving and yearning as I press on towards something which is better and greater than myself,

---

[37] 3 M 295–296, where he takes up a position in advance against the later idealism: 'Je comprends fort bien que l'être objectif d'une idée ne peut être produit par un être qui existe seulement en puissance' (I understand perfectly well that the objective being of an idea cannot be produced by a being that exists only potentially).

[38] 3 M 299.

[39] 4 D 152.

[40] 2 Rp 374–375: 'cette puissance que j'ai de comprendre qu'il y a toujours quelque chose de plus à concevoir' (this power which I have to understand that there is always something more to conceive of): this is Anselm's formula, which we have already encountered in various adaptations in the course of our path through history.

but I understand at the same time that the One upon Whom I depend possesses within Himself all these great things for which I yearn and the ideas of which I find within myself, not only in an indeterminate way or only potentially, but in such a way that He enjoys them in reality now and eternally, and thus is God'.[41] From this emphasis upon the *cogito*, light falls on all the darkness in the surrounding world: from God there flows the light of its being too, and thus of its truth, for in God truth and truthfulness are of necessity one: 'Thus it is plain enough that God cannot deceive' as could perhaps an *esprit malin*. The *cogito* does not reveal a gnostic demiurge, but directly reveals the highest radiance of the Being of the Good (of Plato and Plotinus), under the Christian sign of a free and good Creator who also grounds the practical, biological interrelationship of man and his surrounding world in his own ultimate truth and truthfulness of Being. At the end of the third Meditation, the thinker Descartes worships this God, who is not however Pascal's *Dieu des philosophes*, in the act of philosophical adoration: before passing on to other themes 'it seems to me proper to pause for a moment in the contemplation of this all-perfect God, to take time to consider His wonderful properties, to reflect upon, to wonder at and to adore *the incomparable beauty of this immense light*, at least in so far as the strength of my spirit permits me, for it is struck blind before it'. Descartes speaks here of the 'divine majesty'[42]; the light falls upon him by virtue of an original counterblow, and not at all on account of any continuity or peaceful speculative transition from a likeness to its original.

Thus the book of *Meditations* is composed 'for the glory of God',[43] although Descartes is everywhere careful not to cross the border dividing pure philosophy from theology.[44] He is concerned, as was Augustine, with 'God and the soul' (the

[41] 3 M 299–300.

[42] *Ibid.* 300.

[43] 'Ce traité qui regarde la Gloire de Dieu' (this treatise which is concerned with the glory of God): L (7.1640) 1074; *cf.* 2 Rp 366; 'La Gloire de Dieu à laquelle tout ceci se rapporte' (the glory of God with which all of this is related): accompanying letter to M 259.

[44] L (27.4.1637?) 963–964.

external world, the less certain reality, is deciphered only after the dissolution of this dual unity).[45] Descartes does not dare to face up to the third Kantian idea of 'immortality' because God in His freedom could still destroy the soul, although of itself it outlives the body.[46] God 'in whom all the treasures of wisdom and science are hidden' emerges from the *cogito* as that which is 'most intimately known',[47] and the *cogito*, in order to see it, requires the *grande application d'esprit* mentioned at the beginning, which frees itself by ascetic means from the *divertissement* of the persistently impinging images.[48] This endeavour causes the occurrence of that 'counterblow', by which the *cogitor* becomes visible in man's *cogito* (as Baader felicitously expresses Descartes' idea), and thereby also and for the first time (and not for instance as the inner form of the *cogito*!) the absolute all-grounding *cogito* of God.

The absolute primacy of the Augustinian (and Newmanian) 'God and soul' means however that for me Being, goodness and the *Thou* emerge only in relation to God as the 'Other', and thus there is no way that leads to God *via* the *being* of the world and the human *thou*. The destructive consequences of this exclusion can be felt throughout the whole of the philosophy of spirit which now begins. One reason for this is that the *sum* is not resolved in the *cogito* because all the thought-contents (*idée*, νόημα) which inhabit the thought process (*idée*, νόησις) are never more than objectified 'reality', and never present existence, and the criterion of truth is no longer situated in Being but only in the 'clarity and distinctness' of the idea, which comes to be the entire representation of the thing in itself (*das Ding an sich*).[49] The road to Leibniz, Kant and Hegel is open, and also to Husserl's reading of Descartes in which doubt (ἐποχή) methodically serves the purpose of bringing into light the liberation into existence of the νόημα from the νόησις. Already in Descartes, the idea of truth has become dialectical, for if the

[45] 4 D 151; 3 M 286.
[46] L (24.12.1640?) 1105.
[47] 4 M 301, and already 4 D 151; *cf.* L (3.1637) 962.
[48] 5 M 315.
[49] *Cf.* what was said above about Suarez, pp. 000.

soul is really 'nothing other than thought', then we cannot see why it should not be 'pure thought' and thus contain the criterion for truth immanently within itself, as the relation between the νόησις and the 'clarity and distinctness' of its νοήματα. Nevertheless, Descartes wishes to locate the guarantee of truth in God, where essence (*idée*) and existence are one and thus the creaturely distinction between spirit (subject) and world (object) can be grounded and preserved.[50] The forgetfulness of Being in the thought of the *cogito* should cause the extinguishing of existence (*sum*) within the *cogito*, but now the latter calls the classical hierarchy of Being (the *quarta via* of Augustine and Thomas) to its aid in order to ground thought and being not in the ego but in God. The Ontological Distinction (between finite and infinite existence) is most clearly held by Descartes in his theory that man's reason is finite while his will (striving, eros) is infinite: a Platonic idea, mediated by the Franciscan school, which finds expression in Kant in the distinction between pure and practical reason and in the modern Christian Kantian school (including the superseding of Kant: Blondel, Maréchal, Marc, Rahner *inter al.*) as the distinction between conceptual knowledge and the infinite dynamism of the spirit, *représentation* and *affirmation*.[51]

But there is one other line which must be drawn from this Cartesian thought which is forgetful of Being to the various forms of spiritual metaphysics of his century (Francis de Sales, Lallement, Bérulle, Fénelon), which in a similarly devout immediacy of God to consciousness which was likewise forgetful of Being, was inclined to ignore the world and our fellow men. Because the Thou, which is the hard criterion

[50] 4 D 148, 151.

[51] 4 M 305: 'Il n'y a que la seule volonté que j'expérimente en moi être si grande, que je ne conçois point l'idée d'aucune autre plus ample et plus étendue: en sorte que c'est elle principalement qui me fait connaître que je porte l'image et la ressemblance de Dieu' (There is only the one will which I experience in myself as so strong that I do not at all conceive the idea of another ampler and wider will: so that it is principally this that makes me know that I bear the image and the resemblance of God). *Cf.* 306, 307: all error comes from the fact that the will is broader than the understanding, so that I 'posit' things that I do not know with sufficient clarity.

for truth and for Being, is missing here on both sides,[52] this philosophy and spirituality of divine glory lacks the anti-bodies against pantheism, and hot on its heels logical atheism, in which every kind of classical and Christian glory collapses in favour of a solipsistic universal subject in which freedom and necessity must coincide. The path from Descartes to Spinoza and to Leibniz is a logical one.

2. SPINOZA

Descartes handed the external world over to 'exact' materialistic science as its 'material' in order to preserve the inner world for philosophy and religion as the site of the analogy of Being between God and the soul. This dualism cries out to be superseded all the more in view of the fact that the external world has shrunk to mere extension (which can be dealt with just as easily as 'the form of external intuition' [*Anschauung*]) and truth is reduced to the inner relation between the soul and its ideas ('concept' and 'intuition' [*Anschauung*]). Under such preconditions, it was the task of the two great Baroque philosophers to rethink the classical and traditional Christian metaphysics: Spinoza and Leibniz, of whom Leibniz is by far the stronger and more comprehensive thinker.

Spinoza[1] anchors thought and extension (spirit and body), as the two attributes of God (the only ones known to us), in His unique and absolute substance; all finite essences and their

---

[52] The 'Thou' of one's fellow-man falls likewise under the category of the things in the external world that could be a dream, 4 D 151: all the 'ideas' that are not more perfect in Being than my 'ego' could have been produced by myself; this category includes not only the ideas of the things of nature, but also those of my fellow-men: 3 M 291–292. The problem of intersubjectivity is not posed, but is presupposed as a fact: 'car tous les hommes ayant une même lumière naturelle, ils semblent devoir tous avoir les mêmes notions . . .' (for since all men have one and the same natural light, it seems that they must all have the same notions), L (16.10.1639) 1059.

[1] Spinoza, *Opera. Im Auftrag der Heidelberger Akademie der Wissenschaften* ed. Carl Gebhardt, 4 vols. (Heidelberg, C. Winter, no date). The *Ethica* (in Vol. II) quoted by *Pars* and *Propositio* (e.g., III, 2); *Definitio* = df, *Axioma* = ax; *Demonstratio* = d; *Scholium* = sch; *Corollarium* = c.

variations are the *modi* (or states) of these attributes. In this way, all Cartesian distinctions are assumed into an ultimate point of identity: (1) The distinction between God and the world is levelled out by becoming that between substance and the *modi* (accidents) which inhere within it. (2) The distinction between divine and human knowledge is reduced to that which obtains between precise (i.e. clear and distinct, spiritual) and imprecise (obscure, confused, sensual) concepts, from which the Cartesian distinction between finite intellect and infinite will (eros, dynamism) is expressly deduced.[2] (3) Finally, the distinction between essence and existence, which in God are naturally identical, is reduced to the dependence of the finite upon God directly (existence) and upon the conceptual whole (essence). Since God is spirit as well as extension,[3] He is the unity of *logos* and *physis* for which the Stoa, which dominates in seventeenth-century ethics,[4] provides the model. The contributions of Neoplatonists, such as Leone Ebreo, have to conform to this 'Stoic' identity, i.e. the eros must adapt itself to the dominant form of *apatheia*, all the more so since the Stoic clarity of thought (even in the philosophical and divine realm: as κατάληψις) has now taken on the modern 'exact'-scientific form. Spinoza understands a concept to be an inner conception and spawning of the spirit (*per ideam intelligo Mentis conceptum quem Mens format*);[5] therefore, it can wholly correspond to the object (*adaequata*),[6] even in so far as God is concerned as thought-content, and thus be 'real' (*per realitatem et perfectionem idem intelligo*).[7] In a formal sense (by the affirmation of the infinite attributes of the substance) Spinoza retains the superiority of God over the world, but since God as absolute thought necessarily knows all his *modi* and, on account of the absolute identity of knowledge and will in Him, just as necessarily determines them, everything possible becomes actual, and

[2] II 49 sch.
[3] The last point is justified in detail at I 15 sch.
[4] *Cf.* Vol. III of this work, p. 189 (Eng. tr.).
[5] II df 3.
[6] II df 4.
[7] I df 7.

does so by necessity: God's freedom is only the fact of His not being determined by anything other than Himself.[8] 'Things could not have been created by God in any other way or in any other sequence than they were'.[9] It makes sense to speak of 'contingence', therefore, only with respect to 'our deficient cognitive faculty',[10] for 'things have been created by God in the highest perfection and proceed by necessity from the most perfect existing nature'.[11] Spinoza thus returns to Scotus Erigena's *Natura naturata*.[12] Philosophical *hauteur* has rarely expressed itself in more absolute terms than here; once again there is a preference for speaking of the *vulgus*, the common herd who are incapable of thought and for whom the freedom of God seems despotism; 'what I have to say will not be properly understood by anyone who does not greatly beware confusing the power of God with the power or rights of earthly kings'.[13] Actual power is only the precise knowledge which God (and the man who is a philosopher in God) possesses; no opposition to or assault upon the *demonstratio ordine geometrico* of metaphysical ethics is possible.

Human thinking in constant association with extension or corporality, which is just as absolute and which plays a major role for Spinoza as dietetics,[14] must participate in the absolute thought of the *Natura naturans* within the *Natura naturata*. In the same way that God himself is all his *modi*, and is so in the freedom of his own being, man must raise himself above all the forms of his addictions to his 'attacks' (affections) as passions (παθήματα, *Leiden-schaften*) and must transform them by the clarification of their confusion and imprecision into the spiritual precision of self-possessed actions.[15] The

---

[8] I df 7.

[9] I 33.

[10] *Ibid.* sch. 1.

[11] *Ibid.* sch. 2; *cf.* II 3.

[12] Addition to II ax 5 (Gebhardt II 86).

[13] II 3 sch.

[14] 39 and sch.

[15] III df 3: *si . . . harum affectionum adaequata possimus esse causa, tum per affectum actionem intelligo, alias passionem. Cf. Generalis Definitio* at the end of III. On the form of the active taking-possession: III 1 d.

overcoming of this distinction between *passio* and *actio* (corresponding to the Stoic path towards *apatheia*) is necessarily at the same time rightly ordered love of self (which is the basis of all virtue)[16] *and* love of God (since God is the self of my self, the achieved universal perspective of thought). The virtuous man obeys only himself,[17] and is with good conscience the perfect utilitarian,[18] precisely when he loves God for God's own sake. Altruistic love follows (in a truly Stoic or Buddhist way) only on the basis of identity of generic nature and the closest relationship in individuality.[19] In man, *amor* is identical with *cupiditas*[20] (as is being human itself) in so far as the latter (as 'eros') strives for the totality, preferring it to everything that is only partial. It is precisely for this reason that there is no *amor* in God, any more than there is hatred or joy or sadness, because God Himself is the totality which is complete in itself.[21] The one who loves God cannot, therefore, strive for or expect God to love him in return.[22] In so far, however, as the spiritual love of man for the absolute (*amor Dei intellectualis*)[23] is itself absolute and eternal (and thus also unoriginate), it is 'a part of God's infinite love for Himself',[24] and (only!) to that extent does God love men.[25] But this love remains a limiting concept, adjoining that of cupidity, which in the critical moment eliminates itself on the grounds that in absolute knowledge which is attained and

[16] *Conatus sese conservandi primum et unicum est virtutis fundamentum*, IV 22 c.

[17] *Sibi parere.* V 41 sch.

[18] IV appendix 8.

[19] *Ibid.* appendix 9f.

[20] IV 41 d.

[21] V 17 d, c.

[22] V 19.

[23] V 32 c, V 33.

[24] V 36.

[25] *Ibid.* c. When Spinoza says, *Mentis amor intellectualis erga Deum est ipse Dei Amor quo Deus seipsum amat*, this is (in philosophical pantheism) the same doctrine as that of Karl Barth in theological theopanism, because in each case the only possible mediatory position of the *analogia entis* is rejected. Once again, however, we must draw attention to the dangerous closeness to Fénelon. Leibniz will be aware of this, and will seek to avoid the danger.

contemplated *ordine geometrico*, it is at most only the absolute and contented assent (*acquiescentia*)[26] to the intuition of truth which can prevail, but not love. This is the pathos which predominates in Hegel's absolute knowledge and in Nietzsche's Song of Yes and Amen, and which can just as easily be the pathos of a ('modern'), absolutely emotionless realism that is impervious to all love, all enthusiasm and all wonder.

For the Spinozian 'spirit', the world exists in an extra-human sense only as 'material': it contains 'nothing in which the spirit could find joy', 'the consideration of our interests does not require that we should be concerned to conserve it', rather, we can 'destroy it or turn it to our advantage in every possible way'.[27] The absolute technicisation of our world is demanded on the basis of this mystical form of realism; in the axiom that knowledge is power, the proximity to Hobbes (whom Spinoza has studied exactly) is established. Ethics is both at once: knowledge (as clarification of obscure sentiments) and power as self-mastery and as mastery of the world, in an equitable state of mind which forbids feelings such as compassion,[28] humility[29] and contrition,[30] judging these to be inimical to man's strength. Here, too, the path to Nietzsche lies open.

The geometric armour surrounding Being—not only in terms of method but also of content—eradicates all 'glory': everything is radically comprehended in the 'precise idea'. Unknown attributes of God possess no radiance. Spinoza knows and tolerates *gloria*, but only as justified renown that pertains to God and the saints.[31] When he refers to the biblical *kabôd*, he equates it with the *acquiescentia*.[32] But because ethical achievement, the ascent to God's vantage point, is difficult, Spinoza can conclude his ethics with an adaptation of Plato's

[26] IV appendix and frequently.
[27] IV appendix 26.
[28] IV 50.
[29] IV 53, *cf.* IV appendix 22.
[30] IV 54.
[31] III 30 sch.; IV 58.
[32] V 36 sch.

χαλεπὸν τὸ καλόν, *Omnia praeclara tam difficilia quam rara sunt.*

3.LEIBNIZ

There has surely never been a Christian philosophy with such a triumphalistic claim to totality as that system which knows all things, considers all things and reconciles all things and which is the work of the Baroque *uomo universale*, Leibniz.[1] He is the advocate of God and of his world, who fights tooth and nail for the *causa Dei* (the 'summing-up' in defence of God). In the certainty of victory, the splendour of his intellectual penetration and eloquence irradiates the *gloria Dei*, for which he fights in every area of philosophy and theology, of traditional classical metaphysics, of the Church Fathers and scholasticism, down to the Baroque neoscholastics, as also (and more fiercely) in all fields of modern natural science, in the researches of mathematics, physics and biology, in technology, law and historical science, European politics and, of course, corresponding to his universalistic thinking, in the field of ecclesiastical ecumenism. Only Hegel will make such similar universal claims, but it is Leibniz, before him, who possesses the greater skills as scientific researcher and explorer. The ethos of his creativity is the boundless affirmation of every (partial) truth, the courage and the will for its seamless integration. In the manner of a general, he plans the most comprehensive strategies for the conquest of the whole of reality, like an architect (an image he loves), he orders the measures, the weights and the proportions. For him truth lies in the disposition of things, which dovetail together; it is in the harmony (ἁρμόττω to connect, fit together, order) of the world that its goodness and its victorious beauty lie: *beauté*

---

[1] Leibniz' works are quoted from the facsimile edition (1959) of the *Opera philosophica omnia* by J. E. Erdmann (1840), which now includes *inter alia* the *Discours de Métaphysique*. (References to page numbers and columns a, b.) We use in addition the edition by Gerhardt (=G), *Die Philosophischen Schriften von G. W. Leibniz*, 7 Vols., 1875–1890.

Some abbreviations: *Discours de Métaphysique*=DM (with paragraph); *Essai de Théodicée*=Th (with paragraph); *Principes de la Nature et de la Grâce, fondés en Raison*=NG (with paragraph).

is time and again the key word beside *gloire*, as the final proof of identity of the discovered truth. It is Leibniz, not Spinoza, who gave German Idealism its aesthetic ethos and, though it drew upon him, the intervening Enlightenment never acknowledged his greatness.

Leibniz decisively shoulders the burden of Cartesian dualism, which is the burden of modern natural science for the philosopher. At the age of fifteen, he believes himself to have come out against the 'substantial forms' in favour of atomism, but soon he recognises 'que la source de la mécanique est dans la métaphysique',[2] that even the unity of the atom is not conceivable without interiority or 'energy' and the quality of corporality is in no way to be identified with pure extension, that all things, even including the highest spiritual beings, possess two sides, one mechanical and the other of a total and definitive kind, so that both methods, those of the 'natural' and those of the 'human' sciences (as we would say today) must be applied side by side and without mutual antagonism.[3] This is why he immediately applies himself (in 1669) to reconciling Desartes (and indeed Democritus) with Aristotle,[4] and one year later attacks Nizolius for his nominalism and for his misconception of general concepts, since there are also 'distributive totalities',[5] and no science can be based on pure induction.[6] Now everything takes on a dual aspect, which runs like a vertical intersection through everything to the very threshold of divinity and, because of its verticality, permits an astonishing

[2] Letter to Remond de Montfort (10.1.1714) 702a.

[3] DM 21 (826). Thus, the mechanicists 'qui s'attachent à expliquer la beauté de la divine Anatomie' (who insist on explaining the beauty of the divine Anatomy) should not mock the finalists, just as the latter should not despise the mechanicists. While 'the path of the effective causes is direct, but . . . rather difficult, when it is a matter of the individual entities', so that the philosopher recoils from it; 'the path of the final causes is easier and more frequently permits one to see important and useful truths which one would have had to seek for a long time on the other path; anatomy can offer significant examples of this'.

[4] In the letter to Jakob Thomasius 48–54.

[5] 70 a.

[6] 70 b.

degree of continuity from the highest angel to the last material atom, embracing human, animal and vegetable life. For the highest spirit is indivisible (ἄτομον) as is the lowest material particle (the atom), but so too is every form of reality lying between them, which are only gradated according to the increasing preponderance of consciousness (spirituality) over unconsciousness (materiality), of clarity and distinction (up to the precise and finally the intuitive) over the merely symbolic and the imprecise (ultimately, the confused and the obscure).[7] Spirit retains its base in Nature (and thus an element of 'inertia' as non-absolute spontaneity or *materia prima*), matter retains its spiritual spark: it is 'energy', which is embryonic, dormant consciousness.[8] This Pan-Atomism of the Spirit is paid for by the 'windowlessness'[9] and 'autarchy'[10] of all monads or 'entelechies', since each one is an eternally unique embodiment of Being at its own level, which is possible only on the assumption of the creation by God of a 'prestabilised harmony', as it were through the actualisation in the monads of the order of relations, which is anterior to the world, of all the individual, interrelated world-thoughts of God.

The thorough-going parallelism of quantity (for every monad is univocally *one*) and quality (for none can bear comparison with another) is Pythagorean; as indeed the unity of mathematics and philosophy is primally Greek. To this extent Leibniz is the unsurpassed mediator of tradition to modernity, which can scarcely perceive any more the interrelationship between these two things. It is to this identity also that his attempts belong to create beside the special case of numerical mathematics a kind of spiritual universal language or science of expression (*characteristica* or *mathesis universalis*) in which all that can be the object of thought is ordered and fixed in signs and combinations of signs. Leibniz applied himself to this early on (*De Arte combinatoria*, 1666), worked further upon it all his life and promised himself great

[7] *Meditationes de Cognitione, Veritate et Ideis* (1648), 79–81.
[8] *De ipsa Natura sive de Vi insita actionibusque creaturarum* (1698), 154–160.
[9] M §7.
[10] M §18.

things from it for the progress of man's life in the spirit. But the idea of progress already finds its foundation in the dynamic chain of the universe, which is based upon an increasing drawing-out of the dormant unconscious into the light of ever deepening consciousness. In metaphysical terms everything is prepared here for a total evolutionism; even the step from animal to human life is included by careful and exact thought.[11] Thus Leibniz sees (and thus anticipates Hegel) the history of philosophy as unambiguous progress (including reverses) from its origins in the East and among the Greeks via scholasticism to Descartes (who is the 'antechamber' of truth),[12] and to Leibniz himself (in the 'audience hall' between *l'antichambre et le cabinet*).[13] Every systematic endeavour is thus made in order to forge ahead in the sciences and in philosophy and to smooth out all differences of opinion which serve to hinder that progress,[14] and thus,it is not a static apprehension of God which emerges as the highest bliss in an eschatological vision of eternal felicity but, as for Gregory of Nyssa, an eternal progress of the spirit: for 'of course the highest bliss, whatever enrapturing vision or knowledge of God accompanies it, can never be perfect because God is infinite and cannot be known in His entirety. Therefore our joy can never and will never consist in a full enjoyment of God in which nothing is lacking, for such a thing would dull our spirit, but in a perpetual progression towards new joys and new perfections'.[15] Leibniz already senses an unparalleled degree of progress which is soon to be, when the treasures and blessings of Nature and spirit given by God will be exploited in a much more rational manner.[16] The future of the earth, the perfect kingdom of spirits which is to be

[11] In the 'theory of preformation', with reference to A. van Leeuwenhoek, e.g. Th §91, M §74.

[12] To Remond 702 a, b.

[13] To a friend on Cartesianism (1695) 123 b.

[14] *Cf., e.g. Préceptes pour avancer les Sciences*, 165–171. *Discours touchant la Méthode et la Certitude et l'Art d'inventer, pour finir les disputes et pour faire en peu de temps de grands progrès*, 172–176.

[15] NG §18 (718 b).

[16] *Schreiben an Gabriel Wagner vom Nutzen der Vernunftkunst oder Logik*, 421 b.

founded, fuses with the traits of the eschatological kingdom of God.[17]

Of God: for Leibniz opposes every form of pantheism,[18] whether of the Stoic or Averroistic, Cabbalistic, Spinozean or Quietist kind, and neither Weigel nor Angelus Silesius escapes criticism. The experience of contingency *vis-à-vis* wordly being is fundamental. It is true that there exists in the first stage of his thought, as revealed in the seventeen-year-old's first work on the principle of individuation (1663), a form of nominalism which is never fundamentally recanted (*omne individuum sua tota entitate individuatur*),[19] which is blind towards the Thomist distinction between *essentia* and *esse*, which it presents in a way that gets it wholly wrong;[20] and in later works too the monads are described as (Scotist) *haecceitas*.[21] But the absolute question of Being nevertheless breaks through with vehemence. In *De rerum originatione radicali* (1697) it appears somehow prior to all well-ordered philosophical principles (of 'sufficient reason', as Leibniz himself formulates it): *cur aliquis sit potius mundus, et cur talis?*, (*cur*) *aliquid potius existit quam nihil?* [22] Simply rendering this entire world-content eternal would in no way solve the problem. It cannot even be solved by finding reasons for the

---

[17] Leibniz becomes intoxicated with the thought of the eternal progress of culture, and finds the highest beauty therein: 'In cumulum etiam *pulchritudinis* perfectionisque operum divinorum progressus quidam perpetuus liberrimusque totius universi est agnoscendus, ita ut ad majorem semper cultum procedat. Quemadmodum nunc magna pars terrae nostrae *culturam* recepit, et recipiet magis magisque' (the perpetual and utterly free progress of the whole universe is to be recognised also into the highest peak of the *beauty* and perfection of the divine works. In the same way, the great part of our world now receives *cultivation*, and will receive this more and more). If one were to object that the world would thus become paradise, then Leibniz replies that there remains ever more slumbering Being 'in the abyss of things' that 'is to be awakened', 'nec perinde unquam ad terminum pergressus perveniri' (and hence one would never reach the end of the progress), 150 b.

[18] *Considérations sur la Doctrine d'un Espirit Universal* (1702), 178–182.

[19] §4 (1).

[20] §13f. (3).

[21] DM §9 (819–820).

[22] 147 a, b.

ways things are, why one potentiality rather than another 'forces' its way into reality, 'demanding' existence (*in ipsa possibilitate vel essentia esse exigentiam existentiae*), which is the higher perfection invested in existent things. For it is impossible that pure potentiality should create its own existence: *ratio existentis non est nisi ab existente*. The experience of the non-absolute, merely 'hypothetical' necessity of all worldly being is primordial and cannot be referred to a prior cause; it lies deeper than Leibniz's attempt to support the form of the ontological proof for the existence of God, which Descartes in his eyes had inadequately presented, by seeking to show the conceptual possibility of a wholly perfect essence from which alone its existence can be deduced.[23] For Leibniz, the gulf between absolute (divine) to hypothetical (worldly) necessity can only be bridged by absolute, divine freedom, before which there lies open to its choice—and contrary to the identification of God's knowledge and will which we find in Spinoza—an infinite abundance of possible forms of imitation of the divine essence where the *best* possibility presents itself for realisation, which freedom however is in no way reduced by the choice and realisation of the best. In the *Causa Dei*, Leibniz depicts the 'becoming' of the divine willing of the world (with a brilliant reworking of the late scholastic distinctions between *voluntas antecedens* and *consequens, inclinatoria* and *decretoria*) as the integration[24] of single acts of volition orientated towards partial goals into an ultimate, supreme will (partly accepting, partly excluding), which as such is subject to a single law worthy of God, indeed is identical with this: to create in freedom the best of all possible worlds. The world, that is, which can most reveal God's absolute *grandeur* (i.e. His power and wisdom) and His absolute *goodness* (as love for all creation, desiring the happiness of all).

Thus on the one hand the Christian idea of God is applied here as the idea which is philosophically true, because it is the greatest one possible: 'important truths, of which the ancient

---

[23] *Cf.* the scholion to the sketch *Quod Ens Perfecissium existit* (G VIII, 261–262), which Leibniz read before Spinoza in The Hague.

[24] CD § 24–27, ending in §42 (654 b–655 a, 656 a).

philosophers had insufficient knowledge, were divinely well expressed by Jesus Christ'.[25] Christianity is included in the philosophical process of the knowledge of God, as is the case in Hegel. In the Definitions Ethicae we find sentences such as this: *Justitia est caritas sapientis. Deus omnia creavit secundum maximam harmoniam sive pulchritudinem possibilem. Deus amat omnes. Deus amat amari. Qui non quaerit Dei Gloriam, Deo non oboedit. Qui putat Deum agere optimo modo possibili, iste Deum agnoscit perfectum. Qui Deum amat, amat omnes,* etc. [26] It is metaphysical (Spinozean) and Christian ethics in one. On the other hand, metaphysics predominates in so far as the deduction of God's willing of the best of all possible worlds is considered as *Mathesis quaedam Divina seu mechanismus metaphysicus,*[27] as an intuitively evident law in God's absoluteness which permits the competence of reason to extend to the sphere of revelation in a stricter sense than we find in Anselm or Thomas [28] The transition from Platonic absolute goodness to the Christian love of God appears so simple that the latter has the effect of an 'enlightenment of reason' and of an invitation now to deduce the relationship of God to the world metaphysically on the basis of this principle. A great light is thereby cast, quite unexpectedly, upon the constructions of the theologians, which are often groping, text-centred and fraught with controversy. This is the light which shines forth victoriously in the *Causa Dei,* fades again in the Enlightment, increases in Schleiermacher and Hegel and their schools, and totally triumphs in theological terms in Karl Barth's dogmatic teaching about

[25] DM §37 (833 b).

[26] 670 a, b.

[27] *De Rerum Originatione redicali,* 148 a. The law can be formulated thus: *ut maximus praestetur effectus minimo sumptu* (that the greatest effect may be furnished at the least cost), 147 b. One may question whether these 'economies' in the divine housekeeping do not in fact express precisely the Christian dimension of God's love, i.e. the 'costs' of the passion of Jesus.

[28] *Discours sur la Conformité de la Foi avec la Raison* (as introduction to the *Theodicy*): 'La Raison est l'enchaînement des Vérités, mais *particulièrment* . . . sans être aidée des lumières de la Foi' (reason is the linking of the truths, but *particularly* . . . without the helps given by the lights of the Faith), 479 a.

election. A light in which Leibniz not only perceives all evil
in the world to be comprehended by God's always greater
love,[29] but also discerns the grace of God, won by Christ, as
offered to all people, nations and religions, [30] even to
unbaptised children, [31] a fact that obliges us to cultivate an
open, non-exclusive trust in God [32] that radically negates the
idea of an arbitrary and despotic God to whom it might
occur to predestine certain of His creations to Hell for the
sake of the glory of His justice,[33] or even 'to create poor
wretches in cruel pity in order that there might be beings to
whom He could show mercy: all that is tyrannical and remote
from true glory and true perfection, whose worth is to be
found not so much in majesty as in an abundance of
goodness'.[34] 'Therefore, besides the belief in a despotic God,
I would most like to refute the doctrine of [double]
predestination',[35] for 'Christ is the grounds for the choice',
and is so as Saviour,[36] as 'the head of the created world,
through whom the whole of creation will be set free from
the slavery of sin into the glorious freedom of the children of
God'.[37] In this light, which illumines and shines forth from
the depths of God, the philosophically-recognisable primal
law, according to which God chooses the absolutely best thing
possible, merges with the Pauline exclamation of wonder at
the utter profundity of God's wisdom in the working out of
salvation history; all this incomprehensible power is in any
case contained within this comprehensive primal law, which
follows from the philosophical-theological concept of God.[38]

This triumphalism in the defence of God against all possible
objections by His creatures entirely corresponds to the

[29] CD §33–39 (655), 2nd and 3rd part of the *Théodicée*.
[30] CD §110–112.
[31] CD §87.
[32] CD §48, 133; *cf.* NG §18 (718 a).
[33] §74ff.
[34] CD §76–78, *cf.* §117. On God's justice, which includes equity and
mercy: §50.
[35] CD §131.
[36] CD §134.
[37] CD §49.
[38] DM §31 (830 b–831 a).

philosophical apriorism, which—supposedly without threatening human and divine freedom—assists in the construction of the world in the Divine Spirit itself (between God's intellect and His will) from what is externally necessary. Although Neoscholasticism had long tolerated, permitted and practised such a penetration of human thought into absolute thought, it takes on a new aspect in Leibniz on account of his vertical parallelism in method of mechanism and finalism. This parallelism, which extends from the lowest atom to the highest spiritual monad, should as such be limited to the dimension of created reality; but because this innerworldly space is not dominated by the concept of analogy (from spirit to matter) but by that of identity (in the univocal *unum* of the monad), it is impossible for the law of *analogia entis* to prevail effectively between the absolute monad of God and the created monads. It is impossible, in other words, for the activity of the finite spirit, precisely when it is concerned with numbers, to have a merely enigmatic character in Nicolas of Cusa's sense. The question of destiny which is raised there in conclusion (knowledge as *conjectura* or as 'absolute knowing'?) is decisively answered in favour of the latter term. And from the point of view of logic, this happens not only through permitting the thinking of the natural sciences to enter the province of metaphysics, but also because this realm has already fallen a defenceless victim to a form of mechanistic thought on account of its nominalistic point of departure (which alone makes the monad concept possible) and the neglect of the Ontological Difference of the Thomist school. Herein lies a paradox: the apparent 'turn towards the world' of the natural sciences can only catalogue 'phenomena' which are devoid of Being and for which an aprioristic phenomenism is ready to hand as a saving context.

The windowless monads communicate with the other monads only in God; they do not view Being and their fellow existents from their own standpoint, but rather intuit them from above, in artificial isolation, as an essential totality within themselves: 'Just as if we were stars which see earthly things far beneath'.[39] We meet once again this classical and

[39] *Von der Glückseligkeit*, 673 a.

Dantesque image!

Thus it is the worldly existence of man without the real existence of world, i.e. without the vulnerability of his 'defenceless' being to other beings, primarily his fellow-men. The boundless need to communicate which Leibniz feels is that of a scholar who wishes to gather, order and define the entire culture of spirit in itself. *L'âme doit . . . penser comme s'il n'y avait que Dieu et elle au monde.* This *la met* absolument à couvert *de toutes les choses exterieures, puisqu'elle seule fait tout son monde, et se suffit avec Dieu.*[40] This 'autarchic' 'protectedness', 'non-vulnerability' of human existence lends to Leibniz' 'consciousness of glory' a character untouched by, and beyond the reach of, every kind of tragedy. The finite spirit knows itself to be the *expressio*[41] of God and the primal light shines in its knowledge, so that between (the light of) Nature and (the light of) Grace once again only *harmonia* can prevail, which was already the fundamental innerworldly law between the material and the spiritual side of Being.[42] Indeed, the tension between Nature and spirit coincides precisely with that between 'the realm of Nature and that of the spirits': the 'perfect *civitas* Dei under the best monarch', who inclines towards his subjects and is essentially open to them in love, who shows himself to be humane and gracious (*en cela qu'il s'humaine, qu'il veut bien souffrir des anthropologies*),[43] is no longer the Augustinian *civitas Dei* but has already become the universal, human and divine 'realm of spirits' of Hegel.

Nowhere in the classical Baroque does the thought arise that God might have need of the world or of man in order to attain the full abundance of His own being[44] (Böhme is an outsider, and certain utterances of Angelus Silesius are clearly taken from Eckhart), and even the greatest 'thrusting' into reality of the best of all possible worlds does not eliminate for

---

[40] DM §32 (831 a).

[41] DM §35 (832 b).

[42] NG §15 (717 b); M §87 (712), 'harmonie entre le règne physique et le monde *moral* de la *grâce*' (harmony between the physical kingdom and the *moral* world of *grace*).

[43] DM §36 (833 a).

[44] DM §35 (832 b): 'sa gloire [externe] et notre culte ne sauraient rien

Leibniz the freedom of God, and therefore never permits the coincidence of absolute and hypothetical necessity. On the other hand, man is initiated into the thought of God to such a degree and is able to express it with such strength of spirit that with the progress of his discoveries and inventions he can contribute things 'for the benefit of the human race and to the glory of God' which directly further the cause of true religion.[45] Leibniz wishes to see the direct application to theology too of the *mira theoremata* which he commands, and whose *claritas* and *pulchritudo* fill him with the greatest delight (*voluptas*);[46] and if some thinkers have fallen away from God on account of rigorous science, then it is precisely scientific rigour, taken to its ultimate conclusion, which must lead them back to Him.[47] Here, something of the brilliance of the spirit of great Baroque art is discernible: a certainty in faith, which views the radiance of world harmony as one with the radiance of love of the self-revealing God, which therefore expresses itself in a language which is indistinguishably both of the world and above the world, imposing itself indeed triumphantly, understanding itself to be God's representative, party to all His secrets, and to which it never occurs that the Christian can know not only too little but also too much, thereby forgetting two things: in philosophy Being and in theology the Cross. As in the sacralism of the early Middle Ages, Leibniz constructs an enormous monstrance, but one from which the central *monstratum*, the night of the Passion, is absent.

4. MALEBRANCHE

Malebranche,[1] a disciple of Augustine like Descartes and like Bérulle, whose Oratory he enters in 1660, is seduced by the

ajouter à sa satisfaction, la connaissance des créatures n'étant qu'une *suite* de sa souveraine et parfaite félicité' (his [external] glory and our worship could add nothing to his satisfaction, since the knowledge of creatures is only a *consequence* of his sovereign and perfect happiness).

[45] On the general characteristics: 164 b.

[46] *De vera methodo Philosophiae et Theologiae*, 109 a.

[47] 110 b.

[1] Malebranche, *Oeuvres Complètes*, Vols. 1–20 (Vrin 1858f.), as far as these have been published; otherwise, older editions are used.

play of forces between these two into adopting that extreme form of pre-Kantian philosophy of spirit which turns it into a pious, worldless realm of ghosts which cannot but expose the fundamental flaws of the 'metaphysics of the saints' in the *Grand Siècle*, and which falls foul of the court of the French revolution as necessarily as Hegel's realm of ghosts will fall victim to Feuerbach and Marx.

From Bérulle he has thoroughly learned the pathos of creaturely nothingness before God and the pure adoration of glory, which he experiences and performs in the interior dialogue of contemplation. Descartes on the other hand persuades him of the importance of retreat from the exterior world to the pure ego with its *cogitata*, and of the only possible guarantee of truth through the retreat from ego to God. But now the differences begin. While for Descartes the *idée* is only a (psychological) fact of consciousness, provisionally secured in the *cogito-sum*, for Malebranche it is originally a self-evident form of (Platonic-Augustinian) objectivity which cannot be derived from the ego, something beyond the ego's powers of invention, and objectification already 'given' with respect to the ego, so that even a provisional guarantee in the thinking subject collapses and behind it there at once arises the form of an absolute 'thinker', which gives the self-evident its clarity, or which reveals itself there—as in its *own* ideas. Ideas are that which is objectively revealed by the *intellectus archetypus* to human reason; they are the 'real' in the sense which this word possesses for Descartes and Leibniz: as that which offers itself to the spirit's perception clearly, distinctly and without contradiction. But Malebranche sees more: individual ideas for him are the delimitations of the unlimited divine Being which, as the background to all ideas, is reality itself.[2] But

---

[2] God is absolute Being who knows himself and everything in himself that is imitable. Vol. 15, 21–22. 'The idea of God or of Being as such, of infinite Being, is no mere construction of thought' ... since it is evident 'that Being (I do not say, one particular existing being) has its existence through itself, and that Being cannot be without reality, since it is impossible and contradictory to assert the true Being is without existence'. *Recherche de la Vérité*, IV/II §2 (Vol. 2, 95).

because unlimited, infinite and universal Being cannot be glimpsed by any idea, i.e. by any individual being that is distinct from universal and infinite Being,[3] then it must present itself directly to the cognising spirit: the latter therefore *perceives a priori* (that is, from God's point of view and not from that of worldly experience) *the Ontological Difference* (*Realdistinktion*) and sees thereby truth, which exits primarily in the relation (*rapport*) between Being (God) and essence (the ideas of God) and secondarily in the relation between the ideas themselves.[4]

Whether this idea in God is also 'real', viz. created outside God, need not be a matter of concern for man, first because his cognition is in any case far more immediate in this *cognitio matutina* than it is in any *a posteriori* form of knowledge; second, because the knowledge of ideas is not only intellectual but also imaginative and sensory (since *all* perception of ideas is pure 'receptivity' towards the self-revealing absolute Being and its delimitations and the Divine Being can touch the perceiving spirit both through the mind and through the senses); and third, because according to Malebranche and Descartes alike, existing bodies are pure extension (with their various delimitations), so that the ideas of bodies are also 'pure intelligible extension': but now it is inexplicable, or at any rate insignificant, how a 'thought' pure extension is to be distinguished from a 'real' one. Besides, Malebranche wants God Himself, as the origin of all His body-ideas, to be 'infinite intelligible extension', the (spiritual) archetype of all extension therefore. In this he approaches Spinoza but without going the whole way, since by the notion of divine extension he means only that which is the primal idea in God of all worldly extension, as Baader and Schelling would have it, that in God which (in contrast to the created 'spirit') corresponds to created Nature.[5]

Leibniz will criticise this doctrine above all on account of its passive understanding of spirit; it is the same criticism,

---

[3] *Recherche* III/2, 7 §2 (Vol. 1, 449).
[4] *Médit. Chrét.* IV, 7–8 (Vol. 10, 38–39); *Traité de l'Amour de Dieu* [Vol. 14, 7–8].
[5] *Entretiens sur la Métaphysique* I and II.

though with some justification, which Aquinas made of Augustine.[6] Nevertheless, Leibniz cites both Aristotle and Augustine in support of his argument when he speaks of how through the 'light' of insight truth addresses us as with a voice:[7] and it is this experience of the Divine Being, which reveals itself immediately to us, speaking to and touching us, which is Malebranche's chief concern, as it will also be for Heidegger. Leibniz' criticism may well hold true, for without spontaneity there can be no openness of the spirit to the reception of Being. But even worse is the fact that such a pious theologisation of metaphysics—ultimately it is Jesus, God's Word and Son, who comes to meet us *immediately* in all sensible and intellectual knowledge—is forgetful of every worldly encounter of actual Being and springs over this, if all spirits communicate *only* in God as their common sun. Thus this philosophy of spirit also lacks the decisive experience of reality: the shock of a head-on encounter with *another* ego, a dialogue between an I and a Thou which is radically open to its own vulnerable depths of being. This shock was missing also in Bérulle, Condren and Fénelon, which is why their elevated spirituality retains something spectrally unreal, journeying in a world of ideas without a basis in Nature, crudely stated: something élitist for spiritual aristocrats for which, not without reason, the merciless guillotine of the real 'comrades' stands waiting.

c. Kant

I. GLORY 'UNCRITICALLY'

The solitary figure of Kant stands between the epochs.[1] Prior to the publication of his critical masterpiece in 1781 at the

[6] *Discours de Métaphysique* (Erdmann 829a) and other works about Malebranche.

[7] 'Deus est enim lumen illud quod illuminat omnem hominem venientem in hunc mundum. Et veritas quae intus nobis loquitur, cum aeternae certitudinis theoremata intelligimus ipsa Dei vox est, quod etiam [alongside Aristotle] notavit D. Augustinus' (For God is that light which illuminates every man who comes into this world. And the truth that speaks within us when we understand the theorems of eternal certainty, is the very choice of God, as St Augustine noted) (Erdmann 82b).

[1] Immanuel Kant's complete works in six vols., Grossherzog Wilhelm

age of fifty-seven, the paths of his thinking followed those of Leibniz, Newton and Wolff, in terms not only of morality but also of metaphysics. Thus he fundamentally shared— though under attack by Hume—the Enlightenment's vision of glory: adoration of the absolute divine Ego (Descartes), the beauty of the world order in its progression from matter to spirit as the radiance of God's love (Leibniz), together with the pride of the spiritual autarch, who believes himself to be the representative of the absoluteness of God in the world (Leibniz and Spinoza), matter as 'energy', simultaneously objective and 'phenomenal', the cosmic goal of an eternal progression and the emergence of a world which eternally becomes in an asymptotic relation to God (Leibniz and Lessing). Baumgarten creates for it in addition the first 'Aesthetics' as science: a delimited field of the human καλόν (the confused perception of truth through the senses), which is however progressively 'enlightened', as it emerges into an area of clear and distinct truth, which is still experienced, as with Leibniz, entirely by analogy with the transcendent καλό ν of the classical world. And what Kant takes in with his philosophical mother's milk, he passes on to the generation of Schiller and Fichte, Hegel and Schelling, whose views of the world culminate always in a form of aestheticism in one way or another, in a radiant, eschatological 'world of spirits'. Indeed, Kant himself, who at first acts as a critical interruption in this, constructs the overarching vault of his own work with the *Critique of Judgement* (and with the *Philosophical Theory of Religion*), in which he makes himself at the highest level the link between the Enlightenment and Idealism.

Nevertheless, the critical rupture goes deep; most evidently for us in the fact that together with the fundamental self-

Ernst edition (ed. Felix Gross), Insel, Leipzig, 1921. Some abbreviations: *Kritik der reinen, der praktischen Vernunft, der Urteilskraft* = KrV, KpV, KU; *Anthropologie* = A; *Streit der Fakultäten* = StF; *Allgemeine Naturgeschichte und Theorie des Himmels etc.* = ThH; *Grundlegung zur Metaphysik der Sitten* = GMS; *Die Metaphysik der Sitten* = MS; *Religion innerhalb der Grenzen der blossen Vernunft* = RGV.

limitation of pure theoretical intellect we now see the restriction to the human world of the sphere in which aesthetic utterances are possible: 'Beauty is only for man, i.e. for an existence which though animal is also rational', and not for animals who know only 'gratification', nor 'only for . . . spirits'.[2] The definition of the field of the beautiful, and correspondingly of the material realm of the science of beauty, which begins with Baumgarten (*Aesthetica*, 1750–1758), is radicalised by Kant's quite different critical delimitation of reason: it is in him that we first find aesthetics as a specific science in the modern sense.

Whatever the nature of Kant's concluding emphases, 'critical Idealism' no longer permits space for an experience of worldly Being as an epiphany of God's glory. But when the theoretical horizons of the rational faculty are narrowed, then there is yet more cause for amazement at the unlimited breadth of its practical outreach: 'glory' is replaced by moral *sublimity* (*Erhabenheit*), which finds expression in aesthetic sublimity, and in which the intense experience of glory of the younger Kant is preserved in a wholly positive way. The celebrated sentence in the 'Conclusion' to the 'Critique of Practical Reason' ('Two things fill the mind with a sense of admiration and awe which is ever fresh and ever deepening, the more frequently and persistently it is concerned with them: the star-filled sky above me and the moral law within me . . .; I see them before me and I associate them directly with the consciousness of my existence',[3] can be understood only if we know Kant's growing admiration for the star-filled sky in the *Natural History and Theory of the Heavens* (1755), a work, full of pathos, which was dedicated to the King of Prussia, where we similarly read in the 'Conclusion': '. . . the view of a star-filled sky on a clear night [gives] a kind of pleasure which only noble souls can know. In the universal stillness of Nature and of the senses, the hidden cognitive

[2] KU §5 (Vol. 6, 61). *Cf.* §29: The expression 'intellectual beauty or sublimity' is 'not quite correct because these are aesthetic forms of representation, which, if we were mere intelligences . . . would not be found in us at all' (6, 136).

[3] KpV, conclusion (5, 302).

faculty of the imperishable spirit speaks an ineffable language and conveys inarticulate concepts which cannot be described but only experienced'.[4] Prior to this, he writes: 'The structure of the world inspires in us a state of silent wonder on account of its immeasurable grandeur and the infinite variety and beauty which radiates from it on all sides. When the idea of all this perfection touches the imagination, then the intellect is seized by another kind of ravishment as it reflects on how so much splendour, so much grandeur flows from a single universal rule in an eternal and precise order'.[5] Until the very end, the 'contemplation of the star-filled sky is sublime';[6] it is the example of the 'splendour in which there is something sublime which is at the same time beautiful'.[7] But the young Kant[8] sees in the infinity of the stellar world the process of creation which is never concluded in time or space and which occurs in each present moment; whereas Newton still saw the movement of the constellations as a primal phenomenon which pointed back directly to the guiding hand of the Creator, Kant (and soon after him Lambert and Laplace) takes a step back to the idea of atomistic primal matter, which, however, is understood as energy and is thus of itself the author of its own space.[9] This primal matter is organised

[4] ThH III, conclusion (2, 421–422).

[5] ThH II, 7 (2, 353).

[6] KU (6, 135).

[7] A I, 2 §71 (1, 435).

[8] Since the later Kant reduces the aesthetically sublime sight of the sky to what is truly seen by the sense, excluding that which the understanding presumes to read into this sight: KU (6, 135).

[9] Kant had begun in his first work from this Leibnizian concept of power: 'Thoughts concerning the true estimation of the living powers and the evaluation of the proofs which Herr von Leibniz and other mechanicists have used in the controversy' (1746). The powers bring about their own space: §9 and 10 (2, 30–32); thus 'the dimension of the extension will derive from the laws in accordance with the substances, thanks to their essential powers, seek to unite themselves'. Thus still in ThH II, 7 (2, 355): '. . . the coexistence which makes the space by binding the substances through mutual dependencies', and in the *Monadologia physica* (1756), Proposition 6: 'Monas spatiolum praesentiae suae definit non pluralitate partium suarum substantialium, sed sphaera activitatis . . .' (the monad defines the little space of its presence, not by the plurality of its substantial parts, but by the sphere of activity) (4, 63).

within the universe purely by the natural laws of attraction and repulsion, forming a central body together with the spheres which orbit around it, and in an unending process (because the extension of matter and of space is infinite) gradually draws sphere after sphere into its ordering movement. This step beyond Newton,[10] whereby matter has been given the power to bring itself progressively from chaos into order, seems to Kant to be far more worthy of God, especially when the general qualities of Nature, which is 'fruitful with fruits both perfect and beautiful', do not form a system enclosed within themselves, but 'harmonise well with the interests of men and the glorification of the qualities of God' in such a way that the worlds of Nature and of spirit 'must have their common origin in a single intellect as the ground and the source of all beings'.[11] 'But in a mechanical form of explanation the beauty of the world is glorified no less than the revelation of omnipotence'.[12]

The particular perspective which characterises Kant and which links him to Leibniz (although Kant goes beyond him) is the thought that matter at its (fiery) central point is at its most dense,[13] and then, as it moves from one orbiting sphere to the next, becomes looser and finer so that life-forms which inhabit the (now habitable) spheres,[14] from Mercury and Venus to the Earth and Mars, Jupiter and Uranus, must have ever finer bodies and thus a higher state of intellectual life.[15] A further consequence is that 'sensuality' and 'confused ideas' submerged in matter come to predominate on those spheres which are closest to the sun, while a precarious balance exists between senses and spirit on Earth and Mars and, on the bigger planets, it is spirit which gains the upper hand, for which reason the cause of sin appears to diminish or even to be destroyed.[16] Because the creative process is progressively

[10] ThH II, 8 (2, 390).　　[11] *Ibid*. 384, *cf*. III (417).
[12] *Ibid*. 389.
[13] *Ibid*. III (411).
[14] *Ibid*. (411).
[15] *Ibid*. (412). So that 'the perfection of the world of spirits ... should grow and develop in a correct sequence of stages according to the proportion of their distances from the sun' (413).
[16] *Ibid*. (419–420).

unending,[17] and because life moves on stage by stage by virtue of the infinite 'fertility' of Nature[18] and approaches the Godhead asymptotically[19] so that the kingdom of God is progressively revealed within Creation and 'the Godhead Itself appears ... gloriously ... in all creatures',[20] the human spirit can look with confidence, 'even with a kind of pleasure' into 'these terrible convulsions', cosmic peaks and troughs;[21] indeed, it can endure the fact that the worlds which are involved in the process of becoming also grow old progressively and fall back into their suns, because in this way Nature rises like a phoenix from the deaths of the worlds, as the suns gain new regenerative strength.[22]

'The fully developed world is consequently hemmed in between the ruins of Nature [once again destroyed] and the chaos of nature [as yet] unformed'.[23] This is of course a feeling for the world which leads far away from Leibniz and the Enlightenment and which even anticipates extreme experiences of insecurity manifest in the 19th and 20th centuries. In a truly Enlightenment manner, Kant wishes to view the 'inadequacies' and threats, which he sees in the fertility of Nature, from the divine point of view, as 'total security',[24] for 'the inadequacies themselves are a sign of superabundances'.[25] It is the Platonic-Augustinian vision of that universe 'which is perfect even with its left-hand side': 'It is the same unlimited fertility ... which has produced the inhabited heavenly spheres, as well as the comets, the serviceable mountains and dangerous cliffs, the habitable landscapes and the bare deserts, the virtues and the vices'.[26]

---

[17] *Ibid.* II, 7 (356f.). 'Creation is never accomplished. It has indeed once begun, but it will never cease' (362).

[18] The word returns again and again (361, 365, where he speaks also of the 'unexhausted capacity of generation').

[19] Conclusion of II (381).

[20] *Ibid.* III (413).

[21] *Ibid.* II, 7 (367).

[22] *Ibid.* (370).

[23] *Ibid.* (368).

[24] *Ibid.* (371).

[25] *Ibid.* (390).

[26] *Ibid.* II, 8 (400).

But it is Nature which needs death as the increase of life and as the fertiliser for life, which in its sun-kernel must be an immense combustion which cannot be approached by any living thing, as Kant depicts it for us in a description which is more than a masterpiece of visionary, Dantesque poetry, but is rather a piece of *Welt-Anschauung* in the manner of Giordano Bruno's *universo*, Goethe's Earth-Spirit (*Erdgeist*) or Nietzsche's all-generating, all-destroying universe:

'With a single glance broad seas of fire can be seen, which send their flames up towards the heavens, raging storms whose violence redoubles that of the flames, storms which, while causing the flames to break their banks, at one moment cover the raised regions of this cosmic body and, in the next, force them back within their boundaries; burnt-out cliffs whose soaring peaks emerge from the flaming gorges and which cause the alternating appearance and disappearance of the sun-spots as they are submerged or exposed by the flooding element of fire; thick clouds of steam, which smother the fire and which, fanned by the violence of the winds, form dark rain clouds, which then disgorge fiery squalls pouring from the heights of the fixed terrain of the sun into the flaming valleys as showers of burning rain; the crashing of the elements, the rubble of burnt-out matter and Nature in mortal combat with is own destruction, Nature which with the most horrendous condition of its own devastation effects the beauty of the world and the profit of creatures.'[27]

Kant does not want us to see the Godhead in this cosmic centre, or even merely 'a God-like Being';[28] he wants to sing the praises of the fortunate soul 'which, seated upon a height amongst all the tumult of the elements and the ruins of Nature, can see the devastations . . . roar past at all times as if beneath its feet'.[29] But it is only by chance that he takes so great an interest in earthquakes, in the empty space beneath our feet, and the 'maze of multifarious passages' through all of which 'a blazing fire' passes,[30] and interest too in a theory

---

[27] *Ibid.* II, 7 (377–378).
[28] *Ibid.* (379).
[29] *Ibid.* (370–371).
[30] Second *Erdbebenschrift* (1756) (2, 484–485).

according to which yet more volcanic craters should be artificially created in order to give air to the fire that presses against the earth's thin crust from within,[31] since the fire 'is perhaps increasingly gaining the upper hand beneath the uppermost layer of crust . . . and is already nibbling away at the foundations of the highest vault'?[32] In addition, the enthusiastic analogies drawn with regard to the infinity of other worlds and their similarly infinite evolutions are close to what Kant will condemn ten years later (1766) in Swedenborg as the *Dreams of a Spirit-Seer*, summoning metaphysics back to the small land with many boundaries which it can oversee and (with 'honest Candide') cultivate in a responsible manner.[33]

Leibniz had solved the difficulty which metaphysics experiences in coming to terms with modern natural science by the master stroke of his vertical intersection which lends all monadic worldly being a quantitative (exact scientific) and a qualitative (metaphysical) dimension. This was possible, apart from other questionable matters (such as phenomenism and prestabilized harmony), only on condition of an essentialistic understanding of Being as 'essence' or, in other terms, as a concept which is either distinct or confused. In the *Inquiry into the Distinctions of the Principles of Natural Theology and Morals* (1764), Kant relinquishes this parallelism between science and philosophy in so far as he demands for the latter its own ideal of clarity which can no longer be imitated by exact science (mathematics): while exact science can proceed synthetically with self-constructed definitions, metaphysics can only analyse our given experiences of reality by resolving confused knowledge analytically (or 'phenomenologically' as we would say today).[34] In spite of such modesty of method, Kant does not at first hesitate to portray the possibility of the step from this analysis of experience to the positing of an

---

[31] Third *Erdbebenschrift* (2, 530–531).

[32] The question whether the earth grows older, consider from a physical point of view (2, 467–468).

[33] 1, 156, 160.

[34] 4, 282f.

'absolutely necessary Being', although it is of the kind which he had outlined shortly before in his work, *The Sole Possible Proof for the Demonstration of the Existence of God* (1763): i.e. not from the contingency of human existence (for what does human existence mean in this context?—it is not the predicate of a thing but only its absolute position, which the scholastic essentialists described as *extra causas*), but *a priori* from the concept of possibility: is it not impossible that nothing should exist, for otherwise there would not be any possibility, which however does exist, even if I think away all worldly being. But that, the elimination of which would also eliminate all possibility, possesses necessary existence.[35] This idea implies an experience of Being, of course, which permits existence to be eliminated, even if only theoretically, while 'possibility' still remains, with the result that the superiority of possibility then points to an absolute existence and, at the same time, to a form of thought which conceives only of 'what is possible', whether it exists or not. This late-scholastic, Descartian, Leibnizian essentialism pervades Kant's thought all the more because the phenomenism which follows from it becomes for Kant the most pressing philosophical problem on account of the English empiricists and sceptics; neither Leibniz nor Hume nor even Kant is primarily interested in the reality of the 'external world': everything turns on the importance of mental knowledge and of the 'objectivity' or 'reality' of the concept. The reason why there remains an unknowable thing *an sich* in Kant's critical solution, despite the guarantee of this objectivity, has less to do with a conceptually unresolved remnant in Being itself than with the subjective experience of receptivity, which for the time being remains as the irreducible primal phenomenon of knowledge, until the absolute idealists take the necessary steps for the reduction even of this.

2. THE CRITICAL RECALL AND NEGATIVE THEOLOGY

Could the philosopher not have contented himself with the

[35] 4, 129f.

point of view of the *Inquiry into the Distinctness of the Principles*? Could he not have allowed mathematics its formal triumph, and withdrawn as philosopher to the other, his own, kind of certainty and developed a phenomenology of finitude, with an *a priori* proof of God in the background and, at its side, the foundation of morality in 'feeling' (of value and obligation) in the manner of Shaftesbury and Hutcheson?[36] But that was not enough for Kant; for how would the modest empiricist and analytical work of reason relate to the grandiose *a priori* synthesis of mathematics? And how was a reason of this kind capable of entertaining an *a priori* proof for the existence of God? And how does this (very problematical) proof of ⟨God relate finally to the moral sentiment of absolute obligation? All this demanded a far more consistent architectonics, which Kant is determined to provide for the very first time in the consciousness that while the history of philosophy 'offers edifices', they are 'only in ruins'.[37]

'Mathematics is the outstanding example of a form of pure reason which develops happily of itself without the aid of experience. Examples are infectious . . . with regard to the same capacity', which is reason itself.[38] But if mathematics possesses in space a medium of *a priori* sense experience in which it demonstrates, though solely by means of quantitative elements, 'the self-generation, so to speak, of our intellect (together with reason), without first being impregnated by experience',[39] then the philosopher, who possesses true knowledge of qualitative reality only when he works upon the *a posteriori* experience of the senses (*omnis cognitio incipit a sensu*),[40] may not allow himself to be dislodged from this. The manner of human knowing, the site of human truth, is the interrelationship between the 'chance' experience of the

[36] Kant mentions the latter explicitly at the end of the text: 4, 312.

[37] KrV II, 4 (3, 639). Already in 1763, Kant had spoken of metaphysics as a 'bottomless abyss' and a 'dark ocean without shore and without lighthouses' (4, 115).

[38] KrV II, 1, 1 (3, 543).

[39] *Ibid.* II, 1, 2 (579).

[40] First sentence of the introduction to KrV (3, 35).

senses (mediated by the cognitive forms of space and time) and the 'necessary' related processes of ordering within the cognitive faculty. This is an interrelationship which can be graded in a number of synthesis—simple perception and productive imagination, the phenomenal form of sense and category, the total objective unity of experience and the total unity of consciousness which grounds and connects it; but these can never supersede this reciprocity,[41] only deepen it. Experience becomes human only within the illumining intellect; but the 'reason' of this intellect recognises the inner finitude of this light, without being able to broaden it into an infinity of true knowing. It is 'burdened with questions which it cannot reject, for they are posed to it from the very nature of reason itself, and which it cannot answer either, for they exceed all the powers of human reason'.[42] Kant now dares to clarify this paradoxical situation by recourse to an even more paradoxical analogy which of necessity provokes contradiction: 'If I imagine the surface of the earth (as it appears to the senses) to be like a plate, then I cannot know how far it extends'. But if (with Columbus) I have got as far as establishing by experience that it is a sphere, 'then I can also determine from even one small section . . . the diameter and, on the strength of this, calculate according to *a priori* principles and know the entire limits of the earth, i.e. of its surface area'.[43] In the same way, 'our reason is not a plain of indeterminable dimensions . . ., but must rather be compared with a sphere, whose radius can be deduced from the curve of the arc of its surface (*a priori* to the nature of synthetic principles), but from which one can also state with certainty the content and the delimitation of the same'.[44] A form of reason, therefore, which experiences and even calculates its own finitude, an experience which is far less 'Copernican' than 'Columbian'. Or which is also a version of that

[41] The principle is expressed clearly for the first time in the last pre-critical text, *De mundi sensibilis atque intelligibilis forma et principiis* (1770) (4, 327–368).

[42] First sentence of the preface to the first edition of KrV (6, 690).

[43] KrV II, 1, 2 (3, 575).

[44] *Ibid.* 3, 577.

experience of Being mentioned above which is located 'between the ruins of Nature which has been destroyed and the chaos of Nature not yet formed'. Although there are *a priori* synthetic judgments of understanding (a fact that wards off scepticism), there are no *a priori* synthetic judgments of reason (so that every form of theoretical metaphysics becomes impossible); although reason erects 'secure principles', it does so 'never more than indirectly' by relating the intellectual concepts 'to something quite accidental, namely potential experience'.[45] It is a world of reason which is enclosed within itself but which is also aware of its own indeterminate situation: 'Here we do indeed see philosophy in a precarious position which is supposed to be secure, although it is supported neither by anything in Heaven nor by anything on Earth'.[46]

If reason did not understand the finite nature of its cognitive faculty, and if there were not in this an act of 'peaceful self-gratification' with a 'limited but indisputable possession',[47] 'the sole value of all philosophy: Not to discover truth ... so much as to protect against error', in spite of its 'irrepressible desire to find solid ground somewhere beyond the limits of its experience',[48] then it would not truly be reason, it would not be, in Thomist terms, a *reflexio completa*. But the fact that in this process of taking the measure of itself it no longer knows itself as the faculty of absolutely transcendent Being (as is always the case in the classical period, in the Middle Ages and still somehow in Descartes), but also not as the faculty which causes the generation from itself of all that exists (as later in Fichte and Hegel), because the indispensable half of perception in it is receptive: all this gives the whole dimension of 'transcendentality' in Kant a hybrid character which at no point offers itself unambiguously to interpretation. On the one hand reason, in order to be reason, must perceive the finitude of its theoretical knowledge in

[45] KrV II, 1, 1 (3, 560).

[46] This principle, uttered by the practical reason, holds good first and especially of the theoretical reason. GMS 2 (5, 55).

[47] KrV II, 1, 2 (3, 581).

[48] *Ibid.* II, 2 (3, 600–601).

order to pass beyond it; on the other hand it cannot achieve this as 'pure reason', for it has no experience of that which is beyond the senses and thus no means of objectifying it, but has only unverifiable 'ideas'.

Now according to Kant, this antinomic structure of reason should compel man to leave the field of theory for that of praxis in order to win ontically and by action, in venture and in self-commitment, what he cannot achieve by conceptual and contemplative means—and yet what the nature of reason demands that he must achieve. Herein lies the value, still viewed entirely in Enlightenment terms, of an enforced self-limitation. 'Everything which Nature orders, is good for some purpose. Even poisons serve the purpose of eradicating other forms of poison which are produced by our own fluids, and these should therefore not fail to be included in a complete collection of medicines'.[49] Metaphysics, an area barred to theoretical reason, is not only permitted to practical reason but is even forcefully implied by it, on account of the fact that practical reason can only reach an understanding of itself when transcendent (not transcendental!) presuppositions apply.[50] But the fact that it was not permitted to theoretical reason to be a faculty for the apprehension of Being in general (in whatever way we define the delimitation of the precise object of a 'finite reason'), means for practical reasons that it can only 'postulate' its transcendent presuppositions (because it cannot prove them theoretically), and indeed can do so only on the basis of its own dimensions, as these reveal themselves in its self-apprehension as absolute obligation. But this now means that it is the inner *sublimity* of reason which, despite all its finitude, has penetrated to the Infinite, which reveals God to it, and not for instance God's own sublime glory, which reason in its pure form cannot perceive.

This form of thought points back without doubt to negative theology both classical and Christian. God (together with those human qualities which belong to His realm: eternal decision-making in freedom, eternal existence in immortality)

[49] *Ibid.* II, 1, 2 (3, 564).
[50] GMS 2 (5, 56).

is beyond all superficial familiarity the more profoundly Unknown; in all His revealedness, He remains more profoundly concealed. Since this was the expression of the *analogia entis*, it was not put in question or superseded by the Christian revelation, but rather comes to perfection in it. After all the rationalistic forms of scholasticism and neoclassicism, but also after the metaphysics of spirit in the wake of Leibniz, Kant's critical summoning back brings with it a cleansing and a liberation. But it occurs at a late point in history. Leibniz' vertical intersection through all existing things (quantity—exact science, and quality—metaphysics) has the consequences that setting the limits of natural science automatically means setting the limits also of theoretical metaphysics. The marrying of these two (in the philosophy of spirit) led to phenomenism: even metaphysics 'receives' (in its receptivity) only phenomena, not Being. This is why the practical faculty, when it opens up the way to the Absolute, cannot mediate any objective ('external') knowledge, and if religion exists at all, it can do so only *'within* the limits of pure reason'. The intersection, which in Leibniz was aimed at the highest synthesis (of exact and religious knowledge), now cuts man in half: since he can no longer recognise God objectively as the 'Wholly Other' (and thereby indeed as the 'Non-Other'), the positing of God in the ethical law with its categorical imperative does not lead to a making-present which corresponds (even non-objectively) to the human cognitive faculty. Once again the lateness of the project becomes evident: on the one hand the echo of Ockham's and Luther's mistrust towards the excesses of the whole Reason; but even more clearly the philosopher appears, against his will, to be bound to the form of knowledge which is that of the natural sciences, as being normative for all forms of rational knowledge: the categorical ordering of phenomenal world–matter, knowledge therefore as domination, without any consideration of what it is that 'appears' (since this is in itself unrecognisable) or *why* anything should appear at all. For the category of the 'Why' (causality) merely serves to impose order upon what has already become manifest and is thus not competent to explore beyond this level (the third and fourth antinomies of pure reason).[51] When to know means to dominate, then of course God remains that which is definitively indomitable, and thus unknowable. Under this condition, which however introduces a significant distinction, Kant takes his place among the great representatives of negative theology, echoing in fact Anselm's precise formulation (*rationabiliter comprehendit incomprehensibile esse*)[52] when he says that reason 'cannot render comprehensible' the freedom from contingency of its practical law 'in its absolute necessity ... and so we do not comprehend the practical absolute necessity of the moral imperative, *but we comprehend its incomprehensibility* [and thus the sign of God], which is all that can fairly be demanded of a philosophy which presses on in its principles to the very limits of human reason'.[53]

When Kant says that we can still speak with justification in the 'tone of a firm faith', even if we have been 'obliged to give up' the language of knowledge,[54] then this faith as 'the pure faith of reason'[55] is again to be compared with Neoplatonic πίστις as the highest form (beyond knowledge) of devotion to the Deity. This 'pure faith of reason' or 'religious faith' (Jaspers: philosophical faith) is the highest interpreter of the faith of the Church: it posits that which stands over and against itself and which is essential to it in the ethical self-apprehension of man. But Kant is always concerned that the postulates of practical reason (God, freedom, immortality) should not appear as ('psychological', 'empirical') needs on the basis of inner (religious) 'experiences'—such things are merely forms of enthusiasm. In order to make this distinction clear, he calls them 'transcendental':[56] the pure conditions of the possibility of the ethical act, where the latter is understood in its totality. To the same end, Kant distinguishes time and again between the pure and the empirical ego: the former is nothing other than the unity of perception, the subject of thought, pure

---

[51] KrV I, Dialektik II, 2, 2, 2 (3, 354f., 418f.).
[52] *Cf.* Vol. II, p. 228 (Eng. tr.).
[53] GMS 3 (5, 101).
[54] KrV II, 1, 2 (3, 565).
[55] RGV 3, 5 (6, 516).
[56] KrV II, 2, 1 (3, 605).

spontaneity, while the latter is the experience of self, and thereby the object of empirical perception by the inner senses:[57] and Kant warns against self-encounter of this kind. But this distinction, which has its own good reasons, suffers from a systematic handicap, for what man as a natural being experiences, in his experience of the external world for instance, in his contact with his fellows, is, as such, not the object of metaphysics, which begins only when the transcendental standpoint is taken.[58] This 'purification' of philosophy from all empirical experience turns transcendentalism into an unadulterated formalism.

3. THE ETHICAL–AESTHETIC SUBLIME

THE ETHICAL SUBLIME. No one, with the exception of Eckhart, has conceived with such clarity of the essence of moral freedom as the self-apprehension of the spirit-person and has held to this idea with such persistence as did Kant.[59] And it was by this act, which he though to align with religion, even with Christianity (and against everything that belongs to the ethical eudaemonism of the Enlightenment), that he released the pantheistic speculation of Fichte and Schelling. The central point of morality cannot in its purity be approached 'by any example',[60] nor can it be superseded by anything, even by religion (rather religion can originate only from this central, innermost point):[61] this is where that 'synthetic *a priori* judgment' occurs (of which at a theoretical level not pure reason but only understanding, in opposition to sense experience, was capable); first in so far as this free self-

[57] A I 1 §4 (1, 305 n., 303f.); §7 (314).

[58] 'The question whether I as a thinking being have cause to accept, apart from my own existence, the existence of a totality of other beings (called "world") which stand in fellowship with me ... is not anthropological, but merely (!) metaphysical': (A I, 1 §2 (1, 300). Or: 'Ultimately all moral philosophy rests on its pure part, and when it is applied to man, it borrows nothing at all from the knowledge of man (anthropology)': GMS, preface (5, 11).

[59] Kant speaks of this as a 'disgusting hodge-podge': GMS 2 (5, 36).

[60] *Ibid.* 2 (5, 47).

[61] KU, Allg. Anm. (6, 395).

apprehension removes (inner-ethically) the distinction between obligation (*Sollen*) and desire (*Wollen*),[62] and second because the existence of God emerges *a priori* (in the ethical-religious sense) in the absolute character of the moral imperative.[63] Just as in Plato and Plotinus the eros must raise and purify itself until it loves and strives for the good only for the sake of the good, and as in the 'metaphysics of the saints' from Eckhart and Tauler to Ignatius and Fénelon the detachment and indifference of *amour pur* becomes perfect as love solely for the Beloved, in the same way Kant demands the performance of good for the sake of the good, without a primary consideration of happiness or goal or reward. It is not the material coincidence of commandment and deed ('legality') which serves as the measure here, but only the formal acting from duty ('morality'). Man's understanding of the freedom from ends which is characteristic of the good brings him to an understanding of himself as his own end: in this moment he is 'released from the womb of Nature' (which can be a paradise in its own way: Rousseau is right only thus far) in order then to 'fall' into freedom, the freedom, that is, to apprehend himself—in the choice of the good, and in submission to its law.[64] The fact that the good appears as an imperative for many shows that obligation does not from the outset coincide with desire: 'Thus there are no imperatives for a *divine*, or indeed for a *sanctified* will; "having to" is out of place here because "wanting to" is necessarily of itself in harmony with the law'.[65] But man in history must first actualise himself as his own end (and thus himself as person) by apprehending that which is truly its own end (the good) and identifying himself with it in an act of obedience; though this, since it is a matter of a human deed within the world, happens in such a way that in his action he presupposes in his

---

[62] Therefore the categorical imperative is 'a synthetic-practical principle *a priori*': GMS 2 (5, 49 and note: the obligation cannot be deduced analytically from the act of willing, 'for we do not have such a perfect will').

[63] RGV, preface (6, 406, note).

[64] *Presumed beginning of the history of mankind* (1786) (1, 277f.).

[65] GMS 2 (5, 41).

fellow-man this identity of obligation as the measure of his action: 'Act in such a way that the humanity both in your own person and in the person of everyone else serves as an end for you and never as a means'.[66]

This is curious: from the distinction between the ego which knows obligation and the good which is obligatory there springs in an elemental way the reality of the 'other' (whose self-intention is just as radical as my own); while the eudaemonists are all 'practical egoists'; 'pluralism', the way of thinking 'which is not to see oneself as being the whole world, but to see oneself and to behave as a citizen of the world', is opposed here to egoism.[67] The same event whereby I determine upon being myself makes of me a fellow-man in the ethical and altruistic sense. By apprehending myself through respect for the good,[68] and by making myself an object of this *respect*,[69] on account of my own possession of *value*, I base my action on respect for the value of my fellow-man. The logical generality of this postulate is at the same time of internal necessity a sociological one. Kant puts it nicely: '*Doing good* is duty . . . If it is said: You should *love* your neighbour as yourself, then this does not mean: You should (first of all) love and (then) on account of this love you should do good. What it means is this: Do good to your fellow-man, and this doing good will effect an altruistic love (as practical fulfilment of the inclination towards doing good in general) in you!'[70]

But now, as we have already shown, religion springs from the synthetic element in ethics; only in so far as I *obey* the law, do I become ethically autonomous. The law will exist *within* me if, and as long as, I acknowledge it to exist *above* me. The attribution of identity of the *sacred will* to himself or to man in his historical occurrence, occurs so little to Kant that he postulates rather an unbridgeable gulf at the outset:

[66] *Ibid.* 2 (5, 59).

[67] A I 1 §2 (1, 300).

[68] 'The feeling for the inappropriateness of our capacity to attain an idea which is a law for us, is respect': KU §27 (6, 119).

[69] MS II, *Anfangsgründe der Tugendlehre*, introduction d (5, 539).

[70] *Ibid.* 5, 538–539.

that 'radical form of evil' which does not exist in man by natural derivation (since it is a matter of freedom) and which is enigmatic and inexplicable. Neither the life of the senses as such is evil, nor is reason, nor is the combination of both which is natural in man a fateful one (as if the natural love of the self were bound to oppose the ethical principle), and yet in practice there exists in him an inexplicable disorder as far as the orientation and subordination of the senses to the spirit is concerned. Kant agrees with St Paul: 'There is no difference here; they are all sinners. There is no one who does good (following the spirit of the law), not even one'.[71] Thus morality and religion will represent a continuous struggle for the victory of the good (or the kingdom of God) over the bad in man and in mankind, in an eternal approximation[72] to the idea of the saint whereby an 'ideal image' 'descends' from God and works as grace (embodied in Christ) together with the permanent and struggling principle of the good in man. Although there is an 'imputation by grace', a 'justification' ('as consolation and hope, not as certainty') which derives from that very ideal image to which we contract ourselves in our actions, and which can thereby gain a final predominancy over our 'disordered heart',[73] the very fact that the idea of a 'representation' for the sinner intervenes here in a mediating role, shows clearly enough that a simple identification of obligation and desire has no place in Kant's religious ethics.

Rather, Kant desires at all times to *humble* the human spirit in order to raise it up again in a pure way. In *The Natural History of the Sky* men are 'humbled by the knowledge of their own baseness'[74] at the sight of more highly developed spiritual beings on the higher planets. They are also 'humbled' by great natural catastrophes, such as earthquakes,[75] and

[71] RGV 1, 1–4 (6, 419–448).

[72] '. . . that which in us in our life upon earth, and perhaps in all coming ages and in all worlds, is never more than merely in the process of *becoming*, viz. being a man pleasing to God . . .': RGV 2, 1 (6, 484–485).

[73] *Ibid.* 470f., 483f.

[74] 2, 412.

[75] 2, 483.

man's impotence in the face of nature's superior power despite all his technical resources 'leads him finally to the humbling memory, from which he should begin, that he remains only a man'.[76] But the true 'humiliation' for man is the critique of pure reason, which requires a constant 'discipline', which needs 'as it were a system of caution and self-examination' in order not to exceed its own limits in an excess of enthusiasm.[77] For it is 'humbling for human reason that it can accomplish nothing in its pure application'.[78] Therefore spontaneous 'humiliation' also belongs to the 'purest moral attitude', linked with 'gratitude' and 'obedience';[79] the optimism of moral autonomy, as Kant understands it, altogether retains this perpetual premise and, precisely in so far as it is the consciousness of duty, is not in contradiction to it.

Contrary to the widespread view, Kant greatly esteems the incarnation of morality within social custom, the Platonic-Aristotelian ἐθίξεσθαι (the moralisation of the senses) and not only in the cultural but also in the moral sense, as his considered response to Schiller shows, who believed that he had produced something new in his ideal of an aesthetic harmony between duty and inclination, dignity (*Würde*) and grace (*Anmut*: charm). The question, according to Kant, is only whether the highest ideal can lie in such an aesthetic harmony (which as it were yokes together duty and inclination in order to create a third principle common to both), or whether the absolute character of duty and thus its sublimity, might not in this way be forgotten: 'I am happy to confess that I cannot allow the *concept of duty* any *grace* on account of its dignity. For it contains unconditional necessity, to which grace stands in direct opposition. The majesty of the law (like that on Sinai) fills us with awe (not with shyness, which repels, nor with allurement, which invites intimacy), which awakes the *respect* of the underling for his lord but which, in our case, since the latter lies within us ourselves

[76] 2, 531.

[77] KrV II, 1 (3, 541–542).

[78] *Ibid.* II, 2 (3, 600).

[79] KU §86 note (6, 351).

awakens *a sense of the sublimity* of our own nature, which ravishes us more than any thing of beauty. But virtue, that is the determination to perform one's duty exactly, is also beneficial in its effects, which are greater than those which nature or art can achieve in the world, and the glorious image of humanity, erected in this its form, permits the companionship of the graces ... But when we consider the gracious effects which virtue would have in the world, if it found access everywhere, then reason which is morally oriented immediately involves the senses (through the powers of the imagination)'. And when we enquire concerning the 'aesthetic constitution', the state of mind in which man is supposed to perform his duty, then, according to Kant, 'an answer is hardly necessary': 'the joyful heart' in the performance of duty is a 'sign of the authenticity of a virtuous spirit'.[80] The mention of Sinai is not without significance: the appearance of the absolute nature of the commandment is 'sublimity' in the moral sphere while, in the religious sphere, it is glory, *kabod*. 'When morality recognises an object of the highest esteem in the sanctity of its law, then at the level of religion, in its highest cause which is the fulfilment of those laws, it sets up (!) an object of *adoration* and thus appears in its own majesty'.[81]

Kant speaks in all seriousness of this 'adoration'. If he is full of mistrust of those practices of prayer which are useful in religions, 'thought to be the means of grace', and calls them 'superstitious illusion', because God has no need of formal declarations of the desires and feelings of the one who prays and prayer does not 'serve' him, and further because man believes that he has achieved something with his prayers while in reality it is a question of realising the good in practical living, then Kant demands in place of this the 'spirit of prayer, which can and should take place in us "without ceasing"', and which 'through the *contemplation* of the deep wisdom of the divine creation in the smallest of things and of its majesty in the greatest' effects in us the mood both of 'adoration' and

---

[80] RGV I, note (6, 423–424). Kant's underlinings. Schiller's reaction to this in the letter to Körner, 18 May 1794.

[81] RGV I, preface (6, 407). Kant's underlining.

of 'a power which lifts the soul', 'so that in the face of this words must vanish like empty noise'.[82] In Kant this 'contemplation' bypasses all that is 'statutory' in the positive religions and is transfixed by the mystery of *Da-Sein* (existence), which he sought to defend from the attacks of pure reason by his critique and, by his ethics, to expose to the bold enterprises of practical reason. He makes the decisive statement concerning his intent when he says, 'Enquiry into the inner nature of all forms of belief which refer to religion necessarily comes up against a *mystery*, that is against something *sacred*, which, though it is familiar (*gekannt*) to each individual, cannot be publicly recognised (*bekannt*), which is to say generally proclaimed. As something which is *sacred* it must be a (moral) object of reason and must also be capable of being privately counted adequate for its practical application, and yet, as something which is *mysterious*, not so for its theoretical application: because it would then have to be communicable to everyone and would have to be capable of being recognised outwardly and publicly'.[83] But Kant also knows of the urge in man to make concrete for himself the absolute and thus divine mystery of Being in a 'carved image', through and beyond which he may also glimpse that which hovers before him in its mystery: here there is the justice and the limitation, the necessity and detestability of natural religion: 'It sounds questionable, but it is in no way reprehensible to say that everyone *makes his own God*, indeed, . . . must make one in order to honour in him *the God who made him*. For in whatever way one being is proclaimed and portrayed as a *god* by another, or when even such a being manifests to another in this way (if this is possible), then the latter must first of all hold it up against his ideal in order to ascertain whether he is justified in regarding it and honouring it as a god. There cannot therefore be a religion based on pure revelation, which in its purity lacks for its foundation any *prior* concept as a criterion of judgment, for then all divine worship would be the worship of idols'.[84] Thus we

[82] RGV IV, 2 (6, 625–629).
[83] *Ibid.* III, 2 (6, 558–559).
[84] *Ibid.* IV, 2 §1 (6, 594).

may sum up in conclusion: the absolute Good is manifest within the sphere of practical reason in me (autonomy) and above me (sublimity, which can only be approached and never attained); at the 'religious level' of morality, this absolute Good in and above me appears as mystery (beyond all the carved images of theoretical reason), which in its glory (Sinai) demands adoration, but of which I carry within myself such a consciousness (autonomy) that I can measure all that is statutory-religious against it. But this means that there can be nothing 'supernatural' for Kant (despite all his genuine consciousness of mystery) in the sense that it could be located fundamentally beyond the human spirit in its opening as practical reason. Thus it is man who (in his freedom, which touches and contains the Absolute) finally measures out the space between himself and God: 'There is something in us which we can never cease to wonder at . . . that which raises *mankind* in its concept to a value which one would not suppose to exist on the basis of the *individual* as the object of our experience . . . That we possess the *capacity* to make the great sacrifice of our sensual nature to morality, that we are *capable* of doing what we easily and clearly see that we *ought* to do, this predominance of the *supersensual man* in us over the *sensual man*, the predominance of that man face to face with whom the other is *nothing* (when it comes to conflict), even when the latter in his own eyes is *everything*, this moral structure in us, which is indivisible from our humanity, is the object of the highest *admiration*, which only increases the longer we contemplate this true (and unimagined) ideal: so much so that they are to be forgiven who construe this *supersensual* element in us, on account of its incomprehensibility and its practical nature, to be *supernatural*, that is to be something which neither stands in our power nor is our own possession, but is rather the influence of another and higher spirit; though they are grievously mistaken in this . . .'.[85]

It has already been pointed out that Kant is thus renewing in a much profounder way (and in the general context of the

[85] StF I, 2 (1, 609).

Enlightenment) the concern of Shaftesbury and his school: morality as the criterion of religion. But he adds to this the manner of questioning which belongs to late antiquity, and which was introduced in the image of the 'unfinishable bridge': a human religious project with an orientation towards revelation (since the 'supersensual' element in man opens towards a Divine Absolute), but which serves as the criticism of all revelation on the basis of man's ethico-religious capacity, whereby the whole of positive Christianity (as the highest 'mythical' religion) falls victim to this criticism. With this problem Kant initiates the whole tradition of German Idealist religious philosophy and does so in such a way that *a priori* all theology will be dragged before the judgment seat of philosophy.

THE BEAUTIFUL. If for Kant the core of the person, that which constitutes the 'human' in him or her, is the point where the autonomic-moral opens into the mystery of the relationship of God and man, then it is true also that his aesthetics, as developed in the concluding third critique, which is that of judgment, balances on the concept of the (aesthetically) sublime. But the 'sublime' in its true character becomes comprehensible only in connection with and in contrast to the 'beautiful'. It is the *beautiful* therefore which we must first address.

If theoretical knowledge consisted in the reciprocity of perception and concept in relation to an object, then aesthetic knowledge is that same reciprocity but in relation to the subject. 'We have accordingly two forms of perfection: one that is logical and one that is aesthetic. The first form of perfection obtains when my knowledge coincides with the object, and the second when my knowledge coincides with the subject'.[86] This means in *negative* terms that aesthetic judgment has no 'interest' in the objective existence of the

[86] This short formulation stands in the posthumous *Vorlesungen über die Metaphysik*, Erfurt 1821, p. 169. One should note the expression in this of the equilibrium between both forms of knowledge, which for Kant stand *de facto* (in their critical, although quite different limitations) to the left and the right of the practical reason.

object, and relates to its manifest form 'in a purely contemplative manner'.[87] Yet when this beholding 'pleases' the subject disinterestedly, then 'we *linger* in the contemplation of the beautiful because this contemplation is self-enhancing and self-propagating'.[88] The experience of the beautiful thereby differs from the merely 'pleasant', which arouses a predilection with vested interest for that which gives pleasure; it differs also from the 'true', which is interest in the existence of the object, and from the 'good', which is interest in the *Dasein* of an object or an action. In *positive* terms this means that the judgment of taste makes a secret claim to universal validity, despite its relation to the subject, and thus does not remain purely empirical and subjective as does the judgment of what is appealing to the senses (here, 'Everyone to their own taste' holds true). It touches rather on something in the transcendental structure of the subject, that is, it triggers the 'free play' of the cognitive powers—sensual imagination and intellectual concept—and, affecting them in their inner objective 'harmony', it sets them resonating, the beautiful pleasingly and the ugly displeasingly. This is what accounts for the 'claim to subjective universality'.[89] But it is only the cognitive powers as such which resonate, the understanding only as unity of the concept, without a particular concept being formed (which would immediately lead to 'interest' in the object), and the imagination not found as when receiving a given reality but in its free creative play with it. Therefore this resonating harmony of the cognitive faculty,[90] its 'mood' or 'proportion',[91] also stands in opposition to all forms of the 'schematism' of pure reason,[92] but it derives from a 'deeply hidden ground of illumination in the judgment of forms, which is common to all men'.[93] Thus the aesthetic judgment of taste of the individual is 'suggested' to all, without being

[87] KU 1 §5 (6, 60).
[88] *Ibid.* §12 (6, 76).
[89] *Ibid.* §6 (6, 63).
[90] *Ibid.* §9 (6, 71).
[91] *Ibid.* §21 (6, 96).
[92] KrV, Analytik 2, 1 (3, 152f.).
[93] KU §17 (6, 88).

able or wishing to be 'imposed' upon all (as is the case with moral judgments).[94] This communicability of feeling for the beautiful implies a 'common sense', and it does so without recourse 'to psychological observations', 'but as the necessary condition of the universal communicability of our knowledge, which must be presupposed . . . in every form of logic'.[95]

But now every relation of interest with regard to the object must be set aside in order to isolate the phenomenon fully, that is both *what* the phenomenal thing is in itself (truth) and *what* it is good for (goodness), or whether it corresponds in itself to its own concept (perfection). In thus linking the beautiful with the true and the good, Kant speaks of a beauty which is 'bound' or which 'merely adheres' (*pulchritudo adhaerens*), from which however the distinguishing formal character of 'beauty' does not yet clearly emerge. This occurs only with 'free beauty' (*pulchritudo vaga*), with which a 'consonance of taste with reason, that is of the beautiful with the good' is not presupposed— a consonance however in which 'perfection gains nothing through beauty nor beauty through perfection', despite a reciprocal and accidental 'heightening' of each other,[96] but only the 'form of purposiveness' is presupposed without the concept of a purpose.[97] Pure beauty is *formal* in a double sense here: in so far as it ignores the link between the true and the good (which is unheard-of with respect to the classical, Christian tradition), in order to distil in 'pure' form the concept of the beautiful, and in so far as it correspondingly 'abstracts' (this word is Kant's own)[98] from every object and every ethical interest, in order to enjoy the form, as unrelated and possessing meaning only within itself, with the pure formal harmony of our cognitive powers. In this Kant is without doubt the first theoretician of *abstract art*. Although the scholastics also attempted to expose the distinguishing *ratio* of each

[94] *Ibid.* §8 (6, 65f.).
[95] *Ibid.* §21 (6, 97).
[96] §16 (6, 84–86).
[97] *Ibid.* §10–11 (6, 73–75).
[98] *Ibid.* §16 (6, 87).

transcendental (*unum, verum, bonum, pulchrum*), even when they viewed the *pulchrum* as being *realiter* one with the *bonum*, its distinguishing aspect nevertheless emerged. But there all the transcendentals shared in the common being of which they are the transcendent and universal modalities, which fact served also to distinguish them one from another. This objective communication demands within the field of artistic activity the principle of unification rather than of separation. In Kant the 'transcendentals' relate to the transcendental constitution of reason in its critical self-understanding, and the individual aspect emerges clearly only when we disregard the others. This is so because reason, taken in its purity, *hovers indeterminately* in its finitude (as interrelationship of finite perception and finite concept) and loses every anchorage in in-finite *esse*. Therefore beauty, whose essence is the pure interrelationship of the powers of the subject (an interrelationship which prescinds from the true and the good), possesses exactly the same indefinite character of the finite in itself which, when the rigour of the ethical imperative wanes and is no longer seen, can at some point lead to the pure play of finite existence in nothingness with itself, a play which is not only disinterested and without purpose (*l'art pour l'art*) but also ultimately lacking in meaning.

Because it is the freedom from a specific concept which is the precondition for the beautiful, its universal validity can only be 'by example', the representation not of a knowable content but merely of an 'idea', so that 'the highest pattern, the archetype of taste, is only an idea'.[99] Everything beautiful is only 'the example of a general rule, which cannot be stated'.[100] Thus although regularity, symmetry and so forth can be the 'necessary condition' for the beautiful, they can never be its essence, as Plotinus knew best of all.[101] The true centre of the soul's powers is here the creative play of the imagination, which remains incalculable in concept and which, in theoretical thought, stands at the service of the regulating reason, while 'reason serves the imagination . . . in

[99] *Ibid.* §17 (6, 88).
[100] *Ibid.* §18 (6, 94).
[101] *Ibid.*, general note to the Analytik (6, 100).

the free and indeterminately purposive converse of the mind's powers with that which we call beautiful'.[102] Therefore Kant develops his astounding theory of genius, which alone can be the rule of art—despite all demands for technical skills: it is 'Nature' which is the creative agent in genius 'and through the harmonising of its powers', so that 'originality must be its first quality', whose 'products must be models, that is they must have an exemplary character, though not one that functions through imitation', and yet the author 'does not himself know the origin of his ideas, and does not have the power to have these ideas at will or according to his own plan . . . Thus presumably the word "genius" (*Genie*) derives from *genius*, the particular spirit which is given to man at birth and which defends him and guides him and which is the inspiration of those original ideas'.[103] Thus the poet's images *signify* the truth, but they do not permit themselves to be elucidated as concepts; and for the philosopher Kant 'there has perhaps never been anything said which is more sublime' than 'the inscription above the Temple of Isis (of Mother Nature): "I am all that there is, that there has been and that there will be, and no mortal has uncovered my veil"'.[104] Schiller, who makes his youth lift the veil from Saïs and thus become infected with melancholy, and Novalis, who must also raise the veil in order to discover behind it an erotic mystery of identity, possess for Kant too great a knowledge.

It needs to be stressed concerning the 'adhering beauty' however that its freedom from ends enjoys a particular affinity with man, who alone in Nature possesses himself in moral terms as his own end. But two kinds of idea or ideal can be formed of man: a 'normal idea', which in practice presents his average measure (as of an animal species, in the particularity of the various races, etc.), and for this Kant adduces the aesthetic canons of the Greek sculptors and of the Renaissance (though with their variations on normal expression for the characterisation of psychological personality etc.); and then a 'rational idea', which lies within

[102] *Ibid.* (6, 101).
[103] *Ibid.* §46 (6, 181–182).
[104] *Ibid.* §49 (6, 192–193).

the moral sphere: 'the visible expression of moral ideas' puts new questions to the artist which have not previously been glimpsed in the understanding of beauty,[105] for here the beautiful must be drawn beyond itself into the form of 'sublimity'.

THE AESTHETIC SUBLIME. A glance backwards is called for here. At the beginning of the Christian era, an anonymous treatise. *On the Sublime*, was written with reference to rhetoric which also served to sum up the classical philosophical inheritance. Then the concept disappears. In 1756, the young Edmund Burke published his *A Philosophical Enquiry into the Origin of our Ideas of the Sublime and the Beautiful*; the work, in Garve's translation, immediately attracted the, albeit critical, notice of Lessing, Mendelssohn and Herder, and was a stimulus to Kant: already in his early *Observations on the sense of the Beautiful and the Sublime* (1764), and even more in his mature reflections in the *Critique of Judgement*.

The late classical work *Peri Hupsous*[106] also deserves mention in this connection for it too views the aesthetically sublime as being substantially determined by the ethically sublime of the 'elevated attitude of mind' and 'magnanimity'. Truly elevated speech lifts the soul, filling it with such pride and joy as if it had itself invented what it has heard,[107] and this is so because the soul thus becomes aware of its own nature (πρὸς ἃ γεγόναμεν): man is not only introduced into the entire universe (as citizen of the world) as into a great festive gathering in order to participate eagerly in the sporting competitions, 'but in his soul there is an invincible love (ἄμαχος ἔρως) for all that is eternally great and all that is more divine than we are. So not even the universe can satisfy the flights of human vision and thought, but his mind often soars beyond the limits of the world which houses him'. He inclines by nature to the contemplation not of small rivers, but of the Nile, the Danube and the Rhine; the contemplation not of the

[105] *Ibid.* §17 (6, 87–93).
[106] Text and trans. by H. Lebèque: *'Du Sublime'*, Belles Lettres, 2nd edn. 1952; quoted by chapter and paragraph.
[107] VII, 2.

small lamp, but of the star-filled firmament or of Mount Etna spewing forth rocks and fire.[108] All great men have raised themselves above mortality; all other qualities belong only to the human, while the sublime draws near to divine majesty.[109] But the beautiful and the sublime are not explained on the basis of a polarity but rather of a process of heightening, and so 'a mutal relationship' is striven for,[110] and *'harmonia'* is praised as being 'a wonderful *organon*' of the sublime and the pathetic.[111] Finally, the writer complains that life has become bourgeois and constricted and the world has turned decadent: there is no more room in the world for human greatness and thus for artistic sublimity. At the end of his idealist aesthetic, Hegel too will consign sublimity completely to the (archaic Greek) past.

Burke[112] therefore starts something new in so far as he grasps the sensations of the beautiful and the sublime as pure polarities: in the one 'pleasure' (*cf.* Kant's *Lust*) and in the other initially 'pain' (Kant's *Unlust*) on account of something threatening (and thus terrifying), which then in a second phase, when it becomes evident that no direct danger threatens, finds release in 'delight'. Burke removes the ethical from these fundamental aesthetic experiences, as he does sensual desire and utilitarian interest, in so far as pure consciousness is concerned. Meanwhile he interprets the phenomena against the background of a theory of instinctive drives (self-preservation and sociability, Freud's Ego and sexual drive)[113] and interprets them ultimately in a mechanical and physiological way: the slackening of the fibres (love, pleasure)[114] or their tensing (fear, pain).[115] But this materialism is accompanied by a notion of God; if all that is sublime 'is a certain modification of power', which seems to

[108] XXXV, 2–4.

[109] XXXVI, 1.

[110] XXXVI, 4.

[111] XXXIX, 1.

[112] Edmund Burke, *Vom Erhabenen und Schönen*, trans. and ed. Friedrich Bassenge, Berlin 1956.

[113] 1, 9 (74f.).

[114] Although the desire in love introduces an element of pain into the pleasure.

[115] 4, 6 (174f.).

us superior, then we find in the idea of God the greatest heightening of such a power and thus on the part of the creature an insuperable fear of absolute majesty. In the presence of the thought that the universe lies in the hand of the almighty and 'is everywhere filled with His presence', 'we shrink to the diminutive dimensions of our own nature and are as it were destroyed before God'. And when we are heartened by the thought of God's wisdom and mercy and our elemental terror is dissipated by the awareness that God does not threaten us, 'then we rejoice, but with trembling'. Burke quotes not only Horace and Lucretius but also many passages from the Old Testament. It is only with Christianity that talk of the love of God really begins, as the Platonists had only intimations of it, and the other heathens not even that.[116]

Kant's analysis of the beautiful and the sublime owes much to Burke, above all the principle of opposition (instead of mere heightening), which in his transcendental contemplation becomes a polarity between 'proportion' or 'harmony' (between the cognitive faculties: imagination and reason) and a primary 'disproportion' (now between sensuality and rational idea), which is resolved secondarily in a consideration of the nature of man into a higher harmony which has need of inner contrast. The sublime cannot lie in Nature as such, for the mathematical sublime is so only for the imagination, which when it takes a fundamental measure and imagines what will always be greater than it, can no longer find a place for this latter. But the intellect can consider every solar system as an atom in further systems, and here the sublime is transferred to the subject: 'the sublime is that which, in being able to be thought, proves a capacity of the mind which transcends every measure of the senses'.[117] But it is the fact that this 'being able to be thought' also refers to the unknowable ideas, which arise with the nature of man, that first truly throws light on the 'dynamic sublimity' of Nature, since it appears to physical man as an awesome preponderance of power: this terror is countered in some degree by the

[116] 2, 5 (99–107).
[117] KU §25 (6, 111).

consciousness of not being directly threatened, and space is created for wonder at the 'sublime' drama of Nature; but ultimately and more profoundly man meets this superior power only in reflection on his own moral nature. The failure of the imagination when it encounters the idea is 'displeasure', but it is precisely this 'displeasure' 'which awakens in us the feeling of our supra-sensual nature, according to which it is purposeful, even the source of delight, to find every norm of sensuality inadequate with regard to the ideas of reason'.[118] Thus 'the subjective play of the powers of the mind . . . is itself shown to be harmonious' through their contrast.[119] Now it is no still, contemplative delight, as was the case with the beautiful, but a 'movement' of the spirit: that which is sublime (*das Erhabene*) is at the same time, as Schiller will say, that which uplifts us (*das Erhebende*).[120]

And yet this expression of Schiller's goes one step further than Kant. For it is true for the latter that the dynamic sublimity of Nature raises man up to himself by allowing his ethical nature to emerge; and thus that the sublime is located more in man than in Nature.[121] But Schiller does not speak of God any more, whereas Kant at least takes up Burke's idea of God as absolute power as an objection: do we not imagine 'God in His wrath and, at the same time, in His sublimity too, when we imagine Him in the tempest, in the storm, in the earthquake and the like'? 'Here it is not a feeling of the sublimity of our own nature, rather our subjection, our abandonment and the feeling of our own impotence' which appears to be the proper frame of mind. Kant responds to this in accordance with his notion of the religious as the ultimate dimension of the ethical. Against Burke it needs to be said that the response of the creature, which consists entirely of terror at the total superiority of God's power, is by no means a religious one as yet: 'The person who experiences genuine fear . . . is not in the right frame of mind

[118] *Ibid.* §27 (6, 120).

[119] *Ibid.* (121).

[120] *Zerstreute Betrachtungen über verschiedene ästhetische Gegenstände* (1793).

[121] KU §28 (6, 125).

to wonder at the greatness of God . . . Even humility as the unsparing condemnation of his faults . . . is an elevated state of mind'.[122] But against Schiller Kant would still hold to his 'sense of awe at the sublime' which belongs not only to human nature but also to God, with whose sanctity the human will, which is bound to eternal struggle, can never conceive itself to be one. Thus Kant demands that 'the Good, aesthetically judged, must not only be represented as being beautiful but also as being sublime, so that it evokes the feeling of respect (which spurns charm) more than of love and intimate inclination, because human nature does not accord of itself with the Good, but only through the violence which reason inflicts upon our sensual nature'.[123] Despite all the 'Enlightenment within him', Kant does not cross the threshold of German Idealism with its aesthetics of identity, since he refuses to interpret the 'violence' which must be inflicted upon man as a yet higher form of beauty. He retains a Christian sensorium which, however concealed, still has knowledge of the Cross.

d. The Self-Glorification Of The Spirit
I. SCHILLER

With Schiller, that form of Idealism continues which fundamentally transcends the open-ended non-identity of Kant—between phenomenon and the *Ding an sich*, between finite and infinite intellect, and in particular between ethical duty and desire—in Spirit's ultimate conquest of Being, so that all glory of Being now becomes a self-glorification of the Spirit. This marks the end of that philosophical flight which began with Parmenides: the divine standpoint is taken up for the sake of the truth of Spirit, which must ultimately coincide with the absolute freedom of the Spirit. It is Schiller who clearly signals this, although others took the field at the same time. By discovering antiquity for himself as a thinker and poet, though in such a way as to incorporate it into his own philosophy of Spirit, he takes up a position in the stream

---

[122] *Ibid.* (6, 127).
[123] KU, general note, after §29 (6, 137).

of modern thought which is opposed to that of Goethe: fruitful complementarity within a common fate. Only Goethe remains ultimately more peacefully contained within that classical principle of comprehensiveness which is *physis*, while Schiller must place man beyond it as the Absolute Spirit in a process of becoming, in that he can live only with reference to an end which he himself constructs.

THE FORM OF HIS WORK AND HIS POINT OF DEPARTURE. As a thinker Schiller begins, as did Kant, with Leibniz, whom he understands in terms of pietism and enthusiasm.[1] But the vertical section of the world (devised in order to overcome Descartes and the English and French materialists), which Leibniz extended through all things in order to grasp the world quantitively and materially as well as qualitatively and spiritually, is resolved in the young Schiller's hands (as it will be in those of Jean Paul and the Romantics) into two starkly opposed world-views: on the one hand the day and on the other the night side of the universe, on the one hand Idealism (corresponding to the phenomenism which extends from Descartes to Malebranche), and on the other materialism and radical transience. The abrupt shift from one perspective to the other determines his early lyrics, in particular the odes to Laura.

Since the poetic influence of Klopstock is immense, the pathos of the admiring, moving, adulatory praise of the glory and majesty of God who reigns in the infinite universe initially remains: *The Evening* (1766)[2] multiplies the addresses to God, and Nature is called upon to be silent, thus permitting God to sound through its harp. *The Glory of Creation*[3] leads the poet away like Ganymede into a universe which is alive

[1] Schiller's works quoted from the edition by Fricke-Göpfert-Stubenrauch, Hanser-Verlag, 5 Vols., 3rd edn 1962. The letters according to the critical general edition (F. Jonas, 7 Vols.). Some abbreviations: WL = *Wallensteins Lager*; Picc = *Die Piccolomini*; WT = *Wallensteins Tod*; AW = *Über Anmut und Würde*; EM = *Über die ästhetische Erziehung des Menschen*; NSD = *Über naive und sentimentalische Dichtung*. The verse dramas are quoted by the number of verses, the prose dramas by act and scene.

[2] 1, 9.

[3] 1, 43; *cf.* 'Hymne an den Unendlichen': 1, 83.

with God's presence; he often sees laid out before him 'the whole splendour of Creation, the glory,/ which the All-Highest conceived in the solitude of dark eternity' and listens to 'the great song of praise' of Nature which rings forth from the universe 'lost in harmonies/ like a sweet death'. *The Grandeur of the World*[4] is a poetical counterpoint to the young Kant's enthusiasm for infinity in his *Theory of the Heavens*, while *To the Sun*[5] (first draft in 1773) praises the creative light and 'worships its work'. But this mood of worship was enthusiasm in the spirit of Shaftesbury,[6] behind which, unrecognised but of like kind, the greater figure of Giordano Bruno appears. If it is the case that the *Theosophy of Julius*, which is the subject of discussion in the *Philosophical Letters* (1786) between Julius, the idealist, and Raphael, the sceptical thinker, refers back to Schiller's early life and that thus Leibniz and Shaftesbury, in an enthusiastic combination, set the tone, then the existential consequences set out in his youthful dramas must also be taken into consideration in order to balance the ensuing image. In the *Theosophy* we read: 'All the perfections of the universe are unified in God. God and Nature are two forms of greatness which are perfectly alike to each other.'[7] This is the scheme of Plotinus, Erigena and Nicolas of Cusa: the world as the self-manifestation of God is interpreted here unashamedly in terms of identity. There is equally bold talk of both the division of God into the (Leibnizean) universe of spirits and the synthesis of the latter into deity: prismatically 'the Divine Self has divided itself into innumerable sentient substances', whereby 'a Divine Being emerges from the unification of all these substances . . . If it ever pleased the Almighty to destroy the prism, then the dam between itself and the world would collapse and all spirits would . . . bring forth God.'[8] Significantly, Hegel concludes his *Phenomenology of the Spirit* with a quotation from the poem

[4] 1, 84.

[5] 1, 40.

[6] Schiller came to know him through the mediation of Garve in the school of his first philosophy teacher, Abel.

[7] 5, 352.

[8] *Ibid.*, 353.

which follows this. Love is the name which the young Schiller gives to this unitive force: 'it is only the reflection of the unique primal power . . . founded on a momentary exchange of personality, an exchange of essences'. The category of the Platonic 'moment' (ἐξαίφνης)[9] causes the universe to appear through the 'cyphers' and 'hieroglyphs' of the cosmos, eros anticipates identity and thus demands total selflessness (*amour pur*), the renunciation of reward and the dedication of one's entire life to the point even of losing it.[10] Is that all only a dream 'perhaps real only in the brain of your Julius'? But then can reality be less than the idea? 'Are my ideas then to be more beautiful than those of the eternal Creator?'[11] It is not the finite, conceptual clothing which is important here, for the vision which is darkly expressed therein is divine, indeed unsurpassable (*id quo majus cogitari non potest*): as ideal-idea in us (as the analytical breakdown of God) it is necessarily 'real-idea' therefore within the 'active omnipotence',[12] and therefore merits 'veneration'.[13]

But in existential terms the man who wants to see himself and to move within the scheme of identity enters the dialectic of the *Eroici Furori*: eros becomes the gaining of the self as God, and thus self-destruction; but the prismatic analysis of God can be lived and experienced (in the Christian and the Idealist way) as the spontaneous decline of Primal Being and innocence into alienation, revolt and hell. Thus, and especially in a temperament such as Schiller's, the philosophical contradiction (which inheres in all philosophies of identity) necessarily becomes an existential one: it becomes flaming revolt against all that is non-divine, non-autonomous, alien to the Spirit, untrue and unfree in the world order (*The Robbers*), but also the absolutisation of the same contradiction within man himself (the non-identity of ethical imperative and desire which is heightened to a Promethean No to God: in *The Spiritual Libertarianism of Passion*, where God stands

[9] The word is everywhere in the section 'Idee': 5, 346f.
[10] 'Aufopferung' 351.
[11] *Ibid.*, 355.
[12] *Ibid.*, 348.
[13] *Ibid.*, 355.

accused as a 'Wüterich' and a 'Nero', who feeds Himself on human suffering, because He does not permit the coincidence of duty and inclination).[14]

It is exactly here that the primary orientation of the whole form of his work lies. For here two possibilities emerge from a single root. Either man is measured by his 'heroic' greatness, with which he lives out the tension or the split between God's Being and the being of the world (or the ego), which means that the ideal is given the name 'Prometheus'; then the formal, purely dynamic greatness of the hero, of the (original) genius is determinative, and it is virtually of no consequence whether this greatness is represented as rebellious strength or the strength to effect reconciliation and unity. Or the present fact of his 'no longer' or 'not yet' being God prescribes a 'law' for man, the law which is of course that only of his own freedom and liberation, the prescription of his (individual or social) self-realisation, to which he must subordinate himself in order to win the laurels of true spiritual existence. If it was a question in the former case of a static *dynamis* of formal greatness, then in the latter it is a matter of a final dynamism, which forces a 'process' upon man: that of gaining himself through transcending himself. It can be seen here that this second possibility, which will later lead Schiller to Kant, by virtue of its connection with the former possibility constantly serves to distinguish Schiller greatly from Kant, who as a Christian could never genuinely take the Promethean, Brunoesque attitude into consideration, never seriously having thought in terms of a scheme of identity.

If we consider the form of Schiller's work in general from this point of view, then we see that this dialectic causes a rupture at its heart, in a similar fashion to Goethe but for different reasons. The early period (around 1780–1787, with the fading cry of The Gods of Greece, 1788, and The Artist, 1789) ends with the long-worked-over Don Carlos. Then historical and philosophical studies dominate the poetical interregnum until the late period (around 1797–1805) which begins with the similarly long-worked-over Wallenstein, and

[14] I, 127–129.

which was then to be followed by plays and poems to the very end. Schiller called these two great cornerpieces of his work 'infelicitous', and the wrestling with their meaning always seemed to him a 'deep crisis'. If we substitute for human greatness the Kantian notion of the sublime, then two forms of the sublime wrestle one with the other: the greatness of the soaring flight (Prometheus) and the greatness of humility, obedience and subjection. In the poem *The Knights of Malta* (1795), the uniting of what appears irreconcilable is the preserve only of Christianity:

> Religion of the Cross, you alone unite in *one*
> Wreath the double palm of humility and strength.[15]

Looking back from *Don Carlos* to the early works, we see without doubt that the ideal of formal Promethean absoluteness predominates, which is recognisable in the fact that genius remains identical with itself, whether it takes the form of the complete rebel or of the free hero who subjects himself to the law (Karl Moor, Fiesco). Looking ahead from *Wallenstein*, it is the second version of the human ideal which predominates, but with an increasing artistic formalisation and a consequent loss in the existential force of the scintillating *Wallenstein*. The ambiguous, fragmentary character of *Don Carlos* and *Wallenstein* remains the centre of the work, which casts uncertainty also upon the clarity of the early and late periods. We can now offer an outline of the different periods in their chronological sequence.

The Robbers presents the 'majestic sinner' who plays with 'the dangerous aether ray of genius', the 'bold Phaeton' whose 'shame' is erased in order to make place for 'admiration'.[16] Both brothers are 'honourable villains, majestic monsters: spirits who are attracted by terrible vice for the sake of the greatness which attaches to it, for the sake of the strength which it demands, for the sake of the perils which accompany it'. Schiller wants us 'to learn, even to love, my robber's majesty'.[17] In remembrance of the aesthetic rule 'that the

---

[15] I, 248.

[16] *Monument Moors des Räubers* I, 98–100.

[17] Suppressed preface to the *Räuber* I, 481–484.

good are thrown into sharp profile by the wicked and virtue is at its most life-like when contrasted with vice', he wants to depict vice 'in its colossal grandeur', and its representatives are to be 'detested and loved, admired and pitied'; they are to be like Milton's and Klopstock's Satan, like the classical Medea and Shakespeare's Richard.[18] 'We are more inclined to read the mark of the divine from the grimaces of vice' than we are from a 'harmonious portrait'.[19] In Franz Moor it is the Titanism of a direct struggle against God, the devising and the practice of an evil *quo majus non cogitari potest*, which only has meaning when the deeds are performed at every stage in the face of eternal damnation, which is simultaneously challenged, denied and accepted; the fact that the warrior against God must finally pay for his protest by his succumbing to a whining fear of death is part of his paradoxical greatness. On the other hand, it is Karl's Titanism that makes him wish to impose order, through judging and avenging, on God's hopeless corrupt world. He is the 'arm of higher rulers'[20] and he carries within himself the memory of the lost child's paradise of innocence, which is for him 'Elysium', a 'holy temple' and 'unclouded joy'.[21] He feels the infinite distance that separates him from this lost world: 'And I so unlovely in this beautiful world—and I a monster on this glorious earth'.[22] With a Hölderlin-like pathos he asks whether the 'inspiring green valleys' will ever return to him, the childhood scenes 'ever cool my burning bosom again with sweet sighings'?[23] But the way back is closed, which is why Karl can only crown his Promethean rebellion with a yet more astonishing final act in the purest Promethean style: 'But still there remains for me something with which I (!) can once again reconcile the offended laws and mend the abused order. A sacrifice is needed—a sacrifice which will reveal its inviolable majesty before the whole of humanity (!)—I myself

[18] Preface to first edition I, 484–488.
[19] Self-criticism with reference to the *Räuber* I, 623.
[20] *Die Räuber* IV, 5.
[21] *Ibid.*, IV, I.
[22] *Ibid.*, III, 2.
[23] *Ibid.*, III, 2.

am this sacrifice . . . I go to place myself in the hands of the law.'[24] The Moors are the 'giants and peaks' of 'liberty';[25] they achieve nothing less and feel themselves to be majestic beings who, both in rebellion and in penitence, can act as a counterbalance to the majesty of the world order.

In *Fiesco's Conspiracy at Genoa*, the amphiboly of genius becomes yet more evident as through adaptation of the final scenes the poet chooses first to give the formal 'greatness' of the hero the face of a titanic tyrant and then of a cringing republican. 'The noble head knows temptations not of the common order';[26] 'To win a diadem by struggle is a great thing, but to cast it away is divine.'[27] But also the other way around: 'It is unspeakably great to steal a crown. Shame lessens with an increase in sin.' The greatness of the 'moment', which measures in one leap the abyss between 'obeying and ruling', is the decisive thing, which lends existence its meaning and its form: 'A princely moment has swallowed the whole domain of being . . . (*he walks heroically up and down*)'.[28] All the other major characters are affected by Fiesco's contradiction: Julia, Leonore, even Verrina: at some point the Promethean measure is applied to them all.

In *Intrigue and Love*, the poet himself becomes accuser and avenger on behalf of Moor; the inextinguishable impressions of childhood—the terrible distortions of the world order by the presumptuous majesty of the absolutism of Baroque princes, the obedience to absolute law profaned and reduced to the religiously flavoured drill of Karl Eugen of Wüttemberg's military academy—explain the revolutionary pathos of liberty, which endures from this point to *Carlos* and even to *Wallenstein* and to *William Tell*. Even the *Conquerer* (1777) curses with 'the curse of a burning thirst for revenge',[29] which will one day in the Last Judgment cast the

[24] *Ibid.*, V, 2.

[25] *Ibid.*, I, 2.

[26] *Fiesco* III, 2.

[27] *Ibid.* II, 19. In the Mannheim stage version, this word becomes the expression of the definitive victory over self on Fiesco's part: herewith he breaks the sceptre and throws the pieces among the people. 1, 951–952.

[28] *Ibid.*, III, 2.

[29] 1, 14.

tyrants into Hell. The 'evil monarchs' prowl as 'gods of the earth', as 'the giant puppets of God', and are 'faded royalty', who cover 'high shame with the night clothes of the right of majesty'.[30] Thus in the play the mendacious world of the court is 'abhorrent glory';[31] Luise wishes 'to scream without mercy into the ears [of the rascals who destroyed her love for Ferdinand] that even the lungs of the gods of the earth will rattle in the hour of their death and the Last Judgment will shake both kings and beggars through the same sieve.'[32] Once again Hell must serve to deepen the darkness: the intrigue drives the lovers into the despair of suicide and reveals there their own abysmal depths. The Lady, still of course Promethean, saves herself by simultaneously renouncing intrigue (life at court) and love (for Ferdinand): 'My glory dies with my love.'[33]

This leads to *Don Carlos*, which stands in close spiritual proximity to the former drama: a family tragedy between inflexible absolutism and freedom, the latter for the moment as the 'free love' of a son for his step-mother. Then it expands into a great historical tragedy of the transition between two epochs. The king and the queen are ennobled, Posa appears as 'a delegate of the whole of humanity', and finally (in Schiller's friendship with Körner) the accent shifts completely to Posa's eschatological proclamation of a 'new state' which is worthy of man and to the expiatory and provocative sacrifice of his own life for his friend the Prince, who is thereby to be healed from his love-sickness and made capable of realising his social vision. But the plans do not cohere, the old forms of motivation underlie the new and the whole is played to the last in the context of the court milieu and remains confused intrigue. Posa's death for love lacks motive, the Prince's passion drags meaninglessly and destructively on, the conceptual world of Philip II oscillates between authentic and distorted representation and the religious background too takes on a corresponding form: the Inquisition, which pulls

[30] I, 104–108.
[31] *Kabale und Liebe* II, I.
[32] *Ibid.*, III, 6.
[33] *Ibid.*, IV, 8.

the strings, is a hellish abomination, while Posa is a noble
Knight of Malta. The accent shifts from the formal Prometheus
ideal to obedience to that ideal, but this is still the result of an
enthusiastic self-esteem. Since Posa wishes to die, Carlos,
mindful of the king, calls out: 'No, no! He will not . . . resist
so noble a deed . . . It will move him.'[34] And the words 'God'
(for the king),[35] 'divine',[36] are always close at hand.

Don Carlos reaches across the long gap in Schiller's
creativity to *Wallenstein*; after long hesitation Schiller gave it
preference over *the Knights of Malta*, a drama on the Order
which stresses obedience and love of sacrifice and thus, once
again, favoured the Promethean theme. Why? On the one
hand, the poet wished to create a modern counterpart to
classical tragedy: the revealing of a tragic situation which is
already in existence, of hybris and nemesis; and to this extent
it is a play concerning the blindness (*atê*) of the clear-sighted:

> He went his evil way with soft steps,
> And vengeance followed him as softly;
> It stands, unseen and dark, behind him.[37]

Further, it was to become a central episode in German
national history: the destiny of mankind changes in the
Reformation 'and this is indivisibly associated with the Thirty
Years' War'.[38] But finally it was the Promethean theme
which drew the poet, even if it presented him, now that he
was steeped in the thought of Kant, with an impossible tangle
of questions. Prometheus represented the sublime: 'Great is
he who overcomes the terrible. Sublime is he who, even when

---

[34] *Don Carlos* (last version) 4720.

[35] 'Feel . . . the desire to be God', 790. 'And today God is what man was
only yesterday', 950. 'His divinity lasts as long as his dream', 961. Philipp is
'a god' (2932); he presents himself to men as God (3114); he is a god at the
price of his uniqueness (3123); Posa challenges him to give up 'the unnatural
deification' (3205).

[36] 'The divine Mathilde', 560. Carlos' heart is a 'divine gift' 1833. The
Marquis dreams of 'the divine birth of friendship', 4279. The poet can also
speak of the 'divine appearance of virtue', 1937.

[37] Picc 2477–2479. 'Oh, you are blind with your seeing eyes!', WT 890.
Buttler in *Eger*: 'He is within, led by doom', WT 2428.

[38] To Körner, 28.11.1791 (III 170).

succumbing to it, does not fear it. Hercules was great, when he undertook and completed his twelve tasks. Prometheus was sublime when, though in chains in the Caucasus, he did not rue his deed nor confess transgression.'[39] And still more strongly: 'Tragedy does not make gods of us, for gods cannot suffer; it makes heroes of us, that is divine men, or, if you like, suffering gods, Titans. Prometheus, the hero of one of the most beautiful tragedies, is as it were a symbol of tragedy itself.'[40] And so Wallenstein is depicted thus even in his 'camp':

> He wanted to found a kingdom of soldiers,
> To set the world on fire,
> To dare and to attempt everything . . .[41]

> He has a ruler's soul
> And sits on a ruler's throne.[42]

Thus speaks Max. And Wallenstein himself, as he finally includes his guilt in the uncommon character of his life's form:

> Who calls fortune false? For me it was true
> And raised me from the ranks of men
> With love, bore me with a god's
> Strong arms through life's stages.
> There is nothing common in the ways of my fate,
> Nor in the furrows of my hand. Who could
> Read my life according to the ways of men?[43]

Who is speaking here? The deluded man directly before his death—or the poet? If in the first draft (September 1790–January 1791, concurrent with the develop of the historical work on the Thirty Years' War)[44] Wallenstein was only the ambitious strong man who seeks to avenge himself against the emperor for his demotion to Regensburg, later (1796), under the influence of Goethe, he will emerge at the

[39] *Vom Erhabenen.* 5, 502.
[40] *Tragödie und Komödie* (sketch from the posthumous works), 5, 502.
[41] WL 332–334.
[42] Picc 412–413.
[43] WT 3566f.
[44] 4, 365ff.

psychological level as the realist to balance the idealist, Max, and will finally be idealised (in the 'greatest crisis' of the following winter)[45] as the symbol of humanity as such:[46] who bears within himself his lost paradise (like Karl Moor) as his permanent measure of things. In this sense Max was a part of himself: 'for he stood beside me like my youth,/ he made reality into a dream for me'[47]—for whom of course the way back was open, but who stormed ahead, trusting to his 'star', acquiring guilt, but who, like Goethe's harpist and his Faust, can yet be saved, on the grounds of his dark longing, as *Thekla, a Spirit Voice* (1802) proclaims from the beyond:

> There too is the father, free of sin,
> Beyond the reach now of the bloody murder
> And he feels that he was deceived by no illusion
> When he gazed up at the stars . . .
> Dare to be wrong and to dream:
> Nobility of mind often lies in children's play.[48]

In a seemingly classical manner the blindness of Wallenstein, the consequence of his terrible traitor's guilt, is interpreted in a conciliatory way as 'madness'.[49] The astral world is also seemingly classical (as the epiphany of divinity), as is the destiny which it governs and which for Wallenstein is decisive. The stars are his *daimon*, and he sees the origins of the whole disorder of his betrayal in their macrocosmic order, and places himself on 'The spiritual ladders which rise up out

[45] To Goethe, 24.1.1797 (V 146).

[46] Thus in the *Prolog*, where art is to 'bring' Wallenstein's controversial figure 'nearer to your hearts in a human manner': 'Denn jedes Äusserste führt *sie*, die alles/ Begrenzt und bindet, zur Natur zurück,/ Sie sieht den Menschen in des Lebens Drang/ Und wälzt die grössre Hälfte seiner Schuld/ Den unglückseligen Gestirnen zu' (For all that is most extreme leads *her*, who limits and binds everything, back to nature; she sees man in the pressure of life and attributes the larger half of his guilt to the unhappy constellations); thus art elevates itself in a general manner above the ethical decision: 'nature' and 'constellations' (WL 106), cosmic harmony, is given the last word. We shall return to this theme immediately.

[47] WT 3445–3446.

[48] I, 460–461.

[49] WT 2559 and 2564, and in such a way that even in the case of the boy it was not certain 'whether madness or a god had spoken out of him'.

of this world of dust/ To the world of stars with a thousand rungs/ and along which the heavenly/ Powers wander up and down'[50]— not as clever as Faust, who keeps well clear of the macrocosmic world. And so Wallenstein justifies himself by the coincidence of his empirical person with his universal *daimon* and thus proves Terzky right, who wants to instil in him a good conscience:

> For every character is right who
> Is at one with themselves; there is
> No other wrong but self-contradiction.[51]

Wallenstein submits to this philosophy of the identity of guilt and innocence:

> What must be, must be.
> Destiny still possesses the right, for the heart
> In us is its imperious executor.[52]

He pretends to 'seek peace',[53] and to this end to strive for the 'whole', for the synthesis of Emperor and Swede and with this synthesis to embody the objective world-spirit.[54] It is for this reason that the philosophy of Max Piccolomini, which rests upon the 'tug of the heart' as truth,[55] finally fails with Wallenstein.[56] And the poet wants us to believe that the latter is a great power in the world:

[50] Picc 978f.

[51] WT 600–602.

[52] WT 654–656.

[53] WT 1950.

[54] 1976, Picc 1180f.

[55] 'Der Zug des Herzens ist des Schicksals Stimme' (the tug of the heart is the voice of destiny), Picc 1840. 'Dein Urteil kann sich irren, nicht mein Herz' (your judgment can err, but not my heart), 2547, *cf.* WT 1247. Against this, Octavio says: 'Hier gilts, mein Sohn, dem Kaiser wohl zu dienen,/ Das Herz mag dazu sprechen, was es will' (Here, my son, the important thing is to serve the emperor, no matter what the heart says about it), Picc 2460.

[56] WT 717–718: Max must 'make a decision . . . between you and my heart'. Ultimately he admits that his father is right: 'You have indeed spoken the truth, father,/ I trusted my own heart too much' (2283), and Thekla teaches him one final time to let his heart decide, to follow his 'first feeling', to do his duty' (2342): this makes the separation from the beloved, and from the house of Friedland irrevocable.

For this royal man, when he falls,
Will drag a world down with him.[57]

His evil deed must give birth to yet more evil,[58] and he treads
the happiness of his own people into the dust without
concern, as Max points out to him,[59] but this does not prove
the status of Wallenstein as world-spirit. And so it is not clear
what must finally happen and be proven, and what would
justify such a poetic venture. The lines crisscross and confuse
each other. We must put these questions to the philosophy
which Schiller at the same time pursues and with which he
struggles to ascertain the meaning of existence.

THE NEW INTERPRETATION OF THE SUBLIME. In a laborious,
essentially autodidactic struggle, the young Schiller achieves
an aesthetic credo which he expounds programmatically in
his great didactic poem *The Artists* (1789) and to which in
essence he still holds six years later in the *Letters on the Aesthetic
Education of Man*. Between these two points there occurs his
study of Kant with all its fruits, which extend from the lecture
on aesthetics (1790) to its further elaboration under the
growing influence of Kant (1791), to the *Callias Letters* (1792),
On the Sublime and *On the Pathetic*, and to his masterpiece *On
Grace and Dignity* (1793). The important supplement *On Naive
and Sentimental Poetry*, which first began to mature through
his relationship with Goethe, draws out more clearly the
historical and philosophical aspect which could already be seen
in *The Artists*. Kant, who with his aesthetic teaching is
received in his entirety, finds a place in a scheme of things
which is already present in the earlier sketches (1789): in these
the early enthusiastic and sceptical philosophies, the core of
the medical and the fruit of the historical studies, and finally
the encounter with antiquity had all coalesced into a unity.
Artistic beauty is reserved for man in a vertical universe: he
shares his labour with the animals and his knowledge with
the spirits.[60] But it is also the median point in the horizontal
development of history: between the crude condition of

[57] Picc 2638–2639.
[58] Picc 2451–2452.
[59] WT 2088–2090.
[60] *Die Künstler*, verses 30–34 (1, 174).

nature and the epoch of theory with its scientific analysis of nature. One year previously, *The Gods of Greece* had lamented the 'loss of gods' in the modern image of the world; divine beauty survives only in immortal song, but must perish in life.[61] In *The Artists*, on the other hand, the realm of the beautiful and the poet's office are presented as the comprehensive form even in the face of modernity. What is true historically, above all in relation to Greece:

> Only by passing through the morning gate of the
>   beautiful
> Shall you enter the land of knowledge—[62]

is true also today: man has his centre in the harmony between the elements. The medical writings had sought the same centre between Nature (body) and spirit, but now it is entrusted to the creativity of artists, who alone can incorporate into the material dimension the law of harmonious proportions: only when presented with a perfected form does the Spirit abstract from ends and desires. Through the beautiful it sees and contemplates truth disinterestedly and learns to love. *Only through art does the spirit become religious*, for artists are the first to project the values which are palpable to man into a divine image; they represent for him an ethical world-order in narrative and drama, and by the 'immortality' of their creations they even scale the 'prison wall' of mortal existence, discovering thereby immortality. Finally, human beauty must serve to express that of the gods.[63] The historical *kairos* of the beautiful (*The Gateway of Morning*) remains from now on the ontological centre, which is affected by every spiritual step forward:

> Advancing man bears art aloft
> Thankfully on raised pinions,
> And new worlds of beauty
> Spring forth from enriched Nature.[64]

---

[61] *Die Götter Griechenlands* 127–128 (1, 173).
[62] *Die Künstler* 34–35 (1, 174).
[63] *Ibid.*, 210–265 (1, 179–181).
[64] *Ibid.*, 270–284 (1, 181).

The laws of Nature which the scientist discovers are those of the aesthetic harmony which he already bears within himself; and so 'he lends the spheres his harmony': the latter hovers before him and lights his way in his search as the idea and ideal of a sacred fulfilment. He projects it to the end and bends his path towards it as explorer.[65] This is already that vision which will lead Schelling's early philosophy just a few years later to its final form: art as the inner fulfilment of science and philosophy, beauty as the eschatological ideal of the history of the world and of mankind:

> When his science, matured into beauty,
> Shall be ennobled as a world of art.[66]

The artists are told: 'The dignity of mankind has been put into your hands'; here everything, even moral value, is firstly embraced by 'beauty': as is religion itself. And this is so in Schiller in an emphatically anthropological sense. It is mortal man who 'with endearing deceit paints Elysium on the walls of his prison',[67] and 'brightens wretched life with the cheerful shadow-world of poetry'.[68] In the artistic act, man creates himself as man, leaving pure Nature behind, and thus establishes the harmony of the world which, with his incorporation of the universe into the world of spirits and of men, goes before him as an ideal.

The further Schiller goes, the clearer the premise for such an experience of the world becomes. Man is alone in the universe, and all myths and religions were his own projections.[69] Schiller likes to depict man in his finite condition: beleaguered and under attack, as in the *Knights of Malta*,[70] lonely and exposed to the threat of death as in the

[65] *Ibid.*, 292–293 (1, 182); 383–392 (1, 184).
[66] *Ibid.*, 404–405 (1, 185).
[67] *Ibid.*, 76–77 (1, 175).
[68] *Ibid.*, 339–340 (1, 183).
[69] Love 'likes to believe in gods, because love is divine. The beings of the ancient fables exist no more', and so the heart invents new names, new beings, which it projects into heaven: thus Max to Thekla, Picc 1634f. (2, 368).
[70] 3, 155–189.

Knight's Song,[71] risking all vaingloriously as in *The Diver* ('and plunges down to life or to death'),[72] also as an isolated community left to its own resources, as the sea dramas (*The Ship, The Pirates, Sea Drama*) were to depict,[73] doubly endangered in their passage through history which leads them slowly out of the protection of Nature, as in *The Walk*, leaving them to themselves and leading them into a place from which there is no escape:

> But where am I? The path is hidden. Precipitous depths
> Yawn behind me, and I must go on.
> I have left behind me the familiar accompaniment of the gardens and hedges,
> And every trace of human hands . . .
> It is wild here and fearfully barren. In the solitary sky
> There hangs only an eagle, linking the world and the clouds.[74]

The conciliatory ending with its reference to the comprehensiveness of Nature is both weak and false. Schiller's beauties and ideals flash in the middle of the night, and it is only the projections of the heart that light up and overwhelm this dark. *Tartarus* and *Elysium*, as eschatological possibilities, are just such projections.[75] But in *The Pilgrim*, who wanders in the hope that earthly beings 'would be divinely immortal there', it is finally understood that Heaven has no point of contact with the earth and 'There is never here'.[76] So everything hangs on the 'favour of the moment': 'all that is divine on earth/ is only a dream',

> So every beautiful gift
> Fades like the lightning flash,
> And is quickly enclosed again
> In night's dark grave.[77]

[71] WL conclusion (2, 309–311).

[72] 1, 373.

[73] Fragments: 3, 259–266.

[74] 1, 233.

[75] 1, 90; 1, 103.

[76] 1, 412–413.

[77] 1, 428–429.

Thus the moment is for Schiller not only what it was for Plato, or even for Goethe, which is to say the gracious confluence of the forces of Nature, but is the flash as beauty and Spirit—and in Spirit also as God—of that which remains night beyond man. Therefore there is the repeated statement that truth is terrible and is only endurable when it is clothed in beauty. This is the case in *The Words of Madness*,[78] in *Cassandra*,[79] in *The veiled Statue of Saïs*[80] and in *The Sayings of Confucius* ('The depths are bottomless . . . and truth dwells in the abyss').[81] In addition, there is the insight into the radical impermanence precisely of that which is the basis of all our hope for eternity: in *Nania* ('Even what is beautiful must die . . .')[82] and, in the form of a question, in *To Emma*.[83] The idea of the radical demythologisation and dedivinisation of the world endures to the last—and very clearly so in the poem *The Four Ages of the World*.[84] The ideal becomes real according to the measure of the strength of the human heart (*The Words of Madness*: 'It is *in* you, you bring it eternally out').[85] Significantly we find the symbol of 'Columbus', which anticipates Nietzsche: the coast *must* appear, because it is a projection of the spirit and is its goal.[86]

Before Schiller came into contact with Kant, therefore, he had already grasped the idea of the radical finitude of reason, the unknowability of things *an sich*, the unverifiability of ideas and ideals and also the aesthetic 'median force' between the animal and the spiritual parts of man. Even more, he had understood the vulnerability of man within the universe, and the absolute anthropocentrism of the world is for him the basis of the idea of the sublime: the human heart, that is, which, cast into the void, transcends itself as it ventures forth into an unfathomable reality. This heart is the sole glory. All

[78] I, 213–216.
[79] Verses 57–64 (I, 358).
[80] I, 224–226.
[81] I, 226–227.
[82] I, 242.
[83] I, 406.
[84] I, 417–419.
[85] I, 215–216.
[86] I, 247.

that Schiller learns from Kant, he assimilates into what he already possesses. His introduction through the *Critique of Judgment*, which depicts a third, mediating force between perception and intellect, will assist him in this. Initially Schiller is concerned—while preserving Kant's tension between beauty and sublimity—with emphasising the role of the aesthetic as the (higher) centre of man and of humanity: firstly in the Kantian sense as 'harmony' between Spirit and the senses (grace: *Anmut*), but then, going beyond Kant, as the harmony between the harmony of 'beauty' and the disharmony of 'sublimity' (dignity: *Würde*), and finally as the balance between the historically anticipated totality (of the Greeks) and the totality which is to be retrieved as a higher harmony by passing through the modern disharmony (in the 'aesthetic education'), or as the balance between the naive (Goethe) and the sentimental (Schiller). All four forms of balance are only variants of a single basic rule, which is made possible by the fact that the (Christian) rigour and 'sublimity' of the Kantian categorical imperative which, compelled by the 'radical evil' within man, always orientates the will beyond itself to a transcendent sense of duty (*Sollen*), is rejected in favour of a fundamentally achievable identity, a complete harmonisation of ethical man with himself, whereby in a radical anthropological reduction every apprehension of the theological dimension is made redundant. Here the spirit of Fichte is already present: between the absolute and the empirical subject there is no longer any analogical relationship (of God and creature), but identity in a state of tension. It is now possible to speak as a matter of course of 'our divine nature' as the site of freedom and of 'God in us' as the 'law-giver';[87] 'man bears incontrovertibly within himself in his personality the makings of divinity', while he possesses in his senses 'the path to divinity' within himself in infinite approximation:[88] the absolute point, where the Spirit and the senses bifurcate lies within man himself. The 'predisposition' in man to synthesis is God as Nature ('everything that

[87] AW 5, 483.
[88] EM 11; 5, 603.

wholesome nature does is divine');[89] but it is not the will of man alone (*voluntas ut natura*), but his 'moral will which makes him divine'.[90] Where moral freedom can attain harmony with sensible nature, it can at times even 'unfold an unlovely and oppressed form with divine glory'.[91]

The essay *On Grace and Dignity* attempts to shed some light precisely on this mystery of a harmony between the senses and reason (with its non-sensible ideas and imperatives). The body (in man and beast) has a technical perfection of nature for the purposes of life and spirit: this concerns the intellect and hence, for Kant, not the disinterested enjoyment of aesthetic taste. Being disinterested, the form can be of sensual beauty only when it is viewed as an architectonic structure. And it is only when moral freedom employs this naturally beautiful structure as its means of expression that *Anmut* (grace; harmony) results. But what is the form of the schematism between the two realms if man as a moral person must be capable of renouncing the whole of the sensual realm, and thus no overarching law (which would be natural) can embrace them both—and yet 'where moral sentiment finds satisfaction . . . the aesthetic sense will not be curtailed'?[92] The answer is: 'that the representation of interests and aims in man has turned out to be more beautiful than in other organic formations, is to be seen as an act of *grace* (*Gunst*), which reason, as legislator of the human structure, has shown to Nature as executor of its laws,'[93] a kind of grace or favour, that is, which Nature repays by allowing the Spirit to express itself harmoniously even in herself where, being moral, Spirit is bound to contradict sensuality. What is possible as *Grace*— the representation of the free person through a sense medium by playing with architectonic beauty—bridges even the potential 'contradiction' of the two spheres. And so it is true that 'grace is a form of favour which morality shows to the senses just as architectonic beauty can be considered the

[89] ND 5, 704.
[90] AW 5, 471.
[91] AW 5, 447.
[92] AW 5, 458.
[93] AW 5, 443–444.

consent of nature to its technical form'.[94] In this sense beauty is the 'citizen of two worlds'.[95] Schiller speaks at this critical point, which of course he believes to be governed by a 'law which we cannot fathom',[96] of 'liberality',[97] of 'indulgence'[98] and, naturally, time and again of 'play', where 'freedom governs beauty'[99] without abusing it, where the person takes the place of Nature, and assumes 'together with its rights a portion of its obligations'. It is here without doubt that the deepest mystery of Being for Schiller lies, for it now emerges as *charis*: at once grace, favour, beauty, elegance, felicity, mutual gratitude and enrichment: Pindar seems to be present again. One of Schiller's most beautiful poems, *Fortune*, takes *charis* as its theme: the gift of the beneficent gods, granted to their favourite 'before he has emerged victorious from his labours':

> I call that man great who, his own fashioner and
>   creator,
> Commands the Fates with force of virtue
> But cannot command fortune and, what Charis
> jealously denies him, labouring courage can never
>   win.
> A serious will can protect you from the unworthy,
> The all-highest, a gracious gift from the gods,
> As your beloved loves you, the heavenly gifts
>   descend,
> Grace reigns in Jupiter's realm above as it does in the
>   realm of Amor.

The gods, it continues, love youth but 'only the blind man has seen their glory'. And *charis* is raised above the gods themselves: 'felicity alone has crowned the god'. Grace and beauty are the highest things of all, and so

> Do not begrudge the beautiful its beauty or that,
>   undeserving,
> It is as replendent as the lily's calyx by Venus' gift,

[94] AW 5, 459.
[95] AW 5, 442.
[96] AW 5, 459.
[97] AW 5, 477.
[98] AW 5, 477.
[99] AW 5, 446.

> Let that be blessed which, as you gaze upon it, blesses
> you,
> And transports you by its unearned splendour.

So no one should envy the poet his art:

> Because he is blessed, you can be happy . . .
> Where there is no miracle, there can be no
> happiness.[100]

This highpoint in his understanding of the world is quite different from that of Kant. Schiller stands by the absolute character of the moral imperative; but why 'the imperative form', which 'accuses and humiliates mankind' and 'transforms the most potent expression of moral freedom into a more glorious kind of servility', and which imposes 'the appearance of an alien and positivistic law'?[101] The free person belongs to himself and to no one else. And further: Why the desire to view the ethical only in specific cases as a single absolute deed; is it not better on balance and in the long term to establish the ethical, if possible, rather within the context of the whole man (the Aristotelian *ethizesthai*) and to achieve the *habitus* of the good, the *virtus*: 'Virtue is nothing other than an inclination to duty'?[102] 'For the excellence of man does not at all consist in the greater sum of individual rigoristic and moral actions, but in the greater congruence of the whole of the natural structure with the moral law.'[103] Reconciliation is more than conquering the foe.[104] If the situation of 'sublimity' must reveal the 'great soul' and this situation is precisely the 'infallible touch stone' of the 'beautiful soul',[105] in which it is not 'grace' (*Anmut*) any more, but must prove its 'dignity', and we must show it 'respect' and not only the 'love' of 'benevolence',[106] then the

---

[100] 1, 240–241; cf. also *Das Geheimnis* 1, 404, *Die Gunst des Augenblicks* 1, 428–429.

[101] AW 5, 467.

[102] AW 5, 464.

[103] *Über den moralischen Nutzen ästhetischer Sitten* 5, 787. The entire essay is concerned with *ethizesthai*.

[104] AW 5, 465.

[105] AW 5, 474.

[106] AW 5, 482.

shades and degrees which Schiller erects between grace (*Anmut*) and dignity (*Würde*) show that he regards both as being the forms of play of the one single indivisible sensual-ethical human nature, in which (and nowhere else) the divine appears: both as the enchantment of *charis* and as majesty. Schiller reinterprets this too in anthropological terms: 'The highest degree of grace is the power to enchant; the highest degree of dignity is majesty'. This 'presents a law to us which obliges us to look within ourselves. In the presence of the god we cast our eyes to the floor, become oblivious of everything beyond ourselves and experience nothing but the heavy burden of our own existence. Only the holy possesses majesty. And if a man can represent this to us, then he possesses majesty; and our spirit will fall to the ground before him, even if our knees do not follow'.[107] A portrayal of this kind is quite alien to the spirit of antiquity and to that of Christianity.

In essence, the letters *On the Aesthetic Education of Man* add only the historical dimension to these insights, as this was already revealed in *The Artists* and as it remained normative for Idealist philosophy. It is a paradoxical work because it places a major objection at its centre, which it is scarcely possible to rebut. If the historical division into periods shows the passage of three epochs, which emerge clearly with the Greeks for instance: the archaic and mythic period in which the divine appears primarily as fearsome and 'sublime', followed by a classical and aesthetic age in which the world becomes familiar and is the object of a fearless contemplation (*theôria*) and the gods and their images are characterised by beauty, and finally by a post-classical, philosophical and abstract age in which the gods diminish,[108] then is it not the case that the age of beauty is merely a brief period of transition and in actuality the herald of the end of a truly strong and elevated culture? And can this law not be proven almost without exception: in Athens and Sparta, with the

[107] AW 5, 485–486; cf. *Über die notwendigen Grenzen beim Gebrauch schöner Formen* 5, 670.

[108] EM Letters 9 and 20f.; the division into periods is sketched out more clearly in NSD 5, 708f.

Romans, the Arabs, in Medici Florence and into the present? 'Indeed, it must be a cause for concern that in virtually every historical period in which the arts flourish and taste prevails, mankind is debased, and that there is scarcely a single example of a high degree and great profusion of aesthetic culture existing in a people which possesses both political freedom and bourgeois virtue, where *mores* are both beautiful and good and behaviour is both refined and honest'.[109]

This is an almost fatal objection for Schiller, who has to refrain from going back beyond the classical period of beauty to the world of living myth (when the gods were not only the serene projections of human ideals, but were also truly believed to be divine epiphanies), in order to find there, in authentic myth, to which the authentic Christian revelation in the later West corresponds, the provable source of the aesthetic. Schiller will nevertheless oppose the law which he himself as historian discovered and which as philosopher he must also acknowledge to be an empirical law ('perhaps experience is not the judgment seat before which a question such as this can be solved') and will pledge himself to prove by an *a priori* deduction of the essence of beauty (as the synthesis of man and thus of the world), that it *must*—despite history—be the central concept of all culture.[110] Man is and remains spirit-body, and a culture, which—be it religious, scientific or technological—strives away from the body and towards spirit must be his destruction. The interrelationship of these, anticipated by the Greeks in a way that has become paradigmatic, remains a guiding idea for every potential culture, according to which and in orientation to which mankind must be educated, if we are to be true to ourselves. The names of the poles vary: (the drive to) form and (the drive to) matter, structure (*Gestalt*) and life, state and action, state (*Zustand*) and object (*Gegenstand*), relaxation and tension; but we are concerned always with the same mystery of human wholeness, which remains ultimately the mystery of beauty, in the highest tension between grace (*Anmut*) and dignity (*Würde*). The artist projects this highest synthesis, as

[109] EM Letter 10; 5, 598f.
[110] EM Letter 10; 5, 600.

idea and ideal, into his concept of the god: form that is so dominant as to permeate matter utterly, matter that is so transformed that all sensual desire is banished and everything has become a representation of the Spirit which is the object of a pure and disinterested contemplation. The god is the exuberant and perfected form of man of which Schiller—with 'the glorious countenance' of the goddess in Goethe's reception room before his eyes—speaks with evident passion: 'It is neither grace nor dignity that speaks to us from the glorious countenance of a Juno Ludovisi; it is neither the one nor the other, because it is both at the same time. While the female deity demands our devotion, the god-like woman arouses our love; but even while we yield ourselves utterly to the divine loveliness, the divine self-sufficiency thrusts us back. The whole figure rests and remains within itself, an entirely closed creation, and it does so as if it were quite beyond space, neither yielding nor resisting: here there is no strength which ever fought with others' strength, no vulnerability where temporality could gain entrance. Irresistibly seized and drawn by the one, yet held at a distance by the other, we find ourselves both in a state of the highest stillness and in a state of the greatest movement, and that wonderful sensation is born for which the understanding can find no concept and language find no name.'[111] That which comes closest to this ideal in the human world is the *agôn*, the idea of which Schiller (anticipating Nietzsche) traces through different cultures as 'the ideal of the play instinct', which has assimilated gravity into itself.[112] When he depicts the aesthetic synthesis as *indifferentia*, as 'zero', but precisely thus as the prefiguration of the highest reality, he anticipates Schelling; but this formula gives him the possibility of seeing the human ideal as being both the youth of an individual person and as the historical past of human kind (Greek culture) in so far as this aesthetic *indifferentia* is the true point of departure for the realisation of the True and the Good,[113] and yet also to see it as the eschatological goal for the integration of all distinctions

[111] EM Letter 15; 5, 618–619.
[112] EM Letter 15; 617 and note.
[113] EM Letter 23; 5, 641–643.

in the comprehensive *indifferentia*.[114] Since the latter leading idea imposes law upon all endeavour, art also demands at first the ethical self-realisation of the artist: 'Nothing but that which is already a living deed within us, can become so outside us, and it is the same with creations of the spirit as it is with organic structures; the fruit proceeds only from the blossom.'[115] In his review of Bürger's poems, Schiller, who is clinical to the point of cruelty, highlights this lack of an ethical standpoint as the reason for their aesthetic deficiencies.[116]

On Naive and Sentimental Poetry wrestles with the same anxious question addressed to historical development: does the latter not move hopelessly away from an aesthetic culture to one that is abstract and technical, and does the orientation to antiquity or even our nostalgic love of Nature not remain pure and lifeless romanticism?[117] The reply can point to the miracle of Goethe and, next to him, to the endeavours, almost equal in status, of Schiller. In the one there is the naive attainment of a human totality, a creation from the gift of balance, from the *charis* of abundance; in the other there is a lively integration into the totality which serves as a leading idea. From the point of view of the historian, Schiller can favour the latter form. 'Nature makes him [man] one with himself, while art [i.e., culture] divides him so that he returns to unity through the ideal. But because the ideal is infinite, eternally beyond his reach, the cultivated man can never become perfect in *his* way ... And if we compare the different types with each other, then it appears that the goal which man through culture *strives for* is infinitely preferable to that which he *achieves* through nature',[118] because in infinite 'progress' the real integration of the True and the

---

[114] In this aspect, it will then be quite possible for Schiller—as in his polemical Horen essay against Fichte *Über die notwendigen Grenzen beim Gebrauch schöner Formen* (1795)—to characterise the sober, strictly material truth as the 'source of all true beauty' (5, 686) and thus to remove all playful dilettantism from his idea.

[115] *Über die notwendigen Grenzen*, etc., 5, 682.

[116] 5, 970f.

[117] NSD 5, 708f.

[118] NSD 5, 718.

Good of the total person occurs. Within the naive sphere there is 'the art of limitation' while in the sentimental we have 'the art of the Infinite'.[119] But since the latter too must speak in concrete images, Schiller planned an eschatological idyll,[120] in which the final deification of man was to be portrayed: 'The marriage of Hercules and Hebe would be the content of my idyll. The poet has no material beyond this, for he is not permitted to abandon human nature, and the idyll would deal precisely with this transformation of man into god. The chief figures would themselves be gods, but through Hercules I can bind them to humanity and introduce a sense of movement into the picture. If I succeeded with this undertaking, then I would hope to celebrate thereby the triumph of sentimental over naive poetry'.[121]

Hegel will raise man to the level of absolute spirit, whereby all aestheticism which depends upon the senses remains before the door of the Holy of Holies. But Schiller sees the aesthetic counterpart to the Christian eschatology of the resurrection of the flesh into God: not, however, as the miracle of the grace of the personal God, but as the miracle of the divine *charis* of man (who always has been divine). The sentimental poet leads us 'not backwards to our childhood ... but ... forwards to our coming-of-age' since he 'guides man, who can no longer return to Arcadia, as far as Elysium'.[122] Schiller's Titanic nature comes to the fore again here: man is to become God, not by the eradication of his finitude, but by retaining and transfiguring it. And if we ask what in all seriousness finitude means here, then its ultimately questionable character will emerge, as with Kant. Does this finitude (as beauty's small pool of light) contrast with an 'infinite' dark abyss (of 'truth')? Or is finitude itself the True, since the finite human figure has eschatologically integrated within itself all that is true and good?[123] The answer to this

---

[119] NSD 5, 719.

[120] The three forms of sentimental poetry as satire (distance from the ideal), elegy (alternation of attaining and distance) and idyll (attainment), and their deduction from the human capacity: see the note, 5, 744–46.

[121] To W. von Humboldt, 29.11.1795 (IV 338).

[122] NSD 5, 750.

[123] This must then be the meaning of the well-known verses (429–432)

question will determine whether Schiller's *kalon* is a
transcendental property of Being or not. Kant restricted the
latter to a harmony of the subjective powers; Schiller follows
him in this by making the beautiful the primal measure of
the human (for even the sublime does not vacate the sphere
of human proportions). Now is this primal measure also the
ultimate measure of Being? The origin of Schiller's thought
in Leibniz argues for this, as does the reduction of the infinite
process of the becoming of the world towards God to the
progress of mankind towards its highest (perhaps unattainable,
only approachable) idea,[124] and finally the provenance of the
ideal from the Greeks. Against this, on the other hand, is
Schiller's determined halt at Kant's *ignorabimus*, his refusal to
go the way of absolute Idealism, because he would thereby
be obliged to relativise the beloved finitude of spiritual-sensual
man and finally to abandon it altogether. Thus the inquiry
into Being and God is lost to sight, and the spotlight falls on
man actively involved in the *agôn* and in tragedy: on a being
who possesses ideals but not gods, on a being who possesses
its majesty and its glory within itself. Man has no need of
myth; he is his own myth. And as such, face to face with the
Greek hero, Schiller now leads him on to the stage.

THE REMAINDER OF THE SUM. If beauty is supremely *charis*,
favour and grace, then Schiller is honest enough to pose the
question whom man must thank for this grace which comes
to him unhoped-for and undeserved. The answer is an
incomprehensible universalising principle which, despite the
whole philosophy of Spirit, the philosophical texts
unashamedly call 'Nature' and which, in the action of the
dramas, receives the name 'Fate'. What is the source of this
category which forces its way into an Idealism of freedom?
What are the stars to which Wallenstein entrusts himself?
Above all, what is the inherited curse, unstoppable in its
effects, which forms the tragedy *The Bride of Messina*?

---

in the *Künstler*, that man 'at last, at the mature goal of the ages' will creep
'poor in the truth', 1, 186.
   [124] 'Through ever purer forms, purer tones,/ through ever higher heights
and ever more beauteous beauties': *Die Künstler*, verses 426–427; 1, 185.

'Nature' as sensation obeys the Spirit, although it does not include this (as it does in Goethe or Heidegger, for whom Nature as *physis* represents something quite different). Fate in Schiller can be interpreted only in one way: it is the *form of degeneration*[125] of the mythical and theological reality which determines the existential drama of antiquity. But while the fearsomeness of fate in the classical period together with the obscure guilt which went with it led ultimately to praise of the god, whose glory is affirmed even in what is terrible (and hideous), in Schiller it is man who, in suffering the terrible, makes of it something which is both beautiful and sublime. 'We call an object sublime, the idea of which makes our sensual nature perceive its own limits and our rational nature its superiority, its freedom from limits'.[126] But then man owes the transformation of the fearsome into something sublime not to the glory of the gods but to the glory which he himself possesses. In the *Bride of Messina* oracles become necessary, as in the *Oedipus*,[127] prophecies are made, and the Euripidean curse against the gods and their utterances is spoken by the mouth of the unfortunate princess.[128] And further: the world of the divine is addressed as a person, and is so either in a Christian way—Maria is the 'high Queen of Heaven',[129] she is 'divine',[130] the action takes place between 'monasteries', 'churches', 'high masses', 'requiems', 'pilgrimages'[131]—or in a classical manner as 'gods',[132] a

---

[125] This becomes completely clearly in the follies of the so-called 'dramas of fate' which imitate *Die Braut von Messina*.

[126] *Von Erhabenen* 5, 489; 'All that is sublime comes *only* from the reason' (*Über das Pathetische*, 5, 517). Schiller knows no other concept, in all the variations of the conceptual breadth, than this purely anthropological concept. On the theme: Karl Viëtor, 'Die Idee des Erhabenen in der deutschen Literatur' in: *Geist und Form*, Berne 1952. E. Cassirer, 'Die Methodik des Idealismus in Schillers philosophischen Schriften', in: *Idee und Gestalt*, Berlin 1921.

[127] 'The oracle has a share in the tragedy that is quite incapable of being replaced by anything else': to Goethe, 2.10.1797 (V 271).

[128] *Die Braut von Messina*, 2327–2397 (2, 896–898).

[129] *Ibid.*, 294.

[130] *Ibid.*, 1077.

[131] *Ibid.*, 721, 2618f., 2709f., etc.

[132] *Ibid.*, 2386, 2396, 2508, etc.

suspect *indifferentia*. What is more important is that the mother, who steps before her temporarily reconciled sons, can describe the picture set up for all to see as 'beautiful', 'glorious', 'divine'; that her dead sons can be described as 'gods';[133] that Don Cesar understands his necessary expiation for fratricide to be an act which he alone can perform and which necessarily demands his life.

> Bloody murder is expiated only by blood . . .
> Only free death breaks destiny's chains . . .
> I pay for my guilt first to the gods of death,
> Let another god care for the living . . .
> Honour the head of the luckless one,
> Which is sacred even to the gods . . .[134]

We cannot guess at the meaning of the words 'God', 'gods' and 'divine' here, since there is no longer any distinction between man and God; nor indeed what that Fate is which distinct from men reigns obscurely for itself alone. We may presume that, as in *Wallenstein*, it is first and foremost a projection into the universe of human grandeur and guilt.

The anthropocentrism of *Mary Stuart* and *The Maid of Orléans* is more evident. Although the Christian atmosphere is even more pervasive here, it remains throughout no more than that, an atmosphere which surrounds a Kantian, even a super-Kantian problem. Mary acknowledges her previous guilt,[135] though she denies the ostensible grounds for her being held in captivity,[136] and by rising above herself, after her meeting with Elizabeth and her condemnation, she becomes united within herself and finds that she is able to accept the unjust as a higher form of justice and that 'she will die as a queen and a heroine'.[137] In her death she forgives Elizabeth,[138] as Ferdinand in his death had offered his murderous father his hand. The Catholic sacramental decor

---

[133] Don Cesar to his mother: 'Flee to our grave/ and cry to the divinity of your son,/ for then we are gods and hear you', 2759–2761.

[134] *ibid.*, 2637f.

[135] *Maria Stuart*, 271f.

[136] *Ibid.*, 863f.

[137] *Ibid.*, 3380.

[138] *Ibid.* 3781f.

with confession, Eucharist ('blood'), and crucifix remains metaphor in the realm of the senses for 'sublimity', and all the more so in that Mortimer had allowed himself to be converted to Catholicism in Rome through this decor and had been initiated into Jesuitical sophistry in France. The maid of Orléans remains a purely Kantian saint, who can be God's emissary and the one favoured by Him for as long as she remains united with herself, or can live in her pure ideality; she loses her Platonic identity with herself through a single sensual glance, although she can return to her original 'sanctity' by a process of self-purification through penance and renunciation.[139] This time there is much talk of 'glory': Johanna has seen 'the glory of Heaven';[140] 'The king himself with his crown/ Is no more radiant than you',[141] she has 'perfected all this glory',[142] on coronation day her sisters see her 'in glory',[143] and Margot says to her: 'We come to see your glory',[144] and the king asks her: 'Show yourself in your form of light,/ As Heaven sees you and we in dust/ Honour you devoutly'.[145] But Schiller calls the play 'a romantic tragedy', and the religious clothing together with the miraculous element is again nothing but a folkloristic form of symbolism for the inner action, to which chivalry, sheep-rearing,[146] and the Amazons also belong, as well as speeches about the gods.[147] What is essential is that Johanna is permitted to wear without guilt the avenging sword of God which Karl Moor bore, as long as she 'casts all around the glory of Heaven',[148] as long as she performs His task 'as a

---

[139] The poem *Das Mädchen von Orléans* gives the key to the drama: 1, 460–468.

[140] *Die Jungfrau von Orléans*, 2633.

[141] Ibid., 2666–2667.

[142] Ibid., 2534.

[143] Ibid., 2804.

[144] Ibid., 2880.

[145] Ibid., 1967–2969.

[146] Ibid. I, 2nd scene.

[147] 'Child of the gods', 'voice of the gods', 'gods of death', 'without the gods there falls no hair from man's head', the comparison of Johanna with the 'severe Pallas' etc.

[148] Ibid., 2252.

blind tool of God' and 'with blind eyes',[149] and remains the pure transmitter of divine revelation and action. The Amazonian virginity which is essential for this lacks all the humanity which characterises the Christian and Marian element—as the precondition of motherhood. The frosty air of the Kantian-Fichtean absolute formal Self surrounds her. Thus, unassailed by the 'sinful flames of vain earthly delight',[150] as 'a goddess of war'[151] and 'a woman warrior of the highest God',[152] she can wield the 'avenging sword of my God'.[153] By renouncing earthly love, which tempts her for only a moment, she, who 'has seen the immortal one with her own eyes',[154] can retreat through the experience of divine abandonment into her own ideality,[55] thus becoming united with herself and, like Samson when he was blind and bound, break her fetters[156] and, through her own destruction, conquer for herself and for France, with the result that she is proclaimed a saint already by the king.[157] Rarely has there been a greater distortion of Christian sanctity than here, where the word, which in Christian terms expresses our participation in God's own sanctity, becomes the expression of moral self-sanctification.

Meanwhile, there is a counter-motif which is palpable through the whole of his literary work and which draws Schiller into a close proximity to Christianity. This is the motif of *obedience* which, at least in its dramatic representation, must appear not as obedience to self (of the empirical to the intelligible self), but as interpersonal, truly committed obedience, and which thus contains within itself secretly or openly a point of unconditional love. This motif must have

[149] *Ibid.*, 2578–2579.
[150] *Ibid.*, 412.
[151] *Ibid.*, 956.
[152] *Ibid.*, 2203.
[153] *Ibid.*, 2257.
[154] *Ibid.*, 3191.
[155] *Ibid.*, V, 6th scene.
[156] *Ibid.*, 3470f.
[157] *Ibid.*, 3523.

taken root deep in the poet's soul, if even the drill of the hated military academy could not assail it. It is, corresponding to the amphiboly in the notion of the 'great personality', either a blind devotion to the strong, or the unconditional offering of self to the ideal commandment. Thus its sources lie just as much in the enthusiasm of love and friendship (in the Enlightenment 'Theosophy') as they do in Kant's Prussian categorical concept of duty. Karl Moor demands absolute obedience; 'Who hesitates when I issue a command?'[158] This is even more true of Franz Moor: 'With your blind obedience!'[159] And also Wallenstein:

'The deed is mute, obedience is blind,
These are his very words'.[160]

And his words to Illo: 'They must give me words, in an oath, written down/ that they will devote themselves to my service, unconditionally'.[161] And to Max:

'Duty to whom? Who are you?
If *I* do the emperor a wrong, then it is
My wrong and not yours. Are you
Your own possession? . . .
You are rooted in *me*, I am your emperor'.[162]

Gordon says to Buttler: 'We subalterns have no will', to which Buttler replies: 'But the narrow way of duty is sure'.[163] Formal ethics can cover both elements in these cases: the demonically evil and the objectively justified. Johanna's 'blind obedience' to the 'God' who wishes to work through her also remains formal. The pseudo-Catholic obedience of Mortimer and Philip to the Grand Inquisitor is formal and demonic, not to mention the secret order in *The Man who saw Ghosts*. The situation is different concerning the motifs of *The Knights of Malta*, where Christian themes predominate over the Kantian ideology. Two motifs interprenetrate each

[158] *Die Räuber* II, 3.
[159] *Ibid.*, IV, 2.
[160] WL 340–341.
[161] Picc 897f.
[162] WT 2178–2183.
[163] WT 2507, 2515.

other: the commitment to a religious idea which extends as far as the total obedience of the professed religious—a self-offering of which an ideal love is an essential part—and the devotion of a friend for a friend, as real love and at the same time as ideal imitation. This unconditioned love between friends may take on homoerotic traits in the *The Knights of Malta* (Schiller consciously wanted to introduce a Greek motif, including in this drama the Greek choir), characteristics which are absent from *Don Carlos* or from *The Pledge*, where we find only a pure representative death for love ('Now he will be nailed to the cross').[164] And that obedience which is mediated through that incomparable fatherliness of a spiritual superior, which is glorified in the 'battle with the dragon', can be truly understood only in a Christian way, as Schiller expresses it in the final lines, and almost solemnly confirms in the poem *The Knights of Malta* quoted above. Yet it is not the *Knights of Malta* drama which was performed, but *Wallenstein*, and then the series of dramas in which formalism penetrates the artistic element like mildew. The *Mary Stuart* is good though coldly calculated theatre; the *Maid of Orléans* borders on kitsch, the *Bride of Messina* is hollow and unconvincing; *William Tell* is shallow despite all its pure inspiration and *Demetrius* is only another variant on the *Maid* (like the planned *Perkin Warbeck*): that is to say, only man united within himself can act 'divinely'.

Schiller, the educator of the people, driven by his own dialectic and in contradiction to all his traditional drapery (be it classical or Christian), places man on his own without remainder: as a finite spark of beauty without a containing shelter. In this he is ahead of his time, which however will not hesitate to grasp the premises of his vision and to draw the consequences from it.

2. FICHTE

While Kant and Schiller stop short at the finiteness of the human spirit in a way that might be judged to be more

---

[164] *Die Bürgschaft* 98 (1, 355).

'modern', the three Titans Fichte, Schelling and Hegel want to conceive of man within the wholeness of the Absolute, as its centre. This expressly demands that all philosophy, above all that of antiquity, should be fulfilled and transcended through the philosophical appropriation of the Christian revelation. If the starting point for Fichte is the principle of the self, as perfect free self-possession in action, this is a demonstrably Christian point of departure. It is in the Bible that for the first time God becomes 'I' and man His 'Thou', and a πρᾶξις πράξεως is opposed to the Aristotelian νόησις νοήσεως. But since it is a question of philosophy and knowledge and not of theology and faith, there can be no distinction between 'Nature' and 'Grace' (in the theological sense): the historical (biblical) revelation of God coincides with the revelation of Being, and so the finite becomes the revelation of the infinite, God and world together construct—once again—the totality of simple and complex Being, which in aesthetic terms is that total work of art in which God is the 'light' and the world the 'form', in which God is the life and the world the structure. The categories of artistic (secular) aesthetics is also the prime source, especially in Schelling and Hegel, for the language of metaphysics. The world is the 'expression' of God. But Idealism remains a reading of Kant: it is not objective world-systems which are the focus of attention (as in Erigena or Spinoza), rather, the totality needs to be developed from the transcendental art-structure of the thinking and acting subject. In terms of method this act must remain the principle and the fulcrum; in so far as it is the Absolute in its depths, or in so far as it implies and envisages it, the Absolute is relevant; and this remains true even when it opens itself to thought in revelation. The 'retreat to the man as the centre' is in no way retracted; for the first time it is 'Titanically' pressed home, and is so with an appeal to Christianity as the point of the turning of the world to subjectivity. But this means that even when the idealist systems are at their closest to Plotinus (as the final figure of the classical age), the situation with regard to the open and Advent-like decision, which predominates in Plotinus, does not return; rather, everything is finally decided through the determination to conceive Christianity (in a post-Christian manner) as pure philosophy and ultimately as the potentiality of man, history and culture. Even the (much weaker) opportunity for decision in Nicolas of Cusa (conjecture or absolute knowledge?) is now clearly decided in favour of the latter. The die is cast. It is true that Schleiermacher, who in the spring of 1802 heard Fichte lecture on his philosophy of the absolute sense of dependency, will similarly attempt to interpret this teaching in Christian terms, as Augustine aimed to deepen the teaching of Plotinus by christianising it; but the point of departure for both remains quite distinct, for in Plotinus the decision has not been made (or not clearly so) for the 'living God' of the Bible, while Fichte passionately rejects precisely this form of aliveness. No Christian school of thought, be it Protestant or Catholic (Maréchal, for instance, and his followers), will in the long run be able to resist the strength and the pull of the fundamental acts of decision in the three idealist systems when they 'engage' with the latter in order to effect a dialogue with them. Neither can we be deceived by the fact that, compared with the philosophy of Spirit of the Enlightenment, we find in all the Idealists a feeling for the dimensions of negative theology: God cannot be reduced to an object and yet is precisely as such (*pace* Kant) the One who manifests Himself in the world: does not this draw very close to Plotinus, Erigena and Nicolas of Cusa? But philosophical necessity binds God and his revelation, man, one to the other. Man is himself the manifest God, and therefore these titanic cathedrals must always lack what is decisive in Christianity, although they have absorbed all else from it: viz., that which is called in the Bible 'glory'. Being, God, is ultimately overcome. The Old Testament, which is the site of emergent glory, is rejected in favour of the Johannine final form of the New Testament, disassociated from Paul and the synoptics, in order to be able to reinterpret *agape* directly and freely in the direction of *gnosis*. 'Glory' stands and falls with the unsurpassability of the *analogia entis*, the ever greater dissimilarity to God no matter how great the similarity to Him (Denz.-Schönm. 806). In so far as German Idealism begins with the *identitas entis*, the way back to Christianity is blocked; it cannot produce an aesthetics of 'glory' but only one of 'beauty': and the 'aesthetics as science', which was rampant in the nineteenth century, is its fruit.

Fichte's[1] point of departure is the self which, in the appropriation of its freedom (in its sense of duty) is self-possession (autonomy) and self-contemplation. Thus Fichte radicalises the point of perception and the autonomy which we find in Kant, beyond that the *cogito* of Descartes and beyond that still, though unknown to him, the speculative project of Eckhart.[2] This project, as we stated above, would have been impossible in the classical period, since it presupposes Christianity, not only because the Absolute appears as a self (*ego*) but also because it is not eros (longing) but duty (the will of the Absolute) which determines the autonomous point of freedom. This is a descendant of the 'metaphysics of the saints' and it concentrates the classical ethic of Being (which is distributed through the hierarchical universe, as its immanent order) in an indivisible personhood: man is he who knows and can perform the very will of God.

But if we enquire who that self is which is identical with itself and which serves as Fichte's point of departure, then we shall have to reply: it is neither God nor man. It is not God because it stands beyond every form of reflection which presupposes a non-self and every form of self-appropriation of freedom which presupposes an obligation, and thus cannot ever be conceived of under the motif of self-consciousness or personality. But neither is it man, for he is always finite consciousness of self, never pure itself, to which the philosopher only attains 'by drawing a conclusion',[3] as to 'the basis of all experience'.[4] 'The form of selfhood, reflexive action, lies solely in the self as intellectual perception . . . The

---

[1] Collected works, ed. J. H. Fichte, Berlin 1845f., 8 Vols. (textual form following the edition by Medikus, Leipzig 1908, 8 Vols.). *Cf.* my *Apokalypse der deutschen Seele*, I (1937), pp. 158–203.

[2] *Cf.* above, pp. 000, and note 117.

[3] 2nd introduction to the *Wissenschaftslehre*, I 464.

[4] 1st introduction to the *Wissenschaftslehre*, I 423.

self exists in this form only for the philosopher':[5] a point
necessarily constructed in such a way that a progression is
possible from it as pre-supposition to a real consciousness of
self. In order to possess reality, it requires the world as that
opposing (through the creative powers of the imagination)
non-self, which permits it to achieve self-consciousness through
reflection on itself and freedom through action. And in so far
as this process must always continue in order that
consciousness and freedom should emerge through what is
opposite, the scheme of the pure self remains only at the level
of the 'idea'.

This accounts for the simple *aporia*: how can something
which is not real make the real world a prior premise of
consciousness in order that it should attain self-realisation in
its process? There is no possibility of an appeal here to God as
primal reality, since He is neither a person (and cannot
therefore be Creator), nor—for the young Fichte—does He
attain reality other than through the eschatological 'synthesis
of the world of spirits'. In order to attempt a solution to this
aporia one could say that the world in Idealism is not real in
the sense of a reality which is independent of the Spirit, but
that it is pure appearance from the Spirit and for the Spirit.
Then the difference between unreal and real is reduced to the
inner vitalisation and filling out of an initially hollow idea,
and our manner of thought will then be utterly oblivious of
Being as mere 'essences' or 'concepts' turn into a single
totalising concept. This kind of thinking has predominated
since Descartes, Leibniz and Malebranche: for at least the
(external) world was reduced to mere 'appearance' in the
presence of the Spirit, just as it was for the Empiricists, and
became mere 'material' whereby the Spirit, through
projecting itself and conceiving of itself and acting in a
practical and a technical way, raised itself above the world.
This way of overcoming materialism (*cf.* Hobbes), whereby
matter is either ignored or denied and the 'manifestations' are
then handled as the material of the Spirit, profoundly
influences Fichte and makes him a father of the modern

---

[5] 2nd introduction, I 516. 'In the act thus described, the ego is . . .
transposed into the possibility of self-awareness': I 459.

technical work ethos and of 'domination over the world'. For such an external world is no longer one that God created and thus is *in no way theophanous any longer*, but is only the inner dimension of the self (as it were its entrails) and consequently stands utterly at its disposal: in order to be dominated and subjected. This does not stop Fichte from somehow interpreting the world (as genesis of consciousness) in organic and teleological terms, thus approaching Goethe. But still it is oppositions which predominate: if for Goethe *physis* (with the mystery of God in its depths) remains the comprehensive principle of finite consciousness, then for Fichte it is solely the Spirit (with the mystery of God in its depths) which comprehends all *physis*. It should be noted however that that ethos of the domination of Nature—with which Fichte's entire cultural ethics is linked—remains bound to the presupposition that it is the (absolute) self which imagines Nature for the sake of man (for it is not God who does this) and thus grants him complete power over Nature, so that in this respect Idealism and materialism lead to the same ethos. But it is precisely this presupposition which is problematical.[6]

The young Fichte, who begins with the absolute point of the self, cannot conceive of God above this point (because there can be nothing beyond identity), nor beneath it, because God certainly cannot be placed beneath the concrete, and so he can be conceived only within it, as the convergence point of man's infinite approximation, or rather that of the spirit world together with its necessary morality, for which in Kant and Schiller the individual has to commit his or her entire existence even, if necessary, to the point of the ultimate sacrifice: 'That living and effective moral order is itself God'.[7] When Fichte said by way of explanation that this order is 'absolutely the first kind of objective knowledge', and beyond

[6] On this problema, see my review of Karl Rahner's *Geist in Welt* (*Z. kath. Theol.* 63, 1939, pp. 371–379); Rahner, with Fichte and Maréchal, thinks from the standpoint of the same problem, naturally with the presupposition of a creating God. But even so, one must ask who is ultimately the creator of nature.

[7] *Über den Grund unseres Glaubens an eine göttliche Weltregierung*, V 186.

this that to capture the Absolute in a single concept (such as 'personality' or 'consciousness') is contradictory ('and how could the finite grasp and comprehend the infinite?'),[8] then it was this statement which sparked off the 'atheism conflict', on account of which Fichte lost his chair in Jena and which forced him to revise his fundamental position, although without abandoning it entirely. The result was that the form of seity, which was the basis of all consciousness of self and of the world, found itself dependent for its completion on a base which Fichte now calls 'Being', 'Life' and 'Light', and whose (supra-)reality is again understood best in practical terms: when man takes hold freely of his eternal determination (both personally and in the community of selves) and becomes himself, then that supra-reality is that whereby he is determined in his own determination and is called to his own vocation.

How are we to understand such an idea? The 'metaphysics of the saints' had interpreted the act of reason precisely as this correspondence to the call of God and demanded detachment (*indifferentia*) as its transcendental premise. But who in Fichte's world can call out in such a way that the finite person can know himself to be determined by this call and to be able to take hold of it in total obedience? How can that which is beyond language and beyond all seity possess within itself the ground for the differentiation of the calls? For the differentiations of personal vocations in the 'world of spirits' may not and cannot be determined from below, from the concrete world (*individuum ratione materiae*). Thus the Christian expression 'vocation' and 'summons' are to be taken metaphorically, and their relation shifts definitively towards Plotinus: God as the super-spiritual, super-vital and pure mystery (called 'Being'), and Spirit as the act-perception which emerges from this ground, which strives in eternal movement (longing) from into this ground and, for the sake of this movement, releases the concrete world from itself. The sole essential difference with regard to Plotinus is the fact that the ancient thinker does not go beyond the contemplative

[8] *Ibid.*, 187.

description of the powers—albeit in a kind of deduction and reduction—while the modern thinker conceives of the process—in a way that corresponds to Christian historicity—as evolution (of the self from the universe, which in turn presupposes the principle of self) and as revolution without end: the ever fuller awareness of God in the world and the ever greater self-giving of the world in God.

The view that God is the Unknown, who defies reduction to any concept and who is mysterious even and above all in His creation and revelation, has been the substance of all significant forms of Western metaphysics; and it is unworthy of a Fichte to fancy that he can refute this idea of God through the wholly shallow (really objectified) deistic concept of God which we find in the Enlightenment. The choice of two possibilities characteristic of Western thought did not, as Fichte thought, mean Spinozean fatalism or the Kantian doctrine of freedom, for Augustine and Dionysius implanted by way of explanation the more profound idea of the God of the Bible into the classical notion of God in all above all. Nicolas of Cusa too held firmly to the non-polarity of God and thus to His non-objectification even in the context of the biblical God-world relation; and thus the elevation of the living God of the Scripture with his elevated freedom of love over the God of Plato and Plotinus could in no way threaten His absolute, His all-transcending and all-comprehending nature, but could only enhance it. For only now was every kind of divine dependency upon his appearances both in the world and in the realm of spirits definitively denied, and the sublime light of mystery of the ineffable One becomes the glory of the unapproachably holy God who reaches down to us out of love. If we choose to have nothing to do with this elevation through Christianity (which implies the freedom of the creation), then the *nous*, which is now called the form of the self, or reason or freedom, again becomes the 'necessary' revelation of the One, so that the One forms the Absolute in its greatest possible revelation only in cooperation with the self—in their original identity. In other words: christology becomes the inner form of the philosophical theory of 'creation' (and will necessarily remain so even with Schelling and Hegel). Thus what began with Eckhart has become definitive: the assimilation of the God-man relation back into the inner-divine generation process, which as such is called upon to give formal expression to the God–world relation, or to the schematism of philosophy. Christ is only our elder brother, and we are all capable by virtue of our human nature of standing in his place. But it is Jesus who has the merit of first illustrating this principle within the historical process and of bringing it to the point of breakthrough, which is why 'all intelligent people bow deep before him, and everyone, the more they are themselves, will acknowledge all the more humbly the exceeding glory of this great phenomenon'.[9] The truly glorious aspect of what Christ has shown is the place of human freedom as the expression of the ineffable mystery of Being as love. Love, that is, because the form of the self experiences itself as pure grace in so far as it perceives itself as 'freedom' which has emerged from Being and stands as *Dasein* (existence) before Being, and thus can pay back its debt only by the return of its freedom to Being. Thus Fichte becomes a link between Ignatius and Heidegger. Reflection (Spirit) is accompanied by the sense of indebtedness, 'and since it is a bond', it is 'love', 'and since it is the bond of pure Being and of reflection, it is the love of God. In this love Being and *Dasein*, God and man, are one, wholly fused'. 'Thus alternating love, which is neither his nor ours, but which first divides us into two and binds us into one' is the origin of a concept of God. 'What is it then that leads us beyond all recognisable and specific existence, and beyond the whole world of absolute reflection? It is our love which no specific existence can satisfy.' It does not desire God as object, and leaves Him nothing 'but pure negation of all comprehensibility, side by side with the eternal condition of being loved'.[10] But this statement, since it is not analogy but identity which is the point of departure, necessarily becomes dialectical: first of all God was absorbed into the pure self (first phase, which lasts to around the year 1800), then the self (*Dasein*) is reduced to a pure and empty space in God, even to the extent of sacrificing personal immortality.

[9] *Die Anweisung zum seligen Leben*, 6th lecture, V 485.
[10] *Ibid.*, 10th lecture, V 540.

Quite clearly the veil lifts from you,
It is your Self; let die what can be destroyed
And then only God will live in your striving.
Penetrate with your gaze what survives this struggle,
Then you will see the veil as a veil,
And unveiled you will see the life that is divine.[11]

There can be no doubt about it: where Fichte's teaching is pantheistic, because 'God and man act as vital life' and 'form',[12] we can, as with Hölderlin, suddenly discern—in the middle of the lecture—an authentic note of Christian love and prayer within the existential realm through the dialectic between the finite and the infinite. 'Simplicity, which is child-like and devoted to you, seizes you best . . . You are a father to her, who always means her well . . . Do with me what you will, she says, I know that it will be good, as long as it is certain that you are the one who does it. Brooding reason, which has only heard of you and never seen you, wishes to teach us of your essence in itself . . . I veil my face before you and place my hand on my mouth . . . You differ from the finite not in degree but in kind . . . But your relations with me, the finite, are open to my eyes: let me become what I should be!—and they surround me in a clarity that is brighter than the consciousness of my duty . . . You *know* and recognise the substance of my thought and desire . . . You *desire*, for you desire that my free obedience should have consequences in all eternity . . . But *you* are not a being which I shall be able to conceive throughout all eternity.'[13] And if this dialectic ought really to destroy man, since on the one hand he is, as freedom and act, the necessary 'form' of God and, on the other, he transcends himself in orientation towards God as knowledge of the unknowable, then this dialectic between titanic act and devout contemplation finally undergoes a Christian transfiguration in the thought of a stilled, almost unconscious activity which arises from the ecstatic gazing of the one who has been sent upon the source of his calling. It is in this paradox that for Fichte the heart of

[11] Sonnet VIII 642.
[12] *Anweisung*, 4th lecture, V 454.
[13] *Die Bestimmung des Menschen*, 3rd Book, II 304–305.

the ethical lies, and here too, although he speaks of it rarely, is the aesthetic dimension, which has a distinctly Plotinian tone:

'Think, for instance, of a holy woman, who, raised up to the clouds, borne aloft by heavenly hosts, who gaze at her enraptured, surrounded by all the radiance of Heaven, whose highest ornament and bliss she herself is, who, alone of all, can observe nothing of what happens about her, being wholly taken up and dissolved in a Single Thought: I am the handmaid of the Lord, let it be to me always according to His will; and if you form this Single Thought in these surroundings into a human body, then without doubt you possess beauty in a specific form. Now what is it that makes this form beautiful? Is it its members and parts? Or is it not rather the Single Thought which is diffused throughout all these members?'[14] The ultimate pathos of Fichte is not so much to be the 'possessor of the idea'[15] as 'being seized by the idea';[16] this too is why he sees the 'vocation of the scholar' for the contemporary scientific age as descending from the vocation of the prophets and great artists of an earlier, mythological period.[17] the affinity with the enthusiasm of Shaftesbury is evident, even if it is wholly transposed into the Kantian mode: firstly, because here the ethical becomes the yardstick of man and of his religion, and secondly, because, in consequence of this, the ethical lies absolutely and indivisibly in the love of the good for its own sake. It is a form of Plotinian thought enlightened in the direction of John (or of Augustine too at his purest). This deep piety of Fichte is classical and Christian, and it shines victoriously through his whole idealist form of thought.

But the logic of this form of thought thrusts further: if the self is absolute act and absolute knowledge, and yet possesses an indomitable Being as its 'base', then does not God Himself, in so far as He is conceived of as Spirit, possess an obscure

[14] *Anweisung*, 9th lecture, V 527.

[15] *Über das Wesen des Gelehrten*, VI 353.

[16] *Ibid.*, 355, 382, 423.

[17] *Berliner Vorlesungen über die Bestimmung des Gelehrten* (1811), Vol. III of the posthumous works (1835), pp. 167f.

base from which He emerges? And would this obscure base of all beings and all forms of sensory life not perhaps be the Void, the unconscious Nirvana, and would the things which emerge from it constitute the beautiful, but only as the tragic, which must eliminate and transcend itself (*aufheben*)? How easy a task it is to interpret Fichte in terms of Schopenhauer, for whom there is no longer any glory and for whom in the last instance beauty can lie only in contradiction and in self-elimination!

It was Schelling who bore Fichte's idea of the irrational base through all the transformations of his own thought. The philosophical perspective thus changes from a 'prophetic' one into one that is 'sibylline': it becomes a gazing into the abyss.

3. SCHELLING

The point of identity as point of departure determines everything in Schelling even up to his late period: the point at which the self (as subject) posits itself in the primal act and thus comes to know itself (as object). Here it is 'established that the essence of man consists only in absolute freedom, that man is not a thing nor, in his own being, an object'.[1] He is (as the title of his first book has it) *unbe-dingt* (unreified, unconditioned) which means to say that which 'cannot be turned into a thing . . . certainly cannot be thought of as a thing'.[2] Consciousness coincides with being: 'The self is not conceivable without at the same time conceiving of its being'.[3] The predicates of the Absolute as we find them in ancient metaphysics are attributed to it: freedom, total unity, the embodiment of reality, substance, omnipotence, immortality.[4] It is evident that by this Absolute Schelling centrally means God (*The Absolute or God*).[5] This explains his

[1] Collected works, ed. K. F. A. Schelling, 1st section Vols. 1–10, 2nd section Vols. 1–4 (in what follows, the second section is numbered as Vols. XI–XIV). I 157.

[2] I 166.

[3] I 168.

[4] I 179–202.

[5] V 373.

emphatic riposte to Jacobi, the ineffective advocate of the classical and Christian formulation *si comprehendis non est Deus* ('a God who could be known could not be God'),[6] when he states that an assertion of this kind is unworthy of philosophy, which can have no other object or perspective than that of the knowledge of the Absolute, and that it offers a free passage to atheism. It is not that Schelling lacked a sense of the 'wonderful' and the 'mysterious' aspects of Being; for him philosophy is insight into the 'true mysteries',[7] 'which though celebrated in the brightest light of day still remain mysteries',[8] and whose first act is altogether that of *thaumazein*.[9] He counters the fears of Jacobi 'that science and understanding will destroy what is worthy of wonder' with the words: 'The feeling of the philosopher can be called wonder only in so far as he strives passionately to find what is the ultimate, the absolutely wonderful, which is the point at which science draws to a halt and the unknowing, which clearly you do not *understand*, begins'.[10] Only an 'unknowing' which is understood, a *docta* ignorantia (Nicolas of Cusa), a *comprehendere* incomprehensible (Anselm) is worthy of the philosopher. In his final metamorphosis Schelling appears to want to go beyond this thought when he says that philosophy experiences the drive 'to advance from what it can judge to be necessary and which therefore does not inspire wonder, to what lies beyond and above all necessary understanding and knowledge. In fact it will not rest until it has advanced to that which calls forth absolute wonder . . . to that which by its nature eliminates all further thinking because it transcends all thought . . . God is greater than we think, and has nothing

---

[6] VIII 79.

[7] *Philosophie und Religion*, VI 17.

[8] VIII 111.

[9] 'Existence by itself, without taking into consideration the manner and form of the same, must seem a miracle to whomever looks upon it, and must fill the mind with astonishment: just as it cannot be denied that it was the observation of pure existence that, in the earliest presentiments, struck the minds with terror and a kind of holy fear': *Aphorismen über die Naturphilosophie*, VII 198.

[10] VIII 124–125.

to fear'.[11] And yet this 'positive philosophy' will no more escape the framework of the idealist point of departure than does Fichte's primal life (*Ur-Leben*). What could in principle lie beyond an absolute point of identity? Who could call the self into question in this, its own point of origin, object-ify or otherwise threaten it?

It was Schelling's first intention to introduce the old 'objective' metaphysics, which he believed had found its final form in Spinoza, into the new Idealism and thus to eliminate (*aufheben*) it (*Philosophical Letters on Dogmatism and Criticism*: 1795). If Spinoza's final position was that he conceived himself to be 'identical to the Absolute Object and to be lost in its infinity' (in that *amor intellectualis* in which the self transcends its own limits in order to allow the Absolute, God, to enjoy an absolute predominance), then this contained an element of self-deception: 'By viewing himself as being *annihilated* within the absolute object, he still views *himself*. He could not view himself as being annihilated without conceiving of himself at the same time as existing'.[12] Absolute self-sacrifice to the object (love which is its own reward) is at the same time the highest and freest self-possession; Schelling envisages the point of coincidence of subject and object which is everywhere implied as being also existential: as the blending of two ultimate attitudes in both of which, of course, the self has the final word (for the self is the identity of S and O). 'This step is difficult, difficult: setting forth from the final shore'.[13] In mystical and Eckhartian terms: 'Where the creature disappears to itself and becomes transparent to the Creator, there is reason'.[14] Or in Fichte's terms: 'Only in the highest science does the mortal eye close, and it is no longer man who sees but the Eternal Sight which has acquired vision in him'.[15] It can be stated with reference to Fénelon and to his *entière indifférence même pour le salut* (as Schelling quotes it),[16] so that the highest detachment in orientation to God is then

[11] *Phil. der Offenbarung*, VIX 12–14.
[12] I 319–320.
[13] *Erlanger Vorträge*, IX 218.
[14] *Kritische Fragmente*, VII 247.
[15] *Ibid.* VII 248.
[16] *Phil. der Mythologie*, XI 557.

experienced at the same time as the highest victory after the highest active struggle. Finally we can express it in biblical terms: 'Here all which is finite, which is still an existent, must be left behind, and the final dependence must disappear. Here *everything* must be left behind—not only, as it is said, wife and child, but whatever is, even *God*, for God too at this point is only an existent . . . Here we say: Whoever wishes to keep something, will lose it, and whoever gives it up, will find it. Only he who has left all, and has been left by all, has attained his own ground and has known the full depth of life'.[17] But as we are urged to give up all that exists, be it world, or God, it at once becomes clear that the idea of Being as we find it in Avicenna, Scotus and Suarez (as the univocal and neutral principle which is beyond both God and world) has been transposed to the transcendental mode: the *indifferentia* (of subject and object), wich was essentially Schelling's point of departure, beyond the biblical and Ignatian, Alexandrian (*apatheia*) and Fénelonian form, is now that univocity which is 'oblivious of Being' and on the basis of which it is possible to 'construct' both absolute Being and the Being of the world. The old metaphysics was also oblivious of Being, in so far as it believed that it could establish an abstract concept beyond essence and the act of Being, beyond the real distinction of creaturely being and God's identical Being; and this old obliviousness of Being surfaces in Schelling in a logical progression as idealism which, because it gains an intellectual apprehension of God Himself and can construct Him exactly from His specifications, becomes 'a kind of ideal atheism'.[18]

The irredeemable obliviousness of Being is apparent in the fact that the opposition between the ideal and the real which is fundamental to Schelling's thought (in the dissolving of the original identity of subject and object) cannot be fixed according to its sense content, at least not at a point beyond what is meant by Kant's opposition between concept and perception (or in Husserl's *noesis* and *noema*). The ideal is the

[17] *Über die Natur der Philosophie als Wissenschaft*, IX 217–218.
[18] Emanuel Hirsch, *Geschichte der neuern evangelischen Theologie*, 4 Vols. (1952), p. 414.

universal, 'while contraction is the beginning of all reality'; by contracting Himself from the 'universal' (or from 'Being') to an 'existent', God becomes real, which contraction however is also His 'condescension'[19] from the level of an ideal 'existent' to that of a mere premise or ground or basis for it, namely to 'being', and thus the possibility appears of a 'created' world, to which the possibility of a 'participation' in God's Being is granted, without its thus becoming identical with the 'authentic God'.[20] It follows therefore that God, as the Absolute within identity, is the 'non-real', while 'reality exists in the non-identity of the general and the specific',[21] and that consequently God, in order to be existent, has need of the world as His basis of reality, so that 'the entire process of the creation of the world ... is actually nothing other than the process of a fully developing awareness, the complete personalisation of God'.[22] But the fact that the 'Creation' can be God's 'free' condescension, remains the mystery of this thought which is oblivious of Being, in which everything (ideal and real) ultimately goes its way only in the context of a comprehensive ideality or conceptuality in which that which in the realm of the authentically real would be simply contradictory, appears to be 'constructable' in consequence of the loss of the decisive dimension of Being.

We can make the situation clearer by making a comparison with Nicolas of Cusa. The central problem for him, who thereby only sums up the whole of the classical metaphysics, was how God can be 'everything' when there is also a 'world' (consisting of innumerable finite things); or again: how God can be all in all without being in the formal sense the Being of things. Following Nicolas, Schelling poses the same question in the terms that God cannot be a 'discrete and individual' being—that would be dogmatism, and God would

---

[19] *Stuttgarter Privatvorlesungen*, VII 429.

[20] *Ibid.*, 429–430.

[21] *Philosophie der Kunst*, V 370–371.

[22] VII 433. We remember from Fichte that personality is possible only in the Infinite. Schelling too says: 'In that which is without ground, or indifference, there is of course no personality'. *Philos. Unters. über das Wesen der menschlichen Freiheit*, VII 412.

not be the *Non Aliud*—nor yet can God, according to the 'general pantheistic view', have 'no discrete, individual and self-sufficient existence', such that he would be only 'a general substance', only a 'bearer of things'. Schelling's solution is as follows: 'God, however, is both; He is first and foremost the essence of all essences, but as such He must also exist, that is . . . he must have a basis for himself. This God in his sublime dignity is the universal essence of all things, but this universal essence does not hang in the air but is grounded and is as if borne by God as individual being—the individual element in God is thus the basis or substratum of the Universal'.[24] Clearly the perspective here has changed: the 'highest dignity' is the 'universal essence of things', and the 'individual element', the 'for itself' is only the prerequisite for this. But can God as an 'individual' being still fulfil the requirements of the '*Non Aliud*'? In Nicolas, God is the *Non Aliud* in so far as he *Possest*, the One in so far as He is the Unique One, the Universal in so far as He is the Omnipotent, to whose identity of subject and object, *posse* and *esse*, there belongs power over all that is possible (for Him and through Him). Now if God and the world, each for themselves and according to their own nature, are 'constructed' from the point of an identical point of indifference on reason's part, then God is necessarily projected according to the scheme of the universe, or that of man: 'If we desire a God whom we can see as a wholly vital, personal being, then we must also see him in a completely human way. We must assume that His life has *the greatest analogy* with human life, that there exists in Him not only an eternal Being but also an eternal Becoming, that He . . . has everything in common with man but for dependency.'[25] This 'greatest analogy' contradicts the fundamental law of the classical metaphysics concerning the

---

[24] *Ibid.*, 438.

[25] *Ibid.*, 432. *Cf. ibid.*: '*All* living being begins from unconsciousness . . . Just so does the divine life too begin'. 433: 'God has the same two principles in himself that we have in us . . .' 'The whole life is . . . a process of coming into consciousness at ever higher levels . . .the same is true of God also'. In the Jacobi text (VIII 71–72), the parallel is set out very clearly: while God makes himself the ground of the creature, he also makes himself the ground

'ever greater unlikeness' in the God–world analogy. But this, for Schelling, is the only way it is possible to avoid the decline of our world into an 'unnatural God and godless Nature',[26] in favour of which not only Böhme and Baader, but also 'the great Hamann' is called as witness.[27] But the 'intimacy' (Hölderlin) between God and the world in a common all-embracing Being which is apparently achieved thereby is purchased only at the cost of a duplication or even a triplication of God: God as all-embracing identity ('the undeveloped God'), then 'God *sensu eminenti*'[28] (or 'God in the strict sense'),[29] and finally Nature as a 'divine phenomenon of a lower order'.[30] It is evident that the 'eminent God' who lies enclosed in the universal must give way to the universal in the same way, for instance, that the Demiurge of the *Timaeus* gives way to the universal good. But the clock of history cannot be put back: today it is only the 'irrational abyss', the 'horrendous depths', the Void which can enclose God.

Schelling lets God and man evolve (each in his own way, God above time and man within time) out of their common depths into the light of their ideality; thus, not only does he allow the light and the night to coincide, as does Bruno, but he also allows the night to be the primal womb of the light. This is quite different from the idea of the Christian Romantics that night for the creature is a containing and maternal womb, a darkness which in a mysterious unity is unconscious Nature and the incomprehensible God (the 'brilliant darkness'). In Schelling, God Himself rises as Spirit from His pre-divine dark, which as such He offers at the same time to the 'creature' as the ground of becoming. This ground

of his own self, 'since he lives *above* the world only to the extent that he subordinates this part of his essence (the non-intelligent part) to the higher part, and lives with this part free from the world . . . just as man transfigures himself truly to intelligence, to the ethical life, only by subordinating the irrational part of his essence to the higher part'.

[26] VIII 70.
[27] VIII 114.
[28] VIII 81.
[29] VII 436.
[30] VII 441.

'is *matter* (not of course matter which is already formed) and matter is nothing other than the unconscious part of God'.[31] So the ideal is thus ultimately the 'superstructure' above matter: materialism resurfaces here too (as already with Descartes and his followers) as the logical consequence of the conceptual thinking of a univocity which is devoid of Being.[32] The final stance of the philosopher is thus for Schelling that of a heroic defiance in the face of the sibylline vision of the abyss, which even here (as later in Freud and Scheler) is called 'the anarchic', 'primal instinct', 'hunger', 'dependency', 'dark will' (= 'drive'), and which pours out a form of melancholy over all that is.[33] One must hold out against the 'truly terrible thing', one must 'descend into the horrendous depths',[34] which is why Dante has such importance for Schelling:[35]

> The heart wavered at the fearful word:
> 'Give up all hope, ye who enter here'.
> But still you passed on through the terrible gate . . .
> Through the earth's very heart to the eternal light.[36]

But the ethos remains wholly distinct from that of Dante, who wanders through Hell not as an absolute philosopher but as a Christian pentitent and for whom therefore Hell is anything but the 'base of Heaven'. But Schelling's thought contains the seed of complete materialism as unequivocally as that of Fichte contains the seed of an irrational philosophy of life, as this was called above, with reference to Simmel. And both fall victim to this dialectic in that they seek to render univocal the mystery of the Thomist *actus essendi* in its distinction from the existent and in its mediation between

[31] VII 435.

[32] This is just as true as the closeness, often noted, between Schelling and Schopenhauer. *Cf.* Eduard von Hartmann, *Schellings positive Philosophie als Einheit von Hegel und Schopenhauer*, 1869.

[33] VII 359f., 399.

[34] VIII 124.

[35] *Über Dante in philosophischer Beziehung*, V 152–163 (originally as part of the *Philosophie der Kunst*: V 687, note). Schelling's translations from the *Divine Comedy*: X 441–446.

[36] *An Dante*, X 441.

God and the world by substituting at this point a conceptual identity, while in truth the *actus essendi* is neither God nor the neutral concept beyond both God and world, nor is it the potency of matter, but rather—and here Schelling is right—it is that first mystery in which God gives a share in Himself and which therefore appeared to the ancients as the θεῖον of the world (he names it in a way that serves to make it univocal: 'the divinity of the universe').[37] And it is only from within Being and with reference to Being that can we speak of the existent, which is transposed in Schelling into the principle that it is only possible to conduct philosophy from within the Absolute.[38]

But in so far as the highest point of identity between subject and object, the ideal and the real can be realised only through the process whereby the real becomes idealised step by step and *vice versa*, the whole of philosophy becomes the dialectic of an evolutionary philosophy of Nature (in which the Spirit rises through the realms of the organic until it becomes conscious within man) and a philosophy of Spirit (in which the Spirit becomes ever more actively incarnate in the real world through mores and culture and thus rises above Nature in realisation of itself, thus 'transfiguring' it in itself). Thus within absolute identity distinction is nevertheless postulated and, being transcended (*aufgehoben*) in its very postulation, is 'transfigured': the Infinite appears in the 'form', while the latter is interpreted and understood with reference to the Infinite. But that is the form of the beautiful. More so than any other modern philosophy, the philosophy of Schelling, as a philosophy of the balance between the Infinite and the finite, is an aesthetic one. Though it is not a philosophy of glory (for that is what a philosophy of identity can never be), but emphatically a *philosophy of art*.[39] It can unite the classical

[37] VII 140.

[38]'The unconditional is the element in which alone demonstration is possible ... Only in the absolute can everything be set forth': *Stuttg. Privatvorlesungen*, VII 423.

[39] The principal documents: 1., 'System des transzendentalen Idealismus' (1800, with a concluding section on the 'Deduktion eines allgemeinen

and Goethean perspectives (organic Nature which embraces the Spirit) with those of Schiller and in part those of Hölderlin (Spirit which submerges itself in Nature), and it can harmonise both in that highest identity of consciousness and unconsciousness which, for both schools, constitutes the essence of the genius, whose features now necessarily fuse with those of God.[40] Nothing is more characteristic here than the way in which the Kantian subjective 'sublime' (itself a relic of the objective 'glory') in its distinction from the 'beautiful' is first brought by Schiller to an uncertain state of balance with regard to the beautiful, only to be submerged in Schelling entirely within universalising 'beauty', for within the system of identity there can no longer exist any 'true and objective polarity between beauty and sublimity': 'that which is truly and absolutely beautiful is always also sublime, and the sublime (when it is authentic) is also beautiful'.[41] Thus the vital problem which arose with Kant is extinguished; for Hegel the 'sublime' is only the past. Certainly the *kalon* appears again here—in contrast to its anthropologisation by Schiller—as an absolutely transcendental property of being; following the *Timaeus*, the universe (here including God) is seen 'as a divine work of art', in which once again the chief aspects are total forms of beauty, and Nature is the 'eternal organ and document of philosophy'. 'But in the true work of art there is no single beauty, but rather beauty belongs only to the whole'.[42] Thus Schelling constructs first 'the universe in the form of art, and the philosophy of art as the science of the universe in the form or potency of art'[43] in order to understand the individual instance of beauty as such from this absolute perspective. And thus the mutual interpenetration of

Organs der Philosophie oder Hauptsätze der Philosophie der Kunst': III 612–669), 2., the dialogue 'Bruno' (1802, IV 213–332), 3. the great unfinished 'Philosophie der Kunst' (1802–1805, from the posthumous works, V 353–736).

[40] III 616f.; V 460.

[41] III 621, likewise V 468f.: 'only a quantitative antithesis'. On the whole theme, *cf*. Karl Viëtor, 'Die Idee des Erhabenen in der deutschen Literatur', in: *Geist und Form* (1952), pp. 234–266; on Schelling, p. 264.

[42] V 359.

[43] V 368.

the Transcendentals is again achieved: 'truth and beauty [are] merely two different ways of contemplating the Absolute One',[44] and in *Philosophy and Religion* (1804) in particular the identity of the True-Beautiful and the Good-Holy is highlighted.[45] And it is precisely the aesthetic identity between the Infinite and the finite, between God who is manifest in the world and the world itself which is transparent to God, which becomes for Schelling the true key to the religious dimension, for distinction (*Differenz*) *within* identity (*Indifferenz*) allows the construction of historical religion: aesthetics as the manifestation of the Infinite within finite form (or Nature) is 'mythology', pre-Christian religion, while aesthetics as the assimilation of the finite into the Infinite is 'revelation', Christian religion (and religious philosophy).[46]

This *kairos* of an 'aesthetic theology' in Schelling is decisive for our theme, because it appears (more fundamentally than even in Hegel) as the recapitulation of that which was developed in our first volume (*Seeing the Form*), and also as the idealistic representation of the primary matter of the present volume. 'Mythology' is characteristically the first concern of the young Schelling, with which his first work,[47] 'On Myths, Historical Sagas and Philosophemes of the Ancient World' (1793), is concerned.[48] It is a theme which evolves throughout the complete work[49] until the final 'Philosophy of Mythology and Revelation' (Vols. 11–14). And because God's timeless becoming takes temporal form within world consciousness, therefore the religious principle must initially appear in the finite (Nature) form of mythic

[44] V 370.

[45] But this is already so in the last *Vorlesung über das Akademische Studium*, V 344f. Schelling has therefore every reason (beyond Plotinus) to demonstrate that Plato's struggle against the aesthetic culture of the poets is merely the rejection of a lower form of the beautiful at the service of a higher form which appears in Plato's last works and points ahead to the future Christian 'art of the infinite': V 346–347.

[46] V 430.

[47] After the Latin dissertation for the degree of Magister on the likewise mythical character of the narrative of the fall in Genesis: I 1–40.

[48] I 41–83.

[49] Adolf Allwohn, 'Der Mythos bei Schelling', *Kant-Studien* 61 (1927).

beauty, from which Schelling correctly derives the art of the pre-Christian period, before it becomes transfigured within the infinite (Spirit) form of revelatory beauty in which God first becomes man, authentically suffers in his finiteness, only to return by resurrection to the eternal world of ideas where he assimilates the real man into this new reality. Thus Christ is the end of mythology, 'the summit and the end of the old world of the gods'.[50] For the gods themselves were nothing other than the powers of the Godhead: 'The same unified forms of the general and the specific, which viewed in themselves are ideas, that is the images of divinity, are gods, when viewed in real terms'[51] (when these taken over from the sphere of Nature into the Christian sphere of Spirit, they will appear as 'angels').[52] But in so far as there was a change of direction in Christ, when the 'true Infinite entered the finite, not in order to deify the latter but to offer it in sacrifice to God in his own person and thus to effect reconciliation', religion becomes historical for the first time, the esoteric spiritual kernel of the event becomes decisive while, on the other hand, the mythological, symbolic and sacramental side of the new religion remains 'exoteric'.[53] 'Mysticism is the innermost dimension of Christianity'.[54] It appears here that Schelling's understanding of myth, which was initially wholly influenced by the Enlightenment (myth as an imaginative form of envisaging the divine at a child's level of consciousness), remains rationalistic in his mature period too and that his conception of revelation and faith correspondingly remains a preliminary form contained within philosophical understanding and knowledge. Where the Infinite predominates over the finite (revelation), the finite (which as myth once functioned as the valid vessel of the Infinite) can only serve for its aesthetic contemplation: as 'the outer forms under which religion exists',[55] and as the aesthetic

[50] V 292.
[51] V 390.
[52] V 436f.
[53] V 293–294.
[54] V 443.
[55] *Philosophie und Religion*, appendix, VI 65f.

necessity 'to make exoteric what is esoteric within Christianity',[56] in short: the mythic dimension has been wholly absorbed into the philosophy of art. The ultimate reason for this, as with Fichte and Hölderlin, is the fact that the situation of Christ as the revealing God-Man coincides with the philosophical relationship between God and man, indeed between the Infinite and the finite, which, from the perspective of an ultimate point of identity, from an ultimate common root even of this differentiation, is open to an aesthetic overview. Other 'truly divine men' can also stand where Christ stands, including for example that universal German, whose coming is awaited by Schelling, as it is by Hölderlin, Fichte and Schiller:[57] 'Had he appeared, he would have filled the whole people with reverence as a radiant light and an emissary from Heaven, and he would have suddenly, wonderfully and divinely united those who have been divided.'[58] The distinction between God and the world from their original root is the necessary 'self-duplication of God' in His enduring unity. This can thus be understood both in a trinitarian way and, at the same time, within God as a trinitarian economy. And this is so again both within Nature (as the Son of God who succumbs to finitude and death) and within history, where Christ as the recapitulating man displays the self-stripping of God. The synthesis of all contradictions 'lies only in the idea of a God who endures suffering of His own free will' in contrast to the gods of mythology, for the latter 'do not suffer, but are blessed in their finitude'.[59] Thus all the mysteries of faith have become philosophy, and Hegel is prefigured in his entirety. But this apparent subordination of theology to philosophy was possible only because of the failure to elevate theology above philosophy: in aesthetic terms, because the graciousness and freedom which the divine revelation shows towards man, the creature, has always been included within the necessary

[56] V 294.
[57] 'Deutsche Grösse': 'Every people has its day in history, but the day of the Germans is the harvest of the whole of time': *Werke*, I 477.
[58] Über das Wesen deutscher Wissenschaft, VIII 15.
[59] V 432–433.

process of God's emergence as God and man's emergence as man, which also means that God becomes man and man becomes God. All this talk of 'freedom of will' cannot mean anything more here than the 'fundamental character' of the beautiful, under the systematic primacy of which the truth and the goodness of Being are interpreted.

It is entirely integral to the monistic point of departure that finitude and the division of the earliest distinction which conditions it can also be read as a fall (of the existent from the idea), and thus also as guilt, and the emergence of the ego in the concentration of freedom appears not as pure creatureliness but as the Promethean principle. This is first postulated in *Philosophy and Religion* (1804), and developed in the *Enquiries into the Nature of Human Freedom* (1809). This kind of emphasis inheres within the nature of every system of identity: it can be seen to derive from Plato, is present in Plotinus (although with counterbalancing elements) and emerges sharply and titanically in the work of Bruno. Distinguishing philosophical 'mediation' into identity from Christian 'reconciliation', before synthesising these to form a complete metaphysics, remains the principal requirement of Christian discernment.

The dispute as to whether Schelling—in reaction to Hegelian panlogism—really adopted a new point of departure in the philosophy of his old age, which he describes as the transition from a negative philosophy to a positive one, can hardly be resolved; but the balance (following the researches of Walter Schulz)[60] tips towards a negative answer. For philosophy in Schelling's eyes coincides in its concept with the univocity of reason. It is only at a second stage that reason recognises that it can construct God only as an idea and not as a living reality and, reduced to 'ultimate despair', generates God from itself. For the rational self does not want its idea, but 'God Himself': 'It wants Him, Him, the God who acts, the God of providence . . . in short, He who is the LORD of Being . . . God must *draw nearer* with his help, but it can *desire* Him,

---

[60] *Die Vollendung des deutschen Idealismus in der Spätphilosophie Schellings*, Kohlhammer 1955.

and hope to attain a state of blessedness through Him which
... cannot be a blessedness which is *deserved*, which is
proportionate, as Kant wants, but only undeserved, and
therefore incalculable and immeasurable'.[61] Who can fail to
hear the cry here with which thought asks itself questions it
cannot answer and, acknowledging its own limits, posits
something beyond itself that alone, by drawing near, can
bring it to completion. Of itself, it grasps eternally only the
'How' (the 'existing'), but the 'That' of Being, the 'wholly
transcendental Being',[62] the reality beyond all ideas,
transports reason 'absolutely ecstatically' out of itself,[63] so that
here it must absolutely 'surrender', die to itself and allow
Being precedence. But we must listen carefully to how this
process is described. 'According to its mere nature, it (reason)
posits only what has infinite existence and, inversely, in the
positing of the same it is motionless, as if stunned, *quasi
attonita*, but it is rendered numb by all-conquering Being only
in order to attain by this act of surrender to its true and eternal
content, which it cannot find in the world of the senses, and
to attain to it as to something which is truly known and
which it will now therefore possess in all eternity'.[64] The 'in
order to'[65] shows that this *ecstasis*, this 'taking leave of
everything' and 'allowing its approach' is still ultimately
understood to be an enterprise of reason. In Hegel, Schelling
tells us, reason takes itself as object, to which act there
corresponds as 'content only the infinite potency of Being',
although if Being is taken entirely seriously, then it itself
becomes the act, 'of which no thought can find the ground
or beginning', and to which therefore reason can relate only
as a potency. If it is in its own essentiality, 'then only the
infinite act can correspond to its infinite potency of
knowledge'.[66] Not only Heidegger could agre slumbering

[61] XI 566–567.
[62] XIII 127.
[63] XIII 163; the word *Ekstasis* for absolute transcendence had already
appeared: IX 229–230.
[64] XIII 165.
[65] Which recurs repeatedly on the following pages (*cf*. XIII 170).
[66] XIII 165.

view, but also Thomas, and here Maréchal has no difficulty in transposing both the ontological and the transcendental mode of metaphysics one into the other. But this is so only under the condition that the 'negative philosophy', which extends as far as the construction of the idea of God, is established as the realm of the 'natural doctrine of God' (or fundamental theology), and the historical deeds of the living God who draws near of his own free will are valid as the object of theology and not once again as that of a 'philosophy of revelation'. To proclaim seriously the possibility of a philosophy of this kind—as do the Enlightenment and the entire German Idealist tradition—presupposes that the univocity (identity) of reason also survives the *salto mortale* of 'positive philosophy', making use of it as a form of its own *self-mediation* which is necessary purely in methodological terms. But then this extreme and unique *salto* of Schelling would be nothing other than Hegel's constantly-repeated (with the erection of every serious antithesis) mini-death of reason: the 'speculative Good Friday'.[67]

4. HEGEL

Schelling had made a contribution to the building of the 'uncompletable bridge' by understanding revelation to be a higher form of myth; but where it was necessary to lay the final stone, he became unsure of himself and the measure of the distances eluded him. But Hegel's hand did not waver; he calmly completed the arch, strode across it and dedicated it to the future. Hegel knows that he is commissioned by the World Spirit to open up the future. 'Ours is an important age, a time of fermentation in which the Spirit has jolted forward and outgrown its old form, and acquires a new one. The whole mass of former ideas, concepts, the bonds of the world are loosened and collapse like a dream. A new emergence of the Spirit is underway.'[1] The determined

[67] Hegel, *Glauben und Wissen* (Werke I, 1832), p. 157.
[1] G. W. F. Hegels Werke, complete edition in 18 Vols., 1832–1840. Herm. Nohl, *Hegels theologische Jugendschriften* (= N). Hegel, *Jeneser Logik, Metaphysik und Naturphilosophie* (= *Hegels sämtliche Werke*, ed. G. Lasson

transformation of the entire Christian πίστις into a definitive γνῶσις is thus in Hegel's consciousness not only a long-overdue synthesis of the entire past religious history of the world, but also certainly the laying-bare of the path into the future. His way of thought runs in an opposite direction to that of Fichte and Schelling: if they began with the principle of identity, and, slowly considering their point of departure, struggled back to a Christianity of the Johannine type, Hegel in his early period struggled to make sense of Christ, and the meaning of Christ's life and of the institution he founded, in order then, with clear decision, to absorb that which is of philosophical value within it into his own system and to reject the indigestible remains.[2] He long believed that he could interpret divine life and its evolution in the world under the leading idea of love; but finally this notion disappears modestly into the interior of absolute knowledge, to rule now only as the rhythm and brilliance of its 'bacchantine' movement with which 'there is no limb which is not inebriated'.[3] Hölderlin, his friend from early days in Tübingen, comes close to this change in Hegel around 1800 in the teaching of his fictional character Hyperion: *hen kai pan* is the call. Instead of remaining as if paralysed at the point of identity as do Fichte and Schelling, the 'One' is dissolved into the 'Whole' and emerges thereby simultaneously as abundance of love (πλήρωμα) and exiguous poverty (πενία, κένωσις)[4]—in order finally to return home victorious with its whole full-grown truth and glory into the undivided One. In Hegel as in Hölderlin, Christianity is now absorbed into the element of the omnipresent kenosis of Being in which, for both, the unsurpassable 'glory' of reality occurs. For Hegel therefore glory is nowhere to be found more than in the

---

Vol. 18a, 1923 =J). *Dokumente zu Hegels Entwicklung*, ed. Joh. Hoffmeister, 1936 (=D).–D 352.

[2] 'In Swabia one says about something that happened a very long time ago: it is so long ago now, that it will soon be no longer true. Thus Christ died for our sins such a long time ago now, that it will soon be longer true', D 358.

[3] II 37.

[4] See above on Hölderlin, pp. 000.

totality of the Absolute Spirit itself; absolute thought radiates it in a triumph which can be compared only with that of Leibniz, though it is now no longer theodicy but noödicy.

Viewed retrospectively, therefore, Hegel represents the final conclusion to that interpretation of the world which understands the universe to be the self-manifestation of God: the Stoa, Plotinus, Dionysius, Scotus Erigena, Nicolas of Cusa, Ficino, Spinoza, Herder, Goethe. 'The object of religion as well as that of philosophy is ... God and the explication of God.'[5] 'Philosophy has the aim of knowing truth, of knowing God, for He is absolute truth and therefore nothing else is worth the effort in comparison with God and the explication of God.'[6]. But if we wish to find the particular intuition of Hegel, since all this is still too general, then this can best be understood on the basis of Nicolas of Cusa's *non-aliud* as the name of God. All that is finite is the *aliud* of an 'other' and demands this other in order to be itself, thus it transforms itself, if it is itself to be the object of thought, into the other and, when it is itself the thinking subject, retrieves itself (together with the other) into itself. This movement permeates the universe of finitude and only ceases when the last possible other becomes integrated into the Absolute, which can have no opposition since it comprehends all opposition within itself. The *pan* itself as the fullness of integration can no longer be opposed to the *hen* as its other; rather the *kai* is indicative of their identity. But in so far as the movement which in each case embraces the One together with its Other in a single comprehensive unity is one of truth and knowledge, all knowledge of truth must be rooted in the *non-aliud*, that is in absolute knowledge. That is its point of origin and it is there that it must return. But *non-aliud* means as negation that every *aliud* must be posited in the Absolute in order to be integrated (*aufgehoben*: transcended while Being preserved): positing and transcending (*Aufhebung*) are one and the same process—'appearance is a process of being born and passing away which itself is neither born nor passes away, but which exists *an sich* and constitutes the reality and the

[5] XI 5.
[6] XII 287.

movement of the life of truth'.[7] 'Faith' (or 'representation': religion) and 'perception' (i.e. art) belong to the manifest dimension of God; both see through the finite to the Infinite which appears and is concealed within it. Philosophy as 'knowledge' embraces and supersedes both, without destroying either, and while they look up towards glory, philosophy or the knowledge of God is itself glory. Hegel reaches this conclusion by virtue of the fact, first that his point of departure is the biblical revelation, second that he removes the biblical glory from this in three stages, and third that he equates the surviving doctrine of the 'Holy' Spirit with the 'Absolute' (God-world) Spirit.

1. The *Early Theological Writings* were influenced on the one hand by Lessing (that 'the contingent truths of history' cannot satisfactorily ground the 'necessary truths of reason') and, on the other, by Fichte (that the divinity neither can nor may be conceived of 'objectively'); so that 'everything which is expressed in the form of reflection concerning the divine is meaningless'.[8] God is—as Jesus experienced and taught, and as John understood—pure and eternal love, light, life. He is therefore the absolute unifying principle which transcends (*aufhebt*) the duality (which it presupposes): 'In love man has found himself again in another; because it is a bond of life, it presupposed a separation, an evolution, and the developed multifaceted character of the same. And the more forms in which life becomes vital, the more points there are at which it can unify itself and be sentient, and can be love all the more intensely.'[9] Finitude as such is 'pain',[10] opposition between beings is 'death'; but only when placed within a comprehensive and living whole, which posits the contradiction in order to transcend it. Hegel says in his exegesis of the Prologue of St John's gospel, which begins with the first setting up of an opposition between God and the Logos: 'The infinity of the real is infinite division as the

[7] II 36.
[8] N 306.
[9] N 322.
[10] 'The pain is the course taken by finitude': XII 77.

real, everything is through the Logos. The world is not an emanation of the divinity, for then all reality would be divine; but, as reality it is emanation, a part of the infinite division, but also, in the part . . . life. What is specific, limited, in opposition or dead is at the same time a branch of the infinite tree of life.'[11] *That which is contradiction in the realm of the dead, is not so in the realm of life* . . . It is true only of objects, of dead things, that the whole is different from its parts; but for the living, a part of the same is just as much One as is the whole.'[12] In the parable of the true vine Jesus extends this mystery of the integration of the members to the level of the whole of life.[13] The polarity of the members has meaning only from the point of view of that which unites them, which is the perspective from which they are understood; whereas for the members as such their unification is the object of belief: 'The unification is the activity; this activity, reflected as object, is the object of belief . . . That which opposes can be recognised as such only by virtue of the fact that it has already been united; unification is the measure by which comparison occurs . . . Unification itself . . . is the object of belief; though it cannot be proven, for those things which stand in opposition are dependent, and unification in respect to them is independence.'[14] If we further postulated that 'unification and Being are identical in meaning', then it would follow that 'Being can be only the object of belief'.[15] That means, in his later language: the synthesis, which as truth is the real, surpasses mere (discriminating) reason. Living reason contains the element of love within it and is one with it. Now, in proximity to Hyperion, we can say: 'In love, that which is separated still exists, but no longer as what has been separated—as something standing alone by itself, and the living feels the living . . . Thus lovers can distinguish themselves one from the other only in so far as they are mortal . . . The separable causes the lovers embarrassment. It is a kind of

[11] N 307.
[12] N 308–309.
[13] N 314.
[14] N 382–383.
[15] N 383.

conflict between total devotion, between the only possible annihilation, the annihilation of opposites within unification—and the self-sufficiency which is still present; each feels itself to be hampered by this—love resents what is still separated, what is still a private possession; this indignation of love at individuality is shame.' The promise of inseparability is the child, who testifies to unity as something eternal.[16]

If we raise ourselves in this eros to the absolute standpoint, then 'the vision of God as Himself is . . . the eternal creation of the universe', the 'separation of the real, this grounding of diversity is the goodness of God', the self-transcendence (*Selbstaufhebung*) in love of what has been individualised, 'the absolute turning-point'; it is 'the justice of God, which as absolute power over the real shows its negative side', the reintegration into God's consciousness 'is the eternal wisdom and blessedness' of God, which of course, as the transcendence of the real, is 'the judgment'; but this 'cannot judge abstractly, precisely because the individual is limited: God's heart, as judge of the world, must be brought to breaking point, because He is the absolutely universal totality. He cannot judge the world; He can only have pity upon it.'[17] A comparison between this 'pantheistic' Christianity and that of Origen and Evagrius is instructive and shows the distance of the ages: in the latter, the division of the original divine *monas* into the multiplicity of the world was '*krisis*, judgment', and its reunification through Christ in love is called '*pronoia*, loving providence'. But in Hegel, the self-unfolding of God's 'goodness' and the return, which must break and destroy the particular, is 'judgment': though this judgment too ends by becoming mercy in the mystery of universal integration. The judge's heart breaks, in sympathetic suffering with the limitation of the individual. The new *hen kai pan* has passed far more deeply than the patristic one through the mystery of the Cross.

[16] N 379–381.
[17] D 349; *cf.* in the *Religionsphilosophie*: 'The righteousness is the element of negation, i.e. that the nothingness may be revealed; this righteousness is a determination like the coming into being and passing away of Shiva . . .': XII 48.

But Hegel is no timid thinker. From Schelling he inherits the sibylline glance into the abysmal depths (the only thing which Schlesinger's portrait of the aged Hegel still shows); as in Bruno and the young Goethe, enthusiasm can show its dark side: 'God, who has become Nature, who has extended Himself into the glory and the silent circulation of the formations, becomes aware of His expansion and of His lost precision and becomes enraged at that. He finds . . . his essence is poured out in restless Infinity, where there is no present but only a barren thrusting beyond the limit, which always comes into being where it is transcended. This wrath . . . is the destruction of Nature . . . and is likewise an absolute going into the self, a process of becoming the mid-point. In this, the wrath devours its formations into itself . . . Its limbs are thereby crushed and its flesh pressed into this liquid.' Hegel names the 'wrath of God at Himself in His otherness' the 'fallen Lucifer', who rises up against God and whose beauty makes him arrogant. But finally, as with Hölderlin, 'disfigured Nature rises up in a new ideal form as a realm of shadows', and its new form is 'having endured the fire of pain at the mid-point where, now purified, it has left all the flakes in the pot'.[18] Such sweeping formulations are later moderated; the issue remains the same, even when it is expressed in Christian terms: if God takes finitude upon Himself in Christ, 'this finitude which at its most extreme point is evil', then it is 'infinite love, that God has made Himself identical to what is foreign to Him in order to destroy it. This is the meaning of the death of Christ.' But because it is God who dies, death, the negative, conveys for us that 'the original sublimity is postulated as having been attained', and it is understood 'that the human, the finite, the debilitated, the weak, the negative are all an element within the divine; they are all contained within God Himself'.[19]

In the *Spirit of Christianity* and in the so-called *Fragment of a System* written in Frankfurt in 1800, which is close to Hölderlin and also to Schiller and which forms the transition to the system of the Jena period, the classical and Christian

[18] D 365.
[19] XII 250–253.

dimensions are magnificently combined. Infinite life (God) and finite life (world) now appear as 'Spirit' (already in the elevated sense of the 'vital unity of multiplicity') and 'as its form', which is not 'just dead variety separated off from it', but in which, rather, 'individual lives' become the 'organs' of infinite life. If someone can look at the universe in this way, then he 'prays to God'.[20] But because the individual form as such must nevertheless die, the whole appears to it as 'fate', which it must suffer willingly, and through which it can reconcile itself to God in the spirit of love.[21] Here we have Schiller's unillumined fate whereby the fragmenting human form matures into its ultimate beauty; even more, Hölderlin's 'dumb cliff' against which the heart's wave breaks and becomes Spirit; and for Hegel too the final word at this point is beauty: 'beautiful unification'.[22] It is into this fundamental aesthetic law that Hegel now interprets what is distinctively Christian: the unconditioned openness to reconciliation, the love of our enemy, which can glimpse the life of love through the apparently irreconcilable forms of life and fate and can carry it through. Although the otherness of fate can be construed as 'punishment' for the alienation of the finite consciousness from God, it is precisely this otherness that transforms love, which yields and offers itself, and by suffering and dying makes its peace with fate. That is perfect freedom, and at the same time it is beauty: 'the highest freedom is the negative attribute of the beauty of the soul'.[23]

2. But this reconciliation of the Greek spirit with the Gospel has one precondition: the complete elimination of the Jewish dimension. In his insatiable and hateful polemic against the Old Testament, Hegel pursues the one element for which he has no use in his otherwise all-reconciling system: the sovereign and lordly elevation of God above the world, who acts, elects and rejects in complete freedom of will; and thus he has no use either for the distinctively Old Testament form

[20] N 347.
[21] N 348.
[22] N 351.
[23] N 286.

of the divine glory: the *Kabôd*. It was precisely this kind of anti-semitism which necessarily had to appear at the end of our history of the Spirit in which the elevation of God above the world—first in terms of classical antiquity and then of Christianity—is reduced step by step until it becomes a structure of implication and explication. Even in his maturity, when he no longer engages in polemics, Hegel will tear the Bible down the middle and insert the whole of antiquity between Judaism and Christianity. 'The Jewish principle of opposition' pulls God and the world apart:[24] and thus the idea of God becomes abstract, 'empty and without content', 'lifeless, not even dead, a nothingness' which nevertheless as 'infinite object' claims for itself all truth, freedom and justice so that man is reduced to a 'mere possession of his God', who jealously demands veneration and worship, who hates all other cults and commands then as far as possible to be destroyed, while allowing his own servants to live in a 'sad, unfelt unity' before Him and to serve him, but without beauty and without participating in 'anything eternal'.[25] He stokes up within them the 'demon of hatred'; 'a people who despise all foreign Gods must bear the hatred of the whole of the human race in their hearts'.[26] Accordingly, Israel as a people 'have descended to Hell in the infamy of their hatred', and what remains of this today as a sign among the Gentiles is the 'ideal of the one who is most rejected', like Thersites among the Greek heroes.[27] They are the 'hapless people',[28] as later in the *Phenomenology* the disjunction between God and the world is designated as the 'hapless consciousness'. Israel's religion is pure 'positivity', since it constantly exists in servile dependence upon the tyranny of its abstract God, and that is 'immorality'.[29] Hegel's total rejection is to some degree relativised by his placing of the Jewish tradition within that of the Orient in general with its abstract and empty idea of

[24] N 308.
[25] N 251–253.
[26] N 377.
[27] D 265.
[28] N 350.
[29] N 276.

God (India, Islam) and its multiple compensations for this by 'an acquired and alien splendor' (*Kabôd*): it is from this sphere that the dialectic arises between 'sovereignty over all and the willing surrender to every form of slavery',[30] which was the source later for the greatly influential chapter of the *Phenomenology* on the master and the servant. Here too a place could be found finally for the Jewish tradition, as a wholly relative phenomenon, in the interpretations of the 'philosophy of religion', of 'aesthetics' and the 'history of philosophy'. But this does not change the fact that we find in essence a fundamental rejection of the biblical and theological reality: of the elevation of the God of Israel above every harmonising reciprocity of complication and explication.

Thus the concept of sublimity within classical German aesthetics is definitively allocated to the past. It occupies a place in the great 'aesthetics' after the 'unconscious symbolism' of the Persians, the Indians and the Egyptians, as well as the Islamic 'pantheism of art': in the 'symbolism of sublimity', 'external existence, in which the substance is brought into view, is degraded *vis-à-vis* the substance, since this reduction and manipulation is the sole way in which the one God who is in Himself formless and who resists expression by anything wordly and finite according to His positive nature, can be rendered visible through art.' The external dimension is so subordinated that the internal one 'does not appear within it, but passes beyond it in such a way that nothing can attain expression but an act of being beyond and a proceeding beyond'.[31]

Against the Jewish abstractness, which fosters a loveless and 'godless' legalism and ceremonialism, the Jesus of the *Early Theological Writings* sets up the principle of love: as the inner against the outer, the moral against the legal, the reconciling against the dividing, beauty against sublimity. Whoever believes in Him, whoever grasps the principle which He brings, enters the light; and whoever rejects Him, pronounces his own judgment in that he remains within the zone of contradiction and division.[32]

[30] D 257–261.
[31] X/1 479.   [32] N 261f., 285f., 311.

But Hegel must advance to the point of a second denial: the denial of the Church, which through the tragic dialectic of history is led to the point of objectifying by the divinisation of Jesus the wholly abstract element which shines forth in Him,[33] of introducing a permanent contradiction into Jesus Himself and into devotion to him by the belief in the Resurrection,[34] and from there gradually to fall back into the outdated legalism of the Old Covenant:[35] into canon law which soon necessarily mingles with secular law[36] and thus leads to all the forms of medieval abuses.[37] Hegel thus (N 214–231) strikes a note of invective which is fully equal to that of Nietzsche against Christianity.

But does that not demand yet a third denial, that is, of Jesus Christ himself, who, on closer inspection, sought only to overcome the abstract positivity of the Jewish religion by opposing it with a new form of positivism: the link of faith to his own person? 'This constant, uniform thrusting forward of the self in John is a point of distinction from the Jewish character' and, in Jesus' intention, only a transitional stage on the way to complete unity in love and in the Eucharist with his friends; but then the abandoned group of disciples (as in Hölderlin's late hymns)[38] become attached to this too insistently isolated ego with its unique (and thus historical and positive) experience of God. The Graeco-Roman world of myth is shattered for the sake of this one man, without however creating in its place a satisfactory replacement in keeping with the world,[39] for the ancient Jewish legends are alien to the Western world, and Jesus' attitude to suffering, which in his disciples becomes a flight from the world,[40] lacks force of action and world-form.[41] The sacraments do not

[33] N 156f., 175f.
[34] N 384.
[35] N 208.
[36] N 183.
[37] N 315.
[38] See above, pp. 333f.
[39] N 215.
[40] N 328f.
[41] 'The Christian religion has produced many martyrs, heroes in endurance, but not heroes in action': N 357.

become an authentic form of life (as were the Gods of the Greeks):[42] everything points to an initial deficiency in Jesus himself, which had fateful historical consequences and which today points imperiously beyond itself. In his final judgment of historical Christianity, Hegel shows how the latter has failed in all its forms (Catholic, Protestant, Enlightenment) to create a calm and fulfilled form of beauty between God and the world, since it has not been able 'to find peace in an impersonal and vital beauty', but has hovered restlessly between the 'extremes . . . of friendship, of hatred or of indifference towards the world' and thus turned in a circle.[43] The God-world 'opposition' is nowhere 'transcended in a beautiful unity',[44] and the 'imagination can never synthesise it in beauty'.[45] That which should have effected this unity, the divine consciousness of Jesus Christ, becomes destructive and eternally divisive in the theory of the two natures and in the doctrine of the Resurrection. Instead of vanishing in transparency to God and yielding place solely to the sanctifying and unifying Spirit, the transient historical form of Jesus is made eternal, and thus absolute reason is prevented from ever dealing with the positivity of Christ. From this point on, Hegel is determined to throw away the husk in order to preserve the kernel. In the *Phenomenology of the Spirit* (1807) the 'husk' (the historical Jesus and the historical Church) is dispensed with under the title of the 'hapless consciousness' even prior to its entrance into the realm of 'reason',[46] while the philosophically serviceable kernel, the unity and mutual openness of God and man, is reserved for the highest realms of reason ('manifest religion').[47]

And so it is not the historical and positive element which is philosophically assimilable, but the dogmatic one: christology as the general final formula of the relationship between God

[42] *Cf.* the fine but also dismissive reflections on the Last Supper in: N 299–300.
[43] N 342.
[44] N 351.
[45] N 300.
[46] II 159–173.
[47] II 561–593.

and the world; and thus what in the third book of Nicolas
of Cusa's work (*Docta Ignorantia*) is represented as unification
of the supreme divine principle and the supreme divine-world
principle, but linked to the person of Christ. The uncertainty
evident there (in the relationship between Christ and 'spirit',
between 'conjecture' and 'knowledge' as the fullness of faith)
is clarified in Hegel. What was historically 'revealed'
(*offenbart*), is forever 'manifest' (*offenbar*). 'Revealed religion is
manifest religion, because God has become wholly manifest
in it. Here everything accords with the concept; there is
nothing mysterious any more about God.'[48] 'God is
absolutely manifest'.[49] One can therefore also say: 'Religion
is the Spirit's knowledge of itself as Spirit'[50]—in Christian
terms: as identity of the Holy Spirit in God and in the person
who has been saved, of that Spirit which 'searches the depths
of God' and which 'we have', in which 'we judge all things
and are judged by no one' (1 Cor 2.9–16), and 'know
everything' (1 John 2.21,27). This is the justification for the
'transition of faith into knowledge . . . the transfiguration of
faith into philosophy'.[51] 'For faith is also knowledge, only in
a particular form',[52] which begins with a sense-representation
(in an historical phenomenon, a sacramental symbol, a
dogmatic formula) but which yet already substantially
contains the spiritual knowledge within itself. In this it is
distinguished from myth, where the divine is viewed and
attained only in a finite form. For Christianity the statement
is true: 'The form, the determination, is not only finiteness
. . . it is itself the concept as totality of form, and these forms
are necessary and essential'.[53] This position allows Hegel to
be generous and tolerant in his response to the still remaining
forms of ecclesiastical and positive Christianity. At the same
time he can illuminate them all in his final *Philosophy of
Religion* with the light of absolute knowledge. That God

[48] XI 44.
[49] XII 152.
[50] XII 156.
[51] XII 258.
[52] XII 262.
[53] XII286.

becomes man—and man always means *a* particular, individual person who as such reveals the 'subjectivity', indeed the 'uniqueness' of God;[54] that God dies and 'is dead' (this 'most terrible idea that everything eternal, everything true does not exist, that negation itself is within God, the greatest suffering'[55]: that too is true and must be considered) and that this finally is only the means whereby God gives us His own eternal Spirit,[56] that God shows Himself to be the Three in One in this movement:[57] all this is absorbed into philosophy so that 'it only stands above the form of faith, while the content is the same'.[58]

If God is wholly manifest to man, without any mystery remaining unrevealed, then precisely the thinking of the totality of Being is a form of glory into which all that was previously 'sublime' is submerged. Previously, glory was the fact that 'God is at the same time *above* this manifestation, both *within* it and distinct from it',[59] that God in His 'manifestation *in* the world . . . shows Himself at the same time to be raised *above* this manifestation';[60] this 'in' and 'above' is reduced to a total 'in'. With that, the concept of 'miracle' has also changed: 'The true miracle is the Spirit itself. Even animal life is a miracle beside vegetable Nature, and Spirit even more so beside life, and purely sensate Nature'.[61] But when Spirit is present, there is no further need for any external miracle in order to validate its absoluteness: it is itself sufficient to this end. Its own totality, in which it comprehends itself step by step, is the *id quo majus cogitari non potest*, which has already been proven and attained.[62]

3. Hegel's thought always takes the achieved totality as its point of departure; for him, this is no longer only the formal

[54] XII 236–237.
[55] XII 249.
[56] XII 257–288.
[57] XII 283.
[58] XII 288.
[59] XII 51.
[60] XII 50.
[61] XII 256.
[62] Hegel's loyalty to Anselm: XV 162–169.

point of identity we find in Fichte and Schelling, but something that has integrated within itself all the tragic world-distinctions in the world of Nature and of Spirit. A characteristic of this consciousness of unsurpassable abundance is that it can be approached from all sides and can be developed in all directions: in one instance as a total metaphysics (as in the Jena lectures and in the *Encyclopaedia*), and in another as the genesis of total consciousness (or reason) from the implications of simple consciousness and of the consciousness of self (as in the *Phenomenology of the Spirit*), or again from the inner rhythm of the conceptual laws and structures themselves (as in the great *Logic*), or as the evolution of unconscious into conscious Spirit (as in the *Philosophy of Nature*), or as the increasing development and self-integration of the conscious Spirit (in the *Philosophy of History*), as the self-apprehension of absolute reason through its different stages (as the *History of Philosophy*), and finally as the completed self-contemplation of the absolute and infinite Spirit within the finite worldly-human Spirit: as *Aesthetics*. These are the final forms, whereas the *Philosophy of Religion* has in comparison with these only a provisional character, in so far as the transformation of the religious principle into absolute knowledge contains something more radical than the self-contemplation of thought in the *Aesthetics* or the recapitulation of all the premises of its abundance in the other forms of philosophy. Precisely the *Aesthetics*—one of the richest and most successful of Hegel's works—is virtually no more than the portrayal of an awareness of the radiant blessedness of absolute knowledge itself, which can comprehend all things (even the most difficult and the most painful), justify all things and approve all things.

The fact that the beauty of Nature occupies within this work a minor and quite provisional place is understandable, since it is only in man's struggle for the fullness of spiritual insight that the spiritual gleam of the Absolute breaks forth from finitude: aesthetics becomes—since Schiller and Schelling ever more strongly, and now definitively—the theory of *artistic beauty*. Art is representation of the idea, which means to say 'of the concept which is concrete and absolute to itself',[63] of the spiritual (divine) truth which in its own freedom comprehends itself in the fullness of its finite and natural explication. As with Kant and Fichte, the universe is no longer theophanous, but actually anthropophanous; and man is theophanous not in his natural being but in his creative self-idealisation. He produces himself in art not only as the 'image and likeness of God' but also, as we find fundamentally in Fichte and Schelling too, himself as the God-Man, the unitive centre of God and the world. And yet the aesthetic contemplation of the idea (as the full embodiment of the Infinite in the finite) is for reason not the ultimate thing (as it was for a while for Schelling), but philosophy dissolves this contemplation too by comprehending its true meaning; and so the aesthetic principle has already had its *kairos* in the world history of the Spirit: with the Greeks, when consciousness did not yet strive beyond the contemplation of the beautiful divine form. The very fact that there is a science of art today (from Baumgarten, Kant, Schiller and Schelling onwards) is for Hegel the certain indication that the high point of *art* has been passed: firstly by the (Christian) era of *religion*, then by the (present) era of absolute *science*. We have 'passed that stage at which art is the most sublime way in which we become aware of the Absolute ... Ideas and reflection have outstripped the beauty of art'. Thus 'art in the sense of its highest calling remains for us a thing of the past'.[64] 'One can indeed hope that art will rise ever higher and will perfect itself, but its form has ceased to be the highest necessity of the spirit'.[65] It is at this point, if anywhere, that for Hegel the saying concerning Minerva's owl is true, which begins its flight only in the dusk—and invents aesthetics. And so the happy insouciance of his untroubled three volumes of aesthetics is something like a game of relaxation.

But then where does his seriousness lie? In the idea that when absolute thought occurs in man, the axis of Being runs through him, and his concept comprehends absolute totality within itself. Therefore he can construct 'the realm of pure

[63] X/I 120.
[64] X/I 14–16.
[65] X/I 135.

thought', and 'this realm is truth, unveiled, as it exists in and for itself without concealment', and thus is 'the representation of God, as He exists in His eternal essence before the creation of Nature and of a finite spirit'.[66] The question as to whether this God is real or merely a creation of the mind is just as insoluble in Hegel as it is in Schelling, since for both the concept of 'Being' (or of actuality and reality) can emerge only as a counter and complementary concept to that of Spirit, and thus the question is utterly submerged within forgetfulness of Being. The Being, with which logic begins, and which is unmasked in its absolute emptiness as the void, in order finally to mediate itself into becoming is, like all subsequent mediations, precisely as such a concept. The whole of the metaphysics of Spirit and Being is developed within the framework of the Kantian opposition between concept and intuition, and thus ultimately between the general and the particular, which are—within an unsurpassable univocity—matter and form to each other. It is for good reason therefore that the Jena Logic has an explicitly aesthetic foundation which rises from 'simple association' to 'relationship' (in Being as in thought) and to 'proportion'. And even the primary law of the simultaneity of a posited and a transcended distinction, of stasis and movement, which prevails within it is in its balanced equilibrium (in imitation of true eternity) thoroughly aesthetic. 'Polarity', it is said here, 'is altogether the qualitative element, and since there is nothing other than the Absolute, then it itself exists absolutely and only by virtue of the fact that it is absolute does it transcend itself within itself, and the absolute is in its still state of *being* transcended just as absolutely the movement of Being or the transcending of absolute polarity'.[67] But this self-mediating identity is reason: 'Recognition itself is the universal'.[68] It is inevitable therefore that where reason begins

[66] III 35–36.

[67] J 13; cf. ibid. 31 on the *duplex negatio* (as *affirmatio*): the positing of what is other and, since this is a positing, simultaneously its removal (*Aufhebung*), lead to a reciprocal proportion the members of which are what they are only through the *Aufhebung*.

[68] J 128.

to evolve as Nature, it offers itself as universal matter, also called 'aether', for all the forms which realise themselves from within it, corresponding to the way in which, for Spinoza (and later for Malebranche) pure space (extension) was an attribute of God. 'The aether is the absolute Spirit in its dimension of absolute self-identity . . . not the living God, for it is only the idea of God . . . It is Nature, and the self-identity of this Spirit, this Other of the living God, is absolute matter which, as the absolute universality of Nature, is the essence of life itself . . . it is nothing other than this absolute process of fermentation or absolute turbulence which is that both of being and of not being'.[69] Sentences of this kind show, more than with Schelling, and in the clearest possible manner, that the progression from logical univocity (the 'universal') or from logical materialism to the materialism of the natural sciences is itself both logical and unstoppable. And since man in his own thinking possesses the total concept of reality, there is no reason not to draw the atheistic consequences of the Hegelian Left.

Where in addition the divine has become the 'universal' (and no longer enjoys any primacy over it), it becomes inevitable that the individual thing, which has been posited for the benefit of the self-consciousness of the Spirit, is transcended (aufgehoben) as an individual thing in favour of the whole: physically by its death, and aesthetically by its death, aesthetically by its self-sacrifice to the whole. What lies beneath this act is treated as 'the mental realm of creatures' in the *Phenomenology*, that is as natural forms of individuation which believe they have a claim to absolute value (as 'person'). But the Jena metaphysics already knows: 'For the monad its Beyond is the highest essence, and as individuality it is transcended. But the highest essence is in fact the species in which individuality exists as something transcended, not destroyed, but which has gone through the zero of infinity, although, for the monad itself, it is something which has been destroyed; the self-preservation of the monad is only a longing which seeks to save individuality through that

[69] J 197–198.

zero'.[70] If one considers that Hegel's earliest concern was the concrete (i.e. national) Spirit of the People (*Volksgeist*) which mediates between total Spirit and the monad,[71] and that this indeterminate Spirit of the People appeared to him later as the formed Spirit of the State, then it is clear that Hegel had to become the intellectual point of departure for the later socialism of the Left and of the Right, both of which in their own way have gathered the glory of absolute Being into the absolutist claims of their own 'party'.

5. KARL MARX

While the unnatural combination of the 'Spirit of the People' (*Blut und Boden*: blood and earth) with the abstract Hegelian idea of the State, together with artificially warmed-up myths, could only engender an obstructive form of madness which was contrary to all the authentic tendencies of the age, Karl Marx performed an historically necessary act by turning the Hegelian philosophy 'on its head'.[1] And yet, as is always the case with violent negations, the 'No' remained closely bound to that which was rejected, a fact that decisively influenced the world-wide movement which he began and essentially formed.

Initially linked to the group of Hegelians of the Left, following and furthering 'the decomposition of the absolute Spirit'[2] in the 'break-down of the Hegelian system', he soon pursues his own, solitary path. It is precisely the imposing and impenetrable closeness and perfection of the Philosophy of Spirit which is most suspect; could the 'reality' which the Spirit posits and then transcends be only a phantasmagoria, the striking proof of how alien this whole thinking about Spirit was to actual reality? The absolute philosopher contains

[70] J 177.

[71] *Volksreligion und Christentum*: N 3–71.

[1] Karl Marx, *Die Frühschriften*, ed. Siegfried Landshut, Kröner 1953. *Cf.* M. Lifschitz, *Marx und Engels über Kunst und Literatur*, Henschel, Berlin, 1948; Georg Lukács, 'Einführung in die äesthetischen Schriften von Marx und Engels', in: *Beiträge zur Geschichte der Ästhetik*, Berlin 1956, pp. 191–216.

[2] 343.

the World-Spirit in his head, but he no longer sees the man who stands beside him. But the latter emits the cry of need which sunders all the webs of Idealism. 'Need which can no longer be waved away, which can no longer be glossed over and which is *absolutely imperative*'[3] infinitely outweighs every purely cerebral system. It is not our task to depict the world or to 'construct' it in thought, but to 'change' it.[4] Certainly it was Feuerbach who earlier made the first breakthrough: rational man first really comes into being in his encounter with his fellow-man, where absolute reality appears, and the synthesis is created which engenders the Eternal, the Divine. But according to Marx, Feuerbach is not yet free from the Kantian categories of concept and intuition (object and reality); he 'remains with the abstract "man" and can only acknowledge the "actual, individual, physical man" within his experience . . . as love and friendship, and thus in an idealised form'.[5] He has not heard the cry of need, the need of the proletarian who has become wraith-like in his material and mental deprivation and who represents the physical self-alienation of man in such a way that only the unconditional act, as the active negation of this kind of negation, can be an adequate answer to it. None of the philosophers of Spirit ever encountered Spirit in order for it to reproach him for his own spectral character. Marx is little concerned with unmindfulness of Being as a philosophical problem; but he has encountered the forgotten dimension of reality fundamentally, in the form of need. This is the primal Christian situation, and beyond that the primal Israelite, Old Testament and prophetic situation which Marx, a Jew, rediscovers on behalf of the Christian community and which forms the theological *a priori* of his entire thought, and thus also of his aesthetics. But the need of man who is alienated from himself is again the only point at which he advances to the horizon of Being; for he borrows all his conceptual material again from the Hegelian Philosophy of Spirit, which is 'oblivious of Being', in order to find an answer to that

[3] 318.
[4] 341.
[5] 353.

need. This means in practical terms: his thought takes its point of departure from human need and proceeds forwards (to the remedying of the problem) and backwards (to the reasons for its existence); the question as to why we exist, or the world, or Being is entirely submerged behind this. The problem of (total, material and mental) deprivation keeps his gaze firmly fixed on the sphere of 'material' production.

Man becomes distinct from the animal at the point at which he 'begins to produce his own food, a step which is determined by his bodily organisation'. By doing this, man also 'produces indirectly his own material life itself'.[6] He forms Nature in such a way that it returns to him in a human form and thus furthers man in his own humanity. 'Man as subject [is] both the result and the point of origin of this movement':[7] by divesting himself of himself in his work, he humanises Nature and integrates it again as such into himself. Fichte was thus right to understand man to be the self-positing act which can succeed only by passing through a process of objectification, and 'the great thing in the Hegelian "Phenomenology" together with its end results . . . is . . . that Hegel grasps the self-generation of man as a process, objectification as de-objectification, as expropriation and as the transcending of this expropriation, that he therefore comprehends the essence of *labour* and sees objectified man, who is true because he is real, as the result of his own labour'.[8] Man is expropriated in his work firstly through the giving of himself to the business at hand and secondly, and far more radically, through the law of the division of labour, which make of some masters and exploiters and of others serfs and the exploited. In his *Master and Serf*, Hegel had presented a fundamental delineation of how this second process too leads to self-elimination (*Selbstaufhebung*). Marx's life work consisted in the detailed exploration of this in the material process of the self-actualisation of man as a social being. 'Material' in this context means fundamentally that it is objects which (moved by men!) make history and that these

[6] 347.
[7] 237.
[8] 269.

objects in their man-made reality are more than just 'intuitions' but rather stand in a relation to man of existential effect and counter-effect. It is this, and not a metaphysical materialism, in the sense of the Atomists, which interests Marx. The horizon of his thought is the principle that man produces himself by working himself into Nature and thus working Nature into himself. This interrelationship of man and world is both the Absolute dimension and the *eschaton* of the historical process in which the polarities cancel each other out: 'We observe how it is only in the state of society that subjectivism and objectivism, spiritualism and materialism, activity and passivity lose their mutual opposition and thus their existence as polarities of this kind', and do so through 'the practical energy of man', through the completion of his true life-task, 'which philosophy could not solve'.[9] Marx here calls the 'state of society' that state in which man has fully realised his social being in so far as 'a particular individual (and it is precisely his particularity which makes him an individual and a genuine individual social being)' gives expression at the same time subjectively within himself to 'the ideal totality' of the species,[10] and thus where 'society' is no longer abstractly fixed in contradistinction to the individual.[11] Marx is—hardly surprisingly—held fast by Hegel's horizon of essentialistic thinking between the 'general' and the 'particular' and, at the same time, in an anthropological reduction, through the scheme of expression of the general (the 'idea' as something which has been concretely fulfilled) within the particular (which integrates itself into it), which represents within this unity the Absolute, the Divine.[12] His eschatological ideal is therefore not that of vulgar Marxism. The idea of 'the elimination of private

[9] 243.

[10] 239.

[11] 238.

[12] True 'communism is, as perfected naturalism, humanism; as perfected humanism, it is naturalism; it is the *truthful* resolution of the struggle between man and nature and between men; it is the true resolution of the dispute between existence and essence, between objectification and self-affirmation, between freedom and necessity, between the individual and the genus': 235.

property' is as such 'only a generalisation and completion of the same', as also the idea of a 'community of women' as 'universal prostitution' would be only the completion of the prostitution of the human person by capitalism, 'only the concealed form in which greed is produced and is satisfied only in another way', only an 'abstract negation of the whole world of education and civilisation, the return to the unnatural simplicity of the poor man unencumbered by needs who, far from going beyond private property, has not even arrived yet at that point'.[13] The ideal lies rather in such a total humanisation of Nature that the latter, as the 'concretely developed wealth of human nature' wholly discloses to him, in its return, his five senses in the fully human sense, beyond 'immediate gratification', and 'not only in the sense of possession, in the sense of having'. Here in a grandiose vision Marx glimpses the ultimate meaning of the painful process which has led humanity out into the 'absolute poverty' of self-expropriation: through this poverty, humanity had to learn an attitude to existence as a whole, which leaves mere 'having' behind. 'The simple alienation of all our physical and mental senses, the sense of *possession*, has therefore (through private property) taken the place of all these senses. The being of man had to be reduced to this condition of absolute poverty in order that it should give birth, of itself, to its own inner wealth.'[14] For it is through the labour process that the world is humanised, while man is liberated from the subjective constraint upon him of 'wanting to have and to enjoy': 'The eye has become a *human* eye, as its object has become a *human* and social one ... The senses have therefore immediately become theoreticians in their praxis. They relate to the object for its own sake, but the object itself is a concrete and human form of relation to itself and to man and *vice versa* ... In the same way, the senses and the spirit of other men have become *my own* appropriation.'[15] And so Marx can say: 'The education of the five senses is the work of the

[13] 233–234.
[14] 240.
[15] 240–241.

whole of the world's history to this day'.[16] But this fulfilling encounter between man and world is completed in the archetypal encounter between man and woman; for Marx, for whom his deep, life-long love for his wife Jenny von Westphalen was virtually the one bright area in his terrible existence, it is the exact opposite of the happiness we find depicted in the *Politeia*. 'In this relationship, therefore, there appears at the level of the senses, reduced to a visible fact, the extent to which, for man, human essence has become Nature or Nature has become the human essence of man.' The as yet unveiled, eschatological 'mystery of this relationship' has its 'unambiguous, decisive, manifest and revealed expression' here.[17] In his own way, therefore, Marx has the 'disinterestedness' of the highest Platonic eros and that of Kant's ethical and aesthetic dimension in view, when he wishes to see 'having' and 'enjoying' transcended in interpersonal love.

Of course, man cannot be spared the passage through class division and class conflict, which necessarily becomes ever harsher; for this is the only way in which man can interpret himself to himself. Even the age of the 'universal whore', viz. of money, the power which inverts all things—'it turns fidelity into infidelity, love into hatred, hatred into love, virtue into vice, vice into virtue, the serf into the master, the master into the serf, stupidity into intelligence, intelligence into stupidity'[18]—this too cannot be avoided, any more than the 'universal prostitution of the worker'[19] can. It is through his debasement and humiliation that man attains his true worth.

This is the thrust of the early work, especially the essay on *National Economy and Philosophy* which first became known in 1932, and which represents the high central point between the Hegelian philosophy of the first years and the later economic work on *Capital*. But the question cannot be surpressed: who is ultimately the subject of this real, material process? No unconscious-conscious Spirit as with Hegel (as

[16] 242.
[17] 234.
[18] 299, 301.
[19] 237–238, note.

the relic of a classical–Christian divinity). But neither is it man, since it is only out of necessity that he initiates the labour process, which only leads him into yet greater need before finally releasing him from it. Who then? Marx ceased to philosophise when he renounced Hegel, and so the question of meaning in its entirety is no longer asked. The fact that man *is*, suffices. No light falls upon this fact. And so ultimately, this is a process which only absolute necessity can guide. It is neither God nor man but the logic of the matter, of capital, which directs history, which concentrates the titanic energies of material power and causes them finally to collapse. Nor does the material dimension govern because it has at its base a philosophical Atomism, but because the reduction of reality to the material dimension of the Spirit (within the philosophical tradition from Descartes on) is accepted as a fact and is not corrected by any philosophy of Being. The two main protagonists in the drama, the capitalist and the proletarian, play the utterly passive role of persons who are driven, in their relationship to the sole active power, which is capital. Thus the hour of a world-historical advance is missed: by the Christians, who did not see the presence of need, and by those who wished to teach the Christians a necessary lesson. That it should have been a Jew, Marx, who taught that lesson, is a just riposte to antisemitism of Hegel and— despite Lessing's Nathan—of most of the great figures of the age of Goethe. The very thing which was alone excluded from the Hegelian synthesis, the people that resists integration into any world-historical synthesis, toppled him from his throne. Marx, however, did not enthrone the glory of God, but once again absolute man as the centre of the world and of Being. And so once more the 'beautiful' Jewish synthesis hangs unsupported within the void.[20]

---

[20] *Cf.* the very informative essay 'Zur Judenfrage', 171–207.

7. AESTHETICS AS SCIENCE

That which deserved the name of glory in the sphere of metaphysics has been lost to view. Being no longer possesses any radiance, and beauty, banished from the transcendental dimension, is confined to a purely worldly reality where tensions and contradictions, encompassed only by univocity, still remain to be overcome. It is only under this premiss that aesthetics as a strict science becomes possible. This no longer belongs to the object of our enquiry, which took the 'glorious' as its concern and not the dimensions of an innerwordly beauty (which can extend in one direction to the 'sublime' and in the other perhaps to the ugly'). German academic research has mapped out this area with great precision, from Rosenkranz. Solger and Weisse to Carrière and Schasler and Eduard von Hartmann, from Lotze and Vischer, Zimmermann and Fechner to Häberlin and Nicolai Hartmann. Major contributions by other peoples are rarer; even as his opponent. Chernishevski remains under the influence of Hegel and Croce also radicalises German Idealism, while John Ruskin once again strives to establish the wholly transcendental character of beauty.

While German aesthetic science concerned itself deeply with the criteria of good taste, German and virtually all European art—with the exception of French painting—sank into an unimaginable lack of taste, which can only be explained on the basis of the depths of the metaphysical confusion: as the deluded belief in the secure illumination of the cosy 'room of existence' while it had long since grown dark 'outside'. It was Hegel who lent a good conscience to the awareness of this supposed absolute light—'the spirit has overcome every opposition in its self-consciousness', and it 'has ceased to be a seeking form of knowledge'.[1] And yet Schopenhauer, his dark shadow, soon gains the upper hand:

[1] *Documents, p. 350.*

the whole light-filled and beautiful world of the 'ideas' is only the manifestation of a dark and blind will, and thus the paradoxical and perverse site of the self-denial of Being and its disintegration as a return into nothingness. Schopenhauer's perfumed nihilism of the salon, which was further propagated by Wagner, Eduard von Hartmann and Thomas Mann, gives off an ever greater stench of putrefaction and thus requires the more pungent essences which Nietzsche, the late Scheler, the early Heidegger, Sartre and his disciples provide. It is in fact only against this background that 'Aesthetics as a strict science' can evolve.

For when Being in its classical and Christian sense is understood analogically, together with that elevation of the Infinite and the Divine above the finite and the worldly which remains unsurpassable for all forms of finite being and thinking, when therefore the worldly dimension hovers in an incalculable distinction between Being and entity, there the transcendental properties of Being—the One, the True, the Good and the Beautiful—are so affected by this analogy and by this distinction that any reduction of metaphysics and of the metaphysical doctrine of truth, goodness and beauty to an 'exact science' is rendered impossible. Although, in the domain of aesthetics, the transcendentalising analogy causes worldly beauty gradually to become metaphysical, mythical and revelatory splendour, nevertheless this hovering within the world between Being and entity, as determined by the metaphysics of Thomas and to some extent again by those of Heidegger, again prevents any fixing of beauty to a particular concept or to a readily-grasped system of concepts. It is sufficient to state this negatively, since the concluding section will have to develop this distinction again positively. The deduction for our theme is that every 'exact aesthetics' which treats of the beauty which is to be encountered within the world, still sees only a fragment and an aspect of the total object for which worldly beauty is only a 'part', and can thus necessarily offer only 'fragments' and 'aspects' that cannot become a whole. This incapacity is no objection to the authentic albeit fragmentary, truth which it contains; partial perspectives do yield genuine glimpses of the comprehensive whole, and aesthetic rules can gradually be raised to the level of metaphysics, of myth and ultimately of revelation because, seen from the other perspective, metaphysics, myth and ultimately revelation can in their descent make use of the worldly and the fragmentary in order to become manifest at that level and indeed to achieve self-expression. In this sense, it is also possible to extract benefit from 'exact aesthetics' for the purposes of a theory of glory, but this, of course, does not go significantly beyond those aspects which have been previously developed. Three areas of motif can be distinguished from each other, if not marked off 'exactly'; it is these which will provide the perspectives for the analysis of the theological dimension in Vols. VI and VII of this work.

1. The beautiful is without doubt *appearance* (*Erscheinung*), ἐπιφάνεια. It was viewed from this perspective by the Greeks, Plato, the Stoa, Plotinus and, after them, the great aesthetic theologies of the Middle Ages which understood the world's 'beauty' to be the appearance of the One who does not appear, and who shows His transcendence in the unitive ordering of the Multifold. This idea is developed by the German Idealists, but in such a way that the absolute (God-) Spirit which remains concealed in its appearance coincides more and more clearly with the human spirit, so that the axis of the epiphany runs through man as its centre: man as Spirit appears as body, as the universal (idea) he appears as the particular, as God he appears as man. Corresponding to this anthropologisation of the epiphany, exact aesthetics will go back from Hegel's standpoint to that of Kant and Schiller, that is, to a subjective and psychological idealism whose dimensions extend on the one hand from the 'idea' which is still visible to man to the 'embodiment' of the idea which is made possible by man's sense structure, on the other. It is this path from Hegel to Schiller, from the absolute to the psychological idea, which is followed by Friedrich Theodor Visher, who is the most important German aesthetician of the last century.[2] For him the aesthetic synthesis of idea and

---

[2] *Ästhetik oder Wissenschaft des Schönen*, 3 vols., 1846–57, and many later writings.

appearance, the infinite and the finite, clearly runs through the man as centre and of course, since man is himself microcosm, he secondarily reveals the macrocosm too. From this central axis, exact aesthetics in the most various forms copes with the extremes which require synthesis, since for Solger the beautiful is fundamentally 'constituted by component parts which are self-eliminating and which must be grasped in the 'act of transition':[3] idea and appearance, spirit and body, freedom and necessity, subjective and objective, divine and earthly, sublime and beautiful, tragic and comic, and, in the extreme case the ugly. Precisely this borderline case, which was drawn into the discussion by Rosenkranz's *Ästhetik des Hässlichen* (1853), reveals the problems of 'exact aesthetics' more deeply than it would itself like and realises: can beauty which appears, or that which appears in beauty, make of its own opposite (ugliness) one of the poles of its expressivity? And if not, is then its idea limited, and it itself seriously threatened by the unloveliness of the real or by the dark backdrop of the world? The threads become confused, and this line of questioning points clearly beyond itself to a region where aesthetics must assume a theological form. If the lines point back historically to Schiller (and his universal dark fate), synchronically to Marx and his exposure of (Vische's) aesthetics as bourgeois ideology,[4] and forwards to the attempts of our own time to draw attention to the limits of beauty within the world through the 'ugly' and thus to allow something more profound to come into view, whereby it still remains unclear what that more profound element may be: God, or nothingness.

Nevertheless, the central concept of idealist aesthetics, 'appearance' (*Erscheinung*), is still only the half of itself, as long as it is not explained why that which appears in its *form* is experienced as beauty: And so the aesthetic scene of appearances necessarily gives birth to a complementary

---

[3] Karl Wilh. Ferd. Solger: *Vorlesungen über Ästhetik*, 1829 (repr. 1962), pp. 108–109.
[4] G. Lukács: 'Karl Marx und Friedrich Theodar Vischer', in: *Beiträge zur Geschichte der Ästhetik* (1956), pp. 217–285.

aesthetic science of form. We find it present among the Greeks from Pythagoras onwards: it must be possible to enquire into the aesthetic qualities of formal structure (*harmonia*) in space and in time (*rhythmos*). Thus Schiller knows 'architectonic beauty', to mention only this last figure in the Western theory of harmony (from Boethius to Alberti and Dürer). Herbart and his school endeavoured to interpret this element with exact scientific method. Herbart, whose starting point was the Kantian unknowability of *das Ding an sich* and who chooses to define philosophy as the 'elaboration of concepts', accepts by way of complementarity simple aesthetic judgments which are formed on the basis of an irreducible pleasingness or otherwise in perception (aesthetics in the broader sense) of relations of the will (ethics) or in original forms (aesthetics in the narrower sense). Here, there is born the theory of 'values' which are free both of Being and of concepts, and which have played a mostly fateful role down to our own day: they are in fact nothing but the emergency substitute for Being, together with its transcendental modalities, which has been hollowed out and suppressed by Rationalism and Idealism alike. And so however useful the researchers of the Herbart school have been (above all the contribution of Robert Zimmermann in his *Geschichte der Ästhetik als philosophischer Wissenschaft*,[5] Gustav Theodor Fechner in his *Vorschule der Ästhetik*,[6] Karl Stumpf in his *Tonpsychologie*,[7] as well as the work of Hanslick and others), in that they have sought to expose the primal elements of the beautiful and to describe at least their initial combinations, they have necessarily not advanced beyond a pure science of experience, or 'phenomenology', of the beautiful, since the values are simply 'given' to the forms and their relations without their being in any sense derivable.

Unless, that is, we follow the Pythagorean path of an original identity between the law of quantity (the measurable intervals of the monochord strings) and the psychic law of quality (the hearing of the pitch), whereby the identity of

[5] Vienna, 1858.
[6] Two parts, Leipzig, 1876.
[7] Two vols., Leipzig, 1883–1890.

both would lie in the objective-subjective 'tension'. This is the point of origin for many different possible paths: some lead to Gestalt psychology (which Stumpf was already approaching) and further to a pure functionalism,[8] while others lead to an aesthetic-religious Pythagoreanism, such as was developed by A. von Thimus in the last century[9] and magnificently so by Hans Kayser in our own.[10] The limits of these paths are evident as soon as they are made absolute: the Pythagorean identity of the physical and psychic harmony of the world does not permit in principle anything which is superior to it, and thus no form of epiphany, but rather turns in pantheistic and atheistic circles within itself. Plato, who endeavoured to approach this identity in his old age by equating the Ideas with numbers, and again Kepler (*Harmonices Mundi*, 1619), who depicted the mystery of the world in numbers and attributed to them 'powers' (rather than to the moving intelligences), or Leibniz with his pre-established harmony cannot escape the inner logic of the Pythagorean system: the imprisoning of the freedom of the act of appearing within the ordered structures (*Gesetzlichkeiten*) of the appearance.

The direct, i.e. unmediated, parallelisation of Spirit and matter in Descartes, Leibniz and Spinoza prevents the emergence of that distance by virtue of which the Spirit could create a genuine expressive form of itself within the sphere of the material. Its superiority is expressed at most now in the fact that it groups matter into 'pleasing' configurations. Therein the Kantian ideal of the non-signifying and abstract beauty is foreshadowed with which, as we have said before, the ideal of modern 'abstract art' first consciously appears. In so far as this emerges as a demanding and perhaps exclusive programme, it is without doubt a product of modern thinking which is oblivious of Being and in whose train Spirit has become functionalised and can achieve expression only

---

[8] *Cf.* Vol. IV of this work, pp. 28–32 (Eng. trans.)

[9] *Die harmonikale Symobolik des Altertums,* 2 vols., Cologne, 1868–1876. *Cf.* above, Vol. I of this work, p. 108 (Eng. trans.)

[10] *Lehrbuch der Harmonik* (1950), *Harmonia Plantarum* (Basel, 1943), *Akroasis, Die Lehre von der Harmonik der Welt* (Stuttgart, 1947).

within the counter-image of material functions. Significantly the median point between Spirit and the senses which is touched by beauty does not bear the concrete name of 'heart' in Kant, but the abstract name of a 'harmony of the powers of the mind.' This abstract relation already begins to waver in his work in the face of the forms of abstract art, and thus clearly betrays its deficient and fragmentary character.

The entire aesthetics of form and value remains a fragment within what is a greater, though no less fragmentary, aethestics of epiphany. For this too would have to depart as a whole from its own essential sphere for that of total Being, and answer the question, not what the human spirit on its own can conceive and embody in terms of ideas (before what horizon?), but what Being as a whole epiphanically heralds and brings into view. But precisely in so far as these two questions cannot be made to coincide, the mystery of a total ontology and aesthetics opens up in such a way that it makes impossible any systematic analysis of appearance.

2 If 'appearance' (the appearance of that which does not appear) remains enigmatic—for example: *what* becomes known in a perfectly beautiful person?—then a further principle seems to be of help. We know of the *production* of the beautiful by someone who is capable of achieving this, namely the artist (ποίησις, ποιητής). There exists this primal act of generation and of genesis within the spirit, as an act which is above the rational and discursive faculties of thought, since the form is suddenly present in an original intuition and inaccessible unity (a good deal of testing the way can be involved by way of preparation, but the work never crystallises from below) within a single moment which is experienced as being 'given', in a 'μανία', as Plato has it, in which the Plotinian ἔνδον εἶδος is at once 'found' (*gefunden*) and 'devised' (*erfunden*), 'seen' (Ficino), 'stolen' (Shaftesbury and Goethe), 'posited' (Fichte and Schelling) in the unconcious or super-conscious mind of the 'genius', which Herder, Kant and Schiller described or in the phenomenon of 'inspiration' as described by Nietzsche and Dostoievsky. Chr. H. Weisse developed in his *System der Ästhetik* (1830) a theory

of 'genius' which can be taken as an idealist counterpart to the classical *daimon*. In his *Aesthetics* (1902),[11] Benedetto Croce by idealist means raised this act of aesthetic and creative intuition to the level of the fundamental act of the spirit and thereby again proclaimed the identity of contemplation (*Schau*) and expression (*Ausdruck*): 'Intuitive knowledge is expressive knowledge',[12] 'intuitive activity possesses intuitions to the extent that it expresses them,'[13] 'When we have achieved the world within us, conceived definitely and vividly a figure or statue, or found a musical motif, expression is born and is complete'.[14] Expression is free inspiration.'[15] *Actus purus* and *forma pura* coincide. It is evident that no more space is left here for religion, i.e. for the analogy between the original (*urbildlich*) Creative Spirit (God) and the copy *abbildich*) in creative spirit (man), as Nicolas of Cusa envisaged this. And yet only this analogy contains the true problem which weaves its way through the history of Aesthetics as the question concerning the artist's 'imitation of Nature', the problem that stands in the tension between the artist's gazing upon the 'works of God' in the *Natura naturata*—and the assimilation of the artist's genius into the activity of God in the *Natura naturans*. The instinctive genius we have described above will always incline towards the second, even if no serious artist will lack the first element—that of observation and practice. Goethe shows both of these within himself in a good balance, and transposes both elements (as a 'chain' and 'flash of lightning') on to the twofold unity of 'Nature' and 'God'. But in the Prometheus fragment it was the twofold unity of the poet (as self-discoverer) and of his goddess (as inspiration): the motif which will become central for Spitteler. The analogy with the prophet (*poeta vates*) was drawn even in classical times.[16] Hamann[17] and Karl Philipp Moritz[18] saw

[11] *Aesthetic as Science of Expression and General Linguistic* (London 2nd edn, 1953[2]) trans. D. Ainslie.

[12] *Ibid.*, p. 11.   [13] *Ibid.*, p. 8.

[14] *Ibid.*, p. 50.   [15] *Ibid.*, p. 51.

[16] E. Fascher: *Prophetes* (1927); Th*WNT* VI, 781–782.

[17] *Cf.* Vol. III of this work, pp. 239ff.

[18] *Schriften zur Ästhetik and Poetik*, ed. H. J. Schrimpf (Tübingen, 1962), pp. 46f.

the connection between artistic and sexual generation. And thus it becomes clear that whoever grasps the beautiful in an original manner is directed to a point of the origin of Being, and is caught up close to it. From this perspective, existence as a whole appears justified, whatever terrible things it may perhaps bear in its womb. The eternal striving in the moral sphere, the ceaseless dynamism of reason in search of truth are embraced and mysteriously superseded by the aesthetic gaze which approves and justifies the whole, entirely as it is.

This is the main idea of Paul Häberlin's *Allgemeine Ästhetik*,[19] in which he renews the insight of Schelling's middle period and links the aesthetic affirmation of Being closely to that of religion. But in Schelling the emphasis lay emphatically on the identity of subject and object, and Schiller in his *Letters on the Aesthetic Education of Man* underlined the formal and historical instability of such felicitous *indifferentia* and understood this explicitly to be a pre-ethical stage. Thus the path to Kierkegaard already lay fundamentally open: he views the pre-existent aesthetic totality, where this pronounces itself absolute, as the rejection of the ethical dimension, which is authentic existence. It will therefore be necessary to see the *indifferentia* of creative genius in its inner polarity, as described earlier by Goethe and Spitteler, which is that ambivalence which Plato as philosopher lays at the door of prophetic and poetic enthusiasm. Here Moritz again becomes relevant: the vacillation which he describes between the proximity and the distance of the artist to the macrocosm; and Jean Paul is even more relevant with his theory of genius in the *Vorschule der Ästhetik* (1804), which distinguishes the receptive and passive genius, which apprehends the inner life of the universe in a holy and open soul as a 'mute of Heaven', from that active and divinatory genius which in its apprehension of totality creates an inner form with potential for the future, which, in a state of calm reflection, it brings to concrete expression in an external form.[20] It is Jean Paul

---

[19] Basel and Leipzing, 1929, especially pp. 288–322.
[20] *Vorschule* (1804) I, para. 10–14

too who, while leaving open the tension between self-giving (to the objective) and generation (in the subjective), refrains from constraining the ethical into the aesthetic (in any way whatever) and thus is the first theoretician able to analyse in depth the phenomena of the comic and the ridiculous, of humour and of wit. Long before Kierkegaard and Marx, he sees the impossibility of resolving the tension between the idea and the (individual) existence, and when in Hegel the idea enriches itself through the elimination of existences, then *e contra* the infinite weight of existence can call the idea into question and thus, on the grounds of its own particular incomprehension, show the entire wisdom of the world of ideas to be folly, to be 'infinite incongruity'.[21] This is more than that 'romantic irony' which can be derived from the Fichtean elevation above the world as Non-self (something which never produces true harmony), but implies rather the ultimately Christian dialectic of a 'finitude applied to infinity',[22] which in its whole limitation nevertheless possesses enough weight to unmask the relativity of the 'infinite reason'. 'Humour as the inverted sublime does not destroy the finite . . . there exists for it no single insistence of folly, no fools but only . . . a mad world. It topples the great . . . and raises the small on high, but, contrary to irony, it does so in order to set the great at its side and thus to destroy both, since in the face of the infinite all is one and all is nothingness.'[23] In this sense, Cervantes set his 'twin star of folly over the whole of mankind',[24] not in order to turn his back on the world as a whole but as a 'seriousness which descends' from Heaven to Earth. In contrast to the arrogant claims of the philosophy of Spirit, humour becomes the existential testimony of the unbridgeable nature of the relationship between idea and existence, it is the reason why the true and warm light of Being is preserved and the cold and false light of an absolutist speculation and its consequent destructive irony is held at bay. Jean Paul himself depicted

[21] *Ibid.*, I, 155.
[22] *Ibid.*, I, 174.
[23] *Ibid.*, I, 175–176.
[24] *Ibid.*, I, 178.

the ultimate unbridgeable polarity of genius, indeed of man as such, through his heroes, all of whom are ordered in pairs (Siebenkäs—Leitgeber, Albano—Schoppe, Walt—Vult, etc.). As a theoretican of folly, he also assimilated (more clearly than Erasmus or Hamann) the intuition of Christian artists from Wolfram to Grimmelshausen and Dostoievsky into theoretical aesthetics and thus showed once again the openness of this science to what ultimately belongs to the sphere of religion and theology.

The whole nexus of problems of the 'exact aesthetics' with references to the subjective premises for an apprehension of beauty must be accordingly transposed into this openness. First comes everything which is described by the concept of 'empathy' (*Einfühlung*: Theodor Lipps) as that prerequisite of powers, dispositions and expectations of the subject, whereby it draws the object into its own sphere, clasping and permeating it with its sentient organs which bestow both light and warmth in order thus to enjoy it as its own possession. This point of view, although not false, is so evidently limited that it virtually transcends itself by its own nature, since the open and unresisting self-giving of the subject increasingly guarantees space to the object and allows it to appear in its own aesthetic structure. And so the psychology of empathy becomes virtually of itself so a phenomenology of the self-'giving' object (Moritz Geiger), which in turn can itself receive a stress that is more subjectivistic or more objectivistic and the more profound question occurs here as to in what way and to what extent the subject wishes and is able to be open and to give itself, in order to experience 'strata' of life and of Being as a whole (as Nicolai Hartmann carefully distinguishes them) as beautiful, although these appear uninteresting or ugly to the spectator who is only superficially receptive. The quotation from Rilke which stands at the beginning of this work clarifies once more precisely what is meant here, not only because a progressive aesthetic empathy into the whole of existence is prescribed as possible and feasible, but also by virtue of the fact that this attitude is understood to be a precondition for the capacity of the objective value of Being to become manifest.

This is where there lies the full aesthetic significance of the metaphysical eros which is treated in so many ways in this book. As erotic eros, it is the magical transfigurer of lovers and of the whole surrounding world: 'Everything is glorious for me today—if only it would remain like this! I see the world today through the lens of love.' But all those to whom this lens has been offered and then withdrawn, know its subjective character. But the lover has the freedom to purify the natural love into one which is spiritual and to make it universal: Plato performed this metamorphosis in the *Symposium* and raised eros up to become the contemplation of the absolutely Good and Beautiful, which can be glimpsed through no other lens. In this ascent, he purified it of all forms of egotism—up to the threshold of what we have called 'detachment', which is that positive self-giving of the subject to Being in its entirety (and to all its possible revelatory forms), which has to be interpreted as an *a priori* state of assent, as 'Yes and Amen' to eternity. At the precise point at which the *a priori* 'Yes' mutates from one which is categorical to one which is transcendental, the beauty which encounters us in the world becomes (metaphysical) glory. It is also the point at which, for the religious person, Being becomes theophanous, whether the divine appears in the form of a mythic image (with all the provisional character of such images), or whether his 'mental (*geistige*) senses' (as Marx also called them) as 'spiritual (*geistliche*) senses' make him capable of hearing and of seeing the mystery of Being as a whole. It is only this background of the metaphysical eros which prevents the particular eros from misapprehending itself as a bitter illusion and a scurrilous trick of Nature, on which the individual who has been informed and made a fool of avenges himself through his *a priori* 'frigidity and insolence'.

3. The third element within the beautiful explicitly highlights that characteristic for which the unresisting eros creates a space: *charis*. This word has always processed a certain polyvalence which makes it appropriate for a transcendent application, and which emerges particularly clearly in Pindar. It begins as the victorious loveliness of

youth, before becoming the radiant *aretê* (virtue) of the whole person, in which the grace of the gods once again appears, and then finally the grateful exchange between the gift of victory and the return gift of recognition, especially through the poet. It is loveliness, dignity, brilliance, favour, grace, gratitude all in one. And so *charis* is allegorically open to the more earnest, world-historical *agôn* of *pius Aeneas* and open again to the wholly different *agôn* of the crucified Christ, which is comprehensible only on the grounds of the living God of love. In biblical terms too, *charis* will extend from the eroticism of the Song of Songs and the nuptial psalms—*diffusa est gratia in labiis tuis*—to the justification of the sinner through pure *charis*, which is no longer comprehensible to the understanding of the world.

Charis as the miracle of grace which encounters us remains to such an extent a mystery that the 'exact science' can scarcely dare approach it. The ancient Stoic, Augustinian and scholastic definition sought to take account of this miracle when it added to the mathematical and rational element (*partium convenientia*) one which is intentionally vague (*cum quadam coloris suavitate*). This sweetness of colour, of the *teint*, as indeed the simple qualities of sight and sound, remain an enigma for the aestheticians of form. But this incomprehensible element is only a pointer, and remains so precisely in its fragility (Solger), since if we take hold of it too roughly, it escapes our grasp; it exists only as a breath of wind that has passed by; it does not remain long with the one who thus receives its favour; it is more remembrance and promise than actual presence, more a spur to memory than a gift, offered to Tantalus and yet at once withdrawn from his grasp and, being thus inaccessible to 'exact scientific method', it can only be interpreted from the point of view of the Being which embraces it. If one element within beauty is a fragment, then this is certainly *charis* which shines forth only from within the unbridgeable Ontological Difference and is most properly that which primordially blazes forth through this opening. When it is not remembrance of the mystery of Being itself, it causes the person who views it to sink into the helpless melancholy of eros. It is, as Claudel says, the hook with which the angel draws the bleeding heart towards eternity. And so the 'exact science' of the beautiful would be more a science of the guardian angels than a science of men.

The three elements we have discussed—*epiphaneia, poiêsis, charis*—offer the perspectives from which to discuss a biblical and theological aesthetics.

3. OUR INHERITANCE AND THE CHRISTIAN TASK

A. THE SITE OF GLORY IN METAPHYSICS

1. THE MIRACLE OF BEING AND THE FOURFOLD DISTINCTION

The direction of the meandering historical paths of Western Metaphysics becomes straightforward and simple if we centre the chaotic fragments around the authentic metaphysical question: 'Why is there anything at all and not simply nothing?'. This question is not posed seriously by any 'science' because science always presupposes its subject matter as objectively given thus. But it is also only rarely examined thematically by philosophy or, when thus examined, is not pursued in depth, in that philosophy either begins with description rather than wonder or, if it does begin with wonder, then also with the impulse to answer the astonishing question as to why things should exist at all, from the fact of their existing in such and such a way.

Without doubt the phenomenal world contains on all sides an objective order which is not imposed by man, and thus a beauty; the legitimacy of the premise is repeatedly confirmed for him that there is within Nature a greater objective ordering of things than he had previously recognised. Every theoretical science with a practical application, such as medicine or physics, lives from this perennial assumption which forever proves itself anew. So much is this so, that on this basis philosophy dares to make an ultimate forward leap by projecting a totality of sense upon the totality of the actuality of Being in such a way that now necessity is predicated of the latter. Then Being becomes identical with the necessity to be, and when this identity has been taken up by reason, then there is no longer any space for wonder at the fact that there is something rather than nothing, but at most only for admiration that everything appears so wonderfully and 'beautifully' ordered within the necessity of

Being. This is the beauty of the *theios kosmos* in the late Plato, as earlier in Parmenides and Heraclitus, and again the beauty of the world contained in the Aristotelian *noêsis noêseôs*, and further still it is the beauty of the world order of Boethius and the School of Chartres and of most of what is conveyed in modern times under the titles 'the classical tradition' and 'philosophy of Spirit'. We can also give this 'beauty' the name 'glory' in so far as the total order of phenomena always remains a boundless limiting concept (as for instance K. Ph. Moritz and Goethe put it) for the lived experience of the finite spirit—which strives towards it as 'eros' and proceeds from it as 'intuition'. But 'glory' which is understood in this way is nothing other than the totality of beauty; its 'superiority' over the individual instances of beauty which we encounter derives only from the fact that the categories of rhythm, polarity, the harmonisation (ἁρμονία) of what is apparently lacking in harmony and misshapen, can as yet only be applied to the totality by way of conjecture (in the devout vision of Erigena and Nicolas of Cusa, or in the titanic vision of Heraclitus and Bruno), where they can be monitored in their individual parts by sight and sound (as in a symphony).

A leap forward like this remains in a tension between piety and titanism: a piety which believes that all in essence is good, even when the rhythm of the world and of existence overwhelms that of man, and a titanism because man imposes his own rhythm upon the totality. And if the leap forward in antiquity remained predominantly 'pious', since man experienced above all the superabundance of the universal καλόν and yielded himself to it, in the modern period it becomes visibly more titanic, because man enforces his own καλόν and its rhythm ever more energetically upon the (material) universe.

But such a forward leap towards apprehension of the identity (of Being and meaning), in the very first step of thought, gets the phenomenon wrong. Wonder at Being is not only the beginning of thought, but—as Heidegger sees— also the permanent element (ἀρχή) in which it moves. But this means—contrary to Heidegger—that it is not only astonishing that an existent being can wonder at Being in its own distinction from Being, but also that Being as such by itself to the very end 'causes wonder', behaving as something to be wondered at, something striking and worthy of wonder. Reflection, while holding fast to this primal wonder, must be the fundamental aim of metaphysics; here we are attempting to approach it in four stages, which witness to a fourfold distinction and which together reveal for the first time that which in the realm of metaphysics deserves the authentic name 'Glory'.

1. The fact that I find myself within the realm of a world and in the boundless community of other existent beings is astonishing beyond measure and cannot be exhaustively explained by any cause which derives from within the world. In surveying Western metaphysics in its entirety, we must be amazed at how little the enigma of reproduction—not only of organic natural creatures but above all of man, who is Spirit—has concerned philosophers. From the infinite prodigality of an act of generation—prodigality in the male as well as the female organism resulting in a 'chance hit'—a 'new' being is created which, reflecting upon its personal ego, cannot interpret itself in any way as a product of chance; for it possesses in fact the capacity to view the world as a whole, indeed Being as a whole, from its unrepeatable perspective and thus to effect a unification of what it sees (Leibniz). Nothing within (world-)Being indicates that this had the 'personal' intention of producing precisely this unique and as such irreplaceable person through that game of chance; there is nothing to prove that this unique person receives a kind of necessary place through his incorporation into a (wholly hypothetical) series of monads, as a number receives its necessity within a totality of a series of numbers. I could imagine (and there is nothing to conflict with this idea) that an infinite number of 'others' could have occupied this 'same' place in the universe instead of me. Why it should have been me, I do not know.

Of course, the child does not awaken into consciousness with this question in its mind. And yet it lies, unacknowledged but alive, in the first opening of its mind's eyes. Its 'I' awakens in the experience of a 'Thou': in its mother's smile through which it learns that it is contained, affirmed and loved in a relationship which is incomprehensively encompassing, already actual, sheltering and nourishing. The body which it snuggles into, a soft, warm and nourishing kiss, is a kiss of love in which it can take shelter because it has been sheltered there *a priori*. The awakening of its consciousness is a late occurrence, in comparison with this basic mystery of unfathomable depth. It finally sees only what always has been, and can therefore only confirm it. A light which has been perpetually asleep awakens at some point in to an alert and self-knowing light. But it awakens at the love of the Thou, as it has always slept in the womb and on the bosom of the Thou. The experience of being granted entrance into a sheltering and encompassing world is one which for all incipient, developing and mature consciousness cannot be superseded. Therefore it is right that the child should glimpse the Absolute, 'God' (Parzifal, Simplicius), first in its mother, its parents, and that only in a second and a third stage does it have to learn to distinguish the love of God from the love which it has experienced in this way. It can awake only in Paradise or in what Plato depicts as that Heaven which is the contemplation of the Ideas. The fact that it experiences Being (*Sein*) and human existence (*Dasein*) (why should it make a distinction between the two?) as the incomprehensible light of grace, is the reason why it engages in play. It could not play if—like a beggar at a marriage feast—it had been allowed to come out of a cold and dark outside by the 'grace' of a condescending mercy into a place to which it had no 'right' (these are later experiences, for those who have become guilty, which remain only parentheses within the totality of human experience). It gives itself to play because the experience of being admitted is the very first thing which it knows in the realm of Being. It *is*, in so far as it is allowed to take part as an object of love. Existence is both glorious and a matter of course. Everything, without exception, which is to follow later and will inevitably be added to this experience must remain an unfolding of it. There is no 'gravity of life' which would fundamentally surpass this beginning. There is no 'taking over control' of existence which might go further than this first experience of miracle and play. There is no encounter—with a friend or an enemy or with a myriad passers-by—which could add anything to the encounter with the first-comprehended smile of the mother. 'Unless you become as a child, you cannot enter the kingdom of Heaven': this statement is a tautology. The first experience contains what cannot be surpassed, *id quo majus cogitari non potest*. It is an experience in which distinction slumbers in the unopened unity of the grace of love—at once *before* and *after* the tragedy of its dissolution. However it prevails even there, because that which is 'a matter of course' is not the '*de facto*' with its constraining and finite narrowness, but the graciously-opened whole in which every space is granted to tumble around as much as one wills: existence as play.

Certainly, the distinction will soon become apparent. There is the compulsion of duty, which leads to a divided will, and there is, definitively in puberty, the tragic opposition of a world which goes its own way and in whose constraints I shall have to find my own place if I desire to exist at all, together with my dream of love and of being 'a child of God', which in the face of this world seems the illusion of a fool; and, for my part, I shall despise and reject the world for the sake of my dream and for the sake of the dream I have of the world. But nevertheless, that first mystery prevails even here; it has only unfolded. Neither my parents nor the whole of the surrounding world are substantially that love to which on the grounds of my being and my consciousness I owe the fact of my being in the world, which is to say both myself and the world. That *Angst* which Heidegger depicted, in which Being as such disappears for me and with it my sense of self, becomes the methodical way in which to pose the question as to why Being should exist at all.

In any case, for the thinker nothing would be altered in the first metaphysical distinction, even if the generative act were to be performed in a way which is technically more closely guided and planned: determining the 'character' and the 'conduct' does not reach the point of selfhood where the person knows that he is more than the creation of a genus consciousness which is either accidental or which can be regulated in its contingency. And yet I can never conceive of myself as part of the organism of the world in such a way that this organism could not exist and properly function without me. I cannot attribute to myself the dignity of Being and the degree of necessity which the world as a whole possesses. And thus there occurs an opening within me as Spirit to the light-space of Being, which is in no way directed to the Being of the world as a whole: if in the first aspect my spirit 'nihilates' with respect to the Being of the world into which I find myself to be thrown and constrained, then in the second aspect the Being of the world 'nihilates' within the opening of my spirit, which can attribute to the Being of the world no necessity within itself which would excel our wonder at its existence: both are related to each other, but they do not coincide.

2. But in so far as I am one existent among others, in so far as I am Spirit, I now understand that all other existents stand in the same relation to Being as I do myself. It evidently follows from this that, although all existents partake in Being, yet—to whatever extent we were to multiply them—they never exhaust it nor even, as it were, 'broach' it. In their individual finitude as fragments they can indeed form a greater, perhaps somehow even the greatest whole, which however hangs as much in the air (of Being) as a total configuration as do its constituent parts. I can imagine this total configuration to be quantitatively and qualitatively as extended and as perfect as I will, but still it cannot match my most primitive experience of Being, if indeed I were to see in it the unsurpassable abundance of Being: *id quo majus cogitari non potest*. The nothingness through which all its parts pass does not dissolve within the whole; and on the other hand Being, in which a world totality participates, possesses its own mode of 'nihilating', that is an indissoluble identity with respect to every participation within it (Proclus: *amethektôs metekhetai*). The Neoplatonists are therefore right when they refuse to identify the 'beauty' of the totality of that which is

with the 'glory' of Being itself which prevails beyond it, and who glimpse within the former only a 'reflection' of the latter. And in the same way Thomas Aquinas is right when he attributes to the *actus essendi* its own *bonum-pulchrum* in which the individual *essentiae* and the world which is constituted by them only participate. But if my spirit is conformed to this act of Being in which it participates and also performs the act of thinking (*intellectus agens*) in the light of this superessential (and thus incomprehensible, or as Rosmini has it, 'idea-like') act of Being in order to grasp what is essential, then it understands at the same time that it is not the act of Being which has the responsibility of bringing essences into existence from itself, just as it is not my *intellectus agens* (without the *conversio ad phantasma*) which constructs the real world; not only 'concepts without intuition are empty', but the 'idea' or the 'light' or the 'abundance' of Being remain so too. What this means, once again, is that I cannot appease my primal and overpowering wonder at the fact that 'something is' through gazing at Being, in which those things participate and thus exist. Rather, my wonder is directed at both sides of the Ontological Difference, whether this is construed in Thomist or Heideggerian terms, for the fact that an existent can only become actual through participation in the act of Being points to the complementary antithesis that the fullness of Being attains actuality only in the existent; but the fact that (Heideggerian) Being can only be interpreted within existence (Spirit) points to the complementary antithesis that existence (Spirit) grasps the dependence of Being upon beings and thus its non-substantiality.

3. Precisely by virtue of this dependence (which Thomas, Hegel and Heidegger equally see) of Being upon its explication in the existent (or in the human existent, which is to say man), it is impossible to attribute to Being the responsibility for the essential forms of entities in the world. The *indifferentia* of the abundance which is characteristic of the Being of the existent fundamentally contradicts any form of planning, located within Being, in order to actualise itself

in substance through a specific ascending sequence of stages of essential forms, which contain it first as 'vessels' and then (as Heidegger says) finally shepherd it. For the 'plans' lie in the entity, not in Being, however true it may be that there are no entities which do not participate in Being. Thus all those forms of interpretation must be rejected as 'oblivious of Being' which conceive of the totality of the world–entity–reality as the (self-)explication of Being: whether Being (God) explicates itself statically in a world as the unitive implication of all entities (Plotinus, Nicolas of Cusa, Böhme), or whether Being (God) as the non-subsisting epitome of all entities actualises itself dynamically through a world (Fichte, Hölderlin as philosopher, Schelling, Hegel, the early Soloviev). And correspondingly, the category of 'expression' must be rejected as a precise statement of the relationship between Being which prevails without substance as abundance, and the participating entity; for 'expression' presupposes a responsible decision to express oneself, which Being as such does not make, because it attains such decisiveness only within the existent Spirit. Only in an analogical sense (which however is not considered in the systems mentioned above) can it be said that every form of actuality—whether as individual existent or world totality—expresses something of the fullness of reality (but precisely *without* the latter's expressing 'itself').

A biological and evolutionary sequence of stages—if there ever could be such a thing as a self-sufficient system—would at best be able to allow the ascent of the individual essential form, say that of a bird, from its preformations in an earlier form, say that of the fish, but it would never be able to derive the inherent necessity of a single perfected essential form in which—in a wholly anti-Kantian manner—*pulchritudo* and *perfectio* evidently coincide, from the ends of a total evolution of the whole of life or the whole of Being in movement towards itself. The entities, precisely the sub-intellectual art works of the *prakriti*, of creative Nature, bear the mark of an unconditionedly original imaginative power to which one must be blind if one—I do not say classifies their forms within the evolutionary process, but explains them entirely on the grounds of their position within this process. To this degree the realm of forms of sub-human Nature remains a singularly illuminating touchstone for the value of a metaphysics: anyone like Descartes and the Materialists, who explains animals in a purely mechanical way has already lost, but so too have those who, like Schelling and Hegel, interpret the forms of Nature as the ways and stages of the Absolute Spirit in search of Itself—or in the more ancient version of Erigena and Nicolas of Cusa—as the Absolute Spirit which explicates Itself. The first approach cannot interpret the *glorious* freedom of the essential forms, indeed not even the necessity of such forms, while the second does not explain how the Spirit which is still only in search of Itself achieves such perfection which presupposes, not only a luminous intelligence (and not mere unconscious powers of imagination), but a superior and playful freedom beyond all the constraints of Nature; and the third approach again fails to explain why a divine abundance of Being should explicate itself precisely in beetles and butterflies and not also in entirely different, unpredictably various, forms and figures.

Heidegger also offers us no information regarding the underivability of the interrelation between essential form and Being; in his work, sub-human Nature receives as little metaphysical interpretation as it does with the other thinkers named above. Rather, the 'pivot' of Being and of the existent (*Sein-Seiendes*) receives the whole of its meaning from the pivot of Being and human being (*Sein-Dasein*: man as shepherd of Being). And this interrelation is then so loaded with meaning that the original question as to why there should be something rather than nothing is finally submerged, and metaphysics must yield its place to a *phenomenology* of Being in the realm of its distinction. But this priority of Being over human existence does not mean that responsibility for the essential forms (as 'presuppositions' for the 'essence-less' character of human existence) can be attributed to Being. If we close the circle, no matter how, between Being and essence (the existent), then 'glory' as a metaphysical category is lost: it dissolves on the one hand into the beauty of order that prevails within the world (the totality of which then becomes 'explicated' Being), and on the other it is submerged in the necessity of an ineluctable self-explication of Being, governed by no ultimate form of freedom, in order simply to be itself. In both cases, the primal phenomenon is not treated appropriately, and not even the most soaring metaphysical towers can conceal this; and it is something of this failure which is understood by those Materialists who reject such speculative systems as conceptual dreams. But the Materialists themselves fail even more fundamentally to do justice to the primal experience, since they do not in the least want to enquire into why matter should exist at all in the first place.

Within the world, 'expression' remains a category of the 'beautiful' whose radiance and charm easily brings the word 'glorious' (*herrlich*) to our lips, but which can only inauthentically lay claim to the sense of 'lordship' (*herrschaftlich*) and 'majesty' (*hehr*) which inhere within it: in as much, that is, as the 'ground' of a living entity—be it a plant, animal or person—is always 'more' than what is projected on to the phenomenal surface, and this mysterious More can also be read in a mysterious manner from that surface,[1] most supremely in the free spiritual being which, in expressing itself, remains the sovereign capacity (mendaciously) to conceal itself all the while. And yet this is not at all sufficient to characterise the incomprehensible 'freedom' of Being itself, which plays indifferently over all things and is bound to nothing, and on the grounds of which the elevated, sublime (transcendental) radiance of glory is justified, that radiance which streams intangibly through everything which is. Just as Being does not mould everything which is to itself, but lets it be, in the same way all that is must correspondingly allow Being to dwell in its imperturbability, in order that its light should rise over all. To press oneself too closely against Being, as Hölderlin did, is to conceal it further and to confuse it with God Himself. In the space of the distinction which opens up when Being allows us to be and we Being, two things can happen: first, the elevation of Being above us can cause it to appear to us as

---

[1] *Cf. Wahrheit* I (1942), pp. 233–255.

something which is alien, indifferent and even fearful, and we can be tempted to view it as neutral, value-less, meaningless, and thus to give precedence to non-Being, when the darkening of our human existence in guilt, illness and death, and the horrifying aspects of the existent world as a whole seem to authorise us to pronounce such a curse against Being itself. This fearfulness is no less when we become shudderingly aware of the nameless waste of individual and personal life through the whole, when not only Nature appears as the Calvary of life, but also History as a Golgotha of the Spirit (Hegel), and when man must trample down his own heart in order to justify, against his own self, the World-Spirit which lacerates him. And yet: in the same distance of letting be, Being can appear to us in its glory, for which the relation of expression is now only an image (although the most important one), in a glory which excels in mysterious elevation all the beauty and order of the actual world, although the latter is equally a reflection and an indication of it; possessing a value so infinite and so fundamentally unsurpassable (capable at most of being unfolded) that all lordly 'power' (in the victory over the impotence of what is only-possible), all light (in the victory over the darkness of nothingness), all 'grace' (in the infinite gift of participation) are gathered in it.

The Western metaphysical systems of light ultimately opt for the second possibility, a homage to Being which lets Being in its totality be. Virtually the whole of Greek myth and philosophy is bathed in this enfolding light: Homer's gods and men stand in it together, Pindar's victories, Sappho's devotion, high sculpture is bathed in it, Plato's allegory of the cave expresses it, Aristotle's quintessence, the Stoic primal fire, the Plotinian stream of Being. Throughout Greek patristics, throughout Boethius and Erigena, and again the natural philosophies of Grosseteste, Albert, Ulrich, Nicolas of Cusa, Ficino, Descartes, Patrizzi, the Enlightenment (*siècle des lumières*), Goethe.

But the other, the first possibility of the deepest alienation from Being and darkening of Being can overtake whole epochs; it does so extensively in the period of late antiquity, more tragically in the late Middle Ages, and more fatally still in our own late modernity. It is like a fateful loss of sight which befalls whole generations: the extreme questionability of the existent world distorts our view of encompassing Being, and the primal metaphysical question is no longer asked with regard to the latter, so that the light of Being no longer shines over the world. Too much is demanded of the latter in this case when its own essential light is supposed to suffice for Being as a whole and, since this excessive demand lies clear to view, the forced optimism of the forced worldliness turns perpetually into nihilistic tragedy. The injustice of the world is directly transferred to Being as a whole, which thus itself appears unjust. The scholastic metaphysics which derive from the late Middle Ages and which have achieved only a neutral concept of Being, of which of course the καλόν cannot any more be asserted, no longer form a bulwark against this nihilism.

4. The preceding dimensions of distinction necessarily diverge. I find myself in a world in whose necessity my accidental existence cannot find a place as *pars integralis*. But all existents are in an analogous situation, since they too—either as fragments or as world-wholes—do not fit into Being as *partes integrales*. Here a third point comes into view: namely, that Being as a whole or the actuality of all that is actual does not generate from itself the actual entities, for the responsible generation of forms would presuppose a conscious and free spirit. It is therefore impossible to allow, as Heidegger does, the distinction between Being and the existent to be suspended as an ultimate mystery, resting within itself. It is precisely this which points inexorably beyond itself to the fourth and final distinction, which alone provides an answer to the opening question. One's gaze must seek to penetrate beyond the Ontological Difference (which is not far removed from the Thomist *distinctio realis* in its systematic significance) to the distinction between God and world, in which God is the sole sufficient ground for both Being and the existent in its possession of form. The primal question of the *Da-Sein* (human existence: 'being-there') which finds itself present proceeds from its own non-necessity, and its counterpart,

which is the greater necessity firstly of the world and then that of encompassing Being, does not prove to be strong enough to provide an ultimate foundation for Being, which is thus left suspended, or to overwhelm it by means of integrations (Hegel). It appears rather that the third distinction leaves actual Being just as much, indeed for the first time fully because finally, hanging in the air, as I found myself to be hanging in the air. The consequence is that the grounding in God of this Being which does not depend upon any necessity, points to an *ultimate freedom* which neither Being (as non-subsistent) could have, nor the existent entity (since it always finds itself as already constituted in its own essentiality). And so on the one hand, the freedom of non-subsisting Being can be secured in its 'glory' in the face of all that exists only if it is grounded in a subsisting freedom of absolute Being, which is God; and so, on the other hand, the dignity of an essential form evades being threatened by the encompassing act of Being and thus being swallowed up and devoured as an invalid 'stage of Being' only if its valid contour can be referred back to a sovereign and absolute imagination or power of creation. If the Ontological Difference must already, as bifurcation, be referred back to a *unicum* (as Plotinus correctly and definitively saw), then it will be secured as the authentic 'site of glory in metaphysics' in its deepest affirmation of Being under *the* condition that the 'gloriousness' of its floating in the air, its oscillation, is not hardened into a mathematical necessity (as ultimately happens in Heidegger) but remains the event of an absolute freedom and thus of grace within its open-ended sway, in which each 'pole' has to seek and to find its 'salvation' in the other pole: Being arrives at itself as subsistence only within the entity and the entity arrives at its actuality (and thus at the possibility of its self-generation and *perfectio*) only within its participation in Being.

And so in what is actual there reigns a mystery beyond fullness and poverty,[2] each of which expresses it accurately but still inadequately. Nothing is richer and fuller than Being

[2] For the following see: Ferdinand Ulrich: *Homo Abyssus. Das Wagnis der Seinsfrage* (1961).

in its incomprehensibly glorious and absolute victory over nothingness (Being without this fullness is inconceivable; it would be only spectrally present in the first beginnings of thought), and yet this fullness can unfold absolutely only *once*: in God. But since there is nothing against which it must assert itself (for nothingness is nothingness), it does not need, holding on to itself, to enclose itself in the casing of an entity in order perhaps to break out from this and communicate itself beyond its borders (which it does not have). Rather, fullness as such is pure power (Nicolas of Cusa: *Possest*) from whose potency (*Macht*) all that is potential (*das Mögbare*) proceeds as rich abundance (*das Vermögliche*), which is thus pure freedom and, as freedom which does not hold on to itself (or gather itself together into an 'entity'), is also pure gift and love. This mystery of the streaming self-illumination of Being, which was glimpsed by Plato and Plotinus and which alone explains the possibility of a world (that is, the paradoxical existence 'alongside' Infinite Being which fills all things and which stands in need of none), attains its transparency only when, from the sphere of the biblical revelation, absolute freedom (as the spirituality and personality of God) shines in: but not in such a way that the personal God encounters man as one existent marked off from another existent (with the omission of Being; as one could suppose if one were to interpret the Old Testament without recourse to philosophy), but rather in such a way that the personal and free depths of self-giving absolute Being first bring the mystery of Creation, the 'fourth distinction', into the light. God is the Wholly Other only as the *Non-Aliud*, the Not-Other (Nicolas of Cusa): as He who covers all finite entities with the one mantle of his indivisible Being in so far as they are able to participate in his reality at an infinite remove—as 'entities', which are not Him, but which owe their possibility to His power, and their wealth (to grasp Him as the One who is actual and to shelter in Him) to His creative freedom.

God-given Being is both fullness and poverty at the same time: fullness as Being without limit, poverty modelled ultimately on God Himself, because He knows no holding on to Himself, poverty in the act of Being which is given out, which *as* gift delivers itself without defence (because here too it does not hold on to itself) to the finite entities. But equally, the created entities are simultaneously fullness and poverty: fullness in the power to shelter and to tend (as 'shepherd of Being') the gift of the fullness of Being within themselves, however 'poor' they may be on account of their limitation, and poverty again in a double sense in as much as the container experiences its inability to scoop out the whole ocean with its small bowl and, instructed by this experience, comprehends the letting-go of Being—as letting-be and letting-stream, handing on further—as the inner fulfilment of the finite entity. Here, through the greater dissimilarity of the finite and the infinite existent, the positive aspect of the *analogia entis* appears, which makes of the finite the shadow, trace, likeness and image of the Infinite. And not in such a way that the finite 'first' constitutes itself as a 'closed' entity or subject (through the seizing and hoarding of the parcel of actuality which it is able to take into oneself from the stream of finite Being) in order 'then' (and perhaps for the rounding-out of its own perfection) to pass the surplus on. But rather in such a way that the finite, since it is subject, already constitutes itself as such through the letting-be of Being by virtue of an *ekstasis* out of its own closed self, and therefore through dispossession and poverty becomes capable of salvaging in recognition and affirmation the infinite poverty of the fullness of Being and, within it, that of the God who does not hold on to Himself. Only on this level and in this medium can the event take place which the Bible describes as the process from (God) person to (man) person: predestination, election, vocation, justification, sanctification, glorification (Rom 8, 28–30), for all these are *modi* of radiant and universal love and have as their basis the breadth of the world's creation as a whole (Rom 8, 18–25) and of its painful (painful for God and for the world) concealment in the mantle of the divine Being which encompasses all things (Rom 8, 26–27).

2. THE THEOLOGICAL *A PRIORI* ELEMENT IN METAPHYSICS

If in this manner biblical revelation rests on the basis of the primal God-world distinction, and thus on metaphysics, and radiates from this point, then metaphysics correspondingly attains fulfilment in the event of revelation, if it does not want to make a definitive halt at preliminary stages and thus become fatally fixed. The possibility, sketched out above in the third distinction, of a choice in the interpretation of the detachment of Being still remains unresolved. Could the glory of Being which soars above all that exists not be understood in its unsurpassable alienness in another way: as abandonment, instead of simply letting-be? Where is the guarantee that the finite entity is genuinely sheltered in the infinite indifference of Being? And if it experiences the incomprehensible alienness which prevails within the distinction and yet still gives precedence to its encompassing character, must it not then necessarily petition for its own self-elimination and, in so far as this is its concern, also strive for it, as happens in India and in so many areas of Western metaphysics too?

The 'choice' of the interpretation of Being is not something that can be decided by man, because both sides of the choice (which are mutually exclusive) each commend a truth. Both protective accompaniment and uncanny alienation prevail. It is impossible to merge the two into one on the same level (as Heidegger does); one can see from this that metaphysics in itself defies completion and, in the event that it nevertheless wants to attain completion, must make the different levels of the Ontological Difference identical—as we have shown.[3] The confusion is complete if in the end the negations of Negative Theology, the inner-divine mystery of self-outpouring (as basis for the following two aspects), the

---

[3] *Cf.* above, p. 447.

'noughting' of the communicated fullness of Being in its non-subsistence, and ultimately the kenosis of Christ are partially or wholly equated; thereby the ultimate theologoumenon is totally shorn of its theological character and cannot therefore be fruitful for metaphysics either. There exist at least tendencies towards this in the mysticism of the Rhineland, in Böhme, Hölderlin, Hegel and Heidegger. But such equations absolutise what belongs to the world and reduce God to world. The onset of confusion occurs where the events of historicity between God and man (to which also the event of an alienation of man from God belongs) are equated with the 'event' of the destiny of Being (Heidegger) or with the inner dialectic of the absolute Spirit (Hegel).

But where could metaphysics derive the authority to make a distinction between the levels—essentially those of 'creation' and 'grace'—before the Ground, which releases from Itself both Being and all that is, has manifested Itself as such in a personal and sovereignly free manner? Metaphysics can at most refer back to myth and attempt that hybrid synthesis of the 'unfinishable bridge', which is all the more hybrid in that myth itself persists in indissoluble ambiguity: a spirit-like cry from the depths of Being—or projection of the human personality on to impersonal Being? The claim of metaphysics to critical self-responsibility through reason will necessarily tend towards the latter and will explain man's address from Being as man's address to Being ('eros'). Thus the relationship between 'metaphysics' and still-surviving 'religion' which is not content with a mere transcendence of human longing becomes unclear. But to the extent that it holds to one kind of revelation or other, it alienates from itself the scientistic metaphysics which, as Plato said, tends increasingly to Titanism. Thus this becomes entirely man's own achievement, retrieves eros into itself as man's own potentiality and is no longer essentially distinct from any other science, whereby it effects its own elimination.

In distinction to this, the taking seriously of the address from Being tends in the direction of making the individual myth, as finite myth, transparent to the entire language of Being, which thus does not allow the individual to be submerged in anonymous ordinariness but can draw him out into the hearing of a personal address. This happened most magnificently in Virgil, but it was prefigured in Homer and Pindar, as it was in Greek tragedy. The hero of the *Aeneid* is *pius* as one who listens to and obeys his unique and yet universal task (the founding of the Roman empire), and his devotion to this mission is his achieved self-transcendence. In the same way, Alcestis in her self-sacrifice for her lover accepted an opportunity opened to her by God, Pindar's hero conquered in a grace which flowed from Being, the wandering Odysseus followed a path of providence, which he himself could not see, under the guidance of his protective goddess. This particular path has become integral in Aeneas as 'spoken Being' (*fatum*), containing within itself all the particular utterances of the gods. Virgil recapitulates in this the actual historical fate of the world—beyond the faded possibilities of metaphysics and religion. He unites in his allegorical image what could no longer be fused by the power of thought alone. As a poet, he therefore describes the point at which, without any possible anticipation, God begins to speak from the depths of His own heart.

All the fragments of meaning which inhere in metaphysics are contained in this unforeseeable speech: above all, the first dismayed astonishment at the fact 'that I am', which refuses consolation from any philosophical assertion of its necessity. Then it contains the hovering oscillation of the unbridgeable difference, to which there adheres need as well as glory, poverty as well as the fullness of true reality, and which cannot be grounded anywhere but in an absolute freedom which sanctifies the oscillation as such. And then the other oscillation—comprehensible only within it—between universality and unique personality: every existence in the world, every mission which gives fullness of meaning to a human life, all noetics, ethics and aesthetics. The ineluctable polarity of failure and success, of wound and healing, of sacrifice and happiness which prevails in reality as it is; the deep will to death and self-sacrifice which cannot be outweighed by the simultaneous will to life and self-fulfilment. So much are these concerns of the heart, which have been gained and understood on the basis of the Ontological Difference, contained in the biblical word and forever held open there, that mankind would like above all to appropriate and to interpret this revelation itself as the central projection of his own self-transcending heart. But the word of God prevents this by the unyielding force with which it turns upside-down the person who begins to listen to it. It convicts him first of his disobedience; it makes him responsible for his alienation from God; it imposes upon him an initially quite alien ('positive') commandment and law; it says disconcerting things about him which would otherwise never have occurred to him in his self-reflection. And precisely in this inexorability lies salvation for him, for it is only in this way that it is forcefully impressed upon such a person that 'Another' than himself is concerned about him, and that his famed concern (for himself or for Being) has long been surpassed by the concern which 'Another' bears for him and on his behalf. But the question of which form this concern has desired to take lies quite beyond the realm of metaphysics. We will speak of it in the final volume of this work.

But however at odds revelation may be to all that is foreseeable, and however little it may appear to be the supplying of a missing fragment, it must nevertheless enter into the distinctions as a form of completion: the word of God must be written into the word of Being, the word of Being into the words of creatures which are exchanged as comprehensible words among existent creatures. Thus the distinctions as such are obediently at the disposal of God's revelation. And they are so in so far as the highest distinction (between God and the Being of the existent) is only the oscillation between the giver and the gift, whereby gift signifies the being given (and being received) of the giver. Nothing substantial and subsistent, therefore, but the radiant fullness of God's Being in the condition of its being given to the finite recipient. The scholastics of the Franciscan school tentatively circled around this mystery, nor was it unknown, *via* the Plotinian and Dionysian tradition, to the Dominicans. The non-subsistence of the *actus essendi* is the creative medium which suffices for God to utter His kenotic word of the Cross and of glory and to send it as His Son into the world to experience death and resurrection. This word (which brings with itself its own grace) will ultimately be grasped only by those who hold out within the oscillation of distinction and who do not make themselves guilty of the 'essentialisation' (F. Ulrich) of defenceless and radiant Being—an 'essentialisation' which is the death and paralysis of both Being and the word.

To overlook the noughting of Being in favour of essences which with its help attain the power to be, is inevitably to blind oneself to the mysterious shining which inheres within Being: a shining which in its transparency contains the 'flowing light of the Godhead' (Mechthild) and raises the world of finite essences into its brightness. Being itself is 'not the light' but gives 'witness to the light' in so far as it points to it by virtue of its own non-subsistence. When therefore in Western philosophy Being is posited as the horizon of the cosmos, it is itself either understood to be the sphere of the shining (Aristotle) or better, as the 'first emanation' of a light of the 'Good' which prevails beyond Being, as the absolutised self-emanation. Thus the highest distinction is expressed in words which are still accessible to metaphysics at its extreme limits. But here it becomes clear why the pre-eminent spirit-place from which the shining of Being—in its serene elevation beyond all finite essence—becomes visible, has to be that 'poverty of spirit' which is distinguished in the history of metaphysics as ἀπάθεια—detachment or impassivity—and which is demanded by Plato too for his highest degree of eros: varied forms of self-stripping which, though accessible to false kinds of absolutisation are, as the renouncing of one's own self-interested power for the sake of harmonising with Being, also capable of being changed into evangelical poverty. But where the attitude of renunciation hardens to a defence against pain and death—and thus also against love—it becomes self-deception and deprives itself of its sensitivity to the light. Only rarely do metaphysicians entirely escape this danger; but Christianity by its own nature possesses the power and the responsibility of arming the spirit against this kind of abuse of detachment and to disarm the heart so that it becomes purely receptive—even, and precisely, to pain and deprivation. That which is thus received is not anything neutral, or abstract, but is a food which is worthy of the spirit. We can call it the 'word' of Being, if we understand that to be a communication which points beyond all formulated and formulatable speech to the origin of the communication and thus also to the origin of the facility of speech of spiritual beings. It is only necessary to distinguish this speech of Being clearly from all free revelations of the word from the heart of the Godhead, as well as from the free creative speech of existent beings. The communication of Being lies, as we have already seen, simply enclosed in the child's wonder at reality with the first opening of its eyes: in the fact that it is *permitted* to be in the midst of what exists. This condition of being permitted cannot be surpassed by any additional insight into the laws and necessities of the world. It emerges within the first distinction, communicates itself in the second to all co-existent entities and, in the third, grasps Being itself. Because no existent thing can be deduced by necessity from Being, but nevertheless exists in that it partakes in Being, and because this participation and sharing are two aspects of one and the same incomprehensible (because not able to be grounded within itself) oscillation, therefore the word of Being is itself the permission to be. This is recalled every time man raises his eyes above the pseudo-necessities of his empirical and transcendental activity. It encourages us to believe in an encompassing grace beyond all laws, categories and schematisms. The categorical imperative of Being does not only consider, as does that of Kant, our own human fellow-world upon which the human agent is supposed to impose a law, but it considers Being altogether, since this rises up above every law into grace. In this, it is even more demanding than Kant's system, in which man exists alone and forgetful of Being. Act in such a way, we are now told, as if you yourself, your fellow-man and fellow-object owed your existence to a boundless grace. To a grace in which Being itself bathes in its primal distinction as an emergence both dark and luminous, through which it reveals itself. It is not difficult to see how the language of intellectual beings evolves in descent from this primal word of the world, as the sign of having heard that indication and as its application to the sphere of spiritual freedom, which in speech always opens itself up with grace in its background, while in ascent from it the revelatory Word of God becomes possible, which now first reveals both the *foundation* for the fact that Being proclaims grace, and where the origin lies of the permission to be.

B. LOVE AS CUSTODIAN OF GLORY

I. THE LIGHT OF BEING AND LOVE

Let us consider again the distinction which opens up in four different ways: for the four phases shown were only the ever greater extension of the same thing which is already present in the first act of consciousness of the awakening child. This first act, journeying towards transcendence, immediately touches the final end: there can be nothing more beyond the love which wakens me and shelters me, and which greets me in the smiling face of my mother. Many things can interfere: incomprehensible departure and abandonment, privation, disappointment, not being understood, pain, death. But all that is only an interpolation. Perhaps it will appear infinite, perhaps interrupted by lightning recollections of the origin: but I have been given a measure for all that is called distance and distinction. However excluded I may be, I remain primally someone who has been permitted entry. And then comes the second insight: we have all been permitted entry. Our mother too. And the animals with which I play. There is much that is real, and yet Being overarches everything, sublime and serene; nothing of all this had to be as it is. Everything stands in an open light which is greater and more glorious than the essence of this world with all its terror and beauty. Thus there is the third point: what would happen to this light if none of us existed to see it? Does it stand in need of us? No, I, all of us, are 'accidental' with respect to it. Taken altogether, we are not a sufficient explication of being; it is free to manifest itself in an infinite number of other ways and to be a light for an infinite number of other entities. Nevertheless: what would light be if there were no one to see it? Are we then both necessary to one another: Being to existents and existents to Being? Do we both experience the process of noughting? Is the permission to be, the being given entry, a beginning both for me and for Being? Does it become glorious only by virtue of its being in need? Is it serene only because it has been given entry—into us? Do we then both hover in oscillation, and is this hovering that which has been freed, which is unconditioned? But how can this double dependence, and so mutual conditionedness, produce an Absolute? And so gingerly, almost against our will, we must posit the fourth opening of distinction: beyond the still conditioned, mutually dependent freedom of the existent with regard to Being and the freedom of Being to shine unconstrainedly as a light within the existent: an unconditioned freedom, or one which is at most one which is conditioned through itself, and which is untouched by nothingness, an *actus purus*, which is posited in the first instance only in order to preserve the light of openness between Being and the existent as a free and unconstrained light so that the individual entity is not submerged within the exigencies of a process of explication and Being does not lose its freedom in the same 'Odyssey' of its cosmic evolution towards itself. Otherwise the primal experience of the child is false and is contradicted by the ingenuity of adulthood and the wisdom of metaphysics. But if the most precious thing which must be preserved in Being can only be preserved by God, viz. its miraculous and glorious character, then must not God be pre-eminently the guardian and the shepherd of this glory: in direct contradiction to what the finite spirit imagines as necessity and absoluteness? And then is not that which we experience in the contingent and dualistic nature of the world as possessing the greatest beauty, that oscillation which is wholly unconstrained, both within itself and to others, which comprehends and grounds all justified and satisfying necessities, incomprehensibly, that which we find again, new and different, in God? If He creates the world without constraint and imparts to it, with its unconstraining unconstrainedness, something of the manner of His freedom and sovereign power of gift, and if this bestowing freedom deserves no name but love: then from what other ground could God 'be' than 'from' love? Any attempt other than this to approach the 'Absolute' beyond the Ontological Difference would have to ascribe less to the Absolute than to what derives from it.

The fundamental metaphysical act is love within the Ontological Difference (that is, the third distinction, which includes the first two within itself); the fundamental Christian act is love within the God-world distinction (than is, the fourth, which contains the first three within itself): in each case love means here the total human act which comprehends the totality of mind and body and, in particular, percipient intelligence. As metaphysical intelligence, it perceives the relation of the existent and Being which defies formulation and, as Christian intelligence, it perceives God's free word of absolute love which utters itself as a medium within this relation. But we must guard here against both false distinctions and false equations. We are following the right path when we genuinely locate the metaphysical act within the Ontological Difference—even if it naturally points to God as its depths— and understand the Christian act as a new response to the new word of God which, of course, contains the metaphysical act within itself and, beyond that, contributes also to its fulfilment. It is necessary to elucidate this once again by running briefly through the history of metaphysics. In distinction to the intellectual limitations and impoverishments of present metaphysical thinking, this must above all be a history of metaphysical love. In distinction to all the reductions of the metaphysical act, it is however necessary to pay attention at every point to the distinguishing of the degrees of distinction in order to unmask confusions and over-simplifications.

In *Homer*, the distinction arises elementally between those who are self-luminous (gods) and those who stand in the light (men); the self-luminous gods are at the same time both elevated and unconcerned, *and* illumining and involved in events, while those who receive their light become their true selves (heroes) the more they go beyond themselves (becoming *ek-sistent*) into the divine light through a posture which is prayerful and trusting. The light is common and reciprocal, and the darkness which it encloses (*moira*), though remaining unillumined, is also affirmed.

In the *Tragedians*, the distinction is affirmed in a similarly elemental way, but for man, in the radicality of his exposure, the light turns to darkness: the *moira*-darkness is assumed into the will of the gods and his luminous *ek-sistence* is experienced as the extreme form of unshielded vulnerability. But whatever the outcome of this encounter may be, man's salvation or his downfall, it is at any rate affirmed (tragedy is liturgy), and the ultimate self-sacrifice of man is reckoned in the statement of affirmation.

In the case of *Pindar*, the unity (identity) of the affirmed distinction is attained in the high-point of the *agôn*: the grace of the gods and the achievement of men coincide in the 'victory'. The first philosophers, for their part, pursue the unity of the distinction in proud soarings: *Heraclitus* when he includes the dark remainder within the law of harmony of the Logos, *Parmenides* when he eliminates the darkness of distinction as the non-existent; both do so in order to be able to utter a whole-hearted Yes and Amen to Being. The *Pythagoreans* appropriate the whole for themselves by numbers, in which quantity and quality harmonise.

By means of his questioning, *Socrates* keeps the distinction open and dies on account of his love for the immalleability of truth; *Plato* also holds it open in his *chôrismos* (the division between idea and thing) and stretches between them the eros which, bearing within itself the source (identity) as recollection, yearns for wisdom (*philo-sophia*). On the other hand, comprehending reason (ἐπιστήμη) discovers that the Being which is visible to our eyes is itself inwardly permeated with nothingness (dialectic). The final form (in the *Timaeus*) becomes indecipherable: eros is fulfilled in full affirmation within the perfect and rounded universe (which comprehends both gods and men), whose grounding through the Demiurge in accordance with the ideas can be narrated only in a 'sacred language of images' (myth). And only from its margins does the aroused eros of the entire universe become visible in *Aristotle* as all-grounding and self-reflecting mind together with man's participation from outside in Spirit (θύραθεν). But God, the universe which circles upon itself (κυκλοφορία), and the encompassing Being (οὐσία) together indivisibly form the object of metaphysics, and the second, third and fourth distinctions merge into one another. Not until *Plotinus* does the light arise afresh in greatness, since here the Spirit (the world of the ideas) is moved in a hitherto unheard-of manner by the eros of a yearning which is both needy and not needy: towards the Inconceivable, the Unique and the Good, which is the primal source of all beauty, although it does not itself even 'deign to be beautiful'. Here thought and love are one, and both are the light of the world, although this light breaks forth from an inaccessible place, which as a fathomless ground and source is a non-light or a darkness or a superabundant light. It is true that here Being is equated with thought, but both exist by the grace of the One, both too, in so far as they are eros-like, are permeated by nothingness (the doctrine of intelligible matter), and only in this way are both the ground which generates what exists as 'soul' and 'nature'.

Just as with Homer and the Tragedians love within the distinction was a metaphysical love which was in no way erotic in the sexual sense, and in Plato eros (of the homosexual and then also the heterosexual kind) was also only an image of the metaphysical eros, in the same way *amor* in Virgil becomes light which discloses Being; boyishly tremulous in the *Eclogues*, of manly solidity in the *Georgics*, pan-historically open in the *Aeneid*—love here as the pure *ek-sistence* of man in his obedience to fate, but also as the guiding, gracious, accompanying destiny itself (Zeus, Venus as the voices of Being) in the face of an all-contradicting fate (Juno).

It is *Augustine*[4] who takes over the metaphysics of Being-Light and the metaphysical Knowledge-Love into Christianity and who determines it more profoundly than does Plotinus by the (evangelical) decision of man for or against the light in which absolute love prevails. The light in which our spirit sees and thinks is not directly God, but even less is it the natural light which the creature possesses; rather, it is truth which holds sway as the openness of God, in accordance with which it thinks in orientation towards God

---

[4] *Cf.* Vol. II, pp. 95–143 (Eng. trans.).

an, in turning from which, it loses God. And this turning towards or away is determined by the claims of love and by man's response to them. After Augustine, and without renouncing his direction, the metaphysics of Being is conditioned by the paradoxes of the *Areopagite*: God revealed in the world *as* He who is concealed. The light in the world (which is the distinction between the *archai* and the existent) is the light of the divine eros towards the human eros, but it points as a whole towards the mystery of the more than radiant darkness. This holds also for *Gregory the Great*. It is critically important that those philosophies which work with the model of the God–world relation of implication and explication (*Erigena*, *Nicolas of Cusa*) also fully adopt that paradox and thus escape idealist rationalism, for which the implication (God) will be comprehensible, or even in an evolutionary way constructable, on the basis of the explication. In this way, they preserve space for love and also for that all-grounding awe which characterises above all the love of the founders: *Benedict*, *Francis* and *Ignatius*. If the scheme of interpretation of metaphysical love is determined by the eros of the ancients to such an extent that the *Victorines* do not in essence distinguish it in structural terms from agape, then eros from Augustine on is seen as *desiderium*, i.e., as all that is contrary to a love which victoriously takes possession, rather a love which powerlessly and longingly yearns and which disposes itself for the reception of free grace. As such, it also permeates the first ontological attempts to construe Being and the existent itself as gift: this is what we find in *Boethius* and *Cassiodorus*, for whom all the beauty of the world is received in prayerful thanksgiving as love which flows from the Godhead, in *John Erigena* in his distinction between *datio* (the gift of Being and substance) and *donatio* (the gift of the participation of the existent in the wealth of Being), in *Chartres* and in *Gilbert*, and even more so in *Alexander of Hales*, for whom the existent is understood as pure ('material') indefiniteness for the progressive endowments of Being, as in the doctrine of the real distinction of *Thomas*, in the ontology of *Eckhart* and from this point on within the whole spiritual family which was summed up in the 'Metaphysics of the

Saints'. It is within this context that we must place the medieval metaphysics of light, which only rarely makes the mistake of understanding Being itself (divine or worldly) to be substantial light (*Adam of Paris*), but which either sees the highest analogy to God in the worldly light with its power of revelation (*manifestabilitas*), as do *Grosseteste, Bonaventure* and *Albert*, or alternatively interprets the stages of the world's Being from the point of view of God as the streaming superabundance of light: *Areopagitically* above all as the potency of a loving reception (contemplation) and a loving flowing-on (action). And so even in the brightest of these doctrines of love, the dimension of the Dionysian darkness is never absent, neither in the Franciscan line (where love still presses on into that darkness of God where reason can no longer follow), nor in the Dominican school (since in Thomas negative theology takes precedence throughout).

A kind of testing of metaphysical love came with the epochal darkening of the fourteenth century: here there is a parting of the ways. The philosophers strain and storm *nominalistically* and shatter the web of the world dialectically, while the lovers surrender themselves to the night and discover the existential form of detachment (*Gelassenheit*). This presupposes that man is disposed, as in the literary tragedies of antiquity and in part the Stoa, to see even *the night* as a light (unseen, but therefore only all the more profound). It has to be admitted that here in most places the distinctions that pertain within the ontological distinctions are effaced, not only when Being is straightforwardly equated with God, but already when Being (as the first *arché* from God: *Dionysius*) is interpreted according to the Platonic analogy of the sun as the pure 'flowing light of the Godhead' (*Mechthild*, but also early Augustinian scholasticism) and thus the non-subsistence of the *actus essendi* is dissolved to the point of nothingness, and again when subjectivity is construed as pure (mystical) openness in the sense of a receptivity without any spontaneous act of one's own. *Thomas* erected a first wall here with his clear distinction between God and Being, but also with his doctrine of the spontaneity of the spirit, precisely in order that this can become '*quodammodo omnia*'; *Ignatius* again had to stress this spontaneity so that the fundamental human act of a loving preference for the elective will of God becomes possible. Thus we see that the express sighting of the third distinction (before the fourth one) in *Thomas* with his unlimited *esse* also highlights the positivity of *essentia* as *limitatio* and *capacitas receptionis*, supremely as the individual uniqueness of existence as spirit, underivable as form from *esse* alone and, like the latter, pointing back directly to the eternal ground. And thus also with *Ignatius* the individually unique decision-making freedom of the person is underivable from the 'freedom' of Being which is unattached to any entity or world; rather, it refers back to the eternally decisive freedom of the divine ground (*Kant, Fichte, Schelling*). It is in *Thomas* that the problem between Being and God first arises with this clarity, the problem between the active spontaneity of the human spirit (acting in wisdom) and the contemplative receptivity of the same spirit towards divine wisdom (perhaps mediated by the Church) which, even considered purely metaphysically, can lead to acts of *folly*. Folly no longer as mere acts of penance for the love of God and Christ, folly also no longer as the pure passivity of reason towards God (with the exclusion of all one's own thoughts), but folly as the conscious and loving preference for the unlimited and sovereign will of God, beyond all the spiritual harmony of the cosmos of the cardinal virtues.

These two distinctions conflict with the over-simplifications of the modern period, which must lead of necessity to the loss of the metaphysical act. The rediscovery of antiquity (Renaissance) meant two things: taking the world seriously in the face of a spiritualistic flight from the world, and taking the piety of the world seriously (natural religion) in the face of an over-positivisation of religion in biblical faith. But the pious metaphysical eros of *Ficino* founders as it becomes a primarily sexual one which already in *Gottfried of Strassburg* and later in *Bruno* usurps the place of the Christian and metaphysical eros, or goes no further than the universe (*Goethe*) or else is submerged within itself in an inauthentic melancholia (from Petrarchism to *Leopardi* and Pre-Raphaelism). But wherever love no longer seconds the encompassing metaphysical act, it collapses sceptically and agnostically within itself and limits itself to what is found within the world: the dimension of glory is lost within that of beauty. *Heidegger* represents an attempt to retrieve the classical and Christian form of metaphysical love, as detached readiness for the call of Being; but this attempt must fail, because he projects the fourth distinction into the second and thus turns the oscillation of Being and human existence, which should remain open and pointing beyond itself, into the fixed and indissoluble form of a sphinx, before which and for which man cannot live and love. Hermias (in Aristotle's hymn) dies for the sake of truth: but who would want to die for Being?

The other line, that of the philosophy of Spirit and later of transcendental philosophy, develops more catastrophically: here in a first phase (from *Descartes* to *Leibniz* and *Malebranche*) Being is left out of the picture in a pseudo-Augustinian aprioristic immediacy of relation between God and Spirit, and the metaphysical act is bound up with a somehow mystical love of God. This forgetfulness of Being takes its revenge as the loss of Being in *Kant*, in whom the pious immediacy of relation with God survives only in the moral and autonomous self-appropriation of the will, becoming then, inevitably, a Titanic immediacy of relation between God and the formal Self (the first philosophy of *Fichte*), which in its inner infinity appropriates the divine point of view for itself through the world. Thus not only does 'glory' collapse into the beauty of the world, but it becomes the prayerless self-glorification of the Spirit, which takes not only itself but also all that remains to it under its own control. With this, metaphysics comes to an end and, at the same time, all metaphysical love. There remain at best the substitute forms of a love within the world and a love among men. And because the former must be increasingly dissolved within the latter, as man himself takes control of the world, for which a transcendental and evolutionistic philosophy furnishes the justification to salve his conscience; because he himself has the world in and beneath himself, there remains for him—like the last of his emergency rations—only love among men.

From *Feuerbach* and *Marx* onwards, this interpersonal love has the choice either of understanding itself to be the Absolute within the world, as 'God', for which all else can be sacrificed and consumed as material, or, if that is to be debunked as a mystical utopia, to dissolve itself within the process (as in *Hegel*) in order itself to become material which has been sacrificed to the—no less utopian—future goal of the greatest 'happiness' of the greatest number of people. A highly problematical form of 'happiness' which can be evaluated even now, weighed in the scales and found to be wanting, and to which I am supposed to subordinate the whole of my being-permitted-to-be as a means to an end. If I am no more than a means, then so too is the Thou whom I love, and then we can give nothing to each other by way of grace, since neither of us is unique as an entity nor, as existents, have we really been permitted to *be*. This means that there is no gleam of glory surrounding personal love any more, or at most the deceptive illusion of one, which lovers are always supposed to see through in a melancholy or cynical way—for the glory of love can flourish only within the context of an at least intuited glory of Being. Where personal love has been debased and reduced to the status of being a machine-part in an either transcendental, biological and evolutionistic or materialistic process, then no other value can compensate for this loss, human existence itself lacks all radiance and meaning, and there is no longer any reason why it should be better that something exist rather than simply nothing at all. What kind of gift can the other person be for me? Within the transcendental system he is essentially no different from myself: one aspect of the absolute subject; what he is in 'empirical' and 'psychological' terms is provisional and accidental and certainly undeserving of any absolute commitment. Within the biological and evolutionistic system, he is a fertile (and fertilisable) cell within the whole organism, who can enjoy only a prospective intuition of an invisible evolutionary goal; all human life thus becomes animal life. Within the materialistic and economic process, both my consciousness and yours remain a material product which is in principle constructable by technical means and which can be transformed at will and made into something else, into something which is sub-, super- or near-human, so that there is nothing better for consciousness to do than to ready itself from the outset for its own self-elimination in every possible manageable direction. Every form of metaphysics, therefore, which withdraws the light of Being from man in order to locate the light in its entirety within his self ceases of itself to be metaphysics and becomes 'science' which takes control of (manifest) existence. At the same time, Being and love are extinguished, for the philosophical act lives from both.

2. THE CHRISTIAN CONTRIBUTION TO METAPHYSICS

A Christian has to conduct philosophical enquiry on account of his faith. Believing in the absolute love of God for the world, he is obliged to understand Being in its ontological difference as pointing to love, and to live in accordance with this indication. As suggested above, the mystery of the fact that anything exists at all becomes for him yet more profound and in the most comprehensive sense more worthy of enquiry than it does for any other kind of philosopher. For every philosopher searches Being for a particular—albeit uncomprehended—ground which is presupposed *within it.* Thus the question as to Why becomes one as to What—τί τὸ ὄν or τὸ εἶναι—and thus leads openly (Aristotle) or hiddenly (Heidegger) to an essentialisation of Being. The Christian must deny Being an ultimate necessity and thus allow it to hover in the unheard of oscillation of not-having-to-be if he is to avoid the perilous path of a Leibnizean philosophy of Spirit which would deduce it, even as something created, out of God (whose freedom is love and therefore wills to communicate itself and whose will, being rational, must create the best of all possible worlds, which is the world as it actually exists). In this case the world would acquire the same necessity as God; God would lose his absolute rule over it and human reason, having raised itself to the level of absolute calculation, would combine its own glory with that of God, thus dethroning the latter.

The Christian remains the guardian of that metaphysical wonderment which is the point of origin for philosophy and the continuation of which is the basis of its further existence. Wonderment is constantly on the point of turning into a marvelling at the beauty of existence as a whole, of that order and orderliness of what is already 'adorned' and 'equipped' (κόσμος), and which the individual sciences are only too keen to enquire into. Plato himself seems finally to have lost the sense of wonder (*Verwunderung*) and to have acquired instead a sense of admiration (*Bewunderung*), and thus the way was open that led from metaphysics to the cosmology of the platonic school and that of Aristotle. The sciences now soar proudly aloft in their joy of intellectual discovery, their admiration turning now to the already achieved stock of order within existence and now to the presumed stock of order which is as yet unascertained. But this elevated feeling is not love. Love loves Being in an *a priori* way, for it knows that no science will ever track down the ground of why something exists rather than nothing at all. It receives it as a free gift and replies with free gratitude. Here that light weaves which is the source of all authentic images and cyphers together with the 'sacred words of origin' and thus also of all art which remains close to the origin. Here that metaphysical glory prevails which is higher than and prior to the perception of worldly beauty. It is right to understand eros and beauty as ordered to each other; it is true that it is for the sake of union that Nature adorns herself and that it is eros which makes the eye perceive as attractive that which has been thus adorned. But this play is governed by intentions, and if love were nothing but that, then Nature could still be Goethe's 'ruminating monster', or Hegel's 'horror which consumes its own formations'. The metaphysical eros prevails at a higher and earlier level, and it is ordered not to beauty but to glory. This is surely what Angelus Silesius' Cherubic Wanderer means when he says:

> Beauty comes from love, and even the countenance of
>   God
> Takes from her its beauty, or it would not shine.

Viewed from this elevated perspective, the aesthetic argument of theodicy, which we have encountered so often in the second volume (Augustine, Bonaventure) and in the present one (Plato, Boethius, Leibniz, Goethe, Hegel, etc.), and which has been understood in the main to belong to the 'lower' level of aesthetics, in accordance with its own formulation, acquires a deeper and more fitting significance: the beauty and the terror of this world complement each other like light and darkness in a perfect picture and on account of its total beauty God is justified even as the creator of such a world. But this idea becomes tasteless when it is the language of a contemplation which merely observes for its own satisfaction, in the face for instance of the suffering of this world. And when it is used by Christian thinkers in order to justify eternal damnation, it is wholly intolerable. And yet it has a shattering grandeur when it is the language of a lover who wishes to perceive the reflected glory of the first miracle in all Being's forms, even the most wretched and hideous, or even to believe it to be present. The Greeks, who found a place for Tragedy within their *Weltbild*, were of this mind, as was Virgil in his *Georgics*. But above all it is Christians who are required to adopt this perspective. And they are so on the basis of the special word of God in Jesus Christ, which lays down that the preferred place for the manifestation of God's love and thus for His emergent glory is precisely those areas of darkness which seem to fall out of every aesthetic contemplation. Areas of darkness which are otherwise excluded from any aesthetic view of the world (and thus prove the limitations of these views), or which lead the observer to look with stony gaze at Nature and Being, themselves hard as stone, and which now become precisely the critical touchstones of love and glory: both of the love of God which glorifies itself even and especially when it shows its light in the darkness, and also of the love of man, which then corresponds to this aesthetics of God's glory in so far as it recognises God's love there in its highest glory and worships it accordingly.

The Christians of today, living in a night which is deeper than that of the later Middle Ages, are given the task of performing the act of affirming Being, unperturbed by the darkness and the distortion, in a way that is vicarious and representative for all humanity: an act which is at first theological, but which contains within itself the whole dimension of the metaphysical act of the affirmation of Being. Those who are directed in this way to pray continually, to find God in all things and to glorify Him are able to do so on particular grounds (that is particular graces) which allow them to perform their 'creaturely duty' (as *Ruysbroeck, Bérulle* and *Condren* understood it). But in so far as they are to shine 'like the stars in the sky', they are also entrusted with the task of bringing light to those areas of Being which are in darkness so that its primal light may shine anew not only upon them but also upon the whole world; for it is only in this light that man can walk in accordance with what he is truly called to be.

The way for the Christian to perform this task successfully is clear from what is most deeply his own inheritance. If on account of their advancing blindness to the light of Being men and women have lost the treasure of love with the exception of those inalienable 'emergency rations' of interpersonal relations (as the last source of warmth in an area of cold), then the Christian is truest to his calling when he finds himself in the presence of this poorest and smallest area of love's manifestation. His duty is to experience the presence of absolute love, and himself to actualise it, and to make it visible, within his love for his neighbour; it is his task to effect the miracle of the multiplication of the loaves precisely out of this poverty ('What is that for so many?'). His faith teaches him to see within the most seemingly unimportant interpersonal relation the making present and the 'sacrament' of the eternal I-Thou relation which is the ground of the free Creation and again the reason why God the Father yields His Son to the death of darkness for the salvation of every Thou. The Christian love for our neighbour is therefore something quite distinct from a good and morally upright model for interpersonal conduct; it occurs always as the focal point, as the demonstration (*Erweis*) and realisation (*Vorweis*) of a love which itself wholly transcends man, and thus also as an indicator (*Verweis*) to that love which man cannot appropriate for himself as it has long since shown itself to him to be that which is ever greater than himself. A Christian encounters his fellow-man in grace and in each task of this love which is given both to him and to the brother who meets him, and under the pre-condition of its absolute radiance; it is not he who lifts his brother titanically out of the darkness by the

strength of his own power of love; even in full-blown and active *engagement* (such as that of the Samaritan) he only testifies to the light, as Christ Himself, the Son of the Father to whom the light was given as His own, wanted in all His radiance only to testify to the Father. If the Christian therefore were to give definitively the love he has for his fellow men the character of a purely interpersonal (even if humanly perfect) love, then he would be acting counter to the command to allow his light to shine forth so that people may glorify God (Matt 5.16), and would rather be hiding his light under the bushel. The love which he concentrates like a light through a lens in his encounter with his brother comes from a place infinitely beyond the individual Christian and it reaches therefore infinitely beyond the limited reality of the present situation. He can only prove himself to be a friend of this light by showing that he is its servant. For it is not I who died for this brother, but he who is Lord of us both; and this representative death in love, which has already removed the resistance and the darkness of the brother, has long since been present for him, before I met him. 'Before Philip called you
. . .'

What thus authenticates and points the way forward for the Christian is his faith. Whoever believes accepts a light of salvation which shines for him *a priori* from beyond the limits of pure reason and towards whose glory he is orientated receptively and attentively, seeing and hearing, which is to say 'contemplatively', in a primal break-through. It was not practical reason and its activity which existed in the beginning but the gift that comes from grace. This is the insight which Fichte, transcending Kant and his own titanism, struggled successfully to achieve. The 'destiny' (*Bestimmung*) of man really is his 'being-determined' (*Be-stimmung*), and it is precisely here that the mystery of freedom has its primal seat. And so the Christian faith unveils the metaphysical dimension—without being identified with it. But it is impossible that this determination as the act of the living God should not at the same time reveal the metaphysical dimension. It is the Christian mystery between 'contemplation' and 'action', or rather between being absolutely determined by God and the absolute appropriation of our own nature in freedom, which decisively illuminates the horizon of Being and of humanity who live within it. This fundamental metaphysical mystery can be perceived only within the Ontological Difference, because in the systems of identity the ('perfect') man necessarily coincides with the 'will of God'. Fichte glimpses the mystery for which he allows a place between primal life (Ur-Leben) and the Self. Heidegger sees it too in his own way, which approaches the philosophy of Zen. But for the Christian it is even more luminous, for in the 'Holy Spirit' he can through self-denial open up his own will to that of God. It was towards this passivity, which is the basis for all forms of active appropriation of our own destiny, that the entire 'metaphysics of the saints' was orientated; in their openness the great 'fools' were wiser than the teachers of wisdom, with their closed minds. Christianity casts a mercilessly clear and sober light upon this most inward point; it demands not only detachment from all that is (as did the Stoa), but also detachment from Being from which the primal words and the primal commands spring; and fresh forms of detachment are always needed since God remains free to alter, to develop, to apply and to deepen old commands anew in an unexpected, unhoped-for and unforeseen way. All the maturity of self-appropriation retains here its fertile womb. Whoever does not wish to root himself in detachment is already cut down and desiccated. This fundamental mystery of existence exposes the character of Christian existence. This is the meaning of Christ's command to leave all and to hate all. There is no 'world-task' of man, in particular of 'modern man', which has the right to uproot him from this ground or demand that he give it up. There is no form of worldly wealth which removes from him his poverty in Being. There is no kind of mastery over Nature which belongs to his destiny, that may or can tear him away from the glory in which alone he finds the measure of beauty without losing sight of himself in the context of the whole.

The encompassing glory gives the Christian a freedom with regard to the beauty of the world. In so far as the encounter with the brother (and with him with the whole surrounding

world as it is) takes place in the light of eternal love, guilt
and wrongfulness have a quite different appearance for him
(that is as *sin*) than they have for someone who has *a priori*
balanced all things out aesthetically in a rhythmic law of
beauty. For the Christian, it is impossible to view sin in any
way other than against the background of the eternal love
which dies for it. This is sobering; it breaks the wings of the
'cosmogonic eros', but also those of the 'phenomenology of
the Spirit' in which guilt is at most compensated for by fate
but sin is never eliminated (*aufheben*). Since sin is visible only
for the eye of love, it is only in the gaze of this eye that it
can be drawn through the act of love into the glory of love
which comprehends all things. Translating this greater glory
into the terms of the laws of a beauty of this world can be a
sign of blindness to value (and to its lack). In this way the
καλόν is transposed by the Christian mystery—precisely
because of its recognition of the metaphysical dimension—into
the ultimate sphere which is its due; and is thereby fulfilled in
so far as its true premises are uncovered, and it is negated in
so far as its finite aspects emerge, in which it expels from itself
what is unlovely. But this, in the Christian approach, becomes
precisely the place chosen for the manifestation of the all-
encompassing glory of love. We shall return to this theme in
our final volume.

It is from this point of view that the responsibility for
developing a comprehensive and contemporary metaphysics
falls to the Christian. This task seems to be made more
difficult by the fact that the form of modern life is clearly
influenced by the onesidedness of a metaphysics which has
forgotten Being (with which the Christians too have
collaborated, not without incurring blame). But it also
appears to be made easier by virtue of the fact that this
metaphysics has brought its hidden premises out into the
light of day during this, its final phase, and that the
impoverishment of the times offers the responsibility and the
opportunity to the Christians to yield to their own concept
of poverty and thus authentically to develop the true glory
from within it. Humanity today is struggling with the

material world in order to master it. That is one part of their destiny, which by the ways of metaphysics is given an appearance of wholeness; through the logical materialisation of the concrete, through the removal of God from the classical vision of Being, through the titanic verticalisation of Spirit into the essence of world and also that of Being. Thus according to Hegel's logic, man himself becomes the slave of what he sought to master: matter and the machine. He frees himself from this antithesis and so finds his true destiny (as master of Nature) only by examining again the ground of this mastery, which certainly cannot be secured by unphilosophical theories of evolution (which want to encourage him to endure the present drudgery because things will improve at some later date), but only by a present act of elevation as ek-sistence within the Ontological Difference. In his consideration of the Difference, it becomes immediately clear to him that no possible evolution can surpass it nor even touch it, that no asymptotic approaches of the existent to Being are possible, and that thus no concept of human (individual or collective) wholeness can be constructed from the function of a mastery and domination of the world.[5] If this has been proven not to be the case by an authentic metaphysics, then at the same time the positive side also emerges, which is that of a greater horizon of freedom—in orientation to Being as a whole—and also that distance to his work is given to man without which it cannot ever become masterful. And it is only a distorted, that is partial, metaphysical perspective which prevents him from seeing this, in that it makes him believe that the classical contemplative vision of the θεῖον within the order of the universe was only possible because it was an ontic rather than a transcendental orientation to existence; and for the latter precisely the subhuman is nothing other than a component element within man himself who thereby, in knowing Nature and controlling it, in essence only knows and controls himself. But if man who exists is not Being itself (or indeed God), then it remains no less worthy of wonder for him than it was

[5] Cf. my Das Ganze im Fragment (1963).

for the Greeks that this whole reality of Nature was given to him as a prior basis (for he was not himself there, as God tells Job), and so there is no reason why the harmonious laws of Nature into which he has gained a much more profound insight should not make existence as a whole yet more theophanous for him. It is therefore a superficial reasoning which seeks to make the transition from a natural culture (of farmers and shepherds) to a technical one responsible for the fundamental loss of piety. The former possessed a horizon of Being which was restricted to the surrounding world of Nature, which today has to be broadened to its true—and in man infinitely widened—dimensions.

And so what we are truly concerned with here is a new integration in which Christians must lead the way, an integration of the service of the world into the all-embracing openness of man to Being. 'Service' would mean the responsibility for a destiny whose dimensions lie with Being, which disposes and determines. 'You cannot serve two masters', and so one of them, the service of the world, must take its measure from the other, which itself has no measure (being 'indifferent'). For a man can give himself fully only once. But his gift of self is a response, to the one who is the ground of his being-permitted-to-be; to him who ultimately wants from man not things and objects but his very self. *Fili, praebe mihi cor tuum.* However perfect things may be, man will never improve his heart through them; the world will only be filled with love by making ultimate decisions for love, and never through the ameliorations of technology. Only within the Ontological Difference does the irreducible mystery of fullness and nothingness emerge, as we have seen, and thus an uneliminable *use-lessness* (*Vergeblichkeit*) of all (human) existence, which can experience the *gratuité* of absolute Being only when it has made this *vanité* of its own. It is use-less (*vergeblich*), and so it can be forgiven (*so kann es ihm vergeben werden*), and so forgiveness is possible (*es kann vergeben werden*). And only then can it too speak with the absolute word: 'As we forgive those . . .'

All this will, of course, prove a hard test for Christians; if they want to be the teachers of our times, then they must learn to read the signs of our times. This age cannot be purified by fire if Christians are not ready to allow themselves to be tested in the same fire to see whether they are made of gold or of potash, whether their hearts and their work are of 'gold, silver and precious stones' or of 'wood, hay and straw' (I Cor 3, 13). This is the ultimate truth: that Christians, as guardians of a metaphysics of the whole person in an age which has forgotten both Being and God, are entrusted with the weighty responsibility of leading this metaphysics of wholeness through that same fire. But metaphysics is not a ware which can be bought and sold ready-made: we must ourselves think. And if the Christian is brought by Christ to a place of ultimate and profound decision ('Whoever is not for me, is against me'), then as a serious thinker he is brought to the same point of decision, for there is no 'neutral' metaphysics. Either one sees the mystery of the ultimate oscillation or one does not, and becomes blind. It is in no way a question of facilitating or sparing oneself thought on the basis of a theology that one already knows, and then of juggling with systems *ab extra*. This has often been the view of Christians, who have donned and stripped off metaphysics like a form of outer clothing; and this has been the cause of part of the historical tragedy. But Christians cannot divide their decision any more than they can their gift of self: *as* Christians they are always human beings and thus entities who are determined by the metaphysical act. They can only adequately answer God's universal engagement with the world in the love of Jesus Christ for them by lending their own love, in the *concretissimum* of the encounter with their brother, that universal breadth of Being which—consciously or not, explicitly or not—the metaphysical act possesses and is. If they are called to be the guardians of thought, then they will note the extent to which pre-Christian thought in all its complexity preserved an advent-like openness of the coming of something greater than itself by which it could be determined, and how much post-Christian thought, whether it will or not, has been determined by that which is greater than itself. The Christian sees this but does not become arrogant. As a man among men, he is involved with the destiny of all. It would give rise to a false idea which would be difficult to dispel if we were to say that the metaphysician can only 'ask questions' of Being whereas the Christian brings ready-made answers from revelation, which surpass the act of thinking and destroy it from within. For neither did Aristotle mean that philosophical thought is merely a form of questioning—thought is certainly a form of knowledge, even if it is one which is 'above science'—nor does the Bible primarily exist in order to toss ready answers down to ascending thought. But the way in which Jesus Christ lives in openness towards the Father and in this openness shows both the supreme exposure of the love of God and the supreme decision of man for God, can cause the metaphysician to ask himself whether he already thinks and enquires sufficiently openly, or whether perhaps he has come too quickly to an end. It is in this sense that the Christian is called to be the guardian of metaphysics in our time.

INDEX

230 · 011185 BAL